D1712908

Meditations on the Life of Christ

# THE WILLIAM AND KATHERINE DEVERS SERIES
## IN DANTE AND MEDIEVAL ITALIAN LITERATURE

Zygmunt G. Barański, Theodore J. Cachey, Jr., and Christian Moevs, editors

---

*Winner of the 2017 Aldo and Jeanne Scaglione Publication Award*
*for a Manuscript in Italian Literary Studies,*
*Modern Language Association*

# MEDITATIONS

## on the

# LIFE

## of

# CHRIST

*The Short Italian Text*

Sarah McNamer

University of Notre Dame Press
Notre Dame, Indiana

University of Notre Dame Press
Notre Dame, Indiana 46556
www.undpress.nd.edu

Copyright © 2018 by the University of Notre Dame

All Rights Reserved

Published in the United States of America

*Library of Congress Cataloging-in-Publication Data*
Names: Johannes, de Caulibus, active 14th century. |
Bonaventure, Saint, Cardinal, approximately 1217–1274. | McNamer, Sarah, editor.
Title: Meditations on the life of Christ : the short Italian text /
[edited by] Sarah McNamer; linguistic analysis by Pär Larson.
Other titles: Meditationes vitae Christi. Italian. | Meditationes vitae Christi. English.
Description: Notre Dame : University of Notre Dame Press, 2017. |
Series: The William and Katherine Devers series in Dante and Medieval
Italian literature | Contains the Italian text of Bodleian Library MS. Canon. Ital. 174
and English translation. Scholars dispute whether Meditationes vitae
Christi originated as a Latin or Italian text. |
Includes bibliographical references and index. |
Identifiers: LCCN 2017035599 (print) | LCCN 2017053556 (ebook) |
ISBN 9780268102876 (pdf) | ISBN 9780268102852 (hardcover : alk. paper) |
ISBN 0268102856 (hardcover : alk. paper)
Subjects: LCSH: Jesus Christ—Biography—Meditations.
Classification: LCC BT306.43 (ebook) | LCC BT306.43 .M4312 2017 (print) |
DDC 232.9/01 [B] —dc23
LC record available at https://lccn.loc.gov/2017035599

∞This paper meets the requirements of ANSI/NISO Z39.48-1992
(Permanence of Paper).

ABOUT THE WILLIAM AND KATHERINE

DEVERS SERIES IN DANTE AND

MEDIEVAL ITALIAN LITERATURE

The William and Katherine Devers Program in Dante Studies at the University of Notre Dame supports rare book acquisitions in the university's John A. Zahm Dante collections, funds an annual visiting professorship in Dante studies, and supports electronic and print publication of scholarly research in the field. In collaboration with the Medieval Institute at the university, the Devers program initiated a series dedicated to the publication of the most significant current scholarship in the field of Dante studies. In 2011 the scope of the series was expanded to encompass thirteenth- and fourteenth-century Italian literature.

In keeping with the spirit that inspired the creation of the Devers program, the series takes Dante and medieval Italian literature as focal points that draw together the many disciplines and lines of inquiry that constitute a cultural tradition without fixed boundaries. Accordingly, the series hopes to illuminate this cultural tradition within contemporary critical debates in the humanities by reflecting both the highest quality of scholarly achievement and the greatest diversity of critical perspectives.

The series publishes works from a wide variety of disciplinary viewpoints and in diverse scholarly genres, including critical studies, commentaries, editions, reception studies, translations, and conference proceedings of exceptional importance. The series enjoys the support of an international advisory board composed of distinguished scholars and is published regularly by the University of Notre Dame Press. The Dolphin and Anchor device that appears on publications of the Devers series was used by the great humanist, grammarian, editor, and typographer Aldus Manutius (1449–1515), in whose 1502 edition of Dante (second issue) and all subsequent editions it appeared. The device illustrates the ancient proverb Festina lente, "Hurry up slowly."

Zygmunt G. Barański, Theodore J. Cachey, Jr.,
and Christian Moevs, editors

DANTE

AL    DVS

# Advisory Board

Albert Russell Ascoli, Berkeley

Teodolinda Barolini, Columbia

Piero Boitani, Rome

Patrick Boyde, Cambridge

Alison Cornish, New York University

Claire Honess, Leeds

Christopher Kleinhenz, Wisconsin

Giuseppe Ledda, Bologna

Simone Marchesi, Princeton

Giuseppe Mazzotta, Yale

Lino Pertile, Harvard

John A. Scott, Western Australia

*Alle mie dilette figlie*

*con affetto*

# CONTENTS

# ACKNOWLEDGMENTS

Many forms of support have enabled me to complete this book, and it is a pleasure to acknowledge them here.

For access to materials in their care and for many quiet hours in lovely spaces I wish to thank the curators, staff, and trustees of the Bodleian Library, Oxford; the Biblioteca Riccardiana, Biblioteca Laurenziana, and Biblioteca Nazionale Centrale, Florence; the Biblioteca Nazionale Marciana and the Nuova Manica Lunga, Fondazione Giorgio Cini, Venice; the Biblioteca comunale degli Intronati, Siena; the Biblioteca Apostolica Vaticana; the Biblioteca Universitaria, Bologna; the Biblioteca del Sacro Convento, Assisi; the Bibliothèque nationale de France; the Wren Library, Trinity College, Cambridge; the British Library; Houghton Library, Harvard University; The Snite Museum of Art, University of Notre Dame; the Library of Congress; the National Gallery of Art Library; Dumbarton Oaks Research Library; and not least, Lauinger Library, Georgetown University, where Jeffrey Popovich and the Interlibrary Loan staff have made everyday research a pleasure.

Grants and fellowships from a number of organizations have provided travel funds, time for research and writing, and fruitful intellectual companionship. In 2008, a National Endowment for the Humanities summer seminar on Franciscan history in Italy provided a very stimulating setting for early work on this book; I wish to thank Bill Cook and the seminar participants, especially Sara Ritchey and Mary Dzon, for many rich conversations. In 2010, I received a Craig Hugh Smyth Fellowship from Harvard University's Villa I Tatti. It is one of my great regrets that I was not able to take up the I Tatti fellowship due to a family emergency; I am grateful to Joseph Connors for handling this unforeseen circumstance with kindness and grace, and to Lino Pertile and the library staff at I Tatti for their hospitality at a later date. The Vittore Branca Center, Fondazione Giorgio Cini, offered ideal conditions for intensive work on this project in Venice in 2011. As winner of the Bonnie Wheeler Fellowship in 2013, I not only received material support, but the

energetic encouragement of the Fellowship committee, led by Howell Chickering. It was through the auspices of the Wheeler committee that two experts in the field, Ann Matter and Frances Andrews, were invited to comment on my work in progress; this book is much the better for their astute attention and guidance. From the earliest stages of this project to the end, Georgetown University has provided generous support in the form of summer grants, travel grants, and research assistance (including, especially, the research assistance provided with such diligence and good sense by Alice Maglio). More than this, Georgetown has provided a congenial and stimulating intellectual home, and I am grateful to my colleagues and students and to my department chairs, Kathryn Temple and Ricardo Ortiz, for their confidence and engagement. I would like to express thanks, too, to our stellar staff in 306 New North, especially Donna Even-Kesef and Karen Lautman, for smoothing the way at every turn; and to our president and provosts, John DeGioia, James O'Donnell, and Robert Groves, for their robust support for work in the humanities even in changing times.

Many interlocutors at home and abroad have freely shared their expertise. Chief among these is Pär Larson of the Istituto Opera del Vocabolario Italiano. Pär's generous response to my request, when I knocked on the door of the Accademia della Crusca one spring day, led not only to a quick assessment of the language of MS Canonici Italian 174 then and there, but to the detailed study appearing in this volume as the Linguistic Analysis. In the course of preparing that study, Pär read every word of the Italian text, making many editorial suggestions and noticing specific features of the language that helped improve the translation. As I continued to refine both text and translation over the years, Pär responded to particular queries quickly and with unfailing generosity. Francesco Caruso also merits special thanks for stepping in, late in the day, as copyeditor for the Italian and Latin sections of the book. Francesco's eagle eye and good judgment, his checking of the text against the Canonici manuscript one last time, and his final review of the translation instilled confidence that this volume was ready to send out into the world; his good humor under the pressure of a deadline also brightened the final stages of this project.

Others who have shared their expertise, asked incisive questions, commented on drafts, or engaged in helpful conversations include Alexandra Barratt, Valentina Berardini, Bruce Barker-Benfield, Nicolas Bell, Gino Benzoni, Thomas Bestul, Louise Bourdua, Jessica Brantley, Katie Bugyis, Christopher Cannon, Francesco Ciabattoni, William Cook, Anne Derbes, Mary Dzon, Paolo Evangelisti, Dávid Falvay, Sean Field, Holly Flora, Brad Franco,

Emily Francomano, Rachel Fulton, Tommaso Gramigni, Jeffrey Hamburger, Mark Henninger, John Hirsh, Anne Hudson, Géraldine Johnson, Lindsay Kaplan, H.A. Kelly, Tobias Kemper, Kathryn Kerby-Fulton, Richard Kieckhefer, Lezlie Knox, V.A. Kolve, Marcia Kupfer, Alice Maglio, Sabina Magrini, Pasquale Magro, Susy Marcon, William Marx, William McDermott, Kathryn Blair Moore, Jo Ann Moran Cruz, Laura Morreale, Ronald Murphy, Barbara Newman, James O'Donnell, John O'Malley, Derek Pearsall, Arianna Pecorini, Gabriella Piccinni, Dianne Phillips, Manu Radhakrishnan, Sara Ritchey, Lucia Sardo, Michael Sargent, Neslihan Şenocak, Daniel Shore, Katherine Stern, Noël Sugimura, Peter Tóth, Teresa Webber, Kelley Wickham-Crowley, Lucia Wolf, and Jan Ziolkowski. I am grateful to Carolyn Dinshaw and Chris Cannon and their students for incorporating a draft of this book into their graduate seminar on Medieval Women's Writing at NYU; and I thank the students in my own seminars at Georgetown for their astute comments on the *testo breve* and the hypothesis I have advanced for its authorship and importance. Georgetown's publishing guru, Carole Sargent, helped to shepherd this work from manuscript to press, and I am grateful for her guidance.

At the University of Notre Dame Press, Stephen Little's enthusiasm for this book has been matched by his courtesy and good judgment. That good judgment led to the decision to approach the editors of The William and Katherine Devers Series in Dante and Medieval Italian Literature, Theodore Cachey, Zygmunt Barański, and Christian Moevs. I am deeply grateful to this rare trio of *italianisti*, not only for the risk they have taken in welcoming this book into a series that has prioritized Dante, but for their exacting standards. Their rigorous comments and those of the anonymous readers for the Press caused me to rethink key aspects of the book's argument and style. The production staff at UNDP has also brought astute attention to this project; I wish to thank Matt Dowd in particular for his copyediting prowess. For permission to publish material that first appeared in *Speculum*, I thank the Medieval Academy of America. I also acknowledge the Bodleian Library, University of Oxford, for permission to publish the text of the *Meditazioni* from MS Canonici Italian 174, ff. 1–127r, and to publish the image of folio 1r.

Without practical help on the domestic front, I could not have spent the necessary hours in the archives and at my desk; for this essential form of research assistance, I gratefully acknowledge Ariel Borroff, Lucie Nonin, Iryna Kurbatava, and Marian Fernandez. Many friends have sustained and cheered me, including Emily Francomano, Kate McNamara, Holly Brewer, Roland Stephen, Carolyn Bernstein, Julia Lamm, Jonathan Ray, Katherine Cox, Heather Townsend, Julia Prosser, David Gewanter, Joy Young, Marcia Kupfer,

and Tim Noah; thanks to you all. Francisco LaRubia Prado offered thoughtful conversation and support at a pivotal moment in the course of this project; I am grateful for his generosity, which extended to heroic efforts to recover a precious notebook. My remarkable family offered encouragement at every turn. I thank the entire, far-flung McNamer clan, but I wish to express gratitude to those who live nearby, Bruce McNamer, Amy McNamer, and Jim Neill, for their ordinary and extraordinary kindnesses, solidarity, and good company as this book was brought to completion.

Finally, I wish to thank my daughters, Claire Parker and Ellida Parker, for their lively minds, big hearts, and cheerful presence throughout this journey. Our time together in Siena and Assisi, especially, yielded a store of happy memories to treasure in the mind and savor. *Grazie, dilette figlie.*

# PREFACE

The *Meditations on the Life of Christ* was the single most influential devotional text in Western Europe in the later Middle Ages. Composed in Tuscany in the first half of the fourteenth century for a Poor Clare, the *Meditations* spread rapidly throughout Europe, moving out of the cloister and into the world: more than two hundred manuscripts survive, in multiple versions, in Italian, Latin, and all of the major vernaculars, including Middle English, French, German, Catalan, Swedish, and Irish. With its lively dialogue and narrative realism, its gentle invitations to enter into imagined and embellished scenes from sacred history, its poignant and moving depictions of the Nativity and Passion, and its direct appeals to the reader to feel love, grief, and compassion, the *Meditations* had a major impact on devotional practices, religious art, meditative literature, vernacular drama, and the cultivation of affective experience.

This book seeks to contribute to the scholarship on the *Meditations* in two ways. It presents, for the first time, a unique Italian recension of the *Meditations* witnessed by a long-neglected manuscript, Oxford, Bodleian Library MS Canonici Italian 174; and it builds a case that this short vernacular text, here christened the *testo breve*, is likely to be the sole surviving copy of the original version of this influential masterpiece. Although the most fundamental facts about the *Meditations*—who wrote it, when, and in what language—have never been established with certainty, the traditional view has held that the long Latin text, *Meditationes Vitae Christi*, was composed first, by a Franciscan friar typically identified as pseudo-Bonaventure. This volume reconstructs and offers for consideration a very different history of the text, one that emerges from a careful examination of the *testo breve* and its place in a complex manuscript matrix. Livelier and far more compact than the Latin *Meditations*, more consistent in its affective strategies and incarnational aesthetic, and unencumbered by the copious didactic passages of the Latin text, the *testo breve* possesses a stylistic, thematic, and textual integrity

xvii

that appears to testify to its primacy among the early versions of the *Meditations*. It also appears to have been composed by a woman, a Poor Clare from Pisa. The early textual history of the *Meditations*, then, may—like so many medieval texts, from the *Romance of the Rose* to Gratian's *Decretum*—reflect the sequential work of more than one author. In this case, it seems, a nun who composed the base text was followed by a friar who expanded and altered that text, adding a more learned gloss and adapting it for broad circulation while suppressing some of its more intensely affective and potentially risky passages: risky, that is, in the theological challenge they implicitly offer in their depictions of a very vulnerable, very human Christ and in their open and easy endorsement of imaginative practices as a means of knowing spiritual truths.

This book, then, presents the Italian text, English translation, commentary, and detailed argument that will facilitate a fresh look at the *Meditations* and serve as a foundation for further scholarship and debate concerning a broad array of subjects in Italian and European literary and cultural history, including the development of Italian prose narrative in the early Trecento; the role of women as writers and readers in the invention of genres and devotional practices; the part played by the Franciscans in the cultivation of affective piety; the rise and risks of vernacular theology; and the history of emotion.

# INTRODUCTION

Sometime around the year 1842, in the tranquil haven of Oxford, an intriguing figure appeared on the scene: Count Alessandro Mortara—man of letters, bibliophile, aficionado of falconry, *cavaliere*. Drawn there, it seems, in part by his friendship with an Oxford don and in part by the Bodleian Library's manuscript collections, he made an impression during his decade in residence. "He became a daily reader in the Bodleian," writes the library's chronicler, "where the interest he took in the place, together with his polished, yet genuine, courtesy, made him a welcome and popular visitor."[1] He took a special interest in the Italian manuscripts of the Bodleian's renowned Canonici collection, acquired at great expense in 1817; and because these volumes had not been catalogued, he set to work describing and identifying them, dwelling with particular care on texts by Dante, Petrarch, Boccaccio, and other early Italian luminaries, but dutifully cataloguing, too, the more numerous manuscripts of miscellaneous and anonymous religious writings in the vernacular—including the humble volume bound in plain white leather now designated as MS Canonici Italian 174. Mortara's assessment was swift and decisive. This volume was compiled for a convent of nuns, he deduced, and its first and most substantial text is a version of the famed *Meditazioni della Vita di Nostro Signore Gesù Cristo* once attributed to Bonaventure; "*ma*," Mortara writes—and one can nearly see him furrowing his brow and gesticulating for emphasis—"*nella presente copia barbaramente alterato e guasto*": "but in the present copy barbarously altered and corrupted."[2]

*Barbaramente alterato e guasto.* Given Mortara's judgment, it is little wonder that this short Italian copy of the immensely popular and influential work typically referred to by its Latin title, *Meditationes Vitae Christi*, or

1. Macray, *Annals of the Bodleian Library*, 279.
2. Mortara, *Catalogo dei manoscritti italiani*, 179.

more simply as "the MVC," continued to sit silently on a shelf deep in the Bodleian's stacks after publication of Mortara's catalogue in 1864. Among the many remarkable nineteenth- and twentieth-century philologists, paleographers, and textual critics who sought to make sense of the immensely complex textual history of the MVC, which survives in more than two hundred manuscripts, none thought it worth the trouble to seek out and read this modest volume. Even those who questioned the assumption that the MVC was originally composed in Latin, thinking it may have been written in Italian, did not consider this manuscript a potentially useful witness to the Italian tradition. Given Mortara's description, the late date of the manuscript (ca. 1400), its manifestly impure dialect (Tuscan with a strong Venetian overlay), and the unique structure and style of the text—containing the Infancy and Passion alone, in a compact thirty chapters preceded by a preface—it clearly seemed very *unpromising* in the quest to locate the original version of the MVC, to identify its author, and to determine where and when it was written.

Happenstance and a fresh perspective, however, can sometimes alter the archives. A century and a half after Mortara's sojourn, I too had the good fortune to become a daily reader at the Bodleian. When I took up Canonici 174 one morning and began to read, I too was struck by a distinct sense of this text's difference from the other versions of the MVC. But was this difference due, as Mortara surmised, to barbarous alteration and corruption? As I continued to read, I was not so sure. A strong, clear, compelling voice kept drawing me back. That voice, and the lively, dramatic narrative—unencumbered by long didactic passages—seemed so familiar; seemed to be, in other words, the voice of the familiar MVC, but more fully itself, and *better*: more skilled in its narrative pacing, more adept in its rendering of dialogue, more vivid in its visual imagery, more moving. Visits to many other libraries ensued as I began to make detailed comparisons between this text and the other Italian and Latin manuscripts of the MVC. Patterns of difference emerged, patterns that suggested the greater degree of affective, stylistic, and textual integrity in the Canonici version.

My first hypothesis was rather modest: if the original version was the long Latin text, as the current scholarship held, and the Canonici simply a late adaptation and abridgment, then whoever reworked it was, at the very least, a supremely skilled redactor, capable of locating the lively and dramatic essences in a source text, drawing them out, enhancing the emphasis on women's perspectives and practices, eliminating lengthy didactic passages with systematic efficiency, rewriting the core narratives of the birth

and crucifixion to lend them greater simplicity and pathos, and connecting the resulting abridged sections with graceful, logical transitions. At the very least, this was an elegant revision—not a barbaric one. If this were a late, local adaptation made for a specific community, one of Venetian nuns circa 1400, it would still merit investigation as an instance of textual *mouvance*; or it might provide the basis for a microhistory of the kind that has itself become so interesting in the overlapping fields of religious, textual, literary, and art history.[3] As I continued to look closely at the textual details, review the extensive scholarship, and question basic assumptions, however, this theory of the Canonici version's belated and derivative brilliance made less sense, and an alternative theory continued to press for serious consideration. Could this shorter, simpler Italian text, preserved in a single late manuscript copy, be a rare and valuable witness to the original version of the MVC?

This volume will suggest that it is. Drawing on my earlier work, especially "The Origins of the *Meditationes Vitae Christi*" (2009), I will present a case for the priority of the Canonici text—newly christened here, for the sake of clarity and simplicity, the *testo breve*, or "the short Italian text"—while providing the text, translation, evidence, and reasoning that will allow Italianists, textual critics, and medievalists rooted in other disciplines to engage with the details of the argument in order to evaluate, challenge, contest, confirm, refine, or extend it.[4] Several aspects of this argument have already benefitted from commentary and critique; these counterarguments have prompted revisions to some aspects of my analysis while strengthening my core argument

---

3. On *mouvance* as a fundamental feature of medieval manuscript culture, and on the value of examining disparate recensions for what they might tell us about specific readers and communities, see Zumthor, *Toward a Medieval Poetics*, and Cerquiglini, *In Praise of the Variant*. Representative samples of the fine work on specific communities of religious women and their books, images, and textual cultures include Field, *Isabelle of France*; Poor, *Mechthild of Magdeburg and Her Book*; Flora, *The Devout Belief of the Imagination*; Lewis, *By Women, for Women, about Women*; Hamburger, *The Rothschild Canticles*; and Bornstein, *Life and Death in a Venetian Convent*.

4. See McNamer, "The Origins of the *Meditationes Vitae Christi*"; *Affective Meditation and the Invention of Medieval Compassion*, chap. 3: "Franciscan Meditation Reconsidered," 86–115; "The Author of the Italian *Meditations on the Life of Christ*"; "Further Evidence"; Review of *Iohannes de Caulibus: Meditaciones Vite Christi*; and *The Two Middle English Translations of the Revelations of St. Elizabeth of Hungary*, 10–16.

about the priority of the *testo breve* in the textual tradition.[5] In addition to my primary argument that the *testo breve* is likely to be the original version of the MVC, I also present my related findings, some of them published in earlier iterations but revised and refined here: that the *testo breve* was composed during the first half of the Trecento, most likely between about 1300 and 1325, though possibly somewhat later, and that it appears to have been composed by a woman, a Poor Clare from Pisa, for her fellow nuns. Moreover, I argue that it was taken up soon after its completion, before it had a chance to circulate widely, by a Franciscan friar who clearly valued it and wished to adapt it for wide circulation, but sought to "correct" certain passages, gloss it with more copious and specific citations, expand it in a way that would grant it greater authority and legitimacy, add images and language promoting the specific ideologies of the Franciscan Order, and replace it with three revised versions: first an Italian version of circa forty-one chapters, the *testo minore*, which seems to have gained immediate popularity and wide diffusion in Italy, judging from the number and dates of surviving manuscripts; next, the *testo maggiore*, an Italian version of circa ninety-four chapters, expanded to include the Public Ministry, which did not circulate as widely; and finally the version that allowed the work to achieve international circulation and influence, the circa one-hundred-chapter Latin *Meditationes Vitae Christi*. The long Latin text, then—the work that has acquired canonical status as "the MVC"—is not, I argue, the original form of the work, from which all other versions derive, nor is it the work of a single author. Rather, it is a composite text reflecting distinct layers of compositional effort, built up in successive stages from a short, vernacular core. It contains two distinct stylistic registers

5. See below "Counterarguments," in "Textual History," lxxxvi–xciv. Two jointly authored articles by Peter Tóth and Dávid Falvay have been especially valuable in setting the stage for further debate, debate that can now begin in earnest with the publication, in this volume, of the text and translation of the *testo breve* from the Canonici manuscript, along with my full argument about its place in the textual tradition. (The articles are Tóth and Falvay, "New Light," and Falvay and Tóth, "L'Autore." The second article is essentially a translation and condensation of the first, with some revisions and elaborations. For the sake of simplicity in the discussion that follows, I refer to the authors consistently as Tóth and Falvay; if the material discussed is essentially the same in both articles, I cite only "New Light.") Tóth and Falvay have sought to reinstate the "traditional view" that the Latin text was composed first. I provide a detailed response to their work in "The Debate on the Origins of the *Meditationes Vitae Christi*."

whose presence we can now account for as the voices of two distinct authors, whom I call here simply Author A and Author B.

This book, then, seeks to make visible both a text and a textual history that have long been obscured: obscured deliberately, in the first instance, by Author B's efforts to "improve" the *testo breve* by adapting and absorbing it into a sturdier didactic and theological framework (perhaps even with the consent of Author A, for, if this author was a woman, she may well have wished for the text to benefit from such authorizing measures by a learned Franciscan friar) and obscured passively, in the modern era, by the assumptions and practices that have tended to govern the scholarship on the MVC and medieval textual and literary history more generally, including the granting of priority and authority to Latin over vernacular texts and a default practice of assigning all anonymous medieval texts to men. What is at stake here, then, is a challenge to tradition: not only to the traditional view of the MVC's history, but to traditional views of other histories with which the MVC is entwined, including the history of medieval devotion, the history of the Franciscan movement, and the history of women's writing.

It is worth pausing to dwell for a moment on what the word "traditional" means in this context, in part because not doing so risks perpetuating scholarly stances of deference where they may not be warranted. The formation of what has come to be called the "traditional view" of the MVC's textual history is itself a contingent and patchwork product of history. This view, as we shall see below ("Textual History"), took shape chiefly in the first half of the twentieth century, in studies of varying scope and rigor published between 1921 and 1962; it was this body of work that established the grounds for Stallings-Taney's critical edition of the Latin MVC published in 1997.[6] Even the traditional view, however, was not one of consensus. The authors of the two most comprehensive studies of the Latin and Italian manuscripts, for instance, seriously considered the possibility that the original was to be found among the Italian versions, without reaching definitive conclusions.[7] While early scholarship on the MVC's textual history remains indispensable, then, it is not, itself, the internally consistent, sacrosanct, or

6. Stallings-Taney, ed., *Iohannes de Caulibus: Meditaciones vite Christi*. Full citations for the scholarship preceding the publication of this monumental work are given in "Textual History," below.

7. Fischer, "Die *Meditationes vitae Christi*"; Vaccari, "Le 'Meditazioni della vita di Cristo' in volgare."

firmly established entity that the phrase "traditional view" might conjure. Moreover, fifty years have passed since that first phase of textual scholarship. The broad conceptual shifts and scholarly advances of a half century in various branches of humanistic study have not been negligible, and they both permit and require a rethinking of the evidence in this case. Vernacular theology, for instance, is now a familiar category, one that has opened up so many late-medieval religious texts and contexts for reconsideration while inviting more astute attention to *del basso* perspectives. In addition, we now know of many more medieval women writers than we did half a century ago, and of the diverse ways that religious women participated in the making of devotional literature and culture. The possibility that a Poor Clare composed an anonymous meditative work in the vernacular is now far from the strained theory it might have seemed prior to the 1960s. And not least, the past fifty years have witnessed advances in the theory and practice of textual criticism. Textual scholars of the early twentieth century tended to dismiss as a matter of course late manuscript copies of ancient and medieval texts, on the theory, derived from Lachmann, that they would inevitably be more corrupt. But the principle articulated by Giorgio Pasquali in 1952, *recentiores non deteriores*—"more recent copies are not, for that reason alone, to be considered less reliable witnesses"—has proven to be a sound and very useful guiding principle: time and again, even very late manuscript copies have been shown to preserve earlier, more authentic readings of literary texts.[8]

In a pragmatic vein, we might also recognize that basic conditions for research have changed. Those who first posited the theory of a Latin original lacked the practical advantages we now take for granted, including the ability to travel to distant archives with ease, to obtain reproductions of manuscripts, and to access Internet archives; they relied much more heavily on catalogue descriptions (such as that by Mortara) to take the measure of out-of-the-way manuscript witnesses. These facts should be self-evident, but I mention them here because they help to clarify the state of the question, which, in my view, is not solely that the *testo breve* merits close scrutiny as witness to the original MVC, but that there is no going back. Scholarship on the MVC must move

---

8. "Un *recentior* non è per ciò un *deterior*. L'autorità di un testimonio è indipendente dalla sua antichità" [The authority of a witness is independent from its date]; Pasquali, *Storia della tradizione e critica del testo*, xvi. Pasquali dedicates a full chapter to the explication of this principle: see chap. 4, "Recentiores, non deteriores: Collazioni umanistiche ed editiones principes," 41–108.

*forward*. A reflexive return to the "traditional view," without a reassessment of its foundations, would be precisely that: a recursive retreat to a place of assumed stability and authority that may not merit such confidence as the most reasonable default position. Given serious problems with the theory that the long Latin version was composed first—not least that of the manifest stylistic disjunctions and abrupt shifts of tone and purpose in the Latin text (see "Textual History")—it seems to me that the real question at this stage is which of the two short Italian versions, the *testo breve* or the *testo minore*, represents the earliest form of the work. Close comparison of these two vernacular texts is the kind of precise and diligent labor that is needed now.[9] In this volume, I present the fruits of my own comparisons of these two recensions. It is detailed work of this kind, which takes stylistic features as well as textual variants into consideration, that has led me to conclude that the *testo breve* represents the earliest state of the text, and that the *testo minore* is the first of several revisions undertaken by a different author.

To present a critical edition of a text along with a potentially controversial argument is, from one perspective, an unusual goal. The critical edition as a genre typically seeks to be neutral in its tone and claims. Arguments regarding attribution or the priority of recensions are often conducted offstage, with a general resolution of the issues reaching broad agreement prior to the editing of the text. Yet such an approach would not in this case serve the scholarly conversation. Without a reliable text of the *testo breve*, no genuine debate about it can proceed; yet without an argument that does justice to its potential significance, while offering evidence for this at the detailed level of commentary and notes, the judgment offered by Mortara—that it is a late, eccentric adaptation—would remain, by default, its governing interpretive framework. This book, then, is something of a hybrid volume. In its joint presentation of text and argument, it is (or aspires to be) similar to other books that set forth detailed textual, paleographical, and stylistic evidence that in many respects is beset with uncertainties, yet ultimately take a stand on controversial questions of attribution or textual history rather than adopting a position of neutrality or agnosticism. Recent volumes in this vein include Enrico Menestò's *Angela da Foligno: Il Memoriale* (2013), Jacques Dalarun's *La Vie*

9. I have sought to facilitate this work not only by presenting the text of the *testo breve* here but also by making a serviceable printed edition of the *testo minore*, that by Francesco Sarri, more widely available; see https://repository.library.george town.edu/handle/10822/1042297. There is, at present, no critical edition of the *testo minore*.

*retrouvée de François d'Assise* (2015), and Barbara Newman's *Making Love in the Twelfth Century: "Letters of Two Lovers" in Context* (2016).[10]

The questions that this volume presents merit continuing debate, and I am well aware that I cannot have anticipated all possible angles and perspectives here. Some of my conclusions are more tentative than others, given the nature of the evidence, and I have sought to signal this throughout the volume by using the available spectrum of terms—*possible*, *likely*, *highly likely*, *probable*—with careful consideration. Many of my conclusions, too, are inevitably based on subjective interpretation of the evidence or on conjecture—as so many judgments about medieval texts must be, given the paucity of objective facts available to us. I have sought to mark this more subjective or speculative register as such whenever practical. I have also sought to acknowledge uncertainty wherever it exists—and to gesture towards ways that others might take up questions I have been unable to resolve.

I am aware, too, that certain arguments I advance here may seem circular, or easily "reversible," at the theoretical level. For example, I argue that the *testo breve*'s strikingly focused narrative energy is among the features that testify to its primacy in a sequence of composition; but one might argue instead that, departing from the *testo minore*, the author of the *testo breve* eliminated matter that impeded the text's narrative flow and stifled its affective impact. How can one prioritize one hypothesis over the other? Is this possible at all?

To this important and appropriately skeptical line of reasoning, I would offer two responses. First, it is indeed possible to move beyond arguments that are merely self-confirming. The way to do so is to recognize the possibility of alternative theories and to engage, at a detailed level, with very particular forms of evidence, examining the language and contexts closely while asking a fundamental question: given the equal plausibility of two hypotheses *in the abstract* (in this case, the traditional textual history represented by Table 1, or the revised history that I propose in Table 2, both found in the next section of this volume), which one better accounts for the broadest range of empirical evidence? Both theories cannot be equally valid. Either the MVC was composed initially in Latin or it was composed in Italian. Ei-

---

10. For another exemplary volume of this kind, see Mews, *Lost Love Letters*. The fact that not all scholars have agreed with Mews does not detract from the rigor, sensitivity, or value of his argument that Heloise and Abelard were indeed the authors of these letters; the debate itself has been a very rich site of scholarly exchange in the past two decades, and Mews's work has paved the way for Newman's.

ther the *testo breve* preceded the *testo minore* or vice versa. Since a single truth lies at the bottom of these questions, only persistent and astute empirical analysis will move the question forward. Simplicity and economy of explanation for the presence or absence of particular textual details help us to decide which hypothesis is more reasonable. But the power of any explanatory framework will be its capaciousness: its power, that is, to account for *cumulative* and disparate kinds of evidence. A single, simple question—which theory best accounts for the cumulative evidence of particular details?—has led me to conclude that the *testo breve* came first. I would invite others to assess the argument with this question in mind.[11]

Because the details matter, ultimately there can be no substitute for the independent testing by others of my claims for the priority of the *testo breve* through a careful comparison of the relevant texts in the context of the theory I have proposed for the Italian and Latin versions. In any scientific endeavor, replicating the experiment is essential to the evaluative process. Now that this edition of the *testo breve* is available, my hope is that those with the relevant linguistic and evaluative skills (Italian, Latin, and textual criticism) will test my claims in a rigorous way. To facilitate such testing, I have taken measures to make the complete set of relevant texts, including the best edition of the *testo minore*, available to specialists.[12] At the same time, I have sought to

---

11. Without belaboring the point, I think it is important to emphasize that a certain degree of apparent circularity is to be expected in any scholarly endeavor. We are all, always, working within what philosophers (e.g., Schleiermacher and Heidegger) have called hermeneutic circles, since we can only ever make judgments about particular parts in relation to a contextual whole, and we can only understand the whole in relation to particular parts; for a recent, succinct summary, see Mantzavinos, "Hermeneutics." Virtuous circles are therefore to be expected. To take one obvious example, one sees evidence that the earth revolves around the sun, which confirms the theory that the earth revolves around the sun. A robust testing of core assumptions combined with close evaluation of particulars would seem to be the only way to ensure that one is working within a productive hermeneutic circle rather than presenting a circular argument. This method is what I have sought to abide by, both in my own work and my evaluation of the work of others.

12. Although access to the manuscripts is ideal, my claims about the sequence of recensions can be tested through a comparison of the best available printed editions of the various versions. Those who wish to replicate my findings may compare the following editions in sequence: the *testo breve* (McNamer); *testo minore* (Sarri, as presented in Digital Georgetown); *testo maggiore* (Sorio); Latin MVC (Stallings-Taney; trans. Taney et al.); Paris, Bnf MS ital. 115 (trans. Ragusa and Green).

lay out the argument as fully as possible for nonspecialists—that is, for those who do not identify themselves chiefly as philologists or textual critics. The interrelated arguments I make here do not rely solely on technical knowledge of the language or manuscripts. They depend, in a fundamental way, on skills and sensibilities that most literary critics and historians of art, religion, and culture possess: sensitivity to nuance, agility with logical reasoning, the capacity to detect stylistic and thematic continuities and discontinuities, and a drive to test fixed assumptions in order to recover a more ample and accurate history of the past and its artifacts.

It is true, of course—as it is with any anonymous medieval text, which is to say, most of the literature that survives from the period—that absolute certainty concerning who wrote the MVC, in what form, and when and where, may forever be out of reach: such is the nature of medieval anonymity and of the fragmentary state of the archives. But I hope the discovery of the *testo breve* and its presentation here will not only contribute to our understanding of this important and engaging work, but serve to advance scholarship on aspects of Italian and European literary and cultural history more generally.[13] Before turning to the more technical arguments, then, I would like to gesture briefly towards six broad areas that I see as particularly promising.

1. *The history of early Italian literature.* Religious and devotional prose is typically separated out for independent treatment in the standard histories of early Italian literature, as if it were necessarily a distinct category, and perhaps not quite "literature"; in addition, the division between "major writers" (Dante, Petrarch, and Boccaccio) and "minor writers" of the Trecento has

---

13. I use the term "discovery" with some hesitation, knowing that some may perceive this as an overstated claim; the manuscript, after all, was not found in someone's attic, but has been safely preserved at the Bodleian Library, available to any scholar wishing to see it, for two centuries, and prior to that it was held in the Canonici and Soranzo collections. However, in addition to a paucity of alternative terms, there are precedents for using this one when a text long preserved in archives is newly identified or recognized as more intriguing, rare, or significant than the catalogues have suggested. Ewald Könsgen's identification of the Latin love letters held at the municipal library of Troyes is typically referred to as a "discovery" (Mews, *Lost Love Letters*; Newman, *Making Love*), as is Anders Winroth's identification of two distinct recensions of Gratian's *Decretum* from manuscripts held in multiple archives (Winroth, *The Making of Gratian's Decretum*). Jacques Dalarun has called his recent identification of the Celano text a "rediscovery," since it follows upon his earlier hypothetical reconstruction of what he called the Umbrian Legend from manuscripts in the Vatican Library (Dalarun, *La Vie retrouvée*).

had an enduring fixity.[14] There have been good reasons for these categories, yet they are ripe for reassessment, as recent scholarship on the energetic production of *volgarizzamenti* in the early Trecento, among other things, suggests.[15] Carlo Delcorno, for instance, has called for closer attention to the "arte della narrazione" in the writings of Domenico Cavalca and his *bottega*, observing that the Cavalcan corpus offers a fundamental resource for understanding the development of the genre of the *novella* in the early Trecento as well as a key site for exploring the stylistic affordances of Italian vis-à-vis Latin prose.[16] If the case presented here for the *testo breve*'s origins as a work composed directly in Italian in the early decades of the Trecento is deemed persuasive, how might this enrich current understandings of Italian literary history and the diverse narratives embedded within it?[17]

14. The *Storia della letteratura italiana*, vol. 2, *Il Trecento*, for instance, categorizes devotional prose as a separate domain in its chapter, "Letterature devota, edificante e morale" (Malato, *Storia*, 2:282–84). This practice is, of course, valuable in its own way, but it is worth asking whether other configurations are possible and desirable. Stephen Botterill opens his chapter on "Minor Writers" in the *Cambridge History of Italian Literature*, which divides the Trecento into four sections—Dante, Petrarch, Boccaccio, and Minor Writers—with an acknowledgment of the limitations of this division: "The glittering light of the *tre corone* has traditionally left the rest of the Trecento literature in its shadow. Few of the scholars who have pored so minutely over the voluminous texts of Dante, Petrarch and Boccaccio have spared more than a glance for the work of the canonical threesome's contemporaries. Minor the other writers of the Trecento may be in comparison with the three great Florentines—most writers are—but, for all that, their work offers a richly varied range of literary responses to a historical and cultural situation, that of the Italian peninsula between about 1300 and 1400, which is itself of unusual interest" (Botterill, "Minor Writers," 108). The Italian versions of the MVC do not make an appearance in Botterill's chapter, no doubt due to the traditional view, inherited by Botterill, that they are derivative *volgarizzamenti* rather than original works. At the very least, the argument I present here would seem to present possibilities for enlarging current understandings of "minor writers" of the Trecento.

15. On the reorienting of Italian literary history that closer attention to *volgarizzamenti* invites, see esp. Cornish, *Vernacular Translation in Dante's Italy*; Allaire and Psaki, *The Arthur of the Italians*; and the many articles and editions of religious prose by Carlo Delcorno, including "Cavalca, Domenico," "Diffusione del volgarizzamento," *Domenico Cavalca, Giordano da Pisa*, and "Predicazione volgare e volgarizzamenti."

16. Delcorno, "Cavalca, Domenico." Among other things, Delcorno observes that Cavalca's Italian versions often offer "the most inventive and delicate images" [*le immagini più delicate e fantasiose*].

17. On *diversità* and *varietà* as primary characteristics of Trecento literary history, often occluded in the writing of such histories, see Sapegno, *Storia letteraria del Trecento*, 1.

2. *Women writers in history*. The conclusion I advance here, that the original version of the MVC may have been composed by a woman, will likely be debated very actively, as it should be. Were it accepted or even judged to be plausible, that would have interesting implications. In the context of Italian literary history, it would locate a major woman writer in the heart of the rich artistic innovations of the early Trecento, between the landmark figures of Angela of Foligno and Catherine of Siena.[18] In medieval literary history more broadly, it would place an anonymous Poor Clare in the company of many other talented women writers of the Middle Ages, from Heloise and Hildegard to Marie de France to Julian of Norwich to Christine de Pizan. Perhaps the most fruitful avenue for investigation, however, might be renewed attention to the very question of anonymous authorship itself. What methods are at our disposal to determine whether or not an anonymous text was composed by a woman? How might anonymity have served to enable women's creative endeavors? Do current practices, in which the burden of proof lies so heavily with those who would argue for a woman's authorship, continue to make good sense, or is the default assumption of male authorship an outdated legacy? Does it make a difference to know whether a text was composed by a woman? If so, how does it alter our understanding of literary and cultural history?

3. *Franciscan history*. The MVC features prominently in histories of the "Franciscan revolution," the grand narrative that credits the Franciscans, more than any other group, with fostering affective meditation on the humanity of Christ and devotion to his Passion. My own work has drawn out some of the implications of the MVC's textual history in this context.[19] But this continues to be a promising line of inquiry. There are significant tensions between the *testo breve* and the Franciscan friar's revisions, tensions that may gesture towards more general differences between the Poor Clares and the Order of

18. On early Italian women writers, see Pozzi and Leonardi, *Scrittrici mistiche italiane*; Benson and Kirkham, *Strong Voices, Weak History*, especially the essay by Maggi, "The Place of Female Mysticism in the Italian Literary Canon," 199–215; and Matter and Coakley, *Creative Women in Medieval and Early Modern Italy*, esp. Gill, "Women and the Production of Religious Literature in the Vernacular," 64–104. Women writers usually categorized as "minor" figures of the late thirteenth and early fourteenth centuries include Umiltà of Faenza (1226–1310), Margaret of Cortona (1247–1297), Benevenuta Bojanni (1255–1292), Vanna of Orvieto (1264–1306), Clare of Montefalco (1268–1308), and Villana de' Botti (1332–1361).

19. McNamer, *Affective Meditation and the Invention of Medieval Compassion*, esp. chap. 3, "Franciscan Meditation Reconsidered," 86–115.

Friars Minor and a "counter-revolutionary" impulse within Franciscanism, particularly surrounding Christ's human vulnerability. This text and the possibility that a Poor Clare wrote it bears interest also to the study of the early Franciscan women's movement, which has proven to be a very rich vein for historical research in recent years.[20]

4. *Multiple authorship.* The MVC has been considered to be the work of a single author. This book suggests that was not the case. I argue that the longer versions of the MVC by the redactor, Author B, were built up from a core text composed by the original author, Author A. The MVC can thus be aligned with other influential medieval texts that have been identified as the work of multiple authors, ranging from cases that have long been known and closely studied, such as the *Roman de la Rose*, to Gratian's *Decretum*, which more recently has been recognized as the work of at least two authors—a discovery that, in turn, has raised compelling new questions about the early history of canon law.[21] In this volume, I have sought to initiate work on the systematic differences between the work of Author A and Author B, gesturing towards some of the more consequential textual sites and intriguing avenues for future comparative work.

5. *Intermediality in the early Trecento.* The relationship between the MVC and the art of the early Trecento has always been recognized to be very close, so much so that it was long assumed that the MVC directly influenced Giotto, Simone Martini, Pietro and Ambrogio Lorenzetti, and the artists responsible for the frescoes of Santa Maria Donna Regina in Naples, among others. Here, however, I make a case for greater subtlety and caution in such assessments, in part because the dates of composition for the various versions of MVC remains uncertain; indeed, what I will present here are dates *less* secure than those that have been advanced previously. This uncertainty itself has the potential to spur more incisive investigations into the relationship between this text and the artistic innovations of the Trecento—investigations that could and should become more expansive in scope.[22]

20. For books published since 2000 on women in early Franciscan history, see especially Alberzoni, *Clare of Assisi and the Poor Sisters*; Field, *Isabelle of France*; Field, Field, and Knox, *Visions of Sainthood in Medieval Rome*; Flora, *The Devout Belief of the Imagination*; Knox, *Creating Clare of Assisi*; Catherine Mooney, *Clare of Assisi and the Thirteenth-Century Church*; Mueller, *The Privilege of Poverty*; and Roest, *Order and Disorder.*
21. Winroth, *The Making of Gratian's Decretum.*
22. For a model of how such work might proceed, see Frugoni, *Francesco e l'invenzione delle stimmate.*

The new interest in intermediality across disciplines and historical periods could be brought to bear fruitfully on the MVC and its multiple affiliations with other media as well—drama and performance, sermons, liturgy, architecture, material culture, and social and devotional practices.

6. *The* Meditazioni *as work of narrative art.* Scholarship on the MVC has steered clear of close readings of the work as a literary text. In part, this has been a consequence of the channeling of attention to its importance in religious history in various cultural contexts.[23] But studies of its literary style have been inhibited also by the simple fact that what scholars have been faced with, prior to the publication of this volume, is a set of texts that has not always rewarded close reading from a literary perspective. While the tenderness, pathos, *candore*, or *freschezza* of much of the MVC is often highlighted, there has also been a recognition of the many dry, didactic passages as a stumbling block. In effect, I suggest, this edition of the *testo breve* restores the work to its original form and style, its *vivezza*, *dolcezza*, and *semplicità* unencumbered by accretions. Literary critics will, I think, find much to engage with here, from considerations of the work's generic inventiveness, to its mingling of temporalities through the use of the historical present, to its scripting of affective response through dialogues and exclamations, to its delicate handling of the language of gesture, to its invitations to the reader to enter into imagined drama, to its rendering of sacred narrative from a woman's point of view, to the gentle yet authoritative voice established through this work's distinctive first-person singular. The very artlessness of this narrative art, distinguished by its simplicity and lack of self-consciousness as it seeks to express and elicit feeling, is worth examining more closely and contextualizing more richly.[24]

Other issues will present themselves, no doubt, to those working in disparate fields, from Romance philology to vernacular theology to the history of emotion. My hope is that this book will not only stimulate further debate concerning the origins of the MVC, but rich and lasting *conversazioni* about a humble text long hidden from view.

---

23. Attention to the MVC's influence in England has been especially rich and full; see esp. Watson, "Censorship and Cultural Change in Late-Medieval England"; Johnson and Westphall, *The Pseudo-Bonaventuran Lives of Christ*; and Kelly and Perry, *Devotional Culture*. For a model of how a more literary approach might proceed, see Boulton, *Sacred Fictions of Medieval France*.

24. Auerbach's linking of a simple, unselfconscious Italian literary style and language of feeling to the Franciscan movement is worth revisiting in this context; see "Adam and Eve," in Auerbach, *Mimesis*, 143–73, esp. 172–73.

# TEXTUAL HISTORY

Textual history is not the most fashionable mode of scholarship in the humanities at present. As a form of philology, it can easily conjure up images of the kind James Turner has described in his recent history of the field as "the archetype of crabbed, dry-as-dust, barren, and by and large pointless academic knowledge":

> Philology has fallen on hard times in the English-speaking world. . . .
> Whenever philology shows its face these days in North America or the
> British Isles—not often, outside of classics departments or linguistic
> faculties—it comes coated with the dust of the library and totters along
> with arthritic creakiness. One would not be startled to see its gaunt torso
> clad in a frock coat.[1]

Reconstructing textual histories is a time-consuming activity, requiring patience on the part of those who study the minutiae of the manuscripts and seek to piece together their patterns of affiliation as well as those who seek to read the results, which are typically presented in prose riddled with symbols, abbreviations, tables, and the distinctive *stemmata* that have become the arcane emblem of the discipline ever since Karl Lachmann (1793–1851) developed his genealogical methods of textual criticism in the early nineteenth century.[2] Moreover, the traditional goal of textual history—that of seeking to identify distinct recensions, classify the manuscripts as better or worse witnesses, and reconstruct from these witnesses a text that is as close as possible to the original authorial version—has been seriously questioned. Many medieval works, after all, offer evidence of extensive revision by their authors;

1. Turner, *Philology*, ix.
2. For a useful summary of Lachmann's principles, as well as a history and description of the field, see Greetham, *Textual Scholarship*.

which version, then, is to be declared authorial? More fundamentally, what is an author? For the very concept of authorship, at least as that term is understood in the modern era, does not fit most medieval contexts, in which anonymity is by far the prevailing mode—one that enabled multiple authors and redactors and annotators to elaborate, extend, compress, or adapt a text to the particular needs of a particular reader or textual community.[3] Multiple states of a text are the rule, not the exception. Zumthor famously christened such textual fluidity and dynamism *mouvance*, calling for a fundamental reconsideration of the critical edition as a scholarly enterprise.[4] Cerquiglini, infusing pragmatic considerations with deconstructionist theory, has followed in his wake, arguing that the project of sifting through multiple manuscript versions and variants in order to establish authoritative texts or genealogies is inherently normative and thus ideologically suspect. As he puts it, such work relies on and props up a "bourgeois, paternalist, and hygienist discourse of the family."[5]

Many would argue, then, that it is more interesting and valuable to abandon the quest to identify textual origins, authors, and patterns of affiliation, and to devote attention instead to deep readings of particular manuscripts and the communities that produced and read them. And this would seem to be especially fitting where a devotional text like the MVC is concerned because, as a range of studies have reminded us, it is a feature of this genre to allow for adaptation.[6]

Yet capturing a fresh, more vivid sense of *mouvance* does not necessarily require abandoning the methods of traditional textual criticism, including the effort to locate origins; often, by identifying and describing distinct textual states and their place in a sequence more precisely, *mouvance* becomes newly visible and available to analysis. Nor is textual history inevitably the normative or paternalistic enterprise Cerquiglini assumes. What if, by engaging in close comparisons with a discriminating eye and attributing greater value to some witnesses over others, one finds a surprising story that has been buried—a story that calls into question, rather than perpetuates, a normative, paternalistic narrative of origins?

3. See Foucault, "What is an Author?"; Minnis, *Medieval Theory of Authorship*; McGann, *Critique of Modern Textual Criticism*.

4. Zumthor, *Towards a Medieval Poetics*.

5. Cerquiglini, *In Praise of the Variant*, 49.

6. On adaptations of lives of Christ and affective meditation in the German context, see Ruh, *Bonaventura deutsch*; for England, see Kelly and Perry, *Devotional Culture*; for France, Boulton, *Sacred Fictions of Medieval France*.

This is what we find, I suggest, by seeking to trace the origins of the MVC. Let's turn, then, to the details, engaging in a kind of "textual archaeology" with that fellow in the frock coat as a valuable guide.[7] The technical tools of traditional philology, however—textual criticism, linguistic analysis, paleographical analysis—are not the only tools that are fitting here. For the MVC is not simply a "text." It is a work of meditative literature, one whose prose style is intimately related to its content and its aims: it would not be the text it is without its distinctive mode of engaging with the reader, its colorful inventions of dramatic moments not found in the gospels, its use of the historical present, its invitations to feel and imagine and embellish, its deployment of a woman's point of view, its narrative energy, its lyricism, its lucidity, its pathos. For this reason, the reconstruction of its history cannot afford to set stylistic aspects of the texts aside, as if they are epiphenomena or merely decorative features of the work.[8] In addition to philology, then, we would do well to imagine a complementary guide, one who cares about style: in short, a connoisseur. For although connoisseurship, like philology, has fallen on hard times, some of its core methods and aims can be recuperated to valuable effect, particularly when the kind of detective work at issue requires identifying precise stylistic distinctions and patterns of aesthetic difference, as is the case here.[9]

Since the discussion that follows will focus closely on particular details, it will be useful to provide two illustrations at the outset. Table 1 illustrates

7. I take the term "textual archaeologies" from Dominique Poirel. As he puts it in his eloquent defense of excavating textual histories, this form of intellectual work can, among other things, illuminate the complex and mediated forms of women's writing: "The task of the philologist can never be separated from that of the historian, as is seen in the case of texts as thoroughly enigmatic as the *Liber Angelae* of Angela of Foligno. . . . A historian who prefers to tread water at the surface of these texts rather than dive into their flowing and shape-shifting depths would be deprived of whole currents of information regarding some of the most persistent questions that historians pose" ("The Death of Angela of Foligno," 287–88).

8. In calling attention to stylistic analysis as an integral part of textual criticism and the reconstruction of the MVC's history, my approach differs from that of Tóth and Falvay, who do not engage in any serious way with questions of stylistic differences among the versions or consider the implications this may have for attribution, textual integrity, or a sequence of composition ("New Light"; "L'Autore"). See McNamer, "The Debate on the Origins of the *Meditationes Vitae Christi*."

9. For a classic statement of the value of making such fine discriminations, often first noticed through "intuition," see Ginzburg, "Morelli, Freud, and Sherlock Holmes."

Table 1. Traditional Hypothesis for the Textual History of the MVC Prior to Discovery of the *testo breve*

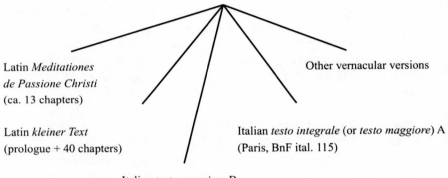

Latin MVC (or *der große Text*)
(composed by a single author, often said to be Johannes de Caulibus)
(prologue + ca. 108 chapters)

Latin *Meditationes
de Passione Christi*
(ca. 13 chapters)

Other vernacular versions

Latin *kleiner Text*
(prologue + 40 chapters)

Italian *testo integrale* (or *testo maggiore*) A
(Paris, BnF ital. 115)

Italian *testo maggiore* B
(prologue + ca. 94 chapters)

Italian *testo minore*
(prologue + ca. 41 chapters)

Table 2. Revised Hypothesis for the Textual History of the MVC

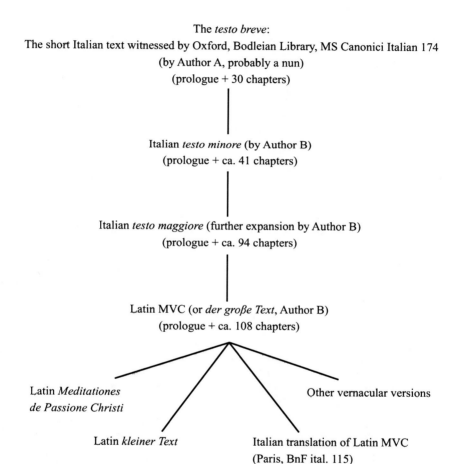

The *testo breve*:
The short Italian text witnessed by Oxford, Bodleian Library, MS Canonici Italian 174
(by Author A, probably a nun)
(prologue + 30 chapters)

Italian *testo minore* (by Author B)
(prologue + ca. 41 chapters)

Italian *testo maggiore* (further expansion by Author B)
(prologue + ca. 94 chapters)

Latin MVC (or *der große Text*, Author B)
(prologue + ca. 108 chapters)

Latin *Meditationes*
*de Passione Christi*

Other vernacular versions

Latin *kleiner Text*

Italian translation of Latin MVC
(Paris, BnF ital. 115)

the traditional hypothesis regarding the relationship of the various recensions of the MVC.[10] Table 2 illustrates my revised hypothesis.

There are several ways one could begin to set forth the reasons for questioning the traditional paradigm and make the case for this revised textual history as the more viable working hypothesis for the origins and early transmission of the MVC. But it seems to me that it is simplest to begin by questioning a basic assumption: is the long Latin text the product of a single author, consistent in design, purpose, and stylistic texture? The traditional hypothesis of the MVC's origins relies on an affirmative answer to this question. But that tacit, affirmative answer has never been demonstrated through a close analysis of the Latin text itself. Indeed, as we shall see below, the simple fact that the long Latin text is the longest of the extant versions has been taken as an indication of its authority and priority. Since it is longest, the reasoning goes, it must be the "most complete" version: therefore, the shorter versions, including those in the vernaculars, must be extracts and adaptations.[11] One of the fundamental principles of textual criticism, however, has been overlooked entirely in textual scholarship on the MVC: *lectio*

10. I use the phrase "traditional hypothesis" here with the caveats mentioned in the Introduction. This hypothesis is briefly summarized in the introduction to the critical edition of the Latin text, Stallings-Taney, ed., *Iohannes de Caulibus: Meditaciones vite Christi*; subsequent references to the Latin text refer to this edition. The most comprehensive list and description of the manuscripts remains that of Fischer, "Die *Meditationes vitae Christi*"; the terms *der grosse Text* and *kleiner Text* were Fischer's. Fischer's work has been supplemented and corrected by Vaccari, "Le 'Meditazioni della vita de Christo' in volgare"; Petrocchi, "Sulla composizione," from whom the terms *testo maggiore* and *testo minore* derive; Gasca Queirazza, "Intorno ad alcuni codici"; Stallings, *Meditaciones de passione Christi*; and McNamer, "The Origins of the *Meditationes Vitae Christi*," which forms the basis for the discussion of the MVC's Textual History that I advance here. Tóth and Falvay have called attention to several additional Italian manuscripts that had not been listed or described in the published articles on the MVC: Florence, Biblioteca Nazionale Centrale MS N.A. 350; Siena, Biblioteca Comunale degli Intronati MS I.V.7; Siena, Biblioteca Comunale degli Intronati MS I.V.9; Siena, Biblioteca Comunale degli Intronati MS I.VIII.6; Siena, Biblioteca Comunale degli Intronati MS I.VIII.24. Certain Italian manuscripts have now been dated with greater precision than the initial dates given them by Fischer, Vaccari, and Gasca Queirazza. See below, "Date and Place of Composition," cxxvii–cxxx, for the most current assessments of the earliest Italian and Latin manuscripts by Bertelli, Flora, Gramigni, De Robertis, Gura, Webber, and McNamer.
11. See below, l–li, for the articulation and transmission of this idea from Petrocchi, "Sulla composizione," to Vaccari, "Le 'Meditazioni della vita de Christo' in volgare," to Stallings-Taney, *Iohannes Caulibus: Meditaciones vite Christi* and "Pseudo-Bonaventure."

*brevior praeferenda.* As Johann Griesbach articulated this principle, "the shorter reading . . . is to be preferred over the more verbose. For scribes were much more prone to add than to omit. They hardly ever leave out anything on purpose, but they added much."[12] Griesbach's principle has generated significant controversy and refinement over the past several centuries, especially in the context of New Testament textual criticism; moreover, in a technical sense, the *lectio brevior* refers to individual textual variants rather than shorter and longer recensions of a work.[13] Yet where medieval devotional prose is concerned, the principle and the insight it reflects have served as important tools. To be sure, we have many clear examples in which longer works were shortened to serve the needs of a particular community. Yet there is also ample evidence of the reverse.[14] The important point here is that the longer text cannot be assumed to be better simply because it is longer ("more complete"); the *lectio brevior* may indeed be the earlier version. Nor can we simply assume that the Latin MVC was composed first simply because it is Latin: the choice of language, too, was often governed by particular audiences and their presumed or expressed needs, and translation into Latin from Italian was not unknown in Trecento textual culture.[15] Several early scholars of the MVC recognized this: Columban Fischer, in his foundational study published in 1932, observed that the manuscripts of the Italian versions are earlier than the Latin manuscripts; he thus raised the possibility that the original may have been Italian, but could not square this with what seemed a fixed fact in his day, the notion that part of the work was composed by Bonaventure himself, who wrote exclusively in Latin. Alberto Vaccari revived the question in 1952, presenting philological arguments and leaning towards the likelihood of a Latin original, but without ruling out the possibility that the work was first composed in Italian.[16]

12. Cited in Kloppenborg and Newman, *Editing the Bible*, 140. Griesbach's principles of textual editing were formulated in the context of his work on the New Testament; they appear in Griesbach, *Novum Testamentum Graece*.

13. Kloppenborg and Newman, *Editing the Bible*, provides the most recent and comprehensive overview of these debates.

14. For evidence of adaptation and interpolation in two texts comparable to the MVC, the *Legenda Aurea* and the *Specchio della vera penitenza*, see Maggioni, *Legenda aurea*, and Auzzas, "Dalla predica al trattato."

15. See, for example, G. Rossi, "La 'redazione latina' dello *Specchio della vera penitenza*."

16. Fischer, "Die *Meditationes vitae Christi*"; Vaccari, "Le 'Meditazioni della vita de Cristo' in volgare." I engage with these and other arguments for an Italian original below, lvii–lxv.

The story that follows, then, will begin by establishing grounds for doubt: doubt, that is, that the long Latin text currently circulating as the original version of the MVC is the first iteration of the work. We will then move on to the evidence that the work may have been composed in Italian; that it contained only the Infancy and Passion sections; and that of the only two viable textual candidates, the *testo breve* and the *testo minore*, the *testo breve* appears more likely to have come first in the sequence. It alone lacks the interpolations evident in every other version—interpolations that can be identified as such in part because they are accompanied by a vocabulary of interpolation.

## SIGNS OF INTERPOLATION IN THE LATIN MVC

The practice of interpolation was, of course, very common in the later Middle Ages.[17] It was conducted with special regularity where works of religious instruction or devotion were concerned; it was facilitated by anonymity as a fundamental condition and concept of authorship; and it was accompanied by a related activity, that of glossing religious texts to give them more ample or accurate alignments with scriptural or exegetical tradition or church doctrine.[18] There was no need to apologize for the practice. The substantial cast of redactors populating this epoch seldom considered their efforts worth mentioning, nor did they typically seek to cover their tracks. Indeed, even the mise-en-page of many manuscripts during this period, which often left ample margins precisely to facilitate commentary on religious or edifying texts, reflects the strong expectation that texts could and should be glossed;

---

17. The term "interpolation" can have several meanings, as Tarrant observes in a classic essay on the subject: "In textual critics' parlance 'interpolation' has two meanings: in its broad sense, which corresponds to the classical meaning of *interpolare*, it denotes any conscious alteration in the wording of a text (including, for example, replacement of an obscure or difficult word by a simpler synonym); in its narrower use, it denotes one kind of such alteration, the insertion of unoriginal matter into the body of a text" (Tarrant, "Toward a Typology of Interpolation," 281). Like Tarrant, I am concerned only with the second of these definitions. The matter of interpolation in medieval devotional prose is in many ways more complex, and I know of no textual-critical study that takes up the matter in a general way; the site for discussion of the phenomenon has typically been the introductions to critical editions of specific texts.

18. The *Glossa Ordinaria* itself serves as a particularly interesting example of the phenomenon of glossing; see Smith, *The Glossa Ordinaria*.

and such glosses could and did find their way from the margins into the body of the text. In the resulting patchwork texts, abrupt shifts of tone, content, and voice are often allowed to stand. "Improvements" to devotional texts, as well as copious expansions, could be made freely in such a context, and in good conscience—at least by learned men in positions of spiritual authority.

It is worth recalling these historical conditions of literary production, for they show how important it is to ask a simple question: are there signs of interpolation in the Latin MVC? There are. Here I will touch briefly on three kinds of evidence while dwelling at greater length on a fourth. The first three are the following: a recurrent vocabulary of interpolation embedded in the text; lengthy quotations from sermons and treatises, especially those of Bernard of Clairvaux, often included at the ends of chapters; and awkward seams between parts of the text. The fourth kind of evidence, the artistic inferiority of the chapters on the Public Ministry, is the most cumbersome and, in itself, the least rewarding to assess. But only an extended look at the stylistic flatness of the Public Ministry chapters can expose their character as additions by a writer with stronger didactic impulses and lesser literary talent than the original author.[19]

## A Vocabulary of Interpolation

Terms that appear to refer to a process of interpolation are scattered throughout the text:

De exposicionibus raro *me intromittere* cogitaui: tum quia ad hoc insufficiens sum, tum eciam quia nimis esset longa materia. (9:41)[20]

---

19. In an early study, Elizabeth Salter observed that the Infancy and Passion sections have an "impressive dramatic and descriptive quality" that the long section on the Public Ministry lack (Salter, *Nicholas Love's "Myrrour,"* 43). Salter did not, however, explore the possibility that the section on the Public Ministry was added by a different author; her focus was on the Middle English translation by Nicholas Love.

20. References to the Latin text are to chapter and page in Stallings-Taney, *Iohannes de Caulibus: Meditaciones vite Christi* (hereafter Stallings-Taney); references to the English text are to chapter and page in Taney, Miller, and Stallings-Taney, *Meditations on the Life of Christ* (hereafter Taney et al.). When the precise wording of the Latin is not at issue, I have cited only from the English text. However, the chapter numbers of the two texts are aligned, and this should faciliate the easy locating of the relevant Latin parallels.

-------

[Concerning the treatises, I have decided *to interject myself* only rarely, on the one hand because I am inadequate for this, on the other because the material would become too long. (9:34)]

Quamuis ad tuam instruccionem talia prout michi occurrunt *interseram,* et eciam moralia et auctoritates sanctorum. (21:101)

-------

[However, for your instruction *I shall intersperse* commentaries, moral teachings, and quotations of the saints as they occur to me. (21:88)]

. . . ideo cogitaui hic ista duo *opponere.* (67:231)

-------

[I have decided *to insert* two events here. (67:218)]

Moralitates autem et auctoritates quas ad tuam erudicionem *in hoc opere posui* non expedit ad meditacionem adduci nisi si qua uirtus amplectenda uel uicium destestandum ipsa prima facie cogitacionis occurrat. (108:350)

-------

[However, it is unnecessary to bring into your meditation the moral points and references *I have interpolated in this work* for your instruction, unless such should occur to you of itself as an immediate means of acquiring some virtue or detesting some vice. (108:332)]

Perhaps the most telling example of this language of interpolation is the following:

Audisti igitur uerba pulcherrima altissimi contemplantis et oracione dulcedinem degustantis. Rumines ea si uis ut sapiant tibi. Ideo autem *libenter ipsius uerba in hoc opusculo intersero et adduco*, quia non solum spiritualia sunt et cor penetrancia, sed et decore plena et ad Dei seruicium exortancia. (36:139)

-------

[You have heard the exceedingly beautiful words of Bernard, a very great contemplative, as he savors the sweetness of prayer. Ruminate on them if you want to taste their sweetness. It is for that reason that I like *to introduce and voluntarily intersperse his words liberally throughout this little work* . . . because they are not only spiritual, and pierce the

heart, but are also full of beauty and of urgings to the service of God. (36:124)][21]

This passage is especially significant because it casts many of the copious quotations from Bernard of Clairvaux in the Latin MVC as "words inserted in this little book." The language here does not definitively prove that a second author is alluding to a process of composition in which he added Bernardine passages to a little book originally written by someone else. It is certainly possible for a writer to insert quotations into a text he or she has already composed or is in the process of composing *ab initio*. But it is also possible that this passage is a frank statement by a redactor about the activities proper to a redactor. Here, then—as elsewhere—we have two plausible hypotheses. What further evidence might we assess as a means of judging between them?

### Quotations from Bernard of Clairvaux and Other Authorities

Even if they were not introduced with what appear to be statements that they are interpolations, the copious quotations from Bernard would invite skeptical scrutiny as passages added at a secondary stage in the composition of the text. Many of these function as didactic digressions from the narrative, typically addressed more to the head than to the heart. Most are not from the emotionally rich *Sermons on the Song of Songs*; they are drawn from Bernard's works more generally, including treatises, letters, and sermons that have little or no affective content and are strongly didactic.[22] Stylistically, the copious quota-

---

21. The ellipsis points in the English passage signify my own deletion of two misleading words in the translation published in Taney et al.: "of mine." There is no textual basis for their addition of these words; the Latin phrase is simply, "this little work" [hoc opusculo] not "this little work *of mine*" (36:124). The correct translation makes a substantive difference in our understanding of the character of the Latin MVC and its place in the sequence of revisions and adaptations.

22. The conclusion of chapter 8, on the Circumcision, offers a typical example: after the narrative section ends, the author draws on Bernard's *In Circumcisione Domini*, his *Dominica Ia post octauam Epiphaniae*, and his *De consideratione ad Eugenium Papam* to construct a lesson on "spiritual circumcision," including the "circumcision of the tongue": "Therefore, we ought to circumcise our tongue, that is, to speak sparingly, and to say only what is useful" (Taney et al., 31). A complete list of the sources used by the author of the Latin MVC, including twenty-seven of Bernard's sermons or sermon collections, is provided in Stallings-Taney, xix–xxi.

tions from Bernard lack the signature techniques of the meditations: the visual painting of a scene from the life of Christ or the Virgin; the frequent use of the present tense; the privileging of domestic detail and realism; the invitations to the reader to enter the scene in order to experience the emotions of intimate love, compassion, and grief. Nor do the Bernardine passages invite the reader to use the text interactively. Instead, they require that she adopt a passive pose, listening, from a subordinate position, to the words of a renowned preacher who is repeatedly designated as a higher spiritual authority. The imaginative stance that is clearly authorized and encouraged by the MVC's vividly dramatized meditations is, from one perspective, compromised by these numerous passages from Bernard, which tell the reader how and what to think. Moreover, the placement of the passages from Bernard, typically at the ends of chapters, is compatible with the hypothesis that they were inserted after the affective meditations had been completed—and by a different author, one with a strong impulse to gloss the text, finding it, as we might say in modern parlance, "undertheorized."

In the long history of scholarship on the MVC, many scholars have observed, in passing, that the quotations from Bernard and other learned authorities are a stylistic problem in need of explanation. Émile Mâle, observing that "there is more scholasticism here than we might have wished," assumed that these and other didactic passages were added later; Livario Oliger described the tract on the active and contemplative lives—a lengthy stretch of thirteen chapters (46–58) consisting almost entirely of quotations from Bernard—as "un peggioramento, una stonatura" [a worsening, a false note] in artistic terms.[23] Stallings-Taney, too, recognized the importance of the question: "Why would anyone add those passages to disrupt an otherwise lively, human, appealing narrative?"[24] The answer given by Stallings-Taney—that the author wished to instruct his reader, even at the cost of disrupting the affective or meditative momentum or diluting the appeal of the narrative—has been the answer repeatedly offered in support of the conclusion that the Bernardine passages belonged to the original version of the MVC. It is worth pointing out, however, that this is pure

---

23. "Nous y trouvons encore, assurément, plus de scolastique que nous n'en voudrions: n'oublions pas toutefois que les plus longues dissertations ascétique ont été ajoutées après coup, au xive et au xve siècle" (Mâle, *L'art religieux de la fin du moyen âge en France*, 28); Oliger, "Le *Meditationes vitae Christi*," 146.

24. Stallings-Taney, "Pseudo-Bonaventure," 259.

assumption.[25] The other possibility—that the passages were added later— has not been seriously investigated.

### Awkward Seams Joining Disparate Sections of Text

There are some very visible and awkward seams between what might be called the core affective meditations and these heavily didactic and more learned passages.[26] I will mention just two such seams here. The first occurs at the end of the Prologue: "Inicium igitur ab incarnacione sumendum est; sed quedam ipsam precessisse meditari possumus" (Prologue:10) [Let us begin, therefore, with the Incarnation; but we can insert certain meditations preceding the Incarnation (Prologue:4)].[27] As narrative—in a text generally

25. This assumption has been based, moreover, largely on a form of circular reasoning in which Stallings-Taney's designation of the Bernardine passages as "authentic" (included, that is, by the original author of the MVC, not a redactor) both derives from and is used to support claims that the Latin MVC was composed first and that the manuscripts containing the better readings of Bernard are "early." For a more detailed critique of this assumption and other principles informing the Corpus Christianorum critical edition of the Latin MVC, see McNamer, Review of *Iohannes de Caulibus: Meditaciones Vite Christi.* Stallings-Taney describes the Bernardine references as "a collective *lectio difficilior*"—without considering the alternatives, that they could be accretions added by a redactor or passages corrected by a copyist with access to better copies of the works of Bernard. Tóth and Falvay have more recently made an argument similar to Stallings-Taney's, without engaging with the possibility that a redactor may have had access to better copies of Bernard; see their "L'Autore," and, for a response to the argument there, McNamer, "The Debate on the Origins of the *Meditationes Vitae Christi.*"

26. By "core" affective meditations, I mean the dramatic passages, rich in affective detail, that are repeatedly singled out as exemplifying the style of the MVC by modern scholars (e.g., Joseph's doubts about Mary, the Visitation, the Circumcision, the return from Egypt, the encounter between Jesus and Mary on the road to Calvary, Christ's appearance to his mother after the Resurrection). The singling out of such passages has medieval precedent; these and similar scenes were the most influential sections of the MVC. They form the basis for many of the English mystery plays, for example, especially those of the N-Town cycle; and they are the sections that tend to be preserved in subsequent translations and adaptations, as for instance in Nicholas Love's *Mirror*, which omits many of the quotes from Bernard and compresses much of the Public Ministry section.

27. The translation of "precessisse" (from *praecedo*, to go before or precede) as "we can insert" is that of Taney et al. I have retained this translation because the

praised, and justly so, for its skillful narration—this is less than elegant. It suggests a reversal, a change of course in which one textual beginning is displaced by another. The fact that the episodes appearing just after this transition differ significantly in style from other passages in the Infancy section underscores the possibility that these were added later. Chapter 2, on the debate of the four daughters of God, is allegory, a stylistic mode foreign to the rest of the MVC, and it is taken almost entirely from Bernard's first sermon on the Annunciation.[28] Chapter 3, on the Virgin's youth in the temple, is composed almost entirely of a lengthy quotation from the *Revelations of St. Elizabeth of Hungary*, followed by a selection from St. Jerome.[29]

Even more deserving of scrutiny is the problematic transition in chapter 18, just prior to the chapters on the Public Ministry. From the point of view of textual criticism, this statement of intent merits especially close attention— for in my view, this awkward transition, more than any other single passage, invites skepticism that the Latin text is the original recension of the work. What we have here is a stark contradiction between what the text states it will do and what it actually delivers. The reader is explicitly told that it would "take too long" to include detailed meditations on the Public Ministry. She is given general directions for how to meditate on this material—and appears to be invited to do so on her own time, as it were, because, this statement of intent tells us, it is more important for this text to treat the events of the Passion:

> Hucusque per Dei graciam uitam Domini Iesu ordinate tetigimus, parum uel quasi nichil de his que sibi contigerunt uel per ipsum facta sunt omittentes. *Sed non sic deinceps facere intendo. Nimis enim esset longum omnia que dixit et fecit in meditaciones redigere,* maxime quia nostre sollicitudinis debet esse facta Christi continue more beate Cecilie portare in secreto pectoris. Igitur aliqua ex gestis eius colligimus, in quibus meditando uersemur assidue, et usque ad passionem; et ex tunc enim

---

term "insert" has narrative warrant: the preceding sentence has indicated that we will start with the Incarnation, but a different intention is then announced; several episodes are placed before the Incarnation. *Precessisse* and the narrative double-take it registers is thus not as clearly an example of a "vocabulary" of interpolation (though it makes good sense in this context as "to place before, insert") as a sign of interpolation in action, in my view; this is why I categorize it as one among several awkward seams.

28. Stallings-Taney, 12–14; Taney et al., 6–8.
29. Stallings-Taney, 9–12; Taney et al., 15–18.

nichil est omittendum. Alia eciam non debemus ex toto omittere quin pro loco et tempore meditemur in eis. *Meditaciones autem non intendo deinceps prolixe tractare, nisi per raro.* Sufficit enim quod rem per eum gestam uel dictam ante mentis oculos ponas, et quod cum eo conuerseris et familiaris ei fias. Nam in hoc uidetur haberi maior dulcedo et deuocio efficacior, et quasi totus fructus harum meditacionum consistere: ut ubique et semper intuearis eum deuote in aliquo actu suo, ut quando stat cum discipulis, quando cum peccatoribus, quando loquitur eis, quando predicat turbe, quando uadit, et quando sedet; quando dormit, et quando uigilat, quando comedit, et quando aliis ministrat, quando sanat egrotos, et quando alia miracula facit. In his autem et similibus considera omnes actus et gestus suos, maxime contemplans faciem si potes eam imaginari, quod super omnia predicta michi uidetur difficilius sed credo quia reficeret iocundius. Illud eciam attende: obserua si forte ipse te cum benignitate respiciat. Et hec tibi sint pro recursu et doctrina omnium que sequuntur; ut ubicumque factum narrauero si aliter non expressero singulares meditaciones uel istas omisero, recurras ad hunc locum et sufficit tibi. Ad narracionem igitur sequencium accedamus. (18:92–93)

---

[So far, by the grace of God, we have treated the life of the Lord Jesus in orderly fashion, omitting little or nothing of what happened to him or what he did. *But I no longer plan to do this from here on, since it would take too long to convert everything he said and did into meditations.* Our special concern ought to be to carry the deeds of Christ continually in the secret recesses of our heart, as was customary with blessed Cecilia. Therefore, we have chosen just some of his deeds for careful meditation; that will be our procedure as far as the Passion, for from then on nothing is to be omitted. Even the other events we must not totally omit, but meditate on them at the appropriate time and place. From now on, however, *I do not intend to treat of the meditations at any great length,* except on rare occasions. It is enough that you place before your mind's eye anything done or said by him, and that you converse with him and become a friend to him. For it seems that you will have greater sweetness and more productive devotion, and it is in this that the whole fruit of these meditations consists: that everywhere and always you contemplate him devoutly in his every activity, as when he is in company with his disciples and then with sinners, when he is speaking to them, when he is preaching to the crowds, when he is walking and when he is sitting; when he is sleeping and when he is awake, when he is eating and when

he is ministering to others; when he is curing the sick and when he is performing other miracles. In these and in similar things, consider his every action and all his deeds, especially contemplating his face, if you can picture it, something that seems more difficult to me than everything already mentioned, but something that I believe would be more joyfully refreshing. Follow that advice carefully too: see if he may gaze on you with his loving kindness. Let these pointers be a learning resource for you on everything that follows; so that wherever I have related an episode, if I have not brought out the patterns of meditations besides, or have left them out, then you can come back to this place and it will suffice for you. Let us get on, therefore, with the narration of the events that follow. (18:80–81; emphasis added)]

What follows this expression of concern about prolixity and commitment to *abbreviatio* is, in fact, a very imposing stretch of text: the next fifty-one chapters—nearly half of the 108-chapter text—treat the Public Ministry. The inclusion of that tract of twelve chapters on the active and contemplative lives (chapters 46–58) in this central section further underscores the discrepancy between what appears to be promised at the end of chapter 18 and what the Latin text proceeds to deliver.

There are versions of the MVC in which this statement of intention functions as a genuine transition and makes perfect sense. These are the short Italian versions—those containing only the Infancy and Passion: the *testo breve* edited in this volume and the *testo minore*. Neither of these texts treats the Public Ministry at all. In these, a transition very similar to that given above provides a graceful and effective bridge to the chapters treating the Passion. In the *testo breve*, the transitional passage, at the end of chapter 13, reads as follows:

Hora perfina a qui, per la gratia de Dio, noi habiamo detto per ordine della vita de miser Iesù Cristo, quasi nulla lassando de quelle cose che gli sono intravenute et che per lui furono facte et decte perfina a questo tempo. Ma io non intendo de fare così da qui inançi, però che el seria tropo longa materia a volere redire per meditatione tuto quello che lui fece overo disse da hora inançi. Ma noi dovemo essere solliciti de quello exempio de sancta Cecilia de portare sempre le opere del nostro dolce spoxo miser Iesù negli chuori nostri. Unde quando tu aldi dire de miser Iesù alcuna opera per lui decta o facta, o in el vangelio overo in predicatione o per altri modi, fà che tu le meti denançi gli ochi della mente tua et

ripensale, però che el me pare che in questi cotal pensieri di facti de miser Iesù Cristo sia maçore dolçeça et devotione che in altri modi. Et tuto il fondamento del spirito [f. 53v] me pare che stia in çiò: che sempre in ogni luocho riguardi lui cum li ochi della mente tua, cum devotione in alcuna sua operatione. Hora come lui e cum li discipoli, hora come va cum gli peccatori, overo quando siede o dorme o vegia, o quando serve altrui o che sana li infermi o quando el resuscita li morti, et che elgi fa altri miracoli someglianti a questi. Adonca considera tuti li soi acti et costumi, et specialmente contemplando la sua faça, se la pòi contemplare—la qualle cosa mi pare malagievole sopra tute le altre cose, ma credo che questo te saria la maçore consolatione che tu potesti bonamente havere. Et stà attento, se lui vegnisse inverso di te, a riceverlo benignamente.

Et questo ti pò bastare de pensare delli acti suoi perfina al çorno che lui començò a congregare li discipoli. Hora da qui inançi parlaremo della Passione. Et començeremo dalla Domenega del Olivo.

———

[Now up to this point, by the grace of God, we have spoken in order about the life of Lord Jesus Christ, leaving out almost nothing about the things that happened to him and that he said and did up to now. But I do not intend to continue like this from now on, because it would take too long to try to retell in the form of meditations all that he did or said from this moment on. But we should always strive to follow the example of Saint Cecilia and carry always the words and deeds of our sweet spouse Lord Jesus in our hearts. So when you hear about any of the deeds and words of Lord Jesus, whether this is through the Gospels or through preaching or in another way, be sure to put them before your mind's eye and reflect on them, because it seems to me that in this way of meditating on the deeds of Lord Jesus Christ there will be greater sweetness and devotion than by other means. And the whole foundation for spiritual growth seems to me to come down to this: that always and everywhere you watch him with the eyes of your mind with devotion in everything that he does. Now how he is with his disciples, now when he walks with sinners, or when he sits or sleeps or wakes, or when he serves others, or when he heals the sick, or when he raises the dead and performs other miracles like this. Then consider all his deeds and manners. And contemplate his face with special care, if you are able to contemplate it, for this seems to me more difficult than anything else; but I believe that this will be for you the greatest experience of solace that you might have. And prepare yourself to receive him kindly, if he should come to you.

And this is enough for you to contemplate concerning his life until the time when he began to call his disciples. Now from here on we will speak about the Passion. And we will begin with Palm Sunday.]

The *testo breve* then proceeds directly—and, given this transition, *logically*—to the events of the Passion. The passage is virtually the same in the *testo minore*, where it also functions logically and gracefully as a hinge between the Infancy and Passion, given that there is no Public Ministry section in that text either (Sarri, 88–89).[30]

The awkwardness of this passage in the context of the long Latin text has been noted by critics who have sought to sort out the relationship between the various versions of the MVC. A certain assumption, however, has operated powerfully in relation to the assessment of this passage, preventing textual scholars from taking it seriously as a relic from an earlier state of the text and a sign that the Public Ministry chapters may have been inserted at a later stage. This is the assumption that a series of meditations on the life of Christ that lacks coverage of the Public Ministry is by its very nature defective because "incomplete." Petrocchi, for instance, asserts that since the miracles of Christ are in themselves "importantissimi," and since the transfiguration and casting of the merchants from the temple are, in his view, essential elements in any text calling itself a life of Christ ("momenti insopprimibili in una vita di Cristo"), he rejects the possibility that the short Italian texts might represent the original form of the MVC.[31] This is puzzling logic, however, for the simple reason that events from the Public Ministry rarely serve as the focus of affective devotion in the fourteenth century. Devotional

30. There is no critical edition of the *testo minore*. My citations from the *testo minore* throughout this volume are thus from the best available edition, that by Francesco Sarri; see Sarri, *"Le meditazioni della vita di Cristo."* As I explain in my note to the digitized version of Sarri's text, Sarri produced a composite version of the *testo minore* and material from the *testo maggiore*; despite this eccentricity, Sarri's edition of chapters from the *testo minore* is more reliable than other editions of the *testo minore* published in the nineteenth-century because Sarri compared his base text, Biblioteca Riccardiana 1419, with four other manuscripts (Biblioteca Riccardiana MSS 1286, 1348, 1358, 1404) and notes some of the variants from these witnesses.

31. Petrocchi, "Sulla composizione," 759. Vaccari's decision to call the long Italian text the *testo integrale* or *testo intero* is based on a similar assumption—taken as a given in no need of critical assessment—that the earliest manuscripts of the MVC must have contained the complete life of Christ (Vaccari, "Le 'Meditazioni della vita de Cristo' in volgare").

literature, drama, art, and practices center nearly exclusively on the Infancy and Passion in the high and later Middle Ages, in Italy and elsewhere.[32] The Infancy/Passion diptych is the norm. To impose a standard of completeness is, in short, to make ahistorical assumptions about the life of Christ as genre. At this time and in this place, a decision not to treat the Public Ministry in order to focus solely on the Infancy and Passion is a very logical choice.

This would suggest that it is best to seek the original text among the short Italian versions, the *testo breve* and the *testo minore*, which contain only the Infancy and Passion.[33] But since the long Latin text has for so long been assumed to be the original text, and the work of a single author, it is important to confront the Public Ministry chapters squarely and adduce stylistic evidence that the entire fifty-one-chapter section on the Public Ministry is likely to be an interpolation by someone other than the original author of the MVC.

### Discrepancies in Stylistic Texture and Implicit Aim in the Public Ministry Chapters

Stylistically, the chapters on the Public Ministry differ considerably from the chapters on the Infancy and the Passion, and in dramatic and affective terms, they are inferior to them. The fact that these chapters are routinely ignored by modern scholars—and appear to have generated little interest or influence in the Middle Ages—is one indication of their relative dullness, their lack of vivacity. Elizabeth Salter has singled out the sections on the Infancy and Passion for their "impressive dramatic and descriptive quality"; Canice Mooney points out that "the nativity, infancy, and passion are minutely pen-pictured,"

---

32. Giotto's cycle of frescoes on the life of Christ in the Arena Chapel (ca. 1305), for instance, contains just two scenes from the Public Ministry, the wedding at Cana and the raising of Lazarus; Pacino di Bonaguida's *Tree of Life* (ca. 1310), based on Bonaventure's *Lignum Vitae*, is typical of historiated crucifixes in depicting a narrative of the life of Christ that gives very short shrift to the Public Ministry. Early religious drama in Italy concentrates on the Infancy and Passion, as do devotional lyrics and the liturgy; see, for example, D'Ancona, *Origini del teatro italiano*, and De Bartholomaeis, *Laude drammatiche e rappresentazioni sacre*.

33. By "Infancy," I mean the events of the early life of Christ, including his adolescence, up to the chapter that treats the Baptism (which casts Christ as one who needs his mother's permission to undertake a long journey) and the Temptation in the desert; by "Passion," I mean the events from the Passion through the Ascension. In this, I follow common usage in discussions of the MVC.

while the chapters on the Public Ministry are not; Luigi Cellucci observes that the long middle section is "less interesting," and states that "less value has justly been attributed to this part."[34]

Neither the scriptural material itself nor the repeated claim that it would take too long to draw out this material, shaping it into affective meditations, can fully explain this difference in artistic texture. Rather, a shift in priorities appears to be evident here, and this shift is accompanied by other shifts: in point of view, voice, tone, purpose. Instruction, in short, is the primary goal in the chapters on the Public Ministry. Scenes from the Gospels are here treated as opportunities for learning, rather than feeling. The author of these chapters is quite willing to quote at great length from the works of Bernard, for instance, or to explicate the moral significance of Christ's words and deeds. But attempts to generate feelings of intimate attachment to Christ, or even to elicit any kind of affective response, are very rare, even when the Gospel narratives themselves contain ample potential for affective elaboration (as is the case, for instance, with the many episodes in the gospels of healing and forgiveness). Little effort is made in these chapters to facilitate the vivid imagining of a scene; indeed, there is a marked impatience with narrative itself. Scenes of intimate human drama from the Gospels are abbreviated or even eliminated so that the writer can get to what is now treated as the more important use of his, and his reader's, time: attending to the didactic or exegetical significance of the scriptural events.

Chapter 37, on the Canaanite woman, exemplifies this impatience with narrative, the flattening out of the drama of the gospels themselves, and the author's privileging of meaning over feeling in the chapters on the Public Ministry. The chapter begins as follows:

Cum Dominus Iesus laborans circuiret predicando et infirmos curando, accessit ad eum mulier Chananea, id est de terra Chanaan, que erat gentilium et non Iudeorum, rogans eum ut liberaret filiam que a demonio uexabatur. Erat enim confidens in eo quod hoc facere posset. Et Domino non respondente, nichilominus instabat et perseuerabat clamans et petens ab eo misericordiam: intantum ut et discipuli pro ea rogarent. Cumque Dominus responderet non debere dari panem filiorum canibus, ipsa se humilians respondit ut saltem sine more canis posset de micis habere, et sic meruit exaudiri. (37:146)

---

34. Salter, *Nicholas Love's "Myrrour,"* 43; Canice Mooney, *Smaointe Beatha Chríost*, 326; Cellucci, "Le *Meditationes vitae Christi*," 41.

[When the Lord Jesus was going about doing his work of preaching and healing the sick, a woman approached him, a Canaanite from the non-Jewish, gentile land of Canaan. She asked him to free her daughter of her demonic possession, and she was confident he had the power to do this. The Lord did not respond; nevertheless she stood her ground and kept on crying and beseeching him for mercy; so much so that even the disciples took up her request. When the Lord answered that it was not right to give the children's bread to dogs, in all humility she rejoined that he at least allow for the custom that a dog could have the falling crumbs; and thus she merited being given a favorable hearing. (37:131)]

This rendition is far less dramatic than the Gospel passage on which it is based, which contains direct dialogue and ends on an intimate and affecting note: "Then Jesus answered her, 'O woman, great is your faith! Be it done for you as you desire.' And her daughter was healed instantly" (Mt 15:28). In the MVC chapter, the author has chosen not only to substitute indirect for direct dialogue, but to omit any mention of the moving conclusion to the story: that the daughter was healed. Instead, there is a brief, general statement that "the woman was commended on that faith by the Lord himself" (37:131). The emotional drama inherent in the story is completely ignored. But this is not because it would "take too long" to develop its affective potential. Length is manifestly not the issue, for what follows this bare summary of the Gospel is a very lengthy sermon on the importance of persistence in prayer, which leads into a sermon on the angels, in which Bernard is quoted copiously. This section is seven times as long as the initial gospel summary. The whole chapter concludes, "And so you have in this passage a commendation of the angels' obedience and help, and also the power of grateful prayer. Try to be faithful to this advice and revere them in every way you can" (37:133). Dispensing advice and drawing out moral lessons are the top priorities for the author of the chapters on the Public Ministry.

In keeping with this decided shift in priorities, there is a shift in voice. The voice in these chapters is the hortatory voice of the preacher, replete with imperatives. The tone of gentle invitation that guides the reader through so much of the Infancy and Passion is virtually absent here. A close look at other rhetorical techniques in the section on the Public Ministry reveals further differences. There is a paucity of the techniques through which the *Meditations* elsewhere elicits emotion: deictic rhetoric, exclamations, the use of the present tense, parataxis, direct dialogue, and the regular deployment of a woman's point of view.

The shift away from a woman's point of view is particularly telling and, in my view, difficult to explain as anything other than evidence that a redactor, rather than the original author, has composed these chapters. In the Infancy and Passion sections, the text regularly places women and the details of women's lives at the center of the drama, even when there is no scriptural basis for this. Thus, the journey to Bethlehem is a matter for compassion not only because it is difficult for a heavily pregnant woman to travel but also because of the cultural convention that there is some embarrassment (an embarrassment that the reader is assumed to understand) at being seen in such a state in public (chap. 7); the Visitation becomes an occasion for Elizabeth and Mary to sit together in an intimate domestic space, and to ask each other how their pregnancies are going (chap. 7); Mary is placed at the Circumcision so her maternal feelings for her child might model such feelings in the reader (chap. 8); Mary's sisters and other relatives and friends hear of her return from Egypt and immediately rush to visit (chap. 13). The Virgin and Mary Magdalene appear in many scenes from the Passion for which there is no scriptural basis. The risen Christ even appears to his mother first; and what the mother wants to know is not how the miracle of the Resurrection happened, but whether her son is now whole and sound and free from pain (chap. 82). Indeed the adoption of a woman's point of view is often hailed as one of the primary narrative achievements of the *Meditations* as a whole. But in the chapters on the Public Ministry, this technique is dropped, apart from a few half-hearted gestures in its direction.

Its absence is most noticeable where the Gospel stories themselves center on women. In chapter 68, for instance, which treats the "Woman Caught in Adultery," the author displays no interest in how the woman might feel, or how this story might serve as a model for affective intimacy between the reader and a Christ who will take compassion and forgive; attention is directed, instead, towards the mysterious words Christ was writing on the ground. Chapter 27, "A Girl Restored to Life and Martha Cured," further exemplifies this obtuseness to a woman's perspective. The chapter treats the story of the woman with a hemorrhage, a distinctly female malady designated as such in the Gospels (as in Mt 9:18–19). Here the detail that the malady is a hemorrhage is omitted; the woman is merely described as being "seriously ill" (*grauiter infirma*, 27:109). Instead of amplifying the affective potential of this scene, the author seizes upon the detail of the "hem of the garment" as an opportunity for a discourse on humility: "Anyone serving God perfectly can be called a hem, as it were, the last part of the Lord's garment, by reason of his humble self-estimate," and so on (27:99). The same chapter concludes with the most perfunctory mention of the story of the rais-

ing of Jairus's daughter: "Finally the Lord Jesus went to the home of that leader, and finding his daughter dead, restored her to life" (27:98). The intimate, moving drama of the Gospel story, in which Jesus, surrounded by those who mock him, takes the hand of the dead girl and gently bids her to arise, is crisply reduced and emptied of emotional content.

Many additional examples could be supplied, but the diminishing of the affective power latent in the story of Martha and Mary is particularly striking. The Gospel itself is dramatic, making use as it does of direct dialogue: "But Martha was distracted with much serving; and she went to him and said, 'Lord, do you not care that my sister has left me to serve alone? Tell her then to help me.' But the Lord answered her, 'Martha, Martha, you are anxious and troubled about many things; one thing is needful. Mary has chosen the good portion, which shall not be taken away from her.'" (Lk 10:40–42). The intimacy and complexity of Christ's repetition of Martha's name, and his recognition of her emotional state, are unimportant to the author of this section of the *Meditations*. The story is presented in a way that flattens out the dialogue, the drama, the affect, the opportunity for entering into the scene: "Martha was annoyed at this and requested the Lord to have her help with the serving. But what she received in response was a contrary opinion, and she heard instead that Mary had chosen the better part" (45:156). Instead, this author treats the story as a convenient peg on which to hang that thirteen-chapter tract on the active and contemplative lives (chaps. 46–58). At the end of the tract, even the author admits that it was long, and a trial to get through—but worth it for its instructional, not affective, utility: "Whew! Thank God we are finally free of the tract on contemplation. It is a subject that is rich and very useful. Through it you will be able to become well-instructed" (58:204).

In short, the signature style of the MVC—those aspects of voice, tone, dramatic detail, and narrative technique that have made this text seem the quintessential work of affective meditation—disappears almost entirely in the Public Ministry section. This, then, is a key instance in which stylistic texture can serve as an important clue to textual history. Given the unrelieved didacticism and stylistic flatness of this section, there is reason to doubt that it was composed by the author who composed the dramatic, moving passages in the Infancy and Passion.[35] Indeed, I would risk putting the matter more assertively:

35. My argument here could be further tested by those with expertise in the stylometric analysis of Latin prose and digital tools for such analysis. These tools have been brought to bear on questions of attribution in other contexts, such as the letters attributed to Abelard and Heloise (see Newman, *Making Love*, xii–xiii, and the work by Jan Ziolkowski, Francesco Stella, and others referred to therein). As I

in the absence of any argument offering a reasonable or more viable explanation for the manifest differences in style and aim in the Public Ministry chapters, I would maintain that this section (more than half of the long Latin text)
can be ruled out as part of the original MVC.[36] Yet there are no other Latin
versions of the MVC that might have been written prior to the long Latin version. Although the *Meditaciones de Passione Christi*, or MPC, was once
thought to have been written prior to the MVC, Stallings has conclusively
proven that the MPC is an extract from the MVC.[37] My own work has demonstrated that the other short Latin version, the forty-one-chapter *kleiner Text*, is
also an extract from the long Latin text.[38]

The possibility that the MVC was originally composed in Italian, then,
requires renewed consideration. This hypothesis was advanced by Adamo
Rossi in 1856 and more assertively by Columban Fischer in 1932, who
pointed out that most of the earliest manuscripts are of the Italian versions.
The brief refutation by Luigi Cellucci in 1938, however, has been surpris-
ingly influential, muting subsequent debate, even after the publication of
Vaccari's more serious study in 1952.[39] It is time to reopen the question, and
to present the evidence that the original text was indeed written in Italian.

---

indicate below, the Latin MVC appears to be a translation and expansion of the Italian *testo maggiore*, so further stylometric analysis would, in turn, need to be conducted on that text. I recognize the challenges involved. Vernacular texts from the
medieval period are often far more difficult to assess than Latin because of variabil-
ity in spelling, dialect, and copying practices. Still, it could be that a stylometric
analysis of the *testo maggiore*, comparing the Public Ministry chapters to the Infancy and Passion (and, further, comparing these to the *testo breve*), might serve to
test my claim that two authors were involved in the composition of the MVC.

36. Tóth and Falvay, who have recently asserted the view that the Latin is the
original text ("New Light" and "L'Autore") do not offer an account for the differences in style and aim in the Public Ministry section; indeed, they do not even acknowledge this aspect of my argument as it was first articulated in "The Origins of
*Meditationes vitae Christi*." In my view, any efforts to reassert the traditional view
that the Latin text was composed first must at least engage with the problem presented by the Public Ministry section. See McNamer, "The Debate on the Origins of
the *Meditationes Vitae Christi*."

37. Stallings, Introduction, *Meditaciones de passione Christi*.

38. McNamer, "Further Evidence," 251–58. Gasca Quierazza, in "Intorno ad
alcuni codici," has identified additional Latin manuscripts similar to the *kleiner Text*
as defined by Fischer; these, too, are clearly extracts.

39. A. Rossi, *Edizione principe*, 8; Fischer, "Die *Meditationes vitae Christi*,"
468–70, and esp. 482; Cellucci, "Le *Meditationes vitae Christi*," 34–35; Vaccari,
"Le 'Meditazioni della vita de Cristo' in volgare."

## THE ORIGINAL LANGUAGE OF THE MVC

There has never been a thorough study of the original language of the MVC. The question of whether the Italian or Latin versions came first has been treated chiefly in passing—often in a single page or paragraph—in various studies and editions published since the nineteenth century. Despite the extreme paucity of linguistic analysis, however, the belief that the text was composed in Latin has had remarkable endurance. No conclusive linguistic, textual, or paleographical evidence has been offered to support this conclusion; the primacy of the Latin has simply been asserted and reasserted.[40]

The foundations for the assumption that the work was composed in Latin are in fact very fragile. In the earliest scholarship on the MVC, it was assumed that the text was written in Latin because it was assumed (erroneously) that the work was written by Bonaventure, who composed exclusively in Latin. But there are stylistic grounds for doubting this. Time and again, the Italian *testo minore*, which exists in many more manuscript copies than any of the Italian versions and was assumed to be an early *volgarizzamento*, has been singled out for its beauty.[41] The Italian is manifestly more dramatic than the Latin. Direct discourse is much more abundant here—a feature that accounts for the greater liveliness of the work. Colorful colloquialisms contribute to this *vivezza*. In the Latin text, for instance, the adolescent Jesus, who has not demonstrated any miraculous or even admirable traits, due to his humility, is mocked by the people as a "useless" idiot: "Iste est quidam inutilis. Ipse est idiota" (15:65). In the short Italian texts, he is not merely "useless," but *pane perduto*: "Questo è dritamente uno pane perduto

---

40. In the introduction to the Corpus Christianorum edition now used as the standard edition of the MVC, for instance, Stallings-Taney states that the edition is of the "original Latin" (ix). Similarly, in their introduction to the English translation, Taney et al. state that "the original language of the MVC is Latin" (xv). Tóth and Falvay ("New Light" and "L'Autore") have more recently offered some textual (not linguistic) arguments in favor of a Latin original, in response to my work ("The Origins of the *Meditationes Vitae Christi*"). I engage with their argument in "The Debate on the Origins of the *Meditationes Vitae Chrsiti*" and more briefly below, lxxxvi–xc.

41. This judgment, based on Tuscan copies of the *testo minore*, has been made on linguistic grounds: in the nineteenth century, the Accademia della Crusca chose it as one of its linguistic texts; and one edition's subtitle declares it to be on a par with the best Italian prose from the "buon secolo della lingua" (Donadelli, *Meditazioni*). To be clear, these assessments of the beauty of the short Italian texts were not based on the *testo breve*, which survives only in an impure linguistic form, Tuscan with Venetian overlay; see below, "Linguistic Analysis."

e uno idiota . . ." (*testo breve*, f. 40v, Sarri, 70). Squaring the superior liveliness of the Italian with the fact that texts usually lose, rather than gain, in
translation, has required significant ingenuity. The explanation Cellucci pro-
poses is not entirely unreasonable. He posits that the original author was
thinking in Italian, even while he was writing in Latin. Thus, "when the *Meditationes* were translated, they perfected themselves, assuming an exterior
garment more in keeping with the way in which they were conceived, and a
more spontaneous and lively diction."[42] But while this argument has some
merit, it is, after all, only conjecture.[43] Why not consider the possibility that
the *Meditations* wore their colorful and lively Italian garb from the very start?
On paleographical grounds, this would seem the more reasonable default theory. Most of the earliest manuscripts—those dating from the fourteenth century, rather than the fifteenth—are copies of the Italian versions, rather than
Latin; and of the eight manuscripts that have been dated to the first half of the
fourteenth century, six are Italian, two Latin (see "Date," cxxvii).[44] On historical grounds, too, it would seem more reasonable to begin with the hypothesis
that the MVC was composed directly in Italian, not Latin: its original readership, after all, was one of Poor Clares, for whom Italian would have been the

42. Cellucci, "Le *Meditationes vitae Christi*," 61.

43. This is not to say, however, that *volgarizzamenti* can never be livelier than
the texts on which the translations are based; see Cornish, *Vernacular Translation in
Dante's Italy*. The Italian *Fioretti di San Francesco*, for example, composed ca.
1370, is widely recognized as a more vivid and engaging story collection than the
Latin original on which it is based, the *Actus beati Francisci et sociorum eius*, composed ca. 1330. Carlo Delcorno's work on the *volgarizzamenti* produced by
Domenico Cavalca and his *bottega* has also demonstrated that translations into Italian from Latin could be more lively and colorful than their originals, incorporating
colloquialisms, dialogue, and anecdotes (see Delcorno, "Cavalca, Domenico," and
*Domenico Cavalca, Vite dei santi padri*). This body of writings, which Delcorno
helpfully calls "Cavalcan," since many of them appear to be conflations of Cavalca's
own translations with those of anonymous assistants and imitators, merits close
study in relation to the early Italian iterations of the MVC—not least because of the
probable Pisan context of textual production and early circulation.

44. See below, "Date and Place of Composition," cxxvii–cxxx. See also Fischer's lists of the Latin and Italian manuscripts, "Die *Meditationes vitae Christi*,"
13–35, 175–87. While the supplementary studies of the manuscripts mentioned
above (xxxviiin10) have corrected and refined some of the manuscript dates Fischer
supplies, Fischer's general observation remains true: the Latin manuscripts as a
group are later than those of the Italian. Manuscripts of the Italian *testo minore* are
far more numerous than those of the *testo maggiore*.

more natural choice for a devotional text in the early Trecento.[45] In addition, an important phrase embedded in the Prologue speaks of the "unlettered," reassuring this category of readers that those who lack Latin can nevertheless gain spiritual wisdom by meditating affectively on the life of Christ: "And in this way many who are unlettered and simple have gained knowledge of the lofty and profound things of God."[46] This phrase appears to legitimize, in a very lucid way, the composition of affective meditations on the life of Christ in the vernacular for those who do not read Latin.

## Alleged "Corruptions" in the Italian Texts

It has been asserted that the Italian versions contain "corruptions"; this, more than anything else, has prevented the theory of an Italian original from gaining traction. The character of these so-called corruptions are of two kinds.[47] First, there are Latinate linguistic forms and phrases in the Italian texts. Second, several scholars have noted what appears to be "garbled" language in the Italian text of Bibliothèque Nationale de France MS ital. 115, the sole surviving medieval copy of what Vaccari has called the "A" version of the long Italian text.[48] These two kinds of evidence have been conflated in the scholarship, but they are actually two forms of evidence that can and ought to be analyzed independently, for they gesture towards two disparate conclusions.

To take up the matter of the Latinate constructions first: Cellucci devotes only a few paragraphs to an assessment of these constructions, in an article

45. The most extensive recent treatment of the literary practices of the Poor Clares is that by Roest, *Order and Disorder*; see esp. "Forms of Literary and Artistic Expression," 283–346.

46. The phrase in the *testo breve* reads, "Et per questo molti sono stadi sança letere et simplici et hano habuto cognoscimento delle alte et profunde cose de Dio" [And in this way many who are simple and unlettered have gained knowledge of the lofty and profound things of God] (f. 3r). The existence of the phrase in the Latin text (Taney et al., Prologue, 3), can, in my view, be best explained as a relic of an earlier, vernacular state of the text; see below, 201n8, for further comment.

47. A third instance of alleged "corruption," one that Tóth and Falvay claim to have noticed in the Canonici manuscript, is not corruption at all; it reflects their erroneous reading of a particular passage in the manuscript. See McNamer "The Debate on the Origins of the *Meditationes Vitae Christi*."

48. Vaccari, "Le 'Meditazioni della vita de Cristo' in volgare," 356–62. As Vaccari notes, the only other copy of the text witnessed by BnF MS ital. 115 is a nineteenth-century copy transcribed directly from ital. 115: Rome, Biblioteca Apostolica Vaticana MS Ferraioli 423.

dedicated primarily to other aspects of the MVC. Cellucci begins with an emphatic statement of belief: "For me, it is beyond doubt that the work was first written entirely in Latin: an Italianized Latin, to be sure, as one often finds in other writers of the time coming from the Franciscan Order."[49] He then notes the presence of what appear to be Latinate constructions in the Italian. One category of these is the occasional use of the subjunctive (*potesse, dicesse*) where the grammar would lead us to expect the indicative (*poteva, diceva*); this would seem to suggest that the phrase derives from a Latin subjunctive imperfect form following an initial *cum* (*cum . . . posset/diceret. . .*).[50] Two other phrases Cellucci highlights are *fece grazie a Dio* and *grazie ti faccio, Dio Padre*, which he describes as "Latinisms deriving from *agere gratias*"; he also asserts that the phrase *non saria stato morto* is a "bad translation of the Latin *non fuisset mortuus*."[51] Cellucci states that each of these examples can only be explained as failures to fully translate a Latin original and even asserts that some examples—examples that he does not cite here, noting only that "many other examples could be cited"—are only comprehensible with reference to a Latin original.[52]

Cellucci's remarks have been cited uncritically in subsequent scholarship.[53] Cellucci's analysis, however, was flawed. He did not take account of the earlier work on the MVC's language by Bartolommeo Sorio, who had argued that such constructions were a legitimate feature of literary Italian in the fourteenth century. In his 1847 edition of the *testo maggiore*, Sorio notes that while the presence of such forms may seem a "strange caprice of the language" to modern readers, it was "not so strange to medieval writers."[54] Sorio

49. Cellucci, "*Le Meditationes vitae Christi*," 34.

50. "Essendo abattuta la umana generazione . . . e nullo . . . *potesse* salire alla patria sua"; "Quando lo Signore predicava nel tempio e *dicesse* intra l'altre cose" (Cellucci, "Le *Meditationes vitae Christi*," 34).

51. Cellucci, "Le *Meditationes vitae Christi*," 34n12.

52. Cellucci, "Le *Meditationes vitae Christi*," 34.

53. Cellucci's remarks are relied upon especially heavily by Stallings-Taney. In the Corpus Christianorum edition of the Latin text, Stallings-Taney does not present new evidence or independent analysis of the Italian texts and their relation to the Latin; instead, she refers the reader to a separate article in which she promises "a treatment of the evidence that the MVC was translated into Italian from Latin, by a writer who often did not understand the Latin" (Stallings-Taney, ed., *Iohannes de Caulibus: Meditaciones vite Christi*, "Introduction," xiin13). But the article in question treats the matter summarily—in a single page that defers to Cellucci as the authority on the subject (Stallings-Taney, "Pseudo-Bonaventure," 263).

54. Sorio, *Cento meditazioni*, 27.

had noticed the use of subjunctive forms (*potesse, dicesse, si disponesse*) where the grammar would lead us to expect the indicative. But Sorio demonstrated that these constructions cannot simply be accounted for as quirks generated by the act of translating Latin into Italian, for they appear in writings originally composed in Italian. He adduces as evidence passages from Catherine of Siena and, significantly, from Boccaccio, who uses verbal forms in the *Decameron* in ways that appear to derive from Latin (e.g., the use of the forms *andassero* and *si disponesse* in phrases that seem to presuppose a Latin subjunctive grammatical construction) but were clearly not translated from a Latin text: Boccaccio was manifestly composing directly in Italian.[55] Sorio notes that constructions such as these in early Italian literature were often assumed to be faulty or suspect readings, in need of editorial correction and emendation. Sorio, however, chose to retain these readings in his edition of the Italian MVC, on the grounds that this feature of fourteenth-century Italian texts is "ben sano ed intero, ed è un bello arnese di nostra lingua" [entirely sound, and a beautiful feature of our language].[56]

More recently, additional evidence supporting Sorio's assessment has become more widely available in the form of the compilation of the Corpus Opera del Vocabolario Italiano (OVI) database and the searches enabled by it. As Pär Larson, senior researcher at the OVI Institute, has observed, one of the ostensibly problematic phrases highlighted by Cellucci, *fare grazie a qualcuno*, is in fact well documented in Old Italian in the thirteenth and fourteenth centuries.[57] Cellucci's claim that the phrase could only be explained in

55. Sorio, *Cento meditazioni*, 27–28. Sorio was not seeking to evaluate whether the Italian MVC was composed first or the Latin; rather, his aim is to evaluate the question of whether these Latinate phrases in the Italian are "corruptions" or, instead, sound features of fourteenth-century Italian that ought to be retained by editors rather than emended.

56. Sorio, *Cento meditazioni*, 28–29.

57. As Larson has pointed out to me (email correspondence, Jan. 13, 2017), the Corpus TLIO presents these examples containing the *fare grazie a qualcuno* construction: Fiore, XIII u.q. (fior.) 1) 195, v. 3 - pag. 392, riga 4, Bellacoglienza la parola prese / E sì rispuose, come ben parlante: / «Gentil madonna, i' vi fo grazie mante / Che di vostr'arte mi siete cortese; Detto d'Amore, XIII u.q. (fior.) 2) , v. 34 - pag. 487, riga 11, o d'oro, / Perch'i' a llui m'adoro / Come leal amante. / A llu' fo graz[z]e, amante / Quella che d'ogne bene / È sì guernita bene / Che 'n le' non truov'; Legg. S. Torpè, XIII/XIV (pis.) 3) cap. 4 - pag. 58, riga 33, paraule dell' angiulo, si levò e fece oratione a dDio e disse: «Io ti foe grasie, Signore Domenedio, che m' ài consolato mandando a mei l' angiulo tuo il quale m'; 4) cap. 9 - pag. 63, riga 11, letto, e ispaventata fece orasione a Dio co molte lagrime e disse: «Io ti foe grasie, Singnore mio, e pregoti che tu debie ampiere lo mio disiderio». E l' altro die;

the Italian MVC as a direct translation from Latin *agere gratias* thus cannot be sustained. The phrase *non saria stato morto*, which Cellucci considered a "bad translation of the Latin *non fuisset mortuus*," also has an alternative explanation, for early vernacular Bibles use this formulation.[58]

To summarize, then, the use of Latinate constructions in the Italian text are not necessarily the "corruptions" that Cellucci took them to be—peculiarities that could only be explained as faulty translations from a Latin text; and the specific phrases Cellucci saw as absolute barriers to positing an Italian original (*fare grazie a qualcuno, non saria stato morto*) are in fact attested in other Italian texts from the period. Indeed, it would be more surpris-

---

5) cap. 20 - pag. 69, riga 8, ella avea fatto, e acordonsi l' uno co· ll' altro, e con grande allegressa fero grasie a Dio e al beato messer santo Torpè. E la molglie rendette pienamente lo voto; Andrea Cappellano volg. (ed. Ruffini), XIV in. (fior.), 6) L. I, cap. 15 - pag. 75, riga 22, pensar di me e del buon volere ch'ài di me servire, sì tti faccio grazie come debbo, ed io altressì penserò di te e tuoi servigi receverò quando sarà tempo; 7) L. I, cap. 15 - pag. 99, riga 4, e colui amerò, saputa e isaminata prima la veritate». Responde l'uomo: «I' ò fatte grazie al potente re dell'Amore, ch'à degnato di revocare vostro proponimento d'errore. Ma; Simintendi, a. 1333 (prat.), 8) L. 2 - vol. 1, pag. 59, riga 17, sopra esso, e rallegrasi di toccare con le mani le date redine; e quindi fa grazie al non voluntaroso padre. Come Feton non seppe menare il carro. Intanto i veloci cavalli; Simintendi, a. 1333 (tosc.); 9) L. 6 - vol. 2, pag. 45, riga 4, madre con questo uccello. Tutti quelli di Trazia si rallegrano di questo matrimonio; e fecero grazie alli dei: e comandaro, che 'l dì nel quale la figliuola di Pandion fu data; Ottimo, Par., a. 1334 (fior.); 10) c. 2 - pag. 40, riga 7; sono manifeste. 46. *Io risposi ec.* Questa è la terza parte, dove l'Autore fa grazie a Dio che l'ha remoto dal mondo, e trae per lo Cielo, e mostra; Niccolò da Poggibonsi, p. 1345 (tosc.); 11) cap. 264 - vol. 2, pag. 237, riga 11, tenemo verso Frigoli; e così penosamente giugnemo a Vinegia. Quando noi la vedemo, sì facemo grazie a Dio, dicendo: *Te Deum laudamus*, con molte lagrime sempre, imperò che di molti pericoli (information available via http://tlio.ovi.cnr.it/TLIO/).

58.  Once again I thank Pär Larson for sharing his expertise on this point (email correspondence, Jan. 11, 2017): "it is true that 'stato morto' in Old Italian usually means 'killed' rather than 'died,' but the construction might stem from a vernacular translation of the Bible and not necessarily from a Latin model; cfr.: Vangelo Giovanni volg., XIV pm. (tosc.), 1) 11 - pag. 51, riga 10, Andò Marta et disse a Ihesù: «Signore, se tu fosse istato qui, il fratel mio non sarebbe istato morto. Ma ora so che tucte quelle cose le quali tu domandarai a Dio, Dio le darà a te»; Bibbia (06), XIV–XV (tosc.), 2) Is 48 - vol. 6, pag. 566, riga 10, [19] E lo tuo seme e la tua generazione sarebbe istata come la rena, e la schiatta del tuo ventre come le pietre piccole e pietre preziose del mare; e lo suo nome non sarebbe stato morto, e non sarebbe stato fracassato nella mia faccia" (information available via http://tlio.ovi.cnr.it/TLIO/).

ing to find no Latinate constructions in a work of vernacular devotional literature from this period. Even in the most cautious assessment, then, one must
conclude that the Latinate constructions in the Italian versions do not rule out
the possibility that the work was first composed in Italian.

The second type of apparent corruption—the "garbled" language in the
A version of the *testo maggiore* (BnF MS ital. 115)—is different in kind. As
Ragusa and Green observe, the A text offers evidence of what appears to be
an inability of the translator or scribe to understand certain Latin passages,
particularly the more complex phrases from Bernard of Clairvaux.[59] However, I believe that this corruption leads to a different conclusion than that
reached by earlier critics. A faulty assumption has governed the reasoning
here: that is, that the manifest evidence of corruption in the A version, corruption which stands as strong evidence that A was translated from the Latin,
implies that the B version was also translated from the Latin. In fact, this
does not follow. It is not a logical deduction because A and B are independent
texts. They do not rely on each other at all. As Vaccari puts it, text A "reflects
the Latin like a mirror"; B does not.[60] While it was Vaccari who established,
conclusively, the independence of these two versions, he did not register the
full implications of his own analysis. What Vaccari's analysis opens up, in
short, is the possibility that while text A is indeed a translation from the
Latin, text B may not be.

Paradoxically, Vaccari does not consider the possibility of B's primacy
because it is, artistically, the better text, "more beautiful and refined" than
both A and the Latin text:

> B is artistically the more beautiful and refined, but it is not faithful; A is
> rough, but very faithful. Literary scholars, who admire the beauty of the
> language, have given their preference to B; but the critic who studies the
> origins and mutual relations of the texts will recognize instantly that A is
> closer to the genuine root of the MVC.[61]

The language here, of course, is reminiscent of the kind of language often
deployed in textual criticism of the nineteenth and early twentieth centuries,
in which certain textual readings are cast as tempting seductresses whose
beauties ought to be resisted. This metaphorical subtext may help to explain

59. Ragusa and Green, *Meditations*, xxvi.
60. Vaccari, "Le 'Meditazioni della vita de Cristo' in volgare," 360.
61. Vaccari, "Le 'Meditazioni della vita de Cristo' in volgare," 360.

Vaccari's conclusion. Considering, for a moment, the possibility that the original may have been written in Italian, Vaccari privileges the principle of fidelity: "If an original Italian text lies behind the Latin version of the MVC," he writes, "this cannot be other than text A."[62] But this is not the only possible way to solve the puzzle. Vaccari assumed, in short, that it would not be possible for a lively, beautiful vernacular text to lose in translation: to become flatter and duller when translated into Latin, in part through the substitution of indirect for direct discourse, in part through the addition of further interpolations from Latin sources by a translator-redactor. But texts of all kinds regularly lose beauty and vivacity in translation.

## A Rationale for Translating from Italian into Latin

Finally, there is the question of the rationality of labor, or presumed lack thereof, where practices of translation are concerned. It has been assumed that the Latin cannot have been a translation from the Italian because a motive for undertaking such labor has been hard to imagine. As Stallings-Taney has put it, "one would have to ask . . . why anyone would undertake the labor and fatigue of translating the very lengthy MVC into Latin if Italian had been the original language."[63]

But the wide diffusion of the MVC itself provides one very obvious and logical answer to this question. Someone undertook the labor of translating the work into Latin in part to "authorize" it, but even more practically, so that it could be disseminated more broadly throughout Europe and translated into other vernaculars. Such dissemination and translation would not have been possible without this intermediary step. Latin was a supremely practical medium for the dissemination of religious texts. Indeed, as Barbara Newman has observed, the "role of Latin as an intermediary between vernaculars" is

---

62. Vaccari, "Le 'Meditazioni della vita de Cristo' in volgare," 361. On the basis of several passages that he claimed were unique to Paris, BnF MS ital. 115, Isa Ragusa asserted that this was the earliest version of the MVC ("L'Autore delle *Meditationes vitae Christi*"). Ragusa's very brief article (six pages), however, does not bring rigorous comparative assessment of the manuscripts or of the various versions of the MVC to the question. Moreover, Ragusa's assertion rests on a fundamental error. As a team of Hungarian scholars has recently shown through detailed collations, Ragusa's claim that there are unique passages in this version (passages Ragusa deems authorial) is factually incorrect: "The argument for the absolute precedence of the Paris MS proposed by Isa Ragusa is simply wrong" (Ertl et al., "The Italian Variants," 8).

63. Stallings-Taney, "Pseudo-Bonaventure," 264.

one of the many complex—and insufficiently recognized—functions Latin served in the later Middle Ages as the vernaculars came into their own as literary languages.[64] Mystical and devotional texts by and for women (including works by Marguerite of Porete, Beatrice of Nazareth, Angela of Foligno, Bridget of Sweden, Mechthild of Magdeburg, and Henry Suso) often originated in the vernacular, and some were "so prized that clerics translated them into Latin, as in Marguerite's case—thus facilitating a multi-ethnic readership, along with the prestige and the implied (if sometimes misleading) seal of orthodoxy conferred by the learned tongue."[65] The progress of Henry Suso's *Little Book of Eternal Wisdom* is perhaps especially relevant to the case of the MVC. Suso composed this work in German for nuns and beguines, then adapted and translated it into Latin as the *Horologium Sapientiae* for a broader clerical audience; the *Horologium* was, in turn, adapted and translated into French, Dutch, Italian, English, Bohemian, Hungarian, Polish, Swedish, and Danish.[66] Even in the local Tuscan context, there are documented cases in which translations were made from Italian to Latin in the fourteenth century, during the same period when the MVC was composed, translated, and disseminated: Bartolomeo da San Concordio (1260–1347) and Jacopo Passavanti (1297–1357) first composed sermons in Italian and circulated them in the vernacular, then translated them into Latin for the clergy.[67] Historical circumstances were such, then, that a process of composing a text in the vernacular and translating it into Latin at a later stage, for broad diffusion, could make very good sense.

## THE PRIORITY OF THE *TESTO BREVE*

Once the seemingly fixed barrier of the priority of the Latin is removed, the Italian versions can once again be assessed for the possibility that they

64. Newman, "Latin and the Vernaculars," 233.

65. Newman, "Latin and the Vernaculars," 231.

66. Newman, "Latin and the Vernaculars," 232–33. On the complexities of language choice in this period, particularly with regard to religious writing by and for women, see also Poor, *Mechthild of Magdeburg and Her Book*.

67. Passavanti is particularly forthcoming about his process, describing how he decided to take sermons that he had preached to the public in Florence in the vernacular in 1354 and to write them in the vernacular "per volgare, come fu principalmente chiesto per coloro, che non sono letterati, e per lettera in latino per gli cherici, a' quali potrà essere utile, e per loro e per coloro, i quali egli hanno a ammaestrare, o predicando, o consigliando, o le confessioni udendo"; see Auzzas, ed., *Iacopo Passavanti*, Prologue; and Rossi, "La 'redazione latina' dello *Specchio della vera penitenza*."

represent earlier states of the text. In what follows, I will present evidence in support of this claim—evidence that shows, in turn, that the text edited and translated here, the *testo breve*, is likely to be the original version of the MVC.

The Italian version in BnF MS ital. 115 (Vaccari's A text) can be set aside, as it gives every indication of having been translated from the Latin. Since the Italian *testo maggiore* (Vaccari's B text) contains the chapters on the Public Ministry that differ so greatly from the Infancy and Passion sections, I will also set it aside here and move directly to a consideration of the short Italian texts, the *testo breve* and the *testo minore*.

At this stage it is important to recall that awkward transition at the end of the Infancy section. As we have seen, the claim made in this transition—that it would "take too long" to present the public life of Christ as material for meditation—does not square with the prolixity of the chapters on the Public Ministry in the Latin text. The transition is equally illogical in the long Italian texts.[68] But its presence makes perfect sense in the *testo breve* and the *testo minore*, for neither of these treat the Public Ministry at all. I have quoted the passage from the *testo breve* above. The transition in the *testo minore* is nearly identical (Sarri, 88–89). Both of the short texts then proceed directly to meditations on the Passion, beginning with sentences that clearly signal the beginning of a new section and move directly into the quintessential mode of the MVC: poignant, dramatic action, in which the worried mother asks Jesus why he intends to go to Jerusalem, and begs him not to go (f. 54r; Sarri, 284). The logical character of this transition from the end of the Infancy to the beginning of the Passion strongly suggests that one of the two short Italian versions is likely to be the original form of the MVC.

Which one? Much is at stake in determining the answer to this question. This is because the two texts are not independent versions; they are so similar, so often, that one must be a redaction of the other.[69] Yet where they differ,

68. As Sorio notes in his edition of the *testo maggiore*, the transition is lacking in the two manuscripts from which he edited the long Italian version (the version of the *testo maggiore* that Vaccari calls "B"), but it is found in the early printed text of this version (Sorio, *Cento meditazioni*, 28). From this Sorio deduced that it was originally part of the *testo maggiore* and was omitted by scribes who noticed that it made little sense in this context.

69. I base this judgment on my examination of virtually all of the extant copies of the *testo minore* in Italian libraries. There is, to my knowledge, no third short text that might have served as intermediary between the *testo breve* and the *testo minore*, nor are there signs of cross-contamination, as far as I have been able to determine.

they do so in such substantive ways that there is only one reasonable deduction: they must represent the work of two different authors.[70] The *testo breve* is far more committed to an incarnational aesthetic, to portraying Christ and the Virgin as vulnerable human actors, and to eliciting feelings of love, compassion, and grief. In what follows, I will present evidence that the *testo breve* preceded the *testo minore*, and that the differences between the two texts can best be explained as additions made by a redactor who recognized the value of the *testo breve* but sought to correct and contain some of its affective energies and implicit vernacular theology while glossing it with additional material, adding many didactic passages and aligning it more fully with the ideals of the Franciscan Order.[71] This redactor appears to have been the same person responsible for composing the *testo maggiore*. The movement from the *testo minore* to the *testo maggiore* is one of expansion, in which the *testo minore* is essentially preserved intact and expanded to include the Public Ministry. The Latin MVC then adds further passages, very similar in kind to the passages added at the earlier stages, without eliminating material from the Italian *testo maggiore*. It is possible, perhaps likely, that the same person who produced the *testo minore* and the *testo maggiore* translated the latter into Latin, adding several additional chapters in the process. As the tables above indicate, I will in due course call the author of the *testo breve* Author A, and the redactor—who composed much additional material as he moved from the *testo minore* to the *testo maggiore* to the long Latin version, shaping the work for various stages of dissemination as a Franciscan text—Author B.[72] At this stage, however, I will hold in abeyance

70. The alternative hypothesis, that a single author may have composed two different versions for two different audiences in response to the perceived needs of those disparate audiences, is one that could and should be tested by other scholars; but my own extended comparative analysis of the *testo breve* and the *testo minore* strongly suggests that this alternative hypothesis does not account for the differences between the texts adequately or persuasively. See my further comments in this volume regarding the deep attitudinal, stylistic, and theological differences between the *testo breve* and the *testo minore*.

71. On vernacular theology, see McGinn, *The Flowering of Mysticism*; Watson, "Censorship and Cultural Change in Late-Medieval England"; Corbari, *Vernacular Theology*; and Boulton, *Sacred Fictions of Medieval France*.

72. I wish to make it clear that I am using the designation "Author B" as a heuristic device, following the model employed by Anders Winroth, who not only identifies "two Gratians" but suggests that the second of the two may not have

that conclusion about the involvement of two authors, allowing the reader to follow the path that I myself initially followed: that of noticing the differences between the *testo breve* and the *testo minore*, seeking to deduce which of the two was composed first, and asking whether these two texts could represent two successive stages in a single author's revisions.

Perhaps the most telling evidence that the *testo breve* came first is its relative lack of specific details concerning the Holy Land. The author of the *testo breve* was clearly interested in the geography of the Holy Land and in the holy sites in Jerusalem, Nazareth, and Bethlehem. But specific distances between places are mentioned far more often in the *testo minore*. The *testo breve* simply states that the angels went to announce the birth of Christ to the shepherds (f. 15v), while the *testo minore* mentions that the shepherds were "presso forse a uno migliaio" ("perhaps about a mile away"; Sarri, 33); the *testo breve* states that Mary travelled from Bethlehem to Jerusalem to present the child at the temple (f. 25r), while the *testo minore* mentions that this was a distance of "cinque miglia" ("five miles"; Sarri, 43); the *testo*

---

been—indeed, is not likely to have been, in the case of the legal texts he examines— a single person (chap. 6, "The Men Behind the *Decretum*," in Winroth, *The Making of Gratian's Decretum*, 175–92). It is not impossible that the successive versions I attribute to "Author B" were the result of more than one Franciscan friar working with similar compositional aims and possibly at the same monastery; it is intriguing that two friars who have been advanced as candidates for authorship, Jacopo of San Gimignano and Johannes de Caulibus, are associated with the Franciscan monastery of San Gimignano. The reference in chapter 77 of the Latin text to the "porta Sancti Geminiani" (Stallings-Taney, *Iohannes de Caulibus: Meditaciones Vite Christi*, 269) has long been recognized as a valuable clue to authorship of the Latin text. In the English translation, the passage reads, "The same person also says that Mount Calvary, where he was crucified, was located about the same distance from the city gate as our place is from the gate of San Gimignano" (Taney et al., *Meditations on the Life of Christ*, 250–51). For those who wish to trace this further, it may be helpful to know that the reference to the *porta Sancti Geminiani* does not appear in the *testo breve*, *testo minore*, or *testo maggiore*. In the fourteenth century, there was a convent of Poor Clares outside the walls of San Gimignano, situated at a distance of what a nineteenth-century source describes as "two arcs of the arrow" from the Porta Quercecchio ["a due tratti di balestra fuori porta Quercecchio"] (Pecori, *Storia della terra di San Gimignano*, 431). Inventories for this convent for the years 1317–41 have been transcribed by Gaddoni; see Gaddoni, "Inventaria Clarissarum." Two missals, two epistolaries, an antiphonal, two psalters, and a hymnal are among the items listed in the inventories of this convent.

*breve* states only that Mary and Joseph returned to Nazareth from Jerusalem, while the *testo minore* notes that this was a distance of "settantaquattro miglia o in quello torno" ("about seventy-four miles, or thereabouts"; Sarri, 63–64); and so on.[73] Similarly, specific place names appear in the *testo minore* that are not present in the *testo breve*. For example, in the *testo minore*, the name of Mount Tabor is given (Sarri, 365), while in the *testo breve* this is simply "el monte" (f. 120v).

The presence of various factual details about the Holy Land in the *testo minore* and their absence in the *testo breve* is clearly a systematic difference. The discrepancies cannot be explained as difficult passages that scribes were unable to understand and thus omitted. Are these changes, then, additions or excisions? To answer this, the question of motives needs to be brought into play. It is difficult to see a motive for excising details of this kind. If doctrinal, pastoral, or even aesthetic issues were at stake, the suppression of a certain category of details might be warranted by a larger principle. But it is hard to imagine what sort of principle would motivate the systematic deletion of distances and place names. Hypothetically, we might posit—if only because of the powerful resonance of stereotypes—that a redactor believed that women readers would not have wished to be bothered by facts and figures about anything, including the Holy Land; or that facts and figures would decrease the affective impact of the imagining a scene. Yet evidence of women's devotional practices from this time suggests the reverse: women appear to have been keenly interested in specific features of the Holy Land in order to more vividly imagine and respond feelingly to the events of sacred history through "virtual pilgrimage."[74] The systematic elimination of distances and place names in the Holy Land, then, is not easy to explain, even as part of a hypothetical process of adapting the text to make it "more affective." A motive for adding such details, however, is readily available: a redactor in possession of details such as distances and place names in the Holy Land is likely to have found it both tempting and valuable to enrich the text by glossing it with facts such as these.

73. Other examples of the precise specification of distances in the *testo minore* appear in Sarri, 76, 83, 338, and 372. Corresponding passages in the *testo breve* appear on ff. 45r, 49r, 104v, and 122v–123r. There are a few references to distances in the *testo breve*: see f. 8r and 14v, and the notes to those passages.

74. On women, meditative practices, and virtual pilgrimage, see Rudy, *Virtual Pilgrimages in the Convent*, and Flora, *Devout Belief of the Imagination*.

There are many other differences between the two texts that also appear to indicate that the *testo minore* reflects changes made to the *testo breve*, rather than the other way around. A highly unusual dramatic detail in the *testo minore*'s Circumcision chapter, for instance, appears as a jarring disruption in the narrative. After we are told, in the *testo minore*, that the Virgin had no pillow on which to lay her son's head, and that it pained her to know that his head would rest on a hard stone, she herself takes up the knife and cuts her son's flesh:

Dei credere che molto volontieri v'averebbe posto uno guanciale, se l'avesse avuto, ma da che non avea altro, con grande amaritudine di cuore vi puose quella pietra. Odi ancora che oggi sparse lo sangue suo preziosissimo e fue la carne sua preziosissima et tenera tagliata dalla Madre sua. Adunque non è bene d'averli compassione? Certo sì, e anche alla sua Madre dolcissima. Pianse dunque oggi lo fanciullo Jesù per lo dolore che sentìo nella carne sua tenera, imperò ch'elli ebbe vera carne e passibile sì come noi. Ma quando elli piagneva, credi tu che la Madre si potesse ritenere di non piagnere? Da credere che no (Sarri, 37).

———

[You must believe that she would very gladly have placed a pillow there, if she had had one, but given that she had nothing else, with great sorrow in her heart she placed the stone there. You hear also that today he shed his most precious blood, and his most precious flesh was cut by his Mother. Isn't it fitting, then, to have compassion for him? Surely yes, and also for his most sweet Mother. The infant Jesus wept today for the pain that he felt in his tender flesh, because he had real, vulnerable flesh as we do. But when he wept, do you believe that his Mother was able to hold herself back from weeping? Certainly not.]

It is a striking departure from the expected narrative, and from the character of the Virgin as she has been portrayed up to this point, for the Virgin to become the agent who causes her son to suffer. And in the *testo breve*, the Virgin does not commit this deed. She does not violate custom or dramatic and affective logic by functioning as the one who inflicts pain with a knife in a male initiation rite. She simply weeps with her son and seeks to protect and comfort him:

Tu poi ben pensare che voluntiera lei li haveria posto uno caveçalle, se la havese habudo. Ma da che lei non ebbe altro, cum grande amaritudine di cuore li messe quella pietra.

Oçi el dolcissimo Iesù, per dolore che lui sentite quando el fo circumciso nella carne sua, si pianse fortemente, imperò che lui havea veramente carne passibile come noi. Sta qui cum la mente et vedi piançere—
colui che fece el cielo et la terra!—ne[l] grembio della Madre sua. Et
vedi anche piançere [f. 20r] duramente la Madre per compassione del
figliolo. O cuore di pietra, piançi anche tu per compassione del tuo Creatore, il qualle per tuo amore spanse oçi il sanctissimo sangue suo, siando
cusì picolino: hàbili uno poco de compassione! Et ancho vedi come la
Madre prese uno panolino et suçoli el viso et poi se lo acostò al pecto et
basiolo, et ogni volta che el piançea secundo l'usança de fançulli, lei
facea el simegliante. Però che piançea per dimostrare la miseria de l'humana natura, et per asconderse dal dimonio, che nol cognoscesse. (ff.
19v–20r)

---

[You may well imagine that she would have gladly placed a pillow
there, if she had had one. But given that she had nothing else, with great
bitterness of heart she placed the stone there.

Today most sweet Jesus, through the pain that he felt in his flesh
when he was circumcised, cried a lot, because he truly had tender flesh
like us. Stay here with your mind, and watch him weep—he who made
heaven and earth!—in the lap of his Mother. And see the Mother weep bitterly too, through compassion for the son. O heart of stone, you too weep
for your Creator, who for love of you shed his most precious blood today,
even when he was so little: have a little compassion! And watch, too, how
the Mother took a cloth and dried his eyes and then drew him to her breast
and kissed him; and each time he cried, as babies do, she did the same. For
he cried to reveal the misery of the human condition, and to disguise himself from the devil, so that the devil would not recognize him.]

This version of the event appears to make far better sense, from the point of
view of both style and affective tenor. The *testo breve*, in short, seems to offer
the better reading—for it is a reading that is of a piece with the gestures and
emotions of the Virgin present elsewhere in the MVC. In my view, the most
reasonable way to interpret this evidence is that the detail of the Virgin's
commission of the act was added later by a redactor who sought to enrich the
symbolic, and Franciscan, resonance of the scene.[75]

---

75. Flora presents an intriguing analysis of this scene, particularly as it is illustrated in BnF MS ital. 115; see "Women Wielding Knives: The Circumcision of Christ
by His Mother," in *The Devout Belief of the Imagination*, 101–15. Flora identifies the

The Nativity chapter contains similar evidence that the *testo minore* is likely to be a reworking of the *testo breve*. An aesthetic of simplicity governs the *testo breve*'s rendering of the scene of Christ's birth:

> Havea in uso la Vergene Maria de sempre levarse nell'hora della meça nocte et stare in oratione. Et approximandose l'ora della meça nocte, levose la gloriosa Vergene Maria et fece secundo el suo costume; et stando lei inçenochiata, véneli uno mirabele desiderio di vedere el Figliolo de Dio in carne humana. Et stando la Dona nostra in [f. 15r] questa contemplatione et desiderio, alora per divina dispensatione el Figliolo de Dio usite fuori del ventre della Madre Vergene Maria sança alcuna molestia. Et sì come lei non lo sentite intrare, così lei nol sentì ussire; et sì come gli era nel ventre della Madre Gloriosa, et così el fue fuori sopra il feno denançi alla Vergene Maria.
>
> Et nasuto ch'el fu, pianse stando sopra il feno a dimostrare l'humana miseria. Et allora la gloriosa Vergene Maria si l'adorò. Et reverentemente si'l tolse cum le sue sanctissime mane et mésselo nel suo gremio; et non havendo panicelli da rivolçerlo, tolse il vello del suo capo et involselo in quello. Et da poi il mese nella mançatoia fra el buo' e ll'asenello, sopra uno pocheto di feno. Et cognoscendo le bestie el suo Creatore, sì se inçenochiono et méssono le loro boche sopra la mançadora et refiadavano sopra il fançulo. E lla gloriosa [f. 15v] Vergene Maria se messe inçenochioni a contemplare il Figliolo de Dio onnipotente, nato in questo mondo in tanta povertade. Et poi rendete lauda a Dio Padre Onnipotente et disse: «Gratia rendo a vui, Padre Eterno, de tanto beneficio, che a me havete dato el vostro Figliolo. Et adoro te Dio Eterno et Figliolo de Dio vivo et vero Dio et vero huomo». Et el simele fece Ioseph. (ff. 14v–15v)

---

[The Virgin Mary was in the habit of rising at midnight to pray. And when the hour of midnight came, the glorious Virgin Mary got up, according to

---

episode as a "theological nuance" that had special relevance for Franciscans (101), one that turns on a typological association between Mary and Zipporah. There are also more general parallels in the medieval period, including narratives in which loving mothers tolerate or cause pain to their children; see Newman, "'Crueel Corage': Child Sacrifice and the Maternal Martyr in Hagiography and Romance," in *From Virile Woman to WomanChrist,* 76–107. In the MVC, however, the act is unexplained, unmotivated by any preceding material in the narrative, and out of keeping with the Virgin's other actions or the way her character has been established; for these reasons, it would appear to be an interpolation.

her custom. And as she was kneeling in prayer, a tremendous desire came upon her to see the Son of God in human flesh. And as Our Lady was meditating with this desire, in an instant, by divine dispensation, the Son of God was born, leaving the womb of the Virgin Mother Mary without any trouble. And just as she did not feel him enter, in the same way she did not feel him exit; and just as he had been in the womb of the Glorious Mother, so he was now out on the hay before the Virgin Mary.

And as soon as he was born, he began to cry, as he lay there on the hay, as a sign of the misery of the human condition. And then the glorious Virgin Mary knelt to adore him. And reverently she lifted him up with her most holy hands and placed him in her lap; and, not having linens to wrap him in, she took the veil from her head and swaddled him with that. And then she placed him in the manger between the ox and the donkey on a little hay. And the animals, recognizing their Creator, knelt and put their mouths over the manger and breathed on the infant. And the glorious Virgin Mary knelt to contemplate the Son of the Almighty God, born in this way in such poverty. And then she gave praise to God the Almighty Father and said, "I give you thanks, eternal Father, for so great a blessing, that you have given me your Son. And I adore you eternal God and Son of the living God and true God and true man." And Joseph did the same.]

The *testo minore* gives a different, more complicated, and disjointed rendering, one that derives from a "revelation given to a brother of our Order," gives a prominent role to Joseph, and places in the scene two unusual objects, a column and a saddle pack, which are not present in the *testo breve*:

Poni ben mente ora ogni cosa, imperò che quelle cose ch'io ti dirò furo revelate e mostrate dalla Donna nostra, secondamente ch'io ebbi da uno santo frate del nostro Ordine, a cui io penso che fossero revelate queste cose, e è molto degno di fede. Adunque, quando venne l'ora del parto, cioè nella mezza notte della domenica, levandosi la Donna sì s'appoggiò a un colonna ch v'era, e Josep stava molto tristo, forse perché non puoteva apparecchiare quelle cose che si conveniano. E incontanente si levò e tolse del fieno della mangiatoia e gittollo ai piedi della sposa, e volsesi in un'altra parte. Allora lo Figliuolo di Dio eterno, sanza alcuna molestia o lesione, si come era dentro nel ventre, così ne fue di fuori sopra 'l fieno, a' piedi della sua Madre. E incontanente la Madre s'inchinò e ricolselo, e con grande dolcezza l'abbracciò e puoselsi in grembo. E ammaestrata da

lo Spirito Santo sì lo lavò e unse tutto quanto col suo latte, lo quale Iddio le diede in grande abbundanzia. E poi lo fasciò con esso 'l velo di capo e puoselo nella mangiatoia. Allora lo bue e l'asino puosero la bocca sopra la mangiatoia, e mandavano fuori l'alito per la bocca e per lo naso sopra 'l Fanciullo, pure come avessero ragione in loro, e conoscessero che l' Fanciullo così poveramente coperto nel tempo di così grande freddo avesse bisogno del loro caldo. Allora la Madre s'inginocchiò e sì l'adorò, e fece grazie a Dio, e disse: Grazie ti faccio io, Dio Padre onnipotente, imperò che tu m'hai dato lo tuo Figliuolo, e adoro te Dio eterno e Figliuolo di Dio vivo e mio. E poi Josep fece lo simigliante, e tolse la sella dell'asino e trassine lo cotal sacconcello di lana o di borra che sia, e puoselo allato alla mangiatoia perchè ella vi sedesse suso, e anche la sella allato. E quella si puose a sedere in su quel sacconcello e 'l gombito teneva in su la sella. E così stava la Reina del mondo, e teneva lo volto sopra la mangiatoia con li occhi fitti, con tutto l'affetto sopra 'l suo dilettissimo Figliuolo. Qui è compiuta la revelazione. (Sarri, 31–32)

―――――

[Pay attention, now, to each thing, because these things I will tell you were revealed and shown by Our Lady herself, according to what I have heard from a trusted source, a holy brother of our Order, to whom I think these things were revealed. When the hour of birth had arrived, that is, at midnight on Sunday, the Lady leaned against a column that was there, and Joseph was very sad, perhaps because he was not able to provide anything more comfortable. And at that moment he rose and took some hay from the manger and scattered it at the feet of his spouse, and then he turned away. Then the Son of the eternal God left the womb just as he had alighted in it, without any harm or lesion, and appeared on the hay at the feet of his Mother. And at once the Mother knelt and gathered him up, and with great tenderness she embraced him and laid him in her lap. And instructed by the Holy Spirit, she washed him with a little of her milk, which God had given her in great abundance. And then she wrapped him with the veil from her head and placed him in the manger. Then the ox and the ass placed their mouths over the manger and breathed out through mouth and nose over the Infant, as if they were possessed of reason and knew that the Infant, so poorly covered in a season of great cold, had need of their warmth. Then the Mother knelt and adored him, and gave thanks to God, and said, "I give you thanks, God the almighty Father, for you have given me your Son, and I adore you, eternal God and Son of the living God and my son." And then Joseph did the same, then

he took the saddle pack from the ass and emptied the pack of whatever stuffing was in it, and placed it beside the manger so she could sit on it, and put the saddle beside it. And in this way she was able to sit on the pack and she rested her elbow on the saddle. And the Queen of the world remained like this, keeping her face turned towards the manger and gazing at her most dear Son with all of her affection. And that is the extent of the revelation.]

Several features of this presentation of the scene suggest that it is likely to be a revision of the version found in the *testo breve*. First, this version draws on the *Historia scholastica* of Peter Comestor for the detail that the time was not only midnight (as the *testo breve* specifies) but "midnight Sunday." Like the matter of distances and place names, it is difficult to locate a motive for the excision of this detail, for it does not seem to disrupt either narrative flow or affective response; it seems simpler to posit that a redactor in possession of this extra detail would simply wish to add it, as part of a practice of glossing the text. Second, the *testo minore* version is based on a source that is not present in the *testo breve*: a revelation given to a "holy brother of our Order." A motive for actively suppressing this source is not easy to identify (though in this case, as in others, I would invite possible explanations that I have not been able to generate). In my view, it is more reasonable to posit that a redactor, upon hearing of this private revelation through conversation with a confrère, would wish to enrich the text by inserting it. Third, the attention given to Joseph here, in his provision of the saddle pack, can best be explained as material that has been added, rather than subtracted. A reason for inserting Joseph into the narrative can readily be supplied, for the cult of Joseph was gaining momentum towards the middle of the fourteenth century, in part as a means of attracting the sympathies of lay men to the practice of affective devotion; indeed, the increased attention to Joseph in the *testo minore* may stand as evidence that the *testo minore* was designed as an adaptation for a readership that would extend beyond an audience of Poor Clares to one that included lay people, including lay men.[76] A motive for the alternative—the removal of the attentive Joseph from the scene—is more difficult, if not impossible, to identify. In fact, this is one of the most significant sites for determining

76. As Phillips has observed, one of the earliest illuminated manuscripts of the *testo minore*, Notre Dame, Snite Museum MS Acc. 1985.25, gives great prominence to Joseph in its many illuminations and appears to have been commissioned by a wealthy Bolognese layman; see Phillips, *"Meditations on the Life of Christ."*

the relative order of the two texts, for this difference, too, is systematic: Joseph is present in the *testo minore* in many scenes where he is absent in the *testo breve*.[77] There is, perhaps, a hypothetical explanation; we might posit, for the sake of argument, that a redactor systematically removed Joseph from the *testo breve* under the assumption that a readership of nuns would find Joseph's presence as a male figure disruptive, detracting from the affective momentum and woman-centered quality of the meditations. But this explanation seems strained compared to the reasons for adding Joseph. Moreover, it lacks internal coherence, for Joseph's presence does not in itself seem to detract from the centrality of women or the affectivity of the text; indeed, Joseph's concern for his spouse in the Nativity scene appears to heighten, rather than decrease, the affective poignancy of the scene, while underscoring, through his supportive role and gestures, the centrality of the woman giving birth.

There are additional differences. Stylistically, the *testo breve* birth narrative is utterly simple, lucid, and unselfconscious. The emotional momentum of this important event is not disrupted by the curious staging of the birth as a scene in which the Virgin stands against a column and the infant appears at her feet. The column itself is, from a narrative point of view, distracting. Since it is clearly not a feature that aligns with a realistic aesthetic, it disrupts the narrative momentum, hinting at a symbolic meaning without explaining that meaning. It does not function, in any immediately obvious way, to heighten the affective impact of the scene.[78] Both the column and the dra-

---

77. In the *testo breve*, the reader is asked to kneel before Mary and Christ at the manger, to kiss the child's feet, to hold the child, and to return him to the mother (ff. 17v–18r). In the *testo minore*, an additional instruction is given, to "reverentemente saluta quello santo vecchio Josep" ("reverently salute that saintly old man Joseph") before kissing the child's feet (Sarri, 34). In the Baptism chapter of the *testo breve*, it is only Mary who gives her son "permission" to leave home to travel to the Jordan ("Or licenciato dalla Madre, mésesse in camino inverso Ierusalem" [f. 45r]); in the *testo minore*, both Mary and Joseph give such permission ("Così dunque reverentemente licenziato da lei e da Josep, cominciò a andare da Nazaret inverso Jerusalem, al fiume Jordan" [Sarri, 76]).

78. In the illustrations of Paris, BnF MS ital. 115, the stylistic difference between the iconography of the column—here, a stout column inside a cave—and the realistic domestic scenes elsewhere in the Infancy section is striking; see Ragusa and Green, *Meditations*, 27. The Cave of the Nativity at the Church of the Nativity in Bethlehem featured a column embedded in the wall, which fourteenth-century pilgrims reported to be the column against which Mary leaned at the time of Christ's birth; see "Notes to the *Meditations*," 205n23.

matic action seem out of keeping with the implicit stylistic principles of simplicity, realism, and affective appeal governing other dramatic episodes of the MVC. From the point of view of these principles, the *testo breve*'s version of the scene would seem to be the earlier text.

## Two Authors?

Differences such as these—small details, but adding up to systematic differences—indicate that the two versions are highly unlikely to have been composed by a single author. Medieval writers often revised their own compositions, of course—issuing a work in multiple versions and expanding or adjusting its contents in light of new thinking or additional sources or the desire to reach different audiences. But as even the brief passages cited above suggest, there appear to be two mentalities behind these two texts. The writer responsible for the *testo minore* is far more intent on adducing authorities— here, a revelation by the Virgin to a holy brother; later in the same chapter, Francis, Bernard, and Augustine. The *testo minore*'s mode of address is often from high to low, vertical in orientation; imperatives are more abundant. The author of the *testo breve* does indeed make use of the imperative: "Hora vàtene anche tu al presepio, et inçenochiate denançi al Signore del Mundo et alla Madre sua" (f. 17v) [Now you, too, go to the crib, and kneel before the Lord of the World and before his Mother]. But injunctions of this kind are often mixed with others more deferential or tentative in nature, where the injunction is preceded by "you may": "Et qui tu poi vedere tre cose molto notabile" (f. 38v) [And here you may see three very notable things]; "Tu poi ben pensare . . ." (f. 19v) [You may well imagine . . .], and so forth. Moreover, the author of the *testo breve* often uses "we" constructions, conveying a sense of shared engagement with the material: "Hora habiamo decto della nativitade" (17r) [Now we have spoken about the birth]. The parallel passage in the *testo minore* begins, in contrast, with establishing distance between writer and reader: "Hai veduto lo nascimento" [You have seen the birth] (Sarri, 32).

Above all, while the author of the *testo minore* clearly accepts the emphasis on Christ's humanity that so pervades the MVC, he is quite concerned about providing reminders of Christ's divinity. The line summarizing the Nativity in the *testo minore* typifies this impulse: "Hai veduto lo nascimento del nostro santissimo Principe Messer Jesù e simigliantemente lo parto della Reina del mondo" [You have seen the birth of our most holy Prince Lord Jesus and similarly the childbirth of the Queen of the world] (Sarri, 32). In

the *testo breve*, a simpler phrase is used, one in which Christ's lordship is accepted as a given, rather than emphasized in a way designed to elicit awe; and no mention is made of the regal status of Mary: "Hora habiamo decto della nativitade del Signore nostro miser Iesù Cristo" (17r) [Now we have spoken about the birth of our Lord Jesus Christ].

Another example of divergent emphasis given to the humanity and the divinity of Christ is the discrepancy in the roles given to the shepherds and the angels in the two renderings of the Nativity. In the *testo breve*, the angels appear briefly at the manger and quickly travel to the shepherds to announce the good news; then the angels disappear from the narrative. The shepherds then talk among themselves and decide to visit the child—"Andiamo in Bethelem et vediamo questo Salvatore del Mondo" (f. 16r) [Let's go to Bethlehem and see this Savior of the World]—and it is the words that the shepherds relate that Mary treasures in her heart. In the *testo minore*, there is no direct speech among the shepherds; their dramatic role is minimal. The angels, in contrast, have a much larger role than they do in the *testo breve*. After announcing the birth to the shepherds, the angels fly up to heaven and announce the good tidings to the celestial court, whereupon all of the angels in heaven descend— rank by rank, in good hierarchical fashion—to see the child and his mother and to adore and praise him in song (Sarri, 33–34).

Was this emphasis on divinity and majesty added by the author of the *testo minore*, or excised by the author of the *testo breve*? This is perhaps the single most important question to ask in order to determine which text is the original version of the MVC. And the answer would seem to be straightforward. Eliminating preexisting textual references to the divinity of Christ would be a risky act, one that even the hypothetical goal of making a devotional text more "accessible" could hardly be said to warrant. The deliberate, systematic excision of any work's references to the divinity of Christ would make a very large statement, one bordering on heresy. Yet the *testo breve* is not a work that assertively presses the boundaries of accepted doctrine; it is a far cry from Marguerite Porete's *Mirror of Simple Souls*. Given this, the alternative hypothesis would seem to be the more logical: reminders of Christ's divinity and majesty were later added in a systematic way—as correctives— to a text perceived by a redactor to dwell too much on the vulnerable, ordinary, human nature of Christ.

Even a brief glance at the contemporary historical context supports the hypothesis that the references to Christ's divinity are likely to have been added later by a concerned redactor. The worry that devotion to the humanity of Christ could be dangerous, in theological and devotional terms, without complementary attention to his divinity, is a note sounded early in the four-

teenth century. A vernacular sermon preached by the Dominican Giordano of Pisa on April 9, 1305, in Santa Maria Novella, was recorded as follows:

> There are many insane people [matti] who wish only to dwell on the humanity of Christ, and on how he was a man. These divide Christ; because we must not only meditate on his humanity, but on his divinity. . . . Therefore it is good to meditate on the humanity of Christ, in as much as he was man; but it is better to meditate on his divinity. There are many who pay no attention to his divinity; they wish only to dwell on his humanity. They are mad: and they divide him, who is indivisible; who always has joined, and continues to join, humanity to the deity.[79]

The Franciscans expressed similar concerns about excessive focus on Christ's humanity as early as the thirteenth century. A particularly interesting instance of this concern is registered obliquely in one of the most important surviving Franciscan processional crucifixes, that by the Master of the Blue Crucifixes (also known as Master of the Franciscan Crucifixes) now held at the museum of the Basilica of San Francesco in Assisi and dated to circa 1250. On one side, the side apparently displayed to the public, the phrase *Rex Glorie* appears to have been added at a secondary stage—as if a reminder about Christ's divinity were necessary for those gazing upon this unusually intimate and sorrowful rendering of Christ's physical and psychic suffering.[80]

There are clear analogues, then, to the impulse to "correct" depictions of a too-human Christ. But I know of no examples of the reverse: the manifest excision, at a secondary stage, of references to Christ's divinity that were originally embedded in a devotional text.

---

79. "Onde sono molti matti, i quali non voglion pensare, se non dell'umanità di Cristo, e come fue uomo. Questi dividono Cristo; perocché non solamente dovemo pensare pur dell'umanità sua, ma della sua deitàde. Odi, che dicono i Santi. Voi vedete, e son molti, i quali pensando l'umanità di Cristo, trovano diletti sommi, e grandi dolcesse nella Croce di Cristo; perocché gli è la miglio cosa a pensare di questa vita, e la più somma, e che più frode fa" ("Sul credo," in Magli, *Gli uomini della penitenza*, 130).

80. Double-sided crucifix, tempera on panel, 109.5 x 77 cm. This processional crucifix is now held at the Museo del Tesoro della Basilica di San Francesco. The theory concerning the later addition of the *titolo Rex Glorie* was relayed to me in person by Pasquale Magro, director of the Museo del Tesoro, who described it as a probable response to the kinds of concerns expressed by Giordano of Pisa in the early fourteenth century (personal consultation, July 2008). The Master of the Blue Crucifixes, who was active in Umbria ca. 1250, may have been an assistant of Giunta Pisano.

## Two Authors: Author A and Author B

At this stage, it seems warranted to begin speaking of two authors: Author A, who wrote a first version of the MVC, the *testo breve*; and Author B, who used the *testo breve* as his base text, but excised certain passages and added much material of his own to create the *testo minore*. Let's look more closely at systematic differences between the two texts.

Clearly, Author B held that the scenes concerning Christ's humanity and vulnerability possessed high devotional value, for he preserved most of them (with important exceptions mentioned below). But there is, in the *testo minore*, a very concerted effort to insert these passages into a theologically correct framework that makes such vulnerability and ordinariness acceptable—acceptable because divinely ordained, willed, and authorized. Such framing is evident at the very beginning. The *testo breve*, for instance, gives no theological justification for the Incarnation. It proceeds directly to concrete dramatic action, in which the Trinity—simply because it is now time for the salvation of humanity to be effected, and because the Trinity is moved by the plight of humankind and by the prayers of the angels—sends Gabriel on his mission to the Virgin (ff. 3v–8r). As drama, this version is exquisite in its delicacy and pacing, particularly in the way it holds in abeyance—as if in freeze-frame—the Virgin's answer while the Trinity and Gabriel await her response (f. 6r). It is, above all, the Virgin's consent to a romantic proposal that is made to matter here; the language and gestures are those of courtly convention, and larger theological questions do not come into consideration. Given this absence of overt theological grounding—along with the quite potent implication that a woman's consent was the action chiefly responsible for the Incarnation—it is easy to understand why a redactor would wish to frame such a momentous event properly. This would explain the presence, in the *testo minore* but not in the *testo breve*, of the allegorical debate of the four daughters of God—cited almost entirely from Bernard and preceded, as we have seen, by that cumbersome transition that appears to register a change of course: "E prendiamo lo principio della Incarnazione. Ma possiamo pensare che alquante cose l'andassero innanzi" [And let's begin with the Incarnation. But we may imagine that certain things happened before this] (Sarri, 6–7). The debate chapter, then, is likely to have been inserted to place on firmer theological ground a text written by one author and perceived as defective—in need of "authorization" and orthodox grounding—by another.

Like the distances and place names cited above, it is the brief, passing references to the divinity or majesty of Christ and the Virgin that serve as the

most telling signs that what we have here are indeed efforts to "correct"—
and that the direction of revision was from the *testo breve*, composed by
Author A, to the *testo minore*, adapted and expanded by Author B. One of
these appears near the end of the Nativity chapter, in a celebrated scene from
the MVC in which the reader is invited to approach the manger, to ask the
mother if she can hold this baby, and then to hold him tenderly. This is the
scene as rendered in the *testo breve*:

> Hora vàtene anche tu al presepio, et inçenochiate denançi al Signore del
> mundo et alla madre sua, la qualle sta inçenochiata al presepio et adora
> el Figliolo de Dio cum ogni riverentia et timore, et basia gli piedi al
> fançulo Iesù che çase nella mançatora, et priega dolcemente la madre
> che lei te'l sporça over ch'ela te 'l lassia tocare over abraçare. Et quando
> lei te l'averà sporto cum ogni reverentia el riceverai, et aliegrate et dilec-
> tatene de lui et cum grande fidutia. Et poi pensa come humelmente elgi è
> conversato cum noi et finalmente ha lassato se medesimo in cibo; unde
> la sua benignità pacientemente se lasserà tocare al tuo volere, et non te 'l
> riputare a presumptione, ma ad amore et a devotione. Et poi riverente-
> mente el rendi alla madre sua, et guarda come lei governa il bambollino
> et come diligentemente ella procura de farli tuti li piacere che lei puote.
> Stàtene adonque cum lei et [f. 18r] aiutela et dilèctate di pensare speso
> del fançullo, però che pensando et dilectando te de lui haverai pace nella
> mente tua.

---

[Now you, too, go to the manger, and kneel before the Lord of the World
and before his mother, who is kneeling beside the manger, and worship
the Son of God with great reverence and awe. And kiss the feet of the
child Jesus who lies in the manger, and gently ask the mother if she will
hand him to you or let you touch or embrace him. And when she has
given him to you to hold, receive him with great reverence, and rejoice
and delight in him with great confidence. And then consider how humbly
he dwelt among us and even finally left himself as food. So his goodness
will patiently allow you to touch him as you wish, and he will not attribute this to presumption but to love and devotion. And then reverently return him to his mother, and watch how she cares for the infant, and how
attentively she tries to do everything she can to please him. Stay with
her, then, and help her, and delight in thinking often of the little child,
because by meditating and delighting in him in this way you will have a
deep sense of peace.]

The *testo minore* is in most respects the same. But at the point just before the reader is asked to hand the baby back to the mother, an extra injunction is issued: "Tuttavia sia reverente e timoroso, *imperò ch'elli è santo sopra tutti i santi*" [Nevertheless, show reverence and fear, *because he is the saint above all saints*] (Sarri 34–35; emphasis added). Small textual differences such as this—applied to both Christ and his mother—are systematic, pervasive, predictable. By the time Christ appears to his mother after the Resurrection, it comes as no surprise that he would address her, in the *testo breve*, with the simple, tender, "Madre mia carissima" (f. 111r)—whereas, in the *testo minore*, he dons dazzling white regalia ("vestimenti bianchissimi") and addresses her as "Madre santa" (Sarri, 347).

There are two additional, and related, patterns of difference between the *testo breve* and the *testo minore*. One is Author B's repeated efforts to depict Christ as teacher. The other is a very striking effort on the part of Author B to tone down the greater pathos of the *testo breve*—and in particular, the emotional responses of the Virgin.

Two examples of the desire to render Christ as teacher in the *testo minore* can be mentioned here. The first occurs in the scene in which Christ sets off to pray in the garden of Gethsemane. An image of chickens, and how they relate to a mother hen, is the image on which this difference turns. In the *testo breve*, the disciples are afraid:

> Alora tuti impauriti, non sapiando dove el se volesse andare. Et strençandose adosso a miser Iesù, sì lo seguitavano fuori de Ierusalem. Or vedi i discipoli, cum quanta paura vano drieto a lui. Tuti si sforçavano de approximarse a lui, sì come fano gli polli alla galina quando hano paura de qualche occello. Così faceano gli discipoli intorno a miser Iesù, però ch'eli non sapeano dove lui andase. (f. 68r)

---

> [And then they were all afraid, not knowing where he wished to go. And crowding around the Lord Jesus, they followed him outside of Jerusalem. Now watch the disciples, how fearfully they follow him. They all strove to draw near him, like chicks do around the hen when they are afraid of some bird of prey. Like this the disciples gathered around Lord Jesus, because they did not know where he was going.]

Here, the chickens are used to heighten a sense of the affective poignancy of the moment, and of the protection and love that Christ affords to his disciples. As inscribed readers of a sort, the chickens also serve to promote the

kind of affective response that the Prologue professes is the aim of the meditations. In the *testo minore*, in contrast, Christ becomes a hen who preaches, and the chickens change:

> Vedi ora i discepoli come li vanno dietro ragunati insieme; e chi più puote li s'appressa, come fanno i pulcini dietro alla gallina, incalciandolo ora l'uno ora l'altro, per lo desiderio ch'hanno d'accostarlisi e d'udire le sue parole. E come elli volentieri sosteneva questa ingiuria da loro. (Sarri, 300)

> [Watch the disciples now, how they crowd together as they follow him; and how each strives to press more closely against him, as chicks do behind a hen, crowding in, now one, now another, impelled by the desire that they have to get close to him and to hear his words. And how he willingly puts up with this mistreatment from them.]

The image of Christ patiently "putting up with" the proximity of his disciples—disciples cast as very competitive chicks, unlike their *testo breve* relatives—seems out of keeping with the familiarity he elsewhere seeks to cultivate with them in this text.

The second example occurs at what is potentially the moment of greatest pathos, the moment when the crucifiers have finished their work and Christ now hangs on the cross. In Author B's *testo minore*, even as he is dying, Christ is described as not being "lazy." He wants to use even these last moments to teach: "Ma lo Segnore stando in su la croce, eziandio insino che lo spirito ne penò ad uscire, non istette ozioso: ma faceva e diceva quelle cose ch'erano utile per noi" [But the Lord, hanging on the cross before he breathed his last, did not remain idle; but he did and said things that were useful for us] (Sarri, 326–27). These words introduce the theme of the seven words spoken from the cross, here presented as a discrete unit abstracted from the narrative, as if Christ himself culled these words from the Gospels to present as a sermon. The parallel passage in the *testo breve* lacks this image. It follows the Gospels themselves more closely, interweaving the seven last words with a moving, pathos-infused narrative (ff. 91r–97v).

As for the tendency to tone down the Virgin's affective responses, the most striking instance occurs after the Deposition. The *testo breve* contains a very ample lament of the Virgin after Christ is taken down from the cross and placed in her lap. It is a scene that is stylistically controlled, with its repetitions and sequence of words and gestures, even as it depicts copious weeping and

lamentation. And it depicts the mother not only gazing at the body of her son while weeping, but kissing that body repeatedly: now his eyes, that had been blindfolded; now his cheeks, that had been beaten; now his mouth, that was forced to drink vinegar; and so on down the body to his feet; "et non se potea saciare de basiarli" (f. 102v) [and she could not cease from kissing him].

In the *testo minore*, the mother does not kiss the body in this unembarrassed and systematic way. Most of the lament, as given in the *testo breve*, has been excised. In what remains, the Virgin simply "looks at" the body in her lap:

Guardava le fedite delle mani e del lato. Ora l'una ora l'altra, e 'l volto e 'l capo, e vedeva le punture delle spine, la barba divelta, la faccia brutta di sputo e di sangue e il capo tosolato; e guardando e piagnendo non si potea saziare. (Sarri, 335)

---

[She looked at the wounds in the hands and side. Now one, now the other, and the face and head, and she saw the punctures of the thorns, the beard pluckings, the face fouled with spit and blood and the shorn head; and she could not stop looking at him and weeping.]

This hesitation where tactility is concerned is apparent in other passages in the *testo minore* as well. In the *testo breve*, when the Virgin passes the cross—still wet with her son's blood—on her return from the burial, she kisses that blood, and the women who accompany her do the same: "Et poi basiò el sangue precioso del qualle ne era tuta bagnata, et simelmente feceno le altre done che erano cum lei" (f. 106v) [And then she kissed the precious blood with which it was completely bathed, and the other women who were there with her did the same]. In the *testo minore*, the women do not kiss the blood: "E quando giunsero alla croce, ella s'inginocchiò e disse: Qui si riposò lo Figliulo mio, e qui è lo sangue suo prezioso. E tutti quanti fecero lo simigliante" [And when they came to the cross, she knelt and said: 'Here is where my Son was, and here is his precious blood.' And the others did the same] (Sarri, 340).

Finally, there is another major textual difference between the *testo breve* and the *testo minore* that, in my view, serves as a valuable clue to their relative positions in the sequence of the MVC's history: their divergent renderings of the crucifixion itself. In the *testo minore* and the more widely known versions of the MVC, the Latin text and its many derivatives, the work offers not just one, but two ways of imagining how Christ was crucified. In the first

scene, Christ mounts a ladder to a cross already fixed in the ground; in the second, he is nailed to a recumbent cross (Sarri, 323–24). Neither of these methods of crucifixion is unique to the MVC; both were in circulation as iconographic and literary *topoi* (*erecte cruce* and *jacente cruce*) in northern Italy by the early fourteenth century. But the juxtaposition itself is highly unusual.[81] In the scholarship on the MVC, this presentation of two modes of imagining the crucifixion has regularly been interpreted as a sign of the "many and diverse ways" that one might imagine scenes from the life of Christ (Sarri, 6), as long as these ways do not contradict church doctrine. However, Author B manifestly privileges the first mode, Christ's mounting of the ladder—a scene that, in the specific details of its language and imagery, can be identified as a distinctly Franciscan rendering of the Ascent of the Cross, one that promotes an understanding of the crucifixion as prototypical martyrdom, as voluntary and necessary sacrifice in which Christ's agency is emphasized: "aperse quelle sue braccia reali, e sparese le sue mani bellissime e eccellentissime, e porsele ai suoi crucifissori" [he opened his royal arms, stretched out his most beautiful and excellent hands and held them out to his crucifiers] (Sarri, 323). Author B not only places this scene first, but dwells on it far longer; the alternative mode, crucifixion *jacente cruce*, is given only very cursory treatment.

The *testo breve*, in contrast, presents just one way of imagining the scene: crucifixion *jacente cruce* (ff. 89v–91v). This narrative draws out the pathos latent in the scene, portraying Christ as vulnerable human victim and punctuating the stages in the action with exclamations of pity: "Or pensa che dolore era quello!" (f. 91r) [Now imagine what pain that was!]. In this text, like the *testo minore*, Christ offers a prayer to the Father accepting the necessity of his death. But the place from which he speaks in the two texts makes a significant difference. In the *testo minore*, the prayer is a public proclamation, made before Christ actively extends his arms up to his crucifiers. In the *testo breve*, Christ offers the prayer after he has been nailed to the cross, while he lies prone on the ground, obscured from view, in a posture of total defeat and submission. The prayer is thus cast as a private communication between Christ and his Father, one that the reader overhears, as it were, and this private resignation to the Father's will increases the pathos of the scene.

---

81. Both scenes appear juxtaposed in Ubertino da Casale's *Arbor vitae crucifixae Jesu*, composed in 1305; see Davis, *Ubertino d Casale*, 317. It is possible that the redactor of the MVC knew of the *Arbor vitae*, but he does not quote from it. Both of Ubertino's scenes are rendered in a highly pathetic mode.

How might this difference between the two texts be explained? Here, as elsewhere, we could generate several hypothetical explanations.[82] But given the multiple, cumulative patterns of difference between the two texts, it seems to me that the most reasonable answer is this: that Author A's rendering of the scene was, to put it simply, too pathetic for Author B. Like the image of the suffering Christ on the processional cross made by the Master of the Blue Crucifixes, it appears that Author A's rendering of *Christus patiens* seemed, to a Franciscan redactor, too risky in its portrayal of a very human, vulnerable Christ. A "corrective" was needed; and that is why we find, in the revised versions of the MVC, a crucifixion scene that credits Christ with agency, heroically mounting the cross and extending his beautiful, royal hands.

Elsewhere, I have presented an extended argument about some of Author B's adaptations, including the way that they call into question the grand narrative of the "Franciscan revolution" in late-medieval culture.[83] The edition and translation offered here will, I hope, facilitate further study of the interesting tensions embedded within the MVC's textual history, including the possibility that the *testo breve*—with its more "naive" texture, its depiction of a perhaps-too-human Christ, and its direct and unapologetic translations of many Gospel passages—was actively suppressed. Such study will depend, however, on the viability of the textual history I have presented here. Is this argument robust enough to withstand trial?

## COUNTERARGUMENTS

The argument above has generated considerable interest since I first advanced it, and the most common response has been one that recognizes the potential impact of this revised history while reserving judgment until the

---

82. There is another Italian version, for instance, that gives only the recumbent crucifixion: Rome, Biblioteca Angelica MS 2213. This is a unique, fifteenth-century adaptation of the *testo minore*. Tóth and Falvay have suggested that in the case of the Angelica manuscript, the first mode of crucifixion was eliminated in order to enhance the pathos of the scene. I agree with this assessment of the Angelica adaptation; however, I disagree with the logic of Tóth and Falvay's deduction that since one manuscript depicting only the recumbent crucifixion (Angelica) can be shown to be a late adaptation, another witness depicting only the recumbent crucifixion (Canonici) is *necessarily* the same in kind ("L'Autore," 419–20). For further discussion of the differences between these two witnesses, and the implications of this comparison for the textual history of the MVC, see McNamer, "The Debate on the Origins of the *Meditationes Vitae Christi*."

83. See McNamer, *Affective Meditation and the Invention of Medieval Compassion*, chap. 3, "Franciscan Meditation Reconsidered," esp. 95–115.

publication of the Italian text and translation.[84] Now that the primary text is available to a wide readership, the real work of evaluation can begin.

Several counterarguments, however, have been published in response to my earliest articulation of this revised textual history. In her 2011 study, *Imagination, Meditation, and Cognition in the Middle Ages*, Michelle Karnes expresses skepticism in some brief but influential remarks; "I am not persuaded," she writes.[85] And in two articles with overlapping content published in English in 2014 and in Italian in 2015, Peter Tóth and Dávid Falvay offer a detailed and sustained argument that rejects, in emphatic terms, my argument for the priority of the Italian *testo breve*: the Canonici manuscipt, they write, "in our opinion absolutely does not represent the closest witness to the original."[86] Tóth and Falvay conclude that the "traditional" hypothesis

---

84. Barbara Newman, for instance, writes: "If McNamer is right, her argument has far-reaching implications. Not only would the nun's Latinized meditation be the most influential text penned by any medieval woman, but the whole narrative of 'Franciscan spirituality' would need to be sharply revised" (Newman, Review of *Affective Meditation*, 524). As Bert Roest has put it, "If Sarah McNamer is correct, our evaluation of Clarissan literary involvement from the later thirteenth century onwards will have to be thoroughly re-evaluated. For the moment, however, the final verdict on the authorship of the 'primitive' vernacular Ur-text of the *Meditationes Vitae Christi* still is out. If we are dealing with the repression of an original female version, subsequently replaced by a 'tamed' male version geared to steer female spirituality into acceptable devotional channels, this would be in line with the views of control over female monastic life expressed by several influential Franciscan theologians, including Bonaventure of Bagnoregio" (*Order and Disorder*, 303–4). For additional responses to my theory of the priority of the short Italian text and the possibility of its authorship by a Poor Clare, see the reviews of McNamer, *Affective Meditation* (particularly "Chapter 3: The Franciscan Revolution Reconsidered") by Caroline Bynum, Fiona Somerset, Benedikt Vadakkekara, Ineke van 't Spijker, Mary Erler, Gail Gibson, Constance M. Furey, Glenn Burger, and A. W. Klink.

85. Karnes, *Imagination, Meditation, and Cognition*, 144n6. It is possible that Karnes's very brief remarks, advanced in a long footnote but not in the main text of her book, have had greater impact than she herself anticipated, due to their incorporation into a Wikipedia article on Johannes de Caulibus. In any case, I am taking them seriously here because they have attained wide circulation, influencing the debate.

86. Tóth and Falvay, "New Light" and "L'Autore." In the discussion that follows, I refer only to "New Light" where the content is similar. The phrase cited here, from the Italian, is "a notre avviso non rappresenta affatto la più vicina all'originale"—with *non . . . affatto* meaning, of course, "absolutely not, by no means"; Falvay and Tóth, "L'Autore," 430. Tóth and Falvay do not refer to the text as the *testo breve* because I referred to this text as the "Canonici version" in my 2009, 2010, and 2014 publications.

regarding the Latin original should be reinstated, while proposing a new candidate for its authorship: "In contrast to what has recently been suggested by Sarah McNamer, the long Latin text of the MVC should be re-established as the earliest version of the work, written about 1300 by the Franciscan Jacobus de Sancto Geminiano, who, we posit, could be identified as the leader of the 1312 revolt of the Tuscan spirituals."[87]

Neither Karnes nor Tóth and Falvay build a renewed case for the priority of the Latin text on the basis of its content or style or internal coherence. Indeed, their studies do not engage at all with the issues I have raised with respect to the Latin text: signs of interpolation, the digressive character of the quotations from Bernard of Clairvaux and other authorities, awkward seams joining disparate sections of the Latin text, discrepancies in style and aim between the Infancy and Passion sections and those of the Public Ministry chapters, and so on. Nor do these studies make a case for the priority of the Latin text by offering linguistic or documentary evidence that the Italian versions must be *volgarizzamenti*, translations from the Latin. Neither Karnes nor Tóth and Falvay undertake careful comparisons between the *testo breve* and the *testo minore* in order to determine which was composed first—a question that has been of overriding importance in my analysis as it was first published in *Speculum* and now, more amply, in the present volume. Nor do these studies engage with my argument for the involvement of two authors, Author A and Author B. If there are weaknesses in these core components of my argument, then, they have yet to be exposed; I welcome direct engagement on these specific issues, but it is important to note that Karnes and Tóth and Falvay do not address them.

Yet these are important studies, meriting close attention and serious response. What, then, are the grounds for these dissenting and skeptical views?

Where the work of Tóth and Falvay is concerned, the answer is complex. Indeed, it is so complex and technical that their full argument, and my response to it, cannot be presented with adequate care in this volume. My article, "The Debate on the Origins of the *Meditationes Vitae Christi*," thus functions as a supplement to the present volume; there, I engage directly and at length with the positions Tóth and Falvay have advanced. Here, however, it is worth summarizing the primary strands of their argument. In part, it is an argument based on their contention that Michael of Massa, who wrote in Paris in the 1320s, cites passages from the Latin MVC; since this would be the ear-

---

87. Tóth and Falvay, "New Light," 93.

liest sign of the MVC's circulation and uptake, the reasoning goes, the Latin must have been composed first. I engage with this part of Tóth and Falvay's argument in this volume (see below, "Date of Composition," cxxxvi–cxxvii). Another strand of their argument has to do with their claim that "the Canonici version, proposed by McNamer as the earliest form of the MVC, shows multiple signs of textual corruptions and simplifications, which are usually interpreted as markers of a later reworking and not of an earlier, more genuine text."[88] However, this claim about "simplifications" begs the question; it does not take into account the possibility that a simpler text was made more complex through redaction, accretion, and glossing. Moreover, Tóth and Falvay's claim about the Canonici manuscript's "corruptions" is based on a misreading of a single word in the manuscript, a word on folio 57v that they construe as "admira."[89] On close inspection, it is clear that the word actually reads "adimra"; and it is also clear that the scribe simply dropped a syllable, "pi," at the site of the hyphen. This is garden-variety scribal error, a category that Tóth and Falvay appear to conflate with the category of textual corruption. In any case, my emendation of the word to "adimpirà," and the unremarkable character of the scribe's slips of the pen, are evident in this volume (see 88); now that a critical edition of the complete text is available, Tóth and Falvay's claim that it is full of "corruptions" will be one that others can evaluate for themselves.

Tóth and Falvay's detailed analysis of the greater precision of the citations from Bernard of Clairvaux in the Latin MVC, and the greater precision of the lengthy quotation from the Latin *Revelations of St. Elizabeth of Hungary* in the Latin MVC, merit careful consideration and response. I offer such response in "The Debate on the Origins of the *Meditationes Vitae Christi,*" concluding that these practices of citation and quotation do not present a barrier to my argument for the priority of the Italian *testo breve.* Finally, Tóth and Falvay argue that Jacobus of San Gimignano, to whom the work is attributed in several copies of the Italian *testo breve* and *testo maggiore* (but not mentioned in any of the Latin manuscripts) can be identified as a leader of the Tuscan Spirituals who led a revolt in 1312. The date of the flourishing of this Jacobus serves as the basis for their conclusion that the work was composed circa 1300; they present no paleographical or other evidence for the composition of the Latin MVC circa 1300. I respond to these arguments

88. Tóth and Falvay, "New Light," 73.
89. Tóth and Falvay, "New Light," 73.

about date and authorship in "The Debate on the Origins of the *Meditationes Vitae Christi*," but here it is important to mention that the attribution to Jacobus of San Gimignano in several Italian manuscripts does not function, as Tóth and Falvay imply, as evidence that my theory of sequential authorship (with a core composed by Author A, and expanded versions composed by Author B) must be wrong. Indeed, I believe it is worth pursuing the possibility that the figure I have identified as Author B may have been called Jacobus of San Gimignano—though I am skeptical of the claim that the Jacobus of San Gimignano mentioned in the MVC manuscripts must necessarily be the same Jacobus who led a revolt of the Tuscan Spirituals in 1312. It is not inherently implausible that a friar aligned with the Spirituals may have served as spiritual director to Poor Clares and even composed moving and imaginative meditations for them.[90] But the general tone and tenor of the MVC, in any of its versions, does not seem compatible with the hypothesis that it was composed by the fiery rebel described in a letter of 1314 as "head and origin of all calamities, disobedience, and schism."[91] Anything is possible, but to my mind the MVC seems too relaxed, too lacking in fierce conviction, too free of anything that might be called Spiritual polemic to be attributed with any confidence to such a man.

As for the skepticism Michelle Karnes has voiced, it is important to note that this skepticism is not based on a reading of the *testo breve* itself nor on independent comparisons of the various Italian manuscripts or editions in relation to the Latin text. Rather, it rests chiefly on her reading of the secondary literature and what she takes to be paleographical evidence contradicting my argument for the origins of the MVC: the evidence presented by a particular manuscript, Cambridge, Trinity College Library MS B.14.7 (which has also been referred to as Trinity College 293 in the scholarship).[92] This manuscript has often been cited as the earliest witness to the MVC. Indeed, that is why I myself gave it special scrutiny in my earliest work on the MVC, so it is important to address its potential relevance here.

Cambridge, Trinity College Library MS B.14.7 contains a copy of the Latin *Meditaciones Passione Christi*, which, as Stallings has conclusively

<hr/>

90. For evidence that Spiritual Franciscans served as spiritual directors to Poor Clares, see Burr, "Appendix: Spirituals and Mystics," in *The Spiritual Franciscans*, 315–46.

91. Tóth and Falvay, "New Light," 89.

92. Trinity College 293 is the number given to the manuscript in the catalogue by M. R. James (*Western Manuscripts*).

shown, is a recension of English origin deriving from the full Latin MVC.[93] In his catalogue of the Trinity College manuscripts published in 1900, M. R. James made the following note on this manuscript: "Cent. xiv early, in a good hand."[94] Karnes observes that my case for the Italian original "depends on her rejecting the traditional dating of one manuscript of the *Meditaciones Passione Christi* . . . to the early fourteenth century. As McNamer notes, the script is typical of early fourteenth-century manuscripts ('Further Evidence,' 245) but she argues that such evidence is inconclusive."[95]

There are problems with Karnes's assessment, however, starting with her characterization of my work. In my article, "Further Evidence," I did not, as Karnes suggests, state that the script is typical of early fourteenth-century manuscripts. Rather, I observed that the script is a *littera textualis*, which, as paleographers know well, can be quite difficult to date. Often, experts can get it wrong by several decades, or even a century, in part because the script aspires to atemporal status. In "Further Evidence," I also noted that Columban Fischer, in 1932, questioned the basis for M. R. James's date; although he cited James's date in his descriptive list of MVC manuscripts, he added a note of caution and observed that several others with paleographical expertise had examined the manuscript without reaching the same conclusion as James: Ephrem Longpré refused to assign a date to it on the grounds that textura scripts such as this cannot be dated with accuracy; Margaret Deansley also refrained from giving it a date; and Fidelis a Fànna dated the manuscript to the fifteenth century.[96]

I also took the paleographical evidence further than James had in his brief description. James had noticed and transcribed a fourteenth-century inscription on f. 197: "Memorandum quod frater Johannes Neuton liberauit R. Thurk istum librum in quaternis non illuminatum nec ligatum et in se vij quaternos" [Memorandum: that friar John Neuton delivered this book to R. Thur[k] in quires, neither illuminated nor bound; seven quires in all]. James did not comment on this inscription. But by drawing on Neil Ker's *Medieval Libraries of Great Britain*, published in 1964 (and thus unknown to James), and drawing on the expertise of Malcolm Parkes and Andrew G. Watson, who generously shared their paleographical expertise with me, I was able to show that the manuscript belonged to the Augustinian Abbey of Leicester,

---

93. Stallings, *Meditaciones de passione Christi*.
94. James, *Western Manuscripts*, 409.
95. Karnes, *Imagination, Meditation, and Cognition*, 144.
96. McNamer, "Further Evidence," 246.

that what appeared to James as "Thurk" was more likely to be an abbreviation for the name "Thurlestone," and that the Thurlestone in question could be identified as Ralph de Thurlestone, a canon at the Abbey of Leicester who is known to have been studying at Oxford in 1339 and was prior of Mottisfont, Hampshire, from 1352 to 1356. The date of Ralph's death is unknown, but the fact that he was alive in 1356 leaves open the possibility that he received the book in the 1350s or even several decades later (for we might set his birth date close to 1320, given that he was a student at Oxford in 1339). The unbound and unilluminated state of the manuscript at the time Neuton delivered it does not necessarily indicate that it was commissioned by Thurlestone, but it does seem to indicate that it was copied not long before it came into Thurlestone's hands.

This kind of paleographical and bibliographical work is typically sufficient to be considered a serious contribution to the scholarship. It has not been contradicted by paleographers; indeed, more recent work on the manuscript and its context by Teresa Webber has confirmed a date of "first half of the fourteenth century," rather than "early fourteenth century," as the most reasonable date.[97] It is puzzling, then, that Karnes would cast the work I present in "Further Evidence" as less certain, thorough, or persuasive than the "traditional dating" of the manuscript.

Indeed, it seems to me that Karnes's approach here epitomizes a methodological problem I have touched on above: the uncritical use of the term "traditional." The ring of authority that the term "traditional" possesses can operate powerfully in assessments of scholarship on the MVC—and it is tempting to defer to it when faced with the complexity of the evidence. But it is worth looking closely at how the term functions in this particular case. What does the "traditional dating" of this manuscript represent?

What it represents, on closer inspection, is a judgment that appears to have been made fairly quickly late in the nineteenth century, by the colorful and prodigious Montague Rhodes James (1862–1936)—medievalist, Cam-

97. Webber, "Latin Devotional Texts," 33, and Webber and Watson, *Libraries of the Augustinian Canons,* 201. There is a discrepancy between the date Webber gives to the manuscript in these publications and the date she gives in another, "s. xiv in." ("The Books of Leicester Abbey," 178). As Webber has explained to me, "the broader dating is the more judicious one," and the one she stands by; the date supplied in "The Books of Leicester Abbey" was influenced in part by M. R. James's catalogue and perceived Italian influence in the hand, but my work in "Further Evidence" and her own independent analysis have led her to be skeptical of the "early fourteenth century" dating (personal email to me and to Nicolas Bell, Librarian of Trinity College Cambridge, August 14, 2016).

bridge don, antiquarian, amateur actor, provost of King's College and of Eton College, author of ghost stories, translator of New Testament apocrypha, director of the Fitzwilliam Museum, and energetic compiler of the *Western Manuscripts in the Library of Trinity College Cambridge: A Descriptive Catalogue*.[98] This four-volume catalogue contains descriptions of 1500 items, descriptions made at the average rate of three hundred per year while James was serving as dean and fellow of King's College; and it is clear that some of the manuscripts, especially those containing illuminations (such as the Trinity Apocalypse), consumed his attention more than others. The plain volume at issue here, Trinity B.14.7, with its copy of the Passion section of the MVC, did not present a manifest puzzle. The date James assigned to it was perfectly compatible with the hypothesis at that time: that Saint Bonaventure himself (1221–1274) composed the text, in Latin, in the thirteenth century. James had no need to think twice about assigning the date "xiv, early" to this manuscript. To be sure, James had a perceptive, expert eye, and he may have based this date on comparable dated or datable scripts he had seen; but we will never know, since he gives no reasons at all for assigning the manuscript to this date. Indeed, with characteristic affability, James himself recognized that the task of describing so many manuscripts, with such speed, could not be accomplished without errors. "In sending out the fourth and concluding volume of my Catalogue," he writes, in the preface to that volume, "I am troubled with many misgivings as to the character of the whole work":

> The man who undertakes the task of describing a large and heterogeneous mass of books, ranging in date from the seventh or eighth century to the nineteenth, and not restricted to one language or even three or four subjects, is necessarily giving many hostages to fortune. He is exposing himself to the onslaughts of every future specialist who has recourse to his laboriously compiled volumes. Absence of references to printed editions of texts, failures to detect the identity of a nameless treatise, omissions of what prove to be important details in the description of miniatures, ignorance of famous heraldic bearings, will all merit and perhaps meet with sharp reproof. . . . To these errors and failings I plead guilty; but I have deliberately preferred risking mistakes and producing the best catalogue I could within five years, to consulting all the available experts and postponing publication until the ninth.[99]

98. Pfaff, "James, Montague Rhodes."
99. James, *Western Manuscripts*, 4:5.

James himself, then, did not expect that his catalogue would be taken as the final word. He knew that it would contain errors that others would notice. And given what we now know about the MVC—that it was not composed in the thirteenth century by Bonaventure, that there is no other Latin manuscript that has been dated securely prior to circa 1350, and that the text contained in the Trinity College manuscript, the *Meditationes de Passione Christi*, is a derivative recension from the MVC—we must conclude that it is well and truly time to set the Trinity College manuscript aside in this debate. It does not contradict the theory of origins that I have proposed.[100]

The textual history of the MVC, then, is indeed complex, and the argument I have presented merits continuing debate. At this stage, we will turn to one of the most intriguing questions to which this reconstruction of the text's history gives rise: if the whole complex edifice of the MVC, with its many versions and adaptations in multiple languages, rests on a core text composed with such freshness, tenderness, and *vivezza* by Author A, who was Author A? How might we identify the author of the *testo breve*?

100. Although I have focused here on responding to Karnes's assertion that the Trinity College manuscript is a barrier to the argument I have made for the priority of the short Italian text, it is worth mentioning that Karnes also expresses opposition to my hypothesis that the original version of the MVC was composed by a woman: "It is more likely that the author was male," she states (13n49). Karnes offers no support for this statement. Indeed, it seems to be a judgment made without recourse to the primary evidence that would seem to be essential in such an evaluation, the text of the *testo breve* itself (to which, evidently, Karnes did not have access, or at least there is no citation of the Canonici manuscript or any of the Italian texts in her work). If judgments about the attributions of anonymous texts can be reduced to statistical probability, then her statement may be correct on a technical level: it is statistically "more likely" that the work was composed by a man than a woman simply because more men in the Middle Ages were trained to write. But this kind of reasoning is itself unhelpful, as Alexandra Barratt has pointed out, for it perpetuates circular arguments based on an "unwritten law of literary scholarship," which Barratt summarizes succinctly: "If most named authors are men, then so too are most anonymous writers" ("The Flower and the Leaf," 2). As Barratt observes, this premise requires critical evaluation, rather than simple repetition; see further my analysis in "Authorship," below. In any case, statistical probabilities are obviously too blunt an instrument for the proper evaluation of the question of the authorship of the various versions of the MVC.

# AUTHORSHIP

Who, then, was the author of the *testo breve,* this shorter, livelier Italian version of the MVC—and the text that may be its core, original form? It is an important question, one with significant implications for Italian literary history and for European cultural history more generally, given the broad circulation and influence the work achieved. Here, I will present evidence that the author is likely to have been a Poor Clare.

Hypotheses concerning women's authorship of anonymous medieval texts often meet with skepticism, of course, and the nature of the evidence in this case is such that it does not admit of certainty. The author makes no overt self-identifying statements within the text, and no external evidence of the author's identity—in the form of documents, convent chronicles, allusions to the author by other writers, or manuscript rubrics—has come to light. In short, there is no hard evidence that proves beyond doubt that the *testo breve* was composed by a woman, nor are ideal forms of proof likely to be discovered. Rather, it is the cumulative weight of disparate kinds of evidence that gestures strongly, as I see it, towards this conclusion.

In what follows, I will take up the question of the author's institutional affiliation first. I will then move on to a direct assessment of the evidence for female authorship.[1]

## FRANCISCAN AFFILIATION

In the better-known versions of the MVC, those that I have identified as the work of Author B, the Franciscan affiliation of both author and reader is

---

1. I adopt this structure of argument in part to make it very clear that I am not taking an "essentialist" position on authorship; institutional structures and social practices are the guiding rubrics here.

made very clear.[2] In the Prologue to the Latin text, for instance, both Francis and Clare of Assisi are presented as spiritual models for the nun for whom the work is intended: "If you were to read about blessed Francis and about your sweetest mother, blessed Clare the virgin, you would discover that they emerged from their many tribulations, wants and infirmities not only long-suffering but even cheerful."[3] In addition, the versions by Author B contain passages that align with motifs and ideologies promoted by the Franciscan Order.[4] In contrast, there is no overt mention of the affiliation of author or reader in the *testo breve*. Neither Francis nor Clare are mentioned in the Prologue. There is only one brief allusion to Francis in the text, in the chapter on the Last Supper. After mentioning that John and Christ exchanged words, which John then kept secret, the author refers to Francis: "Unde si leçe de sancto Francesco, che le revelatione occulte non manifestava de fuora se non in quanto el construe[n]çea la carità del proximo" (f. 62r) [Thus one reads of Saint Francis that he did not disclose secret revelations unless the love of neighbor required it]. This appears to be an allusion to a passage in Bonaventure's *Legenda maior*.[5] It is presented in passing, without any special emphasis. No expression of filial deference or special honor is present in conjunction with it. It would, of course, be possible for a non-Franciscan to cite a legend of Francis, who was, after all, the most celebrated saint in Italy at the time. Religious writers affiliated with one order could and did draw on sources aligned with other orders. As potential evidence of the author's affiliation, then, this single brief reference to Francis is not itself determinative.

But there are other reasons to believe that the author was affiliated in some way with the Franciscan Order. The stance taken in the text is that the author and reader share the same set of ideals—and in particular, an ideal of voluntary poverty. The ideal of poverty was not espoused exclusively by the Franciscans, of course. But the language of poverty in the *testo breve*, especially in relation to the Virgin, whom the reader is asked to imitate, has the

---

2. The other familiar version of the MVC, the Italian translation illustrated in Paris, BnF MS ital. 115, highlights its Franciscan allegiances even more through its pictorial program, which provides images of Francis and Clare and is addressed with particular fittingness to a readership of Poor Clares; see Flora, *The Devout Belief of the Imagination*.

3. Taney et al., 2.

4. In addition to the discussion in the Textual History section above, lxxi, lxxxv, see also "Notes to the *Meditations*," 228n126.

5. Bonaventure, *Legenda maior*, 603.

ring of a specifically Franciscan idealism.[6] A passage at the end of the chapter on the Visitation, for instance, not only depicts the Virgin as poor—returning to a house in which there is no bread, wine, worldly goods, possessions, or money—but calls the reader "spechio di povertade": "O spechio di povertade, hàbili compassione et attendi di amare povertade!" (f. 10v) [O mirror of poverty, have compassion and strive to love poverty!].

Moreover, Christ himself seems to be depicted as "Franciscan" in his enactment of poverty.[7] In the chapter on the Baptism, for instance, Christ walks the long route from Nazareth to the Jordan barefoot (*cum li piedi descalçi*, f. 45v), and the mention of this detail leads directly into a passage that emphasizes Christ's poverty through contrast with the riches and honors he might have possessed—a contrast that inspires, in turn, one of the more moving and poignant expressions of gratitude, and implicitly of the desire to imitate Christ, in the *testo breve* (ff. 45r–v).[8] Later in the same chapter, Christ is cast as one who begs for alms: "Ma di che viveva miser Iesù per camino? Io penso che lui andava cercando elymosina de porta in porta, et la nocte andava a dormire allo spedale. Et tuto questo facea miser Iesù per amore della povertade" (f. 46r) [But you ask how Lord Jesus lived on the road. I think that he went begging alms from door to door, and at night he went to sleep at a hostel. And Lord Jesus did all this for love of poverty.] Indeed, Christ began the practice of begging as a child, according to this author, who depicts the child as "maestro de la povertade," accepting alms from well-wishers as the family sets off from Egypt for the return home to Nazareth:

6. Lambert, *Franciscan Poverty,* remains the most comprehensive treatment of the subject. See "Notes to the *Meditations*," 200n6, 204n20, 209n36, 211n48, for specific references to poverty in the *testo breve.*

7. On the way Francis's life served as template for renderings of the lives of other holy figures in the thirteenth and fourteenth centuries, including Christ himself as depicted in the MVC, see Little, "*Imitatio Francisci.*" For a parallel phenomenon, the tendency among Dominicans to "Dominicanize" Christ, see Newhauser, "Jesus as the First Dominican."

8. This reference to Christ as barefoot may be another way in which he is subtly Franciscanized in the text. There was a contemporary debate between the Franciscans and Dominicans regarding footwear in the early fourteenth century; the question concerned whether the Dominicans could be deemed legitimately "apostolic" if they wore sandals. For a summary of the debate, in which the English Dominican Thomas Sutton defended the wearing of sandals in part by adducing the relic of Christ's sandals displayed at St. John Lateran in Rome, see Jotischky, *The Carmelites and Their Pasts,* 71.

Et alora el Maestro de la Povertade humelmente porse la mano et vergognosamente ricevete la [f. 33v] elimosina loro. O anima la qualle sei
venuta al serv[i]cio de Dio, pensa qui et habi compassione al tuo Signore, el qualle per insegnarti la via del cielo ha voluto eleçerse così
streta povertade! Adonque sforçate de seguitarlo! (ff. 33r–v)

———

[And so the Master of Poverty humbly stretched out his hand and
meekly received their alms. O soul who has come to the service of God,
reflect on this, and have compassion on Our Lord, who, to teach you the
way to heaven, wished to choose such strict poverty! Strive, then, to follow him!]

All of the mendicant orders practiced begging, of course, by definition; and
references to Christ's poverty by writers outside the Franciscan tradition are
commonplace. Here, however, it is not only the special emphasis given to
poverty, but the injunction to the reader to strive to imitate Christ in the practice of voluntary *streta povertade* that stands as strong evidence of the Franciscan affiliation of author and reader, for this was a concept and a phrase
that held special resonance for the Franciscans.[9]

In addition to these references to poverty, special emphasis is given in
the chapter on the Crucifixion to the shame Christ endured through being
stripped naked in the presence of all the people (f. 90r). While this theme was
not exclusively used by Franciscans, it was favored by them.[10] Perhaps more
compelling still is the particular form of one of the writer's exhortations to
the reader: "O soul who desires to glory in the Passion of your Lord, pay attention here" [O anima la qualle desideri de gloriarti nella Passione del tuo

———

9. See Lambert, *Franciscan Poverty*. It is important to note that the concept
of strict poverty is used in foundational Franciscan texts that continued to circulate
in the fourteenth century, including the *Rule of St. Clare* (Armstrong, *Clare of Assisi*,
chaps. 6 and 8). Its use does not imply that a document was authored by a Spiritual
Franciscan. Francis himself is said by Thomas of Celano to have been zealous for
poverty ("Omni studio, omni sollicitudine custodiebat sanctam et dominam pauper-
tatem"; *Vita prima*, cap. 19, in Leonardi, *La letteratura Francescana* 2:110; "He
zealously and carefully safeguarded Lady Holy Poverty"; Armstrong, Hellman, and
Short, *Francis of Assisi* 1:227).

10. See Derbes, *Picturing the Passion*, 138–42, and Trexler, *Naked before the
Father*.

Signore, stà qui attento] (f. 89v). This appears to be an allusion to the Franciscan Order's motto, *Mihi absit gloriari nisi in cruce Domini.*[11]

Other indications of the author's institutional affiliation include glimpses we can catch of the author's relation to others. For example, the author mentions communicating with a friar (*frate*) who has been to the Holy Land (f. 19v). This friar has told the author that there is a stone placed in a wall at one of the holy sites, a stone that is believed to have been used in place of a pillow for the infant Jesus, for his mother was so poor that she had no pillow for him. It is not impossible that the term *frate* refers to a Dominican, or even more generically to a brother of any kind; but given the strong Franciscan presence in the Holy Land and tradition of pilgrimage there, this phrase is likely to refer to news from a Franciscan friar—and therefore to imply that the author was also affiliated with the Franciscan Order. Further, the context makes it clear that this news about the stone was not gathered from a sermon or another form of public discourse, but through what sounds like an intimate, one-on-one conversation about holy things: "according to what I have heard from a friar who told me" [et secundo che io havi da uno frate che mi disse] (f. 19v). Such a conversation is most likely to have taken place within the same Order, whether in the context of friars speaking to each other or a friar speaking to a Poor Clare in the context of spiritual direction.

Another kind of evidence for Franciscan affiliation is largely conjectural. If my reconstruction of the history of the text is correct, then there is a process of textual appropriation and control to account for in some way. Author B, clearly a Franciscan who was a spiritual director of women, came into possession of the *testo breve* and edited and expanded it with an evident sense of entitlement to do so. His acquisition of the text and authoritative approach towards altering it would be easier to explain, it seems, if the affiliations of first and second authors were the same. The suppression of the *testo breve*, too, would have been facilitated if it were produced from within the Order. No evidence has yet surfaced to indicate that the *testo breve* achieved any significant circulation; indeed its survival in a single copy of Venetian

11. The passage itself is a scriptural citation, Galatians 6:14, and as such its use was not restricted solely to Franciscans. It appears, for instance, in the early-thirteenth-century Middle English *Ancrene Wisse*, which is not a Franciscan text (Savage and Watson, *Anchoritic Spirituality*, 176). But by the early fourteenth century, the dominant use of the phrase is its deployment as motto of the Franciscan Order and the encapsulation of the Order's ideals.

provenance—in a location, that is, far from its Tuscan home—appears to be a happy accident of history. Given the *testo breve*'s survival in a single manuscript, it is reasonable to deduce that the circulation of this text may have been actively restricted. It is a text with such appeal in literary terms, and one that so skilfully engages its readers, that it is unlikely to have simply languished until rescued by Author B. It begs to circulate; yet it appears that it did not. Given the Franciscan redactor's concerted efforts to correct the *testo breve*, a motive for its suppression is easy to imagine; and suppression would have been most effective if the author of the *testo breve* and its earliest readers were subject to the control of the Franciscan Order.[12]

All things considered, then, the most reasonable deduction is that the author of the *testo breve* was affiliated with the Franciscan Order. The question can then be narrowed to this: to which Order of the Franciscans did the author belong, First, Second, or Third? The possibility that the author was a Franciscan tertiary is unlikely. Among other things, the author emphasizes the need not to contradict or oppose "our superiors" [*nostri maçori*, f. 30v, f. 46v], especially when they issue correctives. This implies that both reader and author are situated within an institutional hierarchy in which regular correction by superiors is to be welcomed as part of the regular spiritual training of living in a religious community. In addition, the authorial voice and stance towards the reader are those of one who is in a position to give spiritual advice and direction to a nun. It would be highly unusual for a Franciscan tertiary to adopt or be granted this kind of authority.[13]

12. The process by which Bonaventure adapted Thomas of Celano's lives of Francis might be adduced as a parallel. Bonaventure was granted the license to change Thomas of Celano's work so extensively because Franciscan ideals, practices, and institutional identity were at stake. The supremely efficient suppression of Thomas of Celano's *vitae* after the Chapter General of 1266 indicates that censorship, the publication of new official texts superceding the old, and a strict control of the circulation of manuscripts were by no means practices foreign to the Franciscans. The production of Angela of Foligno's *Memoriale* provides another potential parallel. Brother A. states that there was a first draft that he did not circulate but submitted for approval to a Franciscan council, which required revisions. The revised version was issued as the text officially authorized by the Order. No copies of the first version are known to survive and are likely to have been deliberately destroyed. On efforts to suppress women's learning within the Franciscan Order and the resilience of the Poor Clares within such a context, see Roest, "*Ignorantia*," esp. 57–58, as well as Roest's *Order and Disorder*.

13. There are, to be sure, cases in which tertiaries served to inspire others and impart spiritual wisdom. Ubertino da Casale credits the tertiary Angela of Foligno,

Was the author, then, a First Order Franciscan—a Franciscan friar? Or a Second Order Franciscan, a Poor Clare? To frame this as a question about distinctions in institutional history—setting aside, for now, other ways of asking whether the text was composed by a woman—is useful, I believe, in that it can enable us to evaluate internal textual evidence in relation to what is known about the First Order and the Second Order in the first two decades of the fourteenth century and to ask, on that basis, which is the most likely conclusion.

Let's return to institutional affiliation itself as authorial preoccupation, for instance. It is a striking feature of the *testo breve* that the author's Franciscan affiliation is something that needs to be *deduced* from clues embedded in the text; it is never openly announced or asserted. In other words, this appears to be an author who espouses Franciscan ideals but for whom the overt claiming of allegiance and promotion of institutional identity per se is unimportant. This feature of the text, and of Author A's apparent mindset, is especially noticeable when the *testo breve* is situated next to the subsequent versions of the MVC, in which Author B is so plainly intent on asserting the Franciscan identity of his reader and himself and thus of defining the text as a *Franciscan* text, beginning with the direct reference to Francis as spiritual model in the Prologue (Sarri, 4). Indeed, Author B can be seen as a typical Franciscan of the First Order in this regard. For the Order of Friars Minor, defining the Order within and against other forms of religious life, bolstering a strong sense of institutional identity and allegiance, and assertively claiming various texts, practices, and saints as "Franciscan" were central preoccupations for the first century of the Order's history and beyond. In the wake of the fierce debates about poverty taking place during the first two decades of the fourteenth century, it would be very difficult to find a member of the O.F.M. who could be as unconcerned about asserting Franciscan identity and promoting allegiance to the founder of the Order as Author A manifestly is. The most obvious writer to take as basis for comparison would be Ubertino da Casale, who wrote his *Arbor vitae crucifixae Jesu* in 1305, and Ubertino certainly conflates affective meditation on the Passion with Franciscan polemic.[14]

---

for instance, with changing "the whole face of my mind" (Davis, *Ubertino da Casale*, 5). He also mentions seeking instruction on the "arcana" of Christ's life from a certain Peter of Siena, who has been identified as the Franciscan Tertiary Pietro Pettinaio (d. 1289), mentioned by Dante in *Purgatorio* XIII.127–29, and from the "holy virgin Cecilia of Florence," who has not been identified (Davis, *Ubertino da Casale*, 4).

14. See Davis, ed., *Ubertino da Casale*. For other texts by Franciscans dating to the first half of the fourteenth century, see Fleming, *An Introduction to Franciscan Literature*.

For the Poor Clares, however, institutional circumstances were different. From the very beginning, women who belonged to what would become the Second Order had a more ambiguous and flexible relationship to institutional affiliation itself. This is not the place to rehearse the complex early history of the Poor Clares in relation to the Order of Friars Minor, or to trace the shifting institutional affiliations of particular women of the thirteenth and early fourteenth centuries. But it can be confidently stated that there was far greater fluidity in institutional circumstances, identity, and allegiance among women religious at this time, including those we can identify as Poor Clares for at least part of their lives.[15]

To return to the *testo breve*, then, and to the internal clues it provides for institutional affiliation: we are now in a position to recognize these clues as, simultaneously, clues indicating that the author is likely to have been a woman. In short, this author appears to be Franciscan but exhibits no impulses to promote the Order over and against other Orders; nor are there any hints, here, of the fierce debates between the Spirituals and Conventuals that preoccupied the Order of Friars Minor during the early decades of the fourteenth century. These features of the text are compatible with the hypothesis that a Poor Clare wrote the work—and more difficult to reconcile with a theory that it was composed by a Franciscan friar.

## CUMULATIVE EVIDENCE THAT THE *TESTO BREVE* WAS COMPOSED BY A WOMAN

As I have suggested above, the possibility that the *testo breve* was composed by a woman needs to be approached carefully. There is no absolute proof, neither internal to the text nor external to it, that could resolve the question beyond any doubt. Yet there are indications the cumulative force of which gestures strongly towards the conclusion that the text was composed by a woman.[16]

15. See Alberzoni, *Clare of Assisi and the Poor Sisters*; Knox, *Creating Clare of Assisi*; Catherine Mooney, *Clare of Assisi and the Thirteenth-Century Church*; Field, *Isabelle of France*; and Field, Field, and Knox, *Visions of Sainthood in Medieval Rome*.

16. It is interesting to note that one of the most astute and learned authorities on religious writing of the Trecento, Giuseppe de Luca, speculated in the 1950s that the MVC may have been composed by a woman. He devotes only a few sentences to this hypothesis, without arguing a case, but his words are worth repeating here: "To me it appears—or to say it better, I suspect—that the *Meditations* were produced in

One of the most compelling of these indications, in my view, is a single phrase that appears uniquely in the *testo breve*—a phrase whose potential significance can easily be overlooked. It appears in the context of a reference to St. Cecilia. In all versions of the MVC, St. Cecilia is advanced in the Prologue as a model to be imitated. She is then mentioned again in the middle of the text, at that important transitional point in which, as we have seen, the reader is invited to meditate on scenes from the life of Christ even if they are not included in the MVC. In this second context, the wording in the *testo breve* differs from that of the other versions. It presents Cecilia, the author, and the reader as brides of Christ: "Ma noi dovemo essere solliciti de quello exempio de sancta Cecilia de portare sempre le opere del nostro dolce spoxo miser Iesù nelgli chuori nostri" (f. 53r) [But we should always strive to follow the example of Saint Cecilia and carry always the words and deeds of our sweet spouse Lord Jesus in our hearts]. The author is thus mentioning to the reader—in an offhand way, without making this the main point of the passage—that Christ is their spouse: *nostro dolce spoxo miser Iesu*. The phrase is used very matter-of-factly here, as if it refers to a social bond, rather than a mystical or metaphorical union. It thus appears to indicate that both author and reader were nuns.

It is true, of course, that male religious regularly speak of Christ as bridegroom in mystical texts; Bernard of Clairvaux's *Sermons on the Song of Songs*, which cast Christ as the bridegroom and the soul as bride, is merely the most familiar example of a widespread practice. It is true, too, that the relationship between Christ and the church is routinely allegorized as marriage in the later Middle Ages. And indeed, even in the *testo breve*, there are passages that cast the relationship between Christ and a collective "we," signifying all members of the church, as a relation between spouses.[17]

But distinctions among the various usages of the term "spouse" in religious writings can too easily be collapsed—and when they are, certain meanings can be missed. Precise textual and historical contexts matter. And it seems to me that Christ is referred to as spouse in such a matter-of-fact way here because that is exactly what he was for medieval nuns, who took on the social and legal identity *sponsa Christi* at the moment of

---

Latin and the vernacular at the same time. As the work of a female visionary and her confessor—originating from an Agreda or Emmerich of the Duecento—they were hiding the 'dossier' of a mystic, and for that reason were given shelter under the aegis of St. Bonaventure" (de Luca, *Prosatori minori*, 1003).

17. See, for example, the conclusion of the chapter on the Baptism (f. 47r).

consecration.[18] In short, this phrase, in this particular context, reads as if it rests on a *social* base; Christ appears to be referred to as *spoxo* here in the social, institutional, pragmatic sense relevant only to female religious, who took Christ as spouse in rites of consecration. The phrase is indeed infused with emotion: "*dolce* spoxo." But it is a term of endearment that also serves as a reminder of a social bond, "dolce *spoxo*," and the particular obligations attendant upon that institutionalized relationship.

That such a specific social sense existed in fourteenth-century Italy is not in dispute; nuns are so regularly referred to as brides of Christ, simply by virtue of their status as nuns, that there is no need for extensive documentation that this was a widespread usage of the term.[19] It is this semiotic register that appears to be invoked, in this specific context, in the phrase *nostro dolce spoxo miser Iesu*. This is, I would submit, a simple allusion to social status. And if this is true, a simple deduction follows: one nun is writing for another.

Does this single phrase in the *testo breve*, then, stand as incontrovertible evidence that the author of this version was a nun? Not on its own; indeed, a closer look at the phrase, under the pressure of this hypothesis, reveals a further complexity that might, at first glance, appear to refute the claim that this passage refers to nuns. That complexity lies in the ending of the preceding adjective, *solliciti*. This is not the feminine plural form of the word: *sollicite*. Wouldn't we expect to find the feminine plural ending if the speaker, as well as the addressee, were both women? Or, to put it another way, does the masculine plural form (which also functions as a gender-neutral plural) rule out the hypothesis that both speaker and addressee were women?

It is indeed a conundrum worth puzzling over.[20] But one thing that can be said with certainty is that the masculine plural form, *solliciti*, does not *dis-*

18. For sources documenting this social and legal designation, see "Compassion and the Making of a *Sponsa Christi*," in McNamer, *Affective Meditation and the Invention of Medieval Compassion*, 25–57. In his analysis of the legal dimensions of a *sponsa Christi*'s marriage, Thomas Head has put the matter succinctly: "Being a 'bride of Christ' was not *like* marriage to Christ, it *was* marriage to Christ" ("The Marriages of Christina of Markyate," 75). On the parallels between the rites of consecration of nuns and marriage rites, see Metz, *La consécration des vierges*.

19. See Battaglia, *Grande dizionario* XIX, 1016: *sposa*, sf., 3, "Donna consacrata alla vita monastica, monaca, suore" and examples.

20. I would like to thank Richard Kieckhefer for bringing this matter to my attention and thinking it through with me. What the "i" ending does show is that the phrase cannot be the smoking gun (or, as Kieckhefer suggests, the smoking thurible) that could settle, definitively, the question of whether the author was a woman. An "e" ending—*sollicite*—*would* have served as a textual feature approaching the status of clinching evidence.

*prove* the hypothesis that both speaker and addressee were nuns. It does not stand as clinching counterevidence. Why not? There are several reasons, having to do with the practices and assumptions of scribes.

A reminder is in order, here, that the Canonici manuscript was copied in the early fifteenth century in the Veneto, close to a century after the composition of the *testo breve* (see below, "The Manuscript," cxlix). The number of copying stages between the original and the Canonici manuscript is not clear, but it seems that there were quite a few such stages, for the language of the text appears to have been "gradually Veneticized" over some period of time.[21] The default assumption of any medieval scribe faced with an anonymous devotional text would have been that its author was male. Thus, a feminine ending, *sollicite*, even if this were the original form of the work, is highly unlikely to have been preserved. Scribes are likely to have "corrected" this surprising form if they had encountered it.

Further, a tendency towards carelessness in the preservation of feminine forms appears to be a fairly common feature in devotional texts for women. A passage in the Latin text of the *Rothschild Canticles*, copied for a nun at the turn of the fourteenth century, provides an interesting example of this.[22] It appears in the context of the Gospel story of the healing of the woman with a hemorrhage. The Gospel verse reads: "Dixit enim intra se, si tetigero fimbriam vestimenti eius, salva ero (Mt 9:21, Lk 8:44). But in the copy written in the *Rothschild Canticles*, the scribe has written *salvus* for *salva*—even though the character in the Gospels is definitely a woman and the reader for whom the *Rothschild Canticles* was compiled was a woman. The simplest explanation for the masculine form *salvus* in this manuscript, then, is that it is a simple copying error.[23] Indeed, of all the kinds of potential scribal errors, a reflexive substitution of masculine plural forms—understood, then as now, as the default or "neutral" form—is perhaps the most common. Even in the Canonici manuscript itself, there are many instances of the "neutralizing" of a plural as masculine, or of a carelessness or oscillation in grammatical gender. Very early on in the text, for example, we encounter the phrase, "instrumenti delectevoli e belle" (f. 2r). Such inconsistencies in grammatical gender were either introduced by the scribe or, if present in the exemplar, did not bother the

---

21. See below, "Linguistic Analysis," clxxv.

22. On this interesting and amply illuminated manuscript, see Hamburger, *The Rothschild Canticles*.

23. I would like to thank Barbara Newman for sharing this example with me; in her view it is likely to be a wrongly expanded abbreviation (personal correspondence, July 2012).

scribe enough to require correction. For these reasons, then, the manuscript's masculine plural ending of *solliciti* is not an ending that we can confidently trace to the author. To put it another way: if the author had written *sollicite*, there is virtually no chance that this feminine ending would have survived multiple layers of copying, given scribal habits and assumptions.[24]

In addition, there is a striking form of indirect evidence that the phrase originally referred specifically to nuns, and that it testifies to an authorial stance in which one nun is speaking to another. That evidence is this: the phrase *nostro dolce spoxo* is *not present* in the revised versions of the text. In the *testo minore*, the parallel passage reads, "Ma noi doveremo essere solic-iti, ad esemplo di santa Cecilia, di portare sempre l'opere di Cristo ne' cuori nostri" [But we should always be concerned, following the example of saint Cecilia, to carry always the words and deeds of Christ in our hearts] (Sarri, 88). Author B, then, appears to have deliberately omitted the phrase *nostro dolce spoxo*.[25] This is not because Author B has anything against spousal im-agery per se; other references, those that cast the relationship between Christ and all Christians or the church as a marriage, are retained. Why, then, would Author B delete the phrase *nostro dolce spoxo* from its place in the transi-tional passage? The most reasonable deduction is that he omitted it because it did not apply to him. Author B was not a nun; it would make no sense, then,

24. The defaulting to masculine forms of adjectives is evident in other Italian versions of the MVC too, including the copy of the *testo minore* used by Sarri (Flo-rence, Biblioteca Riccardiana MS 1419). Even though the fiction is maintained there that the work is addressed to a solitary female reader, adjectives referring to the reader take masculine forms: the author instructs the reader to be "reverente e timo-roso," for instance, where we would expect *timorosa* (Sarri, 35).

25. In theory, of course, it is possible that the phrase was dropped accidentally. However, this seems unlikely to me, in part because the particular differences be-tween the *testo breve* and Author B's revised texts, beginning with the *testo minore*, do not appear to be accidental or to have casual motives. The differences fall into patterns: Author B adds references to Christ's divinity, omits passages that are overly affective, adds specific distances and place names, adds more material from authoritative sources, adopts a more preacherly stance, substitutes indirect for direct discourse, and so on (see above, "Textual History," and "Notes to the *Meditations*"). Even more significantly, in my view, is the potential for evidentiary power that the phrase *nostro dolce spoxo* contains. In its limpidity, in the lack of attention it calls to itself, I believe it is the closest we have to a serious, clinching clue: an indirect indication—all the more credible *because* indirect—that a nun composed the text. It seems important to ask how likely it would be for such a phrase to be removed *acci-dentally* from the scene.

for him to use the phrase, *nostro dolce spoxo*, as if he, too, were a nun, participating in the kind of social, legal, institutional bond with Christ that was only permitted to nuns. The theory that best explains this suppressed phrase, then, is that the original author was a nun; Author B was not.

## Literacy

What about literacy levels in early Trecento Tuscany, and the compositional skills needed for a woman to compose a work such as this, skills that included reading Latin and writing in Italian? The assumption that medieval women were incapable of composing because they lacked the capacity to read and write has, after all, been the dominant assumption undergirding the default assignment of anonymous texts to men unless hard documentary evidence proves otherwise. But a look at the particular historical context indicates that there is no serious barrier to granting that a Poor Clare could have acquired the skills to write a vernacular meditative text such as this. Evidence of education and book ownership within the order of the Poor Clares indicates that a nun from this order could well have composed a text like the *Meditations* in the early fourteenth century. Women who entered Clarissan convents in fourteenth-century Italy were typically of noble birth and continued to possess books even after entering the convent.[26] Literacy levels in many convents appear to have been quite high. As John Moorman has noted, many licenses for entry "were granted on the grounds that the postulant was an educated girl, *puella litterata*."[27] Bert Roest's more recent study of the Poor Clares provides ample evidence of reading practices and literary and scribal activity in the fourteenth century.[28] Among the chief primary sources for such activity is Fra Mariano da Firenze's early history of the Poor Clares, composed in the early sixteenth century but based on earlier convent chronicles, which paints a picture of an institutional context conducive to reading, learning, and writing, with examples of literary women ranging from Clare herself, whose letters to Agnes continued to circulate long after her death, to a certain Elia dei Pulci of the convent of Monticelli in Florence (as well as many Poor Clares of the late fourteenth and fifteenth centuries who engaged

26. Moorman provides a convenient overview; see "The Clarisses in the Fourteenth Century," in *A History of the Franciscan Order*, 406–16.

27. Moorman, *A History of the Franciscan Order*, 413n1.

28. Roest, *Order and Disorder*, esp. chap. 6, "Forms of Literary and Artistic Expression."

in forms of learning, writing, and instruction). Nothing is known of Elia dei Pulci, apart from records of her existence at Monticelli in 1308, 1315, 1318, and 1320. Yet these dates alone are suggestive, for they would make her a contemporary of the author of the *testo breve*. Mariano describes Elia as one "who, in addition to the ornament of moral and divine virtues with which she was adorned, certainly was adorned also with singular natural genius and with learning in Latin [*di singulare ingegno naturale et di gramaticha*] but much more with perfect observance of the rule and with prayer and contemplation."[29] If the Poor Clare Elia dei Pulci could excel in learning and in contemplation and yet remain unknown to history apart from Mariano's chronicle, it is not far-fetched to suggest that there may have been others like her in Tuscany in the early decades of the Trecento: educated women from noble families, adept at reading Latin, drawn to contemplative practice—and capable of taking up a pen and beginning to write.

That nuns in fourteenth-century Tuscany were often taught to read and to write can be inferred from a number of other sources as well. Literacy levels for girls in Florence in the first half of the fourteenth century appear to have been among the highest in Europe; as Christiane Klapisch-Zuber observes, the *Cronica* of Giovanni Villani "affirms, in an oft-cited passage, that on the eve of the Black Death 60 percent of Florentines between the ages of 6 and 13 went to school, regardless of their sex."[30] And while there may have been some resistance to educating girls among the merchant classes by the middle of the century, daughters destined to become nuns remained the exception— or at least this remained a prescriptive ideal, according to the conduct book penned by the merchant Paolo da Certaldo, who advises fathers not to teach their daughters to write *unless* they wish them to become nuns.[31] Moreover, there is evidence of significant scribal activity among nuns, including Poor Clares, in the later Middle Ages. Although most of the evidence documenting a thriving scriptorium of Poor Clares at Monteripido dates from the fifteenth century, the scriptorium appears to have first emerged in the fourteenth century.[32]

As for the composition of texts by women in Duecento and early Trecento Italy, Pozzi and Leonardi's list of *scrittrici mistiche italiane* includes

29. Boccali, *Mariano da Firenze*, 207.

30. Klapisch-Zuber, *Women, Family, and Ritual*, 108.

31. Schiaffini, *Libro di buoni costumi*, 126.

32. Nicolini, "I minori osservanti di Monteripido e lo 'scriptorium' delle clarisse di Monteluce." See also the pioneering study by Gill, "Women and the Production of Religious Literature in the Vernacular."

ten documented writers prior to the great Catherine of Siena (1347–1380), who has sometimes figured in literary histories as the "first" Italian woman writer. These women include Clare of Assisi (1193–1253), Beatrice d'Este (ca. 1200–1226), Umiliana Cerchi (1219–1246), Umiltà of Faenza (1226–1310), Margaret of Cortona (1247–1297), Angela of Foligno (1248–1309), Benevenuta Bojanni (1255–1292), Vanna of Orvieto (1264–1306), Clare of Montefalco (1268–1308), and Villana de' Botti (1332–1361).[33]

It may also be time to take more seriously the indirect evidence of authorial activity by women, especially in genres related to meditative practices. The shadowy figure of the "most holy virgin Cecilia of Florence" mentioned by Ubertino da Casale, for instance, is intriguing. Nothing is known of her except what Ubertino describes: that he was drawn to her as one who taught him about the *arcana* of Christ's life, those episodes that are not recorded in the Gospels.[34] There is also indirect evidence that Tuscan women were trying their hands at vernacular renderings of, or commentary on, the scriptures. Giordano da Pisa—who was concerned, as the Dominicans of the early Trecento were, to combat heresy—condemns this kind of activity in no uncertain terms:

> There are many crazy people—cobblers, furriers—who would like to explain [or translate] Holy Scripture. Great boldness, and too great offense is theirs! And if this is true of men, so it is all the more true of women, because women are too much farther than men from the Scriptures and from Latin learning [*la lettera*]. There are some women who make themselves expositors [or translators] of the Epistle and of the Gospel. Great is their folly! Too great is their foolishness [*scipidezza*].[35]

Although a source of indignation to Giordano, such women, whose existence Giordano assumes is open knowledge among his audience of Florentines, are likely to have generated a horizon of expecations in which meditations on

---

33. Pozzi and Leonardi, *Scrittrici mistiche italiane.*

34. Of the "deuotissima uirgo cecilia de florentia" who introduced him to "arcana iesu," Ubertino writes: "Nam praefata uirgo quod nunc simul cum praefato petro regnat in celis totum praecessum superioris contemplationis de uita iesu & arcana cordis mei & alia multa de paruulo iesu sepissime me instruxit" (Davis, *Ubertino da Casale*, 4). Since Ubertino mentions that Cecilia is now in heaven, she must have been actively teaching about the life and especially the childhood of Christ towards the end of the thirteenth century, or by any case no later than 1305, when Ubertino composed his book.

35. Quoted in Cornish, *Vernacular Translation in Dante's Italy*, 113; 209n51.

the Gospels could be composed. It is not out of the question that the *testo breve* represents the very kind of text that Giordano railed against, with its imagined scenes from the life of Christ and its vernacularization of entire chapters of the Gospels.[36]

The general stance of the *testo breve*, too, in which the authorial voice is guiding the reader, is a stance that is itself well documented in women's convents. There was an active culture of women instructing women in Tuscany in the early decades of the fourteenth century. Examples include Clare of Montefalco (d. 1308), who "proved her great ability to understand the scriptures" even though she was not an educated woman, and who was lauded in her *vita* for instructing her sisters.[37] More generally it is worth recalling that there was a regular practice in medieval convents in which nuns in positions of authority within the convent (abbesses, prioresses, or those known for their spiritual wisdom) took on responsibility for instructing other nuns within the community; Heloise, Hildegard, the nuns of Helfta, and Clare of Assisi are simply the most well-known figures for what was a much broader medieval phenomenon. It would be false to assume that spiritual direction in general and instruction in prayer and meditation in particular were uniquely configured as a structure in which a superior and literate male instructed an inferior and illiterate female. Women guided other women in the practice of prayer. Since there are well known cases of nuns in other contexts providing devotional texts for other nuns (Gertrude the Great's *Spiritual Exercises*, for instance), it would be surprising if this did not happen in Italy. In the energetic climate of the production of vernacular religious texts in early Trecento Pisa, in particular (see "Date and Place of Composition"), it is reasonable to conclude that both women's literacy and the horizon of expectations were such that the composition of a meditative text in Italian by a nun for her fellow nuns, especially if she were an abbess, was possible.

### Sources

The author of the *testo breve* drew on sources of the kind that might well have been available to a nun capable of reading Latin in the early decades of the fourteenth century. The limited range of frequently cited texts can be

---

36. The *testo breve*, unlike the more familiar versions of the MVC, presents long stretches of vernacularized scriptural passages, uninterrupted by meditative direction or commentary; see below the notes to chapter 18, for example, which is almost entirely a translation from the gospel of John.

37. Cornish, *Vernacular Translation in Dante's Italy*, 119.

identified as the Gospels, especially those of Matthew and Luke, and the *Glossa Ordinaria*; the *Psalms*; Peter Comestor's *Historia scholastica*; the *Legenda aurea*; Bernard of Clairvaux's *Sermons on the Song of Songs* (22, 43, 61); and the *Gospel of Nicodemus*. The ease and confidence with which these sources are woven into the narrative suggests that the author was quite familiar with them and drew upon them directly. It is worth noting that no great library was required; indeed, we need only posit that the author had ready access to four or five volumes, including the Gospels and a psalter. The liturgy is another important source Author A drew upon with ease. Other sources, referred to briefly or in passing, can be identified as Angela of Foligno's *Memoriale*; Bernard of Clairvaux's *In die natali Domini*, *In die sancto Paschae*, *De psalmo "Qui habitat,"* and *Epistula*; John Chrysostom, *Homilies on the Gospel of Matthew*; St. Jerome, *Commentary on Matthew*; Bonaventure, *Legenda maior*; Augustine, *Tractates on the Gospel of John*; St. Ambrose, *In Lucam*; and pseudo-Origen's *Homily on Mary Magdalene*. Given the brevity of the citations in this second category, it is possible, indeed likely, that these latter sources were not drawn upon directly from complete written compendiums by Chrysostom, Jerome, Ambrose, and the others. Rather, some passages, like that from Ambrose, may have reached the author via the liturgy, through sermons, or through spiritual conversation of the kind the author mentions in connection with a certain *frate* who had been to the Holy Land (f. 19v); it is also possible that such passages reached the author at one remove, through their incorporation into the *Glossa Ordinaria*.

Although too little is still known about the contents of nuns' libraries in Tuscany in the decades around the year 1300, the sources used here appear to be compatible with the hypothesis that the *testo breve* was composed by a nun.

## Familiarity with Women's Social Practices

The *testo breve* fully, yet unselfconsciously, privileges a woman's point of view—so much so that it seems to come by this point of view honestly, as it were. There is no element of striving here, no sign that it has been an effort to understand a woman's perspective. That a mother would weep to see her baby in pain, that the Purification should be an event worth a chapter, that Christ should desire his mother's cooking above all else, that the mother would kiss rather than merely "look at" the body of her dead son, that the risen Christ would appear first to his mother, greeting her as *madre mia carissima* (f. 111r)—that such details come across so convincingly would itself suggest that the text was written by a woman.

Could Author A have been a male author who was particularly attentive to a woman's point of view? This is not impossible, of course; gifted writers of any place and time can be credited with expansive imaginative capacities and a heightened degree of attunement to the lives of others. Given this, it can be useful to narrow the issue further, to the matter of specific social practices. Just as evidence of familiarity with certain practices has been taken as a valid clue to the identity of a broad array of anonymous authors in the medieval period (knowledge of legal procedures suggesting lawyers, of priestly rituals suggesting priests, and so on), I would suggest that we can take the *testo breve*'s knowledge of women's practices—knowledge that is, significantly, embedded in the text unselfconsciously—as a potentially valuable clue to the identity of Author A.

Let's look at just one example in this regard, an example that shows how such knowledge of women's practices infuses the *testo breve* with naturalness and ease. It occurs in the chapter depicting the return from Egypt to Nazareth. Jesus is now a small child, one who plays in the road and can speak full sentences; he is capable of walking but cannot walk very far; we also gather that he is still small enough to be carried. Together, these features imply that he is a toddler of about two or perhaps three years old (unlike his designation as age seven in subsequent versions of the text).[38] The meditator is asked to enter this scene as the one who leads the donkey by the halter, while Jesus rides with his mother and Joseph follows behind. As this procession ambles along, an ordinary moment, but one rich in affective potential, is introduced:

> Now, if Our Lady wants to dismount sometimes to go a little on foot, be sure to hold the child Jesus so he doesn't fall. And if the child Jesus wants to get down, take him in your arms and hold him until his Mother comes, and then reverently give him to his mother, because it is a great comfort to her when she receives her son in her arms.

38. In the *testo minore* and subsequent versions, in contrast, we are told at the outset of the chapter on the return from Egypt that seven years have passed (Sarri, 57). It would appear that Author B revised Christ's age upwards, and that he did so because this is the time period specified in the *Historia scholastica*. That this specification of seven years is a later addition, providing further evidence that the textual history I have outlined is correct, can be deduced from the resulting inconsistency: Christ's age has been altered to seven, yet the prior layer of the text, which asks the reader to carry him, and presents Mary as carrying him, is retained (Sarri, 61). Carrying a toddler makes sense, both as a pragmatic everyday occurrence and as an incitement to affective devotion; carrying a seven-year-old boy is harder to imagine on both counts. The *testo breve*'s reading (chap. 9) is manifestly superior here.

[Or se alcuna volta la Dona Nostra volesse desmontare per andare uno puocho a piedi, fà che tu tegni il fançullo Iesù açiò ch'el non cadesse. Et se 'l fançullo Iesù volesse desmontare, fà che tu el pigli in braço et tienlo fin che la madre vegna, et poi reverentemente il dà alla madre, imperò che gran riposo era a lei quando la ricevea il figliolo in braço.] (f. 34r)

Worth pointing out here are the author's awareness of a very young child's vulnerabilities, the pragmatic provision that his mother should ride with him, and the need to "hold the child Jesus so he doesn't fall" should his mother want a break, as she would. It is a small set of details, and easily escapes notice—until it is compared to the revised versions of the text. In the versions I have presented as successive redactions—*testo minore, testo maggiore*, Latin text— Author B first removes the child's mother from the donkey altogether, so that in the *testo minore* he rides alone, with his mother walking behind; in the long Latin text, the meditator's protective hand, holding the child on the donkey, has also been removed. [39] These changes may well have been motivated by a desire to present an image of "Jesus riding alone on a donkey" that could function as a prefiguration of the mature Christ's entry into Jerusalem prior to the Passion.[40] Whatever the motive, the scene as imagined by Author B illuminates, through contrast, Author A's superior degree of attunement to a very young child's limited capacities—and of the specific practices that women typically caring for a child of this age would need to engage in in order to keep such a child safe.

This single scene does not on its own, of course, prove that the *testo breve* was composed by a woman. But there are so many scenes like this. Moreover, the cumulative effect of this kind of evidence of a woman's point of view—the ease and confidence with which women's spaces and domestic rituals are depicted, the lively attention given to how women socialize and share beds and engage in intimate talk, the lack of hesitation in describing aspects of pregnancy and the care of a newborn, and so on—invites attention to more assertive moments in the *testo breve* in which women's status or authority is heightened. Mary, for instance, is a figure with considerable authority in the *testo breve*. Christ wants to do what pleases her when he leaves the learned doctors in the temple (f. 37v); and before he sets out for the Jordan

39. Sarri, 61; Taney et al., 51.

40. The illustrations in Oxford, Corpus Christi College MS 410 bear out this typological understanding of the scene in the Latin text; see the interesting interpretation by Bartal, "Repetition, Opposition, and Invention."

River to be baptized, Mary gives him permission to undertake the journey and this defining step in his life ("Or licenciato dalla madre, mesesse in camino inverso Ierusalem" [f. 45r]). Magdalene, too, is given a very prominent role in the text. In the course of summarizing the various appearances Jesus made after the Resurrection, for instance, the author of the *testo breve* defines Magdalene quite pointedly as Christ's "beloved disciple": "But in a spirit of devotion we may imagine that he, being so kind, appeared many times to his mother—and also to her, his beloved disciple, that is, Magdalene; and to many of his other devoted followers, in order to strengthen them in his love" [Ma noi podemo piatosamente pensare che lui, come benigno, piu volte apparse alla madre sua et anche a quella sua dillecta discipula, çioè Magdalena, et a molti altri suoi divoti per confermarli nel suo amore] (f. 121v). This designation of Magdalene as Christ's beloved is certainly not unprecedented.[41] But it is particularly striking here because the phrase *dillecta discipula* seems to be a direct substitution for the expected *dilecto discipulo*, John, who is not mentioned in this passage; nor indeed are any of Christ's male disciples mentioned. The author of the *testo breve* has placed women at the center here in a way that challenges scriptural authority in its implicit substitution of Magdalene for John as beloved disciple. Could a male author have composed such a thoroughly woman-centered text? Yes; this would be possible. But that possibility should not prevent us from recognizing a compelling alternative: that Author A's demonstrably heightened awareness of women's domestic practices, spaces, and social relationships, combined with a manifest tendency to assert the authority and importance of women, deserves consideration as a possible, indeed probable, indication of female authorship. It may not be naive, in other words, to deduce from this evidence the simplest explanation: that the author was a woman.

## Authorial Self-description

What about authorial self-descriptions in the *testo breve*? Might these serve to identify Author A?

There is one such reference to the author's own lived experience; and this appears, at first glance, to contradict the hypothesis that the work was composed by a Poor Clare. It is a description that locates our author in Rome, at the church of Saint John Lateran, gazing with keen interest at the remnants from the table used at the Last Supper: "Et era quella mensa overo tavola

41. See esp. Jensen, *The Making of the Magdalen.*

quadra et era de più peçi, la qualle io ho veduto a Roma in la chiesia de sancto Çuane Laterano, la qualle io ho mesurata che per quadro la è braço uno et uno palmo et tre dida; sì che sentarebe tre per quadro" (ff. 60r–v) [And this table, or rather board, was square in shape, and made of several pieces; and I have seen it in Rome, in the church of Saint John Lateran, and I took its measure, and each side is the length of one arm and one palm and three fingers; so it could seat three per side].

Given the strict enclosure required of Poor Clares, as well as the issuing of the papal bull *Periculoso* in 1298, this requires some explanation. We might conclude from this detail, for instance, that the work could not have been composed by a Poor Clare, because Poor Clares were not permitted to leave the convent. But there are alternative explanations. A woman might well have traveled to Rome on pilgrimage prior to becoming a nun; such was the case with Clare of Assisi's own mother and sister, so there was clear precedent for this specifically among the Poor Clares. In addition, even after the issuing of *Periculoso*, nuns did in fact leave their convents for a variety of reasons. Abbesses were given special dispensation even within the terms of *Periculoso* itself; it was recognized that they might need to travel to fulfill administrative obligations, and they were permitted to do so as long as they took the appropriate chaperones.[42] It is possible—given the authoritative stance assumed by the author of the *testo breve* in relation to her reader—that if the author was a nun, she may have been an abbess, and thus would have had greater freedom of movement outside the cloister.

Finally, the occasion of the Jubilee year in 1300 may be a relevant consideration in this context. The indulgences offered by Boniface VIII—indulgences formally announced from the Benediction Loggia of Saint John Lateran on Holy Thursday of that year—provided a highly significant incentive for pilgrims to visit Rome in 1300. Villani tells us that more than 200,000 people, "così femmine come uomini," flocked to the city.[43] Nuns were among those pilgrims crowding into Saint John Lateran and the other designated sites in Rome.[44] Although I have found no specific documentation indicating

42. Makowski, *Canon Law and Cloistered Women*, esp. 40–41, 67, 136. *Periculoso* applied to all nuns, of course, not only Poor Clares. Although it was issued in 1298, Makowski observes that its mandates were not fully enforced right away. Makowski helpfully provides the full text of the original bull (133–35), along with an English translation (135–56).

43. Aquilecchia, *Giovanni Villani*, 77.

44. Canaccini, *Al cuore del primo Giubileo*, 46, 107–8. Canaccini provides documentation of the participation of nuns from the *Chronicon parmense ab anno*

that Poor Clares were among these nuns, it is certainly not impossible that they, too, participated in this pilgrimage; indeed it would seem very unusual if they alone, of all categories of lay and religious, were banned from such an important and consequential event. In addition, there were three convents of Poor Clares in Rome during this period.[45]

As for the specific activity mentioned here, measuring the length of a table (or rather a board, which served as a table on the floor), it is interesting that the reason our author wants to take such measurements is to work out what the seating arrangements at an important dinner might have been. The act of measuring can, in this way, be seen as perfectly compatible with the knowledge of women's lives and practical domestic concerns so amply in evidence elsewhere in the *testo breve*. Moreover, the author's perception that the table was *square* is unusual. The remnants from the table on display at the Lateran did not inevitably suggest this conclusion. When this observation that the table was square rather than rectangular is compared to the long "high tables" usually depicted in paintings of the Last Supper at this time, it appears to offer further evidence of a nonhierarchical mentality evident elsewhere in the *testo breve*, especially in the text's attention to shepherds, servants, and women. The eye of the beholder is clearly a relevant factor here; and the square shape of the table here invites consideration as a "gendered perception" of the Last Supper, for it is akin to other images that, as Diana Hiller has shown, appear to have been conditioned by differing practices in male and female religious communities in the later Middle Ages.[46]

### Suppression of the Image of Cecilia Writing

Finally, there is a key textual site that has implications for the authorship of the *testo breve*: the work's opening invocation of St. Cecilia as exemplary figure. The *testo breve*'s depiction of Cecilia includes a detail that is not present in the other versions. Here, Cecilia is not only a devout reader, she is also a writer.

Let's look more closely. Like the many versions and translations of the MVC that enjoyed wide circulation, the *testo breve* presents Cecilia as exem-

*MXXXVIII usque ad annum MCCCIX*, in *Rerum italicum scriptores*, ed. L. A. Muratori, vol. 9 (Milan: S. Lapi, 1727), col. 842. Interestingly, Kessler and Zacharias cast their fictional pilgrim as a woman, though they do not explain the reason for this choice or specify her status as nun or laywoman; see Kessler and Zacharias, *Rome 1300*.

45. Moorman, *Medieval Franciscan Houses*, 655–56.

46. Hiller, *Gendered Perceptions*.

plar of affective meditation: "she always carried the gospel of Christ Jesus hidden in her breast" [ela portava sempre lo evangelio de Cristo Iesù ascoxo nel suo pecto] (f. 1r). Strikingly, however, the *testo breve*—alone of all the extant Italian or Latin versions—goes on to describe Cecilia as a writer. She has not only selected but written out passages from the Gospels for her use in meditation. Expanding on the *Legenda aurea*'s image of Cecilia carrying the Gospel hidden in her breast, Author A continues thus: "And you should consider this to mean that she had written out for herself some of the most moving passages from the life of Lord Jesus Christ, and she meditated on these day and night with all her heart and with all her intention and fervor" [E questo dè' tu intender cusì, che ella se havea scrito algune electe cose più devote de la vita de miser Iesù Cristo, e in queste la pensava dì e nocte cum tutto el so cuore e cum tuta la intentione e fervore] (f. 1 r). Cecilia is thus presented as a woman writer in the *testo breve*—as the maker or author of a meditative Gospel *florilegium*.

This image of Cecilia as writer is not present in the *testo minore* and subsequent versions of the MVC. The *testo minore* credits Cecilia with "choosing" but not "writing" Gospel passages: "ella s'avea iscelte alquante cose più devote della vita di Jesù Cristo" (Sarri, 1) [she had chosen some of the more moving passages from the life of Lord Jesus Christ]. As is the case with other alterations made by Author B, we have two choices: the change was either accidental or it was deliberate. It seems to me implausible that the omission of such a significant detail as Cecilia's authorship of her Gospel *florilegium* could be accidental. For one thing, this is a very significant site: these are the opening words of the text, the tone-setting, disposition-setting mise-en-scène, and opening words are highly likely to receive any author's most careful attention. Beyond this, there is the fact that the image of Cecilia as writer is a strong image: it is not simply a passing phrase that is omitted, but an image of a memorable sort, an image crystallizing an activity, an identity, and a model for imitation.

Is there, then, a reasonable explanation for the deliberate omission of the image of Cecilia as writer? I would suggest that there is. To grant women within the Franciscan fold spiritual authority, even symbolically through the propagation of images of women as writers or visionaries, is something to which the friars were occasionally drawn (as in the case of Angela of Foligno) but far more often found problematic and sought to limit or suppress.[47] The relation between Author A and Author B would seem to fit within this historical context of suppression.

47. Roest, "*Ignorantia*."

In conclusion, I would emphasize that the evidence for a woman's authorship of the *testo breve* is cumulative, and the argument here is certainly open to refinement and debate. But as I see it, a Poor Clare was the original literary artist who created the MVC, and a Franciscan friar actively censored her authorial role and altered her text. To reach this conclusion is not necessarily to conclude that Author B's activities were unknown to Author A, or that they were unwelcome. Indeed, given the difficulty women writers encountered during the period, especially where authority on religious matters was concerned, one of the strategies available to a nun was precisely to remain anonymous—and to willingly hand over her work to a male author who might "improve" and "correct" it and issue it in his own authoritative voice, in this case as a learned and orthodox Franciscan charged with the guidance of Poor Clares. Any potentially problematic traces of its origins in a woman's ideas and imagination would thereby remain hidden; suspicion of the kind so often attendant upon women's writing in the period would be averted; and the text would have a better chance of circulating freely—as, indeed, it so manifestly did.

# DATE AND PLACE
# OF COMPOSITION

## DATE OF COMPOSITION

The question of the date of composition of the MVC has long remained an unresolved, challenging, and compelling subject for research. It is a question with far-reaching implications for understanding the dynamics of Italian cultural history during an especially rich period of innovation. If the MVC was indeed initially composed in Italian, for instance, the question of its date has relevance for the question of the early development of native Italian forms of prose narrative, as well as for a richer understanding of practices of translation in the first half of the fourteenth century, including the practice of translating from the vernacular into Latin. Moreover, as art historians have long recognized, determining when the MVC was written is fundamental to understanding the interplay between this popular meditative text and the innovations in religious art of the early Trecento. Establishing more precise dates for the various iterations of the MVC, then, is essential: this will serve to sharpen and refine discussions about cultural invention and change, about the adoption of one medium's modes into another, and about how a new emotional, realistic, and narrative style came to infuse religious art and literature in the fertile first half of the fourteenth century.

Before we turn to the details, it should also be said that while efforts to date any "variable text" are difficult, the case of the MVC presents a special challenge.[1] The anonymous authorship of the Italian and Latin texts, the fact that no documentary sources have come to light, the likelihood that more than one author played a role, and the lack of certainty regarding the place of

---

1. For an astute discussion of the challenges presented to textual criticism when undated texts appear in several distinct versions reflecting authorial revisions, see Hudson, "The Variable Text."

composition: all of this leaves us with an unusual paucity of secure anchors. Nevertheless, we can narrow the possibilities for the two distinct stages of composition that this study has identified, stages reflecting the work of Author A (the *testo breve*) followed by the work of Author B (the *testo minore*, *testo maggiore*, and the long Latin text). Previous scholarship as well as some new evidence I present here indicates that the *testo breve* is likely to have been composed sometime between about 1300 and 1325, and that the secondary stage of composition, by Author B, is likely to have taken place sometime between about 1325 and 1340.[2]

In what follows, then, my primary aim is to put forward the evidence for the date of the text edited here, the *testo breve*.[3] But given the fact that the *terminus ante quem* for the *testo breve* is intertwined with evidence presented by Author B's revisions, especially the first of these, the *testo minore*, it will be necessary to bring the manuscripts and certain textual details of those redactions into the discussion as well. It is a large and complex puzzle, one that will include working out several particular conundrums, including a reassessment of the date and provenance of a key source quoted by Author B, the *Revelations of Elizabeth of Hungary*, a text that has been recognized as a major clue to the date of the MVC. But only a close look at the details, of course, can reveal the big picture.

### Date of the First Stage of Composition, the Completion of the testo breve: ca. 1300–1325

The basis for a *terminus post quem* for the *testo breve* is a textual source referred to in the chapter on the descent from the cross. In the course of describing Christ's wounded body and face as he lies in the lap of his mother, the author cites the revelations of a certain holy woman regarding one of the injuries Christ suffered: "Io ho trovato in uno luocho ch'el Signore nostro rivelò a una

---

2. The dates I advance here—which remain provisional estimates—build on and revise my previous work ("Further Evidence"; "The Origins of the *Meditationes Vitae Christi*"; "The Author of the Italian *Meditations on the Life of Christ*") while taking account of the work of Tóth and Falvay ("New Light" and "L'Autore").

3. In this analysis, my procedure has been to think through the issues as if my reconstruction of the text's history is accurate, with the *testo breve* preceding the *testo minore*, *testo maggiore*, and Latin texts. If subsequent research by others proves that this sequence of composition is wrong, then the date of the *testo breve* would need to be reconsidered.

sua divota che per derisione lui fo tosato" (f. 103v) [I have found in a certain source that Our Lord revealed to one of his devoted ones that through derision he was shorn].[4] This allusion to a text originating with a female visionary is not unique to the *testo breve*; it also appears in the other Italian versions of the MVC, as well as the Latin, where it appears in slightly different form. In the Latin MVC, the passage reads, "Legi autem in quadam scriptura, quod Dominus cuidam deuote sue reuelauit quod ipse tonsus fuit capillis et depilatus barba."[5] Noticing the allusion in the Latin text, and recognizing its potential as a clue to the date of the MVC, Edmund Colledge proposed, in an article written in 1976, that the source in question was likely to be Mechthild of Hackeborn's *Liber specialis gratiae*, which appears to have begun to circulate shortly after Mechthild's death in 1298.[6] This has seemed persuasive to many, including myself; I have regularly cited it as the best foundation we have for a *terminus post quem* in my prior published work on the MVC.

Yet there are difficulties with identifying this passage as an allusion to Mechthild's *Liber*, not the least of which is the particular injury in question. The passage adduced by Colledge from Mechthild's *Liber* refers to the plucking of Christ's beard; it does not refer to the hair on Christ's head: "Sentiens autem anima ipsum barbam non habere, cogitare coepit si aliquod praemium a Deo Patre pro barbae in passion evulsione accepisset."[7] This has not been recognized as an important distinction in the scholarship. The plucking of the beard has been taken to be the more salient feature of the passage; the MVC's mention of the shearing of the hair has been set aside without comment. Moreover, an important feature of the *Liber*'s framing of the detail has not been registered. In the *Liber*, the image of a beardless Christ is presented as a seductive image. It makes his red mouth more visible; it makes him more inviting to kiss. The full passage reads:

4. The lack of specificity in the phrase "io ho trovato in uno luocho" might make one wonder whether the reference is to a textual source at all. But it clearly is; *luocho* as textual passage is well attested (Battaglia, *Grande dizionario*, *luogo*, sm, 13), and the verb *trovare* in this context indicates a process of finding the detail in a text, rather than hearing about it or seeing a visual image.

5. In the *testo minore*, the passage reads: "Ho trovato scritto in alcuno luogo che 'l Segnore revelò a una sua divota che li fuoro tosolati i capelli e pelata la barba" (Sarri, 335).

6. Colledge, "Dominus cuidam devotae suae."

7. Cited by Colledge, "Dominus cuidam devotae suae," 106, from the *Liber Specialis Gratiae*, ed. Benedictines of Solesmes, 143. For a complete translation of Mechthild's book, with introduction, see Newman, *Mechthild of Hackeborn*.

Contristata quadam vice per orationis subsidium solito more ad Dominum confugit, ipsi cor suum et voluntatem offerens, ita ut non solum hoc, sed etiam quaecumque pro ejus amore libenter sufferet adversa. Ad quam Dominus dulciter se inclinans, os suum roseum illi praebuit osculandum. Sentiens autem anima ipsum barbam non habere, cogitare coepit si aliquod praemium a Deo Patre pro barbae in passione evulsione accepisset.[8]

---

[Once when she was feeling sad, she took refuge in the Lord as usual by means of prayer, offering him her heart and her will—and not only that, but every hardship that she could willingly suffer for his love. At this the Lord sweetly bent down and offered his rosy mouth for her to kiss. Feeling that he had no beard, the Soul wondered if he had received any reward from God the Father because his beard had been pulled out in the passion.][9]

There are two significant differences, then, between the *Liber* passage and that in the MVC. In the *Liber*, the image of the beardless Christ is aestheticized, made attractive, subsumed into an image of the suffering lover leaning towards the devoted one for a kiss—and thus very unlike the image and its affective resonance in the MVC; and there is no mention in the *Liber* of harm to the hair on Christ's head, as there is in the MVC.

There is also the question of the availability and circulation of Mechthild's *Liber* in the early decades of the Trecento. Although it has been frequently asserted that the *Liber* made its way to Italy within a year or two of its completion circa 1299, and that it was well known at the time Dante was writing the *Commedia*, such assertions appear to rest on slim foundations. As far as I have been able to determine, Colledge's claim that copies of the *Liber* "very soon found their way to Italy, where it was widely circulated and highly esteemed" has not been proven or even subjected to rigorous scrutiny.[10] Pend-

---

8. Colledge, "Dominus cuidam devotae suae," 106.

9. Newman, *Mechthild of Hackeborn*, 124.

10. Colledge, in "Dominus cuidam devotae suae," cites M. F. Laughlin's article in the *New Catholic Encyclopedia* IX, 545–46, to support his assertion about the rapid dissemination of Mechthild's *Liber* in Italy. Laughlin, however, makes this claim without citations, mentioning only that this Mechthild may be the Matelda referred to by Dante in the *Commedia*. In the *Purgatorio*, canto 28, when Dante comes to the earthly paradise, he sees a woman there, singing and gathering flowers; Beatrice later names this woman as "Matelda" (*Purgatorio* XXXIII.118–19). Whether this figure was modeled on the historical Mechthild remains an open question. In addition to this

ing the completion of a critical edition or further investigation of the manuscript tradition of the *Liber*, it cannot be taken as a given that Mechthild's
book was widely known in Italy in the first half of the fourteenth century,
much less the first decade or two. Indeed, it appears that the earliest extant
manuscript, which was copied close to Helfa, dates to 1370.[11]

---

brief allusion, there are parallels between Mechthild's *Liber* and the *Commedia*, particularly in the description of the seven-terraced mountain; this has led to the infer-
ence that Dante knew of the *Liber* and was influenced by it. Gardner, in *Dante and the
Mystics* (265–97), offered the first close comparison of thematic parallels in the *Liber*
and the *Purgatorio,* in 1913. Since then, the question has often been taken up (e.g.,
Pecoraro, "L'ora di Citerea"), but it has not been resolved, in part because the inexact
character of the parallels, along with manifest differences between the two texts,
leaves open the possibility that both Mechthild and Dante may have been influenced
by an independent source. Barbara Newman has recently brought renewed attention
to the question and presented a strong argument for Dante's knowledge of Mechthild's book ("Mechthild of Hackeborn and Dante's Matelda"). Newman's argument
is based on internal evidence alone; the question of how Dante may have come by a
copy of the *Liber* remains a puzzle that Newman recognizes as such. Apart from the
potential witness to the presence of Mechthild's book in Italy that Dante may (or may
not) provide, the only other "evidence" often claimed for the wide popularity of the
*Liber* in early-fourteenth-century Florence is a reference in Boccaccio's *Decameron*,
in the first story of the seventh day. There, the friars of Santa Maria Novella are said
to have taught the "Laud of Lady Matelda" to the thick-headed fellow who is the
dupe of this particular story. From this brief reference, some scholars have deduced
that Boccaccio's "laud" existed in reality outside the frame of his fiction, that it relates to Mechthild of Hackeborne, that it derives from her *Liber*, and that the *Liber*
was therefore in wide circulation in the early decades of the fourteenth century (e.g.,
Halligan, *The Booke of Gostly Grace*, 86). To this one might respond that Boccaccio's
story is fiction; that the mention of the "laud" is immediately paired with the phrase
"and other such nonsense" (Musa and Bondanella, *Giovanni Boccaccio*, 86) ["la lauda
di donna Matelda e cotali altri ciancioni," Branca, *Giovanni Boccaccio,* 447]; that the
Matelda named in the laud is named as a lady, not a saint (enhancing the possibility
that the allusion may be a joke); and that there is no real justification for extrapolating
from this reference, in a work completed in 1353, to a conclusion that the *Liber* was
available in Tuscany soon after 1300.

    11.  Schmidt, "Mechthild von Hackeborn," cols. 251–59; see col. 252, on Wolfen-
büttel, Hzg.-Aug. Bibl. MS 1003 Helmst., completed in 1370 by Priester Albert, vicar
of St. Paul in Erfurt. Poor notes that there are 103 extant Latin manuscripts, but does not
specify the dates of these, deferring to Schmidt (Poor, *Mechthild of Magdeburg and Her
Book*, 182–83). The vernacular translations all seem to be from the fifteenth century,
and the only Italian translation appears to be a 1590 imprint (Poor, *Mechthild of Magdeburg and Her Book*, 182–83). At the very least, it is safe to say that there is at present no
*manuscript* evidence to support the assertions about the availability and popularity of
Mechthild's book in Tuscany in the early decades of the fourteenth century.

Could our author, then, have been referring to a different text—one recording the visions of a different *divota*? Here I will propose that we have a far more likely textual candidate: the *Memoriale* of Angela of Foligno (1248?–1309). In the opening summary of the *Memoriale* there is a brief description of the tenth step of Angela's spiritual journey in which Christ reveals to her a particularly shocking detail from the Passion: "Etiam ostendebat pilos barbe sibi evulsos et superciliorum et capitis" [He even showed me how the hair on his beard, eyebrows, and head had been pulled out].[12]

There are several reasons why this passage is likely to be the source for the reference in the MVC. First, there is no doubt that Angela's *Memoriale* was circulating in Tuscany in the early decades of the Trecento. Composed between about 1292 and 1298, it was officially published in 1299 or 1300, after it had been revised by Brother A. and officially approved by the Franciscan Order. The earliest manuscript, held in Assisi, has been dated to between 1306 and 1309.[13] In addition, there are the multiple Franciscan affiliations of this text. Angela was a Third Order Franciscan, Brother A. was a Franciscan friar, the *Memoriale* received an official approbation from the Franciscan Cardinal Colonna and a council of Franciscan examiners, and the earliest manuscripts are of Franciscan provenance. If the author of the *testo breve* was indeed a Poor Clare, then it is easier to explain, given networks of textual transmission, how the author may have come by a copy of Angela's *Memoriale* than to explain the availability and use of Mechthild's *Liber*. It is not necessary to assume that the author of the *testo breve* had a full copy of the *Memoriale*; the work circulated in shortened forms, including truncated versions and extracts. Our author could have encountered the passage by reading only the first few leaves of Angela's book, for the passage on how Christ was humiliated through the defilement of the hair on his head and face appears in chapter 1, the prefatory summary of the text.

What makes this theory all the more plausible in my view is the shocking character of Angela's vision concerning the shearing of Christ. As we have seen, Mechthild's reference is not only limited to Christ's beard, but subsumed into an enticing image of Christ the lover; it is not in itself arresting. Angela's image, in contrast, is one of rough and shameful assault. The

12. Menestò, *Angela da Foligno*, 7.
13. The manuscript, Assisi MS Biblioteca del Sacro Convento MS A-342, is from the Fondo antico comunale; Menestò, *Angela da Foligno*, lxiii. Menestò describes the complex manuscript tradition of the *Memoriale*; see also Lachance, *Angela of Foligno*, 53–54, and Poirel, "The Death of Angela of Foligno."

language of the Latin text, and of modern English translations, has the potential to obscure this brutality. There are too few options: one must translate "pilos . . . evulsos" with the English "plucked"—a verb which can carry with it, for modern readers, the sense of a delicate, careful process; the word does not in itself convey gross violation and humiliation. In the widely used translation by Lachance, the phrase thus appears as "He even showed me how his beard, eyebrows, and hair had been plucked out."[14] But it is clear that what Angela describes—in listing not only the beard and the head, but the eyebrows—is a gruesome affront; Christ has been violated in a particularly humiliating, painful, and ugly way. There is no aesthetic redemption here.

This is what was picked up by the author of the *testo breve*: the total, nearly unimaginable violation of the hair on Christ's head and face. This ugly image, and not simply the detail that Christ's beard was plucked, is clearly what caught the attention of the author of the *testo breve*. It is the revelation to *una sua divota* that "lui era tosato," a comprehensive image of defacement, that shocks, and the affronting character of this image aligns with the image of total violation of the face and head (beard, eyebrows, hair) presented in the early pages of Angela's *Memoriale*.[15]

In the end, however, the question of this allusion's relevance for the *terminus post quem* of the MVC leads us, interestingly, right back to the same *terminus*. The mistaken identification of the allusion as Mechthild's *Liber* has set the MVC's *terminus post quem* at circa 1300. The identification of the passage as a reference to Angela's book does not alter this date, for circa 1300 is the date that the *Memoriale* began to circulate in Tuscany.

The *luocho* whose origin we have traced stands as the marker of the work's *terminus post quem* because no other sources used by the author of the *testo breve* were composed after 1300 (for a complete list, see above, "Sources," in "Authorship," cx–cxi). Significantly, the *testo breve* does not quote from a particular fourteenth-century work that is quoted at length in all other Italian versions of the MVC, as well as the long Latin text: the *Revelations of St. Elizabeth of Hungary*. This text has attracted significant attention for the light it might shed on the date of composition of the MVC. Since an

14. Lachance, *Angela of Foligno*, 127.
15. See below, "Notes to the *Meditations*," 230n138, for further comments on the rough pulling of Christ's beard and hair in the *testo breve*, the connection between these passages and "ugly art" made by and for religious women in the later Middle Ages, and what appears to be the systematic tidying up or elimination of these passages by Author B.

entire chapter in Author B's texts (chapter 3 in the *testo minore, testo maggiore*, and the Latin MVC) is cited directly from the *Revelations*, it is obvious that the date of the *Revelations* serves as important evidence for the dating of those versions of the MVC. Here, what is worth emphasizing is the fact that the *Revelations* is not used as a source by the author of the *testo breve*. The *Revelations*, then, is relevant in this context by virtue of its absence. Its absence in the *testo breve* is, I would suggest, another indication of the *testo breve*'s primacy in the sequence of composition I have outlined in this study.

To summarize, then: in the *testo breve*, the author draws on no sources composed after 1300; nor are there allusions to historical events, devotional or social practices, or *topoi* that originated after the year 1300, as far as I have been able to determine. Therefore, the *testo breve* could have been composed as early as the first decade of the fourteenth century.

### *Terminus ante quem* of the *testo breve*

What, then, is the date by which the *testo breve* was composed? So far, no other fourteenth-century manuscript copies of the *testo breve* have come to light that might help to answer this question on the basis of paleographical evidence.[16] As I have suggested above, the absence of early copies may well be because the *testo breve* was actively suppressed and supplanted by the more "authoritative" versions made by Author B, beginning with the *testo minore*.

If, as I have argued in this volume, Author A's *testo breve* preceded and formed the basis for Author B's *testo minore* and subsequent revisions and translations, the task at hand becomes that of gathering and assessing the various kinds of evidence for the dates of these versions of the MVC. Determining the *terminus ante quem* for the *testo breve*, then, depends on determining the *terminus ante quem* of Author B's campaign of activity, or what I have called the secondary stage of the MVC's composition.

---

16. As Larson has observed, the linguistic evidence suggests that the work was copied several times in the Veneto region prior to the time it was copied into the Canonici manuscript. This suggests that, if more copies (entire, partial, or conflated) are to be found, libraries in the Veneto and libraries in Europe whose collections include manuscripts from the Veneto would be the most promising places to look. I have undertaken a search of the catalogued manuscripts at the relevant libraries in the Veneto (Padua, Venice), but it has not been practical to undertake a comprehensive, Europe-wide search for other Venetian copies of the *Meditazioni* that may have been miscatalogued.

## *TERMINUS ANTE QUEM* FOR THE SECONDARY STAGE OF THE MVC'S COMPOSITION

Evidence for a *terminus ante quem* for Author B's versions of the MVC takes three forms: the dates of the earliest manuscripts; early signs of the MVC's influence on the visual arts, particularly narrative cycles of the life of Christ; and the earliest use made of the MVC by other authors. I will take up each of these in turn.

### Evidence for the Date of the Earliest Manuscripts

Most of the earliest extant manuscripts of the MVC are in Italian, not Latin; and of the Italian versions, most belong to the *testo minore* type.[17] Most of the manuscripts have not been examined closely by paleographers or dated with greater precision than "sec. xiv" or "sec. xv." There are eight manuscripts, however, that have been identified as belonging to the first half of the fourteenth century. My aim here is not to provide detailed descriptions of these manuscripts, but simply to list them here in alphabetical order and provide references to the most recent and reliable descriptions.

#### *Witnesses to Italian Versions of the MVC*

Florence, Biblioteca Nazionale MS N.A. 350. *Testo maggiore*, sec. xiv, second quarter. Parchment. Bertelli has dated this manuscript to the second quarter of the fourteenth century.[18] The first folio has an illumination of St. Cecilia. This illumination appears to be the work of a Tuscan illuminator and is similar in style to the work of Pacino di Buonaguida and of the Master of the Dominican Effigies, both of whom were working in the second quarter of the fourteenth century.[19]

Florence, Biblioteca Medicea Laurenziana Gadd. 187. *Testo minore*; sec. xiv[1]. Parchment. The date of this manuscript has caused some confusion in the scholarship. The rubric above the description of this manuscript in the catalogue recently compiled by Bertelli gives the date as "sec. xiii[ex.]"[20]

---

17. The most comprehensive list of the manuscripts is that by Fischer, "Die *Meditationes vitae Christi.*"

18. Bertelli, *I manoscritti . . . Nazionale*, 42.

19. I thank Dianne Phillips for this opinion on the date and style of the illumination of St. Cecilia; there appears to be no published work on the image.

20. Bertelli, *I manoscritti . . . Laurenziana*, 115.

However, to deduce the date of the *Meditazioni* on the basis of this date would be a mistake. For as Bertelli clearly indicates in his full description, the manuscript is a palimpsest: while the parchment and the writing it once contained (discernible as accounts in the vernacular) clearly date to the thirteenth century, the two long texts it now contains—the *Meditazioni* (ff. 1–75r) and a *Pianto della Vergine* (ff.76r–84r) are copied in a hand that clearly belongs to a later period. Bertelli, who describes the eccentricities of this hand and provides an image of it, dates it to the first half of the fourteenth century.[21]

Florence, Biblioteca Riccardiana MS 1269. *Testo minore*, with opening chapters missing and various lacunae; sec. xiv[1]. Parchment. According to Bertelli, this manuscript is "databile al decennio 1330–40."[22] Gramigni agrees with Bertelli's reasoning, but notes that it is not impossible that it was copied closer to the middle of the century.[23]

Florence, Biblioteca Riccardiana MS 1358. *Testo minore*; sec. xiv med. Paper. This manuscript has been dated to the middle of the fourteenth century on the basis of the dates of its primary copyist, "ser Bonus," and its watermarks,

---

21. Bertelli, *I manoscritti . . . Laurenziana*, 115. There are a number of names and signs of ownership in the manuscript, the earliest of which appears to be that of a certain Lisa Gherardini or de Gherardinis: Explicit liber Meditationibus Christi, qui est de domina Lisa filia olim Lotti de Gerardinis (fol. 84r); Iste liber est de domina Lisa filia olim Lotti de Gerardinis, quia ego Lisa dedi dicto domino Baldo Angeli de Aretio chanonicus Aretinus, qui est amor amor meo (fol. 85r). Tracing these names further could potentially narrow the range of dates for the copying of the *Meditazioni* text in this manuscript. The *Dizionario biografico degli italiani* lists three Florentines who could plausibly be identified as the "Lotti de Gerardinis" in question: Lotteringo Gherardini, leader of the White Guelphs, who was killed in a skirmish on February 8, 1303; another Lotteringo Gherardini, apparently the nephew of the first, who appears in documents dating from 1316 to 1324 as *cavaliere* and a leader of the Guelphs; and a Lottieri di Lapo Gherardini, who is listed as magistrate in documents dating from 1324 to 1339 (see the two entries by G. Ciappelli in *Dizionario Biografico degli Italiani*, "Gherardini, Lotteringo"). The name "Lotti" in the manuscript corresponds rather more closely to the third of these candidates. I have not traced records for Baldo Angeli, canon of Arezzo, whom Lisa refers to so intriguingly as her "amor"; this too could serve to narrow the date of this manuscript further.

22. Bertelli, "Il copista del Novellino," 39–40.

23. Gramigni puts it as follows: "Sandro Bertelli restringe l'arco cronologico al quarto decennio del trecento, datazione che sul piano paleografico ci convince pienamente. Non ce la sentiamo tuttavia di escludere la possibilità di una datazione più prossima alla metà del secolo, se veramente l'originale latino fu prodotto in una data non anteriore al 1335" (Gramigni, *I manoscritti della letteratura italiana*, 148). I would like to thank Gramigni for sharing the relevant pages of his thesis with me.

which are similar to Briquet 3185 (Siena, 1325), and Briquet 3184 (Siena, 1320). See De Robertis and Miriello, *Manoscritti datati*, 54, number 107, and Gramigni, *I manoscritti della letteratura italiana,* 189–96 and Tav. XXI.

Notre Dame, Indiana, Snite Museum MS Acc. 1985.25. *Testo minore*, with 48 illuminations; sec. xiv med. or sec xiv². Phillips has concluded that this manuscript was made for a wealthy Bolognese layman and that its images are likely to be the work of an illuminator working just prior to Stefano Azzi: "For now, a date of ca. 1350 for the Snite illuminations and the anonymous appellation of the Snite Illuminator are the most prudent proposals."[24] The recent catalogue compiled by David Gura for the University of Notre Dame gives the date as "sec. xiv²."[25]

Paris, Bibliothèque nationale de France MS ital. 115. Unique copy of the Italian version translated from the long Latin MVC (Vaccari's "Testo A"), lacking the final chapters; on paper; with 193 ink drawings, the first 113 colored with a tempera wash; sec. xiv. Flora has dated the manuscript to "circa 1340–50" and has identified its provenance as Pisa.[26] My own examination of the manuscript's watermarks, however, suggests that a slightly later date may be likely. Three types of watermarks are visible: (1) a double circle with bar and cross (e.g., f. 162) corresponding most closely to Briquet 3165 (Bologna, 1329; Pisa, 1330–31) or 3168 (Pisa, 1361); (2) fruit (pear or fig) with leaves (e.g., f. 91), corresponding most closely to Briquet 7372 (Siena, 1331–33); and (3) fruit (pear or fig) with leaves, distinctly larger than 7372 (e.g., f. 93) and corresponding most closely to Briquet 7374 (Florence, 1345–54), 7375 (Siena, 1353–54; Florence, 1356–57), and 7376 (Siena, 1355–56).[27]

---

24. Phillips, *"Meditations on the Life of Christ,"* 243.

25. Gura, *Descriptive Catalogue*, 537.

26. Flora, *The Devout Belief of the Imagination*, 249. Flora's conclusions about the date are based chiefly on the stylistic similarities she sees between the manuscript's drawings and the paintings of the Collegiata at San Gimignano, though she recognizes the difficulties of such a comparison, given the difference in media: "The paintings in the Collegiata at San Gimignano represent the most closely related group of comparative material for Ms. ital. 115, although comparisons here are tenuous at best. Style, iconography, composition, and most importantly, elements of narrative and emotional expression link Ms. ital. 115 generally with the Collegiata paintings" (251). Flora also comments on the paper's watermarks: "Based on the dating of the paper via its watermarks, we may speculate that Ms. ital. 115 was produced in Tuscany between 1330 and 1350" (261). The script, as Flora notes, is quite eccentric and has been dated only as precisely as "fourteenth century" (263).

27. Briquet, *Les filigranes*.

*Witnesses to Latin Versions of the MVC*

Cambridge, Trinity College MS B. 14. 7. This manuscript contains a copy of the *Meditaciones de Passione Christi* (MPC), which has been proven to be an extract from the MVC (see Stallings, *Meditaciones de Passione Christi*). Teresa Webber has dated this manuscript to the "first half of the fourteenth century."[28]

Oxford, Corpus Christi College MS 410. Latin MVC; sec. xiv med. Parchment, with 154 colored miniatures. This copy of the Latin text was chosen by Stallings-Taney as one of the base manuscripts for her critical edition of the Latin MVC. Illuminations include Saints Francis and Clare, fol. 1. Stallings-Taney dates it to "mid-fourteenth century" and gives its provenance as "Central Italy; possibly copied for a lady, her likeness and arms (obliterated) on fol. 1."[29] Thomson also dates it to "s. xiv med." and describes the hand as "a single low-grade Italian gothic rotunda bookhand."[30] Bartal has concluded that the manuscript may have been commissioned by a woman affiliated with the Order of St. Clare; she has also noted similarities between the illuminations here and those of the San Lorenzo illuminator working in fourteenth-century Perugia.[31]

Evidence of the Use of the MVC by Trecento Artists

It has long been recognized that there are close similarities between the MVC and narrative scenes from the life of Christ by Nicola Pisano, Giotto, Pietro Lorenzetti, Simone Martini, and other Italian artists of the late Duecento and early Trecento. Early scholarship on the subject, which held that the MVC may have been composed in part by Bonaventure himself in the thirteenth century, assumed that the text preceded and directly influenced these artists.[32] Most contemporary research, however, has recognized the

---

28. Webber, "Latin Devotional Texts," 33; see also McNamer, "Further Evidence," 245–48.

29. Stallings-Taney, *Iohannes de Caulibus: Meditaciones vite Christi*, xiii, xiv.

30. Thomson, *Descriptive Catalogue*, 156–57.

31. Bartal, "Repetition, Opposition, and Invention," 154–56.

32. Émile Mâle's studies, published in the early decades of the twentieth century, have had a long reach in subsequent scholarship. Mâle expresses no hesitation in asserting that the author of the MVC inspired the innovations of early Trecento painting: "Byzantine paintings seem to have suggested to him certain details of his descriptions, but he was mainly served by his own lively imagination and his delicate sensibility. It was he who inspired the Italian artists with the happy touches which

difficulty of determining whether text influenced image or image text. Indeed, to put the matter in terms of image and text alone may be far too constricting; it is perhaps far more fitting to ask to what extent other cultural forms such as drama, sermons, literary narrative, religious rituals, and devotional practices functioned as mediating sources, informing both the MVC and the visual arts and being influenced in turn by them.[33]

The complexity of the subject is perhaps best illustrated by recent work on the frescoes of Santa Maria Donna Regina in Naples, which was built under the patronage of Queen Maria of Hungary for nuns of the Order of St. Clare. In a collection of essays published in 2004, it is taken for granted that the MVC served as a direct textual source for Donna Regina's Passion cycle, as well as for the angelic choirs on the triumphal arch.[34]

However, it is simply not clear that the MVC influenced the frescoes. In the detailed comparison provided by Adrian Hoch, for instance, there are indeed many similarities between narrative scenes in the Latin MVC and those at Donna Regina; both, for example, include the episodes of the Last Supper,

---

contributed to the transformation of the old iconography" (Mâle, *L'art religieux de la fin du moyen âge en France*, 29). Mâle further describes instances of what he sees as the direct influence of the MVC on Giotto's Arena Chapel frescoes and the work of Simone Martini and Pietro Lorenzetti (27–31). Despite the challenges to Mâle's assumptions by Otto Pächt ("Review") and other art historians, however, many quite recent studies continue to simply repeat the assumption that the MVC directly inspired Italian art of the late thirteenth and early fourteenth centuries—without, however, engaging with current debates on the date of the MVC or offering new methodological interventions that might confirm, refute, or add greater nuance to the question of textual influence (e.g., Varanini, *Cantari religiosi senesi*; Houston, "Painted Images"; several of the essays in Elliott and Warr, *The Church of Santa Maria Donna Regina*; Maginnis, *The World of the Sienese Painter*).

33. Chiara Frugoni's questioning of the default assumption that text influenced image, particularly in the Franciscan context, has been particularly influential; see Frugoni, *Francesco e l'invenzione delle stimmate*. Concerning the question of the influence of Franciscan texts on narrative iconography of the Passion, Anne Derbes observes: "These texts need not be taken as the sources of the images to be considered here; relatively few scholars today would insist on the primacy of texts over images. It is more reasonable to understand both as expressions of a larger discourse on the Passion that engaged the Order during the thirteenth century" (*Picturing the Passion*, 21).

34. This stance, evident especially in the essays by Fleck ("To exercise yourself"), Hoch ("The 'Passion' Cycle"), and Yakou ("Contemplating Angels"), resurrects—without comment or critical analysis—the theory of direct influence put forward in 1906 by Émile Bertaux (*Donna Regina*, 129).

the Washing of the Feet, the Agony in the Garden, the First Judgment before Pilate, and so on. However, none of these episodes is unique to the MVC. Hoch also observes that Mary is depicted in many of the fresco scenes in ways that seem to echo the MVC; for example, when Christ is stripped for the third time, Mary wraps her veil around his waist.[35] Even in Hoch's detailed analysis, however, there is a fundamental methodological problem—one that occurs in many other studies that assert the MVC's influence, namely, that similarities are privileged over differences. Immediately after noting the common motif in text and image of the wrapping with the veil, for instance, Hoch observes that Mary is depicted as collapsing from sorrow at the foot of the cross twice, falling to the ground in two different postures.[36] This is not the case in the MVC, in which Mary simply faints into the arms of Magdalene. Hoch notes other examples of narrative differences as well—but in each case, the assumption is that the fresco artist has embellished and altered the source text; the differences are not considered as potential evidence that the MVC did not serve as a source text. Hoch's assertions of influence, then, are not unreasonable or without any foundation. It may well be, too, that the emotional tenor of the MVC inspired the Donna Regina frescoes, as Hoch asserts: "The text deliberately evoked the sympathetic emotional involvement of the reader, and the descriptive quality of the *Meditations* facilitated their visualization in the form of frescoes."[37] But given the insufficient attention to the many *differences* between text and image, it simply cannot be taken as fact that the MVC served as a source for the frescoes at this interesting site.

Interestingly, the Donna Regina frescoes also include many Latin *tituli*, in the form of labels beneath the narrative scenes or as texts on scrolls or books held by figures in the scenes. As Cathleen Fleck observes, these texts are now heavily damaged or effaced, but "the few remaining words reveal telling relationships with the images around them and suggest that many of the nuns were expected to recognize the words and use them when they viewed the images."[38] It seems to me that *tituli*, in this case and elsewhere, could potentially serve as a very useful category of evidence, demonstrating beyond doubt that a particular text served as the source for an image. But such proof is not provided by the *tituli* at Donna Regina. Fleck observes general similarities between the *tituli* and the MVC. For example, the words "lacrimis faciem" appear beneath the Lamentation scene, and as Fleck notes,

35. Hoch, "The 'Passion' Cycle," 134.
36. Hoch, "The 'Passion' Cycle," 134–35, 140.
37. Hoch, "The 'Passion' Cycle," 150–51.
38. Fleck, "To exercise yourself," 112.

the Latin MVC states that "out of the abundance of her tears, she washed the face of her son."[39] Are such similarities—similarities that stop short of direct quotation—sufficient to prove that the MVC was used as source? While Fleck offers them as evidence that the artist drew on the MVC, I am not so sure. Wouldn't such a conclusion require ruling out all other possible influences from art or the liturgy and so on?

Even if the images and *tituli* aligned in such a specific way that the frescoes could be deemed to be "citing" the MVC, however, it is not clear that the Donna Regina frescoes could serve as a firm *terminus ante quem* for the MVC. For the date of the frescoes is, itself, a subject of continuing debate. While certain recent studies contend that most of the frescoes were completed prior to the death of the church's patron, Queen Maria of Hungary, in 1323, earlier scholarship, which had proposed two campaigns of painting—with the second, comprising the Passion cycle, beginning circa 1332—has not been decisively refuted.[40]

The vexed question of the relation between the MVC and the visual arts in the early Trecento is, then, not a question that can be resolved here. And that is a very promising kind of uncertainty: much methodological and empirical work remains to be done regarding the matter of how images and texts circulated, how they influenced each other, and how they were themselves influenced by devotional practices, liturgical and paraliturgical sources, religious processions and other performances, and local customs, communities, and constraints. But to return to the particular matter at hand, we can rest with the simplest and most secure conclusion: given our current state of knowledge, the first examples of the indisputable use of the MVC as direct source text for Trecento artists are the three illuminated manuscripts of the MVC listed above.[41]

## Evidence of the Use of the MVC by Other Writers

Given the prevalence of writings on the life and especially the Passion of Christ by the early Trecento, this category of evidence for the dating of the MVC requires very careful attention to specific textual details. As is the case

39. Fleck, "To exercise yourself," 112.

40. For a summary of the debate, see Elliott and Warr, *The Church of Santa Maria Donna Regina*, 6–7.

41. Even the manuscript illuminations, however, are not simple illustrations of the text; often they depart from it in intriguing ways: see esp. Phillips, "*Meditations on the Life of Christ*," and Bartal, "Repetition, Opposition, and Invention."

with the visual arts, in other words, it is easy to find thematic parallels between the MVC and other writings, or parallels in narrative sequence or motifs or aspects of style. Whether such parallels are sufficient to show the *influence* of the MVC on other texts, texts whose dates we can establish with
some degree of certainty, is the relevant question when it comes to using
such texts as a basis for dating the MVC.

At present, it seems that the first indisputable evidence of the use of the
MVC by other writers appears in the second half of the fourteenth century.
The most securely dated text is a Passion of Christ in *ottava rima* by Niccolò
Cicerchia (b. 1335/1340?) dated in one of the manuscripts to the year 1364,
which follows the MVC very closely in its structure and textual details.[42]
Far better known, but with greater uncertainty concerning its exact date of
composition, is Ludolph of Saxony's Latin *Vita Christi*. Written sometime
between 1348 and 1368, Ludolph's *Vita Christi* draws directly on the Latin
MVC. Ludolph's *Vita Christi* also draws on an intermediary text: a *Vita
Christi* of uncertain date and origin that also makes use of the MVC.[43] There
are three texts, then—Cicerchia's *Passione*, Ludolph's *Vita Christi*, and the
anonymous *Vita Christi* used by Ludolph—that prove beyond doubt that the
Latin MVC was used as a textual source by other writers by the 1360s, and
possibly a decade or so earlier.[44]

<hr />

42. Oliger was the first to notice the dependency of this *ottava rima* Passion on
the MVC. His assumption that this Passion was composed ca. 1320—with the proviso
that "altri mettono questa Passione un po' più tardi" (Oliger, "Le *Meditationes vitae
Christi*," 170)—was subsequently corrected by Varanini, who produced a critical edition of the text and affirmed the attribution to Niccolò Cicerchia, an attribution given
in three manuscripts, including Siena, Biblioteca comunale degli Intronati MS I.VI.11,
which dates the work to 1364 (Varanini, *Cantari religiosi senesi*, 191–305, 483–536).

43. Tobias Kemper has shown beyond any reasonable doubt that the author of
this *Vita Christi* drew directly on the Latin MVC; see Kemper, *Die Kreuzigung Christi*,
104–7. Kemper also provides a clear summary of the conclusion reached, after very
long debate between Baier and Geith, that Ludolph's *Vita Christi* draws on the anonymous *Vita Christi* and not vice versa; see Kemper, *Die Kreuzigung Christi*, 125–31.

44. Two other texts dating from the first half of the fourteenth century have also
been mentioned in the scholarship in connection with the MVC and its presumed influence: the *Satyrica Historia* of Paulinus of Venice, whose precise date of composition is uncertain, and a *Tractatus de passione Domini* by the Franciscan Francis of
Meyronnes (ca. 1280–1328) (Kemper, *Die Kreuzigung Christi*, 104). It is difficult to
assess the evidence concerning the *Satyrica*: the work exists in manuscript only, and
I have not been able to consult the manuscript referred to in the scholarship, Vatican
Library MS Lat. 1960. However, the only basis for the suggestion that the *Satyrica*

That latter text—the *Vita Christi*—remains something of a mystery: while it appears to have circulated anonymously at first, and was subsequently attributed, mistakenly, to Ludolf of Saxony in later manuscripts, a very confident set of rubrics are bestowed on it in a single fifteenth-century manuscript, Leipzig, Universitätsbibliothek MS 800: Incipit deuotissimus libellus

---

may have been influenced by the MVC appears to be the fact that Paulinus depicts crucifixion in the *erecte cruce* mode (Kemper, *Die Kreuzigung Christi*, 104). Given the prevalence of this image by the early Trecento, there is no reason to assume—in the absence of a direct textual quotation from the MVC, which no scholars have adduced—that Paulinus took the idea from the MVC; any number of visual or textual images may have served as his inspiration. For this reason, the *Satyrica* can be set aside as irrelevant to determining the date of the MVC. As for the hypothesis that the MVC influenced Meyronnes's *Tractatus*, this does merit further study. The *Tractatus* exist only in a single manuscript copy, Munich, Bayrische Staatsbibliothek MS Clm 8393, which dates from the fifteenth century. The rubric in the manuscript states that the text is by Francis of Meyronnes; there is no independent evidence that Meyronnes composed this work or other manuscripts that might corroborate this attribution. The lack of a critical edition of this text, or indeed of any printed edition of it, has made the claim for the dependence of the *Tractatus* on the MVC difficult for scholars to evaluate; moreover, the script in the sole manuscript is cramped and the Latin heavily abbreviated. However, having obtained copies of the folios in question (ff. 146r, 151r, 151v, 155v, 156v), as well as the generous assistance of my colleague Mark Henninger, who transcribed the most relevant passages for me, I have concluded that there are indeed very close parallels between the *Tractatus* (as recorded in MS Clm 8393) and the Latin MVC. The wording is nearly verbatim in certain passages on ff. 146r and 155v. Unless a third, unidentified text served as source for both texts, then, the only logical deduction is that the *Tractatus* incorporates passages from the Latin MVC. However, it remains unclear whether Francis of Meyronnes himself was responsible for those passages. Given the late date of the *Tractatus* manuscript, it is possible that a late fourteenth-century or fifteenth-century redactor embellished the *Tractatus*; the passages deriving from the MVC may not have been part of the original text. One reason I suspect that the sole surviving copy of the *Tractatus* contains interpolations is that several of its motifs are more characteristic of Passion texts composed in the late fourteenth and early fifteenth centuries—and have no parallels that I know of dating from ca. 1320. For example, in the *Tractatus*, the house of Mary Magdalene is depicted as being adjacent to the place where Jesus is tortured by Pilate's soldiers, so that Mary, who is staying at Magdalene's house with the other women, actually hears Jesus being tortured, which increases her sorrow and gives rise to a dramatic lament (f. 151r). In any case, having taken the matter this far, I leave it for further consideration by those with relevant expertise in the writings of Francis of Meyronnes or the textual criticism of Latin devotional writing of the fourteenth and fifteenth centuries. It does seem unlikely to me that the earliest textual witness to the

Michaelis de Massa de vita domini nostri Ihesu Christi secundum textum eu-
angelistarum (f. 1r); Explicit libellus deuotissimus de vita Christi Michaelis
de Massa (f. 100r).[45] The attribution to Michael of Massa in the Leipzig manuscript has generated significant debate—one whose byways I will not go into
here, but whose broad outlines are highly relevant to the question at hand: determining the date by which the Latin MVC was composed.

Michael of Massa was an Augustinian friar and one of the most celebrated theologians of the Order in the late medieval period. Born around the
year 1300 in Tuscany, his presence in Paris is attested by the early 1320s. He
taught, preached, and wrote in Paris through the 1320s and 1330s, and died
there in 1337. If any of his authentic writings can be shown to rely on the
Latin MVC, then the Latin MVC must have been in circulation by 1337.

It is not known, however, whether the attribution of the *Vita Christi* to
Michael of Massa in the Leipzig manuscript is reliable. The most thorough
and direct investigation of the question, by Willeumier-Schalij, concludes
that the matter is inconclusive: there simply is not enough evidence to elimi-
nate the uncertainty surrounding the attribution to Michael. To Willeumier-
Schalij, however, the attribution seems doubtful.[46]

Recently, it has been argued by Tóth and Falvay that two sermons by
Michael of Massa, known from their incipits as the *Angeli pacis* and *Exten-
dit manum* sermons, draw on the Latin MVC as source.[47] The attribution of
these sermons to Michael appears to be very secure. However, while Michael's
two sermons exhibit some passages that are similar to the MVC, there are no
verbatim quotations from the MVC. This is an important point. Tóth and Falvay show that there are thematic parallels between certain passages in the
MVC and Michael's sermons, but there are no direct *quotations*. Tóth and

---

MVC would be a work composed by a French scholastic philosopher who spent most
of his career teaching in Paris. However, given that Francis was a member of the
Order of Friars Minor, that he had strong connections with the Angevin court in
Naples, and that he spent his final days in Italy and died there, in Piacenza, in 1328, I
would not entirely rule out the possibility that he was among the first to have access
to the Latin MVC and to incorporate it into his work.

45. A description of Leipzig, Universitätsbibliothek MS 800, is available
through Manuscripta Mediaevalia: www.manuscripta-mediaevalia.de/dokumente/html
/obj31570858.

46. Willeumier-Schalij, "Is Michael de Massa de auteur." I would like to thank
my colleague Fr. Brian McDermott for translating Willeumier-Schalij's Dutch article
for me.

47. Tóth and Falvay, "New Light."

Falvay's repeated claim that there are "quotations" from the MVC in Michael's sermons is not correct.[48] Moreover, there are significant differences between Michael's sermons and the parallel narrative episodes in the MVC.[49] In addition, it remains possible that both Michael and the author of the Latin MVC may have been drawing independently on a text or texts belonging to the genre of "pseudo-apocryphal dialogue" that Tóth has identified.[50] Thus, although Tóth and Falvay's argument for Michael's use of the Latin MVC in his sermons merits further study and debate, it is, to my mind, unpersuasive in its present form.

48. In "New Light," Tóth and Falvay first assert that the alleged similarities are "paraphrased" passages from the MVC (a term that embeds assumptions that the MVC necessarily came first and served as source); then they introduce the phrase "paraphrased quotations," a phrase that they do not explain; and finally, they reduce this complexity by simply using the term "quotations" to refer to the passages from Michael's sermons that they deem similar to the MVC ("New Light," 32). Two subheadings further enshrine the unsupported assertion that the passages are quotations ("The Character of the Quotations" and "Analyzing the Quotations"). But no "quotations" have been established. I thus urge caution in the evaluation of Tóth and Falvay's argument.

49. For example, Tóth and Falvay assert that the use of the word *semimortua* in the MVC and in Michael's sermons is evidence that Michael drew on the MVC. They state that this is an "unusual word," one that "becomes widespread only in later medieval texts, and as a description of the Virgin's sorrow, it is used (four times!) only in the *Meditationes vitae Christi* and its later liturgical and vernacular derivatives" ("New Light," 35). However, they do not provide any evidence for the latter claim for the word's rarity and exclusive use in the MVC; nor do they point out a significant difference between the use of the word in the MVC and in Michael's text. In Michael's sermon, the term *semimortua* appears in the Holy Wednesday episode, as a description of the Virgin's agony. In the MVC, the term does not appear in the Holy Wednesday episode (which they claim Michael was quoting). It only appears in episodes after this, when the Virgin is grieving in the midst of the Passion and in the chapter on the visit to the tomb (chaps. 77, 78, 79, 83). The term *semimortua*, then, does not anchor their claim of the dependency of Michael's text on the MVC. Moreover, the fundamental choreography of the Virgin in the two texts is different. In Michael's sermon, the Virgin throws herself weeping at Christ's feet, collapsing in agony, half dead: "beata virgo Maria fuit in tanto dolore et in tam forti agonia quod pluries illa die cedidit ad pedes sui dilectissimi filii semimortua"; "New Light," 51). But in the MVC, the Virgin is not nearly as dramatic: Christ and his mother are simply sitting together; they embrace as they sit together; Magdalene comes in and sits at his feet; and Mary's weeping is said to be soft and modest (Stallings-Taney, chap. 72). The discounting of such differences makes their argument for Michael's use of the MVC weak, in my view.

50. Tóth, "Pseudo-Apocryphal Dialogue."

The most judicious conclusion to draw from this rather complex array of evidence for a *terminus ante quem* for Author B's work, then, would seem to be that his successive revisions, the *testo minore*, *testo maggiore*, and the long Latin text, were completed by about 1340. The manuscript evidence, which is the strongest type of evidence to hand, suggests that the *testo minore* and the *testo maggiore* may have been put into circulation some years prior to this date; the Latin text may have come along later. We need not assume, as has sometimes been done in recent scholarship, that there must necessarily have been a delay of years or even decades between the completion of the various Italian and Latin versions and their dissemination beyond Italy.[51]

51. In an influential article on Middle English versions of the MVC, Ryan Perry has expressed skepticism of my argument for the textual history and date of the MVC on the grounds that it is implausible that successive versions were produced and disseminated within twenty-five to thirty years, a period he considers to be a very short time span. "If McNamer is right that the Canonici is the original kernel of the MVC, then according to the current dating of the tradition, within only twenty-five to thirty years this text was expanded three times by 'Author B,' twice in Italian and then, in the making of the MVC, expanded and translated into Latin. The MVC was then adapted by the compiler of the *Vita Christi*, which would in turn be extended by Ludolph of Saxony. Here there are five stages of adaptation and translation, involving the text's moving from Tuscany into central Europe, all within a few decades (and less if, as is entirely possible, Ludolph von Saxony completed his text before the final years of his life)" (Perry, "Thynk on God," 426). Perry characterizes a period of twenty-five to thirty years as "startling speed" (426), so startling as to defy credulity. But why? Perry does not explain this. He provides no baseline for how long it typically took medieval authors to revise, adapt, and translate, or for how long it typically took book-toting friars or their couriers to travel from one part of Europe to another. But if the very rapid dissemination of other Franciscan texts throughout Europe (the multiple *Lives of St. Francis* being perhaps the most prominent example) was accomplished quickly—within months or years, not decades—why not the MVC? Pragmatically, too, we might note that Tuscan towns, including San Gimignano, were linked to Europe by the Via Francigena. As for the speed with which our Author B might accomplish his work, my own sense is that a friar living in a quiet monastery in Tuscany, ca. 1340, unencumbered by the demands of the workaday world or domesticity, would have enjoyed ideal conditions for writing, adapting, and translating the work; his Franciscan network would have provided an ideal network for textual dissemination. If modern academics (even those with significant domestic responsibilities) can complete books within two, five, or ten years, why would we need to posit a longer time span for a medieval friar to revise, adapt, and translate a text? This question of how much time it took to write, translate, and circulate books is a larger subject than I can address here; I would simply urge caution in assuming that getting a text from Italy to central Europe would have taken years or decades, or that medieval writers and translators worked more slowly than we do.

An important question remains, however: when did Author B begin his revisions? Determining this can narrow the range of dates for the composition of the *testo breve*. To put it technically: while the *terminus ante quem* for the second stage of the MVC's composition gives us an outer limit for the *testo breve*, determining the *terminus post quem* for Author B's work can help to provide a more accurate *terminus ante quem* for the *testo breve*. And this is a valuable enterprise. Among other things, determining this can help us to situate Author A more clearly and vividly within the vibrant cultural milieu of early Trecento Tuscany. What follows, then, functions as an *excursus*, one that will take us from Tuscany up to Hungary, down to Naples, and back to Tuscany again, as we take up once again the injunction issued by Alexandra Barratt many years ago in this context: *cherchez la femme*—the *femme* in question here being an elusive "St. Elizabeth, daughter of the King of Hungary."[52]

## THE *REVELATIONS OF ST. ELIZABETH OF HUNGARY*: A NEW HYPOTHESIS AND A REVIEW OF THE EVIDENCE

Significantly, as we have seen, the *testo breve* is the only version that does not directly cite a source that is incorporated at length into every other Italian version of the MVC, as well as the Latin version: the *Revelations of St. Elizabeth of Hungary*. This source has been recognized as a key site for establishing a date *post quem* for the other Italian and Latin versions of the MVC, for an entire chapter, on the early life of the Virgin Mary in the temple (chapter 3 in the *testo minore, testo maggiore,* and the Latin text), is quoted entirely from the *Revelations*, which are attributed to "Saint Elizabeth, daughter of the king of Hungary."[53] The Latin text of the *Revelations* that served as source for this extract was identified and edited by Livario Oliger in 1926.[54]

What, then, is the date of composition of the *Revelations*? Resolving this has been a complex matter, for the text's date, country of origin, original language, and author, as well as the identity of the protagonist whose visions

52. Barratt, *"The Revelations of Elizabeth of Hungary*: Problems of Attribution."

53. In the *testo minore*, the passage is introduced in this way: "Essendo la Vergine Maria piccola di tre anni sì fue offerta dal padre e dalla madre nel tempio, e quivi stette infino a quattordici anni. Ma quello ch'ella vi fece possiamo sapere per revelazione ch'ella mostrò ad una sua devota, e credesi che fusse Santa Elisabetta di cui noi faciamo festa" (Sarri, chap. 3, 12–13). The St. Elizabeth who died in 1231 was of course celebrated with special enthusiasm by the Franciscans, both liturgically and otherwise. Her feast date is November 17.

54. Oliger, *"Revelationes."*

it relates, are unknown. The "obvious" attribution is, in the manner of many medieval attributions, false: a straightforward identification of this Elizabeth as the celebrated Franciscan tertiary St. Elizabeth of Hungary (d. 1231) was ruled out long ago.[55] In the course of my own earliest work on the textual tradition of the MVC, I published an article, as well as a critical edition of the *Revelations*, that built on the work of Alexandra Barratt and argued for the identification of the Elizabeth in question as Elizabeth of Töss, daughter of King Andreas II of Hungary (ca. 1294–1336).[56] Like Barratt, I further argued that the text of this lesser-known great niece of the famous St. Elizabeth was quickly swept up into the latter's cult; the two Elizabeths were thereby conflated, and the great-niece's visions served to increase the famous Elizabeth's saintly lustre.[57] Although the *Revelations* record the visions of Elizabeth, the text speaks of her in the past tense and appears to have been composed in final form after her death. Elizabeth of Töss died in 1336. If the protagonist of the *Revelations* can be identified as Elizabeth of Töss, then the date *post quem* for the *Revelations* would appear to be circa 1336. Thus, I have argued that the date of the *Revelations* implies that the MVC—all versions, that is, *except* the *testo breve*, which does not include the citation from the *Revelations*—would have been composed after 1336. This argument has gained wide acceptance as the most persuasive provisional identification of the text in the absence of any alternative theory, particularly since there are many parallels between the figure of Elizabeth in the *Revelations* and the Life of Elizabeth of Töss composed by Elsbet Stagel.[58] Yet it has been difficult for some scholars to envision how a visionary text concerning a Dominican nun in what is now Switzerland could begin circulating within a few years of its composition in Franciscan circles in Tuscany; in addition, Elsbet Stagel does not describe Elizabeth of Töss as one who received revelations.[59]

55. Oliger, "*Revelationes.*"

56. Barratt, "The Revelations of Elizabeth of Hungary: Problems of Attribution"; *The Revelations of St. Elizabeth (of Töss).*

57. McNamer, "Further Evidence"; *The Two Middle English Translations of the Revelations of St. Elizabeth of Hungary.*

58. See M. Arosio, "Giovanni de' Cauli"; Stallings-Taney, "Introduction" in *Ioannes de Caulibus: Meditationes Vitae Christi,* xi; on specific parallels between the *Revelations* and Stagel's *Vita,* see McNamer, *The Two Middle English Translations of the Revelations of St. Elizabeth of Hungary,* 12–14.

59. G. Klaniczay, *Holy Rulers,* 375. It is worth mentioning, however, that Klaniczay's own work amply demonstrates that Central European princesses were very fashionable in Italy at this time; this could explain why *Revelations* by Elizabeth of

Recently, a different theory about the *Revelations* and the identity of its protagonist has been put forward. Dávid Falvay has argued that the Elizabeth of Hungary depicted in the *Revelations* could be simply a fictive figure, rather than a historical person—or, if a historical person, one who was not necessarily called Elizabeth—and that if there is no persuasive basis for attributing the *Revelations* to Elizabeth of Töss, who died in 1336, we no longer need to set the date for the *Revelations* or for the MVC to a point after 1336.[60] It is an interesting hypothesis, and one that has plausible roots in the work of Gábor Klaniczay, who has shown that saintly princesses from Hungary and Central Europe became especially popular in Italy in the late thirteenth and early fourteenth centuries, and further, that legends concerning St. Margaret were embellished with *topoi* culled from other sources.[61] Falvay has further hypothesized that the text was composed in Italy.

Falvay's argument, then—that the *Revelations of St. Elizabeth of Hungary* is not necessarily linked to Elizabeth of Töss, that it could be an amalgamation of *topoi* not linked to any particular historical person, and that it may have been composed in Italy—is interesting, and it has had the value of reopening important questions. At present, however, this theory lacks sufficient grounding to be considered a secure anchoring point, either for a new explanation for the origin of the *Revelations* text or for a revised date for the MVC. Among other things, Falvay provides no evidence in support of his most far-reaching claim: "The *Revelations* was probably written in Latin at the beginning of the fourteenth century."[62] In addition, Falvay posits a hypothetical text

Töss, who was indeed a daughter of the king of Hungary (and thus not just any "Dominican nun"), might have attracted interest in Italy. In addition, Tibor Klaniczay has documented textual networks between Dominicans and Franciscans in Hungary and Italy ("Attività letteraria dei Francescani e dei Domenicani nell'Ungheria Angioina"). Gábor Klaniczay's hesitations in accepting the attribution to Elizabeth of Töss, then, are important, but not decisive.

60. Falvay, "Le rivelazioni" and "St. Elizabeth."

61. G. Klaniczay, *Holy Rulers*. Klaniczay provides a detailed discussion of the way that the mystical revelations of Marguerite de Porète were incorporated into the writings and iconography of Margaret of Hungary, in part because the lack of mystical elements in Margaret of Hungary's life had come to seem a deficit to those who sought to promote her cult (375–84).

62. Falvay, "St. Elizabeth," 143. The claim is repeated in Tóth and Falvay, "New Light," 54. The only citation Falvay provides in support of this claim is a reference to Oliger's 1926 article, "*Revelationes*." Oliger does indeed state that the *Revelations* must have been composed prior to 1305 (Oliger, "*Revelationes*," 24–25). But Oliger's sole basis for this date was, in turn, the date he had taken as a given for the date of the MVC, i.e., 1305. Like other scholars of his era, such as Émile Mâle, Oliger

behind those that actually exist (a version of the *Revelations*, that is, that lacks any internal references to a St. Elizabeth of Hungary), suggesting that the references to Elizabeth were added at a later stage. But the extant manuscripts universally call the protagonist Elizabeth; there is no manuscript that indicates that a pre-Elizabeth stage ever existed.[63] Further, Falvay's hypothesis does not account for the fact that there are two independent Latin versions of the *Revelations*.[64] One wonders, too, how plausible it is that a set of revelations could be wholly fabricated or fictive—lacking a real, historical protagonist as its subject and generative agent—especially when the text itself is not only eccentric in its content and style but insistent on its truth value. In both of the Latin texts, we are told that the *ancilla Christi, Elizabeth* authorized the *Revelations* with an emphatic assertion that the experiences it records truly happened: "she had such great certainty concerning all these things that she would rather choose death than doubt that even the smallest part of it were untrue."[65] If Elizabeth of Töss is not the protagonist or author

---

had assumed that the MVC inspired Giotto's Arena Chapel frescoes, dated to 1305. For Oliger, then, this deduction about the date of the *Revelations* was a logical one to make. Falvay resurrects this out-of-date dating, but provides no additional support in favor of it. There is no manuscript evidence for this early date for the *Revelations*. The only independent bases for the date of the *Revelations*—independent, that is, from its incorporation into the MVC—are a reference to the *Revelations* in a manuscript catalogue dated 1381, Assisi, Biblioteca municipale MS 442 (Oliger, "*Revelationes*," 30–31), and Banfi's estimate that a *vita* of the famous tertiary Elizabeth, which conflates parts of her classic legend with material from the *Revelations*, dates to the fourteenth century (Banfi, *Santa Elisabetta di Ungheria*).

63. It is interesting that the two Latin versions differ, however, in the frequency with which Elizabeth's name is mentioned; in the manuscript tradition known as Group I (edited by Oliger, "*Revelationes*") references to Elizabeth are infrequent; in the Group II manuscripts (edited by McNamer, *The Two Middle English Translations of the Revelations of St. Elizabeth of Hungary*), they are very frequent, incorporated into virtually every episode. This aspect of the manuscript tradition merits further study.

64. Barratt accounted for the two independent Latin versions by positing that the original was a vernacular text from which the two Latin versions were translated. Barratt observes that "in both versions the Latin has the typically pedestrian and laboured feel of a translation from a vernacular, especially a non-Romance vernacular"; she hypothesizes that the work was composed in Middle High German ("*The Revelations of Elizabeth of Hungary*: Problems of Attribution," 6). Falvay does not address this issue.

65. "Dicebat se de hiis omnibus tantam certitudinem habere quod pocius eligeret mortem, quam de predictis vllum modicum quod vera non fuerint dubitaret" (McNamer, *The Two Middle English Translations of the Revelations of St. Elizabeth of Hungary*, 100); cf. Barratt, *The Revelations of St. Elizabeth (of Töss)*, 112.

of the *Revelations*, then, it seems that our search should continue for another saintly woman named Elizabeth.

As it happens, there is in fact yet another Elizabeth, daughter of the king of Hungary, known for her sanctity—one who has not yet been recognized as a potential candidate for identification as the historical figure whose experience is recorded in the *Revelations*.[66] This Elizabeth of Hungary (ca. 1260–1323/26?), daughter of King Stephen V of Hungary and Elizabeth the Cuman, was a Dominican nun. When she was a very young child, she was placed in the Dominican convent founded by her family on the Island of Rabbits in Buda, later renamed Margaret's Island in honor of St. Margaret of Hungary, Elizabeth's aunt, the convent's most illustrious member. After Margaret's death, Elizabeth became prioress and, as Gábor Klaniczay relates, "had held the post for a decade when her life took a rather fantastic turn: King Ladislas, her shameless brother, had her abducted in order to marry her off, in 1288, to Zaviš Rosenberg, a Bohemian aristocrat. . . . Widowed in 1290, Elizabeth went to Naples to the court of her sister, Mary, Charles II's wife, and again donned her nun's habit."[67] In Naples, Elizabeth became prioress of the Dominican Abbey of San Pietro a Castello; she seems to have remained there until the early 1320s, returning to her former abbey in Buda to live out her final days. She died in 1322.[68]

This Elizabeth of Hungary could prove to be the most viable candidate for identification as the Elizabeth of the *Revelations*, given this Elizabeth's early years in a Dominican convent, her life as a nun in Italy, and the confluence of Dominican and Franciscan cultures around the Naples court and Santa Maria Donna Regina. Internal evidence suggests that the *Revelations*

---

66. I thank Dianne Phillips for calling my attention to an image of this Elizabeth in the habit of a Dominican nun, in a single parchment leaf of a manuscript now at the Houghton Library (Cambridge, MA, The Houghton Library, Harvard University, 1943.1866; reproduced in Palladino, *Treasures of a Lost Art*, 43). The manuscript illumination is attributed to the Master of the Dominican Effigies, and dated ca. 1335–40. Palladino identifies it as "from an unidentified antiphonary, possibly intended for Dominican use" (43).

67. G. Klaniczay, *Holy Rulers*, 262.

68. G. Klaniczay, *Holy Rulers*. The date of her death is variously given as 1323 and 1326 by G. Klaniczay (262, 298); but Matthew Clear cites a record of 1322 indicating that she had died by then ("Maria of Hungary as Queen, Patron, and Exemplar," 54, 59n76). According to Tibor Klaniczay, Elizabeth is likely to have played a significant role in promoting the cult of St. Margaret of Hungary in Naples and contributing directly or indirectly to the material contained in Margaret's various legends ("Attività letteraria dei Francescani e dei Domenicani nell' Ungheria Angioina," 28, 37–38).

may have emerged from a Dominican setting. This evidence is certainly not conclusive: it has to do with the frequent references to St. John, who had a special place of honor in Dominican convents.[69] This Elizabeth's Dominican affiliation and her sisterly bond with Queen Maria, a Third Order Franciscan, could explain how a text that appears to show signs of Dominican influence was quickly taken up by Franciscans in Italy.[70] The hypothesis that this Elizabeth was the historical protagonist of the *Revelations* would also explain how a text about a Hungarian princess began to circulate in Italy in its very early stages. For not only did this Elizabeth live in Italy for most of her adult life, there are also well-documented literary networks between Buda and Naples during the Angevin dynasty, with both Franciscans and Dominicans playing important roles in promoting the saintly dynastic line and writing in the three relevant languages, Latin, Hungarian, and Italian.[71]

To return to the question at hand, then, the date of the MVC: if this historical Elizabeth of Hungary, daughter of King Stephen V, was the protagonist/

69. McNamer, *The Two Middle English Translations of the Revelations of St. Elizabeth of Hungary*, 14.

70. Queen Maria of Hungary "balanced her patronage of the different orders" (Kelly, "Religious Patronage and Royal Propaganda in Angevin Naples," 32)—preferring the Franciscans, becoming a Third Order Franciscan, and obtaining papal permission to participate in the life of the community of Poor Clares at Donna Regina, but founding the Dominican convent of San Pietro a Castello where her sister Elizabeth became abbess. "Familial motives," as Matthew Clear observes, "seem to have been at the root of the Queen's desire to found a new female Dominican house. It was enlarged and embellished to accommodate her sister Elizabeth. . . . As late as 1322, Maria's treasurer Ansellotto de Lumiriaco detailed monies 'for certain building work done in the monastery of San Pietro a Castello in the room where lady Elizabeth, sister of the said Queen [Maria], used to reside'. Later the same year, Maria met the costs of her sister's commemorative funerary obsequies" (Clear, "Maria of Hungary as Queen, Patron, and Exemplar," 54).

71. T. Klaniczay, "Attività letteraria dei Francescani e dei Domenicani nell' Ungheria Angioina." Tracing out this possibility further is beyond the scope of this study and beyond my linguistic competence (one would need to know Hungarian in order to conduct a thorough investigation of the secondary literature as well as the finding aids and introductions to the primary sources in Latin); but I invite others to test its plausibility. One approach would be to undertake a detailed comparison of the style of piety in the *Revelations* with that of the *Vita* of St. Margaret of Hungary and to the records of Elizabeth's testimony in the context of the canonization process of her saintly aunt Margaret of Hungary (see Fraknói, *Inquisitio super vito*). There certainly is a great emphasis on weeping in both the *Revelations* and Margaret's *Vita*, but this aspect of women's devotions is perhaps too widely attested by the late thirteenth century to stand as any kind of conclusive evidence that the Elizabeth of the *Revelations* experienced her early religious formation in Margaret's convent.

author of the *Revelations* that are quoted in the MVC, then the *Revelations* could have been in circulation shortly after her death in 1322. The date *post quem* of the versions of the MVC that cite the *Revelations* would then be circa 1322.

In short, then, various hypotheses have been put forward about the origin and date of the *Revelations*, and, given that this text is a lynchpin for dating the MVC, the question deserves further investigation. In this context, the important facts, given the current state of research, are these. First, there is reason to doubt my own earlier argument about the implications of the *Revelations* text for the date of the MVC. If Elizabeth of Töss is not the most plausible protagonist/author of the *Revelations of Elizabeth of Hungary*, then a *terminus post quem* of 1336 for Author B's versions of the MVC is not necessarily a given. The work of Falvay has been helpful in this regard, since it has called into question the basis for a date that—while no hard evidence has emerged to contradict it—has had the "feel," to many, of being too late. However, the alternative proposed by Falvay—that there was no historical Elizabeth, or need not have been, for the work as a whole might be merely a hagiographic *topos*—does not, in my view, seem persuasive, if only for the reason that there are no known parallels for the wholesale invention of a work of women's visionary literature of this kind.[72] Moreover, the style and details of the *Revelations* strike me as too particularized and allusive to be

---

72. Falvay puts the matter quite strongly: in his view, "to be a daughter of the king of Hungary, as we shall see, is nothing other than a hagiographic topos" [essere figlia del re d'Ungheria, come vedremo, altro non è che un topos agiografico] ("Le rivelazioni," 257). Falvay also makes the erroneous, or at least unsupported, statement that the earliest manuscripts of the *Revelations* are "dated to the first half of the fourteenth century" [i manoscritti più vecchi sono datati alla prima metà del XIV secolo] ("Le rivelazioni," 257). One potentially misleading aspect of this claim is that *datati,* "dated," is typically distinguished from *databili,* "datable," in paleographic analysis. More fundamentally, Falvay provides no actual evidence that any of the *Revelations* manuscripts are dated or datable to the first half of the fourteenth century. He states only that a scholar writing in 1932, Florio Banfi, *believed* that the Italian version of the *Revelations* emerged in the first half of the Trecento (Falvay, "Le rivelazioni," 261). In a second adaptation of this article, Falvay also simply asserts a date for the *Revelations* without providing evidence ("The text was probably written in Latin at the beginning of the fourteenth century"; "St. Elizabeth," 143). In "St. Elizabeth," Falvay states that "at least three Italian MSS can be dated to the mid-fourteenth century" (148). But he does not state which manuscripts those might be, nor, even if he did, would the assertion in the earlier article, "Le rivelazioni " hold true. In short, following up Falvay's footnotes and sources has led me to the belief that my earlier expression of confidence in his findings (McNamer, "The Author of the Italian *Meditations on the Life of Christ,*" 122) was misplaced.

purely the product of a literary imagination. If we grant that a real historical figure was the subject of this text, then, that *third* blessed Elizabeth, daughter of the king of Hungary—the Dominican with a Franciscan sister—could be the most plausible candidate for the saintly woman memorialized in the *Revelations*. If this new hypothesis proves persuasive, then the *terminus post quem* for the secondary stage of composition of the MVC—comprising the *testo minore*, *testo maggiore*, and the Latin text—could then be set to the third decade of the Trecento. Author B, then, would seem to have taken up his pen sometime after 1322, revising the *testo breve* and inserting the chapter from the *Revelations*, along with a great many other passages, after that date. To posit a span of at least a few years between the death of the Dominican Elizabeth of Hungary (1322) and the composition and initial circulation of the *Revelations* seems prudent. A reasonable date *post quem* for the composition of Author B's texts, then, would therefore seem to be circa 1325.

The evidence suggests, then, that Author A composed the first version of the MVC sometime between about 1300 and 1325 (possibly somewhat later), and that Author B composed his successive revisions between about 1325 and 1340.

Where might the composition and revision have taken place? Like other pieces of this interconnected puzzle, the date and place of composition may be mutually informing. It is to the question of the *testo breve*'s place of origin, then, that we shall now turn.

## PLACE OF COMPOSITION

The most plausible hypothesis at present is that the *testo breve* was composed by an author from Pisa. Evidence for a link between the author of this text and Pisa derives from a linguistic analysis of the text. As Larson has shown, the Tuscan base dialect includes a number of features that are found only in other texts known to have been copied by Pisan scribes (see "Linguistic Analysis" in this volume). This does not necessarily mean that the work was composed in Pisa. Alternative explanations for the Pisan forms exist. The author may have come from Pisa, for instance, but may have lived elsewhere during the period when the work was composed; or the text may have been copied at a very early stage by a Pisan scribe who introduced the distinctive Pisan forms.

The theory that the author was Pisan, however, is an intriguing one. Pisa, in the first few decades of the Trecento, was certainly a cultural milieu

conducive to the composition of an affective meditation on the life of Christ in Italian designed for use by women religious. Domenico Cavalca's preaching to women in the province of Pisa, and the copious *volgarizzamenti* produced by him and by his *bottega*, made Pisa one of the most open and energetic centers for the production of religious writing in the vernacular in the early Trecento.[73] Whether the reception of Cavalcan writings by women in the region may have spurred the composition of a vernacular meditation on the life of Christ is a question worth investigating more fully, as is the question of women's roles in the development of a Pisan textual community.[74] In terms of its institutional structures, Pisa was robust enough to support two major religious foundations, the Dominican convent of Santa Caterina and the Franciscan convent of San Francesco, each with well-stocked libraries, as well as numerous smaller convents.[75] Pisa's visual culture was vibrant, and there are affinities in terms of style and content between the MVC and Pisan art. Examples of such affinities include the narrative sculptures by Nicola Pisano in the cathedral and baptistry at Pisa. The unusual and specific resonance between the depiction of Simeon in Pisano's pulpit and in the *testo breve* is particularly intriguing (see "Notes to the *Meditations*," 209n39). There are also many painted wooden crucifixes in the pathetic mode that survive from early Trecento Pisa, including historiated crucifixes containing narrative scenes from the life of Christ.[76] The similarities between these visual images and the *testo breve* are not, I would stress, an indication that this art directly influenced the author of the MVC, or that the MVC influenced particular Pisan works of art. But there is a general consonance between the two; more

73. See Cornish, *Vernacular Translation in Dante's Italy*, and Delcorno, "Cavalca, Domenico," "Diffusione del volgarizzamento," and "Predicazione volgare e volgarizzamenti."

74. I have not undertaken a detailed stylistic comparison between Cavalca's *Vite de' santi padri* and the *testo breve*, but this would, I believe, be a fruitful area for further research. Delcorno writes eloquently of the "dolcezza fabiesca" and the "coloriture romanzesche" that infuse the *Vite de' santi padri* (Delcorno, "Cavalca, Domenico"); these qualities also characterize the *testo breve*. While such stylistic similarities are not, themselves, enough to indicate the presence of a distinctive Pisan textual community, they are at the very least intriguing; to my knowledge, no comparative study of Cavalcan writings and the Italian MVC, in any of its versions, has yet been conducted.

75. On the Franciscans, see Ronzani, "Il francescanesimo a Pisa fina alla metà del Trecento."

76. Testi Cristiani, *Arte Medievale a Pisa*, 456–77. Many of these crucifixes are now held at the Museo Nazionale di San Matteo, Pisa.

generally, the narrative litheness and grace of the *testo breve* resembles Pisan and Sienese gothic devotional art (see "Notes to the *Meditations*," 202n11, on the Annunciation).

I have suggested ("Authorship" above) that the author of the *testo breve* is likely to have been a Poor Clare. Because the convent of Ognissanti was the only convent of Poor Clares in Pisa prior to 1331, it seems reasonable to posit that the author of the *testo breve* wrote at this convent, presumably for her fellow nuns.[77] Ognissanti no longer survives. In 1331, the Poor Clares were transferred from Ognissanti to the Pisan convent of Santa Chiara Novella at San Martino in Kinzica. Interestingly, the provenance of the beautifully illustrated Italian translation of the MVC, Paris, BnF MS ital. 115, has been traced to Pisa, and the evidence that it was designed for use by the Poor Clares of Santa Chiara Novella is persuasive.[78] This may testify to a special appreciation for the MVC as a home-grown, Pisan production—even as it was making its way, through the energetic efforts of many translators and copyists, into the major centers of textual production across the far reaches of Europe.

77. There are not enough records surviving from Ognissanti to reconstruct a textual community or library, but see Cignoni, "Gregorio IX e il francescanesimo femminile." It is important to emphasize that the hypothesis I present here for the work's origins at Ognissanti is provisional. It is possible that an author from Pisa may have been writing among or for Poor Clares elsewhere. The convent of Poor Clares at San Gimignano would merit further consideration, given the associations between Author B and San Gimignano. An inventory from the early fourteenth century survives from the Clarissan convent at San Gimignano; land and books are listed in this inventory. A certain Joanna was abbess there during the first two decades of the fourteenth century (Gaddoni, "Inventaria Clarissarum," 300).

78. See Flora, *The Devout Belief of the Imagination*, and Flora and Pecorini Cignoni, "Requirements of Devout Contemplation."

# THE MANUSCRIPT

Oxford, Bodleian Library MS Canonici Italian 174 is a quarto volume containing 154 paper leaves, sec. xiv^ex–sec. xv^in. The binding measures 210 mm x 155 mm, and the dimensions of a typical folio are approximately 199 mm x 137 mm, with the writing space taking up approximately 141 mm x 87 mm. Quiring is simple: 1–15$^{10}$, 16$^{10}$ lacks leaves 5–10 cut away.

The script throughout is a clear *littera textualis* that appears to date to circa 1400; it displays certain forms influenced by humanist script, such as the *d onciale* and the distinctive shape of the letter *g*, but the duct appears to be gothic (see Fig. 1).[1] The hand appears uniform throughout, and there is a consistent practice of ruling and writing twenty-four lines per folio throughout the compilation. All texts are written in a single column. Titles and chapter headings are given in red, with some initials and paraphs in blue or red; in the text of the *Meditazioni*, there are also splashes of yellow over some capital letters. There are no illuminations. The binding of plain white vellum-covered boards is eighteenth-century Italian, with what appear to be seventy-two paper stubs, some of them folded over and uncut, sewn, or pasted into the binding. These stubs appear to have been inserted as a block to fill out the cover and make it possible to use the original boards and spine after a sizable part of the original manuscript was removed.

The watermarks, most clearly visible on ff. 48, 63, and 67, are among the features that indicate Venetian provenance. The design, an anchor within a circle, measuring about 45 mm in diameter, corresponds approximately to Briquet nos. 464–472, which are all Venetian.[2]

---

1. I am grateful to the late Albinia de la Mare for this assessment of the date of the script, and to Sabina Magrini, who examined the script independently and returned the same judgment: ca. 1400. Given the difficulty of dating textura scripts with precision, it is not impossible that the manuscript was copied somewhat later in the fifteenth century.

2. Briquet, *Les Filigranes*, I: 40.

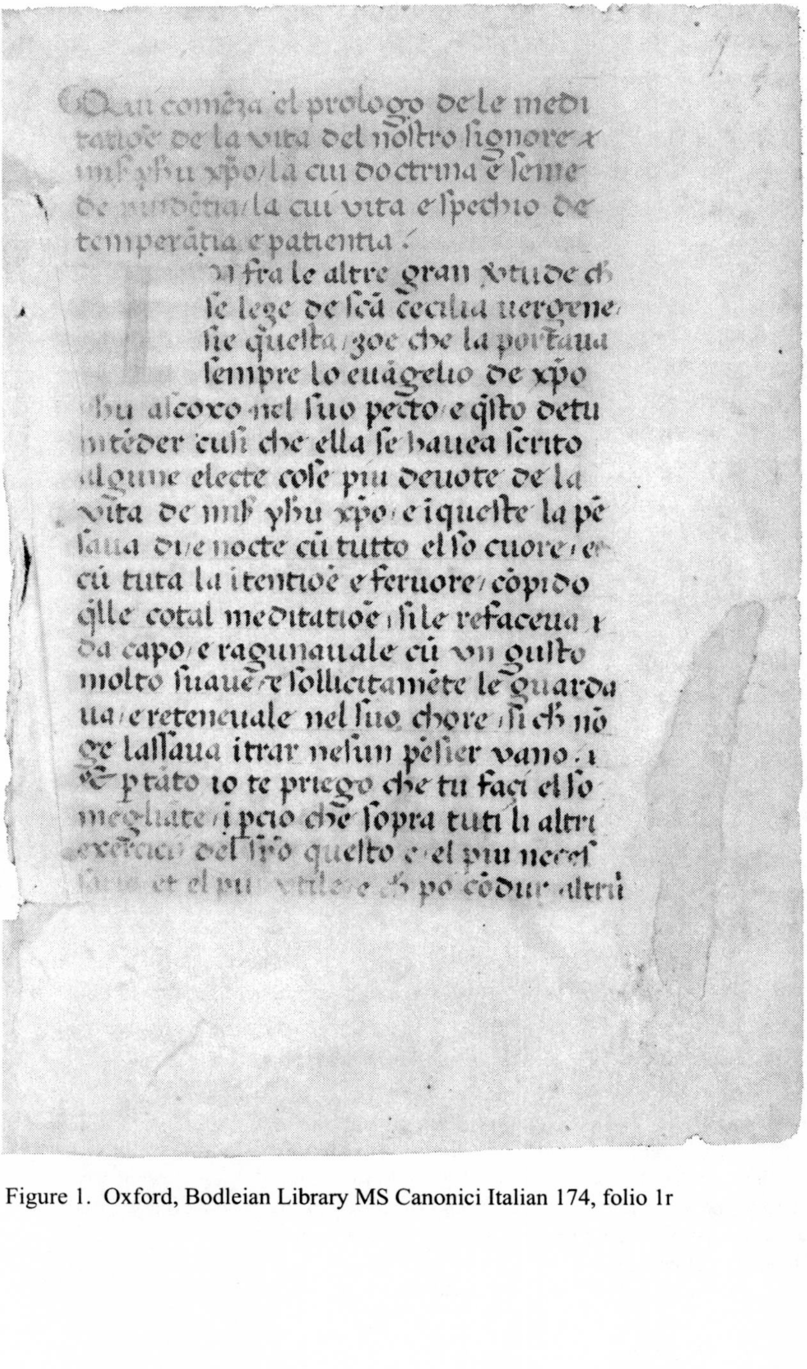

Quan comēza el prologo de le medi
tatioē de la vita del nostro signore ⁊
mīs yhu xpo la cui doctrina è seme
de prudētia la cui vita è spechio de
temperātia e patientia ·

    fra le altre gran virtude cħ
    se lege de scā cecilia uergene
    fie questa zoe che la portaua
    sempre lo euāgelio de xpo
yhu alcoro nel suo pecto e qsto detu
mtēder cusi che ella se hauea scrito
algune electe cose piu deuote de la
vita de mīs yhu xpo e iqueste la pē
saua die nocte cū tutto el so cuore e
cū tuta la itentioē e feruore copido
qlle cotal meditatioē sile refaceua i
da capo e ragunauale cū vn gusto
molto suaue e sollicitamēte le guarda
ua e reteneuale nel suo chore si cħ nō
ge lassaua itrar nesun pēsier vano i
xp̄ptato io te priego che tu faci elso
meghate i pcio che sopra tuti li altri
exercicii del sio questo e el piu neces
sario et el piu vtile e cħ po cōdur altrui

Figure 1. Oxford, Bodleian Library MS Canonici Italian 174, folio 1r

The manuscript was acquired by the Bodleian Library in 1817 in what was, at the time, "a purchase unprecedented in greatness in the history of the Library":[3] the collection of Matteo Luigi Canonici (1727–1806), the Venetian Jesuit who acquired his library of approximately 3550 manuscripts in part by acquiring whole collections, including those of the duke of Modena and of the Venetian Jacopo Soranzo (1686–1761). A number of features indicate that MS Canonici Italian 174 came from the Soranzo collection. These include the plain vellum eighteenth-century binding, the distinctive floral *carta bassanese* paper used for the pastedowns and flyleaves, and the eighteenth-century table of contents, which is written in the hand of Francesco Melchiori, one of Soranzo's librarians.[4] Melchiori's table of contents lists a text which is no longer in the manuscript: "S. Antonini Archiepiscopi Florentini Interrogationis Confessionale, seu Theologia Moralis—vide Tabulam premissam." From this, it can be deduced that the material excised at a later date included the *Summa theologica moralis* by St. Antoninus of Florence, O.P. (1389–1459). It appears, then, that Soranzo bound two quite different manuscripts together, one Italian and one Latin, and that Canonici separated them once he acquired Soranzo's collection.[5] The *Summa* and related texts of S. Antoninus that were once bound with the current contents of MS. Canonici Italian 174 are now contained in Bodleian Library MS. Canonici Misc. 135, preceded on ff. 1–3v by the "Tabulam" mentioned in Melchiori's note.[6] Both compilations (i.e., the Italian collection of texts now in Canonici Italian 174 and the Latin works of S. Antoninus now

3. Macray, *Annals of the Bodleian Library*, 279.

4. The table of contents of MS 174 may be compared with Plate XIV of Mitchell, "Trevisan and Soranzo." Mitchell notes that the "typical Soranzo binding, as Dott. Merolle says, consists of plain vellum-covered boards having a lightly banded spine, and very often with small, stiff flaps on the fore-edges of the boards. The pastedowns and endpapers are of a stiff paper decorated with distinctive floral patterns (*carta bassanese*), or with marbling of a certain type and colour" (130).

5. Mitchell notes that "Soranzo had been in the habit of binding within one cover a number of manuscripts, somewhat unequal in size and discordant in content. Canonici usually broke up these volumes, particularly when a work in Latin was set next to one in Italian" ("Trevisan and Soranzo," 131). There are further indications that Canon. Misc. 135 once formed the second part of Canon. Ital. 174: the quiring of Canon. Misc. 135 is the same ($1–16^{10}$, plus $17^{10}$ but lacks leaf 10), and the catchwords follow the same pattern.

6. The notes by J. B. Mitchell kept at the Bodleian Library, now among the unpublished "Bodley Ref." index cards, indicate that the Italian compilation in MS. Canonici Italian 174 was once designated as Soranzo 735, and that MS. Canonici Misc. 135 was once Soranzo 736. A copy of Soranzo's catalogue is held at the Bodleian Library as MSS Facs. c. 40/1–7; the manuscript of the catalogue is held at the Biblioteca Marciana in Venice as MS. Ital.X.137-9.

in Canonici Misc. 135) can be traced with some confidence to the collection of the Venetian nobleman Bernardo Trevisan (1652–1720), upon whose death the manuscripts passed to his brother, the priest Francesco Trevisan (d. 1732); they were acquired by Soranzo after Francesco's death in 1732.[7]

MS Canonici Italian 174 contains four texts: the *Meditazioni* and three letters of spiritual direction addressed to female religious.

1. Ff. 1r–127r. *Meditazioni della vita di Cristo*, here without attribution to any author and introduced with the rubric, *Qui comenza el prologo de le meditatione de la vita del nostro signore miser yhu xpo la cui doctrina e seme de p[r]udentia la cui vita e spechio de temperantia e patientia.*

*Inc.* Infra le altre gran vertude che se leze de sancta cecilia uergene si e questa zoe che la portaua sempre lo euangelio de cristo iesu ascoxo nel suo pecto e questo de tu intender cusi che ella se hauea scrito algune electe cose piu deuote de la vita de miser iesu cristo e in queste la pensaua di e nocte cum tutto el so cuore e cum tuta la intentione e feruore.

*Expl.* Et molte altre cose fece miser iesu le qualle io non scriuo per[f. 127 r] che seria tropo longo dire. Ma noi posiamo comprehendere et pensare ch'el fece molte cose le qualle io non scriuo in questo libro. Come se puote vedere nelli evangelii ch'el adopero el nostro signore miser iesu cristo. El qualle sia laudato et ringratiato cum la sua benedecta madre vergene maria in secula seculorum. Amen. Deo gratias.

The text of the *Meditazioni* is followed by a colophon: Priegoue sorelle per caritade che quando legereti in questo libero priegate miser iesu per me che me doni cognoscimento (f. 127r).

2. Ff. 127r–137v. *Seguita vna diuota e utile epistola composta da vno venerabile padre e confessore delle venerande done del monasterio de miser sancto aluuixe nella qualle epistola se trata delli auersarii de lanima çioe di quelli che sono buoni e utile aduersarii* (f. 127r). This letter appears to have been composed specifically for the nuns of the Monastero di Sant'Alvise, a convent of Augustinian nuns in the Cannaregio sestiere in Venice, by a priest who served as their confessor. The monastery was founded by the lay noble-

---

7. Mitchell first noted the connection to the Trevisan collection on the basis of a facsimile of Trevisan's catalogue, where, on f. 20v, there is an entry for "Meditazione della vita di nostro Signor Gesu Christo—ms. 1400. miniato in 4°" and on f. 22r there is an entry for "S. Anontini Archieps. Florentini Interrogationum confessionale—De officio divino. De celle. [etc]" (unpublished note, "Bodley Refs." for MS Canonici Italian 174).

woman Antonia Venier, cousin of the doge Antonio Venier, in 1388; she herself retired to this convent and adopted the rule of St. Augustine.[8] To my knowledge, the letter has not been printed, nor has my initial research yielded other manuscript copies.

*Inc.* O choreme per uostra doctrina et conforto in cristo iesu dilectissime figliule. Uno notabel dito Evangelico el qualle scriue sancto Mathio e sono parole del nostro signore. Et dice cussi. Esto consentiens aduersario tuo cito dum es in via cum eo ne forte tradat te iudici aduersarius. Iudex tradat te ministro et in carcerem mittaris. Amen dico tibi non exeas inde donec reddes nouissimum quadrantem. Vulgarmente parlando diçe il signore. Sii consentiente al tuo aduersario tosto perfina tanto che tu se in via cum lui açio che per auentura el non te dia ne le man del Iudice.

*Expl.* [f. 136v] Aduncha ha [f. 137r] biando notitia de cussi vtili aduersarii come appareno gli sopradeti sforciamose de concordarse o essi secundo el consiglio del Iudice perfeto consigliatore cioe de sopra se contiene nella proposta açio loro non ne metano nelle mani del Iudice iusto et esso vedandone discordi cum li deti aduersarii ne meta ne le mano de i tormentatori demonii e loro ne metano nelle infernale pregione la doue mai vssire non si potra perfina atanto che non se renda infina alultimo quadrante çioe perfina che non si compira de satisfare ala diuinia Iustitia. Et questa satisfacione durera per Infinita secula seculorum. Amen. Deo Gratias.

3. Ff. 137v–149r. A letter of spiritual direction by San Girolamo da Siena (1335/6?–1420), corresponding to *Epistola Terza: La Perfetta Monaca*.[9] It is introduced with the rubric, *Incomincia vna diuota e utile epistola di frate ieronimo del lordine di frati romiti di sancto augustino ad vna sua figliola vergene a dio sacrata nella [qualle] se dimostra chi e vera monicha.* San Girolamo preached actively in the Veneto as well as Umbria and Tuscany in the last two decades of the fourteenth century.[10]

*Inc.*: Frate geronimo alla sua cara figliola serua e sposa di dio. Salute e dono di pace cristiano amore notitia di dio chiareça di veritade pentimento verace confusione e odio di vechia vita pasata e nouamento [f. 137r] di virtu. Dispiacimento del seculo costumi religiosi morte al mondo e vita in cristo iesu dolcissimo salvatore. Amen. Charissima in cristo iesu sono stato gia grande tempo in pensiero di douerti scriuere e a questo aspectaua di auere la mente

---

8. "S. Alvise (Venezia)," Archivio di Stato di Venezia.
9. Serventi, *Girolamo da Siena*, 159–72. The existence of the Canonici copy of the letter is not noted in Serventi's edition.
10. Pignatti, "Girolamo da Siena."

quieta e pacifica per potermi asotigliare ad scriuerti quello che dio mi facese intendere che ti fuisse piu necessario.

*Expl.* [f. 149r] Et io che sacrificio non celebro sença la tua memoria sempre cosi il prego che in questa vita el ti riempia di gratia. Et miser iesu cristo figliolo di dio viuo e vero te e me conduca nel sino del suo padre nella cui dextera esso sedendo viue e regna in secula seculorum. Amen. In esso saluatore vaglia e posa l'anima tua e tu serua di dio ora per me peccatore. Deo gratias.

4. Ff. 149r–154v. Letter of spiritual direction concerning ideal qualities that spouses of Christ should strive to embody, qualities similar to those of ideal wives in the secular world. The author is identified here only as a venerable and devout priest, and the text itself is not identified with further precision in the manuscript. My initial research has revealed no additional copies or printed texts. The rubric on f. 149r reads, *Incomincia vna diuota e vtele epistola de uno venerabile & diuocto padre la qualle contien in se le conditione che debbeno auere quelle che sono vere spose di miser iesu cristo a similitudine delle spose mondane.*

*Inc.* [f. 149v] In cristo iesu diletissima figliuola e sorella figliuola dico per ettade sorella per religione. Extimando io voi volere essere tale verso il uestro dilecto sposo qualle gli huomeni del mondo se poteseno tutti uoriano hauere le sue done. Che chome sapeti cerchano quanto li siano possibille hauere done che habino tute queste sotoscripte condictione o piui di quele che posino. Et sel fuse in libertade di cadauna dona mondana di hauerle tute ogniuna se forceria di hauerle per trouare piu marito a suo modo. Et quando trouato lo hauese se forçeria di conseruarsi per eserli grata. La prima cosa he la beleça. La secunda he nobilita. Terço sapie[n]tia. Quarto richeçe. Quinto sanita. Sexto amor e fidelta.

*Expl.* [f. 154v] Et sapiando io voi hauer piui otio che mi apensare di tal cose. Non mi extendero piu oltra. Tanto piu che so per uui medema poreti ben largar queste sie condictione in ogni vestro proposito. Che anchora ho facto piu di quel pensaua quando come[n]çai ascriuere non haue ça tal animo ne so chome mi sia venuto. Se ho in parte satisfacto ri[n]gratio Dio. Se anche mancho chome mi penso pregoue me abiate per escusato. Deo gratias. Amen.

As for the manuscript's origins, there are many indications that the volume was copied in or near Venice for Venetian nuns. This evidence includes the language of the *Meditazioni*, which evinces a Tuscan base text with a heavy overlay of Venetian dialect (see below, "Linguistic Analysis," clvii), the paper's Venetian watermarks, the scribal assumption that the volume's readers will be familiar with the nuns of the monastery of Sant'Alvise (f. 127r),

and the fact that the volume was later owned by Trevisan and Soranzo, both Venetians whose libraries included many volumes made in Venice.

The contents of the *epistole* as well as the concluding colophon of the *Meditazioni* addressed to "sorelle" (assuming that this colophon is scribal rather than authorial) appear to indicate that the volume was made for a community of nuns, rather than for one of the many recluses or *pinzochere* living in Venice at the time or for a group of pious laywomen or widows living in community. Precisely which convent, or even which institutional affiliation, is difficult to determine. There are no overt signs of the institutional affiliation of the manuscript's intended readers in the manuscript or its texts. The spiritual precepts promoted in the compilation could apply to the any of the orders of nuns present in Venice in the late fourteenth and early fifteenth centuries: Augustinians, Benedictines, Poor Clares, or Dominicans.[11]

It is important to exercise caution in deducing the ownership of any manuscript from its contents or even from its rubrics. In this case, two of the texts in the volume identify their first readers or authors as Augustinian ("composta da uno venerabile padre e confessore delle venerande done del monasterio de miser sancto aluuixe" [f. 127r]; "frate ieronimo del lordine di frati romiti di sancto augustino ad una sua figliola" [f. 137r]). This might suggest that the manuscript belonged to Augustinian nuns. However, this cannot be taken as firm evidence that it did. The fact that Augustinian affiliation is considered worthy of mention could be an indication of difference rather than institutional affinity between those authors and readers and the nuns for whom this volume was made. Indeed, given Girolamo da Siena's renown in the region, it would probably go without saying that Girolamo was an Augustinian if the nuns for whom the manuscript was made were also Augustinian.[12]

---

11. The foundational study of Venetian convents, recently reprinted, is that by Flaminio Corner, *Notizie storiche delle chiese e monasteri di Venezia*; see also Zangirolami, *Storie delle chiese*. Marino Zorzi notes evidence of book ownership by the nuns of San Zaccaria, San Servolo, San Alvise, San Girolamo, and Santa Maria degli Angeli di Murano; he further observes that the Dominican nuns of Santa Croce of Giudecca cultivated literary interests at a high level (Zorzi, "Dal manoscritto al libro," 838).

12. An interesting parallel to consider in this context is another manuscript copied in Venice, Biblioteca Nazionale Marciana Ital.Z.7, which contains an Italian copy of the MVC. This manuscript contains an inscription of ownership indicating that the volume belonged to San Girolamo (f. 80v), a convent of Augustinian nuns. It also contains an attribution of the MVC text to "frate Jacobo de l'ordene di frati minori" (f. 1r). Tóth and Falvay discuss the attribution to "Jacobo" at length ("New Light" and "L'Autore"). My point here is that this example provides evidence of the cross-institutional circulation of devotional texts in Venice and of the fact that the mention of an author's order need not imply that the manuscript belonged to those affiliated with that order.

If the convent and institutional affiliation of the nuns for whom the manuscript was made remain a mystery, however, perhaps the openness of the question is itself a revealing feature of women's religious culture at this time, at least in northern Italy. Although the subject requires further study, the fluid circulation of devotional texts originating in varied institutional contexts appears to have been a common practice, far more so than the compiling and reading of texts stemming from a single order, including, significantly, the Franciscan Order.[13] Perhaps it is not an irony at all, then, that the MVC—widely categorized in the modern era as a quintessential "Franciscan" text—is free of any institutional markers in this, the only manuscript bearing witness to what appears to be its earliest form.

13. The presence of scriptoria in Venice in the late Trecento and early Quattrocento, including the famed scriptorium of the Camaldolese monastery of San Michele in Isola, may have facilitated the sharing of texts originally produced by and for those of particular orders. See Zorzi, "Dal manoscritto al libro," on the scriptorium at San Michele and on the production and circulation of manuscripts in Venice during this period. Zorzi observes that the copying of manuscripts was considered an act of piety for the Benedictines; the same was not true, typically, of the Franciscans and Dominicans. However, the Dominican nuns of Corpus Domini appear to have copied manuscripts regularly ("Dal manoscritto al libro," 819); their necrology offers further witness to literary activity there in the early Quattrocento (Bornstein, *Life and Death in a Venetian Convent*). The complex history of the foundation of Corpus Domini provides one illustration of the institutional fluidity among women religious in Venice: its founder, Lucia Tiepolo, a Benedictine nun for most of her life, then Benedictine abbess, set about constructing a church after receiving a vision; her nascent community then became Dominican; two of its earliest recruits, Isabetta and Andreola Tommasini, were initially advised by their guardian's Dominican confessor to become Augustinian nuns; another elderly nun transferred there from an Augustinian convent (Bornstein, *Life and Death in a Venetian Convent*, 4–5). I have not carried out an extensive investigation of the ownership of manuscripts by Venetian nuns ca. 1400, but my initial work confirms that one cannot easily deduce the insitutional affiliation of a manuscript's first readers or owners from a manuscript's contents. As indicated in the prior note, Biblioteca Nazionale Marciana MS Ital.Z.7 was clearly owned by nuns of the Augustinian convent of San Girolamo ("Questo libro è del monastier de miser San Ieronimo," f. 80v); a Franciscan text has thus been absorbed into a collection for Augustinian nuns. Biblioteca Nazionale Marciana It.Z.10 contains writings by a Dominican (Cavalca's *Specchio di Croce*) and by a Franciscan (an Italian copy of the MVC), yet this manuscript belonged to the Benedictine nuns of Santa Croce ("Questo libro xe del monastier de Sancta Croxe dela Çudeche," f. 1r).

# LINGUISTIC ANALYSIS

## by Pär Larson

The reader's first reaction to the Italian vernacular version of the *Meditationes Vitae Christi* contained in Oxford, Bodleian Library MS Canonici Italian 174 might well be one of bewilderment in the face of the mixture of clashing forms and spellings.[1] In fact, the text exhibits Northern, mainly Venetan elements alongside almost perfectly Tuscan forms and constructions.[2] The task of the linguist must therefore be that of trying to ascertain the order in which the different elements entered the text.

The following paragraphs do not pretend to constitute anything even remotely like an exhaustive linguistic analysis of the manuscript. Their only aim is to highlight some features that might be useful for the understanding and the geolinguistic definition of the text.

## BIBLIOGRAPHY

Bertoletti = Nello Bertoletti, *Testi veronesi dell'età scaligera*, Padua: Esedra, 2005 [non-literary texts from Verona, 1268–1387].

1. In chapter 4, f. 14v, a single sentence actually contains as many as four 3rd pers. plur. preterite forms of verbs in *-are*, formed in four different ways: "Et come fu sera, per força *andòno* [< *andare*] fuori della citade forsi doi meglia et qui *trovorono* [< *trovare*] una stalla de pegorari che era fuori della via, et quivi *intrarono* [< *intrare*] per stare et non *trovàno* [< *trovare*] li alcuna cosa se non uno poco di fen per dare all'asino et al buo' et qui non era né lume né fuoco, né lecto né linçuoli."
2. I prefer the term "Venetan" to the more common "Venetian," which refers ambiguously both to the city of Venice and to the entire Veneto region, whereas "Venetan" applies only to the region. A more cautious approach might suggest the wider definition "Padanian," but the lack of more pronounced Emilian or Lombard traits makes this designation less fitting.

Boerio = Giuseppe Boerio, *Dizionario del dialetto veneziano*, 2nd edition, Venice: G. Cecchini, 1856.

Castellani 1980 = Arrigo Castellani, *Saggi di linguistica e filologia italiana e romanza (1946–1976)*, Rome: Salerno editrice, 1980.

Castellani 2000 = Arrigo Castellani, *Grammatica storica della lingua italiana*, Bologna: il Mulino, 2000.

OVI Corpus = *Corpus OVI dell'Italiano antico*, produced by Opera del Vocabolario Italiano and directed by P. Larson and E. Artale, http://gattoweb .ovi.cnr.it.

Paccagnella = Ivano Paccagnella, *Vocabolario del pavano (XIV–XVII secolo)*, Padua: Esedra, 2012.

Rohlfs = Gerhard Rohlfs, *Grammatica storica della lingua italiana e dei suoi dialetti*, Turino: Einaudi, 1966–69 (1st edition in German, Bern: Francke, 1949–54).

Rosa = Gabriele Rosa, *Dialetti, costumi e tradizioni nelle provincie di Bergamo e di Brescia*, Brescia: Fiori, 1870.

Stussi = Alfredo Stussi, *Testi veneziani del Duecento e dei primi del Trecento*, Pisa: Nistri-Lischi, 1965 [non-literary texts from Venice, 1253–1321].

*TLIO* = *Tesoro della Lingua Italiana delle Origini*, online Old Italian dictionary founded and directed by Pietro G. Beltrami, www.ovi.cnr.it.

Tomasin = Lorenzo Tomasin, *Testi padovani del Trecento*, Padua: Esedra, 2004 [non-literary texts from Padua, 1336–80].

Tuttle = Edward Tuttle, *The Veneto*, in *The Dialects of Italy*, edited by Martin Maiden and Mair Parry, 263–70, New York: Routledge, 1997.

Verlato = Zeno Verlato, *Le Vite di Santi del Codice Magliabechiano XXXVIII.110 della Biblioteca Nazionale Centrale di Firenze: Un leggendario volgare trecentesco italiano settentrionale*, Tübingen: Niemeyer, 2009.

All forms cited from the MS are followed by the number of the folio and the indication r(ecto) or v(erso).

## VOCALISM

### Anaphonesis

The vocalic phenomenon known as "anaphonesis" (It. *anafonesi*),[3] consisting (1) in the raising /e/ > /i/ before palatal /ʎ/ or /ɲ/ stemming from -LJ- or -NJ-,

---

3. For the exact definition, see Castellani 1980, I:73–87.

and (2) in the raising of /e/ > /i/ and /o/ > /u/ before velar [ŋ]—characteristic of the Florentine dialect and normative in Standard It.—is largely absent, as is to be expected in a text from Northern Italy, where the above-mentioned vowel raisings do not take place. In the following table non-anaphonetic forms are followed by their anaphonetic counterparts, cited within square brackets:

ĭ > *e*

*conseglio* 'counsel' 54r, 75v, 78v, *consegliati* 70v;

*fameglia* 'family' 13v, 22r, 59v, 64v, 69v, *famegli* 45r, *famegliola* 43r;

*meglia* 'miles' 8v, 14v;

*maravegliosa/-e/-o* 'marvelous' 12r, *meravegli* 38v, *meraveglie* 86v, *meraveglia* 123v, *maravegliandose* 112v, *maravegliare* 2r, *maravegliarse* 39v, *meravegliare* 50r, *meravegliava* 40r, *meravegliavano* 10v, *meravegliàvasse* 40r, *meravegliosa/-e* 6r, 7v, 47v, 62v, 113v;

*simegliante* 'similar' 20r, *somegliante/-i* 1r, 28v, 53v, *someglia* 73v [cfr. *simigliante* 37r, *simigliantemente* 50v];

*intenge* 'dips' 60v [cf. *tincto* 61r];

*spengeva* 'pushed' 75r, *spençando* 75v, *spençea* 81v, 87v, *spenta* 90r;

*strençandose* 'moving close' 68r, *strenselo* 'hugged him' 37v;

*vençere* 'to vanquish' 98v, *vento* 67r, 111v; *convento* 'convinced' 11v [cf. *vincere* 40v, 41r, 49r, 98v, *vinto* 49v (bis)].

ŭ > *o*

*gionte* 'joined' 116r, *çonti* 21v, 25r, 26v, 34v, 68v, 80r, 89v, *çonto* 40v, 73v, 75v, 82r, *zonte* 6v, *cançonse* 7v [cf. g[i]*unta* 4v, *conçunta* 21v, 47r];

*ponto* 'point' 6v, 23v, 51r, 51v, 56r.

There are no examples at all of common Tuscan (and Standard It.) forms such as *consiglio*, *famiglia*, *maraviglia*, *punto*, *spingere*, *stringere* or derivates.

## Dipthongs *ie* and *uo*

The distribution of the rising diphthongs -*ie*- and -*uo*-, resulting from Latin stressed Ĕ and Ŏ, follows fairly closely the Tuscan norm, with diphthongs occurring in stressed position. Accordingly, the MS consistently has <ie> in rhizotonic forms like *viene* 2r, 2v, 9r, etc. (14 ex.), *vieneno* 100v, *adiviene* 2v, *aviene* 51r, *conviene* 2r, 18v, 23v, etc. and *perviene* 1v, 3r (along with *venire*

37r, 52v, 55v, etc., *venero, venite* 20v, etc., and *venuta/-i/-o* 20v, 23v, 29r, etc.), *tienlo* 34r, *contiene* 6v, 48v, 59r, etc. and *mantiene* 52r (alongside with *te(g)nire, sostenere* and *sostenire*), *insieme* 6v, 9v, 12v, etc., *piede/-i* 8v, 9v, 14r, etc., *pietra/-e* 19v, 20r, 49r, etc. A notable exception is the word for 'hay' (Tuscan and Standard It. *fieno*): *fen* 14v, *feno* 15r (ter), 16v (ter).

As for <uo>, we find *buona/-i/-o* 6r, 18r, 18v, etc. (17 ex.), *cuore/-i* 1r, 1v, 2r, etc. (29 ex.), *huomo/-eni* 3r, 5v, 7r, etc. (59 ex.), *luocho, -i* 4v, 11v, 15v, etc. (34 ex.), *puote* 3r, 8r, 11v, etc. (20 ex.), alongside the less frequent *bona/-e* 32v, *bonamente* 53v, *chore* 1r, *homeni* 2v, 18r, 33r.

As regards other lexemes, the balance between diphthongized forms and their non-diphthongized counterparts is more equal: e.g., *nuova/-o* 4v, 50v, 63v, 101r, *rinuova* 97v, vs. *novo* 64r, 65r, 105r, 126r, *rinova* 90r; *rispuose, res-* 5r, 5v, 9v, 35r, 37v, etc., vs. *respose/-eno* 20v, 65r, 72r, 76r; *vintinuove* 'twentynine' 44v, vs. *nove* 'nine' 12v.

On some occasions, the distribution of diphthongs goes decidedly against Tuscan standards. While, for instance, *alegreça* 6r, 7r, 10r, etc. (24 ex.) and the arhizotonic forms of *(r)al(l)egrare* consistently have <e> (e.g., *alegrare* 19v, 109v, 111v, *alegrato/-e* 81r, 115v, *alegremose* 51r, *alegrerà* 66v, *alegreria* 111v, 126r, *alegriamosse* 125v, *alegroe* 9r, *alegrono* 116r, *allegrarse* 8v, *ralegrata* 37v, 111r), the adjective *alegro*, the adverb *alegramente* adv. and the rhizotonic forms of *al(l)egrare* alternate <e> and <ie>: *alegro, -a* 2r, 114r vs. *aliegro, -a* 4r, 6r, 104v; *alegramente* 11r, 12v vs. *aliegramente* 3v, 9v, 26r; *alegrano* 2v, *ralegrate* 7r vs. *aliegrate* 17v. It can be noted that in the OVI Corpus, apart from a dozen examples of metaphonetical *alliegro/-i* in a Neapolitan text, an isolated Umbrian example and three Bolognese occurrences, all remaining 248 diphthongized forms are in fourteenth-century Venetan texts.

Worth noticing are also the forms of the verb *pregare* with <ie> in unstressed position: *priegoe* 7r, *priegavano* 8r, *priegava* 11v, 54r, *priegiamo* 105v, *priegò* 106r. The forms without a diphthong, however, prevail: e.g., *pregiamo* 32v, *pregava* 54r, 57v, 68r, etc., *pregò* 61r, 91v, etc.

In *misier Iesù* 34v (*miser Iesù* 1r, 1v, etc. [319 ex.]) the lone diphthongized form is typically Venetan (cf. Tuscan and Standard It. *messer(e)*): the OVI Corpus contains nearly four hundred examples of *mis(s)ier/mes(s)ier (-e)*, 'sir,' all in texts from the Veneto.

Another characteristically Venetan diphthongized form is the infinitive of the verb 'to take' (cf. the Tuscan forms *togliere, tollere, tôrre*, none of which is present in the MS): *tuore* 34v, 43v, 67r, 71r, 100v, 103r, 112r, 120r, *tuorme* 70v, *tuorli* 97v, *tuorlo* 101r, 114r. The OVI Corpus contains 174 ex-

amples of *tuore*, all in Venetan texts dated between the first half of the thirteenth and the end of the fourteenth century.

Also noteworthy are the forms *buove* 'ox' 13v, 14r, 16r, with the apocopated variant *buo'* 14v, 15r, comparable to Venetan *buò*, documented in the OVI Corpus in texts from Venice and Padua.

Other cases of diphthongs present in positions where Tuscan varieties and Standard It. have -*o*- are *puocho* 34r and *muodo* 101v, both well attested in fourteenth-century Venetan texts in the OVI Corpus.

## Reduction *uo* > *u*

On some occasions the diphthong *uo* is reduced to *u*: *façulo* 'kerchief' 62v [e.g., *façuolo* 62v]; *figlulo/figliulo* 'son' 4v (bis), 5r, 5v (bis), 6v, 7r (bis), 7v (bis), 8r [cf. *figluolo/-a* 3v, 6r, 6v]; *humo* 'man' 40v, 49r, 50r [cf. *huomo/-eni* 3r, 5v, 7r, etc. (59 ex.)]; *linçulo* 'bedsheet' 16v [*linçuoli* 14v, *ninçuolo* 100r, 103r]. In medieval Veneto, this phenomenon is particularly frequent in Paduan texts, but also occurs elsewhere in the region: see Tomasin, 105–7, and Verlato, 65.

It is worth noticing that the issue of Latin FĪLIŎLUS actually presents every possible development: from the Tuscan-type *figliolo/-i/-a* 4r, 6v, 7v, etc. (180 ex.) or *figluolo/-a* 3v, 6r, 6v, to the purely Venetan *fiolo* 3v, 36v, 51v, and *fiol* 4r, 26v, with an example of the intermediate solution *figioli* 73r. However, the types in *o*, *uo*, and *u* coexist only in the first eight folios of the MS, after which *figl(i)olo* reigns unchallenged.

## Treatment of Pretonic *AU*

In the verb 'to hear,' from Lat. AUDĪRE, the Tuscan and Standard It. type *udire* occurs seven times (*udendo* 100v, *udimo* 76v, *udire* 80v, *uditeno* 102r, *udito/-a* 76r, 77r, 97r), but the prevailing type is the Venetan—also common in other parts of Northern Italy—with substitution of the initial Latin diphthong with *al* or *ol*:[4] *aldando* 55r, 104r, *aldendo* 20v, 57r, 80v, 86r, 116v, 121r, *aldendosi* 4v, 6r, *aldeno* 80v, *aldi* 53r, 80r, *aldì* 6r, *aldida* 95v, *aldire* 18v, 46r, 114v, *aldito/-a* 16r, 28r, 39v, 58r, 81v, 113r, 113v, 124r; *oldendo* 22r, 51v, 85v, 94v.

---

4. The forms corresponding to Lat. EXAUDĪRE 'to answer (a prayer)' all conserve the diphthong: *exaudite* 12r, *exaudito* 69r, 69v, 72r, *exaudi* 70r (bis).

The nineteenth-century Venetian lexicographer Boerio, s.v. *aldìr*, considers this form an "antique vernacular word," an opinion confirmed by Stussi (186), who registers the Old Venetian forms *aldìr* and *oldir*. See also Tomasin (228) and Bertoletti (450), who comment on Old Paduan *aldire* and Old Veronese *aldire/oldì*.

### Apocope of Final Vowels after *L, N, R*

A typical Venetan—and generally North Italian—trait is the loss of final unstressed *-e* preceded by *l, n, r*. The examples that follow are all of apocope of *-e* and also of *-o* and *-i* in stressed words:

> "uno tal exemplo *material*" 4r; "façi lo *simel*" 48r;
> "uno poco di *fen*" 14v; "partire *diman*" 32v;
> "non li potea *intrar*" 1v; "Respose *miser* cum grande mansuetudine" 76r;
>     "*miser* non li respondea" 81r; "in pena et *desonor*" 87v; "confermare
>     gli *chuor*" 120r, etc.

## CONSONANTISM

### Voiced and voiceless stops

Notwithstanding the high incidence of Venetan and more generally Padanian forms, spellings, and endings, the intervocalic consonantism appears remarkably Tuscan: the voiced stops /d/ and /g/ and the fricative /v/, which in Northern Italy correspond to Central and Southern (and Latin) /p/, /t/, and /k/, are certainly present, but they do not prevail as might be expected.

### Simple and Geminated Consonants

As is often the case in texts from Northern Italy—where the phonological opposition between long and short consonants, still maintained in Central and Southern Italy and in Standard It., has been absent since late Antiquity—the rendering of long or "double" consonants in the MS is sometimes erratic. A quick look at the first page (= f. 1*r*) finds the pronoun *ela* alongside with *ella*, the verb *leze* 'reads,' *miser* 'sir,' *nesun* 'nobody,' *scrito* 'written,' *spechio* 'mirror,' and finally *tuta* and *tuti* 'all' alongside *tutto*. For almost every spelling of this type, however, counterexamples with "double" consonants can be found in the MS text, since the scribal *usus* is anything but consistent.

The issue of Latin -LL-, usually conserved in Tuscan and Standard It., is frequently expressed by a single <l>. As we have just seen, *ella* 'she' (1r, 4v, 5v, etc. [15 ex.]) and *ello* 'he' (3v, 7v, 28v, 35v, 120v) coexist with *ela* (1r, 2r, 5r, etc. [16 ex.]) and *elo* (4r, 39v, 77r, 121v), and the thirty examples of *fançullo* 'boy' (16r [bis], 18r, etc.) and *fancullo* (25v) are accompanied by *fançulo* (15r, 17v); the diminutive form of *asino* 'donkey' is *asinello* (33v, 54v [bis]), but also *asenelo* (13v [bis], 14r, 16r, 17r), etc.

On the other hand, as is so often the case in North Italian texts,[5] etymological short /l/ is often expressed by a hypercorrect geminated <ll>—so often, in fact, that in some words this spelling is actually majoritarian. This is true for "quale" (Lat. QUALE[M])—with 220 examples of *qualle/-i* against 9 of *quale/-i*—and "tale"/"cotale" (Lat. *[ECCUM] TALE[M]), with 3 examples of *talle* (19r, 21v, 72v) and 6 of *cotalle* (4v, 9v, 10r, etc.) against 3 examples of *tale* (115r, 125r, 125v). Examples of words with hypercorrect <ll> (with counterexamples in square brackets) include the following:

*avillì* 'humiliated' 41v, *avillìte* 41v [cf. *avilisse* 1v, *avilite* 40v];
*bailla* 'nurse' 10r;
*bambollino* 'baby' 17v [cf. *bambolino* 18v, 19r, 27v, 31r];
*caveçalle* 'pillow' 19v;
*eternalle* 86v [cf. *eternale* 45v];
*felle* 89v, *fielle* 'gall' 95r (bis), 102r;
*gentille* 22v, *çentille* 21v [cf. *çentile* 21v];
*malle* 'bad' 71r, 74v, *mallecontenti* 108v [cf. *male* 30v, 31r, 36v, etc. (34 ex.)]
*melle* 'honey' 18r, 119v;
*nobelle* 'noble' 23r [cf. *nobile* 100r, 118r, *nobelissimo* 102v]
*pellava* 'plucked' 75r, *pellata* 85r [cf. *pelargi* 77r, *pelata* 85v, *pelavali* 84v]
*rasonevelle* 'reasonable' 112r;
*revellò* 'revealed' 29v, *revellatione* 29v [cf. *revelare* 62r, *revelatione* 6v,
    62r, *revelato* 62r; *rivelò* 103v]
*salla* 'hall' 77r;
*scalla* 'stairs' 96r, 101v, 102r, *scalle* 101r [cf. *scala* 49v];
*sollo* 'alone' 4v (bis) [18 examples of *solo*]
*stolla* 'stole' 112v;
*vello* 'veil' 15r, 90r, 95r;
*venerabilli* 'venerable' 26v [cf. *venerabile* 125r, *venerabili* 10r];
*ville* 'vile' 16v [cf. *vile* 17r, 22r, 24r, etc. (11 examples)];
*vuolle* 'wants' 118v [cf. *vuole* 43r (ter), etc. (8 examples)].

5. See Stussi, xxx; Tomasin, 93–94.

Another grapheme frequently occurring doubled in hypercorrect forms in Northern Italian texts is <s>:

*batessimo* 21v [cf. *baptesmo* 47r, *batesmo* 21v, 47r, 47v];
*confusse* 49r, *confussione* 108r [cf. *confuso* 49v (bis), 51r; *confusione* 2r, 111v, 118r];
*chasseta* 'small house' 4v [cf. *casa, -e* 8v (ter), etc. (52 examples); *caxa* 21r];
*çosso* 'downwards' 101v [cf. *çoso* 22r, 27v, 49v, 100v, 107v];
*descesse* 95v, 110r, *discesse* 110r [cf. *desceseno* 15v; *discese* 8r, 47r, 110v];
*medessimo* 108r [medesimo 2v, 6v, 11r, etc. (14 examples)];
*permisse* 114r;
*presseno* 90v, 121r [cf. *prexe* 4r; *prese* 7r, 10v, 20r, etc.; *preseno* 74v, 79v, 84r, 87r, 121r];
*pressentia* 90r [cf. *presencia* 50v, *presentia* 51r, 52r, 71v. etc.];
*presside* 82v;
*puosse* 112v [cf. *puose* 42v, 60v, 78v, 98r];
*repossandose* 31r, *ripossase* 9v, *riposso* 12r, 73v, *ripossative* 73v [cf. *riposo* 34r, *riposava* 37v];
*spassemasse* 37v;
*usseno* 89v [cf. *usare, usança*, etc. (14 examples)].

Particular cases are *cossa* (*-e*) 'thing' (9v, 19r, 21v, etc. [12 ex.]) and *cossì* 'thus' 5r, 99v, where the dialectal spelling with <ss>, indicating a voiceless alveolar sibilant, survives to this day.

Double <ss> also occurs in the enclitic pronoun *se* when written as part of the preceding verb:[6] *affligévasse* 37r; *alegriamosse* 125v; *cinçesse* 62v; *dàvasse* 43v; *dicesse* 32r, 34r, 39v; *dolévasse* 69v; *fàçassi* 39r; *levàvasse* 43v; *leviàmosse* 68r; *meravegliàvasse* 40r; *mésesse* 28r, 45r; *podévasse* 30r; *rèndesse* 71r; *senta[n]dosse* 57v; *sotraçévasse* 40r. Here, too, it is possible that the spelling indicates a voiceless sibilant.[7]

6. This list excludes forms with an oxytonic verb form like *hasse* 79r; *levosse* 37v, 62v, *levossi* 76v; *profundosse* 42r; *puosse* 100r, where the corresponding Tuscan forms would also present a geminated <ss>.

7. The grapheme <ss> also occurs in a group of words the Tuscan counterparts of which have <sc> or <sci> = /ʃʃ/: *ambassiata* 'errand' 4r (ter), 6r, 51r (bis), *ambassiate* 124r; *angossa* 'anguish' 100r, *angossia* 72r, 73r; *avilisse* 'debases' 1v; *cognossandoli* 'knowing them' 100v (bis), 114r [cf. *cognoscendo* 5r, 15r, 49r, 62v, 80v];

## MORPHOLOGY

### Verb Forms

Tuscan and Northern It. verb forms coexist in the MS text, but even though the Tuscan elements prevail, many Venetan features are present.

In three very common verbs, a particular kind of oscillation reigns:

"avere": 1st pers. pres. *habo* 66r [cf. *ho/ò* 5r, 26r, 32v, etc. (57 examples)], 1st pers. perf. *havi* 19v, 58v, 104r; 3rd pers. perf. *have* 4r, 17r (bis), 18v, 19v, etc. (20 examples) [cf. *ebbe* 6v, 10r, 19v, *ebe* 76r, *hebe* 10r, 35v, 47v, 52v, 57r, *hebbe* 122r]; 3rd pers. plur. perf. *haveno* 23r, 25v, 77v, 83v (ter), etc. (12 examples) [cf. *hebbeno* 88v, *hebeno* 24r, 34r];
"dare": 3rd pers. perf. *diete* 94r, 99r, *diette* 101v [cf. *dette* 21v, 33r, 63v, 110r, 126r; *deteno* 89v; *diede* 75v, 76r, 86v, 87r];
"vedere": 3rd pers. perf. *vete* 25v, *vette* 79v, 87v; *vite* 101v [cf. *vide* 37v, 113r, 113v]; 3rd pers. plur. perf. *veteno* 112v; *viteno* 56v [cf. *videro* 112v].

The OVI Corpus contains over 1100 examples of the type *(h)ab(b)o* 'I have,' all of which (with the exception of four thirteenth-century Bolognese occurrences) are Tuscan, mainly Sienese and Pisan. The hundreds of 3rd pers. perf. sing./plur. forms *have/hàveno* in the corpus, on the other hand, are typically Northern It., and occur above all in texts from the Veneto and Lombardy. As for the verbs "dare" and "vedere," the 3rd pers perf. forms *diet(t)e* 'he/she gave' and the 3rd pers sing. *vette/vitte* and plur. *viteno/veteno* occur in a number of Lombard and Venetan texts from the thirteenth and fourteenth centuries.

### Metaplastic Forms

In various verbs from the first conjugation, the etymological ending of first-person indicative present plural, *-amo*, has been replaced not only by the

---

*fassoe* 'wrapped' 10r; *lassare* 1r, 8v, 9v, etc. (47 examples); *pesse* 'fish' 21v, 119v, 121r (bis); *prohibisse* 'prohibits' 80r; *ussio* 'door' 75v; *ussire* 'to exit' 15r, 89r, 91r, *ussita* 94r, *ussite -o* 80v (bis), 82r, etc. (10 examples), *ussendo* 47r [cf. *uscito* 18r, 115r, *uscite* 75v, 76r, *uscitero* 113r]. In some cases the spelling <ss> corresponds to what in Tuscan is an intervocalic post-alveolar affricate /tʃ/: *fantessino* 16r, 21r, 22r; *incrossate* 98r; *tredesse* 20r; *vessinança* 33r [cf. Tuscan *fanticino, incrociate, tredici, vicinanza*].

subjunctive ending *-iamo* (as in Florentine and Standard It.), but also by the metaplastic ending *-emo*:

> *alegremose* 51r [cf. *alegriamosse* 125v];
> *amemo* 45v;
> *andemo* 41r [cf. *andamo* 37v, *andiamo* 16r, 58v, 117v];
> *cerchemo* 77r;
> *mançemo* 64r [cf. *mançiamo* 59r];
> *parlemo* 34r, 122v;
> *pigliemo* 51r;
> *tagliemo* 92r;
> *trovemo* 50v [*troviamo* 55v].

Forms like these are well attested in the OVI Corpus in Venetan literary texts from the thirteenth and fourteenth centuries, but they do not appear in the collections made by Stussi, Tomasin, and Bertoletti.

### Third Person Singular and Plural Forms in the Veneto

As the preceding paragraphs suggest, polymorphism can be said to constitute the prevailing linguistic feature of the text. This is true for verb endings as well, and in particular for third person plural forms. For example, it is interesting to observe how the 3rd pers. sing. preterite of *benedire* 'to bless' (< BENEDICERE) occurs as *benedisse* 60r, 106r, 118v (< BENEDIXIT), but also as *benedì* 23r, 25v, 105r, 122v, as if the verb belonged to the regular conjugation in *-ire*. Alongside these two endings, a third type (which will be discussed later on) occurs in the phrase "il Signore sì *benedicete* la mensa" 51v.

In most North Italian varieties the third person singular verb forms are identical to the corresponding 3rd pers. plur. forms: cf. *canta* < CANTAT, *canta* < CANTANT, *cantava* < CANTABAT, *cantava* < CANTABANT, etc.[8] The Canonici MS generally uses different forms for the 3rd pers. sing. and plur., but some undifferentiated forms remain:

> Present indicative: "le altre gran vertude che se *leze*" 1r; "questi magi *viene*" 21r; "alcuni . . . gli vano addoso et sì llo *spoglia*" 89v; "qui se *rinova* le piage" 90r; "perché *torna*, perché *torna* costoro?" 97v–98r;

---

8. See Rohlfs § 532; Stussi, lxv; Tomasin, 183; Bertoletti, 237; Verlato, 423–25.

Preterite indicative: "Come *vene* li magi" 20r; "[gli magi] *feceli* una bella offerta" 22v; "Alora *vene* li sacerdoti" 26v; "così *fece* alcuni delli altri" 33r ; "*vene* li angeli . . . *dise* li angeli" 51r; "doi de li angeli se *mosse* . . . et *feceli* l'ambassiata" 51v; "quelli crudelli ministri . . . sì llo *rivestite*" 84r; "se *fece* grandi teremoti" 96v; "*vene* doi angeli" 124r;

Imperfect indicative: "se *façea* tante vanitade" 2r; "non li *çovava* i molti argumenti" 82v; "i buffeti non li *mancava*" 83r;

Imperfect subjunctive: "che loro se *partisse*" 33r.

### Third Person Plural Endings

As we have observed in the preceding paragraph, the scribe of the MS uses different forms for the 3rd pers. sing. and plur. The plural preterite forms of verbs of the first conjugation are partly of the Tuscan and Standard It. type in -*àrono* (cf. *intrarono* 14v, *cantarono* 18r, *andarono* 20v, *trovarono* 21r, *ritornarono* 23r, etc. [26 ex.]),[9] partly of the type in -*òrono* (*andorono* 14r, 15v, 16r, 17r *trovorono* 14v, *desmontorono* 22r, *domandorono* 22r, *dimandorono* 23r, *ritornorono* 31v, etc. [57 ex.]). The third group consists of forms with the ending -*òno*: *andono* 14v, 31r, 32r, 34r, 59v, *inçenochiono* 15r, 15v, 16r, etc. (11 ex.), *trovono* 16r, 34r, 59v, etc. (44 ex.). To these can be added two possible occurrences of 3rd pers. plur. pret. forms ending in -*àno*: *cridano* 82v, *trovano* 14v.[10]

The second-conjugation verbs are in part formed with the etymological ending -*ero* (*venero* 20v, 76v, 96v, 97v; *çonsero* 21r; *incorsero* 31r; *sostenero* 31r; *fecero* 33r, 34v, etc. [20 examples]), in part with -*eno* (*feceno* 7r, 8r, 33r [bis], 34r, etc.; *steteno* 11r, 31r, 109r, 111v; *poteno* 14r, 103v; *çonseno* 14r, 32r, 97v; *mésseno* 15r, 60r, 75r, etc. [114 examples]).

Alongside these, a third type occurs, forming 3rd pers. pret. plur. forms in -*eteno*, an ending that—notwithstanding the Northern spelling with a single <t>—appears to be formed using the morpheme -*ett*- (see Rohlfs, § 577), which is used in Standard It. preterite forms such as *dovetti*, -*ette*, -*ettero* and *sedetti*, -*ette*, -*ettero*, etc. The corresponding singular forms end in -*ete* (not to be confused with the 2nd pers. plur. pres. ending!).

---

9. There are no examples of the older, etymological type in -*aro*.

10. In both cases, the phrases preceding and following the verb are entirely in the past tense. This fact, together with the presence of the 3rd pers. sing. pret. form of the first conjugation in -*à* (*negà* 77v), render the -*àno* interpretation reasonably probable: see Verlato, 423, who cites the preterite forms *trovà* and *trovàno*.

Here are the complete examples of 3rd pers. sing. and plur. preterite forms in *-ete/-eteno*:

"cadere": *cadete* 88v, 99v; *cadeteno* 74r;
"conoscere": *cognosete* 9r [cf. *cognobero* 118v (bis)];
"credere": *credete* 50r; *credeteno* 22r (bis), 24r;
"rendere": *rendete* 7r, 15v, 37v, 75r;
"ricevere": *recevete* 25v, 51r, 87r; *ricevete* 7v, 21v, 23v, 26r, 28v, 33r, 37v, 72v; *riceveteno* 55r, 126r;
"rompere": *rumpete* 118v; *rompeteno* 99v;
"temere": *temete* 85v; *temeteno* 32r, 34r;
"vivere": *viveteno* 12v.

When we turn to the verbs ending in *-ire*, the situation appears somewhat surprising. The endings *-ìrono* and *-ìno*, which might have been expected to prevail, given *-àrono*, *-òno*, *-àno* in the first conjugation, actually occur only in forms of the verbs *partire* and *aprire*: *partirono* 10v, 16r, 23r, etc. (8 ex.); *aprirono* 22v; *partìno* 21r, 92r, 106r.

The remaining 3rd pers. plural forms, as well as the greater part of the 3rd pers. sing. ones, use the endings *-iteno/-itero* and *-ite* (here, too, <t> corresponds to Tuscan <tt>):[11]

"aprire": *apriteno* 96v;
"avvilire": *avilite* 40v, *avillite* 41v [cf. *avillì* 41v];
"compire": *compite* 9v;
"convertire": *convertite* 21v, 99r [cf. *convertì* 72r, 95v];
"distribuire": *distribuite* 23v;
"empire," "adempire": *impite* 95r, *adimpite* 46v;
"esaudire": *exaudite* 12r;
"fuggire": *fuçite* 75r; *fuçiteno* 75r, *fuçitero* 33r [cf. *fuçì* 27v];
"morire": *morite* 95v, 99r, 107v [cf. *morì* 95v];
"offrire": *offeriteno* 21r [cf. *offerse* 26v, 27r];
"partire": *partite* 8v, 37r, 49v, 52v, 79r, 95r, 95v, 110r, 116v [cf. *partì* 25r, 28r, 52v, 54v, 60v and the cited examples of *partirono* and *partino*];
"partorire": *parturite* 9v, 10r [cf. *parturì* 36r];
"rivestire": *rivestite* 84r;

11. To the forms that follow can be added a 1st pers. sing. pret. in *-iti*: *concepiti* 'I conceived' 37r.

"seguire": *seguite* 60v;
"sentire," "consentire": *sentite* 15r, 19v, 91r, 99v, 111r, 112r [cf. *sentì* 15r];
    *consentite* 6r;
"uscire": *uscite* 75v, *usite* 15r, 110r, *ussite* 80v (bis), 82r, 91r, 99r (bis), 99v,
    111r; *uscite* 76r, *uscitero* 113r, *usitero* 96v; *insite* 27v.

While the *-ett-* morpheme is used in preterite forms of verbs in *-ere* in
various Old Italian dialects and also in Standard It., it is rare to find a text
where the preterite forms of verbs in *-ire* are constructed in the same way.
The 3rd pers. sing. preterite endings *-étte(ro)/-étte(no)* for verbs in *-ere* are
Florentine as well as Pisan, but the coexistence of forms of verbs in *-ere* ending in *-étte(no)* and forms of verbs in *-ire* ending in *-itte(no)* appears to be an
exclusively Pisan trait.[12] This is a fact that must be kept in mind.

## Gerund

A typical Old Venetan feature is the extension of the first conjugation gerund
ending *-ando* to the verbs in *-ere* and *-ire* (see Stussi, lxix, Tomasin, 191, Bertoletti, 249, Verlato, 111). This phenomenon is well documented in the MS:

"avere": *habiando* 22v, 27r, 28r, 31v, 33r, 44v (bis), 47v, 48v, 51r, 79r, 81r,
    85r, 92v, *habiandolo* 69v, 75v, 83v [cf. *avendo* 77r, *havendo* 15r];
"co(g)noscere": *cognosando* 86v, 12r, 66v, *cognossandoli* 100v (bis) [cf.
    *cognoscendo* 5r, 15r, 46r etc. (7 examples)]);
"essere": *siando* 14r, 19r (ter), 20r, etc. (30 examples) [cf. *essendo* 3v, 8r,
    13v, etc. (11 examples)];
"fare": *façando* 5r, 122r, *faciandolo* 89r [cf. *facendo/-ci-/-ç-* 9v, 37v, 39v,
    etc. (13 examples)];
"intendere": *intendando* 32r [cf. *intendendo* 25v, *intendendola* 23v];
"involgere": *involçando* 104r;
"mettere": *metandone* 45v [cf. *metendo* 55v, 121r, *metendose* 9v];
"piangere": *piançando* 97v, 98r, 104r, 104v, 106v [cf. *piançendo* 35v (bis),
    36v, etc. (13 examples)];
"potere": *posando* 58r;
"rompere": *rumpando* 55v;
"sapere": *sapiando* 13v, 14r, 55r, 68r, 73v (bis) [cf. *sapiendo* 22r, 27v, 34v];
"scrivere": *scrivando* 13v;

12. Cf. Castellani 2000, 325–26.

"spingere": *spençando* 75v;

"stringere": *strençandose* 68r;

"tenere/tegnire": *tegnando* 26r, 96v;

"udire/aldire": *aldando* 55r, 104r [cf. *aldendo* 20v, 57r, 80v, etc. (8 examples); *oldendo* 22r, 51v, 85v, 94v; *udendo* 100v];

"vedere": *vedando* 21r, 81v, 82v (bis), 86v, 97v, 98r, 98v, 99v, 101v, 103v, 104v, 108v, *vedandoli* 98r, 100r; *avedandose* 11r, 49v; *revedandome* 66v; *veçando* 81v, 105v, *veçandolo* 37v [cf. *vedendo* 9r, 22r, 35r, etc. (26 examples); *avedendose* 54r];

"venire/vegnire": *vegnando* 104r, *vegnandoli* 13r;

"volere": *vogliando* 5v, 10v, 47v, 62v, 63v (bis), 105v, *vogliandoli* 52r, 82v, *volgliandose* 20r [cf. *volendola* 58r].

Many verbs in *-ere* and most verbs in *-ire*, however, maintain the Tuscan/ Standard It. type in *-endo*, and it is not possible to ascertain which type prevailed in the original text.[13]

## Past Participle

Though most of the past participle forms in the MS are of the regular type in *-ato* (*-ado*), *-uto* (*-udo*), *-ito* (*-ido*), there are two examples of the characteristically Venetan participle forms of verbs in *-ere*: *piacesto* (16v); *apparesto* (98v), documented in the OVI Corpus in Venetian and Paduan texts from the second half of the fourteenth century (Rohlfs § 624, Verlato, 110).

## VOCABULARY

**acombiatarsi** v. 'to take one's leave' (*acombiatandosi* 106r, *acombiatandose* 107r, *acumbiatò* 123r). A variant of Tusc. and Standard It. *accommiatarsi*, this verb clearly derives from *combiato* n. 'leave, parting' (7r, 10v), cf. Lat. COMMEATUS and Standard It. *commiato*. The forms with *-mb-* can be com-

---

13. The following verbs present regular gerund forms in *-endo*: "credere" (1 example), "crescere" (2), "distendere" (1), "dolere" (1), "estendere" (1), "giungere" (7), "intendere" (2), "leggere" (1), "muovere" (2), "rendere" (3), "riprendere" (2), "rispondere" (4), "sedere" (2), "sottoporre" (1), "temere" (2), "vivere" (1); "apparire" (1), "aprire" (1), "benedire" (4), "dire" (22), "dormire" (1), "partire" (4), "sentire" (2), and "uscire" (1).

pared with the more than fifty occurrences of *combiado/-ato* in Venetan texts in the OVI Corpus.[14] The *-t-* in the ending might be considered a Tuscanism: in fact, *-ato* and *-ata* are decidedly more frequent in *MVC* than the genuinely Venetan *-ado/-a* endings.

**ancoi, ancuò** adv. 'today' (*anchoi* 7r, 7v [quater], 8r; *anchuò* 96r, 100r). This typically North Italian term (present in the dialects of Veneto, Lombardy, and, to a lesser extent, Emilia and Liguria) occasionally occurs in Tuscan texts as a poetical form: cf. *TLIO*, s.v. *ancòi* avv./s.m., and Boerio, s.v. *ancúo*. The prevailing term for 'today' in the MS, however, is *oçi* (7v, 8r, 15v, etc. [40 examples]), cognate to Tusc. and Standard It. *oggi* (< HODIE), and totally absent from the Venetan texts in the OVI Corpus.

**assentado,** see **sentare.**

**assunare** v. 'to gather, to assemble' (*assunare* 20v, *assunata* 21v, 81v). The OVI Corpus contains 39 examples of the *assenare/asunare,* all except two (which are Pisan) from fourteenth-century Veneto. Cf. *TLIO*, s.v. *asunare,* and Paccagnella, 47, who registers the three types *arsunare, assunare,* and *asunare.*

**atrigarsi** v. 'to stop, to linger' (*se atrigò* 88r). The noun *triga* 'pause, delay' and the corresponding verb *trigà* are documented in the OVI Corpus in texts from Lombardy and Verona. Rosa registers the verb *trigà* 'to stop' in the dialect of the Lombard city of Brescia. In Teofilo Folengo's macaronic (Latin mixed with Mantuan dialect) narrative poem *Baldo* (1517) occurs the prefixed form *atrigat* 'he lingers' (V, 33: "Baldus eum videt et cupidus novitatis *atrigat*").

**bambolino** s.m. 'baby' (*bambolino, -ll-* 17v, 18v, 19r, 27v, 31r). The OVI Corpus contains five Tuscan (from Florence and Pisa) fourteenth-century examples of this noun, which does not seem to have been in use in the Veneto. Cf. *TLIO*, s.v. *bambolino.*

**briveselo** n. 'bill,' 'placard' (92v). Diminutive of *breve* n. (< Lat. BREVIS), indicating a piece of parchment or paper, cf. *TLIO*, s.v. *brevicello.*

**buso** s.m. 'hole' (90v [*ter*]). Typical North Italian form (constructed on the plural form *busi* [< *buci*] of *buco* 'hole'), present in Venetan, Lombard, and Emilian texts in the OVI Corpus. Cf. *TLIO*, s.v. *buco* (1), Boerio and Paccagnella, s.v. *buso.*

**cariaço** n. 'carriage' (45r). Venetan form—cf. Boerio s.v. *cariàzo*—corresponding to Tusc. *carriaggio.*

---

14. In addition to these, the OVI Corpus contains one Emilian example and two Abruzzese examples of *combiato*; Paccagnella, 152, registers the Old Paduan forms *combiò* and *combià.*

**catreda** 'chair' (84r). The OVI Corpus contains four examples of this metathetic issue of Lat. CATHEDRA in texts from Tuscany and Rome, but the form is also documented in Venetian: cf. Boerio s.v. *càtreda*.

**çerla** n. 'container for carrying water' ("*çerla* di aqua" 59v, 60v). Venetan form of Tuscan and Standard It. *gerla* 'pannier'; cf. Boerio and Paccagnella, s.v. *zerla*. However, in the MS the meaning appears to refer to a slightly different object, as a container used for carrying water could not have been made as a basket!

**combiato**, see **acombiatarsi**.

**cortello** 'knife' (26r, 41v, 42r, 74v, 90v, 100r, 100v [*bis*], 108r). The form with -*r*- is typically Venetan; cf. Tusc. and Standard It. *coltello*, also present in the MS (42r, 74v). See *TLIO* s.v. *coltello*, and Paccagnella, s.v. *corteli/ cortello*.

**cosinato** n. 'cooked food' (51v [*bis*]). Northern It. form: cf. *TLIO* s.v. *cucinato*.

**desficare** v. 'to loosen, to unfasten' (*desficarlo, desficare* 101v). The verb is used for the action of freeing Jesus' limbs from the cross, cf. *TLIO* s.v. *disficcare*, with examples from Tuscan and Roman texts.

**desidar, dess-** v. 'to wake up,' 'to wake somebody' (*desidato* 28r, *dessidò* 73v). Northern Italian form corresponding to Tusc. and Standard It. *destare*: cf. *TLIO* s.v. *descitare* and see also Verlato s.v. *rensedare*.

**desmentigare** v. 'to forget' (*desmentigare* 3v, *desmentigada* 91v, *dismentigada* 9v, *dismentigato* 69r). Typical North Italian form (cf. Tuscan and Standard It. *dimenticare*), of which the OVI Corpus contains more than fifty examples, all from the Veneto. See Paccagnella, 199.

**desmesidare** v.tr. 'to wake somebody' (*desmesidò* 28r). Typical Venetan form, cf. *TLIO*, s.v. *desmissidar*, and Verlato s.v. *rensedare*). Paccagnella, s.v. *desdissiare*, registers the type *desmissiare*.

**façuolo** n. 'kerchief' (*façuolo, façulo* 62v). Cf. *TLIO* s.v. *fazzuolo* s.m. (with examples from the Veneto and from Sicily).

**fantesino** n. 'male baby' (*fantesino* 26r, *fantessino* 16r, 21r, 22r). North Italian form corresponding to Tuscan *fanticino*: cf. *TLIO* s.v. *fanticino* and Verlato, 701.

**freça** n. 'hurry' (*freça* 8v, 75r); cf. the adj. *freçata* 'hurried' 107v. For this typical Northern It. synonym to *fretta* (also present in the MS: cf. *frecta* 79v), see *TLIO*, s.v. *frezza* s.f., Verlato, 703, Paccagnella, 273.

**fregolare** v. 'to rub, to crumble' ("tollevano le spige de grano et *fregolàvale*" 50v, 'they plucked ears of grain and rubbed them [*i.e.*, until the grains came out]'). See Paccagnella, 271, who registers Old Paduan *fregolare* 'to rub.'

**giesia** n. 'church' (18r). North Italian form, akin to the more frequent *chiesia* (21v [*quinquies*], 22v, 26r, 47r [*ter*], 56r, 60r, 109v, 125v), which is closer to Tuscan and Standard It. *chiesa*. Cf. Boerio s.v. *gèsia*.

**giobia** n. 'Thursday' ("il *Giobia* sancto" 'Maundy Thursday' 58v). The OVI Corpus contains numerous examples of the lemma *zobia* in Venetan texts and also in a couple of texts from Lombardy. Cf. Boerio s.v. *zioba*, Tomasin s.v. *çobia*.

**insire** v. 'go out,' 'come out' (*insite* 27v, *insiva* 72r). See Boerio, 347, who observes that the forms *insir* and *ensir* are "antiquated and sparsely used"; Stussi, 221, registers Old Venetian *insida* n. 'exit'. Bertoletti, 475, registers Old Veronese *ensiro* v., and Verlato, 403, registers the forms *ensire* and *enxire*.

**linzuolo**, see **ninzuolo**.

**mangiatoia** n. 'manger' (*mangadora* 17r, *mangiatoia* 16v, *mançadora* 15r, *mançatoia* 15r, *mançatora* 17r, 17v, 56r, *mançatura* 24v). As this list indicates, the MS contains every possible variant of the Tusc. and Standard It. form *mangiatoia*. Verlato, 712, registers the form *maniadora*.

**mesidar, messiar** v. 'to mix' ("vino cum felle *messiado*" 89v, "aceto *mesidado* cum fielle" 95r). The OVI Corpus contains forty-eight examples of the verb *mesedar* (messi-), all but six in Venetan texts. Paccagnella, 428, registers the forms *missiare* and *mesiare*.

**messiar**, see **mesidar**.

**ninzuolo** n. 'bedsheet' (*ninçuolo* 100r, 103r). In the MS, this characteristic Venetan type (cf. Boerio s.v. *niziòl*), coexists with *linzuolo* (*linçuoli* 14v, *linçulo* 16v), which is closer to the Tusc. and Standard It. form *lenzuolo*. Stussi, 224, registers Old Venetian *linçoli*, *ninçoli*, and *niçoli*. Cf. also Paccagnella, s.v. *linzuol/lenciolo/lenzuò/lenzuolo/nenzuolo/ninzuolo* (383).

**oçi**, see **ancoi**.

**pane perduto** n. 'inept person, slacker' (40r). Tuscan expression: cf. the first edition of the *Vocabolario della Crusca* (1612), s.v. *pane*: "*Pan perduto*, si dice d'huomo, che non sia buono a nulla."

**pioba** n. 'rain' (*pioba* 17r). The OVI Corpus contain an example of this form in a Venetan text from the first half of the fourteenth century. Another example is given by Tuttle, 364.

**pugiare** v. 'to lean' (*pugiosse* 112v). Boerio registers this verb in the forms *posar* and *pusar*.

**puto** n. 'boy' (*puto* 16r, 20v, 22r, 22v, 25v, 26r, 27v, 28r, 30r, 31v [*bis*], 33r, 35r, *puti* 27v, 28v, 32v, 81r). Characteristically Venetan form, abundantly present in the OVI Corpus.

**scapuço** 'misstep, error' (*scapuçi* 29v). Typical Venetan term, absent from the OVI Corpus (which, however, registers the Old Milanese verb *scapuzar* 'to stumble'). Boerio registers *scapuzzo* 'stumble, misstep, fault'; see also Paccagnella, s.v. *scapucio/scapuzo/schiapucio/schiapuzzo*.

**sentare** v. 'to sit down,' 'to be seated' (*senta[n]dosse* 57v, *sentadi* 63v, *sentando* 57r, *sentare* 52r, 55r, 62v, 84r, 97v, 102r, *sentarebe* 60v, *sentava* 60v). Cf. Boerio, s.v. *sentàrse*, and Paccagnella, s.v. *sentare* (699). The MS also contains an example of the prefixed past participle form *assentado* 'sitting' (38r).

**sfèndere** v. 'to split open' (*sfendesse* 8r). Typical Venetan form (synonymous to Tuscan and Standard It. *fèndere*), of which the OVI Corpus contains some twenty examples. See Boerio s.v. *sfender*, and Paccagnella, s.v. *sfendre*.

**sguançada** n. 'slap in the face' (*sguançada* 76r, 77r, *sguançade* 84r). Formed from Venetian *sguanza* 'cheek' (see Boerio and Paccagnella, s.v.). For the formation cf. Verlato, s.v. *guançà*.

**smatare** v. 'to mock' (*smatava* 81r). Typical Venetan verb, present in the form *smatta* in a Veronese text in the OVI Corpus. Cf. Boerio, s.v. *smatar*, and Paccagnella, s.v. *smatare/smattare*.

**sotorare** v. 'to bury' (*sotorate* 103v, *sotorato* 60v). The OVI Corpus contains twelve examples of the verb *sotorar* (cf. Tusc. and Standard It. *sotterrare*), all in Venetan texts.

**sparagnare** v. 'to spare' (36r). Cf. Boerio s.v. *sparagnàr* and Paccagnella, s.v. *sparagnare*.

**spudaçato** adj. 'covered with spit' (85r). The OVI Corpus contains two examples of the past participle *spudazado* in a fourteenth-century Venetan text. Cf. Boerio s.v. *spuazza*, who cites the Venetian synonyms *spuazza* and *spuazzo*, both with the meaning 'saliva.'

**suçar** v. 'wipe' ("la madre prese uno panolino et *suçoli* el viso" 20r). Boerio s.v. *suzzàr* registers this verb in the meaning "to suckle" and also the reflexive *suzzarse* "to beautify oneself," but the form *suçoli* might also be an error for *sugoli* 'she wiped his face'(see the following **sugare**).

**sugare** v. 'to wipe, to dry' (*suga* 63v, *sugando* 73r, *sugava* 62v, *sugò* 104v, 105r). Venetan form, corresponding to Tuscan and Standard It. *asciugare*; cf. Boerio s.v. *sugàr*.

**torente** n. 'stream' (73r). Typical Tuscan (*torrente*), non-Venetan form; the example in the MS, however, might depend on the New Testament Latin denomination of the stream in question, *torrens Cedron* (John 18:1).

## CONCLUSION

As we have seen, the copy of the *Meditations* contained in MS Canonici Italian 174 displays many North Italian linguistic features consistent with what we know of the dialects of medieval Veneto concerning orthography, phonology, and morphology (e.g., the diphthongized forms *misier* and *tuore* and the past participles *apparesto* and *piacesto*, all exclusively Venetan) as well as vocabulary. The number of such features is high, and it does not seem possible to attribute them to a single copyist, as the roots clearly go deeper than that.

Theoretically, the mixture of Northern Italian and Tuscan in the Oxford MS might be interpreted in at least three different ways, as the following scenarios show. It is, to use a fitting metaphor, a question of deciding which linguistic variety should be considered as the warp and which as the weft:

(1)  The vernacular version of the *MVC* was originally written by a Tuscan; at a certain point a branch of the tradition was transplanted to the Veneto and gradually Veneticized.
(2)  The vernacular version was composed by a Venetan and copied by scribes from this region; the Tuscan element is due to one or more copyists of Tuscan origin.
(3)  The text was composed and copied by Venetan scribes; the Tuscan elements are the result of a desire to imitate and emulate the language and style of prestigious fourteenth-century Tuscan religious writers such as Bartolomeo di San Concordio, Domenico Cavalca, Jacopo Passavanti, and so forth.

At first glance, these three hypotheses might seem equally plausible. Number (3), however, can be excluded without much ado, as it seems highly improbable that a fifteenth-century Venetan copyist could have possessed the necessary linguistic competence for such an undertaking. As for number (2), I consider it equally improbable that a Tuscan copyist, without doubt conscious of the prestige of her or his own mother tongue, would leave such a bulk of Venetan forms and idioms untouched without even attempting to "correct" them.

This leaves us with scenario number (1) and with the belief that we are dealing with an originally Tuscan text, de-Tuscanized by Northern Italian—most probably Venetan—copyists. This, in my experience, is also the most common condition in similar cases, and explains the fact that even though

most of the Venetan linguistic features are used in a perfectly idiomatic way, they nevertheless seem to have been woven into a straight Tuscan warp. It would be difficult indeed to isolate a completely Venetan phrase in the MS, whereas, on the other hand, consistent portions of the text might pass as acceptable fourteenth/fifteenth-century Tuscan.

This, however, is not enough. Tuscany is a region with mutually intelligible yet different vernaculars: might there be a way to narrow the focus? Perhaps there is.

As we saw in the paragraphs dedicated to verb morphology, the 3rd pers. preterite singular and plural forms constitute a veritable *selva selvaggia* of suffixes. The verbs in -*are* make use of as many as four different endings for the 3rd pers. plur. forms, but the elements that really might help us in our quest appear when we move on to the verbs in -*ere* and -*ire*. The formants -*ete*/-*eteno* and -*ite*/-*iteno*(-*ro*) could, I believe, be the key. As mentioned above, they correspond to the Tuscan and—at least for certain verbs— Standard It. endings -*ette* and -*ettero* in preterite forms such as *cedette* 'he/she gave away' (< *cédere*), *sedette* 'he/she sat down' (< *sedére*) and *dovettero* 'they had to' (< *dovére*), etc.

While it is easy enough to find medieval Tuscan texts making extensive use of forms like these, it is very rare to find texts making use of both -*ette* and -*itte* formations for verbs in -*ere* and -*ire*. But, as I indicated earlier, our MS does exactly this, and for a considerable number of verbs, too.[15] As can be shown searching the OVI Corpus, such a distribution of verb forms is characteristic only of western Tuscany or, to be more precise, of texts produced by Pisan scribes.[16]

15. See above, section titled "Third Person Plural Endings." The verbs are the following: "cadere," "conoscere," "consentire," "credere," "rendere," "ricevere," "rompere," "temere," "vivere" and "adempire," "aprire," "avvilire," "compire," "convertire," "distribuire," "empire," "esaudire," "fuggire," "morire," "offrire," "partire," "partorire," "rivestire," "seguire," "sentire," and "uscire."

16. Before attributing *sic and simpliciter* the text to an author from Pisa, however, it must be remembered that the manuscript also contains many 3rd pers. plur. forms of verbs in -*are* that are formed with the suffixes -*àrono* and -*òrono*, which could not be explained as Pisanisms: they might be attributed to one or more copyists from other parts of Tuscany, or as "literary" forms.

# EDITORIAL PRINCIPLES

Although the copy of the *Meditazioni* preserved in Canonici MS Italian 174 contains many scribal inconsistencies (see above, "Linguistic Analysis"), there are very few manifest difficulties with the text. Little editorial reconstruction of omitted words or phrases has been necessary; where this has been warranted in order for the text to make grammatical sense, interventions are indicated in the notes.

The orthography of the manuscript has been preserved. The only modifications introduced are the following.

The distribution of the graphemes <u> and <v> has been normalized according to modern practice. Examples: MS. *uergene, hauea; vna, vnde* → *vergene, havea; una, unde.*

Word division, punctuation, and the use of accents and apostrophes have been regularized. Thus, the sequence <chel> is rendered as *ch'el* when corresponding to Standard Italian *che egli* or *che il*, but as *che 'l* when corresponding to *che lo*; <de> is rendered as *de* when corresponding to the Standard It. preposition *di*, but as *dè* and *dè'* when corresponding to Standard It. *deve* and *devi* and as *de[h]* when an interjection; <dei> remains *dei* when a prepositional article (= *di* + *i*), but becomes *dèi* when meaning "you must" (Standard It. *devi*); the contracted form of the prepositional article *dei*, <di>, is rendered as *d'i*. Whether or not to place an accent on that most slender and ubiquitous of words, *si*, has required careful consideration, for *si* has multiple functions and meanings circa 1300–1400 (see Battaglia, *Grande dizionario, si* and *se*). In the *testo breve*, it often serves as a shortened form of *così*, but in many cases it is difficult to tell if this meaning (with its deictic character, "like this, like that") is intended and should be indicated as such by an accent; alternatives are possible, including the use of *si* as third-person reflexive pronoun, as ethical dative, or as dative of interest.

Abbreviations have been expanded silently in accordance with the orthographic practice of the scribe, for example, <vtude> with a vertical abbreviation stroke across the <v> → *vertude*; *xpo* → *Cristo*. Where the scribe has

made cancellations, the relevant letters or words have been indicated by angle brackets < >.

Editorial interventions have usually been indicated by square brackets without further explanation, for example, *er[a]no* 30r (MS *erno*), *specia[l]-mente* 31r (MS *speciaméte*). In more complex cases, the situation is explained in a note, for example, *lo[r]o* 31v with a note indicating that the MS reads *lolo*. In some cases an <i> has been inserted between <c> or <g> and a velar vowel to guarantee the pronunciation: *fanc[i]ullo*; *ang[i]olo*, *g[i]on-çere*, *g[i]orno*, *g[i]unta*, *mang[i]adora*.

Modern capitalization has been introduced throughout. This has not been a straightforward matter in every case. Indeed, the decision to capitalize or not capitalize something so fundamental as the names of the central figures in this drama is one that is laden with consequence: *figliolo* or *Figliolo*, *madre* or *Madre*? Because one of the fundamental aims of the *Meditazioni* is to foster a felt awareness of Christ and his mother as *human* son and mother, traditional capitalization, and the reverential distance that it establishes, has the potential to operate as a countercurrent unintended by the author. Yet the alternative, the consistent use of lowercase—*figliolo, madre*—would itself be overly intrusive as an editorial gesture. I have therefore sought to capitalize when it is more clear that the designation is an honorific (*Madre Gloriosa*, 15r), but not when the ordinariness of the kin relationship is what is emphasized (e.g., *crescendo miser Iesù Cristo nel ventre della madre*, f. 11r). But I do so with the reminder that something important is lost in this: where modern editorial convention requires that a decision be made between the two alternatives, *figliolo/Figliolo*, medieval convention allowed for the sustained conflation—even at the level of the grapheme—of the human and sacred.

# A NOTE ON THE TRANSLATION

I have sought to convey the direct and simple style of the Italian as faithfully as possible. Since the text itself is not labored in any way, but rather, at its best, supremely lucid, it does not seem fitting to belabor questions concerning my own theory and practice of translation. There are a few matters, however, that are worth mentioning.

The narrative is marked by a pronounced paratactic style. I have preserved the conjunction "and" throughout, even though its frequent use may strike modern readers as excessive, and even when a subordinating conjunction might better point the logic of a particular sequence of thoughts.

Translation always entails loss. One of the losses I most regret here is the term *miser*, which I have typically left untranslated, given its characteristic placement in this text: it usually occurs in apposition to *signore* in the ubiquitous phrase *miser Signore Jesu Cristo*. A common honorific in fourteenth- and fifteenth-century texts, *miser* is used chiefly in secular contexts, to express respect toward a knight, judge, or secular lord (see Battaglia, *Grande dizionario, messere*, sm.). The most sensible translation in English is "sir" or "lord." The choices here, then, would have been to render the redundancy as a redundancy, shading the difference between the first and second honorifics through the use of lowercase and uppercase lord/Lord—"our lord Lord Jesus Christ"—or to highlight the historical and secular resonance of the term: "Sir Lord Jesus Christ." There would have been merit in either choice; the latter, in particular, would have conveyed the medieval flavor of the text more fully. But in the end, both options seemed unduly distracting.

One further aspect of *miser* is worth noting, however. Although it is often used in contexts where the collective sense "our lord" or the simple term of respect or social status, "lord," is meant (as in the antiquated English term of address, "milord"), literally *miser* means "my lord." A sense of the singular "*my* lord"—with its resonance of personal allegiance—can thus infuse or hover around the term. One particularly interesting example of this

occurs in St. Francis's "Cantico di frate sole" ("Canticle of the Sun"). Translators have rendered the address to Brother Sun—*messor lo frate sole*—variously, as "Sir Brother Sun" or "my lord Brother Sun."[1] In the context of the devotional genre here, it seems important to keep in mind the singular form of address, "my lord," as a meaning that might have carried with it a sense of affective intimacy, devotion, and personal commitment for the readers of the Italian MVC. That such intimacy could be conflated with great respect is an aspect of *miser* that English cannot adequately convey.

Verb tenses have sometimes presented a challenge, in part because of a distinctive feature of this and contemporary narratives, especially romances: the mingling of the past tense with the historical present. Often the oscillation between tenses occurs in especially dramatic passages, such as that of the crucifixion, where it heightens the immediacy and thus the emotional impact of the scene; at other times, the present tense is used to create moments in which time is suspended, thus allowing for more sustained meditation in the midst of the narrative.

Finally, I have sought to highlight the affective resonance of two of the core terms in the *testo breve*, *devoto* and *diligentemente*, and their variants. The initial reflex might be to translate the former term as "pious" or "devotional," and the latter as "diligently." But these terms lack the sense of loving, intimate engagement conveyed by the Italian terms in this context. Thus I have rendered the opening image, in which St. Cecilia selects for meditation "cose più devote de la vita de miser Iesù Cristo" as "the most moving passages from the life of Lord Jesus Christ" (see below, 3), and I have typically translated "diligentemente" as "with loving attention." In doing so, I have been guided not only by etymology, but by the overriding aim of the *testo breve*—which is not to promote "piety" or "diligence" in the modern sense, but, above all, to cultivate intimate affective response.

1. For the Italian text, see C. Leonardi, *La letteratura francescana* 3:217. For translations, Armstrong, Hellmann, and Short, *Francis of Assisi*, 1:113 ("Sir Brother Sun"); Habig, *St. Francis of Assisi*, 1:130 ("my lord Brother Sun").

# MEDITATIONS

*on the*

# LIFE

*of*

# CHRIST

*The Short Italian Text*

---

A critical edition of the *testo breve* from Oxford,
Bodleian Library MS Canonici Italian 174,
with English translation and commentary

# Meditazione della vita di Cristo:
## Il testo breve

[f. 1r] *Qui comenza el prologo de le meditatione de la vita del nostro signore miser Iesù Cristo, la cui doctrina è seme de providentia, la cui vita è spechio de temperantia e patientia.*

Infra le altre gran vertude che se leze de sancta Cecilia vergene, si è questa: zoè ch'ela portava sempre lo Evangelio de Cristo Iesù ascoxo nel suo pecto. E questo dè' tu intender cusì, che ella se havea scrito algune electe cose più devote de la vita de miser Iesù Cristo, e in queste la pensava dì e nocte cum tutto el so cuore e cum tuta la intentione e fervore. Compido quelle cotal meditatione, sì le refaceva da capo e ragunavale cum un gusto molto suave e sollicitamente le guardava e retenevale nel suo chore, sì che non ge lassava intrar nesun pensier vano.

E pertanto io te priego che tu façi el somegliante, imperciò che sopra tuti li altri exerci del spirito questo è el più necessario et el più utile e che pò condur altrui [f. 1v] a più excellente grado; imperciò che tu non troverai mai in algun logo dove tu possi essere così amaistrado contra le vane losenze de[l] diavolo e dei nimici chome ne la vita de Iesù Cristo, la qual fo perfectissima e senza alguna macula. Et imperciò quando l'anima se dispone expressamente de voler pensare e delectase de meditar de la vita de miser Iesù Cristo, perseverando in humilitade, si perviene l'anima in una familiaritade e confidentia et amore de miser Iesù Cristo, intanto che le altre cose avilisse e despreça. Et ancora ne la meditatione de la vita de miser Iesù Cristo sei amaistrado et fortificado de quello che l'omo debe fare e de che se debe guardare.

Dico adonque imprima che la sancta meditatione de la vita de miser Iesù Cristo sì conforta e fa la mente stabile contra le vanitade e malicie del mondo, sì come se manifesta nella decta sancta Cecilia, la quale [avea] lo cuore[1] suo sì pieno de la vita de miser Iesù che neuna vanitade non li potea

1. MS *laquale* v *lo cuore*

2

# Meditations on the Life of Christ:
## The Short Italian Text

*Here begins the prologue of the meditations on the life of Our Lord Jesus Christ, whose teaching is the seed of prudence, whose life is the mirror of temperance and patience.*[1]

Among the other great virtues one reads about concerning the virgin Saint Cecilia is this, that she always carried the Gospel of Christ Jesus hidden in her breast.[2] And you should consider this to mean that she had written out for herself some of the most moving passages from the life of Lord Jesus Christ, and she meditated on these day and night with all her heart and with all her intention and fervor.[3] And once she had finished these meditations, she started again from the beginning, dwelling on them again and savoring their sweetness.[4] And she took them into her heart, keeping and treasuring them carefully there so that no vain thought could enter.

And so I invite you to do the same, because of all spiritual exercises this is the most necessary and the most useful and can lead others to a higher level. For you will never find any place where you can learn better to fend off the seductive tricks of the devil and other foes than in the life of Jesus Christ, which was so completely perfect and without any flaw. And so when the soul prepares in a focused way to meditate on the life of Lord Jesus Christ with loving attention and desire, practicing this with humility, she enters into a state of familiar ease and trust and love with Lord Jesus Christ, and she begins to find other things worthless and unimportant. And also by meditating on the life of Lord Jesus Christ you can learn and gain strength for what to do and what to guard against.

I tell you first of all, then, that holy meditation on the life of Lord Jesus Christ comforts the mind and makes it stable against the vanity and malice of the world, as is evident in the life of Saint Cecilia, whose heart was so filled with the life of Lord Jesus that no vanity could enter it. So when she was in the midst of the great pomp of the wedding, surrounded by so much vanity and by the singing of organs and other pleasing and

3

intrar [f. 2r]. Unde quando lei stava in quella grande pompa de le noçe, dove se façea tante vanitade, cantando li organi et altri instrumenti delectevoli e belli,[2] et ela nel suo cuore stava stabile e ferma, et cantava solamente a Dio, et dicea: «Signore mio Iesù Cristo, fà el cuore et el corpo mio imma-culato, açiò che in me non sia alcuna confusione de peccato».

Ancora la vita de miser Iesù Cristo fortifica l'omo contra le tribula-tione et adversitade, come si vede nelli sancti martiri. E de çiò dice sancto Bernardo che la pacientia del martire sì procede da questo: che li conviene che devotissimamente se volça e rivolça nelle ferite de miser Iesù Cristo e spessamente pensarle e ripensandole si habita in esse per gratia. Sta adon-que el sancto martire tuto alegro, avegna che tuto el corpo sia lacerato. Or dove ène alora l'anima de[l] sancto martire quando el viene martiriçato? Certo ne le piage del suo Maestro Cristo Iesù. E de çiò non te ne marave-gliare, [f. 2v] imperçiò ch'ele sono large ad intrare per la via de la medita-tione de la sua Passione. E dèi sapere che se l'anima è nel corpo del mar-tire quando el viene tormentado, non pensare ch'el podesse sostenire li tormenti; ma stando per carità ne le piage de miser Iesù Cristo, el sta con-stante e fermo a tute le pene. E questo medesimo adiviene di sancti con-fessori et de molti altri sancti homeni i quali se alegrano de le tribulatione et de le adversitade. Et perché questo, se non perché ànno la mente sua continuamente in pensare et meditare la vita e la Passione del Signore suo et qui è tuto el lor studio?

Ancora qui sei amaistrado de sostenere, sì che tu non possi essere in-ganato né cadere nelle mani[3] del diavolo et delli vicii. Et imperçiò qui se trova la perfectione de tute le vertude; et qui troverai exemplo et doctrina de la excellentissima caritade, et de la extrema povertade, et de la profunda humilitade et de sapientia et de oratione et de la mansuetudine [f. 3r] et della obedientia et della patientia et de tute le altre vertude. Unde dice san-cto Bernardo: «Vanamente et sança fructo se afadicha colui che ha spe-rança de aquistare vertude da altrui che dal Signore delle Vertude, la cui doctrina è seme de providentia, la cui misericordia è opera de iustitia, la cui vita è spechio de temperança, la cui morte è segno de forteça». Adonque chi lui seguita non puote errare et non puote[4] essere inganato, la cui vertude

2. MS *belle*
3. MS *man*
4. MS *puole*

beautiful instruments, she stayed stable and steadfast in her heart and sang only to God, saying, "My Lord Jesus Christ, make my heart and my body immaculate, so that no sin may cause me to falter."

And the life of Lord Jesus Christ also strengthens one against tribulation and adversity, as one can see through the holy martyrs. And concerning this, Saint Bernard says that the martyr's patient endurance of suffering comes from this: that by lovingly immersing himself again and again in the wounds of Lord Jesus Christ, meditating on them and reflecting on them often, he learns to dwell in them through grace. In this way the martyr remains completely joyful, even when his whole body is lacerated. Now where, then, is the soul of the holy martyr when he suffers martyrdom? It is, without doubt, in the wounds of his master, Christ Jesus.[5] And you need not be amazed by this, because they are wide enough to enter by way of meditation on his Passion. And you should know that if the soul were to remain in the body of the martyr when he was tortured, he could not possibly bear the torments; but when the soul rests in the wounds of Lord Jesus Christ through love, the martyr remains constant and steadfast through every affliction. And the same is true for those who suffered for their faith and many other saints who rejoice in tribulation and adversity. And how could this be, if it were not that they meditate and dwell on the life and Passion of their Lord without ceasing, keeping their focus solely on this?

Here, too, you can learn to withstand trials, so that you cannot be deceived or fall into the hands of the devil and of the vices. For the perfection of all the virtues is found here; and here you will find the model and doctrine of the most excellent love, and of extreme poverty, and of profound humility, and of wisdom and prayer and meekness and obedience and patience and of all the other virtues.[6] And so Saint Bernard says, "Vainly and without fruit is he who strives to acquire virtue by any means other than from the Lord of Virtues, whose teaching is the seed of prudence, whose mercy is the work of justice, whose life is the mirror of temperance, whose death is the sign of fortitude."[7] So whoever follows him cannot go astray and cannot be deceived, for following him and acquiring his virtues is the summit of perfection. And by doing this one can enter into a state in which the heart is enflamed by the fervor of love and enlightened by divine virtue, so much so that one becomes clothed in virtue, with the power to discern the true from the false.

seguitare et aquistare è summa perfectione. Unde perviene l'huomo in tanto ch'eli accende el cuore per fervore di caritade, et poi illuminato della vertù divina, in tanto ch'el se veste de vertude et discerne el vero dal falso.

Et per questo molti sono stadi sança letere et simplici et hano habuto cognoscimento delle alte et profunde cose de Dio.

*Qui comença la Incarnatione del nostro Signore miser Iesù Cristo. Capitulo primo.*

[f. 3v] Poi ch'el fue compito el tempo nel qualle havea ordinato la beatissima et summa Trinitade provedere alla salute de la humana generatione per la Incarnatione del suo dolcissimo figl[i]uolo, et per la sua habundantissima caritade cum la qualle ello amava la humana natura, movendolo la sua misericordia et ancora i priegi delli ang[i]oli, et essendo çà la Vergene Maria desponsata a Ioseph e tornata in Naçareth, Dio onnipotente chiamò l'ang[i]olo Çabriel et disse a lui: «Và a Maria, dilectissima et carissima nostra figliula sopra tute le altre creature, la qualle è desponsata a Ioseph, et dili che el mio fiolo hae desiderato la sua beleça et ha la ellecta per sua madre. Et priegala che lei el riceva aliegramente, imperçiò che io hoe ordinato di operar per lei la salute humana, et voglio⁵ desmentigare la inçuria recivuta dalla humana generatione».

Attendi bene qui, et stùdiate di esserne presente [f. 4r] cum la mente a intendere quelle cose che qui se dice et se face.⁶ Risguarda cum la mente divota Idio Padre sedere sopra la sedia regale cum uno volto benigno et piatoso, et come paternamente el commete l'ambassiata al servo suo. Et guarda ancora l'angelo ingenochiato riverentemente⁷ ricever l'ambassiata cum una faça aliegra et cum el capo inclinato denançi a Dio Padre onnipotente. Et ricevuta ch'elo have l'ambassiata, incontenente el se levò et prexe forma humana et in un picolo momento el fue denançi alla Vergene Maria, la qualle sedeva serata nella sua cella. Ma l'ang[i]olo non fo sì presto là che Dio Padre fu più tosto là che lui, et co[n]gendo lui si trovò çà g[i]unta la Sanctissima Trinitade inançi che lui. Perché tu dèi sapere che la excellentissima opera della Incarnatione del Fiol de Dio si fo opera de tuta la Trinitade, et avegna che solamente la persona del Figliolo fosse incarnata.

5. MS *volglio*
6. MS *fae*
7. MS *et riveretemēte*

And in this way many who are unlettered and simple have gained knowledge of the lofty and profound things of God.[8]

## Chapter 1. Here begins the Incarnation of Our Lord Jesus Christ.

The time had come when the blessed and supreme Trinity, because of the abundant love he bore towards humankind, wished to provide for the salvation of the human race through the Incarnation of his most sweet Son. So when the Virgin Mary had been betrothed to Joseph and had returned to Nazareth, Almighty God—moved by his own mercy and by the prayers of the angels—summoned the angel Gabriel and said to him, "Go to our most beloved daughter Mary, dearest above all other creatures, who is betrothed to Joseph, and tell her that my son has desired her beauty and has chosen her for his mother. And ask her to receive him joyfully, because I have decided to bring about the salvation of humanity through her, and I wish to forget the wrongs committed by the human race."

Pay attention well here, and strive to make yourself present with your mind so that you can understand the things that are said and done here. Gaze with devotion on God the Father sitting on his royal throne with a benevolent and merciful countenance, and watch how he gives this errand to his messenger in such a kindly, paternal way. And also watch the angel reverently kneeling to accept this mission with a joyful expression and with his head bowed before God the almighty Father. And as soon as he received his mandate, he stood up without delay and took human form, and in an instant he was before the Virgin Mary, who was sitting enclosed in her little cell. But the angel was not so quick that he could get there more quickly than God, and even though he had just taken his leave, he found the most holy Trinity there ahead of him. Because you ought to know that the most excellent work of the Son of God was the work of the whole Trinity, even though only the person of the Son became incarnate.

And I will give you a concrete example of this. Let's say that there is someone who is putting on new clothes, and two other people are helping him to dress. You can see, then, that three are performing the work, even though only one is being dressed. And it was in this way that

Et de çiò te darò uno tal exemplo material. [f. 4v] Poniamo ch'el sia uno che si vesti di nuovo et due altre persone lo aiutasse a vestire. Vedi adonque che tre se adoperano e pure uno sollo rimane vestito, et cusì fu qui che tuta la sanctissima Trinitade se ne adoperò et pure sollo la persona del Figl[i]ulo rimase incarnata.

O chi intrarà in quella chasseta dove cotalle persone vi sono, dove cotalle cose si fano! Ma aveg[n]a che la sancta Trinitade sia in ogni luocho, tu dèi sapere et pensare che qui la fo più singularmente per la singulare operatione che qui si fece.

Intrato adonque l'angelo, dise alla Vergene Maria: *Ave gratia plena, dominus tecum, benedicta tu in mulieribus*. Et ella, secundo che dice lo evangelista, si turbò di queste parole, et pensava qualle fosse la casone di questa salutatione, imperçiò ch'el no era usato di cusì salutarla. Nella qual salutatione aldendosi laudare di tre chose, cioè, Madre del Figl[i]ulo de Dio, et piena di gratia, et ch'el Signore era cum [f. 5r] lei. Non potea quella, che era piena de tuta humilitade, non turbarse de una vertuosa et honesta vergogna, et començò ancho a temere se ciò fosse vero. Et non credere perciò ch'ela temesse che l'angelo non dicesse el vero, ma perçiò ch'el'è propria cosa delle persone humele de non riputarse e de non examinare le sue vertude, ançi ripensano li loro deffeti et cusi façando fano le grande vertude pichole et li picholi defeti grandi. Adonque sì come sapie[n]tissima et honesta, vergognosa et timorosa, non li rispuose.

Et allora l'angelo, cognoscendo la casone della dubitatione, sì li disse: «Non temere, Maria, et non te vergognare delle laude che io te ho dato, imperçiò che cossì ène la veritade; et non solamente tu sei piena di gratia, ma etiandio tu l'ài trovata da Dio a tuta l'humana generatione. Et in segno de çiò tu parthurirai et conceperai el Figl[i]ulo de Dio, el qualle te hae ellecta per sua madre, et sì salverà [f. 5v] tuti quelli che haverano sperança et crederano in lui».

Alora rispuose la Vergene Maria, non tuta via confessando né etiandio negando le commendatione sue, ma vogliando essere certificata della sua vergenitade açiò che lei non la perdesse, della qualle era molto solicita et timorosa de non perderla. Et imperçiò ella domandò a l'angelo del modo della sua conceptione et disse così: «Come puote essere questo, conçosia cosa che io hoe donata fermamente la mia vergenitade al mio Dio et de non cognosere mai huomo?».

Et alora rispuose l'angelo et disseli: «Lo Spirito Sancto descenderà sopra di te et la virtude dell'A[l]tissimo[8] sì te obumbrarà et conceperai

8. MS *dellatissimo*

the entire most holy Trinity did the work, even though only the Son was made incarnate.

Oh, if only one might enter into that little house, where such persons are and where such things are happening! For although the holy Trinity is everywhere, you should know and imagine that the Trinity was present here in a more exceptional way, through the exceptional work that was being done here.

And once the angel had entered, he said to the Virgin Mary: "*Ave gratia plena dominus tecum, benedicta tu in mulieribus.*" And according to what the evangelist says, she was troubled by these words, and wondered what the reason was for this greeting, because she wasn't used to being greeted like this. For in this greeting she heard praise of three kinds, namely, that she was Mother of the Son of God, and that she was full of grace, and that the Lord was with her. Since she was so full of humility, she couldn't help being troubled by a virtuous and honest modesty. And she also began to worry about whether this could be true. And that was not because she doubted the truth of the angel's words, but because it is fitting for humble people not to hold themselves in high esteem or to dwell on their virtues, but on the contrary to reflect on their shortcomings, making little of great virtues and much of small failings. And so, as a most wise and honest, modest and discreet woman, she did not reply to him.

And then the angel, knowing the reason for her hesitation, said to her, "Fear not, Mary, and do not be troubled by the praise that I have given you, because it is the truth. And not only are you full of grace, but you have also found favor from God for the whole human race. And as a sign of this, you will conceive and bear the Son of God, who has chosen you as his mother. And in this way he will save all who hope and believe in him."

And so the Virgin Mary responded by neither fully assenting to nor refusing his words, but by wishing to be assured of her virginity, that she might not lose it, for she was very anxious and afraid of losing it. And so she asked the angel how she would conceive, saying, "How may this be, given that I have firmly pledged my virginity to my God and have pledged never to know man?"

And then the angel replied, "The Holy Spirit will come over you, and the power of the Almighty will overshadow you, and you will conceive, yet you will keep your virginity. And the one to whom you give birth will be called the Son of God. For to God, nothing is impossible. And consider also Elizabeth, your kinswoman, who is old and sterile: six months have already passed since she conceived a son in her womb through the power of God."

et tuta via salverai la tua vergenitade. Et colui che nascerà di te serà chiamato Figl[i]ulo de Dio, imperçiò che a Dio niuna cosa è impossibile. Et vedi ancho Helisabeth, tua cognada vechia et sterile: çà sei mesi sono che lei ha conceputo nel suo ventre, per la virtu[de] de⁹ Dio, uno figl[i]ulo».

Stà fermo qui, [f. 6r] et poni ben mente et guarda la grande caritade de Dio Padre. Et pensa come tuta la Trinitade sta et aspeta la responsione et lo consentimento de questa sua figl[i]uola benedeta, et cum grande alegreça guardando com'ela sta vergognosa et cum buoni costumi. Pensa etiamdio come reverentemente l'angelo sta ingenochioni dina[n]çi alla Dona del Paradiso, et come diligentemente el fa la sua ambassiata cum uno volto aliegro, et come attentamente el considera le parole della Vergene, açiò ch'el sapi bene compire perfectamente la voluntade del suo Signore. Sopra questa opera meravegliosa guarda ancho la donçella, come lei sta vergognosa et humile, cum la faça bassa, la qualle sança providemento se recoverçe sopra queste parole et non se exalta. Et aldendosi dire cose che mai non fue dete ad altra persona, tute le reputa alla bontade de Dio.

Et alla fine la sapientissima Vergene, aldì dele parole dell'angelo, sì li consentite. Et [f. 6v] secundo che se contiene ne le revelatione, devotissimamente se inçenochioe et cum le mane zonte disse: «Ecco l'ancilla del Signore. Sia facto a me secundo la tua parola». Decto che ebbe la Vergene Maria questa parola, incontanente el Figl[i]uolo di Dio, sança dimora, li entroe nel ventre suo tuto quanto et de lei prese carne humana, ma non di meno rimase tuto quanto insieme cum el Padre.

Qui pòi tu piatosamente pensare et imaginare come el Figliolo di Dio, recevudo la obedientia del Padre molto penosa et fatigosa, reverentemente se inçenochioe et divotamente se recomandoe a lui.¹⁰ Et in quel medesimo ponto fue creata l'anima del Figl[i]ulo de Dio et messa in lui et fide facto perfecto huomo. Ma era picolino, et andava crescendo nel ventre della Vergene sì come fano le altre creature naturalmente. Sapi adunque che la infusion dell'anima et la destencion di membri di miser Iesù Cristo [f. 7r] non fue indusiata, sì come si fano ne la creatione delle altre creature, ma incontanente fue facto vero huomo et ancho era vero Dio.

9. MS *uirtu|de dio*
10. MS *allui*

Stay still, here, and pay close attention, and see the great love of God the Father.[9] And imagine how the whole Trinity stays and waits for the response and consent of this his blessed daughter, watching with great gladness how she remains modest and well-mannered.[10] Imagine also how reverently the angel remains kneeling before the Lady of Paradise, and how diligently he performs his mission with a joyful expression, and how attentively he considers the words of the Virgin, for he knows well how to fulfill perfectly the will of his Lord.[11] Above all, in this marvelous scene, watch the young woman, how she remains demure and humble, with her face lowered, and how she instinctively draws back at these words and does not exalt herself. And hearing things said like this that had never been said to another person, she attributes all to the goodness of God.

And in the end, the most wise Virgin, hearing the words of the angel, consented. And according to what is contained in revelation, she knelt with the greatest devotion and, with hands joined,[12] said, "Behold the handmaid of the Lord. Let it be done to me according to your word." As soon as she had said these words, the Son of God, having been without a home, entered her womb at once and took human flesh through her, but nonetheless remained fully joined to the Father.

Here you can imagine with devotion how the Son of God, having received this painful and difficult mission from his Father, reverently knelt and devoutly commended himself to Him. And in that very same moment, the soul of the Son of God was created and placed in him, and he was truly made into perfect man. But he was little, and he grew in the womb of the Virgin as other creatures do naturally. Know, then, that the infusion of the soul and the formation of the limbs of our Lord Jesus Christ did not happen gradually, as it does in the generation of other creatures, but that in a single moment he was made true man, even as he was true God.

And so the angel took his leave of Our Lady, bending his knee in reverence before her. And he took this news to heaven with great exultation and abundant joy, and there the angels had a great celebration. And then the most blessed Virgin Mary, feeling herself more fully inflamed and illumined by divine love than ever before, and feeling that she had conceived the Son of God, knelt reverently and gave thanks to God for so great a blessing, and humbly asked that he deign to teach her so that she might do everything without fail that should be done with respect to his Son.[13]

You should consider how great today's feast is, and rejoice in your heart, and give praise and thanks to God, because today God the Father wedded human nature, which he joined to himself perpetually. Today is

Et alora l'angelo se inçenochioe denançi alla Madona e prese combiato da lei, et portoe questa novella in cielo cum grande festa et grandissima alegreça et qui li angeli feceno grande festa. Et alora la beatissima Vergene Maria, sentendose tuta infiamata et acesa dell'amore divino più[11] che non era in prima et sentendosi havere conceputo el Figl[i]ulo di Dio, se inçenochioe reverentemente et rendete gratie a Dio di tanto beneficio, et humelmente sì 'l priegoe ch'el se dignasse de amaistra[r]la sì ch'ella facesse sança diffeto tute quelle cose ch'erano da fare inverso el suo Figl[i]ulo.

Tu dèi considerare quanta ène grande la festa de ancoi, et ralégrate nel cuore tuo, et referisi laude e gratie a Dio, imperçiò che Dio Padre anchoi feçe noçe cum la humana[12] natura, [f. 7v] la qualle el conçonse a sé perpetualmente. Anchoi sì è la festa delle noçe del Figliulo de Dio nel qualle dì ello naque nel ventre della Vergene gloriosa. Anchoi ène la festa del Spirito Sancto, a cui è appropriada l'opera meravegliosa della Incarnatione, et anche commenciò a demostrare la sua benignitade alla humana natura. Anchoi ène la festa e solenitade della nostra Dona, la qualle oçi fue electa da Dio Padre per figliola, et dal figliulo per madre, et dal Spirito Sancto per sposa. Anchoi fue començada la reparatione della corte del cielo et incomenciose la redemptione dell'humana natura e il reconciliamento cum Dio Padre. Questa novella obedientia[13] ricevete el Figliolo dal Padre per adoperar la nostra salute et rechiusese nel ventre della Verçene Maria et [fu] facto huomo chome noi et ène facto nostro fratelo et advocato e començioe a peregrinare [f. 8r] cum noi.

Anchoi la verace luce discese dal cielo e il verbo di Dio è facto carne. Et etiandio oçi furono adimpiuti li desiderii e chiamori de' sancti propheti et patriarchi, li qualli cridavano[14] et priegavano Idio Padre cum grande desiderio ch'el dovesse mandare questo Agnello benedecto et recomperatore del mondo e che sfendesse i cieli e discendese a noi e che dimonstrasse la sua desiderata façia et saremo salvi. Questi et molti altri simel priegi se trova nel Testamento Vechio che feceno li patriarci e propheti cum grande amore et desiderio de vedere la faça de miser Iesù Cristo.

Et questo basti quanto alla meditatione che se puote fare puramente della Incarnatione del Figliulo de Dio.

11. MS *piui*
12. MS *la lhumana*
13. MS *obedienti*<ꝑ>*a*
14. MS *cridava*

the feast of the marriage of the Son of God, when he entered the womb of the glorious Virgin. Today is the feast of the Holy Spirit, to whom the wonderful work of the Incarnation is attributed, and who began to show lovingkindness to humanity on this day. Today is the solemn feast of Our Lady, who was chosen on this day by God the Father as daughter, and by the Son as mother, and by the Holy Spirit as spouse. Today was the beginning of the reparation of the court of heaven, and the redemption of humankind, and the reconciliation with God the Father. This new mission of obedience was accepted by the Son from the Father to achieve our salvation, and he enclosed himself in the womb of the Virgin Mary, and he was made man like us, and became our brother and advocate, and began to travel on this journey with us.

Today the true light descended from heaven, and the word of God became flesh. And today, too, the desires and exhortations of the holy prophets and patriarchs were fulfilled: they cried out and prayed to God the Father with great desire that he should send that blessed lamb and savior of the world, and that he split the heavens open and descend to us, and that he show his longed-for face, so that we would be saved.[14] These and many other similar prayers are found in the Old Testament and were made by the patriarchs and prophets with great love and desire to see the face of Lord Jesus Christ.

And this will be enough for you concerning the meditations you may undertake purely on the Incarnation of the Son of God.

*Come la Madona andò a visitare sancta Helisabeth.*
*Capitulo secundo.*

Et essendo rimasta la Vergene Maria pregna del Figliolo de [f. 8v] Dio, et recordandose delle parole che l'angelo li havea decto della cognata sua sancta Helisabeth, méssese in cuore de andare a visitarla per allegrarse della sua conceptione. Et prestamente se partite de Naçareth, et andosene in montana cum el sposo suo a casa de sancta Helisabeth, la qualle era da lonçi ben .lxxiiii. meglia. Et non lassoe per aspreça de via né per longeça, ma[15] andò in freça perfine a casa sua, per non esser trovata dalla çente per la via et per non essere veduta in palese. Tu pòi pensare che la Vergene Maria non era niente agravata per la sua conceptione come sono le altre done che sono aggravate della loro[16] gravidança, imperò che miser Iesù Cristo non fue grave alla madre sua.

Vedi adonque chome la Regina del cielo e della terra va lei sola cum el sposo suo a piedi, ma hanno seco la povertade, la humilitade et la honestade et tute le vertude, et anche hanno secco miser Iesù Cristo.

Et çonçendo a casa [f. 9r] de Çacharia, et salutoe Helisabeth et disse: «Dio te salvi, madre mia».

Et vedendo Elisabeth la Vergene Maria, se alegroe et tutta piena de leticia et accesa del Spirito Sancto se levoe suso et tenerisimamente l'abraçioe et per la grande leticia sì cridò et disse: «Tu sei benedecta sopra tute le done et benedecto ène il fructo del ventre tuo. Che è questo, che la madre del mio Signore viene a me?».

Unde quando la Dona nostra salutoe sancta Helisabeth, incontenente sancto Çuane stando nel ventre della madre sì fue repieno del Spirito Sancto, in tanto che soprahabundoe nella madre per gratia del figliolo; et per çiò lei cognosete el Figliolo de Dio nel ventre della madre per la novitade che fece sancto Çuane nel ventre suo. Or vedi quanta vertude fu nella parola della Vergene Maria, che per la sua salutatione è[17] dato il Spirito Sancto alla madre et al figliolo. Et ella ne era sì piena habundevolmente,[18] che per li sui meriti lo Spirito Sancto [f. 9v] fu[19] dato anche ad altrui.

Allora la nostra Dona rispuose ad Helisabeth et dise *Magnificat anima mea Domini*, et tutto quello cantico de laude et de iocunditade compite

---

15. MS *lōgeça <de> ma*
16. MS *lorro*
17. MS *et*
18. MS *habundevelmente*
19. MS *fi*

*Chapter 2. How Our Lady went to visit Saint Elizabeth.*

And then the Virgin Mary, pregnant with the Son of God and remembering the words the angel had said about her kinswoman Saint Elizabeth, took it into her heart to visit her to rejoice with her on the news of her conception. And soon she left Nazareth, and went to the mountain with her spouse to the house of Saint Elizabeth, which was a good seventy-four miles away.[15] And she did not delay because of the roughness of the road or the distance, but went in haste up to Elizabeth's house, so she would not be noticed by people on the road or be seen in public. You may imagine that the Virgin Mary was by no means burdened by her pregnancy like other women are encumbered by their pregnancies, because Lord Jesus Christ was not a burden to his mother.

See, then, how the Queen of Heaven and Earth goes on her own with her spouse on foot. But they have with them poverty, humility, and honesty and all the virtues, and they also have with them Lord Jesus Christ.

And upon reaching the house of Zacharia, she greeted Elizabeth, saying, "God be with you, my mother."

And Elizabeth, seeing the Virgin Mary, rejoiced; and overcome with happiness and enflamed by the Holy Spirit, she rose up and tenderly embraced her, and with great joy she cried out, saying, "Blessed are you among women, and blessed is the fruit of your womb. What is this, that the mother of my Lord comes to me?"

And at this, when Our Lady greeted Saint Elizabeth, suddenly Saint John, resting in the womb of his mother, was filled with the Holy Spirit—indeed filled to overflowing, so much so that the Holy Spirit also infused the mother through the grace of the son. And in this way Elizabeth recognized the Son of God in the womb of his mother, through the remarkable way Saint John announced this news in her womb. Now see how much power there was in the words of the Virgin Mary; for it was through her greeting that the Holy Spirit was given to the mother and to the son. And the Virgin Mary was filled so abundantly with the Holy Spirit that through her merits it was given to others too.

Then Our Lady replied to Elizabeth and said, "*Magnificat anima mea domini,*" and the whole canticle of praise and joy was first uttered then.[16] And then, when they sat down, the Virgin Mary, full of humility, placed herself at the feet of Saint Elizabeth.[17] Elizabeth, however, did not allow her to sit there, but had her sit with her on the same level. And each asked the other about the manner of her conception, and they spoke together about these things happily, praising and thanking God for their pregnancies.

allora. Et poi metendose a sedere la Vergene Maria, piena de humilitade se misse a sedere alli piedi de sancta Helisab[e]th. Ma lei non la lassoe sedere, ma fecela sedere igualmente cum lei. Et domandavase l'una all'altra del modo della sua conceptione, et de queste cosse parl[a]vano insieme aliegramente, laudando et ringratiando Dio de chatuna conceptione.

Et stete la Vergene Maria cum lei perfina che la parturite, facendo alcuni servicii per casa humelmente et divotamente, sì chome se la havesse dismentigada de essere Madre de Dio et di tutto il mondo Regina. O Spechio de Humilitade! Pensa ancho che casa et che camera et che lecto ène quello nel qualle dormeno et ripossase insieme cotalle madre piene di cotalli figlioli, çioè Maria et Helisabeth, Iesù et Çuane [f. 10r]. Et anche ne sono quelli doi venerabili vechi, çioè Çacharia et Ioseph. O che casa piena de ogni bene!

Et approximandose el tempo del parto, sancta Helisabeth si parturite uno figliolo, il qualle la nostra Dona il levò et sì dilige[n]temente el conçoe sì chome se convegniva. Or vedi quanto è grande la nativitade de sancto Çuane, che lui hebe la madre de Dio che 'l levoe, che 'l conçioe et che 'l bassoe[20] et tegnivalo in braçio. Et sancto Çuane sì la guardava fisso, sì che bene parea ch'el cognosesce la madre del suo Signore per Spirito Sancto. Et quando la Madona el volea sporçerlo al[a] madre sua, si volçea el viso pur inverso de lei, et parea ch'el non se volesse partire da lei et solamente se diletava in lei. Et ella volentiera solaçava cum lui, et abraçiavalo et basavalo cum grande alegreça. Considera adonque qui la magnificentia de sancto Çuane, che non fue mai alcuno che havesse cotalle bailla chome ebbe lui in la sua nativitade, [f. 10v] chome fu la Vergene Maria madre di miser Iesù Cristo!

Dapoi çorni octo, sancto Çuane fu circumciso et fu chiamato Çuane, della qual cosa tutti li sui parenti si meravegliavano, però che nel suo parentado[21] non era tal nome. Allora s'aperse la bocha di sancto Çacharia, el qual era stato muto dalla Annunciacione perfina allora, et prophetiçando disse: *Benedictus Dominus Deus Israel, quia visitavit et fecit redemptionem plebis sue,* et disselo tutto infin alla fine. Et la Vergene gloriosa stando drieto una cortina, per non essere veduta dalla gente, et diligentemente ascoltava quel cantico, nel qualle se facea mentione del suo figliolo; et ogni

20. MS *fassoe*
21. MS *parentādo*

And the Virgin Mary remained with her until the birth, performing services in the house with humility and devotion, as if she had forgotten that she was the Mother of God and Queen of all the World. O Mirror of Humility! Imagine the simple house and room in which they rest together, and the bed in which they sleep, these mothers pregnant with such sons— that is Mary and Elizabeth, Jesus and John. And those two venerable old men, Zacharia and Joseph, were also there. Oh what a house, full of all goodness!

And when the time of childbirth approached, Saint Elizabeth gave birth to a son, whom Our Lady took up and lovingly wrapped in linens, as was fitting.[18] Now see how grand the birth of Saint John is, that it was the mother of God who lifted him up and swaddled him and kissed him and held him in her arms![19] And Saint John watched her with such a fixed gaze, as if to say that he knew the mother of his Lord through the Holy Spirit. And when Our Lady wanted to hand him over to his mother, he would turn his face toward her, and it seemed that he did not wish to part from her and only delighted in her. And she willingly played with him, and embraced him and kissed him with great joy. Consider here, then, how greatly honored Saint John was, for no one ever had such a nursemaid at his birth as Saint John did in the Virgin Mary, mother of Lord Jesus Christ!

Eight days after this, Saint John was circumcised and was named John, at which all his relatives marveled, because none of his relatives had this name. And then the mouth of Saint Zacharia opened, which had been mute from the Annunciation until that moment. And, prophesying, he said, "*Benedictus dominus Deus Jerusalem quia visitavit et fecit redemptionem plebis sue.*" And he said all of this to the end. And the glorious Virgin stood behind a curtain, so as not to be seen by the people, and listened attentively to this canticle, in which mention of her son is made, and she reflected on everything in her heart as a most wise woman. And at the end of three months, wishing to return home, the Virgin Mary took leave of Saint Elizabeth and Saint Zacharia. And blessing their son, she left and returned to Nazareth with her spouse.

And here you may imagine the poverty of the Virgin Mary, for she returned to her house in which there was neither bread nor wine nor any worldly goods, and they had no possessions or money. Keep in mind that they had stayed three months with those who were perhaps quite rich; and now they return to their poverty, and by working with their hands they

cosa ripensava nel cuor suo chome sapientissima. Et in capo de mesi tre, vogliando la Vergene Maria tornare a casa, si prese combiato da sancta Helisabeth et da sancto Çacharia, et benedicendo el figliolo se partirono et tornoe in Naçareth cum el suo sposo.

Et qui pòi tu pensare la povertade [f. 11r] della verçene Maria, imperò che tornoe a casa sua in la qualle non era né pane né vino, né alcuno bene tereno, et non haveano né possessione né dinari. Pensa che steteno tre mesi cum loro che forse erano ben richi; et hora tornano alla sua povertade açiò che lavorando cum le sue mane sostegnano la vita loro. O spechio di povertade, hàbili compassione et attendi di amare povertade!


## Come Ioseph volse abandonare la Donna nostra. Capitulo iii°.

Et habitando la Dona nostra cum el sposo suo Ioseph, et crescendo miser Iesù Cristo nel ventre della madre, et avedandose Ioseph che lei era grosa, si conturboe in sé medesimo, et guardandola piui fiade cum grandissimo dolore et turbatione de mente. Et dimonstravali la faça turbata, dubitandose che lei havesse commesso adulterio; et per tanto se pensoe di volerla occultamente lassare. Veramente di costui [f. 11v] si puote ben dire la commendatione che de lui è decta nel evangelio, come era huomo iusto et di grande vertude. Et con çò sia cosa che sia grande vergogna a l'huomo lo adulterio della molgie, niente di meno costui se temperava così vertuosamente che non la volea accusare per non fare vendeta de quella inçuria, ma convento per pietade si li volea dar luocho et occultamente lassarla.

Ma tu dèi sapere che la gloriosa Vergene Maria non era sança grande tribulatione, imperciò che lei se avedea tropo bene che lui era turbato et de çiò lei ne havea gran pena; ma humelmente tacea et occultava el dono de Dio. Et ancho volea inançi essere reputata adultera et rea che palesare el dono di Dio, over dire cosa che tornasse a laude sua, ma humelmente priegava el Signor Dio che se dignasse de metere remedio et ch'el tollesse questa tribulatione tra loro dui. Or vedi in quanta tribulatione ène [f. 12r] colei ch'è piena de ogni gratia! Ma el Signore Dio exaudite le oratione della sua ancilla et mandò l'angelo suo, lo qualle parloe in sonno a Ioseph et disseli come la sposa sua havea conceputo per la vertude del Spirito Sancto, et imperciò dovesse stare cum lei securamente. Unde cessada la tribulatione tornò in grande consolatione; imperò che Idio fa vegnire lo riposso doppoi la tempestade.

make a living. O mirror of poverty, have compassion and strive to love poverty![20]

## *Chapter 3. How Joseph wished to abandon Our Lady.*

And Our Lady continued to live with her spouse Joseph, and Lord Jesus Christ continued to grow in the womb of his mother. And Joseph, having noticed that she was pregnant, became perplexed, and he glanced at her again and again with the greatest distress, troubled in mind.[21] And he took on a worried expression, for he was afraid that she had committed adultery; and so he made up his mind to leave her quietly. Truly the praise given to this man in the gospel is deserved: he was a just man, of great virtue. And even though the adultery of his wife is a great shame to a man, nevertheless he restrained himself virtuously, for he did not wish to accuse her publicly to seek vengeance for this wrong, but, moved by pity, he wished to cede his place and to leave her quietly.

But you ought to know that the glorious Virgin Mary was not without great tribulation, because she saw all too well that he was disturbed, and this pained her greatly; but she humbly remained silent and hid the gift of God. And also she would rather be thought of as an adulteress and guilty than disclose the gift of God or to say something that would contribute to her own praise and honor. So she humbly asked the Lord God that he might deign to provide a remedy and that he might take away this tribulation between the two of them. Now see how much anguish she feels, she who is full of all grace! But the Lord God answered the prayers of his handmaid and sent his angel, who spoke in a dream to Joseph and told him that his spouse had conceived through the power of the Holy Spirit, so he should stay with her without fear. So their tribulation ceased, and it turned into great consolation; for God provides calm after a storm.

Desvelgiato che fu Ioseph, incontenente se ne andò dalla gloriosa Vergene Maria sposa sua et dimandola della conceptione maravegliosa et della salutatione angelicha. Et allora la gloriosa Vergene, cognoscando che era voluntade de Dio Padre, si li manifestò dilige[n]temente el modo della sua conceptione. Rimase adonque Ioseph tuto contento d'ela, et alegramente stete cum la sposa sua benedeta, laudando et regratiando Dio de tanto beneficio. Et amava tanto la Dona nostra che dire non se potria, de uno [f. 12v] amore castissimo, et fidelmente havea cura de lei. Et viveteno insieme sanctamente et alegramente nella sua povertade.

Sta adonque el nostro Signore rechiuso nel ventre della madre sua dulcissima perfina a nove mesi, secundo l'usança delli altri fançuli, benignamente aspetando el tempo debito. Or pensa quanto ène grande la misericordia e lla caritade de Dio omnipotente, che solo per liberarne dalla morte eterna el se à dignado de abassarse intanta profundissima humilitade, çioè che de Dio è facto huomo, de invisibile è facto visibile, de impalpabile hase facto palpabile, de immortale è facto mortale, de signore ène facto servo, et è facto obediente infina alla morte per el nostro peccato! Et questo ène grande beneficio che noi habiamo ricevuto da lui, çioè ch'el stete tanto tempo rinchiuso nel ventre della madre per adoperare la salute nostra. Noi non potemo degnamente [f. 13r] satisfare a tanto beneficio, ma almeno siamone cognoscenti et cum tutto el cuore rendemoli gratia di tanto beneficio, et ch'el s'à degnado de eleçerne dalli altri non per nostri meriti ma solamente per sua infinita caritade. Et hàbilli compassione, però che da l'ora ch'el naque in questo mondo infino alla morte sempre el stete in grande angustia, però che el vedea perdere le anime le qualle el Padre suo havea create alla imagine et similitudine sua, et ancho vedea che li huomeni non honoravano Dio ma adoravano li idoli. Adonque se tu voi sentire in te alcuna dolceça spirituale, fa che speso tu rendi laude a Dio.


*Come miser Iesù Cristo naque in questo mondo.*
*Capitolo quarto.*

Approximandose el tempo della gloriosa Vergene Maria de parturire el suo dilectissimo figliolo, Cesaro Augusto imperadore de Roma vegnandoli voglia de sapere el [f. 13v] numero de tutte le provincie e citade et castelle et ville et anche tute le persone che erano subiecte allo imperio romano. Et vegnudo uno mando per tutto el mondo, li sui vicharii scrivando

As soon as Joseph woke, he went right away to the glorious Virgin Mary, his spouse, and asked her about the miraculous conception and about the greeting of the angel. And then the glorious Virgin, knowing that it was the will of God the Father, described to him in detail the manner of her conception. Then Joseph's faith in her was restored, and he stayed happily with his blessed spouse, praising and thanking God for such a great blessing. And he loved Our Lady, with a truly chaste love, so much that it is impossible to describe.[22] And he took care of her faithfully, and they lived together in a holy way, happy in their poverty.

Our Lord, then, remains enclosed in the womb of his most sweet mother for nine months, just as other infants do, patiently waiting the required time. Now, consider the great mercy and love of almighty God, who, in order to free us from eternal death, deigned to abase himself with the most profound humility, that is, he who was God became man, he who was invisible became visible, he who was impalpable became palpable, he who was immortal became mortal, he who was lord became servant, becoming obedient even unto death for our sin. And this is one of the great blessings we have received from him, that is, that he stayed enclosed in the womb of the mother for so long to achieve our salvation. We can never repay such a great gift adequately, but at least we should be mindful of it and give him thanks in a wholehearted way for giving us such a gift and for deigning to choose us from others not through our merits but only through his infinite love. And have compassion for him, because from the hour that he was born into this world until his death, he remained in great anguish, because he saw the souls whom his Father had created in his image and likeness going astray, and also he saw that men did not honor God but worshipped idols. So if you wish to feel any spiritual sweetness, be sure to give praise to God often.

*Chapter 4. How Lord Jesus Christ was born into the world.*[23]

As the time approached for the glorious Virgin Mary to give birth to her beloved son, the emperor of Rome, Caesar Augustus, decided that he wanted to know the number of all the provinces and cities and towns and villages and people that were subject to the Roman Empire. And an order was sent out through the world, and his officials began to register all the

le persone le qualle erano sottoposte allo imperio romano. Et vegnudo uno de questi vicarii in Bethelem et sapudo ch'el fu per la provincia, tuti vegnivano per farse scrivere. Et essendo Ioseph della schiata et famelgia de David et nato in Bethelem, volse andare alla citade per farse scrivere chome huomo che era sotto a l'imperio romano. Et sapiando Ioseph che tosto era el tempo del parto della sposa sua, non la volse lassare in Naçareth ma menola seco in Bethelem, imperciò che a lui era stata data in guardia; et ancho menoe seco el buove et l'asenelo. Et qui pò' tu pe[n]sare che Ioseph metesse la Vergene Maria sopra l'asenelo, però che lei era çoveneta et etiandio era gravida, avegna che la sua [f. 14r] gravidança non li fosse grave, ma però che el camino era longo et non haveria potuto caminare a piedi. Vedi etiandio grande humilitade, che la Regina del cielo et della terra cavalcha sopra uno asenelo. O povertade sanctissima! Et Ioseph a piedi mena el buove. O superbia humana, che dirai per tua scusa!

Camina adonque la Dona nostra per cusì longo viaço cum il sposo suo Ioseph intanto che çonseno in Bethelem. Et andorono cercando per tuta la terra per havere albergo, et non poteno trovare alcuno che li volesse albergare, però che le case et alberghi erano tuti pieni per la moltitudine della gente che vi erano andadi per farsi scr[i]ver.[22]

O huomo, pensa qui la povertade et la necessitade della Regina del cielo, et siando lei Madre de Dio non trovoe albergo: hàbili adonque compasione! Et anche vedi chome vergognosamente lei va drieto al sposo [f. 14 v] suo per la çente,[23] imperò ch'ela non era usada andare per le citade domandando albergo; et come fu sera, per força andono fuori della citade forsi doi meglia et qui trovorono una stalla de pegorari che era fuori della via. Et quivi intrarono per stare, et non trovono lí alcuna cosa se non uno poco di fen per dare all'asino et al buo' et qui non era né lume né fuoco né lecto né linçuoli. Pensa tu come doveano stare al tempo de tanta fredura! Adonque quando tu hai fredo over alcuna necessitade, ricòrdati della Vergene Maria et habi patientia.

Havea in uso la Vergene Maria de sempre levarse nell'hora della meça nocte et stare in oratione. Et approximandose l'ora della meça nocte, levose la gloriosa Vergene Maria et fece secundo el suo costume; et stando lei inçenochiata, véneli uno mirabele desiderio di vedere el Figliolo de Dio in carne humana. Et stando la Dona nostra in [f. 15r] questa contemplatione et desiderio, alora per divina dispensatione el Figliolo de Dio

22. MS *scruer*
23. MS *p(er) la <p(er)> çente*

people who were subject to the Roman Empire. And one of these officials came to Bethlehem, and, as this became known throughout the province, everybody came to register themselves. And since Joseph was from the lineage and family of David and had been born in Bethlehem, he wished to go to the city to register as a man who was subject to the Roman Empire. And knowing that the time of childbirth of his spouse was near, Joseph did not wish to leave her in Nazareth, because she had been placed in his care. So he took her with him to Bethlehem, and he brought the ox and the donkey too. And here you may imagine that Joseph put the Virgin Mary on the donkey, because she was young and also pregnant; for even though her pregnancy was not a burden, the journey was long and she would not have had the power to travel on foot. See also such great humility: the Queen of Heaven and Earth rides on a donkey. O most holy poverty! And Joseph walks along leading the ox. O human pride, what might you say to excuse yourself?

And so Our Lady travelled on this very long journey with her spouse Joseph until they reached Bethlehem. And they went searching everywhere to find lodging, but they couldn't find anyone willing to take them in, for the houses and inns were all full because of the large numbers of people who had gone there to register.

O human soul, consider here the poverty and need of the Queen of Heaven, and how, even though she was the Mother of God, she did not find lodging: have compassion on her! And also see how modestly she follows her spouse among the people, as one who is not used to going through cities asking for lodging. And since it was getting dark, they had no choice but to go outside the city, and there, perhaps about two miles away, they found a stall for shepherds off the main road. And they went inside, and they found nothing there but a little hay to give to the donkey and the ox. And here there was neither light nor fire nor bed nor linens. Imagine how they must have felt at a time of such cold! So, when you are cold or lack what you need, remember the Virgin Mary and learn to endure it patiently.

The Virgin Mary was in the habit of rising at midnight to pray. And when the hour of midnight came, the glorious Virgin Mary got up, according to her custom. And as she was kneeling in prayer, a tremendous desire came upon her to see the Son of God in human flesh. And as Our Lady was meditating with this desire, in an instant, by divine dispensation, the Son of God was born, leaving the womb of the Virgin Mother Mary without any trouble. And just as she did not feel him enter, in the same way she

usite fuori del ventre della Madre Vergene Maria sança alcuna molestia. Et sì come lei non lo sentite intrare, così lei nol sentì ussire; et sì come gli era nel ventre della Madre Gloriosa, et così el fue fuori sopra il feno denançi alla Vergene Maria.

Et nasuto ch'el fù, pianse stando sopra il feno a dimostrare l'humana miseria. Et allora la gloriosa Vergene Maria si l'adorò. Et reverentemente si'l tolse cum le sue sanctissime mane et mésselo nel suo gremio; et non havendo panicelli da rivolçerlo, tolse il vello del suo capo et involselo in quello. Et da poi il mese nella mançatoia fra el buo' e ll'asenello, sopra uno pocheto di feno. Et cognoscendo le bestie el suo Creatore, sì se inçenochiono et mésseno le loro boche sopra la mançadora et refiadavano sopra il fançulo. E lla gloriosa [f. 15v] Vergene Maria se messe inçenochioni a contemplare il Figliolo de Dio onnipotente, nato in questo mondo in tanta povertade. Et poi rendete lauda a Dio Padre Onnipotente et disse: «Gratia rendo a vui, Padre Eterno, de tanto beneficio, che a me havete dato el vostro Figliolo. Et adoro te Dio Eterno et Figliolo de Dio vivo et vero Dio et vero huomo». Et el simele fece Ioseph.

Et nato che fu miser Iesù Cristo, gli angeli descesono de cielo in terra nel luocho dove era nato el Figliolo de Dio. Et cantando et laudando et iubilando diceano, *Gloria in excelsis Deo et in terra pax hominibus bone voluntatis*. Et adorono il suo Signore in carne, nato per salute de l'humana generatione. Et poi andorono alli pastori annuntiando a loro la nativitade del Salvatore del mondo dicendo: «Noi ve annuntiamo gaudio magno ch'el'è nato oçi el Salvatore[24] del mondo in Bethelem citade de David. Et in segno de çiò andate, che trova[f. 16r]reti il fançullo rivolto nelli paniceli et posto nel presepio».

Et partendose li angeli, li pastori disseno infra loro: «Andiamo in Bethelem et vediamo questo Salvatore del mondo el qualle Dio ne à dimostrato». Et andorono et sì trovono miser Iesù Cristo nel presepio fra el buove e ll'asenelo, et inçenochiandose adorono el fantessino et naroe tuto quello ch'eli havea aldito dalli ançoli. Et la Dona nostra reservava nel cuore suo tuto quello che loro disseno del fançullo. Et alora li pastori, laudando et glorificando Dio, se partirono. Hora sono partiti li pastori et ène rimasta la Vergene et Ioseph cum el puto.

Perfina qui havemo decto della nativitade del nostro Signore miser Iesù et de li ançoli et de li pastori. Hora pòi tu pensare sopra tute queste

---

24. MS *sauāltore*

did not feel him exit; and just as he had been in the womb of the Glorious Mother, so he was now out on the hay before the Virgin Mary.

And as soon as he was born, he began to cry, as he lay there on the hay, as a sign of the misery of the human condition. And then the glorious Virgin Mary knelt to adore him. And reverently she lifted him up with her most holy hands and placed him in her lap; and, not having linens to wrap him in, she took the veil from her head and swaddled him with that. And then she placed him in the manger between the ox and the donkey on a little hay. And the animals, recognizing their Creator, knelt and put their mouths over the manger and breathed on the infant. And the glorious Virgin Mary knelt to contemplate the Son of the Almighty God, born in this way in such poverty. And then she gave praise to God the Almighty Father and said, "I give you thanks, eternal Father, for so great a blessing, that you have given me your Son. And I adore you eternal God and Son of the living God and true God and true man." And Joseph did the same.

And when Lord Jesus Christ had been born, the angels descended from heaven to earth to the birthplace of the Son of God. And singing and giving praise and rejoicing they said, "*Gloria in excelsis Deo et in terra pax hominibus bone voluntatis.*" And they worshipped their incarnate Lord, who had been born for the salvation of humankind. And then they went to the shepherds, announcing to them the birth of the Savior of the World, saying, "We bring news of great joy to you: today the Savior of the World was born in Bethlehem, city of David. And as a sign of this, go and you will find the baby wrapped in swaddling clothes and placed in a manger."[24]

And when the angels had left, the shepherds said among themselves, "Let's go to Bethlehem and see this Savior of the World, whom God has revealed to us." And they went and found Lord Jesus Christ in the manger between the ox and the donkey, and they knelt in adoration before the infant. And they related everything they had heard from the angels. And Our Lady kept in her heart all that they said about the child. And then the shepherds took their leave, praising and giving glory to God. And when the shepherds had left, the Virgin and Joseph remained there with the child.

Up to this point we have spoken of the birth of Our Lord Jesus and of the angels and of the shepherds. Now you may meditate on these things and dwell lovingly on this great gift from God, and on how, in order to free you from eternal death, God deigned to take human flesh and descend into such humility that he became man. And he chose to be born into this world in such poverty and baseness, that is, placed in the manger and in

cose et diligentemente repensare il grande beneficio de Dio, però che el s'à dignato per te liberare dalla morte eterna, prendere [f. 16v] carne humana et descendere in tanta[25] humilitade che de Dio è facto huomo, et ha voludo nascere in questo mundo in tanta povertade et basseça: çioè nel presepio, et in tanta necessitade solamente per adoperare la tua salute. Et ancho pòi tu pensare che miser Iesù havea in sua podestade di nascere in questo mondo in che tempo piacea a lui; et èlgi piacesto de nascere nel tempo di tanta fredura et in tanta povertade che lui non [à] abudo nella sua nativitade pur li panicelli da essere rivoltado. Qui non è lecto né linçulo né alcuno altro bene terreno salvo che uno pocho di feno nel presepio sopra il qualle lui fu messo, et dilectose il Re del cielo et della terra de volere nascere in sì ville luocho come fu nella stalla et essere rivolto in sì poveri paneselli et piançere sopra il feno posto nella mangiatoia tra le bestie. Dice sancto Bernardo ch'el vole che tu sapi per lo fermo che la infantia de Cristo [f. 17r] Iesù et le lacrime et la mang[i]adora et la stalla non dano consolatione a quelli che sono furiosi et inganatori et riditori et a quelli che si dilectano delle pompe et honori di questo mondo, ma dàno consolatione alli afflicti et poveri de spirito. Et questo have in si la Vergene Maria, Madre del Figliolo de Dio, che lei non have in horore la stalla né le bestie né 'l feno,[26] né tute le altre cose vile. Et ancho dice sancto Bernardo: «O Iesù Cristo, che sei povero et bisognoso, primo et ultimo! Forestiero nel casamento della pioba, povero nella mançatora, fugi in Egypto! Sede sopra l'asenelo et cum gli poveri è presentato nel tempio et nudo posto in su la croce». Et qui tu pòi vedere el grande beneficio che tu hai riceputo dal Signore Dio.

Hora habiamo decto della nativitade del Signore nostro miser Iesù Cristo et delli ançoli et di pastori, come andorono adorare miser Iesù Cristo Signore de cielo et della [f. 17v] terra nel presepio. Hora vàtene anche tu al presepio, et inçenochiate denançi al Signore del mundo et alla madre sua, la qualle sta inçenochiata al presepio et adora el Figliolo de Dio cum ogni riverentia et timore, et basia gli piedi al fançulo Iesù che çase nella mançatora, et priega dolcemente la madre che lei te'l sporça over ch'ela te 'l lassia tocare over abraçare. Et quando lei te l'averà sporto cum ogni reverentia el riceverai, et aliegrate et dilectatene di lui et cum grande fidutia. Et poi pensa come humelmente elgi è conversato cum noi et finalmente ha lassato

25. MS <di> ītanta
26. MS nel il feno

such need, solely in order to achieve your salvation. And you can also re-call that the Lord Jesus had the power to be born into this world in what-ever season he wished; and he chose to be born in a time of such cold, and in such poverty that he had nothing to be wrapped in at his birth but a humble cloth. Here there is neither bed nor fine linen nor any other worldly good except for a little hay in the manger in which he was placed; and it pleased the King of Heaven and Earth to choose to be born in such a humble place as a stall, and to be wrapped in such simple cloth, and to weep on the hay, placed in the manger among the animals. Saint Bernard says that he wants you to know for certain that the infancy of Christ Jesus and the tears and the manger and the stall do not give solace to angry and deceptive and foolish people and to those who delight in the pomp and honors of this world, but they give solace to the afflicted and the poor in spirit.[25] And the Virgin Mary, Mother of the Son of God, was poor in spirit, for she was not put off by the stall nor the animals nor the hay nor the other humble things. And Saint Bernard also says, "O Jesus Christ, how poor and needy you are from first to last! A stranger taking refuge in a rain shelter, a poor child in the manger, you flee into Egypt! He sits on the donkey, he is presented in the temple with the poor, and he is placed naked on the cross." And here you can see the great gift you have received from the Lord God.

Now we have spoken about the birth of Our Lord Jesus Christ, and of the angels and of the shepherds, how they went to adore Lord Jesus Christ, Lord of Heaven and of Earth, in the manger. Now you, too, go to the manger, and kneel before the Lord of the World and before his mother, who is kneeling beside the manger, and worship the Son of God with great reverence and awe.[26] And kiss the feet of the child Jesus who lies in the manger, and gently ask the mother if she will hand him to you or let you touch or embrace him.[27] And when she has given him to you to hold, receive him with great reverence, and rejoice and delight in him with great confidence. And then consider how humbly he dwelt among us and even finally left himself as food. So his goodness will patiently allow you to touch him as you wish, and he will not attribute this to presumption but to love and devotion. And then reverently return him to his mother, and watch how she cares for the infant, and how attentively she tries to do everything she can to please him. Stay with her, then, and help her, and delight in thinking often of the little child, because by meditating and de-lighting in him in this way you will have a deep sense of peace. You may imagine these and other beautiful things concerning the birth of Our Lord

se medesimo in cibo; unde la sua benignità pacientemente se lasserà tocare al tuo volere, et non te 'l riputare a presumptione, ma ad amore et a devotione. Et poi riverentemente el rendi alla madre sua, et guarda come lei governa il bambollino et come diligentemente ella procura de farli tuti li piacere che lei puote. Stàtene adonque cum lei et [f. 18r] aiutela et dilèctate di pensare speso del fançullo, però che pensando et dilectando te de lui haverai pace nella mente tua. Queste et altre bele cose pòi tu pensare della natività del nostro Signore miser Iesù Cristo devotamente et secundo chome la sua gratia te amaistrerà.

Oçi è la nativitade del Re de vita eterna, Figliolo de Dio Vivo. Oçi è uscito il Sposo della Giesia del tabernaculo suo, çioè della Vergene Maria. Oçi colui ch'è belissimo sopra tute le creature si ha demostrato la sua desiderata façia al'humana natura. Oçi fide anunciata la pace alli homeni di buona voluntade. Oçi Dio è facto huomo et la Vergene ha parturito. Oçi li cieli per tuto el mondo sono facti dolçi come melle. Oçi li angeli cantarono in terra. Oçi è apparuda la humanità e lla benignità del nostro Salvadore miser Iesù Cristo. Oçi è adorado Dio in similitudine di carne de peccato. [f. 18 v] Et imperciò oçi è g[i]orno di fare grande festa cum alegreça et gaudio. Et però fà che tu vadi speso al presepio a visitare el bambolino et la madre sua, et anche quel buono vechio Ioseph. Et se questo farai, grande dilecto et consolatione ne haverai.

## Come miser Iesù nostro Signore fo circumciso.
## Capitolo quinto.

Compiuto che have miser Iesù Cristo çorni octo el fo circumciso, secundo la voluntade sua. Et manifestose al mondo il nome della nostra salute, çioe Iesù, che tanto viene a dire Iesù come Salvatore. Et questo nome è sopra ogni nome, et in questo nome si conviene che tute le creature—celestiale et terrene et infernale—se inçenochiano. Et non è altro nome sotto il cielo per el qualle possiamo essere facti salvi, se non nel nome de Iesù. Et secundo che dice l'apostolo miser sancto Pietro, questo nome Iesù è quello che rende alli ciechi el vedere, alli sordi l'aldire, alli çopi l'andare,[27] agli muti il parlare, agli [f. 19r] morti la vita, et tuta la potentia tolse al

27. MS lā āndare

Jesus Christ with devotion, according to what he will teach you through his grace.

Today is the birth of the King of Eternal Life, Son of the Living God.[28] Today the Spouse of the Church has come forth from his tabernacle, that is, the Virgin Mary. Today he who is most beautiful over all creatures has shown his longed-for face to humankind. Today peace is announced to men of good will. Today God has become man, and the Virgin has given birth. Today the skies throughout the world are made sweet as honey. Today the angels sing on earth. Today the humanity and benevolence of our Savior Lord Jesus Christ are revealed. Today God is worshipped in the likeness of sinful flesh. And that is why today is a day to celebrate with great happiness and joy. And so, be sure to go often to the manger to visit the little baby and his mother, and also that venerable old man Joseph. And if you do this, you will have great delight and solace.

*Chapter 5. How Our Lord Jesus was circumcised.*[29]

When Our Lord Jesus was eight days old he was circumcised, according to his will. And the name of our salvation was revealed to the world: Jesus, that is to say, Savior. And this name is above all other names, and it is fitting that all creatures—celestial, earthly, and infernal—kneel before it. And there is no other name under the heavens through which we may be saved except for the name of Jesus. And according to what the apostle Saint Peter says, this name Jesus gives sight to the blind, hearing to the deaf, movement to the lame, speech to the mute, life to the dead, and takes all power from the devil.[30] And this name Jesus was established by God from eternity, and by the angel when he came to announce to Our Lady the Virgin Mary that God wished to take human flesh from her. And so, among the other things the angel said to her, he said, "You will call him Jesus."

diavolo. Et questo nome Iesù li fu posto da Dio *ab eterno,* et da l'angelo quando el vene ad annuntiare alla nostra Dona Vergene Maria che Dio volea prendere carne humana de lei. Unde fra le altre cosse che l'ançelo gli disse: «Tu il chiamerai Iesù».

Oçi començoe el dolcissimo Iesù a spandere il suo preciosissimo sangue per noi peccatori, siando sì picolino. O Signore mio Iesù, come per tempo tu incomençi a portare pena per noi! Et voi Signore, che mai non facesti peccato alcuno, oçi havete[28] principiato a portare pena per nostro amore, et siando sì tenerello et picolino! O huomo che hai ricevuto tanto beneficio oçi da Cristo Iesù, pensa sopra questo talle beneficio et hàbili uno poco de compassione, et piangi anche te cum lui, perché siando circumciso elgi pianse fortissimamente. Hàbili compassione donque de Cristo Iesù picolo bambolino!

In questa solenitade noi molto [f. 19v] se[29] dobiamo alegrare per la nostra salute, ma dobiamo havere grande compassione a Iesù picolino per le sue fatiche et tribulatione. Hai veduto quanta afflictione et pena che lui have nella sua nativitade et infra le altre pene si li fu messo una pietra sotto el capo. Et secundo che io havi da uno frate che mi disse che ancora se vedea quella pietra et che la era murada in un certo luocho per ricordamento de questo facto. Tu poi ben pensare che volentiera lei li haveria posto uno caveçalle, se la havese habudo. Ma da che lei non ebbe altro, cum grande amaritudine di cuore lì messe quella pietra.

Oçi el dolcissimo Iesù, per dolore che lui sentite quando el fo circumciso nella carne sua, si pianse fortemente, imperò che lui havea veramente carne passibile come noi. Sta qui cum la mente et vedi piançere—colui che fece el cielo et la terra!—ne[l] grembio della madre sua. Et vedi anche piançere[30] [f. 20r] duramente la madre per compassione del figliolo. O cuore di pietra, piançi anche tu per compassione del tuo Creatore, il qualle per tuo amore spanse oçi il sanctissimo sangue suo, siando cusì picolino: hàbili uno poco de compassione! Et ancho vedi come la madre prese uno panolino et suçoli el viso et poi se lo acostò al pecto et basiolo, et ogni volta che el piançea secundo l'usança de fançulli, lei facea el simegliante. Però che piançea per dimostrare la miseria de l'humana natura, et per ascondersi dal dimonio, che nol cognoscesse.

28. MS <començe> *hauete*
29. MS *molto*|| <*molto*> *se*
30. MS *piãçere* <la>

Today most sweet Jesus, as little as he was, began to shed his most precious blood for us sinners. O my Lord Jesus, how early you begin to suffer pain for us! And you, Lord, who never committed any sin, began to bear pain today for our love, even when you were so tender and little! O human soul, you who have received such a great gift today from Jesus Christ, meditate on this particular gift and have a little compassion! And weep also with him, because when he was circumcised he cried very hard. Have compassion, then, on Jesus Christ, the little baby!

On this feast day we should rejoice greatly for our salvation, but we must have great compassion for little Jesus, for his hardships and tribulations. You have seen how much affliction and pain he had when he was born. And among the other pains, a stone was put under his head. And according to what I have heard from a friar who told me, one can still see that stone, for it was placed in a wall in a certain place to commemorate this fact.[31] You may well imagine that she would have gladly placed a pillow there, if she had had one. But given that she had nothing else, with great bitterness of heart she placed the stone there.

Today most sweet Jesus cried a lot because of the pain that he felt in his flesh when he was circumcised, for he truly had flesh that was subject to pain, like us. Stay here with your imagination, and watch him weep—he who made heaven and earth!—in the lap of his mother. And see the mother weep bitterly too, through compassion for the son. O heart of stone, you too weep for your Creator, who for love of you shed his most precious blood today, even when he was so little: have a little compassion! And watch, too, how the mother took a cloth and dried his tears and then drew him to her breast and kissed him; and each time he cried, as babies do, she did the same. For he wept to show the misery of the human condition and to disguise himself from the devil, so that the devil would not recognize him.[32]

*Come vene li magi adorare miser Cristo cum la sua offerta.*
*Capitolo sexto.*

Et essendo passati ça çorni tredesse da poi la Natività del nostro signore miser Iesù Cristo, volgliandose manifestare alla generatione humana, sì inspirò li tre magi in oriente et dimostroli la stella sua per la
qualle essi comprexeno la sua natività. Unde movendose da casa sua
[f. 20v], venero driedo alla stella fino in Ierusalem. Et andarono al palaço
del re Herodes et dimandono: «Dove è quello che è nato re di Iudei? Ecco
che noi habiamo veduto lo segno ch'el è nato, çioè la stella sua fino in
oriente et siamo venuti per adorarlo». Et aldendo Herodes queste parole,
fu molto turbato, et tuta la çente cum lui. Et incontenente fece assunare
tuti gli principi et sacerdoti del tempio et dimandavali dove Cristo dovea
nascere, et quelli risposeno che dovea nascere in Bethlem città de Iuda,
imperò che cusì era scripto per il propheta che dicea «Et tu Bethlem, terra
de Iuda, non sei la minima tra le principale de Iudea, imperò che di te debe
usire uno duca el qualle reçerà il populo mio de Israel».

Alora Herodes diligentemente domandò quanto tempo era che questa
stella era apparida, et poi disse: «Andiate et cercate diligentemente del
puto, et quando voi lo haveriti trovato venite ad nuntiar[f. 21r]mello, açiò
ch'io vegna adorarlo».

Alora li magi se partino, et eccote la stella la qualle haveano veduta in
oriente, che li andava inançi a lloro perfino tanto che çonsero dove era el
fantessino nato, et là se afirmò in aere. Et vedando li magi la stella fer-
mada, furono tuti pieni de gaudio et di leticia. Et intrando nella caxa, trovarono el fançullo cum la benedecta madre sua Vergene Maria. Et inçenochiandosi adorono el fançullo. Et aprendo gli sui thesori li offeriteno oro,
incenso et mira. Et l'angelo disse a lloro in sonno che non ritornasseno
piui ad Herodes, ma per un'altra via li dovesseno tornare in le loro contrade. Et di questo sancto miraculo cusì ne dice lo evangelio.

Et tu huomo che sei peccatore, pensa et guarda questo miracolo[31]
cum li ochi della mente: come questi magi viene cum grande multitudine
di gente et honorevelmente per honorare il Re de Vita Eterna miser Iesù
[f. 21v] Cristo, il qualle era nato in questo mondo per farne regnare cum
lui in cielo.

---

31. MS *questo miracolo* in margin

*Chapter 6. How the kings came to worship Christ*
*with their gifts.*

And when thirteen days had passed since the birth of Our Lord Jesus Christ, he wished to reveal himself to humankind. So he inspired three kings in the East by showing them his star, through which they might know of his birth. And so, leaving their home, they followed the star until they reached Jerusalem. And they went to the palace of King Herod and asked him, "Where is he who is born King of the Jews? For behold, we have seen the sign of his birth, his star in the East, and we have come to worship him." And hearing these words, Herod was greatly disturbed, and all the people with him. And right away he had all the leaders and priests of the temple gather together, and asked them where Christ was supposed to be born, and they replied that he was to be born in Bethlehem, city of Judah, because it was written by the prophet who said, "And you, Bethlehem, land of Judah, are not the least among the principalities of Judah, because from you will come a ruler who will lead my people of Israel."

Then Herod questioned them intently about how much time had passed since the star had appeared. And then he said, "Go and do your best to find the infant. And when you have found him, come back and relay the news to me, so I can go to pay him homage."

Then the kings left and followed the star they had seen in the East, which went before them until it came at last to where the infant was born, and there it stopped in the air. And seeing the star stand still, the kings were filled with joy and happiness. And entering the shelter, they found the infant with his blessed mother the Virgin Mary. And they knelt to adore the child. And opening their treasure chests, they offered him gold, incense, and myrrh. And the angel told them in a dream that they should not return to Herod, but they must return to their country by another way. And the Gospel tells us about this holy miracle.

And you, human soul, who are a sinner, imagine and watch this miracle with the eye of the mind: how these kings come with a great multitude of people and with reverence to honor the King of Eternal Life, Lord Jesus Christ, who was born into this world to enable us to reign with him in heaven.

And Lord Jesus accomplished many other things on this feast day concerning the Church.[33] The first is that he received the Church in the form of the kings, for the kings were gentiles, and the Church was established and

Et molte altre cosse adoperò miser Iesù in tal çorno inverso la Chiesia. La prima sì è ch'el ricevete la Chiesia in persona d'i magi, però che
gli magi erano del populo çentille, imperçiò che la Chiesia è facta et assunata del populo çentile. La secunda è che in talle çorno fu disponsata la
Chiesia et conçunta cum Cristo per lo batessimo, unde per il batesmo noi
siamo disponsati al[32] nostro dolçe sposo Cristo Iesù. Et anche in tal çorno
elgi fece il primo miraculo, alle noçe, quando lui convertite l'aqua in vino;
et etiandio in tal dì fece miser Iesù el miraculo quando lui dette da mançare a tante persone de cusì poco pane et pesse nel diserto.

Tu pòi pensare alcuna cosa[33] del primo miraculo, çioè degli magi,
però che hora la Chiesia ne fa principale memoria. Da poi che li furono
çonti al casame[n]to dove miser Iesù era cum la madre sua gloriosa et
anche el buo[f. 22r]no vechio Ioseph, desmontorono çoso degli loro cavalli per vedere il Re d'i Çudei. Allora oldendo la Vergene Maria il re-
more della çente, non sapiendo lo facto, començò a temere, et tolse el suo
dolcissimo figliolo in braço. Alora intrando dentro li magi et vedendo la
Dona nostra cum el fantessino in braço, getònose in terra et adorono il Signore nostro miser Iesù Cristo come vero Dio e vero huomo.

Or guarda come fu grande la fede de questi tre magi, che credeteno
che uno fançullo lo qualle era così poveramente vestito, et anche così po-
vera madre, et etiandio trovandolo in luocho così vile—çoè in una stalla e
sança compagnia et sença fameglia et sança alcuno adornamento—fosse
Re de Çudei et vero Dio. Et cum tuto çiò che credeteno niente di meno!

Stando inçenochiati dinanti al Re de Vita Eterna, domandorono alla
Vergene gloriosa della conditione del puto et della sua nativitade et del
modo della [f. 22v] conceptione. Alora la gloriosa Vergene Maria vergognosamente et humelmente gli contò dal principio infina alla fine della
conditione della conceptione et della nativitade; et anche, come inspirada
dal puto, li disse la causa perch'el'era vegnudo, però che gli magi represen-
tavano tuta la universitade della chiesia, la qualle se dovea assunare del populo gentille. Et habiando gli magi inteso tuto il modo dell[a] condicione
del fançullo, aprirono li loro thesori, et[34] distendendo uno pano over tapedo
a gli piedi del miser Iesù et feceli una bella offerta, la qualle fu oro, incenso
et mirra in grande quantitade: l'oro sì como a re, lo incenso sì come a Dio,
la mirra sì come a huomo mortale. Et facta la offerta, si gli basono li piedi.

32. MS al<l>
33. MS *pensare alcuna cosa* in margin
34. MS et|et

taken up by the gentile people. The second is that it was on this feast day that the Church was betrothed and joined to Christ through baptism; so, through baptism, we are betrothed to our sweet spouse Christ Jesus.[34] And it was also on this feast day that he performed his first miracle, at the wedding, when he converted water into wine; and on this day, too, Lord Jesus performed the miracle in the desert, when he provided for so many people to eat from so few loaves and fishes.

You may continue to dwell on aspects of that first miracle, that is, of the kings, for now the Church traces its origins to it. After they had reached the place where Jesus was with his Glorious Mother and the venerable old man Joseph, the kings got down from their horses to see the King of the Jews. And hearing the noise of the people, the Virgin Mary, not knowing what was happening, began to be afraid, and she took her most sweet son in her arms. Then the kings entered, and, seeing Our Lady with the infant in her arms, they threw themselves to the earth and worshipped Our Lord Jesus Christ as true God and true man.

Now behold the great faith of these three kings, who were willing to believe that a baby who was so poorly clothed, and with such a poor mother, and whom they had found in such a wretched place—in a stall, that is, and without a retinue or family and without any adornment—was King of the Jews and true God. Given all that, they believed nevertheless!

As they remained kneeling before the King of Eternal Life, they asked the glorious Virgin about the condition of the child and about his birth and about the manner of his conception. Then the glorious Virgin Mary modestly and humbly told them from beginning to end about his condition, conception, and birth; and also, as if inspired by the child, she told them the reason why he had come, because the kings represented the universal Church, which came to encompass the gentile people. And having understood completely who the infant was, the kings opened their treasure chests, and, spreading out a cloth, or rather a carpet, at the feet of the Lord Jesus, they made him a beautiful offering, which was gold, incense, and myrrh in great quantities. Gold, inasmuch as he was king; incense, inasmuch as he was God; myrrh, inasmuch as he was mortal human being. And having presented this offering, they kissed his feet.[35]

Then the most wise infant, in order to give them greater solace and to confirm them further in his love, extended his hands to them so that they might kiss them; and with great maturity he watched them, like a person understanding but not speaking. And the kings were much delighted by him—as much by their spiritual vision, because they were illuminated by

Alora lo fançullo sapientissimo, per fare a loro maçore consolatione et per confermarli più nel suo amore, si gli porse [f. 23r] ancho le mane açi[ò] che le basasseno; e cum grande maturitade gli guardava, sì come persona intendente non però parlando. Et gli magi molto se dilectavano de lui, sì della visione mentale, però che erano illuminati de lui, sì come etiandio della visione corporale, in çiò che lui era la piui nobelle creatura che mai fosse. Et ricevuta gli magi tanta consolatione et grandissima alegreça, humelmente gli dimandorono la sua benedictione, et il fançullo Iesù si gli benedì cum le sue mane; et riceputa che haveno la beneditione, si partirono in pace, et per un'altra via ritornarono nelli loro paesi.

Et partidi che furono gli magi, incontenente la Vergene Maria, sì come çelatrice de povertade, et etiandio inspirada dal suo figliolo, il qualle l'amaistrava dentro et di fuori monstrava per segni ch'el non volea che se tegnisse quel thesoro, ma che lei il dovesse dispensare [f. 23v] per suo amore a' poveri. Or intendendo la gloriosa Vergene Maria la voluntade del suo figliolo, distribuite a' poveri tuto quello che gli parse. Tu dèi pensare che lei riservasse anche alcuna cosa per loro, ma pocho, et in tanto fu pocho, che quando lei portò el nostro Signore al tempio la non havea da podere comprare uno agnello per offerrire, che gli conviene comprare uno par di tortore over de pipioni, la qualle era la minore offerta che se facesse in quel tempo.

Ricevete miser Iesù Cristo oçi elimosina come povero. Et ancho noi podemo pensare la profunda humilitade di colui che è Signore de l'universo, ch'el volse etiamdio mostrare la sua povertade a gente straniera—et non a' picoli ma a' grandi et a molti, çoè a' magi. Et in tal ponto et tal modo monstrò a lloro che era molto da dubitare, con çiò sia cosa che gli erano venuti per trovare el Re di Iudea [f. 24r], lo qualle pensavano che fosse Dio incarnato, ma l'è da credere che loro credeano trovarlo in grandi honori; ma trovandolo in tanta humilitade, haveano molto da dubitare, reputandose de essere inganati. Et però fu grande la loro fede, et grande fu la gratia che loro hebeno da Dio, che elgi credeteno perfectamente.

Tu pòi pensare ancho della humilitade della gloriosa Vergene Maria, che per dare a noi exempio de humilitade, açiò che sotto specie de apparencia de alcuno bene[35] non se partiamo da la humilitade, et che impariamo di volere parer nel conspecto de altrui vili.

---

35. MS *de alcuno bene de apparencia*, with a *b* superscript above *de* and an *a* above *apparencia*, indicating change of word order

him, as by their corporeal vision, since he was the most noble creature who ever lived. And having received so much solace and the greatest joy, the kings humbly asked his blessing, and the infant Jesus blessed them with his hands; and having received the blessing, they departed in peace and returned to their country by another route.

And as soon as the kings had left, the Virgin Mary, as one who was zealous for poverty, was also inspired by her son, who taught her inwardly and showed her outwardly through gestures that he did not wish her to keep this treasure but to give it to the poor for his love.[36] So the glorious Virgin, understanding the will of her son, distributed to the poor all that seemed right to her. You should imagine that she also reserved something for themselves, but just a little; and in the end it was so little that when she brought Our Lord to the temple, she was unable to buy a lamb for the offering, so they were obliged to buy a pair of turtledoves or pigeons, which were the least one could offer in those days.

Today Lord Jesus Christ received alms like a poor person. And also we can imagine the profound humility of he who is Lord of the Universe: he even wished to reveal his poverty to foreigners—and not only to those of lowest rank, but to the great and powerful, that is, to the kings. And at that moment and in such a manner, he showed them that there was much to doubt. For they had come to find the King of the Jews, whom they thought was God incarnate, and surely they expected to find him surrounded by signs of honor; but finding him in such humble circumstances, they had much to doubt, thinking that they had been misled. Nevertheless their faith was great, and so great was the grace that they had from God that they believed perfectly.

You may also meditate on the humility of the glorious Virgin Mary, who gave us an example of humility so that we will not part from humility even when goods or blessings come our way, and so that we may learn to want to appear to be of little worth in the eyes of others.

The Virgin Mary remained in the stall with her most sweet son and with her spouse Joseph for forty days, as if they were sinners who were obliged to observe the law. You should believe that she cared for her most sweet son with great attentiveness, as much as was possible, because she knew that he was true God and true man, and was made her son and was entrusted into her care; so all her effort and desire was directed towards him. And Saint Bernard says that Joseph often took Lord Jesus in his arms and played with him.[37]

Stete la gloriosa Vergene Maria nella stalla cum il suo dolcissimo figliolo et cum il sposo suo Ioseph perfina a çorni quaranta, sì com'eli foseno peccatori che li convegnisseno observare la lege. Tu dèi credere che cum ogni solicitudine, quanto li era possibile, la governava questo suo dolcissimo figliolo, imperò che lei [f. 24v] cognoscea che lui era vero Dio et vero huomo et era facto suo figliolo et era commesso a lei in guardia; imperò tuto il suo studio et desiderio havea posto in lui. Et sancto Bernardo dice che Ioseph spesse volte tegniva in braçio miser Iesù et solaçava cum lui.

Stando la donque la madre apresso alla mançatura, stàtene ancho tu cum lei et cum il suo figliolo. Et pensa della sua humilitade, imperò che per tuo amore el se ha posto intanta baseça; et ringracialo de tanto beneficio. Et cadauna anima fidele, et specialmente la persona religiosa, dal çorno della Nativitade perfina alla Purificacione doveria almeno una volta al çorno andare a visitare il presepio, çioe la Dona nostra, et adorare el Signore nostro miser Iesù picolino et la madre sua, et pensare della sua povertade et humilitade. Et pensa ch'el se ha dignado per noi recomperare vegnire de cielo in terra!

## Come miser Cristo nostro Signore fo pre[f. 25r]sentado al tempio. Capitolo septimo.

Compidi gli çorni quaranta et observata che have la Vergene Maria la leçe, lei se partì de Bethelem et vene in Ierusalem cum el suo dolcissimo figliolo et cum el sposo suo Ioseph per apresentare il fançullo al tempio secundo la consuetudine della leçe. Ora và ancho tu cum loro, et aiuta a portare il fançullo miser Iesù alla madre sua, et fà che tu sie presente cum la mente attentamente, et fà che consideri tuto quello che qui se fa et che se dice, imperò che qui se fano devotissime cose. Poni mente et vedi ch'el Signore del Tempio viene portado al tempio. Et vedi ancho la gloriosa Vergene Maria, cum quanta reverentia lei porta il dolcissimo miser Iesù.

Et çonti che li furono al tempio, si comprarono uno paro de pipioni per offerire per il fançullo Iesù, però che loro erano poverissimi et non haveano da comprare l'agnello—et anche perché miser Iesù era [f. 25v] amatore di povertade [e] volse fare l'offerta da povero. Comprado ch'eli haveno gli pipioni et intrando nel tempio, et là sancto Simeone, inspirato dal Spirito Sancto, vene contra al suo Signore. Et incontenente che lui el

As the mother stays near the manger, you, too, stay with her and with her son. And contemplate his humility, because for his love for you he placed himself in such humble circumstances; and give thanks to him for such a blessing. And it is good for a faithful soul, especially a person dedicated to the religious life, to go at least once a day to visit the manger, that is, Our Lady, from the day of the Nativity until the Purification, and to adore Our Lord, little Jesus, and his mother, and to meditate on his poverty and humility. And remember that in order to redeem us, he deigned to come from heaven to earth!

## Chapter 7. How Christ Our Lord was presented at the temple.

When forty days had passed and the Virgin Mary had fulfilled the law, she left Bethlehem and went to Jerusalem with her most sweet son and with her spouse, Joseph, to present her infant at the temple according to the custom of the law. Now you go with them too, and help to carry the infant Lord Jesus to his mother, and make yourself present with an attentive mind, and be sure to contemplate everything that is said and done, for things are done here that are very moving.[38] Bring to mind and see how the Lord of the Temple is carried to the temple. And watch the glorious Virgin too, with what great reverence she carries the most sweet Lord Jesus.

And when they reached the temple, they bought a pair of pigeons to offer for the infant Jesus, because they were so poor and did not have enough to buy a lamb—and also because Lord Jesus was a lover of poverty and wished to make the offering of the poor. When they had bought the pigeons, they entered the temple, and there Saint Simeon, inspired by the Holy Spirit, came towards his Lord. And as soon as he saw him, he recognized him through the spirit of prophecy, and he worshipped him in

vete, sì 'l cognobe per spirito de prophetia et adorolo nelle braçe della madre sua. Alora il fançiullo sì lo benedì: alora fo adimpita la promessa facta a lui per lo Spirito Sancto, quando gli fu promesso ch'el non morirebe ch'el vederia el Figliolo de Dio in carne humana. Alora il fanc[i]ullo sì se inclinò, dando segno ch'el volea andare da sancto Symeone. Et la madre, intendendo la voluntade del puto, sì lo porse a sancto Simeone vechiarelo. Et lui sì lo recevete, sì 'l tolse nelle sue brace, benedicendolo, et disse: «*Nunc dimittis servum tuum, Domine, secundum verbum tuum, in pace.*»[36] Io te priego, Signore mio, che tu me lassi morire ormai in pace secundo [f. 26r] la tua parola, imperciò che io ho veduto cum li ochi mei il tuo Figliolo el qualle è nostra salute, il qualle tu hai aparechiato a lume et gloria de tuta la humana generatione». Et etiandio prophetiçò della Passione sua et disse alla madre: «la morte de costui trapasserà l'anima tuo de uno cortello».

Et da poi vene una sancta dona prophetessa, la qualle havea nome Anna, et adorò el Signore et prophetiçò de lui grande cosse. Et la gloriosa Vergene Maria ascoltava tute queste cosse et ritenevale nel suo cuore. Ora tegniva el vechio il fançullo et el fançullo reçea il vechio. Et tegnando el vechiarelo nelle braçe el fantesino et extendendo el puto le mane inverso la madre per volere tornare a lei; et quella, come disiderosa de lui, sì lo ricevete aliegramente. Et poi se missено a fare la processione la qualle ripresenta oçi la Chiesia per [f. 26v] tuto el mondo. Et vano inaçi quelli doi venerabilli vechi, çioè Simeone et Ioseph, cantando et iubilando et laudando Dio cum tanta alegreça che non se poria dire. Dapoi loro seguita la gloriosa Vergene Maria, portando in braço el suo fiol dolcissimo, acompagnata da quella sancta dona cum tanto gaudio et alegreça che non se poria dire.[37]

Vedi che sono pochi a fare questa processione, ma questi pochi representano quasi ogni generatione de çente, imperò che tra loro sono maschi et femine, vechi et çoveni, vergene et vedoe et maritade.

Et quando furono çonti al'altare, la Vergene Maria Madre de Dio riverentemente se inçenoch[i]ò et offerse el suo dolcissimo figliolo a Dio Padre et disse: «Signore mio et Padre excellentissimo, ecco che io vostra ancilla offerisco a voi el figliolo mio». Et elevandose la Vergene Maria, lassolo stare sopra l'altare. O Dio, che offerta è questa! Non fo mai, né mai serà la simele. Poni me[n]te come quello bambino Iesù picolino sta

---

36. MS *Nunc dimittis servum tuum <in pace> Domine*
37. MS *Da poi loro . . . poria dire* in margin

the arms of his mother. Then the infant blessed him; and the promise made to Simeon was fulfilled through the Holy Spirit, that he would not die until he saw the Son of God in human flesh. And then the infant leaned towards him, giving a sign that he wished to go to Saint Simeon. And the mother, understanding the will of the child, handed him to Saint Simeon, the old man. And he received him, taking him in his arms; and blessing him, he said, *"Nunc dimittis servum tuum, Domine, secundum verbum tuum, in pace.* I ask you, my Lord, that you let me die now in peace according to your word, because I have seen with my eyes your Son, who is our salvation, whom you have provided as the light and glory of all humankind." And he also prophesied about his Passion and said to the mother, "The death of this child will pierce your soul with a sword."

And then a holy woman came, a prophetess named Anna, and she worshipped the Lord and prophesied great things about him. And the glorious Virgin Mary listened to all these things and kept them in her heart. Now the old man held the infant, and the infant held the old man.[39] And as the old man was holding the child in his arms, the baby extended his hands toward the mother, wishing to return to her; and she, as one who yearned with desire for him, received him happily. And then they went to perform the procession, which today represents the Church throughout the world.[40] And those two venerable men, Simeon and Joseph, lead the way, singing and rejoicing and praising God with such joy that it is impossible to describe. The glorious Virgin follows them, carrying in her arms her most sweet son, accompanied by that holy woman with such joy and happiness that it is impossible to describe.

You see that there are few to perform this procession, but these few represent nearly all kinds of people, because among them are male and female, old and young, virgins and widows and married people.

And when they reached the altar, the Virgin Mary, Mother of God, reverently knelt and offered her most sweet son to God the Father, saying, "My Lord and most excellent Father, behold, for as your handmaid I offer my son to you." And then the Virgin Mary stood and placed him on the altar. O God, what an offering this is! There was never an offering equal to this, nor will there ever be another like it. Imagine how this baby, little Jesus, lies on the altar as if he were any other infant. And then the priests came and the King of the World was offered for five *dinari* in their currency, according to the custom of that time.

And when the child was returned to the mother, she knelt before the altar with her son in her arms. And as she held the two turtledoves or

desteso[38] in su lo altare si come il fosse un altro fançullo. Alora vene li sacerdoti et fo recomperato il Signo[f. 27r]re del Mondo per dinari cinque de quella moneda, secundo l'usança che era in quella volta.

Et dato che fu el fançullo alla madre, di presente lei se inçenoch[i]oe denançi al'altare cum el suo figliolo in braço, et habia[n]do in mano doe tortore over pipioni levò li ochi al cielo et disse: «O Dio Padre, tollete questa picola offerta che ve fa il vostro unigenito Figliolo della sua povertade». Et tuta via el fançullo tegnìa le mane sue a quelle tortore, et levò li ochi suoi in cielo; avegna ch'el non favelasse, tuta via li offerse insieme cum la madre al Padre suo. O che offeritori sono questi, el Re del mondo e lla Regina del cielo!

Or che festa credi tu che fosse facta nella corte del cielo di questa cotal offerta gradissima![39] Or chi poria narare la singulare alegreça che fo facta dagli angeli et dalli archançoli?

Et levandose la gloriosa Vergene Maria denançi da l'altare, recomandò el suo [f. 27v] dolcissimo figliolo al Padre eterno. Et poi insite del tempio et partise de Ierusalem et tornò a Naçareth. Et qui dimorò la gloriosa Vergene Maria cum il sposo suo Ioseph, vivendo della lor fadicha.[40] Fà che la mente non se parta dal bambolino, et haverai pace.


*Come la Donna nostra fuçì in Egipto cum miser Iesù.*
*Capitolo octavo.*

Tornadi che furuno in Naçareth, credendo qui stanciare in pace. Or passando algun tempo, el re de Ierusalem, il qualle era chiamato Herodes, vedendose essere inganato dagli magi li qualli non erano tornadi a lui, sì come lui havea decto a loro che tornasseno a lui per annunciarli ladove era nasuto el puto. Or non sapiendo in che modo el potesse trovare, instigado dal dimonio di volere al tuto occidere miser Iesù ordinò che tuti li puti de tre anni in çoso in tuto il paese de Galilea fusseno prese[n]tadi a lui; et cose fu facto. Et elgi sì li fece [f. 28r] tuti occidere, pensando per questo modo de occidere miser Iesù.


38. MS *destesto*
39. MS *offerta o\gradissima*
40. MS *<d>fadicha*

pigeons, she raised her eyes to heaven and said, "O God the Father, take this little offering that your only son presents to you out of his poverty."[41] And all the while, the infant kept his hands on those two turtledoves, and he lifted his eyes to heaven; so even though he could not express himself in words, he nonetheless offered them up together with his mother to his Father. Oh, what supplicants these are, the King of the World and the Queen of Heaven!

Now imagine what a celebration was held in the court of heaven for this most welcome offering! Now who could describe the exceptional joy that was shown by the angels and by the archangels?

And rising to her feet before the altar, the glorious Virgin Mary commended her most sweet son to the eternal Father. And then she went forth from the temple and left Jerusalem and returned to Nazareth. And there the glorious Virgin Mary dwelt with her spouse Joseph, living from the work of their hands. Keep your mind focused on that little child, never parting from him, and you will have peace.

## Chapter 8. How Our Lady fled into Egypt with Lord Jesus.

Then they returned to Nazareth, believing they could stay there in peace. But when some time had passed, the king of Jerusalem, who was called Herod, saw that he had been deceived by the kings, for they had not returned to tell him where the child was born, as he had asked them to do. So then, not knowing how he might find the child, and inspired by the devil with a fervent desire to have Lord Jesus killed, he ordered that all boys up to three years old, living in all parts of Galilee, be presented to him; and this was done. And he had all of them killed, thinking he would kill Lord Jesus in this way.

Now when Herod had given the order to do this, an angel appeared to Joseph in a dream and told him that he should take the baby and his mother and go with them to Egypt, because Herod was searching for the child, to kill him. And as soon as Joseph woke, he immediately woke the Virgin Mary and told her the news that had been related to them by the

Or habiando Heredes dato l'ordine de così fare, l'ang[i]olo apparse in sono a Ioseph et disseli che tollesse il puto e lla madre sua et che andasse cum loro in Egypto, perché Herodes l'andava cercando per occidere. Et desidato che fu Ioseph, incontenente desmesidò la Vergene Maria et disseli questa novella che li era stata det[a][41] per l'angelo in sono del fançullo. Et allora levandose la Vergene Maria, tuta smarita per questa novella, imperò che inverso la salute del figliolo non volea essere trovata negligente. Et imperò la nocte medema lei se partì de Naçareth et mésesse in camino inverso l'Egypto per scampare dalle mane de Herodes.

Or sta qui[42] et pensa bene quello che hai aldito, et anche pensa diligentemente la pena che have la Vergene Maria de questa novella del suo figliolo; et etiandio considera quanta adversitade sostenne miser Iesù Cristo per la tua salute. De[h], [f. 28v] habi loro un pocho de compasione, pensando le molte tribulatione ch'el sostene per te! Considera come prima in la persona el ricevete prosperitade et adversitade, açiò che quando el simele intervegnisse a [te], tu[43] non sie impatiente, imperò che al ladi del monte troverai la valle et dapoi la fortuna vegnerà grande tranquillitade.

Vedi che nella nativitade sua miser Iesù fu magnificado dalli angeli et dalli pastori sì come Dio, et pocho stante fo circumciso come peccatore. Et dipoi fu adorato et così magnificamente honorato dalli magi, et cum tuto çiò ello rimase infra le bestie nella stalla et piançea sì come fano il altri puti. Et poi fu presentato nel tempio et fu benedecto et magnificato da sancto Simeone et da sancta Anna, t a mano a mano fu recomprato per cinque denari come peccatore. Et ecco hora è perseguitato et ditoli per l'ançolo ch'el fuça in Egypto. Et de molte altre somegliante [f. 29r] cose potrai trovare nella vita sua, le quale noi potiamo redure a nostro amaistramento.

O anima la qualle sei venuta al servicio de Dio, quando receverai alcuna consolatione non te ne gloriare, ançi te apparechia alla tribulatione, et quando haverai tribulatione habi patiencia imperò che dapoi la tribulatione viene la consolatione. Et imperò non te ne insuperbire quando hai prosperitade nella via de Dio, et non remanere de fare bene. A l'hora della tribulatione daçe Idio la consolatione per mantegnire noi nella sua sperança, et anche per comunichare la sua benignitade a noi come a figlioli. Et ancho çi dà la tribulatione per conservarne in humilitade et açiò che non insuperbiamo, et açiò che noi cognosciamo la nostra miseria, et che stiamo sempre nel timore de Dio.

41. MS *dete*
42. MS *nocta qui*
43. MS *atu*

angel in a dream about the infant. And so the Virgin Mary got up, completely distraught by this news, for she did not wish to be found negligent where the health and safety of her son was concerned. And so, the very same night, she left Nazareth and set out on the road towards Egypt to escape the hands of Herod.

Now pause and pay attention here, and take in what you have heard, and imagine the pain that the Virgin Mary felt concerning this news about her son; and also consider how much adversity Lord Jesus Christ endured for your salvation. Oh, have a little compassion for them, considering the many tribulations that he endured for you! Consider how he received both prosperity and adversity even when he was a young person; so, when the same happens to you, don't be impatient, for beside the mountain you will find the valley, and after misfortune, great tranquility will come.

You have seen how Lord Jesus was honored greatly by the angels and by the shepherds at his birth, and just a little while after this, he was circumcised as a sinner. And then he was worshiped and honored so magnificently by the kings, even as he remained among beasts in the stall and cried just like other babies do. And then he was presented in the temple and was blessed and venerated by Saint Simeon and by Saint Anna, and soon afterwards he was offered for five *denari*, like a sinner. And behold, now he is persecuted and told by the angel that he should flee to Egypt. And you can find many similar things in his life which we can draw on for our learning.

O soul who has come to the service of God, when you receive any solace, do not glory in it, but prepare yourself for tribulation; and when you have tribulation, have patience, for after tribulation comes consolation. And when you have prosperity on your spiritual journey, don't take pride in it, and don't forget to do good deeds. At the hour of tribulation, God gives us consolation to maintain us in his hope, and also to convey his lovingkindness to us as his children. And also he gives us tribulation to preserve our humility, so that we don't become proud, and so that we know our wretchedness, and so that we always remain in reverent fear of God.

Now, let's remember that whatever he did, he did to teach us, and also to hide from the devil. O soul who receives the blessing of solace, don't be ungrateful, and don't act superior towards someone to whom God has not given such gifts. And anyone who does not receive comforts from God should not be dismayed and should not envy whoever receives it, for often people make big mistakes when they receive favors—especially those who don't know how to be discreet about a gift from God. And also one who receives such gifts should not be ungrateful; even if one doesn't have enough of them, or if they are not as one would wish, one shouldn't

Hora pensiamo che çiò che lui feçe, il fece a nostro amaistramento et ancho per asconderse dal dimonio. [f. 29v] O anima che ricevi il beneficio della consolatione, non essere ingrata et non te gloriare sopra di colui a chi Dio non li dae. Et cului che non riceve consolatione da Dio non si smarisca et non habi invidia a cului che le riceve, imperò che alcune volte per le molte consolatione l'huomo dà de gran scapuçi, et specialmente coloro che non sano occultare il dono de Dio. Et ancho colui che le riceve non debe essere ingrato, avegna che non le habi a sua posta et al suo volere non debe però mormorare. Et questo dico io, imperciò che l'angelo revellò tute queste cose pur a Ioseph et non alla madre, con çiò sia cosa che Ioseph nel conspecto de Dio fosse minore de lei. Et anche quello il qualle era sì grande amico de Dio non havea queste cotal revellatione se non in sono.

Ancora Dio permette molte volte agli soi amici de grande tribulatione. Or non dovea essere [f. 30r] questa grande tribulatione alla madre et a Ioseph, quando intesero che Iesù vegniva cercato per essere morto? Io penso che non podevano ricevere in questo mondo la maçore. Unde erano alora in tanta tribulatione che, avegna che loro sapesse che lui era vero figliolo de Dio, niente di meno podévasse la lor sensualitade conturbare et dire: «O signore Dio, voi seti omnipotente! Che bisogno fa che noi scampiamo questo vostro figliolo in Egipto? Non potete voi difendere da Herodes?».

Tute queste cose potevano dare a loro tribulatione. Prima, però che loro andavano in contrade straniere et in paese lontano et per vie molto aspere. La secunda, che non erano aconçi a caminare, sì perché la madre era çovene et havea il puto picolo et Ioseph era vechio, et etiamdio però che er[a]no poveri. Tute queste cose sono de grande tribulatione. O anima che sei tribulata, ricòrdate de Iesù [f. 30v] et della madre sua, et non credere che 'l signore Dio doni a te quel privilegio il qualle non ha voluto dare alla madre sua, neanche a lui! Considera ancho la benignitade et humilitade del nostro Maestro, che lui volse essere perseguitato; et etiandio per darci exempio volse dare luocho al furore de Herodes, con çiò sia cosa che in uno momento lui il potesse occidere, non volse el Signore nostro rendere mal per male. Volse darci exempio contra l'ira, et anche ci dà exempio de non contrastare a' nostri maçori et a coloro che ne riprende et castiga. Et ancho ne dà exempio come çi dobiamo portare inverso coloro che ne perseguita: de non fare vendeta contra di loro, ma pacientemente sostenire et dare luocho al suo furore, et più,[44] che anche pregiamo Dio per loro, secundo che lui çe amaistra nel evançelio.

44. MS <che> piu

grumble. And I say this because the angel revealed all of these things only to Joseph, and not to the mother, even though Joseph was inferior to her in the eyes of God. And also, even he, who was such a great friend of God, only had this revelation in a dream.

So God often permits great tribulations, even to his friends. Now, wouldn't this have been a great tribulation to the mother and to Joseph, when they understood that Jesus was being sought out to be killed? I think that it would be impossible to receive a greater trial in this world. They were in such tribulation that even though they knew that he was the true Son of God, nevertheless their strong feelings must have moved them to distress, causing them to say, "O Lord God, you who are all powerful, what need is there for us to flee with your son to Egypt? Are you powerless to protect him from Herod?"

All these things could cause them discomfort. First, they went to an unfamiliar country, in a distant place, and travelled by difficult routes. Second, they were not prepared to travel like this, because the mother was young and had a young infant, and Joseph was old, and also because they were poor. All these things were such a trial. O soul who is troubled, call to mind Jesus and his mother, and don't believe that the Lord God would give you a privilege that he did not wish to give to his mother or to himself! Contemplate, too, the benevolence and humility of our Master, how he wished to be persecuted; and also, to give us an example, he wished to submit to Herod's anger; for he could have killed Herod in an instant, yet Our Lord did not wish to render evil for evil. He wished to give us an example against anger; and here he also gives us an example not to oppose our superiors, or anyone who reprimands or castigates us. And also he gives us an example of how we should act towards one who persecutes us: not to take revenge but patiently to bear up and endure their fury, and even that we should pray to God for them, according to what he teaches us in the gospels.

The Creator flees, then, before the face of his creature. Have compassion on this little group, and especially on this baby, who was carried along such rough roads and by such a long route; imagine whether these were great afflictions! And it is said that they went through the desert where the sons of Israel had been, and it took them two months to travel a road that a courier could have covered in twelve days.[42] Imagine, then, the hardships that they endured through such a long journey: hunger and thirst and poor sleep. Now have compassion on them, for the Lord made his mother and that elderly man bear all of this hardship for your salvation! So it

Fuçe adonque il Creatore dalla faça della creatura. Ha[f. 31r]bi compassione a quella compagnia, e spetialmente a quel bambolino, el qual fi portado per sì aspere vie et per sì longo camino; pensa se queste era cose de grande afflictione! Et dicesse ch'eli andono per el deserto nel qualle stete gli figlioli de Israel, et steteno nel camino doi mesi la qualle era via de correre in dodece çornate. Pensa adonque la faticha ch'eli sostenero per sì longo viaço: fame et sete et male dormire. Or habi compassione a lloro, imperò che tuta questa fadicha fece il Signore portare alla madre sua et a quel vechio per tua salute! Adonque non çi dè parere grave a fare penetentia per noi, quando per noi è durata tanta faticha[45] da altrui, et specia[l]mente da così facte persone come è il Figliolo de Dio et de la madre sua et de quello buono vechio sancto Ioseph.

De quelle cose ch'egli incorsero per la via dirone solamente queste, che repossandose una volta la madre soto uno arboro de [f. 31v] datoli, et habi[a]nd[o][46] la Verçene Maria fame, per comandamento del fançullo la palma se piegò in terra et poi se driçoe. Et habiando Ioseph sete, per comandamento de miser Iesù naque ivi una bella fontana. Qui se poria introdure molti altri miracoli, ma per non essere tropo longo paserò oltra.

Et quando introno in Egypto, tuti quelli idoli de Egypto se speçarono et ruinarono, secundo che fu propheticato per Ysaia propheta. Et çonçendo lo[r]o[47] a una citade chiamata Onipoli, et ivi se catarono una casa aficto perfina che l'angelo li annunciò[48] ch'eli dovessero tornare in terra de Israel.

## Come la Madona tornò de Egypto in Naçareth. Capitolo nono.

Or morto che fu Herodes, apparse l'angelo in sonno a Ioseph et disseli: «Tolgi il puto et la madre sua et ritorna in Israel, però ch'el'è morto colui che cercava el puto». Et elevandose Ioseph, tolse il fançullo e lla madre sua et ritornorono in la terra de Israel. Et quando [f. 32r] çonseno apresso a Ierusalem, intendando che Archelao regnava in Iudea in luocho del padre suo, temeteno de intrare in Ierusalem. Et ammonidi in sono,

45. MS <d>faticha
46. MS habīd
47. MS lolo
48. MS annunciono

should not seem hard for us to do penance when such trials were endured for us by others, especially by such people as the Son of God and his mother and that venerable old man Saint Joseph.

Of those things that happened to them along the way, I will speak only of these.[43] Once the mother was resting under a date palm. And the Virgin Mary was hungry, and by the commandment of the child the palm bent down to the earth and then straightened up. And when Joseph was thirsty, by the commandment of Lord Jesus a lovely spring appeared there. Here it would be possible to introduce many other miracles, but in order not to take too long I will pass over them.

And as soon as they entered Egypt, all the idols of Egypt broke apart and were destroyed, according to what was prophesied by Isaiah the prophet.[44] And they reached a city called Onipoli, and they lived in a rented house there until the angel announced that they should return to the land of Israel.[45]

## Chapter 9. How Our Lady returned from Egypt to Nazareth.

Now when Herod had died, the angel appeared in a dream to Joseph and said to him, "Take the child and his mother and return to Israel, because the one who sought the infant has died." And Joseph rose and took the child and his mother and they returned to the land of Israel. And when they approached Jerusalem, hearing that Archelaus reigned in Judea in the place of his father, they were afraid to enter Jerusalem. And warned in a dream, they went to Galilee, and they settled in the city of Nazareth. And in this way the words of the prophet were fulfilled: "He shall be called a Nazarene."[46]

Now we know, as it is said above, that God gives tribulations and consolations little by little and not always at the same time, according to

andono nella parte de Galilea et habitarono in la citade de Naçareth, açò ch'el se adimpisse quello che fo decto per el propheta: «Lui sera chiamato Naçareno».

Or vedemo noi, come è decto di sopra, che Dio dà le tribulatione et le consolatione a pocho a pocho, et non tute do' a una volta, sì come desidera. Et di questo tu te ne pòi avedere per questi doi modi, perché[49] in doe volte li disse l'angelo dove el dovesse andare. Et dìcesse per el sponitore che questo fa Dio perché per spessa visitatione se fa la persona più certa. Ora siamone cognoscenti, però che Dio fa sempre[50] dalla sua parte quello che più utile per noi.

Or stiamo sopra il tornare che fece miser Iesù de Egypto. Et che torni in Egypto per visitare il fançullo. Et se tu 'l trovassi [f. 32v] nella via, ch'el zucasse[51] come fanno li puti, fà che ti ingenochi dinançi a lui et basali gli piedi. Et alora elgi te dirà: «Noi habiamo licencia de ritornare a casa et dobiamoçi partire diman, sì che a bona hora sei venuto, imperò che tornerai cum noi indrieto». Et alora fà che tu respondi che de questo sei molto contento et non desideri altro se non de seguitare lui in ogni luocho che lui va. Or vane et dilèctate cum lui in questi tal parlari; e çà io te ho decto che a pensare de queste cose fantolinesche in humilitade molto çovano a conducere a magiore stato nella via del spirito.

Or fà, quando serai denançi alla madre, che te ingenochi et cum grande riverentia saluti lei et Ioseph, et ripòsate cum loro perfina da matina. Et la matina vederai vegnire alcune bone done le qualle, per il buono exempio et conversatione che hano habuto da lei, vengono per acompagnare la Dona Nostra fuori [f. 33r] della citade. Et il simel feceno alquanti buoni homeni. Imperò che loro l'aveano decto per la vesina[n]ça, imperò che non era convenevole che loro se partisse cusì subito sança far sapere a la vessinança. Ma questo non feceno quando fuçitero in Egipto però che temevano la morte del puto.

Or partisse la Dona Nostra de Onipoli dove era stata. Et Ioseph se mise andare inançi cum alquanti buoni homeni, et la Dona Nostra li seguitava cum el suo dolcissimo figliolo a mano, et talhora se 'l mandava dinançi. Et quando furono fuori della citade, Ioseph ritene qui li suoi amici et acombiatosi da loro, et cusì feçe la Vergene Maria. Alora uno de quelli

49. MS *prima perche*
50. MS *semp(er)*
51. MS *zuçasse*

what he sees fit. And you may see this for yourself in two ways, because the angel told them twice where they should go. And as the commentator says, God did this because a person becomes more certain through frequent visitations. Now, let's keep this in mind, because God always does his part to give us what will be most useful for us.

Now we have come to the return of the Lord Jesus from Egypt. So go ahead and return to Egypt to visit the boy. And if you find him in the road, playing as children do, kneel before him and kiss his feet. And then he will say to you, "We have permission to return home and we must leave tomorrow, so you've come at a good time, because you can return with us, following behind." And then be sure to respond that you are very glad about this and desire nothing else except to follow him wherever he goes.[47] Now go ahead and enjoy talking with him like this; as I have already told you, to imagine these childish things with humility helps very much to lead to a higher level in the way of the spirit.

Now when you are before the mother, be sure to bow and greet her and Joseph with great reverence, and rest with them until morning. And in the morning you will see some good women come, who, because of the good example Our Lady had set and the time they had spent with her, wish to accompany her out of the city. And certain good men did the same. For they had announced their departure in the neighborhood, since it was not fitting for them to leave suddenly, without making their departure known to the neighbors. But they did not do this when they fled into Egypt because they feared the death of the child.

Then Our Lady left Onipoli where she had been. And Joseph went ahead, with some of the good men, and Our Lady followed him, taking her most sweet son by the hand, and sometimes she let him walk ahead of her. And when they were outside the city, Joseph paused and took leave of his friends, and the Virgin Mary did the same. And then one of those men, having compassion on the poverty of the child, called him over and gave him some coins, and some of the others did the same. And the women did likewise. And so the Master of Poverty humbly stretched out his hand and meekly received their alms.[48] O soul who has come to the service of God, reflect on this, and have compassion on Our Lord, who, to teach you the way to heaven, wished to choose such strict poverty! Strive, then, to follow him!

And Joseph nodded politely, and Our Lady too, and they took their leave. Now you go with them, and take the donkey by the halter and be

huomeni, habiando compassione alla sua povertade, chiamò il fançullo
Iesù et detteli alquanti denari; et così fece alcuni delli altri, et ancho il
simel fecero le done. Et alora el Maestro de la Povertade humelmente
porse la mano et vergognosamente ricevete la [f. 33v] elimosina loro. O
anima la qualle sei venuta al serv[i]cio de Dio, pensa qui et habi compassione al tuo Signore, el qualle per insegnarti la via del cielo ha voluto eleçerse così streta povertade! Adonque sforçate de seguitarlo!

Et inclinando Ioseph il capo et la Dona Nostra partironsi. Or vàtene
cum loro, et fà che tu prendi l'asinello per la caveça et fà che tu lo meni
per la via buona, et Ioseph vegnirà drieto. Et così andando, fà che pensi
quante fadige il Re del cielo et della terra à voluto portare per te. Et fà che
dichi: «O Iesù dolcissimo, come tosto vui haveti començato a fatigarvi per
me, imperò bene fo prophetiçato de voi quando lo propheta disse: "Io sum
povero et in fatige et in miseria grande infina dalla mia çoventude". Vigo-
rosamente intrasti in le fatiche grandissime et in le afflictione del corpo.
Et havesti voi medesimo quasi in odio per lo nostro amore». Certo questa
faticha della qual hora par[f. 34r]lemo doveria haver bastato alla nostra
recomperatione.

Or se alcuna volta la Dona Nostra volesse desmontare per andare uno
puocho a piedi, fà che tu tegni il fançullo Iesù açiò ch'el non cadesse. Et
se 'l fançullo Iesù volesse desmontare, fà che tu el pigli in braço et tienlo
fin che la madre vegna, et poi reverentemente il dà alla madre, imperò che
gran riposo era a lei quando la ricevea il figliolo in braço.

Et vegna[n]do passono per quel deserto dove stetero li figlioli de
Israel. Et quando hebeno passato il fiume Çordano, dìcesse che i trovono
sancto Çuane baptista, il qualle era çà andato al diserto a fare penite[n]tia.
Et [è] da pensare che sancto Çuane fece a loro grande honore et molta
festa. Et partendose da sancto Çuane se ne andono a casa de sancta Helisabeth et qui feceno grande festa della tornata de miser Iesù.

Et qui inteseno che Hercolao figliolo de Herodes regnava in pe del
padre suo in Iudea, et temeteno de andare in Ierusalem. [f. 34v] Et ammo-
nido in sono dall'ançelo, andorono in Galilea in la citade de Naçareth, imperò che fu detto per il propheta: «lui sera chiamato Naçareno».

Or çonti che furono in Naçareth, se acatono stancia et stetero cum
molta povertade. Et sapiendo le sorelle della Dona Nostra che lei era venuta, andarono a visitarla, et così feceno tuti li parenti della Dona Nostra,
et anche quelli de Ioseph, et ivi fecero grande festa della loro tornata. Et fo
la revocation de miser Iesù de Egipto il çorno drieto la Epiphania.

sure to lead it the right way, and Joseph will walk behind. And walking along like this, imagine what great hardships the King of Heaven and Earth wished to bear for you! And say, "O most sweet Jesus, how soon it was that you began to suffer for me! How right the prophet was when he foretold this of you: 'I am poor and tired and in great misery from the time of my youth.' You entered without hesitation into the greatest hardships and afflictions of the body. It is as if you even despised yourself for love of us." Clearly, this hardship of which we are now speaking should have been enough to accomplish our redemption!

Now, if Our Lady wants to dismount sometimes to go a little on foot, be sure to hold the child Jesus so he doesn't fall.[49] And if the child Jesus wants to get down, take him in your arms and hold him until his mother comes, and then reverently give him to his mother, because it is a great comfort to her when she receives her son in her arms.

And they passed through the desert where the sons of Israel had been. And when they passed the Jordan River, it is said that they encountered Saint John the Baptist, who had already gone to the desert to do penance.[50] And it can be imagined that Saint John did them great honor and welcomed them joyfully. And leaving Saint John, they went to the house of Saint Elizabeth, and they held a great celebration there over the return of Lord Jesus.

And then they heard that Archelaus, son of Herod, reigned in place of his father in Judea, and they were afraid to go to Jerusalem. And warned in a dream by the angel, they went to Galilee, to the city of Nazareth, because it was said by the prophet: "He will be called a Nazarene."[51]

Now when they had come to Nazareth, they found lodgings and settled there in great poverty. And hearing that Our Lady had returned, her sisters went to visit her, and so did all the relatives of Our Lady, and those of Joseph too, and they held a great celebration over their return. And the date of the return of Lord Jesus from Egypt was the day after the Epiphany.

From this time until he was twelve years old, nothing is recorded about what Lord Jesus did. I have learned, and it can be believed, that the well where Lord Jesus went to fetch water for his mother can still be seen.[52] Therefore we know that the Lord humbly performed services such as this, to set an example for us.

Now we have brought the child Jesus back from Egypt, and you have seen what great deprivation and hardship he wished to bear for you up to

Da questo tempo perfin a anni dodece, non se leçe che miser Iesù facesse alcuna cosa. Ho inteso, et è ancho da credere, che anchora si vede il
poço al qualle miser Iesù andava a tuore dell'aqua alla madre; unde el Signore, per nostro exempio, facea humelmente questi cotal servicii.

Or habiamo remenato il fançullo Iesù de Egypto, et hai visto quanta
necessitade et pena infina hora lui ha voluto portare [f. 35r] per te. Et pertanto priegalo ch'el te doni desiderio et grande patire anche ti per lui!

*Come el fançullo miser Iesù rimase in Ierusalem.*
*Capitolo decimo.*

Stando miser Iesù Cristo figliolo de Dio vivo in etade de anni dodece,
si andoe in Ierusalem cum la gloriosa Verçene Maria madre sua et cum Ioseph per honorare la festa del suo Padre, la qual festa durava çorni sette
secundo la consuetudine della festa. Et finiti li çorni, retornò[52] la Vergene
gloriosa in Naçareth et miser Iesù romase in Ierusalem.

Fà che tu attendi qui diligentemente, imperò che qui porai imparare
come se debe trovare miser Iesù quando lo hai perso. Or compiuta la festa
et tornando loro per diverse vie, pensava la Dona nostra ch'el puto fosse
andato cum Ioseph, et Ioseph pensava ch'el fosse cum la Dona nostra. Et
in questo modo perseno miser Iesù; pensa! Or çonçendo la sera insieme,
la Madona, non vedendo miser Iesù, pensa [f. 35v] come lei rimase! Et dimandando a Ioseph: «Or dov'è il mio figliolo?», et lui rispuose: «Non è
llo venuto cum voi?»

Alora la Vergene gloriosa, commossa et de grandissimo dolore piançendo, dese: «Hora ben vedo che ho mal guardato il mio figliolo!». Et in-
continente se mosse la Vergene Maria et andavalo cercando per gli alberghi et dimandava a parenti et amici et a li[53] vicini che erano venuti dalla
festa: «Haveresti voi visto el figliolo mio Iesù?» Et questo diceva cum una
mente tanto afflicta et piena de dolore che a pena fideva intesa. Et così, per
tuta quella sera, honestamente acompagnata da Ioseph, andorono cercando il suo dolcissimo figliolo Iesù. Or alla fine non trovandolo, si ritornorono a lo albergo, pia[n]çendo et lamenta[n]dose. Et non era modo alcuno che la podesse consolare.

52. MS *(et) retorno*
53. MS *li* in margin

this point. And for so much, pray that he will give you the desire to suffer much for him too!

## *Chapter 10. How the child Lord Jesus remained in Jerusalem.*

When the child Jesus, Son of the Living God, was twelve years old, he went to Jerusalem with the glorious Virgin Mary, his mother, and with Joseph, to observe the feast of his Father, which lasted seven days according to the custom of that feast. And when the feast days were over, the glorious Virgin returned to Nazareth and Lord Jesus remained in Jerusalem.

Be sure to dwell on this scene with loving attention, because here you may learn how you should find Lord Jesus when you have lost him. Now when the feast was finished and they were returning by different routes, Our Lady thought that the child was with Joseph, and Joseph thought that he was with Our Lady. And in this way Lord Jesus was lost; imagine! Now when they arrived in the evening, and Our Lady did not see Lord Jesus, imagine how she felt! And she asked Joseph, "Now, where is my son?" And he replied, "Didn't he come with you?"

Then the glorious Virgin, distraught and weeping with great anguish, said, "Now I see well that I have failed to take care of my son!" And immediately the Virgin Mary arose and went looking for him in the inns. And she asked relatives and friends and neighbors who had come to the feast, "Have you seen my son Jesus?" And she said this with a mind so afflicted and full of grief that she was barely understood. And she went searching for her most sweet son Jesus like this for the whole evening, accompanied faithfully by Joseph. And failing to find him in the end, they returned to the inn, weeping and lamenting. And there was no way that they could be consoled.

Now you see what it is to lose the Lord Jesus. Imagine what it is like to lose the spouse of the soul, and what anguish the glorious Virgin Mary endured, having lost Lord Jesus! Have compassion on her, then, because she was in the deepest distress, and up to this point she had never experienced

Or vedi che è a perdere miser Iesù. Poni ben mente çiò che è a perdere
lo sposo de l'anima—et quanto dolore hebe la gloriosa Vergene Maria per
havere perso [f. 36r] miser Iesù! Hàbili adonque compassione, imperò
ch'ela era in grandissima amaritudine, et infina alhora lei non era stata in
tanta tribulatione. Or fà che façi anche tu il somelgiante quando perdi
miser Iesù per tua negligentia, et fà che no cessi de piançere et de andarlo
cercando! Donque non se turbiamo se il Signore ne dà delle tribulatione,
con çiò sia cosa che lui volse andare per la via delle tribulatione, né etiandio le volse sparagnare a colei ch'el parturì, et à voluto tuti li sui sancti
menare per quella via;[54] et imperò godi quando hai tribulatione!

Or finalmente non trovandolo, recorse alle arme della[55] oratione et
della humilitade. Et tuta quella nocte stete in pianto grandissimo. Et disse:
«O Dio Padre omnipotente, a voi piaqua de consolarme et de ricevere la
oratione mia. Piàquave, Padre potentissimo, di darme el vostro figliolo;
ecco che io l'ò perduto et no[n] so dove el sia! O Padre de [f. 36v] misericordia, rendetimelo et tolleti da mi questa amaritudine, et insegnatime el
figliolo mio! Vedete la afflictione del mio cuore et non guardate ala mia
negligentia, però che incautamente me sono portata. Ma voi, Padre, che
sete benigno,[56] priego la misericordia vostra che rendete a me il figliolo
mio, però che io non posso vivere sença lui».

Et tuta via pia[n]çendo dicea: «O figliolo mio dolcissimo, dove se' tu,
et che è di te, et cum chi albergi tu? Or saresti tornato in cielo al Padre
tuo? Io so bene che sei Dio vero et fiolo de Dio, ma come l'averistù facto,
che tu non me lo havessi detto? Or saresti tu retenuto da qualche persona
maliciosamente? Io so bene che tu sei veramente huomo nato di me, tua
ancilla; et un'altra volta te portai in Egypto però che Herodes te andava
cercando per occiderte. Lo Padre tuo si te guarda da male, figliolo mio,
dìme dove sei et io vegnerò a te, overo retorni [f. 37r] tu a me! Or perdona
a me per questa volta, ch'el non me incontrerà più che io te guardi così ne-
gligentemente. Forsi te ho io facta alcuna offesa, figliolo mio, per la qualle
tu fosti partito da me?[57] O figliolo mio, non indusiare de ritornare a me,
imperò che io non steti mai sença te da l'hora in qua che io te concepiti nel
ventre. Et hora sum sença te: tu sei la mia sperança, et la mia vita, et ogni

---

54. MS p(er)<la> via q(ue)la, with superscript b above via and an a above
q(ue)la
55. MS del| <d>la
56. MS be<g>nigno
57. MS da da

such tribulation. Now when you lose Lord Jesus through your negligence, you should strive to do the same; do not cease weeping, and keep searching for him! It should not be surprising to us, then, if the Lord gives us tribulation, since he himself wished to travel the road of tribulation. And he did not even wish to spare the one who had given birth to him; and he wished to lead all of his saints by this road. So rejoice, then, when you have tribulation!

Now, not finding him in the end, she took up the arms of prayer and humility. And for the whole night she continued lamenting bitterly. And she said, "O almighty God the Father, I ask that you give me consolation and hear my prayers. It pleased you, most powerful Father, to give me your son—and look, now, I have lost him, and I do not know where he is! O Father of mercy, send him back to me, and take this bitter sorrow from me, and let me see my son again. See the affliction of my heart, and forgive my negligence, for I have been so careless. But you, Father, who are benevolent, I ask that in your mercy you return my son to me, because I cannot live without him."

And weeping all the while, she said, "O my most sweet son, where are you, and who is with you, and with whom do you stay? Or have you returned to heaven to your Father? I know well that you are true God and Son of God, but how could you have left me like this, without telling me? Or have you been captured maliciously by someone? I know well that you are truly man, born of me, your handmaid; and I once carried you into Egypt because Herod was searching for you to kill you. If your Father is keeping you from harm, my son, tell me where you are, and I will come to you—or return to me! Now pardon me this time, and I will never again be so negligent in your care and keeping. Perhaps I have done you some offense, my son, for which you have parted from me? O my son, don't delay in returning to me, because I have never been without you from the moment I conceived you in my womb. And now I am without you: you who are my hope, and my life, and the source of all goodness. And I cannot live without you! Give me a sign, then, my son, and tell me where you are, so I can find you."

With these and similar words the mother expressed her anguish, lamenting her negligence all night long for love of her most sweet son. And early in the morning she left the inn and went searching for her son everywhere and in various places, because he could have come from Jerusalem by many different routes, and she asked all the relatives and friends that she met.[53] And failing to find anyone who could tell her anything about

mio bene. Et sança te non posso io stare! Insegnami donque, figliolo mio, et dìme dove tu sei, açiò che io te possi ritrovare».

Di queste et simigliante parole la madre se angustiava et affligevasse tuta la nocte per amore del suo dolcissimo figliolo. Et quando fo la matina per tempo, lei se partite da l'albergo et andò cercando del suo figliolo per tuto et in diversi luochi, però che el se podeva venire de Ierusalem per più vie, et dimandava a tuti li parenti et amici che lei trovava. Et non trovando niuno che glie [f. 37v] sapesse dire alcuna cosa, quasi sança alcuna sperança parea che la spassemasse de dolore et non se podea consolare.

Et così tribulata andò il terço çorno in Ierusalem, et trovolo nel tempio in meço degli dotori della leçe. Alora la madre, veçandolo, fu tuta ralegrata et inçenochiosse et rendete gratie a Dio, et il fançullo Iesù, come la vide, levosse et lassò stare li dotori et vene ala madre, et lei lo ricevete nelle braçe et strenselo a si, et cum grande alegreça et dolceça tuto lo basiava. Et così facendo, uno pocho se riposava cum lui. Et era sì grandissima la alegreça et la tenereça che lei havea de haverlo trovato che lei non li podea parlare.

Ma pure li disse: «Che è questo che hai facto a noi? Ecco io dolente et il padre tuo te andamo cercando!».

Et miser Iesù rispuose: «Perché me andate voi cercando? Non sapeti voi ch'el me conviene essere nelle cose del Padre mio?»

Ma elgi non intesero quel parlare, et la madre disse: «Fi[f. 38r]gl[i]olo mio, io volio che noi retorniamo a casa».

Rispuose il Signore nostro: «Io voglio quello che piace a voi».

Alora tornarono in Naçareth, et fu suçeto a loro.

Hora hai veçuto quanta tribulatione et afflictione have la gloriosa Verçene Maria per havere perso miser Iesù. El simele dè fare l'anima che ha perso il dilecto sposo suo Cristo Iesù benedecto.

Or dove pensi tu che miser Iesù mançasse o dormisse questi tre çorni? Sapi, anima, che colui che ha facto il cielo et la terra andava a mançare et dormire a lo hospedale. Andava adonque miser Iesù picholino a domandare[58] de albergare cum li poveri, et non andò a casa de richi per stare ben asiado. O Maestro di povertade! Mançava adunche il Signore del mondo cum li poveri.

Riguardalo anchora, come lui sta assentado in meço de li doctori cum uno volto benigno et savio, et riverentemente ascoltava et dima[n]davali

58. MS <alberg>

him, she began to lose hope. And she was overcome by spasms of grief and could not be consoled.

And on the third day, full of anguish like this, she went to Jerusalem, and she found him in the temple in the midst of doctors of the law. And as soon as she saw him, the mother was filled with joy, and she fell to her knees and gave thanks to God. And when the child Jesus saw her, he stood up and left the doctors and went to the mother. And she received him in her arms and clasped him to her, and with great happiness and tenderness she kissed him. And she rested with him like this for a little while. And she was so overcome by the joy and tenderness she felt at having found him that she could not speak.

But at last she said to him, "What have you done to us? Look at me, so full of sorrow, and your father: we have been searching for you!"

And Lord Jesus replied, "Why have you been looking for me? Didn't you know that I must be going about my Father's business?" But no one understood these words.

And the mother said, "My son, I want us to return home."

Our Lord replied, "I want what pleases you."[54]

And so they returned to Nazareth, and he remained subject to them.

Now you have seen what tribulations and afflictions the glorious Virgin Mary suffered, having lost Lord Jesus. And the same will happen to the soul who has lost her beloved spouse blessed Jesus Christ.

Now, where do you think the Lord Jesus ate or slept those three days?[55] Know, soul, that he who made heaven and earth went to eat and sleep at a hostel. The little Lord Jesus went, then, to ask for shelter with the poor, and he did not go to the house of the rich to stay in comfort. O Master of Poverty! The Lord of the World, then, ate with the poor.

Watch him again, how he remains seated among the doctors of the law with a gentle and wise countenance, reverently listening and asking questions as though he knew nothing. And he did this through humility, for he did not wish to embarrass them through his wise and marvelous responses, since he was just a boy.

And here you may see three very notable things. The first is this, that if one wishes to be close to God, it is necessary not to stay with relatives; and Lord Jesus Christ gives us an example of this, because he left his mother when he wished to attend to the works of his Father.[56] The second is that whoever lives the spiritual life should not be surprised if he sometimes feels hard and dry in his soul, that is, if he seems to have no feeling of devotion and seems to be abandoned by God, since this very thing happened

sì come non sapesse niente. Et questo facea per [f. 38v] humilitade, perché non se vergognassero delle sue savie et maravegliose resposte però che lui era garçone.

Et qui tu poi vedere tre cose molto notabile. La prima si è questa, che chi se vole acostare a Dio conviene che non conversi cum li parenti;[59] et de questo ne dà exempio miser Iesù Cristo, imperò che lui abandonò la madre quando lui volse attendere alle opere del Padre suo. La secunda si è che chiunque vive spiritualmente non se meravegli se alcuna volta rimane cum la mente dura et suta, çioè che non li pare haver sentimento di devotione et parli essere abandonato da Dio, con çiò sia cossa che questo medemo intravegnisse hora alla madre de Dio. Adonca non te smarire et non dive[n]tare pigro in la mente tua, ma diligentemente cerca de lui per continuo exercitio[60] de oratione et de pianto, et in questo modo, humiliandote nel suo conspecto, sì 'l troverai sedere fra li doctori. [f. 39r] La terça si è che noi non dobiamo essere de proprio senno, né di propria voluntade, con çiò sia cossa che miser Iesù Cristo disse alla madre sua ch'el convenia attendere alle opere del Padre suo, et poi mutoe la voluntade et seguitò la voluntade della madre sua et andò cum loro in Naçareth et fu suçeto a loro. Chi adunque vole seguitare Cristo Iesù fàçassi subiecto et negi la propria voluntade et perseveri cum humilitade infina alla morte.

*Come il Signore nostro stette suçeto alla madre sua et a Ioseph da dodece anni perfina alli trenta, et delle cose che se puote pensare ch'el fesse in questo tempo, ben ch'el non se trova per alcuna scriptura che lui facesse alcuna cosa. Capitolo xi°.*[61]

Tornato che fu il fançullo Iesù in Naçareth cum la madre sua, stava subieto a loro perfina anni trenta, et poi començò a manifestarse al mondo. Or che pensaremo adonque che miser Iesù facesse dalli anni .xii. per fina alli trenta? Pare ch'el non si trova nella scriptura [f. 39v] ch'el façesse alcuna cosa. Or stete aduncha miser Iesù cotanto tempo occioso,

59. MS *cum li parenti <quando el vole attendere alle> et*
60. MS *exerticio*
61. MS *Capitol. xii.*

to the mother of God. So do not be dismayed or become spiritually lazy, but seek him intently through the continuous exercise of prayer and lamentation; and in this way, humbling yourself in his sight, you will find him sitting among the doctors. The third is that we should not be acting out of our own wisdom nor of our own will; for Lord Jesus Christ said to his mother that it was necessary to attend to the works of his Father, and then he changed his will and followed the will of his mother and went with them to Nazareth and remained subject to them.[57] Whoever wishes to follow Jesus Christ, then, must make himself obedient to him, and deny his own will, and persevere with humility even unto death.

*Chapter 11. How Our Lord remained subject to his mother and to Joseph from the time he was twelve years old until thirty; and of the things that you may imagine that he did during this time, even though it is not found in any of the scriptures that he did anything.*

When the child Jesus returned to Nazareth with his mother, he remained subject to them until he was thirty, and then he began to reveal himself to the world. Now what, then, can we imagine that Lord Jesus did from the age of twelve until thirty? It seems that it is not found in scripture that he did anything. Now, was the Lord Jesus so lazy for all this time that he didn't do anything worth telling or writing about—he who is our example and our light, and in whom is the perfection of all the virtues? And if he did something, why was it not written about, as his other deeds were recorded? All in all it seems a cause for marvel.

ch'el non façesse nulla la qualle cosa fusse degna de recitare o di scrivere—
lo qualle è[62] nostro exempio et nostra luce et in cui è la perfetione de tute le
vertude? Ma se lui havesse facto alcuna cosa, perché non sarebe lo scripto
come sono scripti gli altri facti suoi? Al tuto pare cosa da marevegliarse.

Ma poni ben mente qui, et porai veder manifestamente che Cristo
Iesù nostro Salvatore, non façendo nulla, fece grande cose; imperò che
tuti li facti de miser Iesù non sono sança grande providentia et tute sono
sancti et vertuosi. Adunca quel summo Maestro il qualle dovea per alcuno
tempo insegnare le vertude et mostrare la via che mena a vita eterna si començò infino da picolino a fare opere vertuose, ma in uno modo marave-
glioso et non cognosuto.

Dicesse che da qui in drieto mai il nostro Signore non fu veduto ri-
dere, et non fo più aldito dire [f. 40r] overo fare alcuna cosa in publico,
rendendose inutile nel conspecto della çente et dispetto del populo. Et so-
traçevasse dalle compagnie et dalle conversatione delle çente, et andava
alla sinagoga et orava molto, et sempre se metea nello più vile luocho che
fusse. Et poi tornava a casa et aiutava la madre. Et andava per la via infra
le turbe, sì come non trovasse persona, in tanto se tenia vile.

Or meraveglàvasse la çente che vedea così belissimo çovene non fare
cosa alguna, imperçiò che aspetavano che lui façesse grande cose, però che
siando lui fançullo cresea in etade et in sapientia dinanci a Dio et delli huomeni. Et ora, cresendo de anno in anno, non facea alcuna operatione che
paresse che fosse degna de alcuna laude o vertude; et perçiò se marave-
gliava la çente et dicea, façendo beffe di lui: «Questo è dritamente uno
pane perduto et uno idiota e da niente et[63] [f. 40v] non inpara a leçere».

Et intanto se avilite che lui vene in proverbio della çente. Et questo fu
il modo del viver suo, rendendose vile et da nulla nel conspecto de
ogniuno. Et questo è quello che fo decto per lo propheta: «Io sum vermo
et non huomo, ma vituperio delli huomeni et dispregio delle çente».

Vedi adonque quello che facea. Pare a te ch'el façesse pocho? Parmi
che façesse assai! Tu dèi sapere che a Cristo Iesù non era bisogno che vin-
cesse se medesimo, né che lui se vilificasse; ma come buono Maestro,
volse prima fare et poi insegnare. Ma noi habiamo bene bisogno nelle nostre operatione vilificarse et riputarse da nulla. Et io reputo ch'el non è
cossa che sia cusì malagievole al humo a fare, come a vincerse si medemo,
et parmi che sia çonto ad altissimo grado colui che sa vincere sí medesimo

62. MS *(et)*
63. MS <dicea> *idiota e da niente (et)* <pare>

But meditate well on this, and you will be able to see plainly that Jesus Christ our Savior, while doing nothing, did great things; because all the deeds of Lord Jesus are not without great prudence, and all are holy and virtuous. So this great Master, who taught the virtues and showed us the way that leads to eternal life, began from the time he was little to do virtuous deeds, but in a marvelous and unexpected manner.

It is said that from this time on, Our Lord was never seen laughing, and he was never heard saying or doing anything in public, rendering him useless in the eyes of the people and considered worthless by the community.[58] And he withdrew from company and from associating with people, and he often went to the synagogue to pray, and he always put himself in the lowest place that there was.[59] And then he returned home and helped his mother. And he went through the streets among the crowd as if he considered himself more worthless than anyone.

Now the people marveled that they saw such a handsome youth do nothing, because they expected that he would do great things, since from the time he was a small child he had grown in age and wisdom before God and men. And then, growing from year to year, he didn't do any deeds that seemed to be worthy of any praise or virtue; and the people were astonished at this, and, making fun of him, they said, "This one is definitely *pane perduto*, and an idiot, and a slacker, and he hasn't learned to read."[60]

And he carried himself so humbly that he became a laughingstock among the people; and this was the way he lived, rendering himself worthless and of no value in the eyes of everyone. And this is what had been foretold by the prophet: "I am a worm, and not a man, but despised of men and considered worthless by the people."[61]

You see, then, what he did. Does it seem to you to be little? It seems to me that he did much! You should know that for Jesus Christ, there was no need to achieve mastery over himself, nor to vilify himself; but like a good master, he wished first to act and then to teach. But we need very much to humble ourselves and to consider ourselves as nothing. And I think that there is nothing that is more challenging for a person to do than to achieve mastery over himself. And it seems to me that the one who has reached the highest level is the one who knows how to conquer himself, and to rule over pride, and to restrain his proud and restive flesh; and to consider all his longing and desire to be base and lowly, as if it is the most vile thing and of no value: this seems to me a greater accomplishment than conquering a city. And as Solomon says, "The patient man is better than the strong man; and better is he who is lord of his soul than the con-

et signoriçare la superba et recalçitrante sua car[f. 41r]ne, et che tuto il suo chuore et desiderio sia essere riputato vile et dispectoso et dispregiato sì come cosa vilissima et da niente: maçor cosa me pare questa che vincere citade. Et secundo che dice Salamone: «Meglio è l'huomo paciente che l'huomo forte, et quello che signoriça l'animo suo del vincitore della citade». Adonque infina a tanto che tu non pervegni a questo grado, non ti parà havere facto alcuna cosa, imperò secundo che dice il Salvatore nostro, che etiandio quando noi haveremo bene facto ogni cosa siamo servi inuteli, imperò che tuto il nostro adoperare viene di sopra. Et ancho che hai tu che tu non habi riceputo? Adonque perfina che non siamo pervenuti a questo grado non siamo ancora in veritade; ançi semo et andemo in vanitade. Et questo ne monstra manifestamente lo Apostolo là dove el dice: «Chi si pensa essere alcuna cosa et è nulla, ingana se medesimo». [f. 41v]

Ma se tu mi dimandi perché se avillì così forte miser Iesù Cristo, io te rispondo che lui se avillite per confondere la superbia del mondo et per monstrarne la via la qualle ne mena a vita eterna, imperciò che non è altra via per la qualle noi se posiamo conçunçere cum lui salvo questa. Imposibile è, se l'huomo non se humilia per qualche modo, ch'el se conçunça cum Dio. Unde se noi habiamo desiderio di conçun[çe]rne[64] cum miser Iesù Cristo, conviene che noi seguitiamo li suoi exemplii et che noi impariamo da lui a humiliarse, et non pensi il servo essere maçore del signore. Bruta cosa è che uno picolo vermisello, et che debe essere cibo de vermi, se lievi in superbia, con çiò sia cosa ch'el Re del cielo et della terra se humiliò per noi infino alla morte.

Et cusì façendo, miser Iesù fabrichò uno cortello de humilitade cum il qualle lui sconfisse il superbo adversario. El non se truova che miser Iesù usasse altro [f. 42r] cortello che quello della humilitade, specialmente nel tempo della Passione sua. Unde lo propheta se lamenta a Dio per lui et dice: «Tu li hai tolto lo adiutorio del suo coltello et non lo aiutasti nel tempo della bataglia». Imprima lui volse fare et poi insegnare, unde lui medemo dice: «Imparate da me, il qualle sono piatoso et mansueto et humile de cuore».

Profundosse adonque miser Iesù Cristo tanto nella humilitade che lui si fece riputare da nulla nel cospecto della çente, intanto che etiandio quando il començò a predicare et a fare miracoli et opere vertuose, si lo svilavano et faceano beffe di lui et diceano «Or non sapiamo noi che costui è figliolo de uno fabro?». Et così era schernito. Et per te il Signore et sposo tuo prese forma de servo.

64. MS *(con)çūrne*

queror of the city."⁶² So, until you reach this state, it will seem to you that
you have not done anything. But according to what our Savior says, even
when we have done everything well, we are useless servants, because all
our accomplishments come from above. For what do you have that you
have not received? So, until we have arrived at this level, we are not yet
living in truth; we are living and going along in vanity. And the apostle reveals this plainly to us, where he says, "He who considers himself to be
something and is nothing deceives himself."⁶³

But if you ask me why Lord Jesus Christ debased himself so completely, I will reply that he debased himself to counter and defeat the pride
of the world, and to show the way that leads to eternal life, because there
is no other way through which we may join him except like this.⁶⁴ If a person does not humble himself in this way, it is impossible for him to become close to God. So if we wish to unite with Lord Jesus Christ, it is necessary for us to follow his examples and to learn from him to humble
ourselves. And a servant should not imagine that he is greater than his lord.
It is an ugly thing if a tiny little worm that ought to be food for worms
raises itself up in pride, especially when the King of Heaven and Earth
humbled himself for us even unto death. And so, in this way, Lord Jesus
made a sword of humility with which he vanquished the proud adversary.
It is not recorded that Lord Jesus used any weapon other than that of humility, especially in the time of his Passion. And so the prophet laments to
God for him and says, "You have taken away the help of his sword, and
you did not help him in time of battle." He wished to practice before he
preached, and so he himself says, "Learn from me, I who am pitiable and
meek and humble of heart."

Therefore Lord Jesus Christ humbled himself so profoundly that he
made himself seem like nothing in the eyes of the people, so much so that
when he began to preach and to do miracles and virtuous works, they re-
viled him and made fun of him and said, "Now don't we know that he is
the son of a carpenter?" And he was mocked like this; and for you the
Lord and your spouse took the form of a servant.

Consider well all his deeds and words, and you will always see humility shining in him, even unto death, as he showed in the washing of the feet
of the disciples and then sustained through the pain of the cross. And when
he was gloriously resurrected, he called the disciples brothers. And after
the Ascension he said to Saint Paul, "Why do you persecute me?" O most
holy Humility, who even after he had ascended into heaven put himself in
the place of his servants! And on the Day of Judgment he will say, "Whatever you have done for the least of my brothers, you have done for me."

Considera bene tuti gli fati et decti suoi, et semper vederai risplendere in lui la humilitade—perfina alla morte, [f. 42v] sì come se manifesta in el lavare di piedi delli discipoli, et poi sostene la pena della croce. Et siando resuscitato glorioso, chiamò gli discipoli fratelli.[65] Et dapoi la Ascensione dissi a sancto Paulo «Perché me perseguiti?» O humilitade sanctissima, che siando montato in cielo se puose in persona delli suoi servi! Et nel Çorno del Iudicio dirà: «Quando voi sovenisti a uno de questi minimi mei fratelli, sovenisti a me».

Non sança casone hamoe questa povertade et humilitade. Sapea il Signore nostro che sì come la superbia è principio et radice de ogni male, così la humilitade è principio et fundamento de ogni bene; et sança questo fundamento indarno si fa ogni[66] edificatione. Unde non te confidare de verçinitade, né di sapientia, né di niuna altra vertude overo operatione se tu non hai la humilitade. Et se tu vòi aquistare questa vertude, conviene che tu seguiti il tuo Maestro miser Iesù [f. 43r] Cristo, il qualle te insegna per questo modo ad aquistare, çioe a vilificarse sì medemo[67] nelli ochi suoi et nelli altrui et per exercitarse[68] in humile operatione. Et secundo che dice sancto Bernardo, «Chi vuole la vertude della humilitade façia humile operatione, sì come chi vuole la pace conviene ch'el sia paciente, et chi vuole havere scientia conviene che prima impari. Quando adonque ti vedi humiliato, hàbilo per buono segno, imperò che l'è argumento che la gratia se approxima a te.»

Hora torniamo a vedere et considerare li acti et costumi della vita del nostro Signore miser Iesù Cristo, nostro spechio, sì come fu il nostro principale proponimento. Co[n]sidera hora questa famegliola benedeta sopra tute le altre, picolina ma molto excellente, la qualle vive poveramente et humelmente. Ioseph vechio guadagnava quello che lui podea de l'arte sua, et la Donna nostra guadagnava de cusire et de filare, et facea ancho delli [f. 43v] altri servigii de casa come era bisogno di fare, et tuto ciò lei era solicita alla oratione et alle vigilie. Convenia adonque alla Regina del cielo et della terra lavorare et fatigarse per vivere! Et anche miser Iesù Cristo la aiutava a fare della cose per casa. Et ora scovava la casa, ora lavava le scudelle, overo andava per aqua et facea delli altri servigii per non stare ocioso, et per questo modo lui se humiliava sì come lui dice nello evangelio: «Io sono venuto per servire et non per essere servito».

65. MS *fratelle*
66. MS *ogni* in margin
67. MS *medeno*
68. MS *exertitarse*

Not without reason did he love this poverty and humility. Our Lord knew that just as pride is the beginning and root of all evil, humility is the beginning and foundation of everything good; and without this foundation, no building can stand. So don't place your faith in virginity or wisdom or any other virtue or deeds if you don't have humility. And if you want to acquire this virtue, you must follow your Master Lord Jesus Christ, who teaches you to acquire it in this way, that is, to lower yourself in his eyes and the eyes of others and to practice humble deeds. And according to what Saint Bernard says, "Whoever wants the virtue of humility should perform humble deeds, just as whoever wants peace needs to be patient, and whoever desires wisdom needs to study first. When you see yourself humbled, then, take it as a good sign, because it is a sign that grace is coming to you."[65]

Now let's return to watching and contemplating the deeds and way of life of Our Lord Jesus Christ, our mirror, as this was our main subject. Imagine now this family, blessed over all others, small but most excellent, living poorly and humbly.[66] Old Joseph earned what he could from his craft. And Our Lady made a living by sewing and spinning, and she also did housework that needed to be done; and even with all that, she was conscientious about prayers and vigils. Thus it was necessary even for the Queen of Heaven and of Earth to work and to toil to make a living! And Lord Jesus Christ helped her to do things around the house. At one moment he would sweep the house, at another he would wash the dishes, and then he went to fetch water and did other tasks so he would not remain idle. And in this way he humbled himself, as he says in the gospel: "I have come to serve and not to be served."

Watch them again, how all three of them remain at one table. And when they have eaten, they rise from the table. Watch as the Lord Jesus clears the table. And then they talk a little about God, and each goes to their room, and they give themselves over to prayer, and then go to sleep. And Lord Jesus Christ rose sometimes and went to the synagogue until it seemed time to go home.[67] And in this way he persevered in humility for that long period when he lived with his mother.

O God, why did you afflict your innocent body like this? It should have been enough for you to spend one night as a pilgrim in this world in order to redeem humankind. But how well you have shown the tremendous love that you feel toward your little lost sheep that you must carry to heaven on your shoulders. You, my Lord, who are King of Kings and Lord of Lords, deigned to die for your servant, to make the servant lord. And also you have given to each according to his need, and you have

Reguardali ancora come stano tuti tre a una mensa, et quando hanno mançato si levano da mensa. Risguarda miser Iesù tuore via la mensa. Et poi parlano uno pocheto de Dio et vano cadauno alla camera sua et dàvasse alla oratione et poi andavano a dormire. Et levàvasse miser Iesù Cristo per tempo et andava alla sinagoga, infina che li parea hora de andare a casa. Et così perseverò in hu[f. 44r]militade per sì longo tempo ch'el stete cum la madre.

O Dio, perché affligevi così il vostro corpo innocente! Bene dovea bastare per una nocte a voi peregrinare in questo mondo[69] a ricomperatione della humana natura! Ma bene haveti monstrato il grandissimo amore che voi portate a questa vostra peccorela perduta, la qualle voi dovevi portare in cielo sopra le spalle vostre. Voi, Messere, che sette Re de gli Re et Signore delli Signori, ve haveti dignato di morire per lo servo per fare lo servo signore. Et etiandio havete dato a catuno secundo la sua necessitade, et per voi riservasti tanta povertade, viltade et aspreça, afflictione et faticha, vegiando, dormendo et façendo abstinentia in tuti gli costumi vostri per così longo tempo.

Adonca quelli che vano cercando la occiositade del corpo et le cose curiose et vane non hanno imparato nella scuola di questo Maestro, il qual [f. 44v] si amaistra cum exempli et cum parole ad amare povertade, humilitade et afflicione del corpo. Seguitiamo adonque questo cotalle Maestro, il qualle per insegnarçi la via della salute à voluto prendere forma humana. Or habiando il vivere et il vestimento secundo la convenevole necessitade di questi, siamo contenti, sì come dice lo apostolo, acostandose sempre alle vertude et sempre faciendo ogni nostra operatione per la via delle virtude.

Or hai visto come miser Iesù se facea riputare vile per insegnare a te la via del cielo.

*Come miser Iesù Cristo Signore nostro andò al fiume Çordano per farse baptiçare da sancto Ioanne. Capitolo duodecimo.*

Habiando miser Iesù compiuti anni vintinuove nelli qualli lui stete in tanta humilitade, et vegna[n]do il tempo suo, dise alla madre sua: «Oçimai

---

69. MS *peregrinare ī q(ue)sto mōdo voi* with a superscript *b* above the first and an *a* above the last word, indicating change of word order

reserved for yourself so much poverty, lowliness, and bitter affliction and hardship, waking, sleeping, and depriving yourself in all your habits for such a long time.

So those who seek ease for the body, and curious and vain things, have not learned in the school of this Master, who teaches with examples and with words to love poverty, humility, and affliction of the body. Let's follow such a master, then, who wished to take human form in order to teach us the way of salvation. Having the basics that we need to feed and clothe ourselves, let's be content, as the apostle says, and rest in virtue, performing all our actions in the way of virtue.

Now you have seen how Lord Jesus acted as if he were worthless in order to teach you the way to heaven.

*Chapter 12. How Our Lord Jesus Christ went to the river Jordan to be baptized by Saint John.*

And when Lord Jesus had lived in such humility for twenty-nine years, his time had come, and he said to his mother, "Today the time has come for me to go, to glorify my Father and to reveal myself to the world and to achieve the salvation of the human race, for which my Father sent me into this world. But take comfort, for I will return to you soon."

è tempo che io vadi a glorificare il Padre mio et manifestare me al mondo et adoperare [f. 45r] la salute della humana generatione, per la qualle il Padre mio me ha mandato in questo mondo. Ma confortàtive, che io tornerò presto a voi».

Or licenciato dalla madre, mesesse in camino inverso Ierusalem, et poi da Ierusalem perfina al fiume Çordano. Hora poni mente qui al tuo Signore che va solo a piedi, descalço et sença niente[70] in capo. O Missere, non sete voi Re delli Re et Signore di Signori? Or dove sono li baroni et cavalieri et li conti et marchesi? Dove sono gli cavalli adornati? Dove sono iscudieri et famegli? Or dove è il cariaço vostro? Dove sono le trombe et li piphari? Or dove sono gli senescalchi che vano davanti a fare aparechiare l'ospicio? Or non se dice che il cielo et la terra sono pieni della gloria vostra? Come andate voi adonque così solo sança alcuno honore? Or non seti voi colui a chi serve la moltitudine del[f. 45v]li angeli et archançoli? Et perché andate voi adonque solo et cum li piedi descalçi? Ma parmi havere trovata la casone, imperò che lo reame vostro non è di questo mondo, et imperò ve havete humiliato voi medemo, pigliando forma di servo et non di re. Facto sete come uno de noi, peregrino et forestiero sì come tuti gli padri nostri. Facto sete servo per fare noi segnori. Vui seti venuto in questo mondo per menare noi al regname vostro, metandone la via denançi alli ochi per la qualle çe possemo noi andare.[71]

Ma perché siamo cosi negligenti a seguitare questa via? Certo però che il nostro reame et desiderio è in questo mondo et amemo le cose false et vane et temporale et lasiamo le eternale; et se così non facessemo, leçiermente noi andaressemo driedo alla via la qual voi, Signore, ne haveti insegnato. [f. 46r]

Hora torniamo a miser Iesù Cristo, il qualle va solo. Or vàtene cum lui. Ma di che viveva miser Iesù per camino? Io penso[72] che lui andava cercando elymosina de porta in porta, et la nocte andava a dormire allo spedale. Et tuto questo facea miser Iesù per amore della povertade.

Or çonçendo miser Iesù al fiume Çordano et siando lì moltitudine de çente che se façea baptiçare et etiandio per aldire la predicatione de sancto Çuane, perché elli il reputavano quasi Cristo et approximandose miser Iesù a sancto Çuane li disse: «Bateçami».

70. MS *miente*
71. MS *andare <et inquesto modo>*
72. MS *penso* in margin

And having been granted leave by his mother, he went towards Jerusalem and then from Jerusalem to the Jordan River.[68] Now contemplate here your Lord who goes alone on foot, barefoot, and with nothing on his head. O Lord, are you not the King of Kings and Lord of Lords? Now where are the barons and knights and counts and marquises?[69] Where are the horses bedecked with adornments? Where are the squires and servants? Where is your carriage? Where are the trumpets and fifes? And where are the seneschals who go to prepare the lodgings? Hasn't it been said that the heaven and earth are full of your glory? Why do you go like this, alone, without any pomp and signs of honor? Are you not he whom the angels and archangels serve? And why do you go alone, and barefoot? But it seems to me that I have found the reason: because your kingdom is not of this world. And that is why you humbled yourself, taking the form of a servant and not of a king. You made yourself like one of us, a pilgrim and a stranger, like all of our forefathers. You made yourself a servant to make of us lords. You came into this world to lead us to your kingdom, setting forth the way before our eyes, so we would know how to go there.

But why are we so negligent in following this road? Surely because our kingdom and our desires are of this world, and we love false, vain, and temporal things, and we lose sight of eternal things; and if we didn't do this, we might easily follow the way that you, Lord, have taught us.

Now let's return to Lord Jesus Christ, who walks alone; now, you walk along with him. But you ask how Lord Jesus lived on the road. I think that he went begging alms from door to door, and at night he went to sleep at a hostel.[70] And Lord Jesus did all this for love of poverty.

Now when Lord Jesus reached the Jordan River, there were crowds of people there who had come to be baptized and also to hear the preaching of Saint John because they considered him to be almost like Christ. And approaching Saint John, Lord Jesus said to him, "Baptize me."

And Saint John, recognizing him through the Holy Spirit, said this to him: "My Lord, I ought to be baptized by you; and you have come to me?"

Then Lord Jesus replied, "Now, let's set that question aside for another time, because this is the way I must fulfill justice," as if to say, "Do not reveal who I am yet, for my time has not yet come. But do what I tell you."

And here he gives us a beautiful example of how not to contradict our superiors through three degrees of humility. The first is to submit to one's superiors and not to be above them; the second is to submit to one's equals and companions; and the third is to submit to one's inferiors. And Lord Jesus fulfilled this here: he raised up his servant and lowered himself; he

Et sancto Çuane, cognoscendolo per Spirito Sancto, sì li disse: «Signore mio, io debo essere baptiçato da voi; et voi seti venuto a me?».

Alora rispuose miser Iesù: «Or lassa andare al prexente questi parlari, imperò che cosi mi co[n]viene adimpire ogni iusticia», sì come a dire «non me manifestare ancora che non è venuto il mio tempo, ma fà quello che io te [f. 46v] dico».

Et qui ne dà uno bello exempio de non contradire a nostri maçori, per tre gradi de humilità. Lo primo si è a sotometerse a suoi maçori et non soprastare; el secundo è a sotometerse al suo equalle et compagno; et lo terço è a sotometerse al suo minore. Et questo adimpite qui miser Iesù, sotoponendose al servo suo, vilificandose se medemo, iustificato il suo servo monstrandose peccatore. Vedi hora come il Signore nostro te insegna la via de aquistare la virtù della sancta humilitade!

Volse etiandio il Signore nostro publicamente essere baptiçato però che lui volea començare a predicare la penitentia aciò che la çente non la despregiasse come peccatore. Et anche volse monstrare ch'el se havea in dispregio per amaistrare noi. Ma noi non faciamo così, ançi volemo essere tenuti buoni siando cativi et peccatori, et se habiamo alcuna vertude in [f. 47r] noi sì la predicamo per le piaçe,[73] et ascondemo li defecti nostri.

Hora torniamo al baptesmo. Cognoscendo sancto Çuane la voluntade del suo Signore si lli obedì. Or vedi il Signore del cielo e della terra spogliarse, sì come lui fosse uno peccatore, et intrare nel fiume Çordano per amore nostro et adoperare la nostra salute. Et ordinando il sacramento del Batesmo et lavando li nostri peccati, desponsò a si la Chiesia universalmente, unde quando noi siamo baptiçati noi semo desponsati a Cristo.[74] Et in segno de çiò canta oçi la sancta madre Chiesia: «Oçi è conçunta la Chiesia al Sposo celestiale, imperò che Cristo lavò oçi nel fiume Çordano li nostri peccati».

Unde ussendo lui dell'aqua, gli cieli se aperse sopra de lui et lo Spiritu Sancto discese in specie de columba, et vene sopra de lui la voce del Padre che disse: «Questo è il Figliolo mio dilecto, nello qualle mi sum molto dilectato». Vedi [f. 47v] ancora, in questa opera meravegliosa, tuta la Sancta Trinitade se manifestò rendendo testimonança come miser Iesù era[75] Figliolo de Dio.

73. MS *piace*
74. MS *a Cristo* in margin
75. MS *erra*

made his servant seem more worthy of respect, and made himself seem like a sinner. Watch, now, how Our Lord teaches you the way to acquire the virtue of holy humility!

Our Lord also wished to be baptized publicly because he wanted to begin to preach penance and did not want the people to disparage it as sinners. And also he wished to show that he considered himself of little worth, for our instruction. But we don't act in this way, because we want to be considered good, even though we are wicked and sinners, and if we have any virtue in us we announce it in public places, and we hide our defects.

Now let's return to the baptism. Saint John, knowing the will of his Lord, obeyed him. Now watch the Lord of Heaven and Earth remove his clothes, as if he were a sinner, and enter the Jordan River for our love and to obtain our salvation. And establishing the sacrament of Baptism and washing away our sins, he married himself to the universal Church.[71] So when we are baptized, we are married to Christ. And as a sign of this, today holy mother Church sings: "Today the Church is joined to the heavenly Spouse, for Christ washed away our sins today in the Jordan River."

And as he was coming out of the water, the heavens opened above him, and the Holy Spirit descended in the form of a dove, and the voice of the Father came down from on high, saying, "This is my beloved Son, in whom I am well pleased." Watch again how, in this marvelous scene, the whole Holy Trinity reveals itself, bearing witness that Lord Jesus was the Son of God.

*Come miser Iesù Cristo deçunò quaranta dì et quaranta*
*nocte in el diserto et come fo tentato da dimonio.*
*Capitolo tercio decimo.*

Or habiando il Signore nostro miser Iesù Cristo adimpiuto lo sacramento del Batesmo et vogliando in prima fare penite[n]tia avanti che la
predicasse, baptiçato ch'el fo se ne andò al diserto et qui començò aspera
penitentia et deçunò quaranta di et .xl. nocte, et poi hebe fame. Dice miser
san Marco ch'el Signore nostro stava qui cum le bestie et cum le fiere sal-
vatiche et dormia in terra. Àbilli compassione, imperò che tuta la vita sua
non fo altro che[76] pena et afflictione! Et tuto questo il fece per nostro
exempio; or seguitiamo adonque Cristo.

Quatro cose se pone qui, çoè solitudine, deçunii, oratione, [f. 48r] et
afflictione de corpo. Fà che tu façi lo simel, ad exempio del tuo dolce
sposo miser Iesù Cristo. Dàti alla solitudine, et, quanto tu pòi, pàrtiti da
ogni compagnia per la qualle tu possi perdere la quiete tua; et quanto tu
pòi guàrdati da parlari ociosi, però ch'el te convegnerà rendere rasone denançi a miser Iesù Cristo. Et ancho guarda gli tuoi ochi che non vedano
cosa illicita, et guàrdate de non prendere tropo amistade cum seculari.
Non sença casone li Sancti Padri fugivano alli deserti et cercavano luochi
che fusseno lonçi dalle çente et insegnavano agli suoi discipoli che se stu-
diaseno di essere ciechi, sordi et muti. Ancora se tu vòi, porai essere soli-
tario stando in congregatione. Fà che ti tragi della mente ogni affecto
mundano, parenti et pensieri vani, et despregia ogni desiderio carnale et
schiva le contentione et non tegnire a mente le inçurie facte. Non essere
de [f. 48v] strania conversatione, et non essere investigatore et çudese
degli difecti altrui. Impara essere de dolce conversatione, et humelmente
supportare il proximo, et sopra tuto schiva la conpagnia occiosa. Et guàrdate dalle mormoratione et da çudegare il proximo. Et fà che tu sie ciego[77]
et non volere veder ogni cosa, et che tu sie sordo a non dare audientia ad
ogni parola, muto a non respo[n]dere ad ogni parola. Et se così non farai,
se tu fossi ben solo, non serai solo.

Vedi adonca che miser Iesù te insegna la vita solitaria: hàti dato la via
et lo exempio de quello che se contiene nella via sua, çioè deçuni, oratione
et temptatione et afflicione di corpo.

---

76. MS *cha*
77. MS *<sordo> ciego*

*Chapter 13. How Lord Jesus Christ fasted for forty days and forty nights in the desert and how he was tempted by the devil.*

Then Our Lord Jesus Christ, having fulfilled the sacrament of Baptism and wishing to do penance before he preached it, went straight from the baptism to the desert.[72] And there he began hard penance, and he fasted for forty days and forty nights, and then he was hungry. Saint Mark says that Our Lord stayed here with the animals and with the wild beasts and slept on the ground. Have compassion, because all his life was nothing but pain and affliction! And he did all this for our example; so let's strive to follow Christ.

He presents four things here, that is, solitude, fasting, prayer, and affliction of the body. Be sure to do the same, following the example of your sweet spouse Lord Jesus Christ.[73] Give yourself over to solitude, withdrawing as much as you can from company, through which you might lose your tranquility. And keep yourself from idle speech as much as you can, because you will have to answer for it before Lord Jesus Christ. And take care that your eyes see nothing illicit, and beware of becoming too friendly with secular people. It was not without reason that the Holy Fathers fled to the desert and sought places that were far from the people and taught their disciples that they should strive to be deaf, blind, and mute. If you wish, you can even be solitary when you are in community. Try to chase from your mind all worldly affections and thoughts of kin and of trivial things, and despise all desires of the body, and avoid contention, and don't hold grudges. Don't participate in conversation about trivial or curious subjects, and don't be an investigator and judge of the defects of others. Learn to be sweet when you engage with those around you, and to support your companions with humility, and above all to avoid idle company.[74] And keep yourself from gossip, and from judging your neighbor. And make yourself blind, so that you do not wish to see everything; and deaf, so you won't give a hearing to every word; mute, so you won't respond to every word. And if you do this, it will be as if you are living as a solitary even if you are not alone.

You see, therefore, that Lord Jesus taught you the solitary life: he has given you the example and path of his own life as one of fasting, prayer, and temptation and affliction of the body.

And having fasted forty days and nights, Lord Jesus Christ was hungry. And the devil, realizing that he was hungry, and wishing to know if he was the Son of God, brought him an armful of rocks and said to him, "If

Et habiando deçunato miser Iesù Cristo quaranta çorni et .xl. nocte lui have fame. Et avedandose il dimonio de questo che havea fame et per volere sapere se lui era Figliolo de Dio, si lli appresentò il seno pieno di [f. 49r] pietre et disseli: «Se tu sei Figliolo de Dio, di' che queste pietre diventino pane». Questa fu la prima temptatione, che è de gola.

Et miser Iesù, cognoscendo la sua malicia, li rispuose per modo che non negò, né anche confirmò, ma disse: «Non vive l'humo solamente di pane ma de ogni parola che prociede della bocha de Dio». Et cum questo confusse il dimonio dando a noi exempio di contrastare al vicio della gola, imperò che d'ella se vole començare se noi volemo vincere, imperò che chiunque se lassa vincere alla gola pare ch'el diventi molto debile in contrastare alli altri vicii. Dice qui lo exponitore: «Se la gola non è rifrenata, indarno se afatica a contrastare agli altri vicii».

Or vedendose vi[n]to, il dimonio prese miser Iesù et portolo in Ierusalem et messelo sopra il pinaculo del tempio. Et qui el tentò de vanagloria et disse: «Se tu sei Figliolo de Dio, gietati [f. 49v] qui de sotto, imperò che l'è scripto che Dio manderà li angeli soi a te, che ti pilgerano nelle mane, açiò che le pietre non offendano agli piedi tuoi».

Alora il Signore nostro disse: «Ell'è scripto, *Non temptarai il Signore Dio tuo*»—come se dicesse, «Se io posso andare çò per la scala, perché mi debo io butare çoso?».

Et alora el dimonio, confuso et vinto, sì lo prese et portolo sopra uno monte altissimo. Et qui il tentò de avaricia, monstrandoli tuti li regnami del mondo e lla gloria loro. Et disse: «Tuti questi te darò se tu te inçenochierai et adorera' me».

Alora rispuose miser Iesù: «Và via, Sathanas. Scripto è 'il Signore Dio tuo adorerai et a lui solo serivirai'». Alora vedendose il dimonio vinto et confuso se partite. Considera qui la humilitade et benignitade del nostro Salvatore, come se lasò maneçare da quella bestia!

Et dice qui miser san Bernardo perché il Signore [f. 50r] nostro non monstrò alchuna possança divina, il dimonio credete ch'el fusse puro huomo, se non la ultima volta.

Or impariamo noi per lo suo exempio a resistere alle tentatione. Hai veduto quante volte miser Iesù Cristo fu tentato; et imperò non te meravegliare se tu sei tentato. Fo ancora miser Iesù Cristo tentato altre volte, ma dice sancto Bernardo ch'el non se leçe del Signore la quarta tentatione[78] però che la Scriptura dice che la tentatione è vita dell'humo sopra la terra.

78. MS *tetātione*

you are the Son of God, order these rocks to become bread."[75] This was the first temptation, that of gluttony.

And Lord Jesus, knowing his malice, responded to him in a way that neither denied nor confirmed this, saying, "Man does not live by bread alone, but on every word that proceeds from the mouth of God." And with this he defeated the devil, giving us an example of triumph over the vice of gluttony. Because we have to start from there if we wish to succeed, for whoever lets gluttony triumph will be too weak to fight against the other vices. Here the commentator says, "If gluttony is not restrained, in vain does one labor to conquer the other vices."

Then, seeing himself defeated, the devil took Lord Jesus and carried him to Jerusalem and set him on the pinnacle of the temple. And there he tempted him with vainglory, and said, "If you are the Son of God, jump down from here, because it is written that God will send his angels to you, who will catch you in their hands, so the stones will not harm your feet."

So Our Lord said, "It is written, 'You should not tempt the Lord your God'"—as if one might say, "If I can go down by the stairs, why should I throw myself down?"

So then the devil, confused and defeated, took him and carried him up to a very high mountain. And there he tempted him with avarice, showing him all the kingdoms of the world and their glory. And he said, "I will give you all of these if you kneel and worship me."

So Lord Jesus replied, "Get away, Satan. It is written that you shall adore the Lord God and serve only him." So then the devil, seeing himself defeated and confounded, departed. Consider here the humility and benevolence of Our Lord, when he allowed himself to be harrassed by that beast![76]

And here, Saint Bernard says that because Our Lord did not show any divine power, the devil believed that he was pure man, at least at this stage.[77]

Now let's learn through his example to resist temptation. You have seen how many times Lord Jesus Christ was tempted, so don't be surprised if you are tempted. Lord Jesus Christ was also tempted another time, but Saint Bernard says that nothing specific is written about the fourth time because scripture says that the temptation is the life of man on earth.[78] And for the fourth temptation you may understand all the other temptations that Lord Jesus endured. And the apostle says that Christ was tempted like us in all things, without sin.[79]

Now when the devil had left, multitudes of angels came and served him attentively. But if you ask me what kind of food the angels served him,

Et per la quarta tentatione si puote intendere tute le altre tentatione che fu facte a miser Iesù. Et lo Apostolo dice che Cristo fu tentato per similitudine in tute le cose, sença peccato.

Or partito che fo il dimonio, vene moltitudine de angeli et servìlo diligentemente. Ma se tu me adimandi di che vivanda li angeli lo servisse, di questo non fa mentione la divina Scriptura. Ma noi potemo [f. 50v] sopra di questo pensare come ne piace. Ma se noi volemo considerare la sua potentia la qualle dà il cibo a tute le creature, expedita è la questione nostra; imperò che lui potea havere delle cose le qualle havea create al suo volere. Ma se noi non trovemo che miser Iesù usasse questa potentia per si né per li soi discipoli, ma ùsola per la turba quando el saciò tante persone de così poco pane. Et anche si leçe de gli discipoli che nella sua presencia tollevano le spige de grano et fregolàvale et poi le mançavano per la fame. Et simigliantemente essendo lui affatichato per l'andare, sedea sopra il poço et parlava cum la Samaritana. Et non se dice ch'el creasse cibo de nuovo, ma elgi mandò li discipoli suoi nella citade per acatarne. Adoncha non è da credere che qui el se provedesse de cibi miracolosamente, però che el non facea miracoli se lui non era [f. 51r] in presentia de molta çente per rendere testimoniança come lui era vero Figliolo de Dio. Qui non era altri che li angeli et lì dintorno non era habitatione alcuna né altri cibi aparechiati, sì come aviene a Daniel propheta che, habiando Ab[a]cuch propheta aparechiato da mançare a soi lavoradori, l'ançelo de Dio portò lui et quella vivanda in Babilonia a Danielo et poi reportò lui in uno ponto de Babilonia in Iudea.

Ma soprastiamo qui et pigliemo questo modo et alegremose cum il Signore in questo suo mançare et pensiamo così piatosamente. Confuso che fu il dimonio, vene li angeli et cum grande riverentia el salutono dicendo: «Dio ve salvi, Signore nostro». Et miser Iesù li recevete humelmente, pensando che lui era huomo in alcuna cosa minore delli angeli.

Alora dise li angeli: «Signore, molto havete deçunato, che ve piace che noi ve apparechiamo da mançare?».

Et rispuose [f. 51v] miser Iesù: «Andate alla mia carisima madre, et domandateli se lei ha alcuna cosa da mançare, che la ve 'l dia».

Alora doi de li angeli se mosse et in uno ponto forono dinançi alla Madona. Et cum ogni riverentia la salutarono et feceli l'ambassiata del suo dolcissimo figliolo. Oldendo questo, la Vergene gloriosa molto fu contenta, et incontenente li aparechiò in una sportella del pane et delle altre cose che lei havea, et mandoli uno pocho de cosinato il qualle lei havea facto per Ioseph et per lei et disseli: «Ricomandatime al mio dolcissimo fiolo».

holy scripture makes no mention of this.[80] But we may imagine this as we please. But if we wish to consider his power, which gives food to all creatures, our question is answered more easily; for if he wanted anything, he could have created it himself as he wished. But we do not find that Lord Jesus used this power for himself or for his disciples, but used it for the crowd when he satisfied the hunger of so many people with so few loaves of bread. And also it is written of his disciples that in his presence they plucked stalks of grain, rubbed them, and then ate them when they were hungry. And similarly, when he was tired from travelling, he sat on a well and spoke with the Samaritan woman. And it is not said that he created food out of nothing, but rather that he sent his disciples into the city to acquire it. So it isn't likely that he provided food for himself miraculously, because he did not do miracles if he was not in the presence of many people to witness that he was the true Son of God. Here there were no others but the angels, and in the surrounding area there was no human habitation; nor was there other food prepared as it was for the prophet Daniel, when the prophet Habbakuk, having prepared food for his laborers, was taken by the angel of God to give this food to Daniel in Babylon and then taken back from Babylon to Judea in an instant.[81]

But let's pause here, then, and consider this way of thinking about it, and rejoice with the Lord at this meal, and imagine it with devotion like this. When the devil had been defeated, the angels came and with great reverence they greeted Lord Jesus, saying, "God be with you, Our Lord." And he received them humbly, thinking that as a man he should behave as though his status were lower than that of the angels.

And then the angels said, "Lord, you have fasted much. What would you like us to prepare for you to eat?"

And Lord Jesus replied, "Go to my dearest mother, and ask her if she has anything to eat that she can give you."

And so two of the angels set off, and in an instant they were before Our Lady. And they greeted her with great reverence and made the request on behalf of her most sweet son. Hearing this, the glorious Virgin was very pleased, and without delay she prepared a basket for him with some bread and other things that she had, and she sent him a little cooked food that she had prepared for Joseph and herself. And she said to them, "Give my greetings to my most sweet son."[82] And then the angels returned to Lord Jesus with the food, and when they had delivered the mother's message, they presented the basket to him. Then they laid everything out on the ground in a festive way; and one served him bread, and another wine,

Alora li angeli tornarono cum quella vivanda da miser Iesù, et facta l'ambassiata della madre si li appresentorono quella sportella. Alora tuti cum
grande festa gli aparechiò in terra, et chi el servia di pane, et chi di vino,
et chi de cosinato, et chi cantava. Alora il Signore sì benedicete la mensa
et sentosse in terra il Re del Paradiso. O anima che desideri de [f. 52r]
stare bene asiada, non hai imparato alla scola di questo Maestro, il qualle
è stato çà quara[n]ta çorni in penitentia! Et hora non ha altro reduto dove
podesse mançare ad axio ch'el conviene sentare in terra a mançare.

Or stà anche ti alla presentia del Signore nostro et riguardandolo
mançare in terra,[79] pensa che lui è il tuo Dio et Signore et Creatore de tuto
lo mondo. Et è colui che nudriga et mantiene cum la potentia sua tute le
creature. Et hora lo vedi così humiliato che lui ha bisog[n]o de sosteni-
mento de cibo corporale. Et pensando questo, hàbili compassione! Et sì
credo certamente che se tu affetuosamente il guarderai cum tuto il cuore
così stare, et vogliandoli bene, penso che per grandissima compassione
diresti «O Signore mio, quante cose per mi facesti! Tute le operatione vostre sono piene de stupore. Donàtime, gran Signore mio, che io patisca alcuna cosa per voi, lo qualle hai sostenuto [f. 52v] tante cose per me!».
Certo solo questo te doveria tirare al suo amore!

Et poi che hebe mançato et ringratiato Dio Padre, dise a li angeli che
reportasseno le cose alla madre sua et che li dicesseno ch'el tornarebe presto a lei. Et tornati che furono gli ançóli al signore, lui si li licentiò, et
disse: «Tornàtive alla patria vostra, che io convegno ancora peregrinare in
questo mondo».

Et dapoi queste cose, començò miser Iesù a descendere del monte per
tornare in Naçareth. Or vedi come va solo[80] a piedi descalçi. Et çonçendo
al fiume Çordano et vedendolo sancto Çuane venire, si el dimonstrò col
dito et disse: «Ecco lo Agnelo de Dio. Ecco colui che tolle il peccato del
mondo. Ecco colui sopra il qualle vidi venire il Spirito Sancto quando io
el baptiçai». Et poi se partite da sancto Çuane et vene inverso Naçareth et
andò alla madre sua. Et poi se partì da lei et andò a congregare gli disci[f.
53r]poli suoi.

Hora perfina a qui, per la gratia de Dio, noi habiamo detto per ordine
della vita de miser Iesù Cristo, quasi nulla lassando de quelle cose che gli
sono intravenute et che per lui furono facte et decte perfina[81] a questo

79. MS _māçare īterra_] in margin
80. MS _ua|<scal> solo_
81. MS _p(er) <ordine> fina_

and another food, and another sang. Then the Lord blessed the meal, and the King of Paradise sat on the ground. O soul who desires to be well fed, you have not learned at the school of this Master, who did penance for forty days! And now he has no other place where he might dine in comfort, so he has to sit on the ground to eat.

Now you, too, stay in the presence of Our Lord. And watching him as he sits on the ground to eat, remember that he is your God and Lord and Creator of the whole world. And it is he who nourishes and sustains all creatures with his power. And now you see that he is so humbled that he needs the sustenance of bodily food. And as you imagine this, have compassion! And I certainly believe that if you watch him lovingly like this with all your heart as he sits there, desiring what is good for him, I think that through great compassion you will say "O my Lord, how much you did for me! All your deeds are full of wonder. My great Lord, grant that I may suffer something for you—you who have endured so many things for me." Surely this alone will draw you towards his love!

And then when he had eaten and thanked God the Father, he told the angels to carry the things back to his mother and to tell her that he would return to her soon. And after the angels returned to him, he gave them leave to go, saying, "Return to your homeland, for it is necessary for me to complete my journey in this world."

And after these things, Lord Jesus began to descend the mountain to return to Nazareth. Now watch how he walks along on his own, barefoot. And as he approached the Jordan River, Saint John, seeing him draw near, pointed to him and said, "Behold the Lamb of God. Behold the one who takes away the sins of the world. Behold the one upon whom you saw the Holy Spirit descend when I baptized him." And then he left Saint John and went to his mother. And then he took his leave of her, and he went to gather his disciples.

Now up to this point, by the grace of God, we have spoken in order about the life of Lord Jesus Christ, leaving out almost nothing about the things that happened to him and that he said and did up to now.[83] But I do not intend to continue like this from now on, because it would take too long to try to retell in the form of meditations all that he did or said from this moment on. But we should always strive to follow the example of Saint Cecilia and carry always the words and deeds of our sweet spouse Lord Jesus in our hearts.[84] So when you hear about any of the deeds and words of Lord Jesus, whether this is through the Gospels or through preaching or in another way, be sure to put them before your mind's eye

tempo. Ma io non intendo de fare così da qui inançi, però che el seria tropo longa materia a volere redire per meditatione tuto quello che lui fece overo disse da hora inançi. Ma noi dovemo essere solliciti de quello exemplo de sancta Cecilia de portare sempre le opere del nostro dolce spoxo miser Iesù nelgli chuori nostri. Unde quando tu aldi dire[82] de miser Iesù alcuna opera per lui decta o facta, o in el vangelio overo in predicatione o per altri modi, fà che tu le meti denançi gli ochi della mente tua et ripensale, però che el me pare che in questi cotal pensieri di facti de miser Iesù Cristo sia maçore dolçeça et devotione che in altri modi. Et tuto il fondamento del spirito [f. 53v] me pare che stia in çiò: che sempre in ogni luocho riguardi lui cum li ochi della mente tua, cum devotione in alcuna sua operatione. Hora come lui e cum li discipoli, hora come va cum gli peccatori, overo quando siede o dorme o vegia, o quando serve altrui o che sana li infermi o quando el resuscita li morti, et che elgi fa altri miracoli somegliantii a questi. Adonca considera tuti li soi acti et costumi, et specialmente contemplando la sua faça, se la pòi contemplare—la qualle cosa mi pare malagievole sopra tute le altre cose, ma credo che questo te saria la maçore consolatione che tu potesti bonamente havere. Et stà attento, se lui vegnisse inverso di te, a riceverlo benignamente.

Et questo ti pò bastare de pensare delli acti suoi perfina al çorno che lui començò a congregare li discipoli. Hora da qui inançi parlaremo della Passione. Et començeremo dalla Domenega del Olivo. [f54r]

### Come miser Iesù Cristo Signore nostro andò in Ierusalem la Domenega de l'Olivo sopra l'asina. Capitolo qu[a]rto[83] decimo.

Approximandose il tempo nel qualle il Signore nostro miser Iesù Cristo volea dare salute alla humana generatione per la Passione del suo proprio corpo et adimpire le Scripture. Siando lui in Bethania il sabbato inançi la Domenega del Olivo, et apparechiandose de volere andare la matina in Ierusalem et avedendose de çiò la madre, si el priegava cum uno piatoso modo et dicea: «Figliolo mio, dove voleti voi andare? Io so che voi sapeti lo mal conseglio che è determinato de voi tra li Çudei. Perché volete adoncha andare fra loro? Priegove, figliolo mio, che no çe ne andati!».

82. MS *dire* in margin
83. MS *quiiato*. It appears that the scribe first sought to write *quinto decimo*.

and reflect on them, because it seems to me that in this way of meditating on the deeds of Lord Jesus Christ there will be greater sweetness and devotion than by other means. And the whole foundation for spiritual growth seems to me to come down to this: that always and everywhere you watch him with the eyes of your mind with devotion in everything that he does. Now how he is with his disciples, now when he walks with sinners, or when he sits or sleeps or wakes, or when he serves others, or when he heals the sick, or when he raises the dead and performs other miracles like this. Then consider all his deeds and manners. And contemplate his face with special care, if you are able to contemplate it, for this seems to me more difficult than anything else; but I believe that this will be for you the greatest experience of solace that you might have. And prepare yourself to receive him kindly, if he should come to you.

And this is enough for you to contemplate concerning his life until the time when he began to call his disciples. Now from here on we will speak about the Passion. And we will begin with Palm Sunday.

## Chapter 14. How Jesus Christ Our Lord entered Jerusalem on Palm Sunday on a donkey.

The time approached when Our Lord Jesus Christ wished to fulfill the scriptures and to give salvation to the human race through the Passion of his own body. And when he was in Bethany the Saturday before Palm Sunday, he resolved to go to Jerusalem in the morning.[85] And when she heard about this, his mother implored him piteously, saying, "My son, where do you wish to go? I know that you are aware of the Jews' bad opinion of you. Why do you wish to go among them? I beg you, my son, not to go there!"

And Magdalene beseeched him similarly. And the disciples, too, said to him, "You know that the Jews wish your death, and you wish to go among them. They will achieve their intention!" O God, how tenderly they loved him!

Et simelmente il pregava la Magdalena. Et etiandio gli discipoli li dicevano: «Voi sapete che li Çudei desiderano la morte vostra, et voi volete andare tra loro. Elli haverano [f. 54v] la loro intentione!». O Dio, come teneramente lo amavano!

Ma colui che desiderava la salute della humana generatione si determinava altramente, et rispuose a loro et disse: «La voluntade del Padre mio è che io vada in Ierusalem, et imperò io voglio andarge. Et non temete, che noi tornaremo qui questa sera».

Alora il Signore se partì cum la sua picola compagnia et andosene inverso Ierusalem. Et approsimandose miser Iesù appreso il Monte Oliveto, mandò dui delli soi discipoli inançi, decendo, «Andate nel castello che è contra di voi, et incontenente trovareti una asina ligata cum uno asinello. Desligatela et menàtella a me. Et se alcuno ve dicesse alcuna cosa, diceteli ch'el signore ne ha bisogno». Et questo fo facto per adimpire quello che fu decto per il propheta, che dice, «Figliola de Ierusalem, ecco il tuo Re che viene a te mansueto, sedendo sopra l'asina et l'asinello».

Et gli discipoli [f. 55r] andorono et menorono le bestie a miser Iesù. Et poi miseno le vestimente sue sopra l'asina et poi feceno sentare miser Iesù desopra. Et in questo modo cavalcava il Re del cielo et della terra. Et avegna ch'el fosse degna cosa che lui fosse honorato, et lui sapiando ch'el dovea ricevere tanto honore, si volse usare cotal despresii per confondere la gloria et la pompa de questo mondo. Imperò che le erano bestie vile, non destrieri, et non erano ornati de freni d'oro o de selle indorate, né coperte delicate, secundo la cativa usança del mundo vano, ma erano adornati de vili pani et doe corde che se usavano[84] per freni, con çiò sia cosa che lui fosse Re di Re et Signore delli Segnori et sopra di lui non è maçore né in cielo né in terra.

Et aldando la turba come miser Iesù venia, sì lli vene incontra come a re. Et sì lo ricevete come re, cantando et iubilando[85] [f. 55v] [et] metendo le lor vestimente per terra. Et altri rumpando li rami delli arbori et çitandoli per terra et facendo grande alegreça et gran festa della sua venuta. Ma io voglio che tu sapi ch'el nostro Signore non volse ricevere cotanto honore che nol mescolase cum tristicia. Unde quando el çonse apresso a Ierusalem si pianse sopra de lei et disse, «O Ierusalem, se tu cognoscesi[86] lo pericolo che dè venire sopra di te, tu pançeresti meco!».

Unde noi troviamo che miser Iesù pianse tre fiade. La prima si è quando resuscitò Laçaro, et qui el pianse la humana miseria. La seconda

84. MS *scusauano*
85. MS *Iubilando* <*metendo le*>
86. MS *cognosesci*

But he who desired the salvation of the human race determined otherwise, and he replied to them and said, "The will of my Father is that I go to Jerusalem, and so I wish to go there. And do not be afraid, because we will return here this evening."

So the Lord left with his few companions and went toward Jerusalem. And approaching the Mount of Olives, Lord Jesus sent forth two of his disciples, saying, "Go to the next town, and there you will find a female donkey tethered with her young colt. Untie her, and lead her to me. And if anyone says anything to you, tell them that the lord needs them."[86] And this was done to fulfill what was said through the prophet, who says, "Daughter of Jerusalem, behold your King who comes to you meekly, riding on a donkey with her colt."

And the disciples went and brought the animals to Lord Jesus. And then they put their cloaks on the donkey, and then Lord Jesus sat upon it. And the King of Heaven and Earth rode in this way. And even though he was worthy to be honored and knew that he would receive much honor, he wished to use such humble means to counter the glory and the pomp of this world. For these were base animals, not prized steeds, and they were not adorned with gold reins or with ornate saddles, or covered delicately according to the wretched ways of the vain world, but they were adorned with rough cloths and two cords which served as reins, even though he was King of Kings and Lord of Lords, and above him none is greater, neither in heaven nor on earth.

And the crowd, hearing that Lord Jesus was coming, came to meet him as they would a king. And they welcomed him as a king, singing and rejoicing and putting their cloaks on the ground. And some were taking palm branches from the trees and scattering them on the ground and rejoicing and making a great celebration for his coming. But I want you to know that even as Our Lord gladly welcomed such honors, he couldn't help feeling sadness too. For when he reached Jerusalem, he wept over her, and said, "O Jerusalem, if only you knew the danger to come, you would weep with me!"

And so we find that Lord Jesus wept three times. The first was when he raised Lazarus, when he wept over the misery of the human condition. The second was when he wept over Jerusalem, when he wept for human blindness and ignorance, because they did not recognize the sweet visitation, that is, that he came to visit to give them salvation. The third time was at the time of the Passion, when he wept for human sin and the malice of the Jews, who were reprobates and hardhearted and did not repent for the offenses that they committed toward God the Father. One can read about these three times in

quando lui pianse sopra de Ierusalem, et qui el pianse l'humana cecitade et ignorantia, però che loro no cognoscea la dolce visitatione, çioè ch'el vene a visitare per dargi salute. La terça volta fu al tempo dell[a] Passione, et qui el pianse la humana colpa et la malicia de' Iudei, li qualli erano reprobati et indurati et non se pentivano [f. 56r] della offesa che faceano a Dio Padre. Di queste tre si leçe in lo evançelio, ma la Chiesia trova che lui pianse una altra volta, çioe quando lui giaçea nel[a] mançatora et pianse per abscondere il misterio della Incarnatione al dimonio. Or se tu lo amassi ponto, tu piançeresti cum lui del pericolo de Ierusalem, sì come feceno coloro che erano cum lui.

Hora intrando miser Iesù Cristo in Ierusalem, tuta la citade fo commossa della vegnuta sua. Et intrando nel tempio, caçiò fuori tuti coloro che vendeano et compravano cose corporale. Et questa fo la secunda fiada ch'el caçiò fuori del tempio coloro che vendea et comprava.[87] Et stete tuto quel çorno nel tempio, predicando publicamente a tuto il populo, disputando cum gli pri[n]cipi et farisei perfina a la sera. Et avegna che li fosse facto così grande honore nella sua venuta, cum tuto çiò non fo persona che in tuto quel çorno lo i[n]vitase pure a bere uno fiato di aqua; et questo fo grande segno della[88] loro perdicione. Stete adunca [f. 56v] miser Iesù cum la sua compagnia tu[t]o quel çorno sença ma[n]çare per adoperare la salute nostra, dandone qui exempio che noi dobiamo cercare più tosto la salute de l'anima nostra che il cibo del corpo.

Or poni ben mente come el torna la sera in Bethania, e come el passa humelmente per la città, il qualle era venuto la matina cum tanto honore! Et de çiò ne dà exempio che pocho çi doviamo curare delli honori di questo mondo, li qualli dura pocho. Tu poi ancora pensare come la madre et la Magdalena et li discipoli erano contenti de l'honore che fu facto a miser Iesù, et specialmente quando il viteno ritornare in Bethania.

*Come el nostro Signore miser Iesù nel Mercoredì sancto cenò cum li soi discipoli in Bethania*[89] *in casa della Magd[a]lena. Capitolo quintodecimo.*

Qui podemo noi pensare una devota meditacione della qualle la Scriptura non fa mentione. Cenando miser Iesù il Mer[f. 57r]core sancto

87. MS *cose corporale . . . comprava* in margin
88. MS *dalla*
89. MS *bthetania*

the Gospel, but the Church finds that he wept another time, that is, when he lay in the manger, and he wept to hide the mystery of the Incarnation from the devil. Now, if you loved him even a little bit, you would weep with him for the destruction of Jerusalem, like those did who were with him.

Now as the Lord Jesus Christ entered Jerusalem, the whole city was in a commotion over his arrival. And entering the temple, he cast out all those who sold and bought material things. And this was the second time that he cast out those who bought and sold. And he stayed for the whole day in the temple, preaching publicly to all the people, disputing with the chief priests and Pharisees until the evening. And even though such great honor was given to him as he entered the city, not a single person among them offered him even a small sip of water the whole day; and this was a clear sign of their ultimate perdition. So Lord Jesus remained with his companions for the whole day without eating in order to achieve our salvation, giving us here an example that we should be more diligent about seeking salvation for the soul than food for the body.

Now imagine well how he returns to Bethany in the evening, and how he passes humbly through the city, he who had entered it in the morning with such honor! And in this he gives us an example that we must care little about the honors of this world, which do not last long. You may also imagine how glad his mother and Magdalene and the disciples were about the honor that was shown to Lord Jesus, especially when they saw him returning to Bethany.

## Chapter 15. How Our Lord Jesus dined on Holy Wednesday with his disciples in Bethany in the house of Magdalene.

Here we may imagine a moving meditation about something that scripture does not mention. When Lord Jesus was dining on holy Wednesday in Bethany in the house of Mary and Martha, and Our Lady was in another part of the house with the other women, Magdalene went to Our Lord Jesus Christ and said, "Master, I want to ask you a favor, and I beg you not to deny it."[87]

And Our Lord replied, "Tell me what you desire."

in Bethania in casa de Maria et de Martha et anche la Dona nostra in di-
sparte cum le altre done, andò la Magdalena al nostro Signore miser Iesù
Cristo et disse: «Maistro, io ve voglio domandare una gratia et priegove
non me la negati».

Et rispuoxe il nostro Signore: «Di' çiò che tu voli».

Alora disse la Magdalena: «Io vi priego ch'el ve piaça di fare qui cum
noi la Pasqua cum li discipoli vostri».

Respuose miser Iesù: «Io sono venuto in questo mondo per fare la voluntade del Padre mio. Et però voglio andare a fare la Pasqua cum li discipoli mei in su el Monte Syon».

Aldendo la Magdalena la risposta che miser Iesù li fece, tuta adolorata se ne andò piançendo alla madre de miser Iesù, et disseli questo facto
et pregola che ancho lei il pregasse ch'el stesse a fare la Pascqua cum loro.
Et compiuto che hebe de cenare miser Iesù, si vene alla madre sua, et sentando [f. 57v] da parte cum lei e parlando cum lei, però ch'el sapea bene
che lei non li poria parlare più. O che compagnia è questa!

Et parlando così insieme miser Iesù cum la madre sua, ecco che la
Magdalena andò a loro e senta[n]dosse alli piedi de miser Iesù et dise:
«Madona, io pregava qui il Maestro mio che lui mi facesse una gratia,
ch'el facesse la Pasqua cum noi, et lui dice ch'el vuole andare a farla in sul
Monte Sion. Pregove che voi nol lassiate andare, però che lui serà perso!».

Alora disse la madre: «Figliolo mio, io ve priego che voi non⁹⁰ çe andiate, ma che voi facte qui la Pasqua cum noi. Voi sapeti, figliolo mio, che
li Çudei [hanno]⁹¹ hordinato e posto li aguaiti per pigliarve».

Respuose miser Iesù: «Madre mia carissima, la voluntade del Padre
mio è che io vadi a fare la Pasqua in Ierusalem imperò che l'e venuto il
tempo della redemptione de Israel. Hora se adim[ple]rà⁹² tute le scripture
le qualle sono [f. 58r] scripte di me. Et farano di me çiò che vorano».

Alora tuti furono adolorati, però che inteseno che lui dicea della morte
sua. Disse la madre, apena posando parlare: «O figliolo mio, tuta sum sbi-
gotita de quello che io ve ho aldito dire e pare ch'el cuore me habia abandonato. O Dio Padre, provedete sopra questo facto,⁹³ imperò che io non so
che me dica. Non li voria contradire. Ma se a voi piace, voi podete bene
provedere per altra via de ricomperare la humana generatione sança la
morte del mio figliolo, imperciò che io so che a vui ogni cosa è possibile».

90. MS *non* in margin
91. MS *çudei|hordinato*
92. MS *adim|ra*
93. MS *fcto* with a titulus over *ct*

So Magdalene said, "I ask you to please have Passover here with your disciples."

Lord Jesus replied, "I have come into this world to do the will of my Father. And so I wish to go to have Passover with my disciples on Mount Syon."

Hearing the reply that Lord Jesus gave her, Magdalene, filled with sorrow, went weeping to the mother of Lord Jesus and told her this, and asked her, too, to try to persuade him to stay and have Passover with them. And when Lord Jesus had finished eating, he went to his mother, sitting to one side with her and speaking with her, because he knew well that she would not be able to speak much longer with him. Oh what a union is theirs![88]

And as Lord Jesus was speaking quietly with his mother like this, Magdalene went to them and sat at the feet of Lord Jesus and said, "My lady, I begged my Master here that he do me a favor, that he have Passover with us, and he says that he wants to go to Mount Syon to celebrate Passover. I beg you not to let him go, because he will be lost!"

And then the mother said, "My son, I beg you not to go there, but to have Passover with us here. You know, my son, that the Jews have ordered your arrest and men are lying in wait to capture you."

Lord Jesus replied, "My dearest mother, the will of my Father is that I go to have Passover in Jerusalem, because the time has come for the redemption of Israel. Now the scriptures that were written of me will be fulfilled. And they will do with me what they wish."

So they were all filled with sorrow, because they understood that he spoke of his death. His mother, scarcely able to speak, said: "O my son, I am overcome with fear about what I have heard you say, and it seems that my heart has abandoned me. O God the Father, do what needs to be done, because I do not know what to say! I do not wish to contradict him. But if it pleases you, you certainly have the power to provide another way to redeem the human race, without the death of my son, because I know that to you all things are possible."

Now if you had seen the mother, and Magdalene too, weep with great sighs, perhaps you would not hold back from weeping with them.[89] Now imagine what anguish they must feel! But Lord Jesus, seeing the mother weeping and wishing to console her, said to her, "Do not weep, my mother, but know that it is necessary for me to carry out the mission of my heavenly Father. But fear not, for I will return to you soon. Know that I will rise from the dead on the third day, free from the wounds of this world. And so I wish to celebrate Passover on Mount Syon according to the will of my Father."

Or se tu vedesti la madre et anche la Magdalena piançere cum grandi sospiri, forsi che tu non te poresti tenire de piançere cum loro? Or pensa come doveano stare tribulate! Ma vedendo miser Iesù pia[n]çere la madre et volendola consolare gli disse: «Non piançeti, madre mia, ma sapiate ch'el me conviene compire la obedientia del Padre [f. 58v] mio celestiale. Ma state securamente, però che io tornerò tosto da voi. Sapiate che io resusciterò il terço çorno, sença alcuna macula de questo mondo. Et imperò voglio fare la Pasqua in su el Monte Syon secundo la voluntà del Padre mio».

Alora disse la Magdalena: «Da poi che noi non lo potemo tenire, andiamo anche noi cum lui in Ierusalem in la casa nostra. Ma io credo, Madona, che io non havi mai Pasqua così amara come serà questa!».

*Come miser Iesù fece la cena il Giobia sancto cum li discipoli suoi sopra el Monte Syon. Capitolo sextodecimo.*

Approximandose[94] il tempo della misericordia de Dio, in el qualle havea ordinato de dare salute alla humana generatione et di ricomprarla non de oro né de arçento ma del suo precioso sangue, si volse fare cum li discipoli suoi una notabel cena avanti ch'el se partisse da loro per morte corporale, in segno de perpetual memoria, et etiamdio per compire li misterii che [f. 59r] erano rimasti a compire. La qualle cena è molto magnifica, et grande cose fece il Maestro nostro in essa cena. Et in questa cena se contiene quatro cose molto excelle[n]tissime. La prima si è la cena corporale; la secunda, lo lavare dilli piedi; la terça, como lui ordinò il sacramento del suo sacratissimo corpo; la quarta si è il belissimo sermone ch'el fece agli soi discipoli. Ma se tu vòi bene vedere queste quatro cose, el fa bisogno che tu ne sie presente cum la mente tua. Et se questo tu farai degnamente et sollicitamente, habi per fermo che colui il qualle è pieno de ogni cortesia non sostegnerà che tu ritorni deçuno da questa cena.

Approximandose li çorni della festa delli açimi, disse miser Iesù a sancto Pietro et a san Çuane: «Andate et apparechiate a noi la Pasqua aciò che la mançiamo».

Et disseno a lui li discipoli: «Dove vi piaçe che noi v[e l]a[95] apparechiamo»?

94. MS *Apporximādose*, with the letters *or* expunged and a mark added below the first *p*, to change it to *p(ro)*

95. MS *va*

Then Magdalene said, "Since we can't keep him here, let's go with him to Jerusalem, to our house.[90] But I believe, my lady, that I have never had a Passover as bitter as this will be!"

## Chapter 16. How Lord Jesus celebrated the supper on Holy Thursday with his disciples on Mount Syon.

When the time of God's mercy approached, which he had ordained to save the human race and to redeem it not with gold or with silver but with his precious blood, he wished to celebrate a special supper with his disciples before he left them through corporal death, as a sign for them to remember forever, and also to fulfill the mysteries that remained to be fulfilled. This is a very splendid supper, and our Master did great things at this supper. And this supper includes four most excellent things. The first is the supper itself; the second, the washing of the feet; the third, how he established the sacrament of his most sacred body; the fourth is the most beautiful sermon that he gave to his disciples. But if you wish to see these four things well, you need to make yourself present there with your mind. And if you do this worthily and attentively, rest assured that he who is full of all courtesy will not allow you to return hungry from this supper.

When the days of the feast of unleavened bread approached,[91] Lord Jesus said to Saint Peter and Saint John: "Go and prepare the Passover for us, so we can eat it together."

And the disciples said to him: "Where do you wish us to prepare it?"

And Lord Jesus said to them, "Look, then: as you enter the city, you will find a man carrying a jar of water. Follow him into the house he enters. And say to the father of the family of this house, 'The Master asks you where the room is where he should eat the Passover meal with his disciples.' And he will show you a large and spacious room, and you can set the table there."

Et disse miser Iesù a loro: [f. 59v] «Ecco, come voi intrareti nella citad[e], voi trovareti uno huomo il qualle porterà una çerla di aqua: seguite lui nella casa dove lui intrerà, et dicete al padre della fameglia della casa: «Dice a te il Maestro dove è il luocho nel qualle el debe mançare la Pasqua cum li discipoli soi». Et lui si ve monstrerà uno luocho grande et spatioso, et lì apparechiate».

Andono gli discipoli et trovono come miser Iesù li havea detto, et qui apparechi[a]rono la Pasqua. Et cerca l'hora del vesporo vene meser Iesù et intrò nella casa dove elgi havea mandato li discipoli a preparare la Pasqua. Et ecco il padre della fameglia venire incontra a miser Iesù, et menolo nell'albergo[96] dove li discipoli haveano apparechiato. Et ecco sancto Pietro disse: «Maestro, el non è ancora apparechiato: conviene che voi indusiate uno pocho».

Ora riguarda cum tuta la mente tua miser Iesù stare in [f. 60r] alcuna parte de[l] cenaculo cum li discipoli suoi, amaistrandoli perfina ch'el fosse apparechiato. Et guarda sancto Pietro et san Çuane, come se affaticano a preparare le cose che sono necesarie,[97] et alquanti altri discipoli delli setantadoi, li qualli erano venuti lì per servire a miser Iesù et ali soi discipoli. Et apparechiato che fo, ecco san Çuane vene a miser Iesù et disse: «Signore, [e]l'è apparechiato; voi podeti cenare quando ch'el ve piace». Or poni ben mente qui, però che queste sono cose da tochare il cuore per li excellentissimi segni ch'el nostro Signore miser Iesù monstrò in questa benedecta cena.

Alora levose miser Iesù cum li discipoli et andose a lavare le mane. Et poi benedisse la mensa et se messeno a sedere. Et qui è da sapere che quella mensa era posta in terra, secundo la usança delli antichi che sedevano in terra. Et era quella mensa overo tavola quadra et era de più peçi, la qualle io ho veduto a Roma in la chiesia de sancto Çuane Laterano, [f. 60v] la qualle io ho mesurata che per quadro la è braço uno et uno palmo et tre dida; sì che sentarebe tre per quadro. Et miser Iesù si sentava penso in uno d'i cantoni della mensa, sì che tuti mançavano in uno catino, et per questa casone non lo inteseno quando el disse «Colui che intenge la mano in lo catino cum me, elgi me tradirà», però che tuti çe metevano la mano: perciò non inteseno chi lo era.

---

96. MS *nella albergo*

97. MS *necesarie ch(e) sono* [*sono* in margin] with a superscript *a* above the first word and a *b* above *ch(e)* (probably an error)

The disciples went and found just what Lord Jesus had described to them, and there they set the table for the Passover. And around the hour of vespers, Lord Jesus came and entered the house where he had sent the disciples to prepare Passover. And there the father of the family came to greet Lord Jesus, and he led him to the room where the disciples were getting things ready. And there Saint Peter said, "Master, it isn't ready yet, so you will need to wait a little."

Now watch with all your mind your Lord Jesus sitting in some part of the room with his disciples, teaching them until the Passover meal was ready. And watch Saint Peter and Saint John, how they work hard to prepare the things that are needed, along with some from the group of the seventy-two disciples, who had come there to serve Lord Jesus and his disciples.[92] And when it was ready, Saint John came to Lord Jesus and said: "Lord, it is ready, you may begin the meal when you please." Now, concentrate well here, because these are things that touch the heart, through the most excellent signs that Lord Jesus showed in this blessed supper.

Then Lord Jesus rose with his disciples and went to wash his hands. And then he gave the blessing and they sat down to eat. And here it should be known that this table was placed on the floor, according to the custom of the ancients, who sat on the floor. And this table, or rather board, was square in shape, and made of several pieces; and I have seen it in Rome, in the church of Saint John Lateran, and I took its measure, and each side is the length of one arm and one palm and three fingers; so it could seat three per side.[93] And I think Lord Jesus seated himself at one of the corners of the table, so that all could eat from one dish; and for this reason they did not understand him when he said, "The one who dips his hand in the dish with me: he will betray me." Since all were dipping their hands there, they did not understand who it was.

And when the meal had been blessed, they sat down. And Saint John sat at the left side of Lord Jesus, even though he was more worthy than the others. And from this time on, he never parted from Christ; so when he was captured, he followed him as far as the house of the high priest, and similarly when he was crucified, and until the moment he was buried he never abandoned him.

Then they began to eat. And then the Passover lamb was brought out and placed in the middle of them.[94] And Lord Jesus, like one who serves at table, carved it, and with great gladness he served it to the disciples, and he invited them to eat it.

Et benedecta che fo la mensa, se meseno a sedere. Et san Çuane se puose alla mano mança de miser Iesù, et avegna che fosse da più che li altri. Et da qui inançi mai non se partì da Cristo; unde quando el fo preso lui lo seguite perfina a casa del pontifice, et così quando el fo crucifixo, et perfina ch'el fo sotorato[98] non abandonò mai.

Ora començono a mançare. Et ecco che fo portato lo agnello[99] pasqualle, il quall[e] fo messo in meço de loro. Et miser Iesù, come servitore, si 'l speçò, et cum grande alegreça si 'l porse alli discipoli, et confortoli che mançaseno.

Et disse: «Longo tempo [f. 61r] ho desiderato de fare questa Pasqua cum voi avanti che io sostegna passione». Et poi disse: «In veritade io ve dico che uno de voi me tradirà».

Questa parola[100] si passò gli chuori loro, et resteteno de mançare. Et come smemorati guardavano l'uno l'atro. Et sancto Pietro disse: «Signore, sono mi colui»? Et così disero tuti.

Ma Iuda traditore, perché paresse che quelle parole non tocasse a lui, non restò de mançare. Et poi disse anche lui: «Sono io desso, maistro»?

Et respuose il Signore: «Tu l'ài detto».

Alora sancto Pietro disse a miser Iesù: «Chi è colui che te dè tradire»?

Et miser Iesù non ge lo volse dire. Alora sancto Pietro pregò san Çuane ch'el domandasse al Signore: «Chi è colui?».

Et san Çuane per priegi de san Piero sì disse a miser Iesù: «Chi è colui che ve debe tradire?».

Alora miser Iesù, come a persona che lui amava più singularmente che li altri, sì li disse: «A colui che porçerò il pane tincto, [f. 61v] colui è desso». Et tuta via porse el bochone del pan a Iuda.

Alora san Çuane tuto tramortito si repuose il capo in sul pecto de miser Iesù Cristo et non disse niente a sancto Pietro. Né etiamdio il Signore non gel volse dire, imperò che secundo che dice sancto Augustino, che se sancto Pietro lo havesse saputo, lui lo haveria squarçato cum li denti.

Et è da sapere che per[101] sancto Pietro se intendeno tuti coloro che serveno a miser Iesù Cristo nella vita activa, et per san Çuane se intendeno color che hano gratia de vita contemplativa. Unde qui hai exempio

---

98. MS *fo torato* with *so* inserted between the two words
99. MS *la agnel\lo*
100. MS *porola*
101. MS *sapere p(er)<o>* with *che* added between the two words

And he said, "For a long time I have desired to celebrate this Passover meal with you before I undergo the Passion." And then he said: "In truth, I tell you that one of you will betray me."

These words passed into their hearts and they stopped eating. And astonished, like those who are dazed, they looked at one another. And Saint Peter said, "Lord is it me?" And all the others asked the same.

But Judas the traitor continued eating, so it would seem that these words did not touch him. And then he too said: "Am I the one, Master?"

And the Lord replied: "You have said it."

Then Saint Peter said to Lord Jesus: "Who is it who will betray you?"

And Lord Jesus did not want to tell him. So Saint Peter asked Saint John to ask the Lord, "Who is it?"

And Saint John, at the urging of Saint Peter, asked Lord Jesus, "Who is it who must betray you?"

Then Lord Jesus, speaking to him as if he loved him more specially than the others, said to him, "The one to whom I will pass the piece of bread dipped into the sauce: he is the one." And just then, Jesus passed a morsel of bread to Judas.

Then John, completely stunned, leaned his head on the breast of Lord Jesus Christ, and said nothing to Saint Peter. Nor did the Lord want to tell him, because according to what Saint Augustine says, if Saint Peter had known, he would have torn him apart with his teeth.[95]

And it should be known that Saint Peter stands for all those who serve Lord Jesus Christ in the active life, and Saint John stands for those who have the grace of the contemplative life. So here you have an example that the contemplative should not seek to intervene in worldly affairs, not even for offenses against God. He must not seek revenge, but give himself over to mourning and weeping, and turn to God to handle things, and draw near him and lean close to him more fully through contemplation, and leave everything to the will of God.

Watch again how Saint John did not disclose the answer to Saint Peter, even though he had asked his question. And you can take this to mean that the contemplative should not reveal the secret things of God the Father. Thus one reads of Saint Francis that he did not disclose secret revelations unless the love of neighbor required it, or that he revealed only what had to be disclosed.[96] See, then, how great the lovingkindness of Lord Jesus is, how he welcomes the beloved John on his breast. See also the other disciples, how sad they are because of these words that Lord Jesus has spoken, wondering what will happen next.

ch'el contemplativo non se dè intrametere nelle operatione corporale né ancho delle offese de Dio; non dè rechiedere vendeta, ma dèssene dolere et piançere et convertirse a Dio per operatione et approximarse et acostarse a lui più stretamente per contemplatione, et ogni cosa remetere nella voluntade de Dio.

Vedi ancora che sancto Çuane nol manifestò [f. 62r] a sancto Pietro, avegna ch'el ne havesse dimandato a sua peticione. Et per questo pòi intendere che il contemplativo non debe revelare le cose secrete de Dio Padre. Unde si leçe de sancto Francesco, che le revelatione occulte non manifestava de fuora se non in quanto el constre[n]çea la carità del proximo, o che li fosse revelato che la dovesse manifestare. Vedi quanto è la benignitade de miser Iesù, come el riceve il dilecto Çuane in sul pecto suo! Vedi ancora[102] li altri discipuli come stano tristi per quelle parole che miser Iesù li havea decto, aspectando il fine de queste cose.

Et questo sia decto quanto alla cena co[r]porale. Et da qui inançi diremo de[l] secundo misterio, çioè dello lavare delli piedi degli discipuli.

*Come el nostro Signore miser Iesù Cristo lavò gli piedi alli suoi discipuli, et come el compuose el sacramento del suo proprio corpo [f. 62v] et diello ai soi discipuli. Capitolo septimodecimo.*

E cognoscendo miser Iesù Cristo che il tempo era breve e vogliando lui compire quello che restava, levosse da cena et andò cum li discipuli suoi in uno altro albergo il qualle era desotto da quello, secundo che dice coloro che la hano visto. Et qui gli fece tuti sentare. Et poi si trasse la vestimenta sua et cinçesse il façuolo. Et poi misse de l'aqua in una concha e portola denançi alli discipuli soi. Et poi se inçenochiò denançi a loro et començavali a lavare li piedi, et poi li sugava cum il façulo ch'el tenia denançi, et poi li basava.

Et quando el fo per meço sancto Pietro, disse san Piero: «Signore, tu me laverai li piedi?».

Respuose il Signore: «Quello che io faço, tu nol sai hora, ma tu lo saperai poi».

102. MS *vedi <quanta> ancora*

And this much may be said concerning the supper itself. And now we will speak of the second mystery, that is, of the washing of the feet of the disciples.

*Chapter 17. How Our Lord Jesus Christ washed the feet of his disciples, and how he established the sacrament of his own body and gave it to his disciples.*

And knowing how little time remained, and wishing to complete what was left to be done, Lord Jesus Christ rose from the supper and went with his disciples to another room, which was beneath that one, according to those who have seen it.[97] And there he had them all sit down. And then he took off his tunic and tied a cloth around his waist. And then he poured water in a basin and brought it before his disciples. And then he knelt before them and began to wash their feet, and then he dried them with the cloth that he had around him, and then he kissed them.

And when he came to Saint Peter, Saint Peter said, "Lord, are you going to wash my feet?"

The Lord replied, "You do not understand what I am doing now, but you will understand later."

And Saint Peter, because this seemed very serious and astonishing to him, replied, "You will never wash my feet!"

The Lord replied, "If I do not wash your feet, you will have no part of me."

Et rispuose sancto Pietro, però che questa cosa li parea molto grave et meravegliosa: «Tu non mi laverai li piedi in eterno!».

Rispuose el [f. 63r] Signore: «Se io non te laverò, non harai parte mecho».

Disse sancto Pietro: «Signore mio, non solamente li piedi, ma le mane et il capo!».

Alora disse il Signore: «Colui che è lavato non li fa besogno se non lavare gli piedi, ma è mondo tuto. Et voi sieti mondi ma non tuti». El sapea bene chi 'l dovea tradire et perciò disse: «Non sieti mundi tuti».

Et dapoi che have lavato li piedi loro, tolse le vestimenta sua et ritornò alla mensa, et disse a loro: «Sapeti voi quello ch'io ho facto a voi. Voi me chiamate Maestro et Signore et dicte bene, però che io sum. Se io ho lavado li piedi vostri, io che sum Maestro et Signore, et voi dovete lavare gli piedi l'uno a l'altro. Et io ve ho dato exempio: così come ho facto a voi, et così facete anche voi».

Or pensa bene ogni cosa et examinale cum devotione et dì: «O Dio mio, quanta è grande la humilitade vostra: che voi che havete facto il cielo et la terra, ve [f. 63v] havete dignato de lavare li piedi a gli discipoli vostri per monstrare la via del reame de vita eterna! Li pescatori sono sentadi, et Dio omnipotente sta inçenochiato in terra denançi a loro et lava gli loro piedi, et poi li suga cum le sue sanctissime mane et basiali cum la sua sanctissima bocha. O Dio, come fo profunda la vostra humilitade, a lavare li piedi a quel Iuda traditore, per darne exempio che io fesse el simele!».

Or reposto che fo il nostro Signore a mensa et vogliando meter fine alli sacrificii della leçe et vogliando començare il testamento nuovo, si tolse il pane nelle sue sacratissime mane et levò li ochi al cielo et compose lo altissimo et sanctissimo sacramento del corpo suo sacratissimo. Et poi il rumpè et dettelo a li suoi discipoli et dise: «Tollete et mançate, che questo è il corpo mio il qualle serà tradito per voi». Et poi tolse il calice et dimandò gratia et detelo alli discipoli soi et disse: «Bevete de questo tuti. Questo è [f. 64 r] il sange mio del novo testamento, il quale serà spanto per molti in remissione di peccatori».

O carità de Dio, il qualle se à dato se medemo in cibo delle anime nostre! Et disse: «Facte questo in mia memoria». Et questa è quella memoria che fa l'anima cum Dio quando lei el riceve degnamente. Et pensando sopra de çiò, l'anima devotamente tuta se doveria transformare in lui per grandissimo amore, imperò che Dio non çe possea lassare maçor cosa, né più cara, né più utile, come lassare se medemo. O quanto havete amato questo huomo, che voi per lui ve havete dato alla morte della croce! Et

Saint Peter said, "My Lord, not only my feet, but my hands and head!"

Then the Lord said, "The one who has washed has no need to wash his feet, but is entirely clean. And you are clean, but not all." He knew well who would betray him, and for that reason he said, "You are not all clean."

And after he had washed their feet, he took his tunic and returned to the table. And he said to them, "You have seen what I have done for you. You call me Master and Lord, and rightly so, because that is what I am. If I have washed your feet, I who am Master and Lord, you must also wash each other's feet. And I have given you an example: just as I have done this for you, so should you do this for others."

Now imagine everything well, and contemplate it with devotion, and say: "O my God, how great is your humility: that you, who have made heaven and earth, have deigned to wash the feet of your disciples, to show the way to the Kingdom of Eternal Life! The fishermen are seated, and almighty God remains kneeling on the ground before them, and he washes their feet and then dries them with his most holy hands and kisses them with his most holy mouth. O God, how profound was your humility, to wash the feet of Judas the traitor, to give an example that I might do the same!"

Then Our Lord took his place at the table again. And wishing to complete the sacrifices of the law and wishing to initiate the new testament, he took the bread in his most sacred hands and raised his eyes to heaven and created the most high and most holy sacrament of his most sacred body. And then he broke the bread and gave it to his disciples and said: "Take this and eat it. It is my body, which will be given up for you." And then he took the cup and gave thanks and gave it to his disciples and said: "Drink this, all of you. This is my blood of the new testament, which will be poured out for many for the forgiveness of sins."

O love of God, who gave his very self as food for our souls! And he said: "Do this in memory of me." And this is the memory that the soul fashions with God when she receives him with reverence. And meditating on this, the devoted soul can be fully transformed through great love. For God could not leave us anything greater or more precious or more useful than to leave us himself. O, how greatly you have loved mankind, that for us you have given yourself up to death on the cross! And also you have left yourself in your food. So this bread that we eat in the sacrament of the altar is he who was made flesh in the glorious Virgin Mary, and when he was born he was placed between two animals in the manger, and in the end he suffered death for us sinners, and rose in glory from the dead, and then ascended to heaven and is seated at the right hand of God the

anche ve havete lassato in suo cibo; unde quel pane che noi mançemo in lo sacramento dello altare si è quello il qualle se incarnò nella gloriosa Verçene Maria, et nato che 'l fo, fu posto tra doe bestiole in lo presepio, et alla fine sostene morte per noi peccatori et gloriosamente resuscitò et poi montò in cielo et siede [f. 64v] alla dextera de Dio Padre omnipotente. Lui è quel pane vivo il qualle ha creato el cielo et la terra et tute le cose che se contiene in essa, et quello che ne pò dare vita et morte, paradiso et inferno.

Et dapoi che lui have comunicato tuti li soi discipuli et etiandio Iuda traditore et siando intrato il dimonio in Iuda, miser[103] Iesù disse a lui: «Quello che tu hai a fare, fàlo tosto». O carità divina, quanto siati voi sollicito alla salute della humana generatione! O caritade sancta!

### Del bel sermone che fece miser Iesù Cristo alli soi discipoli dapoi la comunione, et la partita de Iuda. Capitolo octavodecimo.

Et dapoi che Iuda fo partito, disse miser Iesù: «Hora è clarificato il Figliolo de l'Huomo». Or andò il traditore a gli principi et sacerdoti, alli qualli esso lo havea çià venduto per trenta denari, et dimandò a loro la fameglia per pigliare miser Iesù Cristo.

Et in questo meço miser Iesù fece el bel sermone alli [f. 65r] discipoli soi. Et disse: «Novo comandamento ve faço, che ve amiate l'uno l'altro come io ho amato voi. Et in questo cogn[o]scerano tuti che seti mei veri discipuli, se ve havereti caritade insieme».

Alora dise sancto Pietro: «Or dove andate voi, Signore?».

Rispuose miser Iesù: «Dove io vado, tu non çe poi venire al presente, ma vegnerai dapoi».

Alora disse sancto Pietro: «Perché non çi posso io venire hora? Io ponerò l'anima mia per voi!».

Respuose miser Iesù: «L'anima tua per me ponerai? Et io te dicho in veritade, che inaçi ch'el galo canti do fiade, tu me negarai tre.

«Figlioli, non havete tribulatione per me, se credete in Dio et in me credete. Io vado apparechiarve il luocho vostro, et poi tornerò et menarove mecho. Et dove serò, et voi sempre sareti».

Alora disse li discipoli: «Signore mio, noi non sapiamo dove voi andiate; come potremo noi sapere la via?».

103. MS *et miser*

almighty Father. He is this living bread: he who has created heaven and earth and all things that are contained in it, and he who is able to grant us life or death, paradise or hell.

And after he had given communion to all of his disciples, even to the traitor, Judas, the devil entered Judas. And Lord Jesus said to him, "What you have to do, do quickly." O divine love, how solicitous you are for the salvation of the human race! O holy love!

*Chapter 18. Of the beautiful sermon that Lord Jesus Christ gave to his disciples after communion, and the departure of Judas.*[98]

And after Judas had left, Lord Jesus said: "Now the Son of Man is revealed." Then the traitor went to the leaders and priests, to whom he had already sold him for thirty silver pieces, and asked for a group of them to come and arrest Lord Jesus Christ.

And while this was happening, Lord Jesus gave a beautiful sermon to his disciples. And he said, "I give you a new commandment, that you love one another as I have loved you. And in this all will know that you are my true disciples, if you love one another."

Then Saint Peter said, "Now where are you going, Lord?"

Lord Jesus replied, "Where I am going you cannot come now, but you will come afterwards."

Now Saint Peter said, "Why can't I come there now? I will lay down my life for you!"

Lord Jesus responded, "You will lay down your life for me? I tell you truly that before the cock crows twice, you will deny me three times.

"Sons, do not be troubled for my sake, but have faith in God and have faith in me. I am going to prepare your place for you, and then I will return and take you with me. And where I am, you will be too, forever."

Then the disciples said, "My Lord, we do not know where you are going. How can we know the way?"

The Lord replied, "I am the way, the truth, and the life. No one comes to my Father except through me, and whoever knows me knows my Father.

Respose el Signore: «Io sum via, veritade [f. 65v] et vita. Niuno viene al Padre mio se non per me, et chi cognosce me, cognosce il Padre mio. Et chi crede et ama me, l'opera ch'io façio farà lui, et quello che domandareti al Padre mio, farà a voi.

«Non ve lasserò orphani, io vado et sì tornerò a voi. Chi me amerà serverà li mei comandamenti et lo Padre mio amarà etiandio lui, et vegneremo a lui et staremo cum lui. Chi non amerà me, non serverà li comandamenti mei.

«La pace mia vi lasso, la pace mia vi dono, ma non a quel modo che dà il mondo. Io sum vite vera et voi seti le palmite. Et così come le palmite non puote fare fructo da se s'ele non sta nella vite, così sança me non podeti fare nulla.

«Sì come il Padre mio ama me, et così io amo voi, se servareti li comandamenti mei et stareti fermi in lo amore mio, sì come io ho observati li comandamenti del Padre mio et si stago fermo nello amore suo. Etco [f. 66r] lo comandamento mio: che ve amate l'uno l'altro come habo amato voi. Magiore amore non puote l'huomo havere che ponere l'anima sua per li amici soi. Non ve ho oçimai per servi, ma per amici: el servo non sa li secreti del suo signore. Ma voi sieti detti amici, perché çiò che io ho del Padre mio ve ho manifestato: çioè, la Divina Trinitade.

«Non elegesti voi me, ma io ho electo voi. Et se voi siati odiati dal mondo, habiate patientia, che imprima ha habuto in odio me. Se voi fosse del mondo, il mondo ve ameria; ma perciò che non seti mo[n]dani, lui ve ha i[n] odio.

«Non è il servo magiore che el signore. Se hanno perseguitato me, et ancho voi perseguiterano, et questo fano però che non cognoscono me, né il Padre mio. Ma l'è venuto tempo che chi[104] ve porà occidere si crederà fare sacrificio a Dio. Et imperò ve dico hora queste cose, açiò che quando vegnirà el tempo della tribulatione ve aricordate [f. 66v] che io ve ho detto. Al pri[n]cipio non ve 'l dissi, perché io era cum voi, quasi dica questa humanità era vostro cibo et conforto. Ma io ve dico il vero: egli è bisogno che io mi parti da voi, et se io non mi partirò, lo Spirito Sancto non vegnerà a voi, ma se io anderò io ve llo ma[n]derò et lui ve insegnarà ogni veritade et monstrarave ogni cosa.

«O figlioli mei, per uno pocho non mi vederete, et ancho uno pocho me vederete, perché io vado al Padre mio».

104. MS *ch(e) chi* in margin

And whoever believes in me and loves me will do what I do, and what you ask of the Father, he will do for you.

"I will not leave you orphans. I am going away, and then I will return to you. Whoever loves me will follow my commandments, and my Father will love him also, and we will come to him and remain with him. Whoever does not love me will not follow my commandments.

"I leave my peace with you; my peace I give to you, but not in the way that that world gives. I am the true vine, and you are the branches. And just as branches cannot bear fruit by themselves if they do not remain on the vine, so too, without me, you can do nothing.

"As my Father loves me, so I love you, if you follow my commandments and stay steadfast in my love, just as I have fulfilled the commandments of my Father and have stayed steadfast in his love. Here is my commandment: that you love one another as I have loved you. Greater love has no man than this, that he lay down his life for his friends. From now on, I do not consider you as servants but as friends. The servant does not know the secrets of his lord. But you are called friends, because what I have from my Father I have revealed to you: that is, the divine Trinity.

"You have not chosen me, but I have chosen you. And if you are hated by the world, have patience, for it first hated me. If you were of the world, the world would love you; but because you are not worldly, it hates you.

"The servant is not greater than the master. If they have persecuted me, they will also persecute you, and they do this because they do not know me or my Father. But the time has come when the one who might kill you will believe he is making a sacrifice to God. And so I tell you these things now, so that when the time of trial comes, you will remember what I told you. At the beginning, I did not wish to tell you this, because I was with you (as if to say, this humanity was your food and comfort).[99] But now I tell you the truth: that it is necessary for me to leave you, and if I do not leave you, the Holy Spirit will not come to you. But if I go, I will send him to you, and he will teach you every truth and reveal everything.

"O my sons, for a short time you will not see me, and then you will see me only for a short time, because I am going to my Father."

And they did not understand him. And the Lord, knowing that they wanted to ask him what these words meant, said to them, "In truth I tell you that you will lament and weep, and the world will rejoice; but your sorrow will turn to joy. A woman at the time of childbirth suffers because

Et egli non lo inteseno, et cognoscando il Signore che loro il voleano domandare de questo parlare, disse a loro: «In veritade ve dico che voi pia[n]çereti et lacrimareti, et el mond[o] se ne alegrerà; ma la tristicia vostra tornerà in alegreça. La femina all'hora del parto ha tristicia però che lei sta sul morire; ma poi ch'è nato lo figliolo non se aricorda del dolore per la alegreça del figliolo, et così voi haverete tristicia, et revedandome voi haveti alegreça, et [f. 67r] niuno ve pot[r]à tuore la alegreça vostra.

«Alora quello che domandareti al Padre mio nel nome mio, io ne pregarò il Padre mio per voi; imperò che esso ama voi perché voi havete amato me et creduto che io sia. Et sapete che io veni dal Padre mio nel mondo, et hora lasso il mondo et ritorno al Padre. Et l'hora se approxima che cadauno de voi vadi in dispersione, et laseretì me solo; ma io non sum solo imperò ch'el Padre è semper cum me. Et voi haveretì tribulatione nel mondo; ma confortative, et habiate fede che io ho sconfito et vento il mondo».

Et poi levò li ochi al cielo et disse: «Padre, mo' è hora che dimonstri che io sum tuo figliolo, açiò che io possa manifestare et darli vita eterna. Et questa è vita eterna: che cognoscano te solo Idio vero et Iesù Cristo tuo figliolo, el qualle tu mandasti. Compiuto ho questo mio peregrinaço, che me commandasti et ho manifestato [f. 67v] el nome tuo alli huomeni che me hai donato: elli erano tuoi, et dati li hai a me. Io ho servati i commandamenti tuoi et sì so che io sum da te. Et però io prego per loro, et non per lo mondo, ma per quelli che tu me hai dato che sono tuoi. Et ciò che io ho si è tuo, et quello che tu hai si è mio. Io te priego per questi orphaneli che sono nel mondo, perché io me ne vegno a te. Infina che io sum stato cum loro, io ne ho habuto cura, ma hora li recomando a te. Et niuno non è perito se non Iuda traditore, figliolo della perditione, sì come dice la Scriptura. Tu sai ch'el mondo li hano in odio, et stano nel mondo et io me parto dal mondo et sì vegno a te. Non te priego che tu li tolgi del mondo, ma che tu li guardi da male. Et sì come tu m'ài nel mondo ma[n]dato a predicare et a combatere et a morire, così mando io loro. Et però ti priego per loro et offerisco me alla morte della croce; et non solamen[f. 68r]te per loro, ma etiandio per tuti coloro che crederano in me et viverano secundo la doctrina loro. Sì che tuto siano uno in me, sì come tu et io siamo uno. Et cognosca el mondo che tu me hai mandato et che tu ami loro come ami me. Et sì voglio, Padre, che dove sum io siano anche loro, et che veçano la gloria mia, che me hai dato et che me amasti inançi ch'el mondo fosse. Et sì voglio: che quello amore cum lo qualle tu ami me, sì ami loro».

Et compiuto el sermone disse a loro: «Leviàmosse de qui». Alora tuti impauriti, non sapiando dove el se volesse andare. Et strençandose adosso

she is at the brink of death; but after a son is born, she no longer remembers the suffering because of her joy at the birth of her son. And in the same way, you will have sorrow, and when you see me again, you will rejoice, and no one will be able to take away your joy.

"And whatever you ask of my Father in my name, I will ask the Father for you; for he loves you because you have loved me and believed in me. And you know that I came from my Father into the world, and now I am leaving the world to return to my Father. And the hour draws near when you will all scatter, and leave me on my own; but I will not be alone because the Father is always with me. And you will have tribulation in the world; but take heart, and have faith that I have overcome and vanquished the world."

And then he raised his eyes to heaven and said, "My Father, the time has come for you to show that I am your Son, so that I can reveal and give eternal life to them. And this is eternal life: that they may know you, the only true God, and Jesus Christ, your Son, whom you have sent. I have completed this, my pilgrimage, which you have commanded of me; and I have revealed your name to men whom you have given to me; they were yours, and you have given them to me. I have fulfilled your commandments, and in this I know that I come from you. And so I pray for them; not for the world, but for those you have given me that are yours. And what I have is yours, and what you have is mine. I pray to you for these little orphans who are in the world, because I am coming to you. All the time that I have been with them, I have taken care of them, but now I commend them to you. And not one has been lost, except for Judas the traitor, son of perdition, as scripture says. You know that the world hates them, and they remain in the world, and I am leaving the world and coming to you. I do not ask that you take them from the world, but that you keep them from harm. And just as you sent me into the world to preach and to fight and to die, so I send them. But I pray to you for them, and I offer myself up to death on the cross; and not only for them, but also for all of those who believe in me and live according to their teaching. And all will be one in me, just as I am one with you; and the world will know that you sent me, and that you love them as you love me. And so I wish, Father, that where I am, they may be there also, and that they may behold my glory, which you have given me, and see how you have loved me since before the world began. And so I wish this: that you love them with the same love with which you have loved me."

And when this sermon was finished, he said to them, "Let us rise and go from here." And then they were all afraid, not knowing where he

a miser Iesù, sì lo seguitavano fuori de Ierusalem. Or vedi i discipoli, cum quanta paura vano drieto a lui.[105] Tuti si sforçavano de approximarse a lui, sì come fano gli polli alla galina quando hano paura de qualche occello. Così faceano gli discipoli intorno a miser Iesù, però ch'eli non sapeano dove lui andase.

## Come miser Iesù Cristo andò nel orto. [f. 68v][106]
## Capitolo nonodecimo.

Or çonti che furono miser Iesù cum li discipoli alla villa che [si] chiamava Gethsemani,[107] dove era l'orto nel qualle lui andava a orare, et passato che have el torrente Cedron, intrò nel orto. Et poi disse alli disipoli: «Sedete qui et aspetatime, ch'io voglio andare ad orare». Vedi che discretione lui have alli suoi discipoli: non volle che li vedesseno la pugna et la aff[l]ictione sua, perché non manchasseno in la fede et anche per non darli più afflictione. Ma chiamò secretamente Pietro, Iacomo et Çuane, però che questi erano più forti nella fede, et anche haveano çà visto la gloria della sua transfiguratione; et menoli secho. Et poi se començò a contristare et impaurire nella façia. Et disse a loro: «Trista è l'anima mia perfina alla morte. Rimanete qui et vegiate mecho».

Et partisse da loro forsi uno trare di pietra, et humelmente se inçenochiò [f. 69r] orando et disse: «Padre mio, se l'è possibile, tolle da mi questa Passione; ma veramente non come voglio io ma come piace a voi».

Or stà qui uno pocho, et ripensa cum la mente piatosa la sua grandissima humilitade, con çiò sia cosa ch'el sia Dio equalle al Padre suo, et hora pare che lui se habi dismentigato de esere Dio, imperò ch'el priega hora il Padre celestiale sì come persona bisognosa. Et molte altre volte miser Iesù ha orato, ma alora pregava el Padre per noi sì come nostro advocato. Et hora el priega per lui: veramente è da averli compassione! Considera ancora la sua profundissima obedientia, che lui se lassò nella voluntà del Padre a determinare questa questione et non è exaudito secundo alguna voluntade che era in lui, imperò che in lui erano più voluntade, delle quale io dirò de drieto. Et qui dice sancto Hieronimo che questa

---

105. MS *silo seguitavano . . . a lui* in margin
106. MS *Come miser Iesù Cristo andò nel orto et come el fo preso da' Giudei et menato a casa* [68v] *de Anna.*
107. MS *Geth<e>semani*

wished to go. And crowding around the Lord Jesus, they followed him outside of Jerusalem. Now watch the disciples, how fearfully they follow him. They all strove to draw near him, like chicks do around the hen when they are afraid of some bird of prey. Like this the disciples gathered around Lord Jesus, because they did not know where he was going.[100]

## Chapter 19. How Lord Jesus Christ went to the garden.

Then Lord Jesus and his disciples went to the place called Gethsemane, where there was a garden where he used to go to pray. And when they had crossed the stream of Cedron, he entered the garden. And then he said to the disciples: "Sit here and wait for me, for I want to go and pray." See what concern he had for his disciples: he didn't want them to see his struggle and anguish, so that they would not lose faith, and also because he didn't want to give them more affliction. But he quietly called only Peter, James, and John, because they were the strongest in faith, and also they had already seen the glory of his transfiguration; and he took them with him. And then he began to grow sad, and to take on a fearful expression. And he said, "My soul is in anguish, even unto death. Remain here and watch with me."

And he went off a little way from them, perhaps a stone's throw away, and he humbly knelt to pray and said, "My Father, if it is possible, take this Passion from me; but truly, let it be not what I desire, but what is pleasing to you."

Now pause here a little, and reflect with compassion on his great humility. For even though he is God, and equal to the Father, it as if he has forgotten that he is God, for he prays to the heavenly Father as a person in need. And Lord Jesus had prayed many other times, but he had always prayed to the Father for us, as our advocate. And now he prays for himself: truly, this is cause for compassion! Consider also his most profound obedience: how he left it to the will of his Father to determine the answer to this question, and he was not answered according to his own will, for there were several kinds of will in him, as I will describe later. And here Saint Jerome says that the sorrow and fear that Lord Jesus felt showed the truth of his humanity, contrary to the opinion of many heretics.[101] And he also grieved for his desolate companions, and for the damnation of Judas and for the destruction of Jerusalem, and also for the suffering of his most sweet mother.[102] And wise commentators also say that Lord Jesus prayed

tristicia et questa paura che have miser Iesù[108] monstrò [f. 69v] la verità della sua humanitade contra la opinione de molti heretici. Et dolévasse etiandio per la desolata fameglia et per la danatione de Iuda et della destructione de Ierusalem, et anche per lo dolore della madre sua dolcissima. Et ancho diceno gli savii expositori che miser Iesù pregava più el Padre per compassione del populo çudaico che per paura che lui havesse, perché el vedea la perditione de' Iudei per la morte sua, però che non haveano niuna casone per la qualle il dovesseno fare morire. Unde Pilato, habiandolo diligentemente examinato de ogni cosa, disse al populo: «Io non trovo casone alcuna in lui per la qualle el deba morire».

Pregava ado[n]que miser Iesù il Padre che «Se fare si puote cum salute de' Iudei, che creda la moltitudine delle gente, io refuto la Passione, et se li Çudei deno essere damnati açiò che li altri credano, fia la tua voluntade et non la mia». Et non fo exaudito la prima [f. 70r] volta.

Et tornado alli discipoli, trovoli dormire. Et disse a Pietro: «Non hai tu poduto una hora vegiare mecho, che dicevi de morire per me? Vegiate et orate, açiò che non intrate in tentatione: lo spirito è pronto, ma la carne è inferma. Ma guai a colui per cui io sum tradito. Meglio seria per lui ch'el non fosse mai nasuto».

Et partisse da loro et tornò la secunda fiada ad orare. Et disse: «Padre mio, s'el non pò passare ch'io non beva questo calice, sia facta la voluntade tua. Ma io vi priego che exaudi la oratione mia et che voi non despresiate li priegi mei. Intendi a me et exaudi la mia oratione, imperçiò che io sum contristato in questa bataglia in la qualle me conviene intrare, et lo spirito mio è anxiato et fatichato in me, et lo cuore mio è turbato in tanta pena quanta io me veço denançi apparechiata. Inclina aduncha a me le orechie tue et inte[n]di la voce della mia oratione». Et questo dicea in quanto [f. 70v] vero huomo. «A voi, Padre, ve piaque di mandarme in questo mondo açiò che io satisfacesse alla inçuria ricevuta dalla humana generatione. Et ecco che io ho decto et annu[n]tiato la veritade et la salute tua. Et sum stato semper in povertade et fadiche et in tribulatione infina dalla mia çoventude, facendo sempre la tua voluntade secundo ch'è scripto di me per lo propheta: ch'io façia la tua volu[n]tade. Io sum apparechato de compire quello che resta a fare. Ma tuta via io te priego, Padre, s'el pò essere che tu tolli via da me questa pena et amaritudine la qualle m'è apparechiata dali mei adversarii, imperò che voi, Padre, vedete bene quante iniquitade li hano ordinato contra de me maliciosamente et quante falsitade me apponeno, et sono consegliati de

to the Father more out of compassion for the Jewish people than from his own fear, because he could forsee the perdition of the Jews for his death; for they had no just cause to put him to death.[103] And this is why Pilate, after he had questioned him intently about everything, said to the people, "I find no cause for which he deserves to die."

So Lord Jesus asked the Father, "If it is possible for the multitudes to believe while granting salvation to the Jews, I will refuse the Passion. And if the Jews must be damned so that others may believe, let it be your will, and not mine." And his prayer was not answered the first time.

And returning to the disciples, he found them sleeping. And he said to Peter, "Were you not able to watch an hour with me, you who said you would die for me? Watch and pray, so that you do not enter into temptation: the spirit is willing, but the flesh is weak. But woe to him by whom I am betrayed. It would be better for him had he never been born."

And he left them and returned the second time to pray. And he said, "My Father, if I must drink from this cup, and it cannot be otherwise, let your will be done. But I ask that you answer my prayer, and that you not despise my requests. Listen to me, and answer my plea, because I am sorrowful in this battle which I must enter, and my spirit is anxious and weary, and my heart is so troubled by all the torments I see prepared for me. Incline your ears toward me, and listen to the voice of my prayer." And he said this inasmuch as he was true man. "It pleased you, Father, to send me into this world so that I might make satisfaction for the wrongs committed by the human race. And behold, I have spoken and announced the truth and your salvation. And I remained in poverty and toil and tribulation from the time of my youth, always doing your will according to what was written of me by the prophet: that I do your will. I am prepared to complete what remains to be done. But nevertheless I ask you, Father, if it is possible that you take from me this torment and bitter pain that is prepared for me by my adversaries. For you see well, Father, how many charges of iniquity they have maliciously brought forward against me, and how many falsehoods they attribute to me, and how they have decided to take my soul. But you, Father, know well whether I did these things, and whether I ever committed iniquities, and whether I have rendered evil for evil or evil for good; and if this were true, I would deserve to fall into the hands of my enemies. But you know that I have always done what pleases you. And they have planned to render me evil for good, and hate for love. And they have corrupted my disciple, and he has become their guide to betray me into their hands. I have been appraised and

tuorme l'anima mia. Ma voi, Padre, save bene se io ho facto queste cose et se io fici mai iniquitade et se io ho renduto male per male o male per bene; et se così fosse, [f. 71r] degnamente caçeria nelle mane de' mei inimici. Ma tu sai ch'io sempre ho facto il tuo piacere. Et elli hano ordinato contra di me malle per bene et odio per amore. Et hano corroto el discipolo mio et è facto loro guida a tradirme in lor mane. Io sum stimato et appreciato trenta denari d'arçento. Pregote adoncha, Padre mio, che tu togli da me questo calice, çioè questa Passione. Ma se a voi pare altramente, sia facta la voluntade tua et non la mia, ma apparechiati de aiutarme et non me indusiare.

«Or poniamo[109] che elli non sapesseno che sia tuo figliolo; ma poniamo ch'io sia vivuto cum loro innocentemente et ògle facto de molti beneficii—non doverebbeno essere così crudeli inverso de me. Recordate, Padre mio, ch'io sum stato denançi al tuo conspecto per pregare per loro et per tuore via la tua indignatione da loro; or doncha rèndesse male per bene. Et certo [f. 71v] hano ordinato de tuore l'anima mia et hanomi apparechiato una vituperosa morte. Et tu vedi bene, Padre mio, la obedientia mia et la loro iniquitade, la patientia mia et la loro crudelitade; unde non indusiare a dare la sententia, ma fàmi iudicio, et non te partire da me in questa tribulatione, imperçiò che la Passione se approxima et non è chi me aiuta. Et ecco che çà sono appresso alla tua presentia coloro che me tribulano et che vanno cercando l'anima mia».

Et dapoi queste parole, tornò agli discipoli la secunda volta. Et trovoli dormire per tristicia et sì li dessidoe. Et confortoli de stare in oratione et di vegiare cum lui. Et poi tornò la terça fiata ad orare, et disse: «Padre mio, se io non posso scampare questo calice, che io non beva, sia facta la tua voluntade. Ma ricomandove la madre mia dolcissima et li mei dilecti discipoli: Padre mio, guardali da ogni male».

Et orando così [f. 72r] prolisamente, vene in tanta agonia et bataglia ch'el suo sanctissimo sangue se convertì in sudore, et insiva del suo corpo a modo de sudore abundantemente, in tanto che ne bagnò la terra. O anima ingrata, pensa l'angossia del tuo Signore, et aricordati spesso de così duro et amoroso martirio come fu questo suo, ancora exemplo contra la impatientia nostra, imperò che miser Iesù orò tre fiade inanti ch'el fosse exaudito.

Et stando lui in tanta agonia et anxietade, vene l'angelo Michaelo et confortandolo disse: «Dio ve salve Iesù Cristo, Signore mio et Dio mio. La oratione vostra e il sudore del corpo vostro io l'ò app[r]esentado[110]

109. MS poniamo <chio sia venuto> che
110. MS appeesentado

valued at thirty pieces of silver. And so I ask, my Father, that you take this cup from me, that is, this Passion. But if you decide otherwise, let your will be done, and not mine. But prepare to help me, and do not delay.

"Now we might grant that they do not know that I am your Son. But even so, I have been living among them innocently and have done many good things for them, so they should not be so cruel towards me. Remember, my Father, that I have come before your gaze to pray for them, and to turn your anger away from them; yet evil is rendered for good. And without doubt they have planned to take my life, and they have prepared a shameful death for me. And you see well, my Father, my obedience and their iniquity, my patience and their cruelty. So do not delay in giving the sentence, but give me justice, and do not abandon me in this tribulation, because the Passion draws near and there is no one to help me. And look, they are already in your presence, those who seek to harm me and come to take my life."

And after these words, he returned to the disciples the second time. And he found that they had fallen asleep because of their sorrow. And he woke them, and he asked them to remain in prayer and to watch with him. And then he returned a third time to pray, and said, "My Father, if I must drink from this cup and cannot avoid it, let your will be done. But I commend to you my most sweet mother and my dear disciples. My Father, protect them from every harm."

And praying with many words like this, he entered into such agony and strife that his most holy blood turned to sweat, and it poured out from his body as copiously as sweat, so much so that it soaked the earth. O ungrateful soul, imagine the anguish of your Lord, and call to mind often what a hard and loving martyrdom this was! It was also an example against our impatience, because Our Lord Jesus prayed three times before he was heard.

And while he was in such agony and anguish, the angel Michael came and comforted him, saying, "God be with you, Jesus Christ, my Lord and my God. I have spoken of your prayers and the sweat of your body before your Father and the entire heavenly court, and we all knelt before your Father, and we asked that he might have pity on such a hard and shameful death.[104] Then your Father answered and said: 'My most beloved Son knows well that the human race cannot be redeemed fittingly without the shedding of his precious blood. He knows well how much we have desired this redemption. And so, if he desires the salvation of the human race, it is necessary for him to die for them.' So, my Lord, what have you determined to do?"

denançi al Padre vostro et a tuta la corte celestiale, et tuti se inçenochiassemo denançi al Padre vostro et pregassemo lui ch'el ve havesse misericordia de così dura et opbrobriosa morte. Alora el Padre vostro ne respose et disse: "Lo diletissimo figliolo mio sa be[n] che l'humana [f. 72v] generatione non se puote convenientemente recomperare sança el spargimento del suo precioso sangue. El sa bene quanto noi havemo desiderato questa talle restauratione, et imperò se lui vuole la salute de l'humana generatione, conviene ch'el mori per loro". Adonque, Signore mio, che havete determinato de fare?»

Alora respuose el Signore nostro miser Iesù Cristo: «Io voglio al tuto la salute de l'humana natura. Et imperò io eleço de morire per le anime le qualle il Padre mio ha create alla sua imagine. Sia facta aduncha la voluntà del Padre mio».

Alora disse l'angelo [Michaelo]:[111] «Confortàtive, et state securamente ch'el Padre vostro dice ch'el è sempre cum voi, et che la madre vostra gli serà sempre ricomandata et etiandio li discipoli vostri».

Or qui fo dato contra la superbia nostra: che lui che era Creatore ricevete humilmente conforto dalla sua creatura in quanto huomo. Et partito che fo l'angelo, humelmente se levò tu[f. 73r]to bagnato de sangue. Et netandose la faça, tornò alli discipoli suoi.[112] Risguardalo quando el torna alli discipoli, come el se va sugando il volto cum la vesta sua, et forsi ch'el se va a lavare nel torente? O anima, habi compassione al tuo Signore de tanta pena che lui portò per te solamente per amore!

Et è da sapere che in Cristo Iesù erano quatro modi de voluntade. La prima fo la voluntade della carne, et questa per niuno modo non volea morire né patire pena. La secunda si era la sensualitade, et questa rememorava et temea. La terça era la voluntade de la rasone, et questa obediva et consentiva. Et de questa dice Ysaia propheta de Cristo: «fo facto sacrificio secundo la sua voluntade». La quarta era la divina, et questa comandava et dava la sentencia. O anima che cerchi gli dilecti et fuçi le pene, non mi pare che habi imparato da questo maestro, il qualle per farne de servi figioli se fece lui servo, et [f. 73v] per liberare noi, lui se condenò!

Et çonto ch'el fo alli discipoli, disse a loro: «Hora dormite et ripossative». Et così feceno. Et lui, come buono pastore, vegiava quella sua picola grege. O cum quanto amore lui amava questa sua creatura, che siando lui in tanta angossia et tribulatione era sollicito della loro salute et riposso!

111. MS *Gabrielo*
112. MS *suoi* in margin

Then Our Lord Jesus Christ replied, "I desire, above all, the salvation of humankind. And so I choose to die for the souls who my Father created in his image. Let it be done according to the will of my Father."

Then the angel Michael said, "Take courage, and stay strong in the knowledge that your Father says that he is always with you, and that your mother will always remain in his care, and your disciples too."

Now here an example was given against our pride: that he who was the Creator humbly received comfort, as a man, from his creature. And when the angel left, he humbly rose, completely bathed in blood. And wiping his face, he returned to his disciples. Watch him as he returns to his disciples, how he dries his face with his garment, and perhaps goes to wash in the stream. O soul, have compassion for your Lord, who bore so much pain for you only for love!

And it should be known that in Christ Jesus there were four kinds of will.[105] The first was the will of the flesh, and this in no way wished to die or to suffer pain. The second was the will of the emotions, and this hesitated and was afraid. The third was the will of reason, and he consented to and obeyed this. And of this Isaiah the prophet says of Christ, "He became a sacrifice according to his will." The fourth was the divine will, and this governed and rendered the judgment. O soul who seeks pleasures and flees pain, it seems to me that you have not learned from this Master, who, to make sons of servants, became a servant himself, and to set us free condemned himself!

And when he reached his disciples, he said to them, "Now sleep and rest." And they did so. And he, like a good shepherd, watched over his little flock. Oh, with what love he loved the human beings he had created, that even when he was in the midst of such anguish and tribulation he was so concerned about their health and repose!

*Come Iuda vene per pigliare miser Iesù nel orto cu[m]*
*i principi di sacerdoti cum arme et lance et lanterne.*
*Capitulo vigesimo.*

Et sapiando Iuda che sancto Iacobo Minore somegiava molto a miser Iesù, disse agli Iudei: «Or siate cauti a pigliare Iesù, però ch'el è uno delli discipoli suoi a chi molto si someglia, et perçiò io ve do questo segno: quello che io baserò è[113] desso».

Et approximandose Iuda cum li Çudei al luocho dove era miser Iesù, disse a catuno: «Venga cum silentio et siati cauti. Io anderò inançi».

Et sapiando miser Iesù la venuta loro, si dessidò gli [f. 74r] discipoli dicendo a loro: «Or non dormite più. Ecco che viene l'hora che io serò tradito nelle mane de' peccatori, et ecco il traditore che li guida».

Et cum questo parlare si fece inverso di loro et disse: «Chui cercate voi»?

Et in questo decto Iuda traditore el basò et disse: «Dio ti salvi, Maestro».

Disse miser Iesù: «Amico, a che sei venuto?», come se dicesse «de discipulo traditore?». Et dimandando el Signore chui cerchasseno, rispuoseno: «Iesù Naçareno».

Et lui rispuose: «Io sono desso».

Alora cadeteno tuti in terra; et così feceno per tre volte. O Signore, chi poterà resistere a voi nel dì del Iudicio?

Et anche dimonstrò qui il Signore che se lui non volesse essere preso de sua voluntade, egli non lo potriano pigliare. Et in questo decto si fece apresso di loro, quasi dica: «Eccomi, fate di me quello che vi piace». Et qui monstrò el Signore nostro el grande amore ch'el ne portava [f. 74v] et anche la prompta voluntade che lui havea de morire per noi. Alora gli Iudei si'l preseno.

Or vedendo sancto Pietro ch'el maestro suo venia preso così furiosamente, per dolore che lui havea si trase fuori uno cortello et tagliò la orechia drita a uno servo del summo pontifico. Alora disse miser Iesù a sancto Pietro: «Meti el tuo coltello nella vagina. El calice che m'à dato el Padre, mio non vòi tu ch'io el beva? Come se adimpirà le scripture de' propheti che così conviene essere?».

Et poi se fece menare quello servo denançi il quale havea tagliato l'orechia, et distese la mano sua et sanò l'orechia al suo inimicho.

113. MS *(et)*

*Chapter 20. How Judas came with the high priests
to capture Lord Jesus in the garden with weapons
and lances and lanterns.*

And Judas, knowing that Saint James the Minor looked very much like Lord Jesus, said to the Jews, "Now be careful when you come to capture Jesus, because there is one of his disciples who looks very much like him. And I will give you this sign: the one whom I kiss is he."

And as Judas and the Jews drew near the place where Lord Jesus was, Judas said to them, "Come silently, and be careful. I will go ahead."

And Lord Jesus, knowing of their approach, woke the disciples, saying to them: "Now sleep no more. Behold, the hour comes when I will be betrayed into the hands of sinners. And behold the traitor who leads them."

And with those words he turned to them and said, "Who is it that you seek?"

And at this, Judas the traitor kissed him and said, "God be with you, Master."

Lord Jesus said, "Friend, how did you come this far?" (as if to say "from disciple to traitor?"). And when he asked them who they were seeking, they replied, "Jesus of Nazareth."

And he replied: "I am he."

And they all fell to the ground; and they did so three times.[106] O Lord, who will be able to withstand you on the Day of Judgment?

And the Lord also showed here that if he had not wished to be taken of his own will, they would not have been able to capture him. And as he said these words, he drew near them, as if to say, "Here I am. Do with me what you please." And here Our Lord demonstrated the great love that he bore us, and also his ready willingness to die for us. And then the Jews took him.

Now Saint Peter, seeing his Master seized with such fury, out of anguish drew a knife and cut off the right ear of a servant of the high priest. And then Lord Jesus said to Saint Peter, "Put your knife away in its sheath. The cup that my Father has given me: don't you want me to drink it? How else will the scriptures of the prophets, which say that it must of necessity be like this, be fulfilled?"

And then he asked that the servant whose ear had been cut off be led before him; and he extended his hand, and healed the ear of his enemy.

O Christian soul who seeks vengeance for offenses received, behold your Creator, and learn from him to render good for evil and not evil for

O anima cristiana che cerchi di fare vendeta della offesa ricevuta, risguarda qui il tuo Creatore, et impara da lui de rendere bene per male et non male per male! Et risguarda anchora la benignitade del nostro Salvatore che, siando preso per essere morto, non volse rendere malle per male [f. 75r], ançi sempre rendete bene per male.

Et poi disse alli Iudei sì come a ladrone: «Seti venuti a pigliarme cum arme et lance et lanterne. Io sempre sum stado cum voi nel tempio a predicare et manifestare la salute vostra, ma hora è tempo delle tenebre vostre».

Alora tuti li discipoli fuçiteno et lassorono miser Iesù agnelo innocentissimo tra quelli lupi et cani affamati. Ma uno giovane seguitava lui, vestito de pano lino sopra le carne, et quelli il tenero; et egli lasiò il mantello et nudo fuçite da loro.

Alora quelli ministri cum furore ligorono le mani drieto a miser Iesù, et al colo li messeno una corda sì come fosse uno latrone. Et così ligato cum ogni vituperio et furia el menarono in Ierusalem cum gran freça et cum molte inçurie. Alcuni di loro el tirava cum la corda et facevalli inchinare el capo, et altri il spengeva et tirava per li capelli, et alcuni lo biastemava et façevalo volçere et rivolçere, et altri gli pellava la barba et tirava per li capelli. Et altri [f. 75v] di loro l'andava spençando, et diceano: «Viene oltra, malfactore, tu sei pure stado çonto questa volta!».

Et cum[114] queste inçurie el fo menato prima a casa de Anna, ch'era suocero de Cayfas lo quale era pontifice in quello anno. Certo Cayphas era quello che diede conseglio alli Giudei che gli era di bisogno che uno huomo morisse per lo populo. Ma Pietro seguitava Iesù et un altro discipulo il qualle era cognoscente del pontifico, et entrò cum Iesù nella casa. Et Pietro stava de fuori al ussio, et l'altro discipulo, ch'era noto del pontifice, uscite fuori et parlò a l'hostiaria et menò dentro Pietro. Et essendo aceso il fuocho nel meço della salla, gli servi et ministri stavano al fuocho et scaldavase, però che era gielo. Et Pietro stava nel meço di loro; et essendo veduto dalla ancilla hostiaria che sedeva al lume et habiandolo guardato disse: «Or et tu non sei discipulo di questo huomo?».

Et Pietro il negò denanci a tutti, dicendo: «O femina, io nol cono[f. 76r]sco et non so quello che tu dichi». Et uscite fuori dinanci alla salla, et il gallo cantò.

Poi lo po[n]tifice adimandò miser Iesù delli discipoli suoi et della sua doctrina. Rispuose Iesù et disse: «Io palesemente ho parlato al mondo, et

114. MS *cum* in margin

evil! And behold also the benevolence of Our Savior, who, even as he was being captured to be killed, did not wish to render evil for evil, but always to render good for evil.

And then he said to the Jews, as if to thieves: "You have come to capture me with weapons and lances and lanterns. I have always been among you in the temple, preaching and showing the way to your salvation; but now your time of darkness has come."

And then all of the disciples fled, and left Lord Jesus, the most innocent lamb, among those wolves and greedy dogs.[107] But one youth followed him, wearing nothing but a linen garment over his flesh; and they seized him, and he left behind his cloak and fled naked from them.

And then those guards violently tied the hands of Lord Jesus behind his back, and they put a cord around his neck, as if he were a thief. And they led him, bound like this, with all kinds of insults and fury to Jerusalem in great haste and with many injuries. Some of them pulled him by the cord and made him bow down his head, and others pushed him and pulled him by the hair, and others insulted him and spun him around, and others plucked his beard and pulled his hair, and others went on pushing him and said, "Come here, evildoer, you're really caught this time!"

And with these insults, he was led first to the house of Annas, who was the father-in-law of Caiphas, who was the high priest that year.[108] Indeed, Caiphas was the one who counselled the Jews that it was necessary that a man be put to death for the people. But Peter followed Jesus and another disciple who was known to the chief priest, and he entered with Jesus into the house. And Peter stayed outside, and the other disciple who was known to the high priest went outside and spoke to the woman who kept watch at the door, and led Peter inside. And since a fire had been lit in the middle of the hall, the servants and soldiers stayed near the fire and warmed themselves because it was cold. And Peter stayed in their midst; and the doorkeeper, who was sitting near the light and had been watching him, said, "Now, aren't you a disciple of this man?"

And Peter denied it in front of everyone, saying, "O woman, I do not know him, and I don't know what you are talking about." And he went out of the hall, and the cock crowed.

Then the high priest asked Lord Jesus about his disciples and his teaching. Jesus replied and said: "I have spoken very openly to the world, and I have always taught in the temple and the synagogue there where the Jews gather, and I have said nothing in secret. Why do you ask me, then? Ask those who have heard me and know what I have said."

sempre io ho amaestrato nel tempio et nelle sinagoge là dove li Giudei si ra-
gunavano, et in occulto niente ho parlato. Adonque perche me adima[n]di
tu? Dimandane coloro che me hano udito, et loro sano quel ch'i' ò detto».

Et dette ch'ebe queste parole, uno degli min[i]stri astante li diede una
grande sguançada et disse: «Respondi tu così al pontifice»?

Respose Miser cum grande mansuetudine: «Se io ho parlato male, dà
testimoniança del male, ma se ho detto bene, perché me percuoti tu?».

O anima superba, impara havere patientia dal tuo Maestro!

Et poscia Anna il mandò legato ad Cayphas pontifice, dove li scribi et
pharisei erano radunati. Ma Pietro seguitava miser Iesù dalla longa insino
al palacio [f. 76v] del pri[n]cipe de' sacerdoti et intrò dentro et sedevasi
cogli ministri per vedere il fine. Et li principi de' sacerdoti et tutto il con-
cilio cercavano falsa testimoniança contra Iesù per farlo morire, et non
trovava il modo, quantumque havesseno molti falsi testimonii, però che
non si acordavano insieme. Finalmente venero dui falsi testimonii dicendo: «Noi l'udimo dire, 'Io posso disfare questo tempio facto manual-
mente et dipoi tre giorni rehedificarlo,». Et non era conveniente la loro testimoniança.

Alora levossi el summo sacerdote nel meço, et dimandando Iesù et
disse: «Tu non respondi a queste cosse che costoro dicono contro di te?».
Ma Iesù taceva et a niente rispondea. Et anchora gli disse il summo sacerdote: «Io ti sconçuro per Dio vero che tu çi dichi se sei Cristo Figliolo de
Dio vivo benedetto».

Disse miser Iesù: «Tu l'ài detto. Ma io vi dico per verità che voi vederete il Figliolo della Vergene sedere dalla dextra della virtù de Dio et venire [f. 77r] nelle nuvole del cielo».

Alora el principe de' sacerdoti squarciò le vestimenta[115] sue et disse:
«Ecco che adunca cerchemo testimoniança. H[a]vemo[116] udita la biste-
mia: che ve ne pare?». Et rispuoseno che lo era degno de morte.

Or chi havesse veduto quelli cani Giudei brancarlo nella faça, et velarli
li ochi, et darge le sguançade et di pugni et spudarli nella faça et darli di buffeti et dire «Indivina, chi è stato colui che t'à percosso?», et poi pelargi la
barba et tirarlo per li capelli? Et per derisione lo adoravano dicendo: «Dio ti
salvi, re de' Giudei». Et chi el tirava in qua et chi in là, et altri ge ficava el
dido nel volto dicendo: «O figliolo de uno fabro, perché dicevi che eri Re
de' Giudei? Hora parerà se tu sei Re de' Giudei o no!».

115. MS *veue|stimēta*
116. MS *houemo*

And when he had said these words, one of the guards standing by gave him a great slap and said, "You respond like this to the high priest?"

The Lord replied with great humility, "If I have not told the truth, give evidence of it; but if I have told the truth, why do you strike me?"

O soul full of pride, learn to have patience from your Master!

And then Annas sent him bound to the high priest Caiphas, where the scribes and Pharisees had gathered. But Peter followed Lord Jesus from a distance as far as the palace of the high priest and entered and sat with the guards to see what would happen. And the high priests and the whole council sought false testimony against Jesus, to make him die. And they could not find a way, even though they had brought many false witnesses, because they did not agree with one another. Finally two false witnesses came, saying, "We heard him say, 'I can destroy this temple made by human hands and rebuild it in three days.'" But their testimony was not sufficient.

And then the high priest rose in their midst and questioned Jesus, saying, "You do not reply to these things that they are saying against you?" But Jesus remained silent, and did not respond to anything. And again the chief priest said to him, "I implore you, by the true God: tell us if you are Christ, Son of the living God."

Lord Jesus said, "You have said it. But I tell you in truth that you will see the Son of the Virgin sitting at the right hand of God and coming in the clouds of heaven."

And then the high priest tore his robe and said: "Behold, here is the evidence we have sought. We have heard the blasphemy. What should be done about it?" And they replied that he deserved to die.

Now who could have borne it, to have seen those Jewish dogs grab his face, and blindfold his eyes, and give him slaps and blows and spit in his face and give him buffets and say, "Tell us, now, who gave you that blow?," and then pluck his beard and pull him by the hair? And in derision they paid him homage, saying, "God be with you, King of the Jews." And one pulled him here, and another there, and another stuck his finger in his face, saying, "O son of a carpenter, why did you say that you were the King of the Jews? Now we'll see if you are King of the Jews or not!"

And as Peter was in the hall below, warming himself, a serving woman of the high priest came.[109] And having seen Peter warming himself, she said to someone who was there, "This man was with Jesus of Nazareth."

And another time he denied it, swearing, "I do not know this man!"

And after another hour had passed, one of the servants of the high priest, who was a relative of the one whose ear Peter had cut off, said,

Et essendo Pietro nella salla dissoto et scaldavasi, vene una ancilla del summo sacerdote, et avendo veduto Pietro che si scaldava, disse a quelino che yvi erano: «Et costui era con Iesù Naçareno». [f. 77v]

Et un'altra volta il negà con iuramento, dicendo: «Io non conosco questo huomo!».

Et stando per spatio de una hora, disse uno de' servi del po[n]tifice, ch'era parente di colui al qualle Pietro havea tagliato l'orechia: «Veramente costui era con lui, imperò che li è Galileo. Or non ti vidi io nell'orto con lui?».

Alora Pietro comincio a biastemare et giurare dicendo: «Io non cognosco questo huomo et non so che tu dichi». Et tuta via cantò el gallo. Et dice qui lo evangelista ch'el Signore risguardò sancto Pietro. Alora se aricordò sancto Pietro della parola ch'el Signore li havea detto «Prima che il gallo canti duoe fiate, tu me negarai tre». Et andò fuori et pianse amaramente. Et qui dice uno sancto ch'el risguardare del Signore nostro si è perdonare, però che li ochi suoi sono ochi de pietade et de misericordia.

Et dapoi che lo haveno così[117] conço, sì 'l menono in uno albergo. Et qui, così descalço, lo li[f. 78r]garono ad una colona et feceno farge la guardia ad alcuni ministri, li qualli tuta la nocte el tribularono et facevano derisione di facti suoi, et facendo beffe de lui diceano: «Come sei stato ardito de aprire la bocha contra di principi nostri. Or credevi tu essere più savio di loro? Hora se vederà el tuo senno. Tu stai hora come sei degno, et ben sei degno de morte. Et si parerai uno paço, el te stae molto ben». Et cum queste et altre inçurie, così tutta nocte facea beffe di lui cum parole et cum facti, dandoli di pugni et spudandoli nella faça. Et cum queste inçurie stete miser Iesù, tuo dolce sposo, ligato a quella colona perfina al alba.

Risguarda adonque al tuo Signore, come el sta mansuetamente ad ogni inçuria che li è facta et detta per pagare el tuo debito. Hàbili compassione et dì: «O Signore mio, in le cui mane seti venuto? O quanta paciencia è la vostra!».

Et in questo meço ch'el Signore nostro stete ligato [f. 78v] a quella colona cum quelle inçurie, el summo pontifico si fece adunare tuti li scribi et pharisei, et feceno conseglio come loro il potesseno accusare a Pilato.[118] Et ordinono alguni falsi[119] testimonii et ordinarono de menarlo la matina per tempo a Pilato.

117. MS *cosi* in margin
118. MS *Piliato*
119. MS *falfi*

"Truly, this man was with him, because he is Galilean. Now didn't I see you in the garden with him?"

And then Peter began to curse and swear, saying, "I do not know this man, and I don't know what you are talking about." And at that moment the cock crowed. And the evangelist says that at that moment the Lord looked at Saint Peter. And then Saint Peter remembered the words that the Lord had said: "Before the cock crows twice you will deny me three times." And he went out and wept bitterly. And here a saint says that the gaze of Our Lord is as good as a pardon, for his eyes are eyes of pity and mercy.[110]

And after they had abused him like this, they led him to another room. And there, barefoot like that, they tied him to a column and gave him into the custody of some other guards, who for the whole night tormented him and mocked him, and made fun of him, saying, "How bold you were to open your mouth against our leaders. Did you really believe that you are wiser than them? Now your wisdom will be revealed. Now you are getting what you deserve, and well do you deserve death. And if you look like a fool, it suits you well." And with these and other insults, they made fun of him all night with words and deeds, giving him blows and spitting in his face. And with these insults Lord Jesus, your sweet spouse, remained tied to that column until dawn.

Behold, then, your Lord, how he endures humbly every abuse said and done to him, to pay your debt. Have compassion and say, "O my Lord, into whose hands have you fallen? Oh how great is your suffering!"

And while Our Lord was tied to the column enduring such insults, the high priest had all the scribes and Pharisees gather, and he held counsel with them as to what they might accuse Jesus of before Pilate. And they rounded up some false witnesses, and made plans to lead him early in the morning to Pilate.

Meanwhile, Saint John went to the mother of Lord Jesus, who had come to Jerusalem and was staying at the house of Mary Magdalene with her sisters. And with many sobs and tears, he told them everything that had happened to Lord Jesus. Imagine how she must have felt! O what a lament rose up among them! Behold Our Lady falling into a swoon; behold Magdalene weeping and crying, "O my most sweet Master, into whose hands have you fallen?"

And then Our Lady in her anguish turned to prayer, and said, "O God, omnipotent Father, I know that all things are possible to you. I beg you, most sweet Father: if you wish to redeem the human race, I beg you, just Father, that you redeem it without spilling the precious blood of my most

Et in questo meço san Çuane andò alla madre de miser Iesù, la qualle era venuta in Ierusalem et era arivata in casa de Maria Magdalena cum le sue sorele. Et cum gran pia[n]to li disse ogni cosa per ordine di quello che era advenuto a miser Iesù. Pensa come lei dovea stare nella mente sua! O che pianto se levò tra loro! Risguarda la Madona cadere tramortita; guarda la Magdalena pia[n]çere et cridare: «O Maestro mio dolcissimo, in cui mane sete voi venuto»?

Alora la Dona nostra cum dolore se puose in oratione et disse: «O Dio Padre omnipotente, io so che ogni cosa è possibile a voi. Priegove, Padre dolcissimo, se voi volete recomperare l'humana [f. 79r] generatione, priegove, Padre iusto, che voi la recomperate sança el spargimento del precioso sangue del mio dolcissimo figliolo. Priegove, Padre piatoso,[120] che voi el liberate delle mane di peccatori, açiò ch'el non muora. Elgli per la vostra obedientia non se adiuta, et hasse habandonato se medesimo, et è sì come huomo sança potentia. Se ha messo nelle loro mane per lo amore ch'el porta a questo huomo. Et imperò ve priego che voi non dispregiate li mei priegi, et aiutatelo voi».

O, cum quanta amaritudine et pianto stavano queste donne, et specialmente la Vergene gloriosa! Et habiando orato, se partite de casa per andare a vedere el suo figliolo miser Iesù, acompagnata da Maria Magdalena et da Iohanne et altre done. O come el fo amaro questo partimento!

## Come miser Iesù fo menato a[121] Pilato nel'hora de prima. Capitolo vigesimo primo.

La matina in hora de prima gli principi et Pharisei si feceno [f. 79v] menare miser Iesù denançi, et disseno: Or ecco il Re[122] de' Giudei», et poi li feceno ligare le mani de drieto et cum la corda al collo, et dicevano: «Vieni ladro, al iudicio!».

Alora li servi el preseno cum furore et stretamente lo menavano inverso el palaço de Pilato. Et essendo così menato, se scontrò cum la madre et cum le altre compagne che veniano per lui trovare. Pensa che ferita fu

120. MS *piatoso* in margin
121. MS <*l*>*a*
122. MS *re* erroneously inserted above the line between *de* and *giudei*

sweet son. I beg you, merciful Father, that you free him from the hands of sinners, so he will not die. Through obedience to you, he is not helping himself, and he has abandoned himself, and he is like a man without power. He has put himself in their hands for the love that he bears to humanity. And so I ask that you do not despise my prayers, and that you help him."

Oh what bitter sorrow and affliction did these women endure, especially the glorious Virgin! And having prayed, she left the house to go see her son Lord Jesus, accompanied by Mary Magdalene and by John and other women. Oh how bitter was this moment as they set forth![111]

## Chapter 21. How Lord Jesus was led to Pilate at prime.

Early in the morning, at the hour of prime, the princes and Pharisees had Jesus brought before them.[112] And they said, "Now, behold the King of the Jews." And then they tied his hand behind his back, and put a cord around his neck, and they said, "Come, thief, to the trial!"

Then the henchmen seized him with fury, and led him harshly towards Pilate's palace. And as he was being led like this, he came upon his mother and the other companions who had come to find him. Imagine what a blow that was, and what affliction when she saw Lord Jesus being led along so shamefully! This was a torment borne of great compassion, because they led him in such a hurry that she couldn't even speak to him. And Lord Jesus felt the anguish of compassion because he saw the great suffering that his mother and the other women bore for him.

quella, et che dolore quando lei vette miser Iesù così vilmente menare! Questo fo dolore de grande compassione, imperò che lei non li podea parlare in tanta frecta lo menavano. Grande pena de compassione havea miser Iesù, imperò che lui vedea el dolore grande che sostenia la madre et le altre done per lui.

Et così fo menato inverso la casa de Pilato. Et la madre lo andava seguitando dalla longa, però che la non se potea aproximare a lui, tanto era la pressa della çente. Hora riguarda quello agnello innocentissimo, come il viene menato al macel[f. 80r]lo furibondamente, et come el va col capo inclinato!

Et çonti che furono denançi a Pilato, sì lo començorono accusare de molte cose falsamente, dicendo: «Noi habiamo trovato costui che subverte la gente nostra et prohibisse ch'el sia dato il tributo a Cesare, et dice se essere Cristo Re».

Alora disse Pilato a miser Iesù: «Non aldi tu quante cose testimoniano costoro contra de te?» Et miser Iesù non li rispuose ad niuna parola, in tantum che Pilato se meraveiò granmente. Et disse ali Giudei: «Tolletelo voi et secundo la vostra leçe iudicate lui».

Rispuoseno gli Giudei: «A noi non è licito de occidere alcuno», açiò ch'el se adimpisse la parola de Iesù ch'el disse significando de qual morte el dovea morire.

Alora Pilato andò dentro et chiamò a se miser et disse: «Sei tu Re de' Giudei?»

Rispuose miser Iesù: «Di' tu questo da te medemo o altri te ha detto di me?».

Rispuose Pilato: «Çià non sono io Giudeo. La gente tua et [f. 80v] gli pontifici tuoi me te hano tradito. Che hai tu facto?».

Rispuose miser Iesù et disse: «Lo regno mio non è de questo mondo. Se de questo mondo fosse el regno mio, certo li ministri mei me haveriano diffeso che non saria tradito da' Giudei».

Dise Pilato: «Adonca è tu Re?».

Rispuose miser Iesù: «Tu dici che io sono Re. Io sum nato in questo [mondo], et in vi sono venuto in questo mondo per rendere testimonia[n]ça della veritade, et tuti quelli che sono della verità aldeno la voce mia».

Disse Pilato: «Che cosa è verita?». Et in questo ussite fuori[123] a' Giudei. Et qui dicono i sancti che Pilato non era degno de udire che cosa è verità, et imperò ussite fuori et disse a' Giudei: «Io non trovo in lui niuna casone».

123. MS *fuori* in margin

And in this way he was led to the house of Pilate. And his mother followed behind him from a distance, for the crowd was so great that she could not get close to him. Now behold that most innocent lamb, how he is led with such fury to the slaughterhouse, and how he goes along with his head bowed.

And when they reached Pilate, they began to accuse him falsely of many things, saying, "We have found that he incites our people to subversion, and prohibits paying taxes to Caesar, and says that he is Christ the King."[113]

Then Pilate said to Lord Jesus, "Do you not hear how many charges they bring against you?" And Lord Jesus did not give a single word in reply, which caused Pilate to marvel greatly. And he said to the Jews, "Take him, and judge him according to your law."

The Jews replied, "It is not lawful for us to kill anyone," so that the words Jesus had spoken could be fulfilled, indicating the kind of death he had to die.

Then Pilate went inside and summoned the Lord to him, and asked, "Are you king of the Jews?"

Lord Jesus replied, "Do you ask this of your own accord, or have others said this to you about me?"

Pilate replied, "I am not a Jew. Your people and your priests have handed you over to me. What have you done?"

Lord Jesus replied, saying "My kingdom is not of this world. If my kingdom were of this world, certainly my followers would have defended me, so that I would not be handed over by the Jews."

Pilate said, "So, are you king?"

Lord Jesus replied, "You say that I am king. I have come into this world to testify to the truth, and all those who are committed to the truth hear my voice."

Pilate said, "What is truth?" And at this, he went outside to the Jews. And here the saints say that Pilate was not worthy to hear what truth is, and because of this he went out and said to the Jews, "I do not find any case against him."

Then the Jews accused him saying, "He stirred up the people, preaching his message from Galilee to here."

And Pilate, hearing Galilee named, and knowing that he was under the jurisdiction of Herod, sent Lord Jesus, bound like that, to Herod, who had come to Jerusalem for the feast days. And seeing him, Herod was elated. This Herod was the son of the one who had put the young children to death.

Alora li Giudei lo accusono dicendo: «Costui sì à comosso el populo predicando la sua da Galilea infina qui».

Aldendo Pilato nominare Galilea et cognoscendo che lui era sotto la signoria de Herodes, sì mandò miser Iesù così ligato ad [f. 81r] Herodes, el qualle in quelli giorni era venuto in Ierusalem. Et vedendolo Herodes, fo molto alegrato. Questo Herodes fu figliolo di quello che fece morire i puti. Et habiando grande voluntade di vedere fare a lui qualche segno o miraculo, et dimandandolo de diverse cose, miser Iesù non li respondea a niuna cosa. Ma li prencipi de' sacerdoti stavano costantemente ad accusarlo. Et vedendo Herodes che miser non li respondea, fo molto turbato et riputolo per mato. Et si lo smatava cum i suoi cavalieri, et fecelo vestire de uno vestimento biancho facto a modo de una camisa,[124] per dispregio. Et facendo beffe de lui, sì lo remandò a Pilato. Et furono facti amici Herodes et Pilato in quel giorno, però che prima erano nimici.

O anima che vai cercando honore, resguarda el tuo Creatore et vederai come per te l'è despregiato! Vedi come colui ch'è Maestro de ogni huomo è reputato paçço et pacientemente porta ogni [f. 81v] cosa per tuo amore. Vedi come el va cum la testa i[n]clinata humelmente. O quanta çente era assunata per vedere Iesù, non per compassione ma per fare beffe de lui!

Or chi havesse veduto et aldito le derisione et vilanie che li erano facte et dette! Chi ge butava le immondicie adosso, et altri lo spençea et davali di pugni, dicendo: «Và oltra, paçço». Et altri cridavano: «Ecco colui che se dicea essere Re de Giudei!». Et cum queste et molte altre ingiurie el fo rimenato a Pilato.

O anima che desideri de havere compassione al tuo Signore, resguardalo qui e pensa el dolore ch'el dovea sentire, veçando la sua dolcissima madre essere tanto angustiata, et anche per el suo dilecto Çuane et per le altre done le quale el seguitavano. Et come fo grande pena questa a miser Iesù!

Or chi potria dire la pena che sentiva la Madre Gloriosa vedando el suo dolcissimo figliolo così deriso et beffato? «O Gloria del Paradiso, come te vedo beffato et [f. 82r] deriso?» Inverso del cielo lei[125] cridava, «O Alta Sapientia de Dio, come te vedo vilmente tratare? Io non solea sentire mio pensier duro. Hora sono facta del pianto maistra». Queste et altre parole[126] la madre dicea piançendo, et drieto sempre li andava.

124. MS The first letter seems to have been modified from a *p*
125. MS *io*
126. MS *parore*

And he had a great desire to see Lord Jesus perform some sign or miracle. And as he asked many things, Lord Jesus replied to nothing. But the high priests continued to bring accusations against him. And Herod, seeing that Lord Jesus did not reply to him, was very disturbed, and took him for a madman. And he had him mocked by his soldiers, and he ordered him to be dressed in a white tunic made in the style of a fool's garment to increase his shame. And humiliating him in this way, he sent him back to Pilate. And Herod and Pilate became friends on that day, having been enemies before.

O soul who goes in search of honor, behold your Creator, and see how he endures shame for you! See how he who is Master of every man is considered mad, and patiently bears everything for your love. Watch how he goes along with his head humbly bowed. Oh, how many people flocked to see Jesus, not out of compassion, but to make fun of him!

Now who could bear to have seen and heard the derision and vile things that were done and said to him? One threw filth on him, and others pushed him and struck him, saying, "Keep walking, fool!" And others shouted, "Behold the man who claimed to be King of the Jews!" And with this and many other insults, he was taken back to Pilate.

O soul who desires to have compassion for your Lord, behold him here, and imagine the sorrow that he must have felt for his most sweet mother, seeing her in such anguish, and also for his beloved John, and for the other women who followed him. And what great pain that was to Lord Jesus!

Now who could express the pain that the Glorious Mother felt, seeing her most sweet son so derided and mocked? "O Glory of Paradise, how is it that I see you mocked and derided like this?" Towards the heavens she cried, "O High Wisdom of God, how is it that I see you treated so wretchedly? I used to know nothing of grief. Now I have become the *maistra* of lament."[114] The mother lamented with these and other words, weeping as she continued to follow him.

And then they reached the house of Pilate. And seeing him so derided like this, Pilate went outside to the chief priests and the people and said, "You have presented this man to me as if he had incited and deceived the people. And I questioned him here in your presence, and I did not find any cause for him to be put to death. Neither did Herod, to whom I sent him, and not finding a reason to bring charges against him, he sent him back to us. I will discipline him and let him go."

Then Pilate said to the people, "It is the custom that I release a prisoner to you for the feast of Passover. Do you want me to release to you the King of the Jews?"

Et çonto ch'el fu a Pilato et vedendolo Pilato così deriso, ussite fuori a' principi et al populo et disse: «Voi me havete presentato questo huomo sì come lui havesse subvertito et inganato el populo. Et ecco che io l'ò dimandato in presentia vostra et non trovo casone in lui per la qualle egli deba morire; neanche Herode, al qualle io lo havea mandato non trovando casone in lui, sì lo à rimandato a noi. Io lo coreçerò et lasserolo».

Alora disse Pilato al populo: «L'è consuetudine che io ve lassi uno pregione per la festa della Pasca. Voleti voi chio vi lassi el Re de' Giudei»?

Alora el populo començò a cridare: «Non costui, ma Barabas!», [f. 82v] el qualle era ladro et per omicidio era posto in pregione.

Disse Pilato: «Che voleti che io façi del Re de' Giudei?».

Tutti dissero: «Ch'el sia crucificato!».

Disse a quelli il presside: «Che male ha facto costui?».

Alora i Giudei magiormente cridano, dicendo: «Crucifigilo! Cruci-[fi]gilo!». Et vedando Pilato il clamore del populo, vogliandoli satisfare al populo sì ge lassò Barabas, et commandò che miser Iesù fosse flagellato.

### Come miser Iesù Cristo Signor nostro fo ligado nudo a una colona et come el fo duramente flagellato. Capitolo xxii°.[127]

Hora vedando Pilato ch'el non li çovava i molti argumenti che lui havea mostrati per voler lassare miser Iesù, comandò ch'el fosse flagellato, pensando de potere satisfare al volere del populo per quello. Alora gli ministri de Pilato menarono miser Iesù dentro nel palacio, et introno in una salla in la qualle era una colona. Et qui gli ministri de Pilato[128] despogliarono[129] [f. 83r] miser Iesù cum impeto et furore et si['l] ligarono[130] a quella colona stretamente et crudelmente et tuta via cum parole ingiuriose, et i buffeti non li mancava. Et poi doi ministri de Pilato tolseno doi flagelli asprissimi et sì llo començono a flagelare duramente. Et tanto lo flagellavano aspramente et cum furore che si stancorono che no[n] poteano più. Alora començono doi altri malvagii ministri, i qualli così crudelmente el baterono che non li lassono nulla de sano adosso.

127. MS *Capitolo xxiii*
128. MS *gli ministri de Pilato* in margin
129. MS *desplogliarono*
130. MS *si li\garono*

Then the people began to cry, "Not that man, but Barabbas!," who was a thief and had been put in prison for murder.

Pilate said, "What do you want me to do with the King of the Jews?"

They all said, "Crucify him!"

The presiding judge said to them, "What harm has he done?"

Then the Jews cried out more loudly, shouting "Crucify him! Crucify him!" And seeing the clamor of the people, and wanting to satisfy the people, Pilate released Barabbas, and he ordered that Lord Jesus be flogged.

*Chapter 22. How Our Lord Jesus Christ was bound naked to a column, and how he was harshly flogged.*

Now Pilate, seeing that the many arguments he had made to release Lord Jesus had not worked, ordered that he be scourged, thinking that with this he could satisfy the desires of the people. So Pilate's men took Lord Jesus into the palace, and they entered a room in which there was a column. And here Pilate's men stripped Lord Jesus with haste and fury, and they bound him to this column harshly and cruelly, insulting him the whole time, and there was no lack of blows. And then two of Pilate's guards took two very sharp whips and began to whip him harshly. And they flogged him so harshly and with such fury that they became too tired to continue. Then two other wicked men began to whip him so cruelly that they left none of his flesh unharmed.

O soul who desires to have compassion for your Lord, who, to liberate you from the scourges of eternal death, wished to be so harshly scourged: behold him here, bound naked to the column, completely beaten and full of wounds! Behold him from head to foot, and you will see nothing but wounds. Behold his most holy blood, which pays for your iniquities, streaming down his legs to the ground. And behold that most innocent

O anima che desideri de havere compassione al tuo Signore, el qualle per te liberare dalli flagelli della eterna morte volse essere così duramente flagellato: or riguardalo qui esser ligato nudo[131] alla colona et tutto batudo et impiagato! Guardalo dal capo perfino ai piedi, et non vederai se non piage. Risguarda el sangue suo sanctissimo, il qualle paga le tuoe iniquitate, correre çò per le gambe in terra. Et [f. 83v] risguarda quel corpo innocentissimo, tuto negro per le molte[132] bote recevute, tuto insanguinato.

O Signore mio, chi fo colui tanto ardito, che have animo de spogliarve? Et chi fo quello tanto argumentoso che have animo de ligarve a quella aspra colona? Et chi furono quelli crudelissimi che haveno tanto argumento de flagellare voi che sete Re di Re et Signore di Signori? Ma io so ben perché egli haveno tanto ardimento de fare queste cose contra de voi: perché voi, Sole de Iusticia, abscondesti i raçi vostri, cum li qualli voi illuminate cadauno, et imperciò le tenebre haveno gran podestade contra di voi che sete vera luce. O quanto è lo amore che portate a questo huomo: che per lui liberare voi ve[133] havete condennato a morte! O anima che non porti amore a questo amante il qualle per te à sostenuto tante batiture, grande rasone tu ne haverai a rendere![134]

Or habiandolo così flagellato per [f. 84r] uno grande spatio, sì llo desligono cum molta inçuria et fecello rivestire. O anima risguarda qui el tuo Creatore, tanto humiliato per te et rivestirse cum tanta pena! O Iesù, quanto è grande il vostro amore!

Or rivestito che fu, li ministri si disseno a Pilato: «Misere, costui se fa Re de' Giudei: vestiamolo a modo di re». Alora quelli crudelli ministri s'il preseno et dispogliolo, et questa fo la secunda volta che miser Iesù fo despogliato; et sì llo rivestite de porpora rossa. Et poi el messeno a sentare sopra[135] una catreda, et qui li messeno una aspera corona de spine crudelissime in capo et una canna in mano et una binda denançi alli ochi. Et alora li ministri de Pilato sì llo començarono a schernire et fare beffe di lui. Et chi li spudava nella faça, et chi ge dava le sguançade et buffeti, et altri se inçenochiavano denançi a lui per derisione dicendo: «Dio te salvi, Re de' Giudei!»; et altri li dava nella [f. 84v] faça dicendo: «Prophetiça: chi è chi t'à percosso?». Et altri ge facea le fiche et pelavali la barba et i

---

131. MS *ligato <a una> nudo*
132. MS *molte* in margin
133. MS *ue* in margin
134. MS *renderere*
135. MS *sppra*

body, completely black from the many blows received, completely bathed in blood.

O my Lord, who was so bold, who had the gall to strip you? And who was so ruthless that he had the nerve to tie you to that hard column? And who were these most cruel ones so bold as to take up arms to flog you, you who are King of Kings and Lord of Lords? But I know well why they were so bold as to do these things to you: because you, Sun of Justice, hid your rays, with which you illuminate everyone, so the darkness had great power against you who are true light. Oh how great is the love that you bear for humankind: to set us free you have condemned yourself to death! O soul who does not bear love for this lover who has suffered such beatings for you, you will have quite an excuse to render for this!

Now, having scourged him like this for a long time, they untied him with many insults and had him get dressed. O soul, gaze here on your Creator, so humiliated for you, dressing himself with such pain! O Jesus, how great is your love![115]

Now, when he had dressed, the guards said to Pilate, "Sir, this man presents himself as King of the Jews; let's dress him as a king." Then those cruel soldiers take him and strip him. And this was the second time that Lord Jesus was stripped. And they dress him in a purple garment, and then they make him sit on a chair like a throne; and then they place a sharp crown of the cruelest thorns on his head, and a reed in his hand, and a blindfold over his eyes. And then Pilate's men began to jeer at him and mock him. And one spit in his face, and another gave him slaps and blows, and others knelt before him mockingly, saying, "God be with you, King of the Jews"; and others slapped his face, saying, "Play the prophet: who is it that hit you?" And others made obscene gestures and plucked his beard and his hair, and others took the reed from his hand and struck it hard on his head, saying, "Behold the King of the Jews!"

O soul who desires to see the King of Paradise, behold him here among these rapacious wolves, who surround him to devour him with many injuries. But he, like the most gentle lamb, suffered everything patiently. Behold him here and have compassion, and remember that he bore this pain for your love!

Now watch how they dress him in a garment of purple silk to make fun of him, and they put the crown of the thorns on his head in derision, and in place of a regal scepter, a reed. And all of this was done as if to a person who wished to reign but could not. Now how heart-wrenching it must have been to see the King of Kings and Lord of Lords with a crown

capelli, et alcuni li tollea la canna de mano et forteme[n]te li dava sopra la testa, dicendo: «Ecco il Re de' Giudei!».

O anima che desideri de vedere el Re del Paradiso, risguarda qui tra questi lupi rapaci, i qualli li stano dintorno per divoralo cum molta inçuria, ma lui come agnello mansuetissimo ad ogni cosa stava patiente. Risguardalo qui et hàbili compassione, et pensa che per tuo amore el sostenne questa pena!

Or vedi come l'è vestito de vestimento de seda rossa per fare beffe de lui, et anche la corona de spine li fo messa in capo per derisione et, in luoco del bastone regale, la canna. Et tutto questo li fo facto sì come a persona che volesse regnare et non podesse. Or che compassione dovea essere a vedere el Re di Re et il Signore delli Signori cum una corona de spine in capo et catuna spina passare perfina [f. 85r] al cervello et il sangue correre per lo volto, et anche vederli li ochi velati a modo che si fa ai ladri et malifactori! O Gloria del Paradiso, come te vedo beffato et deriso! O Viso Relucente, come te vedo pieno de sangue et de sputi! Vedi ancora la bella barba tuta pellata, li belli capelli tuti scuarciati fuori della testa. Pensa, o anima misera, tute queste pene sono quelle che pagano el tuo debito!

Hora habiando li ministri de Pilato così beffato et deriso miser Iesù, et pe[n]sando Pilato per questo havere satisfato al populo, sì llo fece menare defuori al populo, et disse a loro: «Ecco che io ve l'ò menato fuori, açiò che voi cognosciati che io non trovo in lui casone alcuna de morte».

Or stava miser Iesù in presentia del populo, vestito de porpora et cum la corona de spine in capo, et cum la canna in mano et cum gli ochi velati, et tuto spudaçato et flagellato, et havea la barba tuta [f. 85v] pelata. O anima, risguarda el tuo Signore qui denànçi a tanta çente così vituperosamente stare, col capo inchinato, cum tanto dolore et pena, per te liberare dalla pena infernale. O spechio de patientia!

Or stando così miser Iesù in presentia del populo, disse Pilato: «Ecco l'huomo», quasi dica: «Che volete ch'io facia de lui? Ecco che l'è castigato, adonca lasserolo».

Alora li pontifici et gli scribi et Pharisei cridavano dicendo: «Crucifigilo! Crucifigilo!».[136]

Disse Pilato a' Giudei: «Tolletelo voi et crucifigetelo».

Respuose i Giudei: «Noi habiamo leçe, et secundo la lege el debe morire, però che el se fa Figliolo de Dio».

136. MS *crucifigilo* in margin

of thorns on his head, and each thorn piercing through his head to the brain, and blood flowing down his face, and to see his eyes blindfolded in a way done to thieves and criminals. O Glory of Paradise, how is it that I see you insulted and mocked? O Resplendent Face, how is it that I see you covered with blood and spit? See, too, the beautiful beard completely plucked, the beautiful hair all torn from his head. Imagine, O wretched soul: all these pains are those that pay your debt!

Now when Pilate's soldiers had mocked and abused Lord Jesus in this way, Pilate, thinking that he had satisfied the people through this, had him brought before the people, and he said to them: "Behold, I have brought him here before you, to show you that I find no cause for putting him to death."

Now Lord Jesus stood before the people, dressed in purple, and with the crown of thorns on his head, and with the reed in his hand, and with his eyes blindfolded, and covered with spit and scourged, and with his beard plucked. O soul, behold your Lord, standing here so shamefully before so many people, with his head bowed and in so much suffering and pain to free you from the pain of hell. O mirror of patience!

Now as Lord Jesus stood like this in the presence of the people, Pilate said, "Behold the man!," as if to say, "What do you want me to do with him? Now he has been punished, so I will release him."

And then the high priests and scribes and Pharisees cried out, saying, "Crucify him! Crucify him!"

Pilate said to the Jews, "Take him yourselves and crucify him."

The Jews responded, "We have the law, and according to the law he must die because he says he is the Son of God."

Hearing these words, Pilate became much more afraid. And he entered the palace and said to Jesus, "Where do you come from?" And Lord Jesus said nothing. Then Pilate said, "You do not answer me. Don't you know that I have the power to release you and I have the power to crucify you?"

Then Lord Jesus replied, "You would have no power over me if it were not given to you from above. And that is why those who have handed me over commit the greater sin."

Then Pilate tried to find a way to release him. But the Jews, seeing that Pilate wanted to release him, began to cry out and say, "If you release him you are not a friend of Caesar, because those who call themselves kings become rivals of the emperor."

Now hearing these words, Pilate had Jesus taken outside, and he took his seat at the judge's bench at a place called Gabbata, in the Hebrew

Oldendo Pilato queste parole, temete molto più. Et intrò nel palaço et disse a miser Iesù: «Donde sei tu»? Et miser Iesù non li rispuose niente. Alora disse Pilato: «Non me responde tu? Non sai tu che io ho podestade de lassarte et ho podestade de crucifigerte»?

Alora respuose miser Iesù: «Tu non haveresti podestade nulla [f. 86r] inverso di me s'ella non te fosse data de sopra. Et imperciò coloro[137] che me te hano tradito ne hano magiore peccato».

Alora cercò Pilato de lassarlo. Ma gli Giudei, vedendo che Pilato el volea pure lassare, sì començarono a cridare et a dire: «Se tu lassi costui, tu non serai amico de Cesaro, imperò che coloro che se fanno re contradicono allo imperio».

Or aldendo Pilato questo parlare, se fece menare miser Iesù fuora et poi se messe a sedere sul tribunale in lo luocho el qualle se chiama in lingua hebraica Gabbata. Et era la vigilia della Pascua quasi sull'hora de sexta. Et disse Pilato agli Giudei: «Ecco el re vostro».

Alora i Çudei cridavano: «Tolle, tolle costui et crucifigilo!».

Disse Pilato: «Volete voi ch'io crucifiga il vostro re»?[138]

Alora respuosero li pontifici: «Noi non habiamo altro re salvo cha Cesaro». O malicia et ingratitudine granda che fo in questo parlare! O Giudei maledeti: chi ve liberò dalle mane de Pharaon? Chi fo colui che vi fece la via per meço el Rosso Mare et mando denançi a voi la [f. 86v] colona de fuocho? Chi fu colui che con tanti segni et meraveglie ve ha menati in Terra de Promissione? El [è] stato questo Cesaro? O generatione perversa et ingrata!

*Come Pilato diede la sente[n]tia contra el Salvatore nostro miser Iesù Cristo della morte della croce, et come el portò la croce in spalla et come lui fece, et come la nostra Donna andò per vederlo. Capitolo xxiii°.*[139]

Or vedendo Pilato ch'el non li giovava i molti argumenti che lui havea monstrati et facti per potere liberare miser Iesù, et vedando che quanto più el cercava la liberatione de miser Iesù Cristo, tanto più el populo se indignava contra a lui, et temendo de perdere la signoria temporale si

---

137. MS *coloro* in margin
138. MS *Alora . . . re* in margin
139. MS *Capitolo xxiiii*

language. And it was the day before Passover, around noon. And Pilate said to the Jews, "Behold your king."

Then the Jews shouted, "Take him, take this man and crucify him!"

Pilate said, "Do you want me to crucify your king?"

Then the high priests replied, "We have no king but Caesar." Oh what great malice and ingratitude were in those words! O wicked Jews, who freed you from the hands of Pharaoh? Who was it who made a path for you through the middle of the Red Sea, and sent a pillar of fire before you? Who was it who, with so many signs and wonders, delivered you to the Promised Land? Was it Caesar? O perverse and ungrateful people![116]

*Chapter 23. How Pilate sentenced our savior Lord Jesus Christ to death on the cross, and how he carried the cross on his shoulders, and what was done to him, and how Our Lady went to see him.*

Now Pilate, seeing that the many arguments that he had produced and presented to free Lord Jesus had not worked, and seeing that the more he sought to free Lord Jesus Christ the more the people became set against him, and fearing to lose his worldly authority chose to lose eternal lordship instead; for he had already said that he found no reason why he deserved to die. And this was the sin of Pilate: knowing that he was committing evil, and that it was wrong to condemn him to death, he chose to please the people rather than God. And sitting on the judge's bench, he

elesse più tosto de perdere la eternalle, imperò che lui havea già detto
ch'el non trovava casone neiuna in lui che dovesse morire. Et questo fo el
peccato de Pilato, cognosando che facea male et che a torto el mo[f.
87r]riva, elesse più tosto de compiacere al populo che a Dio. Et sedendo
sopra el tribunal diede la sententia contra a miser Iesù, ch'el fosse crucifixo secundo la voluntà de' Giudei.

Alora i ministri de Pilato el menarono dentro et si lli despogiorono la[140]
porpora et fecelo vestire delle sue vestimente; et poi se messeno in ordine de
menarlo al luocho della iusticia, et qui feceno vegnire i latroni. Et in questo
meço fo apparechiata la croce. Or siando in ordine tuta la gente de Pilato, et
anche li ministri erano molto sollicitati da' Giudei, et per compiacere a' Giudei molte ingiurie li feceno. Or siando in ordine la cavalaria et gli ministri, si
preseno miser Iesù Cristo et si lli messeno al collo una corda, overo catena,
et poi li messeno al collo el venerabel legno della croce in sulle spale, et lui
come agnello mansuetissimo la recevete volentiera, siando cusì afflicto,
perché ça molto tempo [f. 87v] l'havea desiderata.

Alora cum molto impeto et furore se mossero menando fuori miser
Iesù nel meço de doi ladroni. Et tutti i ministri de Pilato li furono dintorno,
et chi el spençea inançi et chi el tirava per la corda che ell'havea al collo et
facevallo inclinar el capo, et a questo modo era tratato el Signore del cielo
et della terra. Et li Giudei li cridavano drieto et biastemavalo, et cum questi et altri desonori el fo menato per la terra tra doi latroni, et questi li furono dati per compagni ma non compagni in pena et desonor, però che a
miser Iesù li feceno portare la croce et questo non feceno ai latroni.

Or per la pressa grande che era[141] intorno a miser Iesù, la madre piena
de dolore non potea vedere il suo dolcissimo figliolo. Alora lei se mise andare per un'altra via per scontrarse in lui. Et come l[o][142] vette apena lei el
cognoscea, et risguardandose insieme, tuta fu piena de dolore.

Alora lei disse alla Mag[f. 88r]dalena: «O Magdalena quale è il mio
figliolo»?

Et lei cum gran pia[n]to disse: «El è quello de meço che ha la croce in
spalla et la corona de spine in testa et cum la corda al collo[143] et el volto
pieno di sangue et di sputa: quello è il vostro figliolo, Madona mia».

Or passando el nostro Signore oltra et vedendo piançere la madre sua
et le altre done de Ierusalem, si se atrigò et disse: «Figliole de Ierusalem,

140. MS <del>la
141. MS era in margin
142. MS la
143. MS al collo in margin

gave the sentence against Lord Jesus: that he would be crucified, according to the will of the Jews.

Then Pilate's guards took him inside and took off the purple garment and made him dress in his own clothes. And then they formed ranks to lead him to the place of justice; and they had the thieves brought there. And in the middle of this, the cross was prepared. Now all of Pilate's people stood at the ready, and his guards, too, were urged by the Jews; and to please the Jews they insulted him repeatedly. Now, when the mounted soldiers and guards were ready, they took Lord Jesus Christ and put a cord, or rather a chain, around his neck. And then they laid the venerable wood of the cross on his shoulders. And like the most meek lamb he received it willingly, afflicted as he was; for he had long desired this.

Then with much haste and fury they set out, leading Lord Jesus between the two thieves. And all the soldiers of Pilate surrounded him. And one pushed him, and one pulled by the cord around his neck and made him bow his head; and this is how the Lord of Heaven and Earth was treated. And the Jews shouted at him and cursed him. And with these and other insults he was led outside between two thieves. And these two were given to him as companions, but not as companions who shared his pain and dishonor, because they made Lord Jesus carry the cross and they did not make the thieves do this.

Now because of the large crowd surrounding Lord Jesus, his mother, full of sorrow, could not see her most sweet son. So she set out to meet him by another route. And when she saw him, she could hardly recognize him. And as they beheld each other, she was filled with sorrow.[117]

Then she said to Magdalene, "O Magdalene, which one is my son?"

And she, with great lamentation, replied, "He is the one in the middle, who has the cross on his shoulders, and the crown of thorns on his head, and the cord around his neck, with his face covered with blood and with spit. That one is your son, my lady."[118]

Now Our Lord, moving further along and seeing his mother and the other women of Jerusalem weeping, stopped and said, "Daughters of Jerusalem, do not weep for me, but weep for yourselves and for your children. For the time will come when you will say, 'Blessed are those who are sterile, and who have not given birth, and the breasts that have not given milk'; or when you will say to the mountains, 'Fall on us,' and to the hills, 'cover us.'" And he foretold to them the destruction of Jerusalem.

Now imagine the sorrow that the mother of Lord Jesus must have felt, seeing him so afflicted. And then behold your Lord, how disfigured he is, and how he goes gasping under the cross, so completely afflicted by its

non piançete sopra di me, ma sopra de voi piançete, et sopra li vostri figlioli. Però che el vegnerà tempo che direte: "Beate quelle che sono sterile et che non hanno parturito, et le mamelle che non hano lactado," o quando direte a' monti "cadeti sopra noi," et colli "cooperite noi"». Et predisse a loro la destrutione de Ierusalem.

Or pensa el dolore che dovea sentire la madre de miser Iesù vedendolo così afflicto, et poi risguarda el tuo Signore come l'è desfigurato et come el va ansiando sotto la croce, tutto afflicto per el gran [f. 88v] peso della croce.[144] Et tanto era indebelito, si' per el molto sangue el qualle li era ussito et si' per la croce la qualle era molto grande, et etiamdio per la doglia ch'el sentiva della sua dolcissima madre et anche delli suoi dilecti discipoli, i quali erano divisi per paura che haveano, tuti pieni de amaritudine. Et in tanto vene meno che più volte quasi cadete in terra per la debilitade et stancheça.

Or vedendo li Giudei che non potea portare la croce, et scontrandose in uno huomo el qualle vegnia dalla villa et havea nome Simon Cireneo, si llo sfo[r]çorono che tollesse la croce de miser Iesù et portassela per fino al Monte Calvario. Et sapi che li Giudei non feceno questo per compassione che loro li havesseno, ma per no[n] indusiare la morte sua. Et tolto che li hebbeno la croce de spalla, si lli ligarano le mane de drieto, et furiosamente lo menavano al monte cum molte in[f. 89r]çurie, faciandolo andare più ch'el no potea, quasi strasinandolo. Et a questo modo el nostro Signore miser Iesù Cristo, et cum asai più vituperio che non dicho, çonse[145] al Monte Calvario.

O anima la qualle desideri de havere compassione al tuo Creatore et sentire delle pene che sente la madre sua et in parte piançere cum lei, risguarda qui el tuo Creatore et Signore cum li ochi della mente ussire fuori de Ierusalem cum la croce in spalla et in testa una aspera corona de spine, le qualle erano ficate per fino al cervello! Et poi resguarda quella faça gloriosa, la qual solea essere così splendida, hora è piena de[146] sangue et de sputi. Dove è la bella barba? Dove sono i belli capelli et li begli colori che havere solevi nella faça tua? O Iesù dulcissimo, quanta pena hai portata per noi!

O quanta compassione era a vedere vegnire miser Iesù in meço doi latroni cum quella gra[n] croce in spalla, la [f. 89v] qualle,[147] secundo la opinione de alcuni doctori, era longa quindese piedi! Or pensa, anima, per te liberare volse morire de morte così vituperosa et crudelle!

144. MS *corce*
145. MS *çōseno*
146. MS *de* in margin
147. MS *la | la qualle*

great weight. And he was weakened so much, both by the great quantity of blood that had flowed from him and by the cross, which was so very large; and also by the sorrow that he felt for his most sweet mother, and also for his beloved disciples, who had fled because they were so afraid and full of bitter sorrow. And he became so depleted that he nearly fell to the ground many times out of weakness and exhaustion.

Now the Jews, seeing that he was unable to carry the cross, came across a man coming from town named Simon of Cyrene, and they forced him to take the cross from Lord Jesus and to carry it to Mount Calvary. And you should know that the Jews did not do this out of any compassion that they felt for him, but so that his death would not be delayed. And as soon as the cross was taken from his shoulders, they tied his hands behind him. And they led him roughly to the mountain with many abuses, making him go faster than he was able, nearly dragging him. And in this way Our Lord Jesus Christ was led to Mount Calvary, with so much shame that I cannot tell it.

O soul who desires to have compassion for your Creator, and to feel the pain that his mother feels and to share in her weeping, behold here with the eyes of the mind your Creator and Lord going out of Jerusalem with the cross on his shoulders, and on his head a sharp crown of thorns, which pierced through to his brain.[119] And then behold his glorious face, which was once so radiant, now covered with blood and spit. Where is the beautiful beard? Where is the beautiful hair, and the beautiful color that used to be in your face? O most sweet Jesus, what pain you bore for us![120]

Oh how heart-wrenching it was to see Lord Jesus going between two thieves with such a huge cross on his shoulder, which, according to the opinion of certain scholars, was fifteen feet long.[121] Now imagine, soul: to set you free, he wished to die such a shameful and cruel death!

*Come miser Iesù fo messo in croce in meço de doi latroni per piui sua vergo[g]na. Capitolo xxiv°.*[148]

Et çonti che furono al Monte Calvario, inançi che lo despogliasseno, li deteno a bere vino cum felle messiado, et miser Iesù non ne volse bevere. O anima la qualle desideri de gloriarti nella Passione del tuo Signore, stà qui attento et risguarda cum gli ochi della mente tua li acti et facti li qualli i Giudei usseno inverso de meser Iesù Cristo.

Or pòi vedere quelli maledeti exercitarse in le cose le qualle pertegnia a crucifigere miser Iesù. Or chi apparechiava la croce et chi i chiodi et chi fa la fossa per metter el piede della croce et chi facea una cosa et chi un'altra. Or vedi alcuni che furiosamente gli vano addoso et sì [f. 90r] llo[149] spoglia nudo in pressentia de tuto el populo, per più maçor sua vergogna. Et questa fo la terça fiada che miser Iesù fo despogliado, et qui se rinova le piage delle batiture però che i pani se tegniano alla carne et tutto començò a piovere sangue. O quanto dolore era questo alla madre sua de vedere el suo dolcissimo figliolo cusì nudo stare come agnello tra quelli lupi maledeti!

Alora la madre piena de dolore se fece ina[n]çi apresso al suo dolcissimo figliolo et tolse el suo vello del capo et si llo cinse intorno a miser Iesù Cristo cum grande amaritudine. Et non so come lei non cadesse in terra morta, et per el gran dolore che haveano dentro non se podeteno parlare. Et anche perché lei fo presto spenta indrieto da quelli Giudei maledeti.

Et poi lui fo menato lì dove era la croce destesa. Et qui così nudo furiosamente fo branchato et desteso sopra della croce cum molte ingiurie. Et qui erano [f. 90v] apparechiati i chiodi. Et alora gli ministri presseno la mano drita et si la messeno per meço el buso della croce et poi li messeno el chiodo nella mano et començóno ad inchiodarla. Et haimé, come fo gran pena questa a miser Iesù! Et sapi etiandio che ogni botta de martello era una bota de cortello alla sua dolcissima madre.

Et inchiodado che haveno la mano drita, si branchorono la sinistra et quella non çonçea al buso. Alora quelli maledeti sì començorono a tirarla per força per farla g[i]onçere al segno. Et tanto gli tirò quello braço che tutti i nodi se largono, et tanto feceno che per força el feceno açonçere al suo luocho. O come grande dolore sostene qui el Signore nostro! Et inchiodade che li haveno le mane, el branchorono furibondamente per li piedi et començorono a tirarli per fargli çonçere al buso che haveano fo-

148. MS *Capitolo xxv*
149. MS *sil*‖*lo*

*Chapter 24. How Lord Jesus was put on the cross between two thieves to increase his shame.*

And when they reached Mount Calvary, before they stripped him they told him to drink wine mixed with gall, and Lord Jesus did not wish to drink it. O soul who desires to glory in the Passion of your Lord, pay attention here, and behold with the eyes of your mind the acts and deeds that the Jews committed against Lord Jesus Christ.[122]

Now you can see those evildoers devote themselves to everything that pertains to crucifying Lord Jesus. Now one gets the cross ready, and one the nails, and one digs the hole for the base of the cross, and one does one thing, and another does something else.[123] Now watch some who rush up to him and strip him naked in the presence of all the people to increase his shame.[124] And this was the third time that Lord Jesus was stripped, and here the wounds were opened again, because the cloth stuck to the flesh; and they all began to flow with blood. Oh what anguish this was to his mother, to see her most sweet son naked like this, standing like a lamb among these wicked wolves!

Then the mother, full of sorrow, went up close to her most sweet son and took the veil from her head and wrapped it around Lord Jesus Christ with bitter sorrow.[125] And I do not know how she did not fall dead to the earth. And because of the great sorrow that she felt, they could not speak with each other—and also because she was quickly pushed back by those cursed Jews.

And then he was led to the place where the cross was laid out.[126] And there, naked like this, he was brutally taken and stretched out on the cross with many injuries. And then the nails were prepared. And then the soldiers take the right hand and place it over a hole in the cross, and then they place the nail over the hand and begin to hammer it in. And ah!, what great pain that was to the Lord Jesus! And know, too, that every blow of the hammer was a blow of the knife to his most sweet mother.

And when they finished nailing the right hand, they seized the left, which did not reach the hole they had drilled for it. So these wicked men began to stretch it by force to make it join up to the place they had marked. And so violently did they pull the arm that all the ligaments were stretched, and they forced it to stretch to join up with the place they had drilled. Oh what great pain Our Lord endured then! And when they had nailed his hands, they grabbed him violently by the feet and began to pull them to make them reach the hole they had drilled. And they pulled so hard that it

rato. Et intanto tirono che parea che li membri et le osse tute se desnodas [f. 91r]seno. Et poi li messeno uno piede sopra l'altro et cum uno grosso chiodo gli ficharono. Or pensa che dolore era quello! Et nota qui che quelli maledecti cani per darge più dolore[150] haveano despontati i chiodi, et erano grossi. Et furono inchiodati in luocho più nervoso che luocho che sia nel corpo. Et per queste tre rasone sentite miser Iesù Cristo più dolore—et etiandio per el molto sang[u]e ussite del suo corpo, però ch'ell era tanto distesa quello sanctissimo corpo che per força convegnia ussire del sangue.

Or desteso che fu il Signore nostro sopra la croce, haperse le sue sanctissime braçe et porse le sue sanctissime mane alli crucifixori suoi et levò li ochi al cielo et disse: «O Padre mio, ecco che io som qui. A voi è piaçuto che io me sia humiliato perfina alla croce per amore della humana generatione. Ecco ch'io ho ricevuto la nostra obedientia et hove offerito me medesimo per coloro[151] i qualli voi haveti [f. 91v] electi che siano mei fratelli. Se voi recevete questo sacrificio mio, prigove che da qui inançi siate placabile per lo amore mio a l'humana generatione et sia desmentigada ogni offesa vechia; et io morirò».

Et in questo el fo levato la croce in alto et fita in terra. Or pe[n]sa che dolore dovea essere quello, et che pena dovea sentire el Signor nostro siando levato in alto; et tanto era constreto ch'el non podea movere se non el capo. Et tanto era quello sanctissimo corpo desteso per força ch'el non era osso che non se podesse numerare sì come fo detto per lo propheta: *Dinumeraverunt omnia ossa mea.*

Et siando levato in alto miser Iesù Cristo, la prima parola ch'el dicesse si fo che lui pregò il Padre per gli suoi crucifixori et disse: «Padre mio, perdona a loro, imperò ch'eli non sano quello che si facino». Le qualle parole fo segno de gra[n]dissimo amore et benignitade et patientia, dandone qui exempio de quello ch'el ne admonisse [f. 92r] nello Evangelio dicendo: «Pregate per coloro che ve perseguitano et non rendete male per male». O anima la qualle cerchi de vendicharte, non mi pare che habi imparato da questo Maestro, però che tu non seguiti lui!

Et poi sono crucifixi cum lui doi latroni, uno al lato drito et l'altro a[l] lato sinistro, per più sua vergogna. Et qui fo adimpito quello che dice el propheta: *Et cum iniquis reputatus etc.*

Or quando elli lo haveno crucifixo, li tolseno le vestimenta suoe et si le partìno la vesta sua in quatro parte, a cadauno cavalier la sua. Et poi

---

150. MS *p(er)darge piu dolore* in margin
151. MS *p(er) loro* with *co* in margin

seemed that the limbs and the bones were completely torn apart. And then they put one foot on top of the other, and with one huge nail they affixed them. Now imagine what pain that was! And note here that these wicked dogs, to increase his suffering, had made the nails rough, and they were huge nails, and they were nailed into the most sensitive places in the body. And Jesus Christ felt more suffering for these three reasons, and also for the copious amount of blood that streamed from his body, because his most holy body was stretched in a way that forced much blood to flow.

Now when Our Lord was stretched out on the cross, he opened his most holy arms and offered his most holy hands to his crucifiers. And he raised his eyes to heaven and said, "O my Father, here I am. You have wished me to humble myself even to the cross for the love of the human race. Behold, I have accepted this mission of obedience, and I have offered myself for those whom you have chosen to be my brothers. If you receive this, my sacrifice, I ask that from now on you be merciful to humankind for the sake of my love, and that all old offenses be forgiven; and I will die."

And at this, the cross was raised up and affixed in the earth. Now imagine what suffering this must have been, and what pain Our Lord must have felt being raised up. And he was so constrained that he couldn't even move his head. And his most holy body was so stretched by force that there wasn't a single bone that couldn't be counted, as the prophet had said: "*Dinumeraverunt omnia ossa mea.*"

And when Lord Jesus Christ had been raised up, the first words that he said were these: he prayed to the Father for his crucifiers and said, "My Father, forgive them, because they do not know what they do." And these words were a sign of tremendous love and goodness and patience, giving us here an example of what he preaches to us in the gospel, saying: "Pray for those who persecute you, and do not render evil for evil." O soul who seeks revenge, it seems to me that you have not learned from this Master, for you do not follow him![127]

And then the two thieves were crucified with him, one on the right and the other on the left, to increase his shame. And what the prophet said was fulfilled: "*Et cum iniquis reputatus etc.*"

Now when they had crucified him, they took his clothes and divided his robe in four parts, one for each soldier.[128] And then they took his tunic, which was woven in one piece, without a seam. And seeing that it had no seam, the soldiers said one to another, "Let's not tear this garment, but decide whose it should be with dice." And they did this. And what the prophet said was fulfilled: "*Partiti sunt vestimenta mea sibi, et super vestem meam miserunt sortem.*" And it was the mounted soldiers of Pilate who did this.

tolseno la gonella, la qualle era integra sença cosidura, et vedendo i cavalieri che l'era sança cosidura si disseno l'uno al altro: «Non tagliemo questa vesta, ma çugiamola de cui la debe essere cum i dadi», et così feceno.
Et qui fo adimpito quello che disse el propheta: *Partiti sunt vestimenta
mea sibi et super vestem mea miserunt* [f. 92v] *sortem*». Et questo feceno
gli cavalieri de Pilato.

Or habiando Pilato data la sentientia contra la iusticia, el fece scrivere
uno briveselo el qualle dicea: *Iesu Naçarenus Rex Iudeorum*. Et queste letere erano de lingua hebraica, greca et de latina, et questo fece Pilato açiò
che catuno la potesse leçere, et fecella poner sopra il capo a miser Iesù
Cristo. Et legendo li Giudei questo titolo furono molto turbati et disseno a
Pilato: «Mal hai scripto. Tu non dovevi scrivere "Re de' Giudei" ma che
"Lui dicea, io sum Re de Giudei"».

Rispuose Pilato: «Quello che ho scripto, scripto sia», quasi dica: «Se
io ho mal giudicato, io voglio ben scrivere». Et questo è il loro peccato,
che loro cognoscevano che li haveano facto male et non se mendavano.

Or quelli che passavano per la via si lo biastemavano dicendo: «O tu
che dicevi[152] de desfare el tempio de Dio et in tre dì reedificarlo, salvo te
fà hora ti me[f. 93r]desimo, se tu è Figliolo de Dio! Descendi della croce
et sì te crederemo».

Et così dicevano gli pri[n]cipi de' sacerdoti, facendo de lui con lli
scribi et seniori, dicea:[153] «Lui ha facto salvi altri et se medesimo non può
fare salvo! Cristo, Re de Israel, desmonta çò della croce açiò che noi possiamo credere che tu se' Figliolo de Dio electo». Et tuto questo diceano
per fare beffe di lui et non per credere.

Et uno de quelli ladroni i qualli erano cr[u]cifixi[154] cum lui sì començiò
a biastemare miser Iesù, dicendo: «Se tu è Cristo, salva te medemo et noi».

Et rispondendo l'altro et reprehendendolo sì disse: «Et ancho tu non
temi Idio; et però tu sarai dannado cum loro, però che noi receviamo degnamente questa morte per li nostri mali che haviamo facto. Ma costui
non ha facto alcuno male per el qualle el meriti questa pena».

Et poi se rivolse inverso miser Iesù et disse: «Signore mio, ricordate
de me quando [f. 93v] veg[n]erai nel tuo regno».

Et qui il nostro Signore disse la secunda parola, et fo parola de grande
misericordia, dicendo: «Io te dico che oçi serai mecho in Paradiso». O

152. MS <doueue> diceui
153. MS dicea in margin
154. MS cricifixi

Now Pilate, having given the sentence contrary to justice, had a placard made, and it said *Jesu Naçarenus Rex Iudeorum.* And these letters were in the Hebrew, Greek, and Latin languages. And Pilate had this done so that everyone would be able to read it, and he had it placed above the head of Lord Jesus. And the Jews, reading what was written here, were very upset, and said to Pilate: "You have written this badly. You should not have written 'King of the Jews' but 'He said "I am King of the Jews."'"

Pilate replied, "What I have written I have written," as if to say, "If I have judged badly, at least I wish to write well." And this is their sin: that they knew that they had done wrong, and they did not correct themselves.

Now those who were passing by the way jeered at him, saying, "O you who said you could destroy the temple of God and rebuild it in three days, save yourself now! If you are the Son of God, descend from the cross and we will believe you!"

And the high priests said similar things, along with the scribes and elders, saying: "He said that he would save others, and he can't even save himself. Christ, King of Israel, come down from the cross so we can believe that you are the chosen Son of God!" And they said all this to make fun of him, and not in order to believe.

And one of the two thieves who was crucified with him began to taunt Lord Jesus, saying, "If you are Christ, save yourself and us."

And the other responded and reprimanded him, saying, "And even you have no fear of God. And for this you will be damned with them, because we deserve this death for our wrongs that we have committed, but he has done no wrong for which he deserves this pain."

And then he turned towards Lord Jesus and said, "My Lord, remember me when you enter into your kingdom."

And then Our Lord said the second words, and they were words of great mercy, saying, "I tell you that today you will be with me in paradise." O words of the greatest hope! Through these words, the mercy of Our Lord Jesus Christ was openly shown, when he so generously pardoned a thief who repented at the hour of death. And here you can truly see and understand how Our Lord is most generously prepared to pardon, as long as we turn and repent of the evil that we have done and place hope in his mercy.

Now, near the cross stood his mother and her sisters and Mary Magdalene. And seeing his mother and also the disciple whom he loved, Lord Jesus said to his mother, "*Mulier ecce filius tuus.*" And then he said to his disciple, "*Ecce mater tua.*" And these were the third words that Lord Jesus spoke from the cross, and they were words of the greatest compassion, when he

parola de grandissima sperança! Per questa parola se monstra manifestamente la misercordia del nostro Signore miser Iesù Cristo, quando che ad
uno latrone el qualle se pentì su l'hora della morte el ge perdonò così lar-
gamente. Et qui veramente si puote vedere et comprehendere come el nostro Signore è largissimamente apparechiato a perdonare, pure che noi vo-
gliamo tornare et pentirse del male che noi habiamo facto et sperare nella
sua misericordia.

Or stando apresso la croce la madre et le sorele della madre et Maria
Magdalena et vedendo miser Iesù la madre et etiam el discipulo el qualle
amava, disse alla madre sua: *Mulier, ecce filius tuus*. Et poi disse al discipulo: *Ecce mater tua*. Et questa fo la terça [f. 94r] parola che disse miser
Iesù sopra la croce, et fo parola de gra[n]dissima compassione quando el
disse: «Dona, ecco el tuo figliolo», et a sancto Çuane: «Ecco la madre tua».
Et non li disse: «Madre» perché ella non sentisse più dolore per lo grandissimo amore che lei gli portava. Però che se lui l'avesse chiamata «Madre»,
lei sarebe ussita di sé per il grande dolore. Et qui se intende per sancto
Çuane tuti gli el[e]cti i qualli miser Iesù diete alla madre sua per figlioli. Et
da l'hora in qua la Verçene Maria è nostra Madre.

Et ne l'hora de sexta per tuto il mondo se fece scuritade et tenebre. Et
cercha l'hora de nona, miser Iesù Cristo cridò cum grande voce et disse:
*Hely hely lamaçabathani*, che vuole dire «Dio mio, Dio mio, perché me
hai tu abandonato?», quasi dica: «O Padre mio, tanto tu hai hamato el
mondo che hai dato el tuo figliolo a morte per lui!». Et questa fo la quarta
parola, et fo parola de grande compassione però [f. 94v] che el se sent[i]va
essere per admirabile modo abandonato dal Padre. Et anche è d'averli
grande compassione, però che el fo abandonato da tuti gli suoi amici ch'el
seguitavano, salvo che dalla madre et dalla Magdalena et da sancto Çuane,
li qualli non gli potevano dare alcuno conforto, ançi li acresevano più dolore, et specialmente la madre però che la vedea essere in tanta pena per la
pena che lei vedea portare al suo dolcissimo figliolo iniustamente.

O che pianto facea la Magdalena et le altre done et Çuane carissimo
discipulo! Et tuti questi pianti creseano pena a miser Iesù Cristo. Et quelli
che stavano dintorno, oldendo chiamare «*Hely hely*» dicevano «Ecco
ch'el chiama Helia: vediamo s'el vegnirà Helya a liberarlo!».[155]

O sapiando el nostro Signore che çia erà consumado ogni cosa et per
impire la scriptura, si disse: «*Sitio*». Et questa fo la quinta parola, et fo parola de grande compassione et de grande pena alla madre et a' Giudei fo
de grande a[f. 95r]legreça però ch'el vedeano stentare. Alla madre et alli

_____

155. MS *aliberaro* with the second *r* corrected to *l*

said "Woman, behold your son," and to Saint John, "Behold your mother." And he did not say "Mother," for he did not want her to feel more pain for the great love that she bore him. Because if he had called her "Mother," she would have fainted for great sorrow. And here Saint John stands for all those who are chosen, whom Lord Jesus gives to his mother as children. And from that hour on, the Virgin Mary has been our Mother.

And in the sixth hour, the whole world was covered with darkness and shadows. And around the ninth hour, Lord Jesus Christ cried out with a loud voice and said, "*Hely hely lamaçabathani,*" which means, "My God, my God, why have you forsaken me?"—as if to say, "O my Father, so greatly have you loved the world that you gave your son to die for it!" And these were the fourth words, and they were words worthy of great compassion, because he felt that he had been abandoned by the Father, in an astonishing way. And it is also cause for great compassion because he was abandoned by all his friends who had followed him, except for his mother and Magdalene and Saint John, who were unable to give any comfort to him and even increased his pain, especially his mother because he saw her in such great suffering for the suffering that she saw her most sweet son bear unjustly.

Oh what a lament Magdalene and the other women made, and John his dearest disciple! And all of this lamentation increased the pain of Lord Jesus Christ. And those who stood near him, hearing him cry "*Hely, hely,*" said, "Listen! He cries 'Helia.' Let's see if Elijah comes to liberate him!"

Then Our Lord, knowing that everything was finished, and to fulfill the scriptures, said "*Sitio.*" And these were the fifth words. And they were words of great compassion and of great pain to the mother. And to the Jews, this was cause for rejoicing, because they saw that he was struggling. To his mother, and to his other friends, it was cause for great sorrow, because they had nothing to give him to drink. Then one of the soldiers took a sponge and dipped it in vinegar mixed with gall, which was prepared in a jar, and he put it on the end of a stick and then raised it to the lips of Lord Jesus.

And when Our Lord had tasted the vinegar mixed with gall, he said, "*Consummatum est.*" And these were the sixth words that Lord Jesus said on the wood of the cross, as if to say, "I have accomplished everything, and I have carried out to the end the mission of obedience that you ordained for me. I am ready to do even more if necessary, but I affirm that I have fulfilled all that is written of me."

And in the ninth hour the sun grew dark, and the veil of the temple was torn in two. And then Our Lord Jesus Christ cried out with a loud

altri amici suoi era de grande dolore però che loro non haveano da darli
da bere. Alora uno de quelli ministri sì tolse una spongia et si la impite
de aceto mesidado cum fielle el qualle era apparechiato i[n] uno vaso, et
messela in capo de una canna et poi la porse alla bocha de miser Iesù.

Et come el Signore nostro tolse l'aceto cum el fielle mixto disse:
«*Consumatum est*». Et questa fo la sexta parola che disse miser Iesù sopra
il legno della croce, quasi dica: «Io ho consumato ogni cosa et ho adimpiuto ogni tua obedientia che tu me hai imposta perfectamente. Io sono
anchora apparechiato a fare più se el[156] bisogna, ma tanto dicho che habo
consumato tuto quello ch'è scripto di me».

Et ne l'hora de nona il sole se schurò et il vello del tempio se partite
per meço. Et alora el signore nostro miser Iesù Cristo cridò cum grande
voce et disse: «*Pater, in manus tuas commendo spiritum meum*». Et hec
dicens expiravit. [f. 95v] Et questa fo la septima parola ch'el nostro Salvatore disse cum grande voce et cum gran lacrime: «Padre, nelle tue mane
aricomando el spirito mio». Et rimase col capo inclinato sul pecto, quasi
dica: «Io te rendo gratie, Padre mio, che tu m'ài chiamato a te».

Et questo crido convertì quel centurione el qualle era capo[157] di cavalieri de Pilato, el qualle era presente quando el nostro Signore morì. Et vedendolo morir cridando, et anche gli segni, miracoli et terremoti, glorificò
Dio et disse: «Veramente questo huomo era Figliolo de Dio».

Et fo sì grande questa voce de miser Iesù che la fo aldida infina allo
inferno. Et incontenente che Cristo morite, l'anima descesse al limbo alli
Sancti Padri, che cum grande gaudio lo aspetavano. O morte benedecta,
per la qualle l'humana generatione fo liberata dalle mane del diavolo! O
morte per la qualle a' peccatori fo aperto el paradiso! O peccatore, risguarda adonca in questo confalone che oçi fo levato in alto, in el [f. 96r]
qualle la nostra salute et la vita nostra pende. Questa è lla bandiera del paradiso, la qualle oçi è despiegata. Questo è l'agnello della nostra redemptione. Questo è quello desiderato thesoro del paradiso el qualle non vegnerà mai meno, çioè il sangue precioso de miser Iesù Cristo, el qualle
esso anchuò ha spanto per la nostra liberatione. Queste sono le fenestre
del cielo, çioè le piage de miser Iesù, per le qualle fenestre noi potiamo intrare nel reame del cielo. Questa è quella scalla per la qualle el peccatore
puote montare in cielo. Questo è quel spechio nel qualle li peccator se dee
spechiare. Questo è quello arboro el qualle è fiorito de tute le vertude, el
qualle conforta gli peccatori et chiamali a via de salute et niuno puote

156. MS *sel el*
157. MS *capo* in margin

voice and said, "*Pater in manus tuas commendo spiritus meus.*" And saying this, he breathed his last. And these were the seventh words that our
Savior said, with a loud voice and with a great cry: "Father, into your
hands I commend my spirit."[129] And he remained with his head bowed towards his breast, as if to say, "I give you thanks, my Father, for calling me
to yourself."

And this cry converted the centurion, who was the leader of Pilate's
soldiers, who was present when Our Lord died. And seeing him die while
crying out, and also the miraculous signs and tremor of the earth, he gave
glory to God and said: "Truly, this man was the Son of God."

And it was so loud, this cry of Lord Jesus, that it was heard even down
in hell. And as soon as Christ died, his soul descended into limbo to the
Holy Fathers, who welcomed him with great joy.[130] O blessed death, through
which humankind was set free from the hands of the devil! O death, through
which the gates of paradise were opened! O sinner, behold, then, this banner
that today was raised on high, in which our salvation and our life is displayed! This is the banner of paradise, which today is unfurled. This is the
lamb of our redemption. This is that longed-for treasure of paradise, which
will never fail: that is to say, the precious blood of Lord Jesus Christ, which
he poured out to set us free. These are the windows of heaven: that is to say,
the wounds of Lord Jesus, through which we may enter into the Kingdom
of Heaven. This is the stairway by which the sinner may climb to heaven.
This is the mirror in which sinners may see themselves reflected. This is the
tree that blossoms with all virtues, that comforts the sinners and calls them
to the road of salvation, and no one is able to enter into the Kingdom of
Heaven if not by means of it. Therefore, O sinner, plant this tree, that is, the
Passion of your Creator, in the middle of your heart, and remember that he
suffered this most bitter death for you! And prepare yourself to follow him
by the road of penitence and the denial of your own will. And this is the banner with which the sinner wins all battles.

And when he had breathed his last, the earth quaked, and the rocks
split open, and tombs opened. And many holy bodies revived and came
forth from the tombs, and after their resurrection went into the holy city,
where they appeared to many.

Now, rightly are they considered to have hearts of stone who, at this
moment, do not show compassion for their Lord, whether through laments
or through other signs of love, seeing that all the creatures and the elements
showed, through signs, lamentation and sorrow for the death of Our Lord!

Now who could bear to have seen the Virgin Mary fall to the earth,
swooning from the great sorrow that she felt for the death of her most

intrare nel regno del cielo se non per meço di lui. Adonca, o peccatore, pianta questo arbore nel meço del tuo chuore, cioè la Passione del tuo Creatore, et pensa che per te l'à sostenuto questa asprissima morte! [f. 96v] Et fà che tu il seguiti per la via della penitencia et negatione della propria voluntade. Et questa è quella insegna cum la qualle el peccatore vince ogni bataglia.

Et spirato ch'el fo, se fece grandi teremoti et le pietre se speçavano et gli monumenti se apriteno. Et molti corpi sancti resuscitorono et usitero di monumenti et dapoi la resurretione sua venero nella sancta citade et aparseno a molti.

Or bene se puote reputare havere il cuore de pietra colui che a questo passo non ha compassione al suo Signore o per pianti o per altri segni d'amore, vedendo che tute le creature et li elementi per segni monstrorono pianto et dolore della morte del suo Signore!

Or chi havesse veduto alora la Vergene Maria cadere in terra tramortita per el grande dolore che lei sentiva della morte del suo dolcissimo figliolo, et la Magdalena destruçerse per dolore grande del suo Maestro carissimo, et san Çuane pia[n]çere durissimame[n]te et tuta via tegnando la Madona [f. 97r] per el braço et guardando hora el suo dolcissimo Maestro in croce morto et hora la madre tramortita nelle sue braçie; or chi havesse udito il pianto che faceano le sorele della Madona et le altre done che erano alla croce del nostro Salvatore, credo ch'el non se potria tenire ch'el non pianç[e]se[158] cum loro amaramente per dolore che sentiria.

Or vede[n]do gli cavalieri de Pilato et anche i Giudei li segni che erano stati, et vedendo che Cristo era çà morto, tuti se partirono et lassorono il corpo del nostro Signore solo. Et poi che partita fu tuta la çente, la Dona nostra et le altre done che erano cum lei se misseno a sedere apresso alla croce. Et contemplavano il nostro Salvatore, et qui se rinovò el pianto et dolore della madre et etiandio[159] delle altre done.[160]

Or recordandose gli principi et pharisei ch'el corpo del nostro Signore et quelli degli ladroni erano rimasti sopra la croce si andorono da Pilato et disseno: «Misere, costoro sono rimasti sopra le croce [f. 97v] et non sapiamo se loro sono morti o no. Et però te priegiamo che tu mandi a rompere a loro le gambe et sepelirli, açiò che essi non romagnino in croce dimane ch'è el giorno della Pasqua». Alora li cavalieri et ministri de Pilato venero al luocho per occiderli, et rompere a lloro le osse delle gambe, et sepelirli.

158. MS *piãçase*
159. MS *etiãdio dio*
160. MS *dono*

sweet son, and Magdalene defacing herself for the tremendous sorrow she felt for her dearest Master, and Saint John weeping so bitterly, even while holding Our Lady in his arms and gazing first at his most sweet Master, dead on the cross, and then at his mother, who had fainted in his arms! Or who could bear to have heard the lament that Our Lady's sisters made, and the other women who were at the cross of our Savior? I believe that it would have been impossible to keep from weeping bitterly with them, for the grief that they must have felt.

Now, seeing the signs that were made, and seeing that Christ was already dead, Pilate's soldiers and the Jews departed, and left the body of Our Lord Jesus alone. And as soon as all the people had left, Our Lady and the other women who were with her sat down near the cross. And they contemplated our Savior; and then the lamentation and grief of the mother and the other women was renewed.

Then the high priests and Pharisees, recalling that the body of Our Lord and those of the thieves remained on the cross, went to Pilate and said: "Sir, those men remain on the cross, and we do not know if they are dead or not. And so we ask you to order that their legs be broken and that they be buried, so that they will not remain on the cross tomorrow, which is the day of Passover." So the mounted soldiers and guards went to the place to kill them, and to break their legs, and to bury them.

## Come i cavalieri de Pilato çonseno al Monte Calvario per romper le gambe alli ladroni et a miser Iesù. Capitolo xxv°.[161]

Arivando costoro al Monte Calvario, trovono la Dona nostra cum le suoe compagne sentare al lato della croce del suo dolcissimo figliolo. Or vedando la Vergene Maria vegnire gli cavalieri de Pilato, non sapiando che se vegnisseno a fare, començò molto a temere che elli vegnisseno per tuorli el suo dolcissimo figliolo. Ora se rinuova el pianto et crese el dolore, et non sa quello che la debia fare! Et così piançando, la se rivolse al figliolo et disse: «O figliolo mio dolcissimo, perché torna, [f. 98r] costoro?[162] Or te vogliono elli fare più male? Or non te hano ça morto? O figliolo mio, priega el Padre tuo che li faça piatosi inverso di te, et io dalla parte mia farò quello che io potrò».

Alora la Dona nostra cum le compagne se puose a sedere inaçi la croce del suo dolcissimo figliolo, pia[n]çando fortissimamente. Et aprosimandosi gli cavalieri alli latroni furiosamente, vedandoli anchora vivere, gli rompeno le osse delle gambe et tolseli çió della croce, et poi li gittorono in una fossa la qualle era lì appresso. Et poi alquanti se volseno inverso la croce de miser Iesù per fare el simele a lui. Et vedando questo, la madre angostiava, et temendo che loro volesseno fare così al suo dolcissimo figliolo, cum gran pianto corse alle arme della humilitade. Inçenochiandose denançi a loro cum le braçe incrossate, piançendo amaramente, disse:[163] «O fradeli, io ve priego per lo solo Dio altissimo che voi non tormentiate più questo mio [f. 98v] dolcissimo figliolo. Non vedete voi che lui è gia morto? Io sum l'adolorata madre sua, la qualle mai non ve feçe inçuria niuna. Et se 'l mio figliolo v'è apparesto contrario a voi, lo havete morto. Io ve 'l perdono fatime pure questa gratia: non rompete a lui le osse delle gambe, açiò che io el possia soterare integro; et non vogliati usare più crudelitade verso de lui». Et simile dicea Ioanne e lla Magdalena et le sorele della Dona nostra. Stando tuti inçenochioni denançi a quella çe[n]te, piançendo amaramente.

Et sancto Çoane, vedando la pocha pietade[164] che costoro haveano alla Dona nostra, sì disse: «O madre de Dio, non state voi inçenochiati agli piedi di questi maledecti. Or credete voi vençere per priegi piatosi

---

161. MS *Capitolo xxvi*
162. MS *perche torna costoro*
163. MS *disse* in margin
164. MS *pietade <de questi maledeti>*

## Chapter 25. How the soldiers of Pilate came to Mount Calvary to break the legs of the thieves and Lord Jesus.

When those men arrived at Mount Calvary, they found Our Lady with her companions sitting beside the cross of her most sweet son. Now the Virgin Mary, seeing the soldiers of Pilate approaching and not knowing what they might be coming to do, began to be very afraid that they might be coming to take away her most sweet son. And Our Lady begins to lament again, and her sorrow increases, and she does not know what to do. And weeping like this, she turned to her son and said: "O my most sweet son, why do they return? What more do they want to do to you now? Haven't they killed you already? O my son, ask your Father to make them show pity toward you. And I for my part will do what I can."

Then Our Lady sat down beneath the cross of her most sweet son with her companions, weeping most bitterly. And with great noise and violence, the mounted soldiers rode up to the thieves, and seeing them still alive, broke their legs and took them down from the cross and then threw them in a ditch which was nearby. And then some turned towards the cross of Lord Jesus to do the same to him. And when she saw this, the mother grew more anguished; and fearing that they wished to do the same to her most sweet son, in her great distress she hastened to arm herself with humility. She fell to her knees before them with her arms crossed over her breast, and weeping bitterly she said: "O brothers, I beg you, in the name of the one Almighty God, not to torment this my most sweet son any longer. Don't you see that he is already dead? I am his sorrowful mother, who never did any harm to you. And if my son seemed to be a threat to you, you have killed him. I will forgive you, if only you grant me this request: do not break his legs, so that I can bury him intact. And do not inflict any more cruelty on him." And John said similar things, and Magdalene and the sisters of Our Lady too. They all remained kneeling before those people, weeping bitterly.

And Saint John, seeing how little pity those men felt towards Our Lady, said, "O Mother of God, do not remain kneeling at the feet of these cursed men. Now do you really believe you can persuade with piteous prayers those who are full of cruelty, and to conquer with humility those who are full of pride? O my Mother, humility is a worthless thing to the proud, so you labor in vain."

Now one of those soldiers, a very proud man named Longinus, disregarding the prayers of Our Lady, approached the cross of Our Lord with a

quelli che sono pieni de ogni crudelitade, et cum humilitade vincere coloro che sono pieni de superbia? O madre mia, vile cosa è alli superbi la
humilitade, sì che indarno ve [f. 99r] affatichate».

Or uno de quelli cavalieri, che se chiamava Longino, molto superbo,
despregiando gli priegi della Dona nostra, acostandose alla croce del nostro Salvatore cum una lança in mano sì lli diete nel costado, della qualle
apertura incontenente ussite sangue et aqua; per la qual cossa questo Longino se convertite et poi morite martire per amore de Cristo Iesù.

Et in questa apertura me pare comprehendere tre notabele et degne
cose. La prima sì è che lo evangelista dice ch'el fo aperto el costado de
miser Iesù Cristo, per la qualle apertura me pare intendere che Cristo Iesù
qui ne vuole monstrare ch'el sia la porta per la qualle noi dobiamo intrare
nel regno de cielo. Unde lo evangelio dice: «Io sum la porta». Et in uno
altro luocho ch'el dice: «Io sum la via». La secunda cosa sì è ch'el ne ussite
sangue, per la qualle cose noi dobiamo sapere che questo fo contra natura,
unde è da sapere che questo fo miracolosamente facto a demonstrare che
lui era vivo et vero [f. 99v] Figliolo de Dio. La terça sì è che non solamente
ne ussite sangue, ma etiandio aqua, a dimonstrare che la Passione de Cristo
è quella per la qualle noi siamo lavadi da ogni macula de peccato.

Alora vedando la madre cossì aperto il costado del suo dolcissimo
figliolo, sì cadete tramortita nel[e] braçe della Magdalena. Alora sancto
Çuane, constreto per dolore ch'el sentite, prese ardimento et disse inverso
a loro: «O huomeni maledecti et sança pietade, perché fati voi questa
gra[n]dissima crudelitade? Or non vedete voi ch'ell'è çià morto? Non ve
basti havere morto lui, che anche voleti alcidere questa sua [a]dolorata
madre»?

Alora come piaque a Dio, quelli cavalieri se partirono et non gli
rompeteno le gambe. Et qui fo adimpita la Scriptura, che dice: «*Os non
comminuetis ex eo*». Et così rimase miser Iesù sopra la croce perfina dapoi
vespero.

Et poi vene Ioseph a Pilato, il qualle era discipulo de miser Iesù, ma
occulto per timore [f. 100r] d'i Giudei; et dimandò il corpo de miser Iesù.
Et sapiando Pilato che lui era già morto, sì ge lo concesse come a huomo
nobile. Alora Ioseph vene et chiamò secho uno il qualle havea nome Nicodemo. Et per fare secundo l'usança si portono cum sí quasi libre çento de
mirra et aloe et uno ninçuolo mondissimo. Et approximandose costoro al
monte, et vedandoli Ioanne et le done venire, sì tocorono la madre la
qualle non era ancora rivenuta. Et quella, rivegiandosi, dimandò del suo
dolcissimo figliolo. Et quelli rispondendo che non li era sta' facto alchuna
cosa dapoi l'apertura del lato.

spear in his hand and struck him in the side. And through that opening, suddenly blood and water flowed out. And through this Longinus was converted, and later died as a martyr for the love of Christ Jesus.

And this opening seems to me to signify three notable and worthy things.[131] The first is that the evangelist says that the side of Lord Jesus Christ was pierced, which seems to me to mean that Christ Jesus wishes to show us here that he is the door through which we must enter into the Kingdom of Heaven. Thus the Gospel says: "I am the door." And in another place he says: "I am the way." The second is that blood flowed out, and by this we ought to know that what happened here was not natural. Thus it should be known that this was done miraculously, to show that he was the true and living Son of God. The third is that not only blood flowed out, but also water, to show that it is through the Passion of Christ that we are washed from all stain of sin.

And then the mother, seeing the side of her most sweet son pierced in this way, fainted into the arms of Magdalene. And then Saint John, compelled by the anguish that he felt, stood up to them and boldly said, "O wicked men without pity, why do you inflict this great cruelty? Don't you see that he is already dead? Isn't it enough that you have killed him, or do you also want to kill this woman, his sorrowful mother?"

And then, as God would have it, those soldiers left and did not break the legs. And here the scripture was fulfilled which says, "*Os non comminuetis ex eo.*" And Lord Jesus remained on the cross like this until after vespers.[132]

And then Joseph, who was a disciple of Lord Jesus, went to Pilate, but secretly, for fear of the Jews. And he asked for the body of Lord Jesus. And Pilate, knowing that he was already dead, granted this to him as a noble man. And then Joseph came and brought with him a man named Nichodemus. And in order to perform the burial rites, they brought with them nearly a hundred pounds of myrrh and aloes and a pure white linen cloth. And as they approached the mountain, John and the women saw them coming and began to pat the mother gently, for she had not yet awakened from her swoon. And once she had revived, she asked about her most sweet son. And they replied that nothing had happened to him after the piercing of his side.

Oh how many times the sorrowful mother swooned today! Indeed, she fainted in anguish as many times as she saw an injury done to her most sweet son. So today the words spoken of her by the prophet Simeon were fulfilled, when he said, "The sword of your son will pierce your soul." And it might well be said here that the blade of the lance pierced the

O quante volte è anchuò l'adolorata madre tramortita! Certo tante
volte lei è caduta in angossa, quante volte la vedea fare ingiuria al suo dolcissimo figliolo, unde adimpito fo oçi in lei quello che li fo detto da Simeone propheta quando el disse: «Il cortello del tuo figliolo passerà
l'anima tua». Et puosse ben dire qui [f. 100v] veramente ch'el cortello
della lança forò il corpo,[165] çioè il costato del figliolo, et passò l'anima
della madre. Et per questo cortello se intende la Passione del nostro Signore miser Iesù Cristo.

## Come Ioseph et Nicodemo arivono al Monte Calvario per tuore el corpo de miser Iesù çonso de croce. Capitolo xxvi°.[166]

Approsimandose Ioseph al luocho, et vedendoli la Dona nostra et li
compagni vegnire et non cognossandoli, haveno grande paura. Et Ioanne,
cognossandoli, sì disse: «Non habiate paura alcuna, però che io cognosco
tuti costoro. El è Ioseph et Nicodemo che vieneno in nostro adiuto».
Alora la Dona Nostra [era] uno poco[167] confortata, udendo che loro veniano in suo adiutorio. Et quando furono apresso la croce se inçenochiorono et adorono el suo Signore, fortemente lacrimando. Et poi furono rice-
puti rivere[n]temente dalla Dona Nostra et dalle compagne, cum grande
pianto. Et disse la Dona Nostra: «Benedecto sia Dio, el qualle ve ha [f.
101r] mandati in nostro adiuto». Et poi disse a loro: «Bene haveti facto che
ve siati ricordati del Maestro vostro, inperò ch'el ve amava molto. Et veramente ve dico ch'el me parse vedere una nuova luce quando io ve viti venire, imperò che noi non eravamo atti a tuorlo gió della croce. El figliolo
mio ve ne renderà buona mercede». Et questo dicea cum grande lacrime.
Alora rispuose Ioseph et Nicodemo: «Madona nostra, noi ne havemo
habuto grande pena et dolore per amore del vostro figliolo et della iniusti-
cia che lli è stata facta et che noi non lo habiamo potuto adiutare, però che
li maligni hano habuto potentia sopro el iusto. Ma noi almeno ge faremo
questo picolo servicio: che noi el toremo gió della croce et sì llo sotera-
remo, avegna che questo sia servicio de grande dolore».
Or sta qui attento cum la mente tua et vederai cosse de grande compassione. Et riguarda Ioseph et Nicodemo metere doe scalle apogiade alla
croce [f. 101v] del tuo Creatore per desficarlo gió della croce. Hora monta

165. MS corpo <d>
166. MS Capitolo xxvii
167. MS poco in margin

body, that is, the side of the son, and passed through the soul of the mother. And by this blade is meant the Passion of Our Lord Jesus Christ.

## *Chapter 26. How Joseph and Nichodemus came to Mount Calvary to take the body of Lord Jesus down from the cross.*

As Joseph approached the place, Our Lady and her companions, seeing them coming and not knowing who they were, became very afraid. And John, recognizing them, said, "Don't be afraid, for I know these men. It's Joseph and Nichodemus, who are coming to help us."

And so Our Lady was comforted a little, hearing that they were coming to her aid. And when they arrived at the cross, they knelt and paid reverence to the Lord, weeping copiously. And then they were greeted with reverence by Our Lady and by her companions with great lamentation. And Our Lady said: "Blessed be God, who has sent you to our aid." And then she said to them: "You have done well to have remembered your Master, because he loved you much. And truly I tell you that I seemed to see a new light when I saw you coming, because we could not take him down from the cross by ourselves. And my son will reward you well." And she said this with many tears.

Then Joseph and Nichodemus replied, "Our lady, we have felt great pain and sorrow because of our love for your son and for the injustice that was done to him, and because we were not able to help him, since the evildoers have had power over the just. But at least we can do this small service: we will take him down from the cross and we will bury him, although this will be a very painful task."

Now pay close attention here as you imagine this, and you will see things worthy of great compassion.[133] And watch Joseph and Nichodemus put two ladders against the cross of your Creator to take him down from the cross. Then Joseph mounts the ladder and begins to loosen his right hand. And Nichodemus went up the left side. And with great effort Joseph released his right hand.

Ioseph et sì comença a desficare la mano drita. Et Nicodemo montò al lato [m]ancho.[168] Et cum grande fadicha Ioseph cavò quello della mano drita.

Or vedando sancto Çuane el chiodo cavato, sì feçe segno a Ioseph che il dovesse abscondere per amore della Dona Nostra, açiò che lei non vedesse. Alora Nicodemo, essendo dal ladi sinistro, cavò fuori cum bel muodo l'altro chiodo et porsello a Ioseph, per modo che lla Dona Nostra non ne vite niuno d'essi chiodi. Et Ioseph sì branchò el corpo de miser Iesù nelle sue braçie et sì llo sostene infin a tanto che Nicodemo cavò el chiodo d'i piedi. Et diette quello a Ioanne, et poi dismontò gió della scalla. Et così romase il corpo de[l] Signore sopra le spalle a Ioseph. O buono Ioseph, bene sei aventurato, che meritasti di sostenere el Figliolo de Dio nelle tue braçie! Et dismontado Ioseph, uno d'i braçi de miser Iesù sì pendea çosso. Alora la Dona [f. 102r] nostra sì llo prese et basiò la mano et cum grande pianto sì 'l tene perfina che Ioseph fo desmontado della scalla.

Alora la madre se misse a sedere in terra, et Ioseph gli misse el suo dolcissimo figliolo in gremio. Pensa hora tu che pianto dovea fare alora la madre, però che io non posso dirlo! Et poi risguarda la Madalena sentare agli piedi, et le sorele della Madona et poi Ioanne et Ioseph et Nicodemo. O che pianto se començiò fra loro, et che cridi et lamentatione de grande compassione—et specialmente l'adolorata madre sua, la qualle el tenia denançi.

Et hora gli basiava la bocha sua sanctissima, et poi el capo incoronato de crudelissime spine; et poi basiava li ochi suoi sanctissimi che furono velati da' Giudei, et quelle orechie beatissime che tanti obprobrii uditeno. Et poi basiava quella façia angelica che tanto fo consputata da' Giudei,[169] et poi quella bocha preciosissima, che da quelli iniqui fo beverata d'aceto et di fielle et da quello traditore [f. 102v] basiata. Et poi basiava quelle [g]ote[170] che da quelli maledecti Giudei furono percosse, et quello collo nobelissimo che da' Giudei fu tutto inbratato et cum la corda ligato.[171] Et poi basiava le braçie et quell'innocentissime mane le qualle erano così crudelmente vulnerate, et il pecto sacratissimo che fo aperto da quella cruda lançia, del qualle ussite sangue et aqua, et quello corpo sanctissimo il qualle fo tanto batuto et lacerato, et quelle gambe benigne che furono così flagellate. Et poi vene a quelli piedi beatissimi gli qualli furono conficti nella croce cum quello asperissimo chiodo, et non se potea saciare de basiarli.

168. MS *stancho*
169. MS *da Giudei/* in margin
170. MS *bote*
171. MS *ligalto*

Now Saint John, seeing the nail that had been removed, signaled to Joseph that he should hide it for the love of Our Lady, so that she would not see it. And then Nichodemus, being on the left side, gently took out the other nail, and passed it to Joseph in such a way that Our Lady would see neither one of these nails. And Joseph lifted the body of Our Lord Jesus in his arms and held him until Nichodemus removed the nail from the feet and gave it to John, and then he descended the ladder. And the body of Our Lord rested like this on the shoulders of Joseph. O good Joseph, how fortunate you are, that you were deemed worthy to hold the Son of God in your arms! And when Joseph descended, one of the arms of Lord Jesus was hanging down. And Our Lady took it and kissed the hand, and with much weeping she held it until Joseph had descended the ladder.

And then the mother sat on the ground, and Joseph put her most sweet Son in her lap.[134] Imagine, now, how the mother must have lamented then, because I am unable to describe it! And then behold Magdalene sitting at the feet, and the sisters of Our Lady, and then John and Joseph and Nichodemus. Oh how they began to weep then, and with what cries and pitiful lamentations, especially his sorrowful mother, who held him before her.

And then she kissed his most holy mouth, and then the head crowned with the most cruel thorns.[135] And then she kissed his most holy eyes, which were blindfolded by the Jews, and those most blessed ears, which heard such insults. And then she kissed that angelic face, which was so covered with spit by the Jews, and then that most precious mouth, which was made to drink vinegar and gall by those evil-doers and was kissed by that traitor. And then she kissed those cheeks, which were struck by those wicked Jews, and that most noble neck, which was completely defiled by the Jews and bound by the cord. And then she kissed the arms, and those most innocent hands, which were so cruelly wounded, and the most sacred breast, which was pierced by that rude lance and from which issued blood and water, and that most holy body, which was so beaten and lacerated, and those blessed legs, which were so cruelly flogged. And then she came to those most blessed feet, which were nailed to the cross with the sharpest of nails, and she was not able to stop kissing him.

And she said, "O my most sweet son, O King of Glory, how is it that you are crowned with thorns?[136] O mirror and beauty of the angels, how is it that you are now pierced full of wounds? O my son, you never offended anyone. Why, then, have you been so cruelly wounded? O life of all creatures, why have you been so cruelly killed without cause?"

Et dicea: «O figliolo mio dolcissimo, O Re de gloria, come sei de spine coronato? O spechio et beleça de gli angeli, come sei tu ora disforato?[172] O figliolo mio, tu non offendesti mai alcuno; perché te hano adoncha così crudelmente vulnerato? O vita de tutte le creature, come sei stato crudelmente morto sança casone»?

Alo[f. 103r]ra le sorele della Madona, per lo grande dolore, non li potevano rispondere, ma piançendo l[a][173] abraçiavano et faceano gran lamento. Et poi disse la madre alla Magdalena: «È questo il figliolo mio? Ben el doveresti cognoscere, però ch'el te amava molto et albergava molte volte nella casa tua».

Alora la Magdalena disse cum gran p[i]anto: «O Madre de Gloria, questo ch'è morto è il tuo figliolo et è il Dio mio. Questo è il figliolo tuo et è il maestro mio».

Or approsima[n]dose la sera, Ioseph, vedendo gli dolori acerbissimi et le angustie della Dona nostra, dolcemente la pregava che lei dovesse uno pocho restarre de tanto affliçerse et che lei lo lassasse involçere nello ninçuolo et portarlo al sepulchro. Alora la madre rispondendo dicìa: «O Ioseph, non me tuore questo mio figliolo! Lui sì è il Dio mio et sposo mio, l'amore mio et refugio et consolatione mia. Lui è la vita dell'anima mia. O fratelli mei, non me lo tollete, o voi me [f. 103v] sotorate cum lui». Et queste parole dicea la Vergene Maria cum grandissimi pianti et sospiri, guardando le ferite del suo dolcissimo figliolo: ora alle mane, ora allo costado, ora li piedi, ora il capo incoronato de spine, ora el volto pieno de sputi et di sangue. Et poi guardava tuto el corpo lacerato, et tuta via pia[n]çendo non se potea consolare.

Io ho trovato in uno luocho ch'el Signore nostro rivelò a una sua divota che per derisione lui fo tosato. S'el fu vero, non so, ma dovemo noi sapere che li Giudei gli feceno ogni ingiuria che li poteno fare. Et perçiò Ysaia in persona de miser Iesù Cristo disse: «El corpo mio ho dato a coloro che me percuoteno et le guançie mie a coloro che le isvelano».

Or vedando sancto Çuane ch'el se facea sera, sì disse alla Dona Nostra: «Madona, el se fa sera et l'è meglio, s'el ve piace, che lassiate involçere el Signore nostro et sepelire, però che se Ioseph et Nicodemo stesseno qui [f. 104r], tropo potriano ricevere danno da' Giudei».

Aldando la Dona Nostra queste parole, sì come persona savia et discreta, pensando come lei era stata data in guardia a Çuanne, non volse

172. MS *disforāto*
173. MS *lo*

Then the sisters of Our Lady could not reply because of their great sorrow, but, weeping, embraced her and lamented bitterly. And then the mother said to Magdalene, "Is this my son? You ought to recognize him well, because he loved you well and stayed many times at your house."

Then Magdalene said, with much sobbing and weeping, "O Mother of Glory, this man who is dead is your son and my God. This is your son and my Master."

Now when evening approached, Joseph, seeing the most bitter sorrows and the anguish of Our Lady, gently asked that she rest after so much affliction, and that they shroud him in linen and carry him to the tomb. And the mother replied, saying, "O Joseph, do not take my son from me! He is my God and my spouse, and my refuge and consolation. He is the life of my soul. O my brothers, do not take him from me—or else bury me with him!"[137] And the Virgin Mary said these words with great sobs and sighs, gazing at the wounds of her most sweet son: now at the hands, then at the side, then the feet, then the head crowned with thorns, then the face covered with spit and blood. And then she beheld the whole lacerated body, all the while weeping so much that she could not be consoled.

I have found in a certain source that Our Lord revealed to one of his devoted ones that through derision he was shorn.[138] Whether or not this was true I don't know, but we should know that the Jews inflicted every kind of injury that they could inflict. And for this reason, Isaiah, speaking as if in the voice of Lord Jesus Christ, said, "My body was given to those who beat it and my cheeks to those who exposed them."

Then Saint John, seeing that the evening had come, said to Our Lady, "My lady, evening is coming, and if you please it would be best to allow Our Lord to be shrouded and buried, because if Joseph and Nichodemus remain here too long they might receive censure from the Jews."

Hearing these words, Our Lady, as a wise and discreet person, recalling that she had been given into the care of John, did not wish to contradict this, but, making the sign of the cross over him and blessing him, allowed him to be shrouded. But she wished to wrap his head, and Magdalene the feet.

And when they had shrouded the body of Lord Jesus, Magdalene, gazing at the feet, said, "O my brothers, let me wrap these feet, through which my sins were forgiven." Then she began to shroud the feet, weeping bitterly. And what she had once washed with tears of contrition she now washed with tears of compassion. It was for this that the Lord said of her, "She loved much and therefore she wept much," especially in this final service that she performed for her Master who had been so cruelly

contradire ma, signandolo et benedice[n]dolo, sì lo lassò conçare. Ma lei gli volse conciare el capo et la Magdalena li piedi.

Or involçando costoro el corpo de miser Iesù et vegnando ali piedi, disse la Magdalena: «O fratelli mei, lassiateme involtare quelle piedi per li qualli io havi remission d'i peccati mei». Alora lei comenciò a involçere gli piedi, piançando amaramente, et quelli gli qualli lei altre volte havea lavati cum lacrime de contriçione, hora li lava cum lacrime de compassione. Unde de lei disse il Signore: «Ella amava[174] molto et perçiò lei pianse molto», et specialmente in questo ultimo servicio che lei fece al suo Maestro così afflicto et crudelmente morto, sì che a pena lei ge involse i piedi per el gran dolore [f. 104v] che lei sentia del suo Maestro. Et però maçormente gli lavò cum lacrime de conpassione che lei non fece cum le lacrime de contricione, et poi gli sugò cum li suoi capelli et sì lli involtò duramente piançando.

Or vedando la Madre Gloriosa che la Magdalena havea involtadi li piedi del figliolo et che lei non potea indugiare, cum grande pianto lei messe el volto suo sopra quello del figliolo. Et disse: «O figliolo mio, io te tegno morto nel grembo mio et hora non te posso più tegnire. O figliolo mio, la conversatione nostra è stata molto delectevole, ma lo partimento è molto amaro, unde, figliolo mio, in questa tua bataglia io non te ho possudo adiutare perché le tenebre hano habuto grande possança contra el sole. Et tu, Sole de Iusticia, abandonasti te medesimo per amore de questa humana generatione. Duro et penoso m'è stado questo recomperamento, ma aliegra sum per la loro salute. Ora figliolo mio, è spartita [f. 105r] la nostra compagnia. Ora me conviene partire da te et soterarte. O figliolo mio, la trista madre dove andaràla? Come potrò io vivere sança te? Ma io me soterarò cum techo et così sempre serò cum te. Se non posso col corpo, io soterarò l'anima mia cum te. A te, figliolo mio, lasso et a ricomando l'anima mia. O figliolo mio, come è fatigosa questa separatione!».

Et questo dicea cum tanto pianto, che molto più lavò el volto del suo dolcissimo figliolo che non fece la Magdalena gli piedi. Et po li sugò el volto et basandolo sì llo involse et benedilo, et disse: «O figliolo mio, chi darà più consolatione a questa vedoela»?

Alora Nicodemo, Ioseph et Iohanne cum grandissima reverentia tolseno el corpo del nostro Signore et cum gran pianto sì llo portono inverso el monumento novo el qualle Ioseph havea fato fare per lui in uno suo orto, el qual orto era apreso el luocho dove Cristo fu crucifiso, in el qualle messeno el corpo del nostro [f. 105v] Salvatore. Et sepelito ch'el fo, la madre cum grande pianto se butò adosso al figliolo et disse: «Sepeliteme

174. MS *ama<ua>*

afflicted and killed, so that she could hardly shroud the feet for the great sorrow that she felt for her Master. And she washed them much more with tears of compassion than she had with tears of contrition. And then she dried them with her hair and wrapped them with linen, sobbing uncontrollably.

Now the Glorious Mother, seeing that Magdalene had finished wrapping the feet of her son and that she was not able to delay any longer, pressed her face against that of her son with much weeping.[139] And she said, "O my son, I hold you dead in my lap, and soon I can hold you no longer. O my son, our life together was most sweet, but our separation is most bitter.[140] For in this battle of yours, my son, I was unable to help you, because darkness had great power over the sun. And you, Sun of Justice, abandoned yourself through love of the human race. This redemption was hard and painful for me, but I rejoice for their salvation. Now, my son, our union is divided. Now I must leave you and bury you. O my son, where will your sorrowful mother go? How can I live without you? But I will bury myself with you, and that way I can always be with you. If I can't bury my body, I will bury my soul with you. To you, my son, I relinquish and commend my soul. O my son, how painful is this separation!"

And she said this with so much weeping that she washed the face of her most sweet son more than Magdalene did his feet. And then she dried his face, and, kissing it, wrapped it with linen and blessed it. And she said, "O my son, who will now give consolation to this widow?"

Then Nichodemus, Joseph, and John took the body of Our Lord with the greatest reverence, and with much weeping they carried it toward the new tomb that Joseph had made for him in his garden, which was near the place where Christ was crucified. And they placed the body of Our Savior there. And when he had been laid in the tomb, the mother collapsed over her son, weeping bitterly, and said, "Bury me with him!" And kissing him all the while with the most bitter lamentation, she said, "My son, now I remain a widow, without son and without spouse."

Then Saint John, seeing that she was destroying herself over her son, gently led her away and had Joseph put the stone over the tomb.

Now Our Lord is buried. Now the Creator of Heaven and Earth is placed in the earth. Now all the scriptures are fulfilled.

Then Joseph and Nichodemus, wishing to return to Jerusalem, said to Our Lady, "We know well, my lady, that you do not have a house of your own. And so we ask, for love of your son, that you come to our house and consider it yours."

cum lui!», tuta via basandolo cum grandissimo lamento, dicea: «Figliolo mio, hora rimango vedoa, sança figliolo et sança sposo».

Alora veçando sancto Çuanne ch'ela se destruçea adosso il figliolo, dolcemente sì lla levo via et poi fece che Ioseph metesse la pietra adosso al monimento.

Ora è soterato el nostro Signore. Or'è messo in terra el Creatore del cielo et della terra. Ora è adimpito ogni scriptura.

Or vogliando Ioseph et Nicodemo tornare in Ierusalem, sì disseno alla Dona Nostra: «Noi sapiamo bene, Madona, che voi non haveti casa che sia vostra, et però noi ve priegiamo per amore del figliolo vostro che voi vegnite al nostra casa et fati rasone che la sia vostra».

Alora la Madona humelmente li regratiò et disse: «Fratelli mei, io sum commessa a Çuane et imperò io non faria se non quello che lui vuole». [f. 106r]

Et Ioseph et Nicodemo molto ne priegò Iohanne, ma sancto Çuane, contradicendoli, dicea che la volea menare al Monte Syon in la casa dove il Signore fece la cena.

Or acombiatandosi costoro dalla Madona cum grande pianto et inçenochiandosi si adorono il sepulchro, et poi se partino. Et dapoi alquanto disse Çuane alla Madona: «El me pare hora che noi torniamo in Ierusalem avanti ch'el se façia nocte».

Alora la Maistra del'Humilitade se levò in piedi, et cum gran pianto et lamento se inçenochiò denançi al sepulchro et disse: «Figliolo mio, io non posso più stare cum te». Et levando li ochi al cielo sì disse: «O Padre eterno, io ve ricomando el figliolo mio et l'anima mia, la qualle io lasso cum lui nel sepulchro». Et poi lei benedisse il sepulchro et partisse. Et quando lei çonse alla croce se gitò in çenochioni et adorola et disse: «Sopra di te è oçi morto el figliolo mio. Sopra di te oçi è spanto el suo precioso sangue [f. 106v]. Sopra di te oçi è restaurata l'humana natura». Et poi basiò el sangue precioso del qualle ne era tuta bagnata, et simelmente feceno le altre done che erano cum lei; sì che la Madona fo la prima che adorò la croce del suo dolcissimo figliolo, et anche lei fo la prima che lo adorò in carne humana.

Et poi andorono inverso la citade. O quante volte lei se volçea indrieto per vedere el sepulchro et etiandio per vedere la croce, et tuta via piançando et sospirando! Et quando furono arivati appresso alla citade, la Magdalena cum le altre done sì coperseno la Dona Nostra sì come dona vedova. Et intrando nella citade molto forte piançendo, sì che lei facea p[i]ançere ogniuno che la vedea, et molte done per compassione l'acompagnavano per confortarla, et diceano: «Grande torto è stato facto al figliolo de questa donna, et Dio per lui ha mostrato molti segni et miracoli».

Then Our Lady humbly thanked them and said, "My brothers, I am entrusted to John, and because of this I will not do anything if he does not wish it."

And Joseph and Nichodemus earnestly issued their invitation to John, but Saint John declined, saying that he wished to take her to Mount Syon to the house where the Lord had held the supper.

Then those two took their leave of Our Lady with much weeping. And they knelt before the tomb in adoration, and then they departed. And after this, John said to Our Lady, "It seems to me that we should return to Jerusalem now, before it becomes dark."

Then the *Maistra* of Humility rose to her feet, and with much weeping and lamentation she knelt before the tomb and said, "My son, I can no longer stay with you." And raising her eyes to heaven, she said, "O eternal Father, I commend to you my son and my soul, which I left with him in the tomb." And then she blessed the tomb and departed. And when she came to the cross she knelt before it and adored it and said, "On you, today, my son died. On you, today, his precious blood flowed out. On you, today, humankind was redeemed." And then she kissed the precious blood with which it was completely bathed, and the other women who were there with her did the same.[141] And in this way Our Lady was the first to adore the cross of her most sweet son, just as she was the first to adore him in human flesh.

And then they went towards the city. O, how many times she turned back to see the tomb, and also to see the cross, weeping and sighing all the while! And when they reached the city, Magdalene and the other women covered Our Lady with a veil as if she were a widow. And they entered the city weeping so bitterly that she made everyone weep who saw her. And many women, out of compassion, accompanied her to comfort her.[142] And they said, "Great wrong was done to the son of this lady, and God revealed many signs and miracles through him."

And they arrived at Mount Syon at the house where Lord Jesus had dined the evening before with his disciples. And Our Lady turned and thanked the women who had accompanied her. And having taken leave of them with great weeping, they entered the house and locked the door. And then great lamentation and weeping began. And Our Lady, turning and looking about the house, said with a great cry, "O my son, where can you be, that I do not see you? John, where is my son? O Magdalene, where is your Master? O my sisters, where is my son? From me is gone my happiness, my consolation, the light of my eyes. You see well that he was separated from me with great anguish. And this increases my sorrow: that

Et çonçando al Monte Syon alla [f. 107r] casa dove miser Iesù havea
la sera denançi cenato cum li discipoli suoi et rivoltandosi la Donna nostra
indrieto si regraciò le donne che l'avea acompagnata. Et acombiatandose
da loro cum gran pianto, introrono nella casa et fu serata la porta. Et qui se
començiò il grande pianto et lamento. Et rivoltandose la Donna Nostra et
guardando per la casa cum gran pianto dicea: «O figliolo mio, dove sei tu
che non te veço? Çuane, dove è il figliolo mio? O Magdalena, dove è il
maestro tuo? O sorele mie, dove è il figliolo mio? Partito è da me la alegreça mia, la consolatione mia, il lume delli ochi mei. Voi vedete bene
ch'el'è partito da me cum grande angustie. Et per questo più mi acresce el
dolore, ch'el'è partito da me tutto afflito et tuto lacerato, tuto affadigato et
assedato, et io non l'ò potuto adiutare né sovenirlo de niuna cosa. Et da
tuti è stato aba[n]donato, et anche el Padre suo non ha vogliuto [f. 107v]
adiutare. Et come queste cose sono facte, tosto voi lo havete veduto. Or
dove se trovò mai niuno sì scelerato peccatore che la morte sua fosse così
freçata come è stata quella del figliolo mio sança casone? El figliolo mio
in questa nocte passada fo da Iuda tradito, da' Giudei presso et ligato et
menato a casa de Anna. Et poi nella meça nocte a casa de Cayphas el fo
menato, qui infina alla matina fo flag[e]llato. Et nell'hora de prima nelle
mane de Pilato el fo dato; nella meça terça fo menato a casa de Herodes;
et in l'ora de terça el fo da Pilato giudichato. Et nell'ora de sexta fo ficto in
croce; et nell'hora de nona morite; et in l'hora de vespero fo tolto çoso
della croce; et nell'hora de compieta da noi involto et posto in sepultura.
O figliolo mio, come è amara questa separatione tua a l'anima mia! Et
anche la tua vituperosa [f. 108r] et crudelissima morte si ha trapassata
l'anima mia de uno cortello crudelissimo, sì come me disse Symeone». Et
in questo pianto et dolore stava la Dona Nostra cum le compagne sue.

### Come el Sabato stando la nostra Donna serata in casa per paura dei Giudei, et come se congregorono li discipoli. Capitolo xxvii°.[175]

Or stando el sabbato la Donna nostra cum le compagne et cum Çuane
dileto in casa serati per paura de Giudei in sul Monte Syon, et qui staveno
cum grande afflictione et pianto. Et ecco ch'el vene sancto Pietro. Et

175. MS *Capitolo xxviii*

he was taken from me completely afflicted and lacerated, completely exhausted and beset, and I did not have the power to come to his aid or relieve him of anything. And he was abandoned by all, and his Father did not wish to help him. And you saw how quickly all of these things were done. Now where could one ever find even the most wicked criminal whose execution was carried out with such cruel haste as that of my innocent son? Last night my son was betrayed by Judas, and taken by the Jews and bound and led to the house of Annas. And then in the middle of the night he was led to the house of Caiaphas, where he was scourged in the morning. And at the hour of prime he was delivered into the hands of Pilate; at the hour of half-terce he was led to the house of Herod; and at the hour of terce he was condemned to death by Pilate. And at the hour of sext he was nailed to the cross; and at the hour of none he died; and at the hour of vespers he was taken down from the cross; and at the hour of compline he was shrouded by us and placed in the tomb.[143] O my son, how bitter is this separation to my soul! And your shameful and most cruel death has pierced my soul like the sharpest sword, just as Simeon told me." And lamenting and grieving in this way, Our Lady remained with her companions.

*Chapter 27. How on Saturday Our Lady remained at the house with the doors locked for fear of the Jews, and how the disciples gathered together.*

Now on Saturday, Our Lady was staying with her companions and John the beloved disciple at the house on Mount Syon with the doors locked, for fear of the Jews. And they remained there in great affliction and weeping. And suddenly Saint Peter arrived. And entering with great shame and distress, he fell to his knees before Our Lady. And he was sobbing so

intrando dentro cum grande vergogna et pianto se inçenochiò denançi alla Madona, et tanto fu il pianto ch'el non potea parlare per confussione et vergogna che lui havea de havere così vilmente negato il suo maestro. Et essendo stato ricevuto benignamente dalla Dona nostra et dalli altri, molto lacrimando disse: «Io mi confondo in me medessimo, et non doveria [f. 108v] havere[176] ardire de comparere denançi a voi né a huomo che viva per la mia viltade, imperò che io negai colui el qualle tanto me ha amato per paura de una ancilla».

Alora la Madona, per confortarlo, disse: «Il maestro nostro et buono pastore sì è partito da noi per così aspera morte et hane lassati orphani. Ma io spero et ho ferma fede che esso resuscitarà da morte, secundo che lui çi à predicto. Or stà adoncha forte nella fede, et spera nella misercordia del mio figliolo el qualle è benigno et gracioso, el qualle te hama molto, et sono certa ch'el te perdonerà el tuo peccato». Et per questo modo lei si llo ferma nella fede del suo maestro.

Et stando loro in questo parlare, ecco[177] ch'el sopraçonse li altri apostoli, et qui per loro furono facto grande pianto. Et vedando la Madona che loro erano mallecontenti de havere abandonato el suo maestro in tanti affani, sì li consolò et confortoli de stare fermi nella fede.

[f. 109r] Et poi disse a sancto Pietro et ali altri: «De necessitade era, figlioli, che voi lo abandonasti però ch'el'è scripto "*Percutiam pastorem et dispergentur oves gregis*"».

Et stando in questi parlari, disse la Dona nostra tuta tribulata: «Io voria volentiera sapere quello che el figliolo mio fece et disse nella cena».

Alora sancto Pietro començiò a narare ogni cosa per ordine. Et començando da Iuda, et poi del lavare di piedi, et della comunione et del bel sermone ch'el fece a loro, et poi come andò nell'orto et qui orò tre fiade, et come sudò sudore di sangue, et poi come fu preso. Et steteno in questi tal parlari infina a sera, imperò che la Madona se delectava molto in questo tal parlare.

O cum quanta diligentia ascoltava la Magdalena! O quante volte lei dicea: «O maestro mio, dove sete voi?»

O quante volte la Madona cum gran sospiri dicea: «O figliolo mio, cum quanta pena sei partito da me!».

Molto è [f. 109v] da havere qui de loro grande compassione, imperò che stavano cum molta tribulatione et cum grande angustia. O che è a

---

176. MS *doueria || doueria hauere*
177. MS *Etco*

much that he could not speak because of the confusion and shame that he felt for having denied his Master in such a cowardly way. And when he had been received kindly by Our Lady and by the others, he said, with much weeping, "I am so ashamed of myself, and I should not dare to come before you or any man alive on account of my vile behavior. For I denied the one who loved me so greatly, for fear of a serving woman."

Then Our Lady, to comfort him, said, "Our Master and good shepherd has parted from us through such a bitter death, and he has left us orphans. But I hope and firmly believe that he will rise from the dead, according to what he predicted to us. Now stay strong in the faith, and place hope in the mercy of my son, who is benevolent and gracious, and who has loved you so much, and I am certain that he will pardon your sin." And in this way she strengthened him in the faith of his Master.

And as they were speaking, suddenly the other apostles arrived, and at this there was more weeping. And Our Lady, seeing that they were so upset with themselves for having abandoned their Master, consoled them and encouraged them to stay firm in the faith.

And then she said to Saint Peter and the others, "It was necessary, sons, for you to abandon him, for it is written, *Percutiam pastorem et dispergentur oues gregis.*"

And as they were talking with each other, Our Lady, overcome with sorrow, said, "I wish very much to know what my son did and said during the supper."

Then Saint Peter began to tell the whole story in order. And he began with Judas, and then the washing of the feet, and the communion, and the beautiful sermon that he gave to them. And then he described how he went to the garden and prayed there three times, and how he sweated blood, and then how he was captured. And they continued talking in this way until evening, because Our Lady wanted very much to hear all of this.

Oh with what loving attention the Magdalene listened! Oh how many times she said, "O my Master, where are you?"

Oh how many times Our Lady said, with great sighs, "O my son, how painful it is that you are separated from me!"

There is much to feel compassion for here, for they were filled with much tribulation and great anguish. Oh what a sight to behold: the Queen of Heaven and Mother of God, and also the leaders and rulers of the Church of God, staying locked inside for fear of wicked men! O most sweet Jesus, how much you have suffered, and how much you have also allowed others to suffer, that is, your mother and your disciples, only to

vedere la Regina del cielo et Madre de Dio et anche gli principi et gover-
natori della chiesia de Dio stare serati per paura de huomeni malvagii! O
Iesù dolcissimo, quanto havete voi patito et anche facto patire ad altri,
çioè alla madre vostra et agli discipoli vostri, solo per liberare questo
huomo dalle mane del dimonio! O Dio, quanto è grande la caritade et la
misericordia vostra!

O tuti li discipoli et le altre done staveno cum grande tristicia et cum
pocha fede et sperança della resurretione; ma la Madona se confortava per
la ferma sperança che lei havea della resurrectione del suo dolcissimo
figliolo. Et in lei sola rimase la fede nel giorno del Sabato sancto, et imperò a lei è atribuito el dì del sabato. Ma lei non se potea alegrare per la
memoria della morte del suo dolcissimo fi[f. 110r]gliolo.

Or facto che fo sera dapoi tramontato el sole, perché l'era licito de lavorare, Maria Magdalena et Maria Iacobe et Salomè sì se ne andoron ad
una botega et lì comprarono specie per fare unguento da unçere il corpo
de miser Iesù Cristo.

*Come l'anima de Cristo andò al limbo et come el resuscitò
et come apparse alla madre et alle tre Marie et altre
operatione che lui fece. Capitolo xxviii°.*[178]

Hora qui parleremo come l'anima de miser Iesù Cristo descesse al
limbo per trare fuori gli Sancti Padri i qualli erano morti nel testamento vechio. Unde dèi sapere che incontenente che l'anima de miser Iesù usite del
corpo, discesse al limbo et lì trovò molto ben serate le porte, però che gli
demonii sentivano la sua venuta. Et come el Signore ço[n]se, dete del piede
nella porta et apersela et intrò de[n]tro cum el confalon della croce in mano
per [f. 110v] el qualle se intende la vitoria habuda cum el dimonio.

Considera qui la humilitade de Cristo Iesù, et anche la sua superna
caritade, ch'el se dignò de descendere al limbo de l'inferno per trare fuori
gli servi suoi, possando lui mandare el messo suo. Ma discese lui medesimo, non come a servi ma come ad amici, et trasseli fuori et menoli nel
paradiso deliciano; et qui stete cum loro fino alla domenega. Et qui pòi tu
pensare la alegreça et el gaudio che haveno quelli Sancti Padri. Or pensa

---

178. MS *Capitolo xxviiii*

free humankind from the hands of the devil! O God, how great is your love and mercy!

Now all the disciples and the other women remained there in great sorrow, with little faith and hope in the Resurrection. But Our Lady stayed steadfast through the firm hope that she had in the Resurrection of her most sweet son. And she alone was the keeper of the faith on Holy Saturday, and for that reason, Saturday is dedicated to her.[144] But she could not be glad, because of the memory of the death of her most sweet son.

Now after the sun had set, when it was permissible to work, Mary Magdalene and Mary Jacobus and Salome went to a shop and bought items to make ointment to anoint the body of Lord Jesus Christ.

## Chapter 28. How the soul of Christ went to limbo, and how he rose, and how he appeared to his mother and to the three Marys, and other things that he did.

Now here we will speak about how the soul of Lord Jesus Christ descended into limbo to rescue the Holy Fathers, who were dead under the old law.[145] So you ought to know that as soon as the soul of Lord Jesus left the body, he descended into limbo. And there he found the gates firmly shut, because the demons sensed his approach. And as soon as the Lord arrived, he kicked the gates open, and he entered carrying the banner of the cross, which stands for the victory he won against the devil.[146]

Consider here the humility of Christ Jesus, and also his supreme love, for he deigned to descend to limbo in hell to rescue his servants, even though he could have sent a messenger. But he descended himself, as though he were not rescuing servants but friends. And he brought them out from there, and he led them into the paradise of delights, and he remained with them there until Sunday.[147] And here you may imagine the happiness and joy that the Holy Fathers felt. Now imagine how these prophets and patriarchs celebrated with songs and praises and rejoicing before Our Lord Jesus Christ. And at dawn on Sunday, the Lord took his leave of them. And

che canti et laude et che festa faceano quelli propheti et patriarchi davanti al Signore nostro miser Iesù Cristo. Et la domenega all'aurora el Signore se partite da loro. Et egli el pregóno ch'el ritornasse presto a loro, però che loro haveano grande desiderio de vedere el glorioso corpo de miser Iesù Cristo, et per vedere le piage sue sanctissime per le qualle elli riceveano gaudio grandissimo.

Et alora l'anima de miser Iesù Cristo se par[f. 111r]tì da loro e ritornò nel corpo suo, el qualle iaceva nel sepulchro. Et per potentia sua si resuscitò el corpo et ussite fuori glor[i]oso, el qualle fora messo dentro tuto lacerato et vulnerato.

In questo meço Maria Magdalena et le altre Marie se partirono dalla nostra Dona per andare a unçere el corpo de miser Iesù Cristo et lassorono la Madona in casa, la qualle stava in oratione. Et pregava el suo figliolo che li piacesse de consolarla cum la presentia sua. Et stando lei in questo desiderio, ecco miser Iesù li fo presente et disse: «Dio ve salve, madre mia carissima». Alora la madre vedando el suo dolcissimo figliolo così splendidissimo, tuta fo ralegrata et tutta piena de summo gaudio et leticia et più non sentite pena né tribulatione alguna.

Et poi lei el domandò s'el sentiva più alcuno dolore, et per che casone lui havea reservato le piage. Et miser Iesù Cristo respuose: [f. 111v] «Madre mia, io ho riservate le piage mie a conforto et a consolatione de quelli che farano la mia voluntade, et per confusione de quelli che non crederano in me. Et nel Giorno del Iudicio io le monstrerò ai danandi per confunderli et agli iusti per alegrarli. Et in testimoniança mia a dimonstrare che io sono colui che fo morto sopra la croce per gli loro peccati. Io ho vento el mondo e lla morte et ogni dolore è partito da me».

Alora la madre se gitò inçenochioni et adorolo et disse: «Benedecto et laudato sia sempre el Padre tuo eterno che tanta gratia ha facto alla ancilla sua che mi te ha renduto, figliolo mio dolcissimo». Et qui steteno insembre per spacio di alcuna hora.

Ora qui tu pòi pensare devotamente del modo et della alegreça che lei have de havere veduto el suo dolcissimo figliolo resuscitato et etiandio del parlare che lei feçe cum lui. Et pòi pensare qual fosse più, o el dolore che lei have del[f. 112r]la sua morte o la alegreça che l'have della sua resurrectione. Del dolore alguno non sentite maçore de lei; et ancho la alegreça è da pensare che lei l'have più delli altri. Adoncha fu rasonevelle ch'el Signore nostro prima apparesse alla sua madre che a niuno de gli altri, av[e]gna che la Scriptura non façi mentione. Ma noi possiamo pensare devotamente che prima apparesse alla sua madre per tuore da lei ogni dolore.

they implored him to return to them soon, because they had a great desire to see the glorified body of Lord Jesus Christ, and to see his most holy wounds, through which they might receive the greatest joy.

And then the soul of Lord Jesus Christ parted from them and returned to his body, which lay in the tomb. And through his power, the body that had been placed in the tomb completely lacerated and wounded came back to life, and he went forth from the tomb in glory.

And in the midst of all this, Mary Magdalene and the other Marys left Our Lady to go to anoint the body of Lord Jesus Christ. And they left Our Lady at the house, where she remained in prayer. And she asked her son if it might please him to console her with his presence. And as she was praying with this desire, suddenly Lord Jesus appeared and said, "God be with you, my dearest mother."[148] And the mother, seeing her most sweet son so resplendent like this, was overcome with happiness and filled with the greatest joy and gladness, and she felt no more pain or tribulation at all.

And then she asked him if he still felt any pain and why he had kept the wounds. And Lord Jesus Christ replied, "My dear mother, I have kept my wounds as a comfort and a consolation to those who do my will, and as a cause for confusion to those who will not believe in me. And on the day of Judgment, I will show them to the damned to confound them, and to the just to make them glad, and to demonstrate that I am he who died on the cross for their sins. I have conquered the world and death, and all suffering has parted from me."

So then the mother knelt and adored him, and said, "Blessed and praised be always your eternal Father, who has given such grace to his handmaid that he has returned you to me, my most sweet son." And they remained together there for a few hours.

Now here you may meditate with devotion on how happy she was to see her sweet son resurrected, and also on the sweet conversation they had together. And try to consider which was greater, the grief that she felt at his death or the happiness she felt at his Resurrection. Of the pain, no one could feel more than she did. And as for the joy, it should be imagined that she feels this, too, more than others. Therefore it was reasonable that Our Lord appeared first to his mother before others, even though the scriptures make no mention of this. But we may imagine with devotion that he appeared first to his mother to take every sorrow away from her.

Meanwhile, Mary Magdalene and Mary Jacobus and Mary Salome went with precious ointments to anoint the body of Lord Jesus. And as soon as they were outside the gates of the city, they began to bring to mind

Et in questo meço Maria Magdalena et Maria Iacobi et Maria Salome sì andorono cum unguenti preciosi per unçere el corpo de miser Iesù. Et come furono fuori delle porte della citade, se riducevano a memoria le pene et le afflictione del suo maestro. Et in tuti li luochi nelli qualli era stato facto alcuna inçuria al suo maistro, se inçenochiavano et duramente piançendo diceano:[179] «Qui el scontrassemo cum la croce in spalla», et piançendo basiavano la terra. [f. 112v] «Et qui se rivolse et disse alle donne de Ierusalem, *Non piançeti sopra di me, ma sopra de voi et sopra di vostri figlioli*; et qui per molta faticha puosse gió la croce et pugiosse a questa pietra».[180]

Et così perveneno al Monte Calvario dove da' Giudei el fo spogliato nudo et crucifisso. Et cum grandissimi pianti et sospiri se gitorono in terra et adorono la croce et basonola, la qualle era ancora tuta adornata de quello precioso sangue de miser Iesù Cristo; et qui fo posto in braço alla madre.

Et poi se ne andorono al monimento. Et qui pensavano de trovare el corpo del suo Maestro et andando parlavano insieme et dicevano: «Or chi ne rivolçerà la pietra dalla porta del monimento?».

Et guardando, veteno la pietra rivolta. Et intrando nel monumento, videro uno giovene sedere alla dextra parte, el qualle era coperto de una stolla bianchissima et l'aspecto suo *quasi fulgure*, çioè splendidissimo. Et maravegliandose le [f. 113r] donne disse a loro: «Non habiate paura. Io so che cerchiate Iesù Naçareno il qualle fo crucifixo. Ell'è resuscitato, el non è qui. Venite et vedete il luocho dove el fo messo. Ma andiate et dicete agli discipuli soi et a Pietro ch'el'è resuscitato, et qui el vederano secundo ch'el disse a voi».

Et vedendose le donne non trovare el corpo de miser Iesù Cristo, si uscitero fuori del monimento cum grande paura, et andorono inverso la citade Maria Salome et Maria Iacobi per annunciare agli discipuli quello che haveano veduto et aldito.

Et Maria Magdalena, per grande dolore che la havea che lei non trovò el suo dilecto maistro, sì rimase a piançere al sepulchro. Et guardando lei anchora nel sepulchro, vide dui angeli i qualli erano vestiti de vestimenti bianchissimi, gli qualli disseno a lei: «Che cercate voi el vivo cum gli morti? El non è qui, ell'è [f. 113v] resuscitado. Non ve recordate voi come el ve parlò in Galilea, ch'el convegnia el Figliolo de l'Huomo essere tradito et morto et il terço dì resuscitar da morte»?

179. MS *diceano qui*
180. MS *(et) pugiose a questa piestra* in margin

the pain and the affliction of their Master. And in all the places in which some harm had been done to their Master, they would fall to their knees, and weeping bitterly they said, "Here we encountered him with the cross on his shoulders," and they would kiss the earth, weeping. "And here he turned and said to the women of Jerusalem, 'Do not weep for me, but for yourselves and for your children.' And there, because he was exhausted, he put the cross down and leaned against this stone."[149]

And finally they came to Mount Calvary, where he had been stripped naked by the Jews and crucified. And with the greatest laments and sighs the women threw themselves to the earth and adored and kissed the cross, which was still adorned with that precious blood of Lord Jesus Christ. And it was here that he was placed in the arms of his mother.

And then they went to the tomb. And here they thought they would find the body of their Master, and as they went they said to each other, "Now who will roll back the stone from the entrance to the tomb?"

And as they looked more closely, they saw that the stone had been rolled back. And entering the tomb, they saw a young man sitting at the right side, clothed in a brilliant white garment, and his face was *quasi fulgure*, that is, radiant in its splendor. And as the women looked on in amazement, he said to them: "Fear not: I know that you seek Jesus of Nazareth, who was crucified. He has risen from the dead, and he is not here. Come and see where he was placed. But then go and tell the disciples and Peter that he is risen, and here they will see that it is just as he told you."

And the women, not finding the body of Lord Jesus Christ, came out from the tomb very much afraid, and Mary Salome and Mary Jacobus hastened toward the city to tell the disciples what they had seen and heard.

And Mary Magdalene, through the great sorrow that she had when she did not find her beloved Master, stayed to weep at the tomb. And still gazing at the tomb, she saw two angels dressed in the most brilliant white, who said to her: "Why do you seek the living among the dead? He is not here; he has risen. Don't you remember how he told you in Galilee that it was necessary for the Son of Man to be betrayed and killed and on the third day to rise from the dead?"

And because she was burning with such desire to see her Master, she didn't take in what the angels were saying. And she stayed there, lamenting and crying and searching for her Lord. And she looked in the tomb again, because she really believed she would find him there. And she saw two other angels, one at the head and the other at the foot where the body of Jesus had been placed, who said to her, *"Mulier quid ploras?"*: "Woman, why are you weeping?"

Et lei, tuta accesa de amore de vedere il suo maistro, non curò de intendere quelli angeli; et pur lamentandose et piançendo rimase qui cercando pur el suo Signore, et riguardando ancora nel sepulchro però che lei pure credea trovarlo. Et ella vide doi altri angeli, l'uno dal capo et l'altro da' piedi dove fu posto el corpo de Iesù, gli qualli disseno a lei: *Mulier quid ploras?* «Dona, perche piançi tu?».

Et lei respuose: «Però che me hano tolto el Signore mio, et io non so dove l'ànno posto».

Or vedi meravegliose operatione d'amore, che pocho avanti havea lei aldito dalli angeli come lui era vivo et non morto et come lui era resuscitado, et cum çiò ella dicea: «Io piangio però che m'ànno tolto el mio maistro». Et perché era questo, et donde ve[f. 114r]gnia? Solo da l'amore, perché dice qui uno expositore che lei non havea l'anima sua cum lei, ma l'havea nel luocho dove fu posto el corpo de miser Iesù Cristo.

Et colui ch'è tuto benigno non permisse de lassare in longa tribulatione coloro che l'amano. Disse alla madre sua: «Madre, io voglio andare a consolare Maria Magdalena, la qualle non fa se non piançere perché lei non mi trova», de la qual cosa la madre ne fo molto alegra.

Et partendose miser Iesù dalla madre, vene ne l'orto dove era el sepulchro, et trovò Maria Magdalena apresso el sepulchro la qualle parlava cum doi angeli. Et apparse a lei in forma de ortolano et disse a lei: «Dona, perché piangi tu?»

Et ella, non cognossandolo et pensando ch'el fosse ortolano, sì disse a lui: «Dè, misere, se tu lo hai tolto di me, dove tu l'hai posto che io anderò a tuorlo?».

Or guarda cum che volto pieno de lacrime lei priega el buono ortolano, [f. 114v] el qualle cognosce tute le radice degli cuori nostri, ch'el ge insegni quello che lei va cercando, imperò che lei sperava sempre de aldire qualche cosa del suo maistro. Alora el Signore, vogliandola consolare disse a lei: «Maria».

Et lei incontene[n]te[181] se rivoltò inverso lui et disse: «Maistro!».

Et cum grandissimo amore li disse: «Tu sei colui ch'io vo cercando! Perché me sete voi tanto tempo acelato?».

Et gitandosi alli piedi et vogliandoli basiare, sì come lei era usata de fare inprima. Ma el Signore, vogliando levare l'anima sua alle cose celestiale, açiò che la non cercasse più de lui in terra, disse a lei: «Non mi tochare, imperò ch'io non sono ancora montato al Padre mio, quanto nel

181. MS *incontentiete*

And she replied, "Because they have taken my Lord from me, and I do not know where they have put him."

Now see the marvelous way love works: for just a little earlier she had heard from the angels that he was alive and not dead, and that he was risen, and still she said, "I am weeping because they have taken my Master." And why was this, and where did it come from? Only from love, for, according to what a commentator says about this, her soul was not within her, but it was where the body of Lord Jesus Christ had been placed.

And he who is full of kindness would not allow those who love him to remain troubled for long, so he said to his mother, "Mother, I wish to go to console Mary Magdalene, who can do nothing but weep because she cannot find me." And his mother was glad at what he said.

And leaving his mother, Lord Jesus came to the garden where the tomb was, and he found Mary Magdalene near the tomb where she had spoken with the two angels. And he appeared to her in the form of a gardener, and he said to her, "Woman, why are you weeping?"

And she, not recognizing him, and thinking that he was a gardener, said to him, "Good sir, if you have taken him from me, tell me where you have placed him, so I may go to bring him back."

Now watch how, with a face full of tears, she beseeches the good gardener, who knows all the roots of our hearts, to teach her about what she was seeking, because she always hoped to hear something of her Master.[150] And so the Lord, wishing to console her, said to her, "Mary."

And at that instant she turned to him and said, "Master!"

And with the greatest love she said to him, "You are the one I have been seeking! Why have you hidden yourself from me for so long?"

And she threw herself at his feet, wishing to kiss them, as she used to do before. But the Lord, wishing to lift her soul to heavenly things, so that she would no longer go on searching for him on earth, said to her: "Do not touch me, because I have not yet ascended to my Father, although I have ascended to your heart. For I am living and immortal, and you went searching for me among the dead; and for that you are not worthy to touch me. Now don't you remember that I told you that I would rise on the third day? Then why did you seek to find me in the tomb?"

And she replied, "I tell you, my Master, that my heart was so overcome with sorrow for the cruelty that was done to you in your Passion and your death that everything went out of my mind except for your body and the place where you were laid to rest. And that is why I brought this ointment, to anoint your body."

cuore tuo; imperò che io sono vivo et immortale, et tu me vai cercando morto, et però tu non sei degna de tocarme. Or non te aricordi che io ti dissi ch'io resusciteria el terço giorno? Et come mi cercavi tu nel sepulchro?»

Et lei rispuose: [f. 115r] «Io ve dicho, maestro mio, ch'el cuore mio era sì pieno di dolore della crudelitade la qualle ve fo facta nella vostra Passione et della morte vostra ch'el m'era uscito de mente ogni cosa se non del corpo vostro et del[182] luocho dove voi fosti posto. Et imperò havea portato questo unguento per unçerlo».

Or stando lei in questo parlare l'havea grande leticia, avegna ch'el Signore li rispondesse al principio asperamente, apena posso credere che lei nol[183] tochasse familiarmente et basasege gli piedi et ancho le mane avanti che lui se partisse da lei. Ma per divina providentia fece così nel principio, imperò che tale se lli monstrò come lui era nel suo chuore, imperò che lei l'andava cercando morto et non credea fermamente et però el disse: «Non mi tochare». Et secund[o][184] la commune expositione come piatosamente se puote exponere, lui fece per levare l'anima de Maria alle cose celestiale, açiò che lei [f. 115v] cercasse vivo et non morto, secundo[185] che dice sancto Bernardo. Unde piatosamente se pò credere che colei la qualle el Signore singularmente se degnò de visitare avanti de tuti li altri, che se trova scripto che lui fece per consolarla et non per turbarla. Adonque materialmente et non pertinacemente el disse quella parola, «Non mi tochare».

Et alhora el Signore disparse a lei. Et lei se messe a corer drieto alle doe Marie le qualle andavano inverso Ierusalem, per annu[n]ciare[186] a loro la risposta habuta dalli angeli[187] e come lei havea veduto il suo maestro. Et zonçendole, Maria Magdalena si'll narrò ogni cosa per ordine et come el Signore li era apparso. Alora quelle molto alegrate delle parole della Magdalena et della resurretione del suo maistro ma molto dolendose che non l'haveano veduto.

Or andando loro verso Ierusalem, colui el qualle non puote sostegnire che coloro che lo amano habino tribulatione si apparse [f. 116r] a loro nella via et disse: «Avete voi». Et quelle, piene de leticia, se li gitorono alli piedi et sì lo adorono et qui molto se alegrono de lui. Et lui rispuose a

---

182. MS *del il*
183. MS *nōl*
184. MS *secund*
185. MS *seundo*
186. MS *ānuciare*
187. MS *la risposta habuta dalli angeli* in margin

And as she was talking with him she felt great happiness, even though the Lord responded to her harshly at first. And I can hardly believe that she did not touch him in a familiar way and kiss his feet and hands before he left her.[151] But it was through divine providence that he acted like this at the beginning, for this revealed what was in his heart when she went searching for him among the dead and did not believe firmly. And that is why he said, "Do not touch me." And according to the common interpretation, which one can take as a compassionate explanation, he did this to lift the soul of Mary to heavenly things, so that she would search among the living and not the dead, according to what Saint Bernard says.[152] Therefore in a spirit of compassion one can believe this: since she was the one whom the Lord deigned to visit in a special way before the others, as scripture attests, the Lord did this to console her, and not to disturb her. So it was in a simple, matter-of-fact way, and not to be obstinate, that he said those words, "Do not touch me."[153]

And then the Lord disappeared from her. And she hurried to join the other two Marys who were walking towards Jerusalem, to tell them about what the angels had said and about how she had seen her Master. And as soon as she caught up with them, Mary Magdalene told them the whole story in order and how the Lord had appeared to her. And they rejoiced greatly on hearing what Magdalene had to say about the Resurrection of their Master, but they were sad that they had not seen him.

Now as they were walking toward Jerusalem, he who cannot bear that those who love him be troubled appeared to them on the road and said, "Greetings to you." And the women, full of joy, threw themselves at his feet and adored him, and they rejoiced greatly in him. And he replied to them and said, "Go and tell my brothers to go to Galilee, where they will see me just as I promised them before my death." And then the Lord disappeared, and the women proceeded to Jerusalem.

Now think a little about the humility of Our Lord, who, even though he was God, called his disciples "brothers" and always retained this humility. And if you wish to have consolation and wisdom, recall what I said to you above, which is this: where all the sayings and deeds of Lord Jesus are concerned, be sure to place yourself there as if you were present there with mind and body.

Now as soon as the three Marys reached the place where the disciples had gathered, they told them with great joy how the Lord was risen, and how he appeared to Mary Magdalene and then to all three, and how he had told them to go to Galilee where they would see him. And Saint Peter,

loro et disse: «Andiate et nunciate alli frateli mei che li vadino in Galilea, che lì me vederano sì come io li promissi avanti la morte mia». Et alora disparse il Signore, et quelle si andorono in Ierusalem.

Or pensa un pocho della humilità del nostro Signore, che siando Dio chiamò gli suoi discipuli «fratelli» et mai non lasò questa humilitade. Et se tu vòi havere consolatione et intelligentia, aricordate de quello che io te dissi de sopra: çioè che in ogni decto et facto de miser Iesù, fà che tu mecti lo animo tuo sì come tu çi fossi presente cum la mente et cum il corpo.

Hora che furono gionte le tre Marie là dove erano li discipoli congregati, cum grande alegreça disse a loro come el Signore era resuscitato, et come lui apparse a Maria [f. 116v] Magdalena et poi a tute tre, et come gli havea detto che loro dovesseno andare in Galilea che lì el vederaveno. Et aldendo sancto Pietro ch'el suo Maistro era resuscitato, se partite cum sancto Çuane et andorono verso el sepulchro. Et sancto Çuane corse inançi che sancto Pietro. Et alora el Signore li apparse et disseli: «La pace sia con te, Symon Pietro». Et sancto Pietro se gitò in terra et cum lachrime li adimandò perdono. Et miser Iesù, come benigno, lo consolò, et levolo da terra et confortolo de stare fermo nella fede et ch'el non dovesse havere paura, che sempre el saria cum lui; et cum questo il Signore disparve. Et sancto Pietro tornò cum grande alegreça alli apostoli et contoli ogni cosa per ordine.

Or partendose miser Iesù da sancto Pietro, sì apparse a Ioseph Aburimathia el qualle era messo in pregione da' Giudei per amore de miser Iesù et dapoi le feste el voleano fare morire. Et miser Iesù el liberò da quella pregione et conduse[f. 117r]lo in casa sua sano et salvo. Ancora apparse el Signore a sancto Iacomo Minore, el qualle havea giurato de non mangiare et non bere perfina a tanto ch'el non vedesse el Figliolo della Vergene resuscitato da morte. Et il Signore, vedando la sua fede, si gli apparse et confortolo de stare fermo nella fede. Questa apparitione narra sancto Ieronymo.

Et dapoi il Signore apparse a quelli doi discipoli che andavano in Emaus, gli qualli andavano parlando di facti de miser Iesù cum grande tristicia et delle cose che li erano state facte. Et miser Iesù se acostò a loro nella via in forma de peregrino et andava ragionando cum loro parole de salute sì come se contiene nello Evangelio. Et finalmente, constreto da loro, intrò nel albergo cum loro. Et poi se manifesta a loro nel rumpere del pane et altre cosse ch'el fece, le qualle per brevità non scrivo.

Or atte[n]di qui diligentemente, et considera la sua bontade, ch'el non puote sostegnire che gli soi discipoli [f. 117v] v'andasseno erando, et poi dimandò loro qualle era la casone de tanta tristicia. Et li expuose la

hearing that his Master had risen, left with Saint John, and they went towards the tomb. And Saint John ran ahead of Saint Peter. And then the Lord appeared to Peter and said, "Peace be with you, Simon Peter." And Saint Peter threw himself on the ground and with tears he begged pardon. And Lord Jesus, being so benevolent, consoled him and bid him to rise, and he exhorted him to stay strong in the faith and not to be afraid, for he would always be with him. And with that, the Lord disappeared. And Saint Peter returned with great joy to the apostles and recounted everything to them as it occurred.

Now when he had left Saint Peter, Lord Jesus appeared to Joseph of Arimathea, whom the Jews had put in prison because of his love for Lord Jesus. And after the holy days, they wished to put him to death. And Lord Jesus freed him from that prison and led him back to his own house safe and sound. And then the Lord appeared to Saint James the Minor, who had sworn not to eat or drink until he had seen the Son of the Virgin raised from the dead. And the Lord, seeing his faith, appeared to him and encouraged him to stay firm in the faith. Saint Jerome tells the story of this apparition.

And after that, the Lord appeared to his two disciples who were going to Emmaus, who were walking along speaking with great sorrow about the deeds of Lord Jesus and about the things that had been done to him. And Lord Jesus met them on the road in the form of a pilgrim, and he walked along with them discussing the words of salvation as contained in the Gospel. And finally, in response to their entreaties, he entered an inn with them. And then he revealed himself to them through the breaking of the bread and other things that he did, which for the sake of brevity I will not write about.

Now dwell on this scene with loving attention, and consider his generosity, how he could not bear that his disciples continue wandering in error, and he asked them the reason for their distress. And there he revealed the scripture, enflaming their hearts and removing all the rust from their minds. And he does the very same with us every day. When we are burdened, there is no doubt that if we meditate on him, suddenly he comes to us, comforting and strengthening and illuminating our hearts and enflaming us with his love. And therefore the prophet said it well when he said to the Lord, "Your speech pleases me; it is so sweet that it surpasses all sweetness." And meditating on God is like this.[154] And the same prophet says, "My heart seems all enflamed, thinking of you; and in my

Scriptura, infiamando li cuori loro per caçare via ogni ruçene della mente loro. Et questo medemo el fa cum noi tuto el giorno integramente. Unde quando noi siamo alquanto gravati, non è dubio alcuno che se noi andiamo rasonando de lui, incontenente el viene a noi confortando et illuminando gli cuori nostri et infiamane del suo amore. Et però ben disse il propheta, parlando al Signore, «El tuo parlare mi piace ch'el è sì dolçe ch'el trapassa ogni dolceça». Et cusì è 'l pensare de Dio. Unde dice questo medemo propheta, «Lo cuore mio pare tuto infiamato pensando di te. Et nelli mei pensieri pare che sia acceso uno fuocho». Unde sempre se voria parlare de Dio over pensare, açiò che fosse sempre cum noi.

Pòi ancora pensare la sua profundissima humilitade, imperò ch'el-l'andava cum loro sì come compagno con[f. 118r]çosia cosa ch'el sia Re di Re et Signore di Segnori. Or non te pare ch'el sia tornato alla sua prima humilitade in questo altro grado ch'el non se desdegnò de acompagnarse cum questi doi discipuli li quali non erano dei dodece ma erano del numero de gli setantadoi? Certo non fano così gli superbi, li qualli vogliono semper conversare cum potenti et persone nobile, però non hano imparato da questo Maestro Cristo Iesù. Monstrò ancora la sua humilitate, imperò ch'el predicò a questi doi discipoli et disse a loro le cose secrete de Dio a confusione di coloro che non vogliano predicare se non hanno grande populo.

Reguardalo ancora, come el se infinçe de andare più oltra. Et questo el fecce per crescere el lor desiderio et per essere invidato et riceputo da loro. Or invidato et quasi isforçiato intrò benignamente cum loro in casa. Et posti che furono alla mensa, cum le sue sanctissime mane tolse il pane [f. 118v] et benedisselo et il pane se rumpete et poi il porsse a loro et egli el cognobero nel rumpere del pane. Unde sapi ch'el Signore vuolle essere invidato et sforçiato cum desiderio et cum oratione et sancti pensieri. Et però el ne conviene sempre orare et mai non restare, secundo il suo amaistramento, però che non cessa de orare chi non resta de ben fare.

Et incontenente ch'el fo cognosuto da loro, el disparve dalli ochi loro. Et egli dicevano insieme: «Non erano ben gli cuori nostri ardenti quando parlando cum noi nella via ne apriva le Scripture et non lo cognosessemo».

Et incontenente se levorono dalla mensa. Et non guardando ch'el fosse sera, ritornorono in Ierusalem et trovorono li discipuli congregati et le done cum loro. Alora li discipuli disseno a questi doi: «El Signore è resuscitato veramente et è apparuto a Simone Pietro». Et loro disseno tuto quello che ad essi era intravegnuto et come lo cognobero nel rumpere del pane, et [f. 119r] qui fo facta grande alegreça et festa.

thoughts it seems that a fire is ablaze." And it can always be like this if one wishes to speak of God or think of him, for he is always with us.

You can also consider his profound humility, because he walked along with them like that as a companion, even though he is King of Kings and Lord of Lords. Now, doesn't it seem to you that he returned to his original humility, in that he did not consider it beneath his dignity to keep company with those two disciples, who were not among the twelve but belonged to the seventy-two? The proud surely do not act like this. They always wish to associate with powerful people and those of noble rank because they have not learned from that Master, Christ Jesus. He revealed his humility even further when he preached to those two disciples and told them secret things of God, to the confusion of those who do not wish to preach unless they have a great crowd.

Watch him again, how he acts as if he intends to go further. And he does this to increase their desire and to be invited and welcomed by them. Invited and pressed, he entered graciously with them into the house. And once they were seated at the table, he took the bread with his most holy hands and blessed it and broke the bread and then gave it to them, and they recognized him in the breaking of the bread. So through this you know that the Lord wishes to be invited and persuaded to come in with desire and with prayers and holy thoughts. And indeed according to his teaching, it is necessary to pray always, without ceasing, since he who does not stop praying does not stop doing good deeds.

And as soon as he was recognized by them, he disappeared from their view. And they said among themselves, "Our hearts were not ardent enough when, speaking to us on the road, he revealed the holy scriptures to us and we failed to recognize him."

And at once they rose from the table. And paying no heed to the fact that it was evening, they returned to Jerusalem and found the disciples gathered and the women with them. And then the disciples said to those two, "The Lord is risen, truly, and has appeared to Simon Peter." And they told them all that had happened, and how they had recognized him in the breaking of the bread. And at that there was great rejoicing and celebration.

*Come miser Iesù aparse a' soi discipoli nella septimana della Resurrectione stando loro serati in casa, et altre cose che se puote compre[n]dere che lui fece. Capitolo xxix°.*[188]

Or siando sera uno giorno della septimana della Resurretione et siando le porte serate della casa dove erano gli discipuli congregati per paura d'i Giudei, vene miser Iesù et stete nel meço de loro et disse: «La pace mia sia cum voi. Non habiate paura, ch'io sum desso». Alora gli discipuli, come huomeni increduli, se conturbono et temevano ch'el non fusse fantasma, però che el stimavano lui essere spirito. Et alhora disse miser Iesù: «Perché sete voi turbati et perché pensati nelli cuori vostri ch'io sia spirito? Vedete le mie mane et gli piedi mei, ché io sum esso. Attastateme, imperò ch'el spirito non ha carne né osse sì come me». Et monstroge le mane et il lato aperto. Et vedando che ancora [f. 119v] non credea, per meglio confermarli nella fede disse: «Havete alcuna cosa da mangiare?» Alora gli discipuli ge presentorono una parte di pesse arostito et del favo di melle.

Et sancto Thomaso non era cum loro quando miser Iesù apparse la prima fiada alli discipuli. Et tornato ch'el fo a casa, gli discipuli li dissero: «Noi habiamo veduto el Signore et havemo mangiato et bevuto cum lui, et hane monstrato le mane et il costato aperto».

Et sancto Tomaso disse: «Se io non vederò le mane soe forate et che io metti el dido mio nelli forami delli chiodi et ch'io metti le mie mane nel costato suo, non credo».

Et dapoi giorni octo, siando ancora serati gli discipuli et sancto Tomaso cum loro, vene miser Iesù siando le porte serate; et stete in meço di loro et disse: «La pace mia sia cum voi». Et poi se voltò inverso san Thomaso et disse: «Vedi le mane mie, et meti le mane tue nel lato mio. Et non volere essere in[f 120r]credulo ma fidele».

Alora sancto Thomaso rispuose et disse: «Tu sei lo Signore mio et lo Dio mio». Rispuose miser Iesù et disse: «Tomaso, perché tu me hai veduto, tu m'ài creduto; ma beati sarano quelli che non me vederano, et crederano».

Or sapi che questo non fo sença grande dispensatione de Dio che sancto Tomaso dubitasse, açiò che la Resurrectione fosse più chiaramente manifestata per più modi. Or risguarda diligentemente et considera la sua bontade, come humelmente el monstrò qui alli suoi discipuli le sue ferite per tuore via da loro [o]gni incredulitade—et anche per nostra utilitade.

188. MS *Capitolo xxx*

*Chapter 29. How Lord Jesus appeared to his disciples*
*the week after the Resurrection while they were staying*
*at home with the doors locked; and other things that*
*one can conclude that he did.*

Now one evening during the week after the Resurrection, while the
disciples were staying at home with the doors locked for fear of the Jews,
Lord Jesus came and stood in their midst and said, "My peace be with
you. Do not be afraid, for I am he." And the disciples, being skeptical
men, were very troubled, and they feared that he was a phantom, because
it seemed to them that he was a spiritual being. And then Lord Jesus said,
"Why are you troubled, and why do you think in your hearts that I am a
spirit? See my hands and my feet: I am he. Touch me, because a spirit
does not have flesh and bones, as I do." And he showed them his hands
and the opening in his side. And seeing that they still did not believe, to
better confirm them in the faith he asked, "Do you have anything to eat?"
So the disciples gave him part of a cooked fish and some honeycombs.

And Saint Thomas was not with them when Lord Jesus appeared to
the disciples the first time. And when he returned to the house, the disciples
said to him, "We have seen the Lord, and have had something to eat and
drink with him. And he showed us his hands and the opening in his side."

And Saint Thomas said, "If I do not see his pierced hands and put my
finger in the wounds made by the nails and put my hands in his side, I will
not believe."

And eight days later, while the disciples and Saint Thomas were still
staying together inside the house, Lord Jesus entered, even though the
doors were locked. And he stood in their midst and said, "My peace be
with you." And then he turned to Saint Thomas and said, "See my hands,
and put your hands into my side. And do not persist in your unbelief, but
believe."

Then Saint Thomas answered, saying, "You are my Lord and my
God!" Lord Jesus replied and said, "Thomas, because you have seen me,
you have believed in me. But blessed are those who will not see me, yet
believe."

Now, know that this was not without a great dispensation from God
that Saint Thomas doubted him, so that the Resurrection could be more
clearly manifested in more ways. Now watch carefully, and consider his
goodness, how humbly he showed his wounds here to his disciples to alle-
viate all their doubts, and also for our benefit.

Unde tu dèi sapere che miser Iesù se reservò le sue piage sanctissime per tre c[a]sone.[189] La prima per confermare gli chuor' delli suoi discipuli. La secunda per monstrarle al Padre suo celestiale per pacificarlo cum noi et pregarlo per noi, imperò che lui è nostro advocato tra Dio et noi. La terça si è per monstrarle al Di del Giudicio a coloro che serano [f. 120v] giudicati davanti a lui.

Et dapoi alquanto ello gli disse che li dovesseno andare in Galilea, et che qui el vederaveno; et questo dicendo,[190] disparve.

Et dapoi li discipoli se partirono de Ierusalem et andorono in Galilea, et qui el Signore li apparse sopra el monte dove lui gli havea ordinato ch'eli dovesseno andare. Et vedendolo, gli discipoli si lo adorono. Et poi disse a loro: «A me è data ogni podestade et signoria in cielo et in terra. Et però andate et amaistrate ogni çente [et][191] baptiçateli nel nome del Padre et del Figliolo et del Spirito Sancto, et amaestrateli de observare ogni cosa che io ve ho comandato. Et confortative et state securamente, imperò che io sono sempre cum voi, infina alla fine del mondo».

Or considera quanta è la bontade del Signore, che qui el manifesta ogni cosa di quello ch'el à ricevuto dal Padre suo. Et el dà a loro la libertade de andare predicando, et come el ge insegna el modo de baptiçare et anche li dà vigore et ardimento, però ch'el disse [f. 121r] «Io sono sempre cum voi». O quanta è la caritade de Dio, et imperò ne dà gran fiducia de resistere allo adversario nostro; imperò che quello ch'el disse a loro, disse a noi.

Et manifestose ancora miser Iesù a sete delli suoi discipuli, gli qualli erano andati a pescare al mare de Tiberiadis. Et pescando tuta nocte, non presseno niente di pesse. Et la matina per tempo stete miser Iesù in suso el lido del mare, et nientedimeno gli discipuli non lo cognosceano. Et disse a loro Iesù: «Non havete pigliato niente di pesse?» Et rispondendo loro de non, disse miser Iesù: «Mettete la rete nella drita parte della nave et pigliaretine». Et metendo loro la rete in la parte drita, preseno tanto pese che nol potevano tirare nella nave.

Et alora san Çuane disse a sancto Pietro: «Ell'è il Signore». Et aldendo sancto Pietro ch'el era el Signore, se messe a corere per lo mare et andò al Signore. Et li altri discipoli andorono a terra cum la navicella, et qui [f. 121v] mançorono cum miser Iesù et feceno qui grande pasqua.

189. MS *cosone*
190. MS *qusto* with an *e* added above the line and *dicēdo* added in margin
191. MS *te*

Therefore you should know that Lord Jesus kept his most holy wounds for three reasons. First, to strengthen the hearts of his disciples. Second, to show them to his celestial Father, in order to make him more merciful towards us and to intercede with him for us, because he is our advocate before God. The third is to show them at the day of Judgment, to those who will be judged before him.

And after this he told them that they must to go to Galilee, and that they would see him there. And saying this, he vanished from view.

And after that, the disciples left Jerusalem and went to Galilee, and there the Lord appeared to them on the mountain where he had instructed them to go. And seeing him, the disciples knelt in adoration. And then he said to them, "All power and dominion in heaven and on earth has been given to me. So go and teach the nations, and baptize them in the name of the Father and of the Son and of the Holy Spirit, and teach them to observe everything that I have commanded you. And take courage and be at peace, because I am with you always, until the end of the world."

Now consider how great is the goodness of the Lord, who reveals everything here that he received from his Father. And he gives them liberty to go preaching, and he teaches them how to baptize, and he also gives them courage and ardor, because he said, "I am with you always." O how great is the love of God! And he gave us great confidence to resist our adversary; for what he said to them, he said to us.

And Lord Jesus also appeared to seven of his disciples who had gone to fish in the Lake of Tiberias. And fishing all night long, they caught no fish at all. And early in the morning, Lord Jesus stood close by at the edge of the sea, yet the disciples did not recognize him. And Jesus said to them, "Haven't you caught any fish?" And when they replied that they had not, Lord Jesus said, "Cast the net on the right side of the boat and you will catch them there." And casting the net on the right side of the boat, they caught so many fish that they were not able to pull them all into the boat.

And then Saint John said to Saint Peter, "It is the Lord." And Saint Peter, hearing that it was the Lord, jumped into the water and swam to the Lord. And the other disciples came ashore in the little boat, and then they ate with Lord Jesus and had a big celebration there.

Lord Jesus also appeared to more than five hundred people at one time, according to what Saint Paul says, but in what place and in what manner is not recorded.

You have seen how many times Our Lord Jesus Christ appeared to his friends. Now you know that in the Gospels, one finds that the Lord

Apparse etiandio miser Iesù a più de cinquecento persone in una volta, secundo che narra sancto Paulo, ma in che luocho et in che maniera non è scripto.

Hai veduto quante volte el Signore nostro miser Iesù Cristo se ha manifestado a' suoi amici? Or sapi che in li evangelisti se trova ch'el Signore apparse diece volte dapoi la Resurrectione inançi la Ascensione, ma come lui apparse alla madre non mete niuno evangelio. Et come lo apparse a Ioseph se trova scripto nel'evangelio di Nicodemo, et com'el apparse a sancto Iacomo, sancto Paulo el mete in una sua epistola, et anche sancto Ieronimo el dice. Ma noi podemo piatosamente pensare che lui, come benigno, piu volte apparse alla madre sua et anche a quella sua dillecta discipula, çioè Magdalena, et a molti altri suoi divoti per confermarli nel suo amore. Pòi ancora considerare sopra la sua [f. 122r] benignitade et humilitade della quale noi habiamo facto spesse volte mentione nelli suoi facti.

Unde dapoi che lui hebbe così gloriosamente combatuto et sostenuto così vituperosa et obprobriosa morte, lui podea ascendere in cielo et mandare uno overo molti delli suoi angeli a manifestare la sua Resurrectione alli apostoli, ma non volse fare cosi la sua benignitade, ançi volse la sua caritade personalmente conversare cum loro et manifestamente monstrare come lui era resuscitado da morte, et façando a loro molte pruove et argumenti et segni manifesti della sua resurretione et apparendo a loro del regno del cielo.

O quanto ne ha amato questo Signore, non amando noi lui! Et imperò non s[o]lamente[192] el doveressemo amare, ma etiandio tuto bramare et inflamarse de la sua dilectione!

## Come el nostro Signore miser Iesù ascendete in cielo et finì la sua peregrinatione. Capitolo xxx°.[193]

[f. 122v] Hora qui noi parlemo della Ascensione del nostro Signore miser Iesù Cristo; et impero noi dovemo stare molto attenti in questa solenitade della Ascensione del nostro Signore.

Or siando el nostro Signore nel paradiso teresto et siando compiti gli quaranta giorni, lui se partite del paradiso et menò secho gli Sancti Padri.

192. MS *salamente*
193. MS *Capitolo xxxi*

appeared ten times between the Resurrection and the Ascension. But not one of the Gospels tells how he appeared to his mother.[155] And how he appeared to Joseph one finds written in the Gospel of Nichodemus. And how he appeared to Saint James, Saint Paul records in one of his letters, and also Saint Jerome mentions it. But in a spirit of devotion we may imagine that he, being so kind, appeared many times to his mother—and also to her, his beloved disciple, that is, Magdalene; and to many of his other devoted followers, in order to strengthen them in his love.[156] Then also meditate on his benevolence and humility, which we have mentioned many times in describing his deeds.

And so, after he had so gloriously fought against the world and suffered such a humiliating and shameful death, he could have ascended to heaven and sent one or even many of his angels to reveal his Resurrection to the apostles. But his lovingkindness did not wish it to be this way; and his love too, wished to converse with them in person, and to demonstrate clearly how he was resurrected from the dead, giving them many proofs and arguments and manifest signs of his Resurrection and revealing to them the Kingdom of Heaven.

Oh how greatly this Lord has loved us, even when we have not loved him! And so we should not only love him, but long for him ardently and set ourselves ablaze for his love!

*Chapter 30. How Our Lord Jesus ascended into heaven and finished his journey.*

Now from here on we will speak about the Ascension of Our Lord Jesus Christ; and we should pay close attention to this feast of the Ascension of Our Lord.[157]

Now after Our Lord had been in the earthly paradise and forty days had passed, he left paradise and brought the Holy Fathers with him. And he blessed Enoch and Elijah and went to Jerusalem, to Mount Syon, where the disciples were, and Our Lady with the other women. And while the eleven disciples were eating, Lord Jesus appeared to them, chastising them

Et benedì Enoch et Elia et vene in Ierusalem in sul Monte Syon dove erano gli discipuli et la Madona cum le altre done. Et mançando li undece discipoli, si li apparse miser Iesù et reprehendendoli della loro incredulitate et duricia de cuore, perche e' lo haveano veduto resuscitato da morte et non credeano; et poi mangiò cum loro in grande leticia. Et mangiando disse a loro: «Andiate nello universo mondo predicando lo evangelio mio a tute le creature; et baptiçateli, et quelli che serano baptiçati et crederano in me serano salvi, et quelli che non crederano serano dannati».

Et disse alla madre et [f. 123r] alli discipuli che egli dovesseno andare in sul Monte Oliveto. Et qui li apparse el Signore et confortoli et amaistroli et disse: «Non ve turbati et non habiate paura, imperò che serò sempre cum voi perfina alla fine del mondo».

Alora la madre et li discipuli et le altre done che erano lì et la Magdalena[194] se inçenochiorono in terra dimandando la sua benedictione. Et la madre, abraçandolo cum grandissime lacrime, se acumbiatò da lui; et così feceno tuti gli altri. Et tuti inçenochiati a terra parlando cum lui, et la madre et la Madalena et anche le altre donne dicevano: «Signore nostro et Maestro nostro, aricordiative de noi orphani».

Et li apostoli dicevano: «Signore, per te noi habiamo abandonato ogni cosa; solo a voi se recomandiamo».

Alora benedicendoli disse: «Stati forti et combatiate valentemente, che io serò sempre cum voi».

Et vedando loro, levò le mane in cielo cum la façia chiarissima se ne andò in cielo. Et quella turba andò cum lui, cantando et [f. 123v] iubilando, cum grande leticia montavano in verso el cielo. Alora tuti li ançoli et archangeli desmontorono per vegnire incontra al Signore della Vitoria et vegniano cantando: *Sanctus sanctus Dominus Deus Sabaoth*. Et inscontrandose nel Signore, cum tuta reverentia el salutorono, et tuti canta[n]do andorono in cielo in quella vita dolcissima. Or chi poria quella leticia dire et quelli canti narrare che in quello ascendere? Or chi havesse veduto gli angeli invitare li Sancti Padri a cantare et laudare Dio per lo grande beneficio ricevuto!

Hora torniamo al nostro Signore el qualle andava in cielo pianamente per dare più consolatione alla sua compagnia che 'l guardava per meraveglia. Or chi havesse veduto ascendere in cielo el nostro Signore, et la madre et li apostoli guardare in alto perfina ch'el poteano vedere chiaramente! Et poi vene una nebula bianchissima et tolselo dalli ochi loro, et in

194. MS *(et) la Magdalena* in margin

for their disbelief and hardness of heart, because they had seen him resurrected from death and did not believe; and afterwards, he ate with them in great joy. And while they were eating, he said to them, "Go out into the whole world, preaching my gospel to all creatures; and baptize them, and those who will be baptized and believe in me will be saved, and those who do not believe in me will be damned."

And he told his mother and the disciples that they must go to the Mount of Olives.[158] And there the Lord appeared to them and comforted them and taught them and said, "Do not let yourselves be troubled, and do not be afraid, because I will be with you always, until the end of the world."

And then the mother and the disciples and the other women who were there and Magdalene knelt on the ground, asking for his blessing. And the mother, embracing him with many tears, took leave of him; and all of the others did the same. And kneeling on the ground, they all continued to speak with him, and the mother and Magdalene and the other women said, "Our Lord and our Master, remember us orphans!"

And the apostles said, "Lord, for you we have abandoned everything; only to you do we commend ourselves."

Then, blessing them, he said, "Remain steadfast and fight valiantly, for I will always be with you."

And as they watched, he raised his hands to heaven with the most radiant expression and rose up to heaven. And that crowd went with him, singing and rejoicing with great happiness as he ascended towards heaven. And then all of the angels and archangels descended to greet the Lord of victory, and they came singing, "*Sanctus sanctus Dominus Deus Sabaoth*." And coming to meet the Lord, with great reverence they saluted him, and they all went singing to heaven, into that most sweet life. Now who would be able to describe that joy, and to describe those songs as he ascended? Now, if only one could have seen the angels invite the Holy Fathers to sing and praise God for the great benefit they received!

Now let's return to Our Lord, who went to heaven fully in order to give more consolation to his companions, who watch him with wonder. Oh, if only one could have seen Our Lord ascend into heaven, and the mother and the apostles gaze upward as long as they can still see him clearly! And then a very white cloud came and hid him from their view. And in an instant, he arrived in heaven with all of the angels and with all of the Holy Fathers of the Old Testament.

And as the mother and the apostles stayed there gazing up at the sky, two angels came in very white robes, and standing before them said,

uno momento çonse in cielo cum tuti li angeli et cum tuti gli [f. 124r] Padri del Vechio Testamento.

Et sta[n]do la madre et li apostoli et guardando in alto, vene doi angeli in vestimenti bia[n]chissimi et stando apresso loro disseno: «O huomeni di Galilea, perche stati così amirativi guardando in cielo? Questo Iesù el qualle è tolto da voi et è asceso in cielo, così el vegnirà, al modo che lo havete veduto ascendere, a giudicare el mondo. Tornàtive in Ierusalem et aspetate la promissione sua».

Hora considera qui uno pocheto la charitade del nostro Signore et Salvatore, che siando lui in tanta gloria non se domentigò delli sui servi, ançi ne fo molto sollicito. Unde incontenente ch'el fo partito dalli ochi loro, mandò doi angeli a dirli che non dovesseno più stare lì, ma che dovesseno andare in Ierusalem et aspetare la promessa sua.

Or aldita l'ambassiate, la Dona nostra et li apostoli disseno alli angeli che li dovesseno recomandare al Signore. Et cum questo gli angeli disparseno, et loro ritornorono in Ierusalem et qui aspetavano la [f. 124v] sua promissi[o]ne.

Or ascendendo el Signore miser Iesù cum[195] quella turba magna, se aperse el cielo el qualle infina alhora era stato serato a l'humana generatione. Et intrando dentro cum grande triumpho, reverentemente[196] se inçenochiò denançi al Padre suo et disse: «Padre mio, io ti rendo gratia che me hai dato vitoria contra tuti gli adversarii mei, et ecco ch'io te apresento tuti questi nostri anunci i qualli erano impregionati. Et ricomandove gli fratelli mei, li qualli io ho lassati nel mondo et òli promesso de mandarli lo Spirito Sancto, et imperò io ve priego che adimpiati la promessa mia».

Alora lo Padre s'el fece sedere al lato drito et disse: «Figliolo mio benedecto, io te do ogni podestade et ogni giudicio in cielo et in terra. Et imperçiò de questi toi discipuli ordina et fà come te piace». Hora qui fo grande leticia infra gli angeli et propheti.

Et imperò sì come io te dissi nel principio che questa solenitade era sopra tute le altre, considera adonque [f. 125r] et cerca bene ogni casa et vederai che te dicho la veritate. Grande è la solenitade et è da fare grande festa della Incarnatione de miser Iesù Cristo et è principio de ogni nostro bene; ma questa solenitade è nostra, et non sua. Grande solenitade è quella della Nativitade del nostro Signore; ma le è nostra, et non suo, imperò che l'è d'averli grande compassione, però che in tale giorno lui

195. MS *el signore cū mis(er) (Ies)ù cū cū*
196. MS *reuēretemēte*

"O men of Galilee, why do you stay here so full of wonder, gazing at the heavens? This Jesus who was taken from you and ascended into heaven will come to the world in the same way as you have seen him ascend, in order to judge the world. Return to Jerusalem and await his promise."

Now reflect a little here on the love of Our Lord and Savior, who, even when he was in such glory, did not forget his servants but instead was very solicitous for them. And so, as soon as he was hidden from view, he sent two angels to tell them that they should not stay there any longer, but that they should go to Jerusalem and await his promise.

Now having heard the message, Our Lady and the apostles asked the angels to commend them to the Lord. And with this, the angels departed. And they returned to Jerusalem, and waited there for his promise to be fulfilled.

Now when the Lord Jesus had ascended with that great crowd, heaven opened, which until now had been closed to humankind. And entering with great triumph, he reverently knelt before his Father and said, "My Father, I give you thanks, for you have given me victory against all of my adversaries. And here I present to you all of our messengers who had been imprisoned. And I commend to you my brothers whom I left in the world and to whom I promised to send the Holy Spirit. And so I pray that you fulfill my promise."

And then the Father seated him on his right side and said, "My blessed Son, I give you every power and every jurisdiction in heaven and on earth. So as far as your disciples are concerned, do as you please." Then there was great rejoicing among the angels and the prophets.

And so, as I told you in the beginning, this feast is greater than all the others. Consider this, then, and examine all the reasons well, and you will see that I tell you the truth. Great is the feast of the Incarnation of Lord Jesus Christ, deserving of great celebration, and it is the beginning of all our good; but that feast is ours, and not his. Great is the feast of the Nativity of Our Lord, but it is ours and not his, because it is matter for great compassion, since on that day he was born into this world in great poverty. Great is the feast of his Passion—to us, and not to him; to us because on that day all of our sins were washed away, and not his, because he underwent the most cruel death and suffering. But out of compassion for him, it should not be a feast of joy to us, but of lamentation and mourning for his Passion, and of giving thanks to him for our redemption.

Another very great feast and celebration is the Resurrection of Our Lord: to him and also for us. To him, because he was resurrected in glory

naque in questo mondo in grande povertade. Grande è la festa della sua Passione—a noi et non[197] a lui. A noi però ch'in quel giorno fu lavato tuti gli nostri peccati, et non sua però ch'el sostene crudelissima morte et Passione. Ma per compassione de lui, a noi non debe essere festa de gaudio, ma de pianto et dolerse della Passione sua, et rendere gratie a lui della nostra restauratione.

Ancora grandissima solenitade et festa è la Resurrectione del nostro Signore: a lui et etiandio a noi. A lui imperò ch'el resuscitò glorioso et cum vitoria, a noi però che per la sua Resurrectione siamo iustificati. Et imperçiò molto è venerabile [f. 125v][198] il giorno della Pasqua, et imperò la Chiesia in tale dì canta «Questo è il giorno che ha facto el Signore, cantiamo et alegriamosse in esso».

Ma magiore solenitade me pare la Ascensione, imperò che avegna ch'el nostro Signore miser Iesù Cristo sia resuscitato, conviene che per nostro amaistramento el sia ancora peregrino in terra. Et anche la porta del Paradiso era ancora serata, et ancora li Sancti Padri non andorono alla patria sua. Et tute queste cose sono adimpite nel giorno della Ascensione.

Unde se tu poni ben mente çiò che ha fato il Signore Dio perfina hora, l'à facto per venire a questo giorno, et sença questo dì tute le sue operatione erano imperfecte. Imperò ch'el cielo et la terra et tute le cosse che se contiene in loro sono facte per l'huomo, et l'huomo è facto per havere la gloria; et a questa gloria niuno gi andava dapoi el peccato del primo nostro parente, *quantumcumque* fosse iusto o sancto. Vedi adonca come [f. 126r] è grande el giorno de oçi; et è propriamente festa de miser Iesù, imperò che oçi lui començiò a sedere alla mano dextra del Padre et dette fine alla sua peregrinatione.

Et anche oçi fu grande festa alli angeli, imperò che riceveteno novo gaudio della humanitade del nostro Signore; et etiandio oçi fo el primo giorno dello loro restauratione. Et pertanto el me pare maçore festa oçi che giorno de sia nell'anno. Et per confirmatione del mio ditto, io ti do per testimonio sancto Bernardo, el qualle in uno sermone dice: «Questa solenitade è sopra tute le altre, et è seratura et fine de tute le altre solenitade; et è compimento de tuto el viaço de miser Iesù Cristo». Ecco che io te ho monstrato manifestamente come el giorno de oçi è più solene de tuti li altri. Unde l'anima che bene amasse miser Iesù più se alegreria nel dì de hoçi che in tuti gli altri giorni de l'anno. Unde el Signore nostro

197. MS *Et nō sua . . . passione* in margin
198. MS *e venerabile* ‖ *e*

and with victory; to us because through his Resurrection we are redeemed. And for this reason, the day of Easter is very worthy to be venerated. And so the Church sings on this day, "This is the day that the Lord
has made, let us sing and rejoice in it."

But it seems to me that the greatest feast is the Ascension because, even
though Our Lord Jesus Christ had risen, it was necessary for our instruction
that he be still a pilgrim on earth.[159] And also the gate of paradise was still
shut, and the Holy Fathers still could not go to their fatherland. And all of
these things reached their fulfillment on the day of the Ascension.

And so if you meditate well on what Our Lord God did up to this
point, he did it to reach this day; and without this day, all his works were
imperfect. Because heaven and earth and all of the things contained in
them were made for man, and man was made to have glory; and no one
could attain this glory after the sin of our first parent, no matter how just
and holy they might be. See, then, how magnificent today's feast day is;
and it is really the feast belonging to Lord Jesus, for today he began to sit
at the right hand of the Father, and he brought an end to his journey.[160]

And also today was the great feast of the angels, for they received new
joy from the humanity of Our Lord; and also today was the first day of
their restitution. And for all these reasons, it seems to me that today is the
greatest feast day of the year. And to confirm my argument, I give you the
testimony of Saint Bernard, who says in a sermon, "This feast is above all
others, and it is the conclusion and fulfillment of all the other feasts; and it
is the completion of the entire journey of Lord Jesus Christ."[161] There,
then: I have shown you clearly how this is a more solemn feast day than all
the others.[162] And so the soul who would love Lord Jesus well will rejoice
more on this feast day than on all the other days of the year. For as Our
Lord said to his disciples, "If you love me well, you will rejoice that I am
going to my Father." And so I believe that I am right when I say that there
is no feast day so greatly celebrated in heaven than the day of the Ascension of Lord Jesus Christ.

And so we may imagine that the first day after the Ascension, the angels held a very special celebration for Lord Jesus Christ; the second day,
the archangels; the third, the powers; the fourth, the virtues; the fifth, the
principalities; the sixth, the dominions; the seventh, the thrones; the eighth
day, the cherubim; the ninth, the seraphim.

The tenth day the Lord Jesus sent the Holy Spirit to his apostles
and fulfilled his promise. And having received the Holy Spirit, they went
throughout the whole world, preaching the name of Lord Jesus Christ, and
they subjugated the whole world to the faith of Lord Jesus.

disse [f. 126v] alli suoi discipoli: «Se voi me amasti bene, voi ve alegrere-
sti, imperçiò ch'io vado al Padre mio». Et imperò me credo havere dicto
bene ch'el non fo mai alcuno giorno cusì solenniçato in vita eterna come è
el dì della Ascensione de miser Iesù Cristo.

Unde noi possemo pensare che il primo giorno dapoi la Ascensione li
angeli facesseno una singularissima festa a miser Iesù Cristo; el secundo dì
li Archançoli; el terço le Podestade; el quarto le Vertude; el quinto giorno li
Principati; el sexto le Dominatione; el septimo gli Throni; l'octavo giorno
li Cherubini; el nono li Seraphini.

El decimo giorno el Signore miser Iesù mandò el Spirito Sancto alli
suoi apostoli et impite la sua promessa. Et ricevuto che li haveno el Spirito Sancto, andorono per tuto el mondo predicando el nome de miser Iesù
Cristo, et sottomesseno tuto el mondo alla fede de miser Iesù.

Et molte altre cose fece miser Iesù le qualle io non scrivo, per[f. 127r]
ché seria tropo longo dire. Ma noi posiamo comprehendere et pensare
ch'el[199] fece molte cose le qualle io non scrivo in questo libro, come se
puote vedere nelli Evangelii ch'el adoperò el nostro Signore miser Iesù
Cristo: el qualle sia laudato et ringratiato cum la sua benedecta madre Vergene Maria *in secula seculorum. Amen. Deo gratias.*

*Priegove sorelle per caritade*
*che quando legereti in questo libero,*
*priegate miser Iesù per me*
*che me doni cognoscimento.*

199. MS *che* corrected to *ch(e)l*

And Lord Jesus did many other things that I am not writing about because it would take too long to tell. But we may understand and imagine that he did many things that I do not write about in this book, as you can see in the Gospels that treat of Our Lord Jesus Christ: to whom be praise and thanks, with his blessed Virgin Mother Mary, forever and ever. Amen. Deo gratias.

*I ask you, sisters, for charity,*
*that when you read in this book*
*you pray to Lord Jesus for me,*
*so that he might grant me recognition.*[163]

# NOTES TO THE *MEDITATIONS*

The notes to the text are keyed to the English translation even though in some notes a specific phrase in the Italian is at issue. They are intended to explain interesting or potentially puzzling features of the text, to gesture towards potentially fruitful avenues for future research, and to call attention to some of the differences between the *testo breve* and the Italian text to which it is most closely related, the *testo minore*. Close comparisons between the *testo breve* and the *testo minore* provide the essential foundation for the conclusions advanced in the Introduction: that the *testo breve* was composed by one author (Author A) and that the *testo minore* is a redaction completed at a secondary stage by another author (Author B).

1. **Here begins the prologue of the meditations on the life of Our Lord Jesus Christ, whose teaching is the seed of prudence, whose life is the mirror of temperance and patience.** The opening rubric refers to the four cardinal virtues, but omits one of the four, justice; this omission is likely to be a scribal error (the four virtues are listed, complete, in the body of the prologue). Interestingly, this rendering of the cardinal virtues also substitutes *patientia* for *forteça*—and in doing so makes explicit a redefinition of fortitude implicit in much Passion literature of the period: that patience—the ability to suffer, to bear up—is a primary form of strength. I have translated the Italian *providentia* as "prudence," since this is the standard English rendering of this particular cardinal virtue (*prudentia* is originally a contraction of *providentia*). The primary connotations of English "prudence," however—cautious action, aversion to risk, or even prudishness—are clearly not the senses intended here. Prudence as a cardinal virtue is, as Thomas Aquinas defined it, following Aristotle, "right reason in action" (*recta ratio agibilium*; *Summa theologiae* II:I, 61).

2. **she always carried the Gospel of Christ Jesus hidden in her breast.** This detail is given in the *Legenda aurea*; see Ryan, *Jacobus de Voragine* 2:318; *Breviarum Romanum*, 22 Nov. There has been speculation in the scholarship on the MVC that the opening reference to St. Cecilia may indicate that the intended recipient or author was named Cecilia, or that the original convent was dedicated to Cecilia. But this opening invocation makes very good sense on its own terms, which is to say, in generic terms. By the early fourteenth century, St. Cecilia had

come to be thought of as the primary exemplar of affective meditation, as the ideal *sponsa Christi* whose affective fervor bound her in marriage to Christ. St. Cecilia is among the figures depicted in a fresco in the lower church of Santa Chiara in Assisi by an early follower of Giotto. On the evolution of the saint's significance in Italy, see Connolly, *Mourning into Joy*. The reference here to Cecilia's book seems to indicate a very small volume akin to the small books of hours and gospel books in use among female religious in the thirteenth and fourteenth centuries—volumes whose portability (they could indeed be carried next to the breast) and softness (a feature of the "uterine vellum" from which they were often made) served to enhance the affective and sensual dimension of devotional reading; see Oliver, "A Bundle of Myrrh"; McNamer, *Affective Meditation and the Invention of Medieval Compassion*, 130–31, 249n42; and de Hamel, *The Book*, 114–39. The particular formulation in the Italian, *ascoxo nel suo pecto*, conflates the experience of reading and feeling; just as Cecilia carries the gospel florilegium next to her breast in a hidden, intimate way, like the "bundle of myrrh" of the *Song of Songs*, she also has its contents hidden within, known by heart and with feeling.

3. **she had written out for herself some of the most moving passages from the life of Lord Jesus Christ.** There is a significant difference here between the *testo breve* and other versions of the MVC. Here, St. Cecilia writes out the Gospel passages she has chosen; in the other versions, she simply selects them. In the *testo minore*, the parallel passage reads "e questo si dee così intendere, ch'ella s'avea iscelte alquante cose più divote della vita di Jesù Cristo" (Sarri, 1). Given contemporary suspicions of women who sought to write about spiritual matters, it is possible that the author of the *testo minore* actively suppressed this image of a woman writer.

4. **dwelling on them again and savoring their sweetness.** The Italian *ragunavale cum un gusto molto suave* implies that the sweetness comes as much from an active savoring by the reader (*cum gusto*) as from the inherent sweetness of the text (more specifically, from the selected Gospel passages gathered together in Cecilia's *florilegium*). Monastic practices of *lectio divina* lie behind this image, but on sweetness itself in a broader devotional and cultural context, see Fulton, "Taste and See," and Carruthers, "Sweetness."

5. **And concerning this, Saint Bernard says . . . in the wounds of his Master, Christ Jesus.** Bernard, *Sermones super Cantica Canticorum* 61, 8 (Leclercq et al., *Sancti Bernardi Opera* 2:153).

6. **and here you will find the model and doctrine of the most excellent love, and of extreme poverty.** The reference to strict poverty here (*extrema povertade*) is the first among the text's many allusions to the ideal of voluntary poverty. This ideal was fundamental to Clare of Assisi and is enshrined in the Rule confirmed by Innocent IV in 1253 ("De promissis beati Francisci et de non habendis possessionibus"; C. Leonardi, *La letteratura francescana* 1:316–19). On St. Clare's struggles to obtain the "privilege of poverty," see Catherine Mooney, *Clare of Assisi and the Thirteenth-Century Church*.

7. **And so Saint Bernard says, "Vainly and without fruit . . . sign of fortitude."** The four cardinal virtues; Bernard, *Sermones super Cantica Canticorum* 22, 11 (Leclercq et al., *Sancti Bernardi Opera* 1:137).

8. **And in this way many who are unlettered and simple have gained knowledge of the lofty and profound things of God.** The term "simple" in late medieval religious writings has connotations of virtue, incorporating the qualities of innocence, humility, and modesty; in Franciscan contexts, it also implied an attitude towards learning, i.e., a means of attaining wisdom without traditional, scholastic education. St. Francis links wisdom to simplicity in his "Salutation of the Virtues": "Hail, Queen Wisdom! May the Lord protect you, with your Sister, Holy pure Simplicity!" (Armstrong, Hellman, and Short, *Francis of Assisi* 1:164–65). See Şenocak, "Voluntary Simplicity," on the importance of this concept in early Franciscan history. The term "simple" in this phrase is linked to "unlettered" (*sança letere*), which means those who are not readers of Latin and by extension, in this context, those without clerical education. It is a resonant note on which to end the prologue, since it confers a form of authority to the intended reader of this Italian text, a nun who presumably has limited knowledge of Latin. It also appears to license the author's project of composing the ensuing meditations in Italian. In the early decades of the Trecento, a historical period of literary activity that was, as Boterill observes, often very self-conscious about the vernacular/Latin divide ("Introduction," in *Dante Aligheri*), the lucidity and directness of this sentence in the *testo breve* merits notice. Finally, this sentence may also merit attention for its evidentiary value regarding the question of whether the MVC was originally composed in Italian or Latin. The phrase exists in the Latin text (see Taney et al., Prologue, 3); but the mismatch between the endorsement there of the "unlettered" and the ensuing text offered in Latin suggests that, in the Latin text, the phrase is a relic from an earlier, vernacular state of the text. Structurally, the phrase makes better sense in the *testo breve*: it functions fittingly as a justification for the use of the vernacular in a prologue preceding a vernacular text.

9. **Stay still, here. . . . And in the end. . . .** The exquisite delicacy and pacing of this scene, in which momentous divine action is held in abeyance pending the Virgin's consent (*lo consentimento de questa sua figliuola*), may owe something to early drama or *sacre rappresentazioni* associated with the divine office on the Feast of the Annunciation, which became known throughout Europe as the Missa Aurea or Golden Mass. On early dramatizations of the Annunciation in liturgical and paraliturgical contexts, see Young, *Drama of the Medieval Church*, 2:245–50. A manuscript of a fourteenth-century play from Padua is one of the few to contain rubrics; as Jacobus observes, these rubrics convey an "impression of sustained stasis" ("Giotto's *Annunciation*," 98).

10. **watching with great gladness how she remains modest and well-mannered.** The term *vergognosa* is famously untranslatable. Here, I give the English "modest" as the best available approximation, though it lacks the emotional resonance of *vergognosa*, which suggests a hint of shame, readiness to blush, and

a holding back of latent sexual consciousness and desire. The image of the modest and well-mannered Virgin, and of a Trinity pleased to observe how she remains *vergognosa et cum buoni costumi*, merits comparison with contemporary Tuscan protocols and courtesy books, such as Francesco da Barbarino's *Reggimento e costumi di donna* (ca. 1309); see "On the Conduct and Manners of a Lady," 130–58, in Stoppino, "The Italian *Reggimento e costumi di donna*."

11. **with a joyful expression.** The particular detail of Gabriel's happy and expectant expression, his *volto aliegro*, is one that early fourteenth-century Pisan artists were especially adept at conveying in sculptural form; see, for example, the polychromed and gilded wood sculpture from Pisa, ca. 1325/1350, now held at the National Gallery of Art, Washington, D.C. (Middeldorf, *Sculptures from the Samuel H. Kress Collection,* 8). The solemn expression of Giotto's angel of the Annunciation in the Scrovegni Chapel, as well as the solidity and monumentality of Giotto's scene more generally, provide an interesting parallel; they reveal, through contrast, the Gothic elegance and litheness of figure and action that infuses both this Pisan image and the *testo breve*. For an intriguiging reading of Giotto's Annunciation scene as a depiction of a *sacra rappresentazione*, see Jacobus, "Giotto's *Annunciation*."

12. **And according to what is contained in revelation, she knelt with the greatest devotion and, with hands crossed, . . . .** Both the gesture (*mane zonte*) and its source (*revelatione*) require a word of explanation here. As for the gesture, the Italian phrase *cum le mane zonte* can signify the joining of hands in prayer. In this case, however, it is more likely that the crossing of the hands on the chest is intended. This is the gesture of Giotto's Virgin at the Annunciation in the Scrovegni Chapel. As Barasch observes, in a chapter devoted to the subject ("Crossing the Hands on the Chest," *Giotto and the Language of Gesture*, 72–87), it is a gesture with a rich history, and one that experienced a resurgence in the visual arts of the late thirteenth and early fourteenth centuries in Italy. Although the gesture can carry multiple meanings, Barasch identifies the Virgin's crossing of her hands in Giotto's painting of the Annunciation as "in its essence, a liturgical gesture" (86) signifying humility. As for the source mentioned here, the phrase "secundo che se contiene ne le revelatione" is ambiguous, and it is an important crux in the *testo breve*. One difficulty it presents is that of a plural article, *le*, joined to a singular noun, *revelatione* (not plural *revelationi*). "Revelation" has several potential meanings: in its singular form, it can refer to sacred scripture, or more generally to anything revealed by God; in its plural form, it can refer to visions or to a text about visions. The simplest explanation here, given the fact that the term is presented in the singular, would seem to be that the reference is to the scriptural passage that follows: "Ecco l'ancilla del Signore. Sia facto a me secundo la tua parola" (Lk 1:38). However, it could be that the choreography of the scene—the Virgin kneeling with devotion, with hands crossed—was perceived to be the more salient feature of the passage, and the one implicitly in need of authorizing with reference to *revelatione*; for there were multiple, competing ways of depicting the Annunciation

scene in the early decades of the Trecento. Giotto's image of the kneeling Virgin in the Scrovegni Chapel, for instance, differs from the scene as it is scripted in the contemporary Missa Aurea, or Golden Mass: in stage directions that survive from fourteenth-century Padua, *Maria* stands, raises her arms, and proclaims the line *Ecce l'ancilla* loudly: "Hoc finito, Maria se elevet, et stando brachiis apertis alta voce incipiat *Ecce ancilla*" (Jacobus, "Giotto's *Annunciation*," 106). In the *Legenda aurea*, Mary also raises her hands to heaven; the author of the *Legenda* cites Bernard of Clairvaux as the authority for this gesture (Ryan, *Jacobus de Voragine* 1:200). It seems that the choreography of the Annunciation may have been a contested arena, then, with varying versions in need of "authorizing." It is possible that the word *revelatione* in the *testo breve* originally read *revelationi* in an anterior version of the text, and thus that it served as an allusion to written revelations that authorize an image of the humble, kneeling Virgin—including, potentially, the *Revelations of Elizabeth of Hungary*, which depicts the Virgin in this way: "prostravi me in terram et genibus flexis ac manibus iunctis adoravi et dixi: Ecce ancilla Domini, fiat mihi secundum verbum tuum" (Oliger, *Revelationes*, 68). The question would seem to be, then, whether this textual reference to the Virgin kneeling and crossing the arms was so unusual as to have the *Revelations of Elizabeth of Hungary* as its most likely source or whether there were other sources known as *revelatione* or *revelationi* circulating in Tuscany in the early fourteenth century that gave authority to this way of imagining the scene. Given how pervasive the image of the kneeling Virgin becomes in Trecento art, it seems to me that there may have been a common source behind the *Revelations* and the *testo breve*.

13. **and humbly asked that he deign to teach her so that she might do everything without fail that should be done with respect to his Son.** In the Italian, it is not clear whether the meaning is "his" or "her" son; the phrase *el suo figliulo* leaves this open. I have translated it as "his Son" because the preceding phrase seems to me to indicate that the Virgin is anxious to care for the Father's child in the most fitting way. But the way that the Italian formulation allows for the meaning "*her* son" is worth pondering, especially given Mary's emphasis on "*my* son" in the chapters on the Passion.

14. **Today is the feast of the marriage of the Son of God. . . . that he show his longed-for face, so that we would be saved.** This chapter's concluding passage, with its rhythmic and celebratory repetion of *oggi . . . oggi* and its image of the Incarnation as the moment when God wedded human nature, has the ring of a liturgical hymn, though I have not been able to trace a specific source. The feast of the Annunciation was celebrated on March 25 and typically also in December on the Wednesday of the third week of Advent.

15. **and went to the mountain with her spouse to the house of Saint Elizabeth, which was a good seventy-four miles away.** A small but interesting difference is evident here between the *testo breve* and the *testo minore*. The *testo minore* gives Joseph greater prominence by mentioning his name: "collo sposo suo Josep"

(Sarri, 24). This is the first example of a systematic difference between the two texts (for additional examples, see below, 205nn21, 23, 213n52, 215n68, 218n80, 229n133). The most plausible explanation for this difference, in my view, is that the *testo minore* is a revision and expansion of the *testo breve* by an author who sought to highlight Joseph's presence and to insert him into more scenes—perhaps in response to increased enthusiasm for the cult of St. Joseph in the first half of the trecento, or perhaps in anticipation of a wider readership for the MVC, one that would include lay men, for whom St. Joseph served as ideal model. One of the early illuminated manuscripts of the *testo minore*, Notre Dame, Indiana, Snite Museum MS Acc. 85.25, clearly highlights the figure of Joseph in its visual language and is very likely to have been commissioned for use by a wealthy Bolognese layman; see Phillips, "*Meditations on the Life of Christ.*" As for the specific distance mentioned in this passage, the detail that the house of Saint Elizabeth was "da lonçi ben .lxxiiii. meglia" appears to derive from Peter Comestor's *Historia scholastica*, though perhaps not directly, as further calculations are needed to yield seventy-four miles: Peter Comestor states that this house was "quarto milliario a Jerusalem" (col. 1538B) without specifying the distance from Nazareth (Peter Comestor, *Historia scholastica*, col. 1538B).

16. **and the whole canticle of praise and joy was first uttered then.** The *Magnificat*, based on Luke 1:46–55, one of the most ancient and venerable of canticles, was sung during the Liturgy of the Hours.

17. **placed herself at the feet . . . conception.** The intimate and very human drama here, in which two women sit together and share details about their pregnancies (a rare instance of private girl talk about the experience of conception in medieval literature), is captured in an illustration in Paris, BN Ms. Ital. 115; see Ragusa and Green, *Meditations*, 23.

18. **whom Our Lady took up and lovingly wrapped in linens, as was fitting.** The detail that the Virgin lifted John from the earth at his birth is included in the *Legenda aurea* (Ryan, *Jacobus de Voragine* 1:200; 1:330) and the *Historia scholastica* (col. 1538B), both of which cite the *Book of the Just* as source. The motif of Mary assisting Elizabeth at the birth appears in visual images from the early Trecento, but many of the details in this chapter—including the way the infant turns his face towards Mary as she hands him to Elizabeth, generating a poignant, affective moment of narrative *contrapposto*—appear to be original to the MVC.

19. **and swaddled him and kissed him and held him in her arms!** I have emended the Italian *fassoe* to *bassoe* here. It is possible that *fassoe* (swaddled) was intended, forming a sort of dittology with *conçioe* (swaddled, dressed). But Mary kisses the child a few lines further on (*basavalo*); *bassoe* thus seems to make better sense.

20. **O mirror of poverty, have compassion and strive to love poverty!** This address to the reader is one of the chief indications that the work was originally intended for a Poor Clare. While poverty was a widespread ideal among various orders of female religious, as well as for *pinzochere* and laywomen who took no vows, the phrase "mirror of poverty" in this context appears to signify not just

an ideal but Clarissan identity. Clare of Assisi used the image. In her *Fourth Letter to Agnes of Prague*, Clare writes of Christ as the mirror into which Clare and her sisters should gaze in contemplation: "Look, I say, at the border of this mirror, that is, the poverty of Him Who was placed in a manger and wrapped in swaddling clothes. O marvelous humility! O astonishing poverty!" (Armstrong, *Clare of Assisi*, 56). Clare extends this imagery to the Poor Clares themselves; in her *Testament*, she writes that the sisters "whom the Lord has called to our way of life" are to be "a mirror and example to those living in the world" (Armstrong, *Clare of Assisi*, 61). On Clare's persistent efforts to build "a life of religious perfection with poverty at its core," see Roest, *Order and Disorder*, 287, and Catherine Mooney, *Clare of Assisi and the Thirteenth-Century Church*.

21. **Joseph, having noticed that she was pregnant, became perplexed . . . troubled in mind.** A version of the story of Joseph's doubts about Mary appears in the Gospel of Pseudo-Matthew; see Ehrman and Pleše, *The Other Gospels*, 48–49. The MVC author has enriched the emotional drama of the story by depicting the compassionate anguish of the Virgin when she sees Joseph's anguish. The humor latent in the episode was recognized by later dramatists, especially in England, where it was conflated with the standard fabliau plot; see the York version of "Joseph's Trouble About Mary" in Walker, *Medieval Drama*, 32–37. The MVC circulated widely in England in its Latin and Middle English forms and is likely to have served as source for this and other English versions of the play.

22. **with a truly chaste love.** On marriage without sexual relations as an ideal in the later Middle Ages, with Joseph and Mary as ideal exemplar, see Elliott, *Spiritual Marriage*.

23. **How Lord Jesus Christ was born into the world.** There are important differences between this rendering of the narrative of Christ's birth and the version in the *testo minore*. Here, the narrative is simpler and more lucid; it follows the gospel of Luke more closely; and more attention is paid to the shepherds than to the angels. In the *testo minore*, there is an additional passage that relates a vision "mostrate dalla Donna nostra, secondamente ch'io ebbi da uno santo frate del nostro Ordine" (Sarri, 30–31). This vision introduces two unusual elements: there is a column in the stall, against which the Virgin stands as she gives birth; and Joseph, feeling helpless, makes himself useful by supplying a saddlepack for the Virgin to rest against after the birth. Both are illustrated in the Paris manuscript (Ragusa and Green, *Meditations*, 33, 35). The detail of the column in the friar's vision corresponds to descriptions of the Cave of the Nativity at the Church of the Nativity in Bethlehem. The basilica erected there by Justinian in 585, and reconstructed in various stages, included columns built on the foundation of the cave said to be the site of Christ's birth. In his description of his visit to the Holy Land, 1346–50, the Franciscan Niccolò da Poggibonsi describes the Cave of the Nativity: "At the end of the manger is walled up a piece of a column against which the Virgin Mary leaned when she was delivered" (Bellorini and Hoade, *Niccolò da Poggibonsi*).

24. **And then they went to the shepherds.** Another significant difference between the *testo breve* and the *testo minore* occurs here. In the *testo minore*, the jubilation of the angels is drawn out at greater length, and the entire hierarchy of angels descends, rank by rank, to see and adore Christ and his mother, singing praises; the role of the shepherds, meanwhile, is confined to a single line in which their speaking part is eliminated: "Poi vennero li pastori e adoraro lo Fanciullo e redicevano quello ch'aveano udito dalli angeli" (Sarri, 34). This difference between the two texts, which has distinct ideological and aesthetic dimensions (the *testo breve* more concerned with humility, the *testo minore* more concerned with hierarchy), is, in my view, one of the chief indications that the *testo minore* is likely to be a revision of the *testo breve* by a different author. It is similar to the differences in depicting the humanity vs. the divinity of Christ, as remarked upon above, "Textual History," lxxvii–lxxix. The emergence of what Salter has aptly called "shepherd space" in the visual arts, literature, and drama of the later Middle Ages had the potential to challenge traditional hierarchies and aesthetics; see "The Annunciation to the Shepherds," in Salter, *English and International*, 272–92.

25. **Saint Bernard says that he wants you to know.** Bernard of Clairvaux, fifth sermon on the Nativity (Leclercq et al., *Sancti Bernardi Opera* 4:269). The author's citation style is interesting not only in its informality (chapter and verse are irrelevant to this author), but in the relationship it posits between Bernard and the reader, conjured here as a relationship of spiritual direction between familiars.

26. **Now you, too, go to the manger and kneel.** This is one of the most celebrated passages from the MVC. It exemplifies the signature style of the author of the *testo breve*, while encapsulating the affective designs of the text as a whole in its gentle invitation to the reader to enter into the drama of Christ's life as an intimate and feeling participant. The license to hold, touch, and feel the child, and the way tactility is recognized as a way to foster love and devotion, is taken for granted by Author A. The scene is preserved in the *testo minore*, but a cautionary note is inserted after the sentence aligning touch with love and devotion, before the reader hands the child back to his mother: "Tuttavia sia reverente e timoroso, imperò ch'elli è santo sopra tutti i santi. E poi lo rendi alla Madre sua" (Sarri, 35). This is part of a larger pattern evident in the differences between the two texts, one that suggests that the *testo breve* preceded the *testo minore* and that the author of the *testo minore* sought to insert reminders of Christ's divinity, to establish greater distance and awe between the reader and Christ, and to limit or suppress certain passages from the *testo breve* that emphasize touching or holding the body of Christ, including, especially, the Virgin's handling and kissing of the body after the Deposition; see n135 below.

27. **kiss the feet.** The earliest image of kissing the feet of the Christ child in Italian art appears to be Nicola Pisano's sculptural rendering of the Adoration of the Magi on the pulpit of the Cathedral in Siena, completed between 1266 and 1268. On the act of kissing the feet of a superior as an act of ritual submission, and more specifically on the development of this practice in relation to the Virgin and the

Christ child in devotional art of the late Duecento and early Trecento, see Cannon, "Duccio and Devotion to the Virgin's Foot." Cannon makes the intriguing observation that the foot of the Christ child (and that of his mother) is proffered for adoration by the beholder in many devotional images in Tuscany during this period, and devotees may actually have kissed these images, or imagined kissing them. In the MVC, then, the author's invitation to the reader to kiss the feet of the child is not, in itself, unprecedented; but it is worth noticing that the author appears to minimize the traditional ritual significance of the act, as a sign of abasement and submission to the greater power and authority of a superior, in favor of facilitating a simpler and more intimate gesture of affectionate love for a real human baby. As Bartal observes, the feet of the Christ child represented his humanity ("Repetition, Opposition, and Invention").

28. **Today is the birth of the King . . . today is a day to celebrate with great happiness and joy.** This passage, like the conclusion to Chapter 1, has the ring of a liturgical hymn or canticle, though I have not been able to trace a specific source.

29. **How Our Lord Jesus was circumcised.** The *testo breve* is the only text that contains this version of the circumcision. The *testo minore* and other versions depict the Virgin herself performing the rite, cutting her son's flesh with a small knife (Sarri, 36–38; cf. Taney et al., 30–31). As Flora has observed, the image of "women wielding knives" has typological resonances, linking Mary to Zipporah and Christ to Moses, and it may have held special if relatively obscure meaning for the Franciscans (Flora, *The Devout Belief of the Imagination*, 101–15). While the image of Mary cutting her son's flesh may have enriched the symbolic dimensions of the episode, it clearly does so at a cost to the momentum of the affective narrative: the *testo breve* maintains greater consistency of characterization and emotional tenor in its depiction of a mother who suffers to see her son in pain and does not, herself, inflict that pain. Interestingly, Nicholas Love's *Mirror*, the popular Middle English translation of the MVC, omits the image of the Virgin's committing of the deed—in effect, it would seem, restoring the more emotionally consistent and authentic reading of the *testo breve* (though Love could not have known of this version); see Sargent, *Nicholas Love*, 41–43.

30. **and according to what the apostle Saint Peter says.** The citation practices of the author of the *testo breve* suggest that this author did not have formal training in how to cite scripture. Here, for instance, the citation is not only loose, but technically incorrect. The preceding sentence, "there is no other exalted name under the heavens . . . name of Jesus" does indeed come from a speech by Peter in Acts 4:12, but it is the next passage ("this name Jesus gives sight to the blind . . . takes all power from the devil") that the author attributes to St. Peter, incorrectly. The author of the *testo minore* evidently noticed this and corrected the passage by attributing the first phrase to Peter and deleting the second. It is also possible that the author of the *testo breve* was working from a biblical gloss or from a canticle on the name of Jesus, rather than directly from the Bible. The *Glossa Ordinaria* is

used elsewhere by Author A, and may be the relevant source here; but the lack of a critical edition of the *Gloss Ordinaria*, which was itself so variable (see Smith, *The Glossa Ordinaria*), makes tracing this passage difficult. In any case, this is one of the small but telling differences between the *testo breve* and the *testo minore* that appears to indicate that the *testo breve* was taken up and revised by someone with formal training in citation practices and a more thorough knowledge of the Bible.

31. **And according to what I have heard from a friar who told me.** This is one of the few direct first-person statements by the author of the *testo breve*. If the author was indeed a Poor Clare, she would have had regular contact with Franciscan friars, since the friars were responsible for performing the offices and sacraments for the Poor Clares as well as providing spiritual direction. The friar mentioned here, who has clearly been to the Holy Land, appears to be the source for a few additional details about the Holy Land mentioned in later chapters, such as the passage in chapter 9: "I have learned, and it can be believed, that the well where Lord Jesus went to fetch water for his mother can still be seen" (chap. 9, f. 34v). The Franciscans established a "Province of the Holy Land" at the general chapter of 1217 and continued to maintain a presence at the Christian shrines there after the fall of Acre and the loss of Christian control of Palestine in 1291. Although pilgrimage was less frequent in the decades prior to the 1330s, Franciscans continued to travel between Italy and Jerusalem and to bring news of the holy sites to a populace eager to learn of the historical and geographical features of the Holy Land; see Morris, *The Sepulchre of Christ and the Medieval West*. Pilgrimage increased from the 1330s on, generating many written accounts; see Chareyon, *Pilgrims to Jerusalem in the Middle Ages*, and Bellorini and Hoade, *Niccolò da Poggibonsi*. Women religious, including the Franciscan tertiary Margaret of Cortona (1247–1297), were among those who developed the practice of "virtual pilgrimage" to the Holy Land; see "Margarita filia Ierusalem" in Papi, "*In castro poenitentiae*," 141–68; Cannon and Vauchez, *Margherita of Cortona and the Lorenzetti*; Rudy, *Virtual Pilgrimages in the Convent*; and Flora, *The Devout Belief of the Imagination*, 117–42.

32. **to disguise himself from the devil, so that the devil would not recognize him.** The motif of Christ's deception of the devil derives from writings of the early Christian fathers; see MacCullough, "The Deception of Satan," in *The Harrowing of Hell*, 199–216.

33. **And Lord Jesus accomplished many things on this feast day concerning the Church.** The *Legenda aurea* is the likely source for this passage, since the chapter on the Epiphany observes that each of these events occurred on the same day (Ryan, *Jacobus de Voragine* 2:78–84).

34. **the Church was betrothed and joined to Christ through baptism.** The custom of the bridal bath preceding a wedding appears to lie behind the development of the concept of Christ's baptism as betrothal to the Church (Vidal, "*The Infancy Narrative*," 267).

35. **And having presented this offering, they kissed his feet.** On the ritual act of kissing the feet, see n27 above.

36. **the Virgin Mary, as one who was zealous for poverty.** The particular phrasing here—*sì come çelatrice de povertade*—suggests the kind of zeal for poverty that marked the Poor Clares (see above, n20). Just as Christ is "Franciscanized" in various passages in this text (accepting alms, for instance, in this chapter), so too is the Virgin a model Clare.

37. **And Saint Bernard says that Joseph often took Lord Jesus in his arms and played with him.** Bernard of Clairvaux, *Sermones super Cantica Canticorum* 43 (Leclercq et al., *Sancti Bernardi Opera*, 2:44).

38. **Now you go with them too, and help to carry the infant Lord Jesus to his mother.** The reference here and elsewhere to carrying the infant Christ invites attention to the relationship between the devotional practices of imagining holding the child and that of literally holding holy dolls—effigies of the Christ child that were sometimes used in conjunction with cradles and other material trappings; see "Holy Dolls," in Klapisch-Zuber, *Women, Family and Ritual*; and Hale, *Imitatio Mariae* and "Rocking the Cradle."

39. **Now the old man held the infant, and the infant held the old man.** The verb used in the second half of this phrase, *reçea*, from *reggere*, to hold or keep from falling, has a metaphorical significance as well, signifying "to support" or "to guide." The *Legenda aurea* contains this image in a chapter on the Purification: "he, who upholds all things by the word of his power, on this day allowed himself to be carried in an old man's arms, although he upheld the one who carried him, as it is said: 'The old man carried the child, the child governed the old man'" (Ryan, *Jacobus de Voragine* 2:147). This line is also contained in the liturgy for the Presentation and is said to derive from a sermon by St. Augustine on the Nativity: "Simeon senex ferebat Christum infantem, Christus regebat Simeonis genectutem" (*Patrologia Latina* 39, col. 1998; qtd. in Gilbert, "Pisa Baptistry," 17). As Dianne Phillips has pointed out to me, there is a unique visual image of the scene in Nicola Pisano's pulpit at the baptistry in Pisa, which features two narrative moments from the Presentation; one of them depicts a man being held rather awkwardly by a child. Gilbert provides a detailed explication of this image as part of the complex programme of the baptistry in "Pisa Baptistry." Interestingly, the line occurs uniquely in the *testo breve*; it does not appear in the *testo minore* or other versions of the MVC. It is possible that the author of the *testo minore* removed it because, on its own, it makes little sense. The fact that Nicola Pisano's image was not copied, and that it perplexed many generations of art historians in the modern era, suggests that the notion of Christ "holding" Simeon may have been a stumbling block to medieval readers and beholders as well. The presence of the image in the *testo breve* may add some weight to the hypothesis that the author of the *testo breve* was from Pisa and was influenced in part by the Pisan pulpit.

40. **And then they went to perform the procession.** The *Legenda aurea*, which depicts a similar procession, explains that the Presentation and Purification are celebrated as the feast of Candlemas, in which the faithful form a procession bearing candles (Ryan, *Jacobus de Voraigne* 1:149).

41. **And as she held two turtledoves or pigeons.** This detail derives from Luke 2:24, "a pair of turtledoves, or two young pigeons" (par turturum, aut duos pullos columbarum). In the *Legenda aurea*, the following rather confusing explanation is given about the birds: "So, since Christ was of the tribe of Judah, one of the twelve tribes, he should be redeemed, and they offered for him to God a pair of turtledoves or two young pigeons, these being the offering of poor people: rich people offered a lamb. Scripture does not say 'young turtledoves' but 'young pigeons,' because young pigeons are always available while young turtledoves are scarce, though the mature doves can always be found. Nor are two pigeons called for, but two turtledoves, because the pigeon is a lascivious bird and therefore God did not want it offered to him in sacrifice: the dove, on the other hand, is a virtuous bird" (Ryan, *Jacobus de Voragine* 1:149).

42. **And it is said that they went through the desert where the sons of Israel had been.** This detail appears in the *Legenda aurea* and the *Historia scholastica*; see Ryan, *Jacobus de Voragine* 1:57; Peter Comestor, *Historia scholastica*, col. 1543B.

43. **Of those things that happened to them along the way, I will speak only of these.** The author's source for the episode of the date palm and of the spring appears to be the Gospel of Pseudo-Matthew (Ehrman and Pleše, *The Other Gospels*, 55). The chapters neighboring this episode in the Gospel of Pseudo-Matthew contain fantastical stories in which dragons, lions, and leopards worship Jesus and are joined by other beasts who demonstrate their allegiance by wagging their tails (54). These are presumably among the miracles that our author is omitting in the interest of brevity.

44. **And as soon as they entered Egypt, all the idols of Egypt broke apart.** This detail appears in the *Legenda aurea* (Ryan, *Jacobus de Voragine* 1:57) and in the *Historia scholastica* (Peter Comestor, *Historia scholastica*, col. 1543A). Both of these sources also mention the reference to Isaiah.

45. **a city called Onipoli, and they lived in a rented house there.** The detail that the city was called Hermopolis is mentioned in the *Legenda aurea* (Ryan, *Jacobus da Voragine* 1:57). That the family lived in a house they did not own, but rented, is in keeping with a Franciscan practice of *usus pauper*. At this point in the parallel chapter in the *testo minore*, additional information is specified: that the family remained in Egypt for seven years, a detail related in the *Legenda aurea* (Ryan *Jacobus de Voragine* 1:57) as well as Peter Comestor, *Historia scholastica,* col. 1549C; "E andaro a una città che si chiama Ermopoli, e accattaro una casetta a pegione, e quici stettero sette anni come peregrini avveneticci, come poveri e bisognosi" (Sarri, 51). Immediately following this phrase, the *testo minore* continues: "Ma qui si puote interponere una bella e pietosa e molto compassiva meditazione: ponci ben la mente tua. E donde e di che pensi che vivessero costoro cotanto tempo?" (Sarri, 51; cf. Taney et al., 44). A lengthy passage follows in the *testo minore* that turns into what seems very much like a sermon—one spun by an experi-

enced preacher—on the dangers of *superbia, cupidità, curiosità,* and *vanagloria* (Sarri, 51–57). In its language of interpolation ("si puote interponere"), preacherly style, and citation of a source never used by the author of the *testo breve* (the *Sermons* of Gregory the Great), this passage in the *testo minore* is part of a larger pattern of textual differences that appear to indicate that the *testo minore* is an expansion of the *testo breve* by a different, more learned author.

46. **Now when Herod had died, the angel appeared in a dream to Joseph ... "He shall be called a Nazarene."** Like many passages in the *testo breve*, these lines follow scripture very closely, so closely that the passage is in effect a simple translation of the relevant biblical verses (Mt 2:19–23). This is not true of the parallel passage in the *testo minore*, which includes the detail from the *Legenda aurea* and *Historia scholastica* that the family stayed in Egypt for seven years, omits the biblical prophecy "He shall be called a Nazarene," and adds the comment from the *Martyrologium Romanum* that the date of the return from Egypt was the second day of the Feast of the Epiphany (Sarri, 57–58; cf. Taney et al., 49). The fact that the *testo breve* often follows the gospels more closely, offering a straight translation (cf. chap. 18) appears to be another indication that it came first in the sequence and was subsequently revised by a different author. This pattern of difference may also suggest that the composition of the *testo breve* merits consideration in the context of Italian translations of the Bible in the early Trecento—and the concern among some learned authorities that such translations, including those by women, were potentially dangerous and could lead to heresy. On early Italian translations of the Bible, see L. Leonardi, *La Bibbia in italiano,* esp. the essays by Stefano Asperti, "I vangeli in volgare italiano," and Edoardo Barbieri, "Domenico Cavalca volgarizzatore." Iacopo Passavanti, in the 1330s, was one of the more prominent opponents of vernacular translation of the Bible, speaking out against the problem of the "ineptitude" of translators, among other risks (Barbieri, 311, 314). On Cavalca and his workshop in the context of biblical translation in the early fourteenth century, see Delcorno, "Cavalca, Domenico."

47. **follow him wherever he goes.** Revelations 14:4. This line is included in the rite of consecration of virgins (Metz, *La consécration des vierges,* 211). It is thus likely to have had special significance for Poor Clares betrothed to Christ as *sponsae Christi.*

48. **And so the Master of Poverty humbly stretched out his hand and meekly received their alms.** Christ's acceptance of alms, as Master of Poverty, is one of the more overt instances of the Franciscanization of Christ; see Little, "*Imitatio Francisci.*" Worth noticing here is the absence of tension around the act of accepting coins. This is among the features of the text that make it unlikely, in my view, that the MVC was, as Tóth and Falvay have recently suggested, authored by a leader of the Spiritual Franciscans (Tóth and Falvay, "New Light," 89–93). Although Tóth and Falvay imply in their article that my research on the MVC has gestured towards authorship by a Spiritual Franciscan ("New Light," 92), this is not

at all what I have stated or intended. Although poverty is indeed an important emphasis, as it would be for all Franciscans, I see no basis for attributing any version of the MVC to a Spiritual Franciscan; indeed, the absence of any overt polemic in the MVC would seem to stand as strong evidence that the Spirituals, whose writings are typically fiery and fierce, had no hand in it. On the Spirituals and debates about poverty among Franciscans in the early fourteenth century, see Burr, *The Spiritual Franciscans*.

49. **Now you go with them, and take the donkey by the halter. . . . be sure to hold the child Jesus so he doesn't fall.** As I have related elsewhere ("The Author of the Italian *Meditations on the Life of Christ*," 130–31; "Authorship," above), this passage has potential to illuminate both the textual history and authorship of the MVC. Here in the *testo breve*, the scene of Christ riding on the donkey has a consistency of narrative detail that is lacking in the other versions of the MVC. The child's age at the return from Egypt is never given in the *testo breve*, but the actions, dialogue, and gestures all appear to indicate that the child, in this version, is about two or three years old—able to talk, but still quite small. In particular, the meditation asks the meditator to carry the child, and to hand him back to his mother, who happily receives him in her arms ("fà che tu el pigli in braço et tienlo fin che la Madre vegna, et poi reverentemente il dà alla Madre, imperò che gran riposo era a lei quando la ricevea il figliolo in braço"). In the *testo minore* and other versions, the author stipulates that the child was seven years old—a detail that comes from learned sources, the *Historia scholastica* and the *Legenda aurea*, but that generates narrative incongruity in this context. The *testo breve*'s image of carrying the child and handing him back to his mother is retained, for instance, by the author of the *testo minore* ("ricevilo allegramente nelle braccie tue e tiello uno poco in collo," Sarri, 61), but it is difficult to square this action with the size of a seven-year-old child. This difference between the texts would seem to stand as evidence, then, that the version in the *testo minore* was composed at a secondary stage, and imperfectly integrated into the base narrative, by an author who also sought to highlight the potential typological significance of Christ riding on a donkey; in the *testo minore* and other versions of the MVC, Christ rides alone, without his mother, in a way that prefigures his entry into Jerusalem (Sarri, 61; Taney et al., 51).

50. **it is said that they encountered Saint John the Baptist, who had already gone to the desert to do penance.** There is no scriptural foundation for this scene, but the story of Christ and his mother encountering the child John doing penance in the desert was in circulation in various forms in the first half of the Trecento. As Marilyn Aronberg Lavin has observed in her studies of early visual images of the child John the Baptist as penitent, an anonymous Italian *vita* of John the Baptist (published by Manni, *Volgarizzamento delle vite*, 184–266) appears to have been in circulation in Tuscany in the first half of the fourteenth century, possibly as early as the first decade, though this date is speculative; it is based on a study of the structure of the language of the text by Leonardi Salviati (see esp. Lavin's "Gio-

vanni Battista: A Supplement," 321n12). Although this *vita* has often been attributed to Cavalca in scholarship since the eighteenth century, there is no foundation for this attribution; the work is not included in Delcorno's critical edition of Calvaca's *Vite*. Lavin initially suggested that the anonymous Italian *vita* served as source for the scene of the young Baptist in the wilderness on the doors by Andrea Pisano on the Florence Baptistry, commissioned ca. 1322 and completed in 1330, but her "Supplement" registers greater uncertainty about this. See Lavin, "Giovanni Battista: A Study," incl. figures 6, 7, and 9, and "Giovanni Battista: A Supplement."

51. **And then they heard that Archelaus . . . "He shall be called a Nazarene."** This passage repeats nearly verbatim the passage at the opening of the chapter. I have let it stand because the repetition may be authorial rather than a copyist's mistake.

52. **I have learned. . . that the well where Lord Jesus went to fetch water for his Mother can still be seen.** The Italian *ho inteso* can mean "I have heard," and it is possible that the author is conveying information about the Holy Land related in conversation, perhaps by the same friar who is mentioned elsewhere in the text (e.g., chap. 5) as the source of details about Christian sites in the Holy Land. Another possible source is Peter Comestor, *Historia scholastica*, col. 1550A Additio 1: "Dicitur ibi fons esse parvus, de quo puer Jesus hauriebat, et ministrabat matri, dum subditus erat ei." It may be significant for the question of textual history that the detail is introduced with a first-person statement of the author's experience: "Ho inteso." The *testo minore*, in contrast, introduces the detail with the phrase "it is said": "dicesi e puotesi credere che ancora si vede la fonte donde Jesù portava l'acqua alla madre" (Sarri, 62; cf. Taney et al., 52). The particular wording of the *testo breve*, then, suggests that the author of the *testo breve* learned of this detail and incorporated it into the episode, whereas the author of the *testo minore* found it already embedded in the chapter that he then revised; it would thus make little sense for the Author B to include the anecdote of personal experience, "I have learned." This is one of the microdifferences between the two texts that, in my view, adds cumulative force to the plausibility of the theory that the *testo breve* preceded the *testo minore*.

53. **And early in the morning she left the inn. . . . she went to Jerusalem.** Although we hear later that the Virgin was accompanied by Joseph during this search ("and your father: we have been searching for you"; 59), the narrative focuses solely on her agency and movements in this passage. This emphasis on the Virgin as actor distinguishes the *testo breve* from other versions of the MVC and is consistent with its more woman-centered narrative quality. In the *testo minore*, the verbs are pluralized to indicate that she is accompanied by Joseph throughout the search ("cercavano per lui intorno alla contrada," Sarri, 66; Taney et al., 54).

54. **"I want us to return home." . . . "I want what pleases you."** This scene offers a significant departure from the Gospel on which it is based (Lk 2:48–52). The gospel version gives no indication of Christ's readiness to leave his Father's

house and the new community of learned male scholars he has found in favor of returning to his mother's house and doing what pleases her.

55. **Now where do you think the Lord Jesus ate or slept those three days?** This is another instance of the Franciscanization of Christ; see Little, "*Imitatio Francisci.*"

56. **if one wishes to be close to God, it is necessary not to reside with relatives.** On the efforts of laywomen in late thirteenth- and early fourteenth-century Tuscany to create domestic spaces within their homes in order to attain a minimal sense of separation from relatives, see Lansing's study of Umiliana dei Cerchi's "cell" in *The Florentine Magnates*, 109–24; on forms of religious life for women more generally in this period, see Papi, "*In castro poenitentiae*," and Bornstein and Rusconi, *Women and Religion in Late Medieval Italy*. See Luke 14:26, Luke 18:29 and Matthew 19:29 for the scriptural foundations on which this injunction to leave family to follow Christ is based.

57. **he . . . remained subject to them.** That Christ remained "subject" to Mary and Joseph in Nazareth during this time has scriptural foundation (Lk 2:51), but the repeated emphasis on his subjection to his parents in the *testo breve* (chaps. 10–12) resonates in interesting ways with contemporary Italian social and legal practices. On the power of the male head of household, or *patria potestas*, see Julius Kirchner, "Family and Marriage"; and for the apparent assumption of this power by the Virgin in the *testo breve*, see n68, below. Christ's subjection to his earthly parents in the MVC also underscores his humility, which received special emphasis in Franciscan writings and images; see Şenocak, *The Poor and the Perfect*, and Cook, *Francis of Assisi: The Way of Poverty and Humility*.

58. **It is said that from this time on, Our Lord was never seen laughing.** I have not found a likely source for this detail, which is not scriptural. It is interesting that this line does not appear in the *testo minore* (Sarri, 68–69; cf. Taney et al., 56–57).

59. **And he withdrew from company. . . . acted as if he were worthless to teach you the way to heaven.** Much of this chapter appears to be the author's invention; it is offered unselfconsciously, without concern about the lack of scriptural or other authoritative foundation. The author of the *testo minore*, however, expresses concern at this point, and refers to his earlier justification, in the Prologue, for imagining scenes from the life of Christ: "Tuttavia quelle cose ch'io ti dico, le quale per autorità della santa Scrittura o di santi dottori non si possono provare, pigliali in quel modo ch'io ti dissi di sopra" (Sarri, 69; cf. Taney et al., 56).

60. **definitely *pane perduto.*** The phrase in the Italian presents a challenge to translation. *Pane perduto*—literally, "wasted bread"—has two distinct meanings: stale or day-old bread, or a person on whom the nutritive value of bread is lost because the one consuming it does nothing productive (see Battaglia, *Grande dizionario, pane*, s.m., *pane perduto*, and the related *panepèrso*). Either option conveys the sense of a useless or inept person, a slacker. I have chosen to retain the Ital-

ian here in order to avoid flattening out the colorful, colloquial quality of the phrase and the images associated with it. The Latin version's "Iste est quidam inutilis" (Taney et al., 65) is a less vivid phrase lacking a concrete image. This is among the small differences that suggest to me that the Latin is likely to be a translation from the Italian. The other term of reproach in this sentence, *idiota*, could mean simply lacking formal education and Latin learning, though it is clearly infused with derision in this context. St. Francis and his early companions embraced the designation *idiota* as an ideal consonant with humility; see Şenocak, *The Poor and the Perfect*.

61. **"I am a worm, and not a man."** Psalm 21:7.

62. **and as Solomon says.** Proverbs 16:32.

63. **and the apostle revealed this plainly.** Galatians 6:3.

64. **But if you ask me why . . . I will reply that. . . .** The phrasing here resonates with a formula used in romances circulating in Italy in the early Trecento, "and if someone were to ask me. . . I would tell them. . ." A passage in the *Tristiano Riccardiano*, for example, reads, "If anyone were to ask me what the palace was called, I will say that it is called the manor of the Wise Damsel" (Psaki, *Italian Literature*, 181). M. J. Heijkant observes that in the Tristan texts this formula "reinforces the complicity between storyteller and audience in typical *jongleur* fashion" ("From France to Italy," 49). The presence of the formula in the *testo breve* may testify to its author's familiarity with romance, or it may be a more general indication of the *testo breve*'s proximity to oral tradition. This phrase is not present in the *testo minore* or other versions of the MVC.

65. **And according to what Saint Bernard says, "Whoever wants the virtue of humility should perform humble deeds, just as whoever wants peace needs to be patient, and whoever desires wisdom needs to study first."** Bernard of Clairvaux, *Epistula* 87 (Leclercq et al., *Sancti Bernardi Opera* 7:230).

66. **Imagine now this family, blessed over all others . . . lived with his mother.** To work and to pray—or indeed to conceive of work as a form of prayer (*laborare est orare*)—is the ideal of monastic life, here extended to a Franciscan-inspired family. On the Holy Family as exemplary image in the later Middle Ages, see Newman, "Intimate Pieties"; Herlihy, *Women, Family and Society*; and Klapisch-Zuber, *Women, Family, and Ritual*, 326–29.

67. **And Lord Jesus Christ rose sometimes and went to the synagogue.** This is one of several expressions of interest in Christ's Jewishness in the *testo breve*. Peter Comestor was influential in awakening interest in Jewish history and customs; the *Historia scholastica*, however, is not the direct source for this particular detail. On the *Historia scholastica*'s influence, see Morey, "Peter Comestor."

68. **And having been granted leave by his mother.** The parallel phrase to the *testo breve*'s "licenciato dalla Madre" in the *testo minore* is "licenziato da lei e da Josep" (Sarri, 67; cf. Taney et al., 62). This is one of the many passages in which Joseph does not appear in the *testo breve* but is present in the *testo minore* and other versions of the MVC. The term *licenciato* in this context is ambiguous.

The gesture could refer simply to courtesy or good manners. But it could mean that Christ is given permission to go by his mother in a way that registers her parental authority. The passage is thus worth considering in the context of parental authority in fourteenth-century Tuscany, and even potentially as a substitution of maternal for paternal power, given the widespread currency of the *patria potestas* in fourteenth-century Italian communes. Kirchner observes that wives and widows were "absolutely denied the capacity to wield paternal power. Lacking *patria potestas*, they could not adopt, legitimate, or emancipate children, share the husband's authority over the children," or exercise authority in a wide range of capacities with legal significance ("Family and Marriage," 88). In any case, it would appear that the author of the *testo minore* perceived the Virgin as possessing too much authority in this scene—and added Joseph to temper that authority and align it with more familiar familial protocols of power (perhaps as part of an effort to adapt the text for an audience that would include lay men).

69. **Now where are the barons and knights and counts and marquises?** The *ubi sunt* motif that structures this passage has a distant parallel in Jacopone da Todi's *De Contemptu Mundi*: "dic, ubi Salomon, olim tam nobilis / vel ubi Samson est, dux invicibilis," etc. (Raby, *A History of Christian Latin Poetry*, 434–36). The inversion here, which turns on the voluntary relinquishing of riches and status, appears to have been given a subtle Franciscan cast through the image of Christ walking to the Jordan "cum li piedi descalçi." Christ is typically depicted barefoot in visual images of the period, of course, so this could be simply a matter-of-fact detail; but there was a contemporary debate between the Franciscans and Dominicans regarding footwear in the early fourteenth century, one that hinged on whether the Dominicans could be deemed legitimately "apostolic" if they wore sandals. For a summary of the debate, in which the English Dominican Thomas Sutton defended the wearing of sandals in part by adducing the relic of Christ's sandals displayed at St. John Lateran in Rome, see Jotischky, *The Carmelites and their Pasts*, 71.

70. **I think that he went begging alms from door to door. . . . love of poverty.** The author's "I think" in the *testo breve* is absent in the *testo minore*, which has the reading, "Va dunque Messer Jesù Cristo continuando le giornate sue e cheggiendo lemosina per la via per l'amore della povertà" (Sarri, 78; cf. Taney et al., 63). This textual comparison appears to support the hypothesis that the *testo breve* preceded the *testo minore*. It is easy to see why a redactor might wish to suppress the phrase, as it did not record his own thought process; moreover, it makes visible a broader pattern in which many "I" statements in the *testo breve* appear to have been eliminated in the *testo minore* (cf. n52 above), a pattern that supports the hypothesis that the two texts were the work of different authors. As for the actual scene of begging: although all of the mendicant orders begged for their sustenance, the explanation that Christ did this "for love of poverty" ("per amore della povertade") appears to mark such devotion as Franciscan; this love was famously allegorized by Francis in his love of Lady Poverty.

71. **he married himself to the universal Church.** See n35 above.

72. **went straight from the baptism to the desert.** Here the *testo minore* has the reading, "Incontanente che Cristo fue battezzato, se n'andò nel diserto sopra uno monte, lo quale era ivi presso a quattro miglia o in quello torno, che si chiama Quarentana" (Sarri, 80; cf. Taney et al., 73). The additional details in the *testo minore* come from Peter Comestor, *Historia scholastica* (col. 1556D Additio 1). This small difference between the two texts is among the microdifferences that suggest that the *testo breve* came first in the sequence of composition. Subjective interpretation needs to be brought to bear here, of course, but in my view, it is easy to see how a reviser would wish to add an informative gloss from Peter Comestor; it is more difficult to conceive of a motive for the alternative possibility, i.e., that these details may be absent in the *testo breve* because the author removed them. Details such as the name of the mountain and the distance of the journey are not offensive details; they do not take up much space; they do not appear to detract from the work's affective appeal; and the author of the *testo breve* elsewhere displays a keen interest in knowing facts about the Holy Land. In my view, it is thus unlikely that the line would have been deliberately deleted because it was deemed irrelevant or uninteresting. Moreover, this kind of difference between the two texts is evident elsewhere; the presence of additional place names and distances in the *testo minore* and the absence of these at the same sites in the *testo breve* is a systematic difference (cf. "detto monte di Quarentana, a due miglia," Sarri, 83). It would seem logical to deduce, then, that the *testo breve* came first and the *testo minore* is a revised version in which additional details were inserted by an author familiar with the practice of glossing texts and with greater knowledge of and access to a wider range of textual resources.

73. **following the example of your sweet spouse Lord Jesus Christ.** This reference to Christ as "tuo dolce sposo miser Iesù Cristo" is not present in the *testo minore* or other versions of the MVC (Sarri, 81; cf. Taney et al., 73). In this context, the phrase appears to refer to the social status of the original reader, since Poor Clares were betrothed to Christ as *sponsae Christi*. It could be that Author B omitted the phrase because he was envisioning a broader readership for the *testo minore*, one that included not only Poor Clares, but lay people, including lay men.

74. **Learn to be sweet when you engage with those around you.** The Italian *conversatione* has a broader meaning than English "conversation"; it incorporates a more general sense of interacting with others, often in settings of close familiarity, via gestures and actions and attitude as well as through speech (L. Leonardi et al., *Tesoro della Lingua Italiana delle Origini, conversazione* [1], s.f.).

75. **And the devil, realizing that he was hungry, and wishing to know if he was the Son of God, brought him an armful of rocks.** The *testo breve*'s depiction of the devil is more concrete and dramatic than that in the *testo minore*. Here, the devil is called simply "il dimonio," not "lo tentatore, cioè lo diavolo" (Sarri, 82; cf. Taney et al., 75), and he is imagined as having "il seno pieno di pietre," a striking image, which the *testo minore* omits. Visual images of the scene

seem to be rare, but the depiction of the Temptation in a twelfth-century mosaic in San Marco, Venice, includes a scene in which the devil carries the rocks in a bundle against his breast. (I wish to thank Dianne Phillips for pointing this image out to me.) One might ask whether the reference to the devil with the rocks was added by the scribe of the Canonici manuscript. This is possible. The image, however, did have circulation in other contexts in Europe. See, for example, the rendering of the Temptation of Christ in a stained glass window made ca. 1170–80 in Champagne-Ardennes, France, now held at the Victoria and Albert Museum; or the window depicting the Temptation at the Sainte Chapelle, Paris.

76. **And there he tempted him with vainglory . . . harrassed by that beast!** The *testo breve*'s energetic dramatization of the devil in this scene, and of the devils and the dramatic action of the Harrowing of Hell (see chap. 28), merit further investigation in relation to early drama, including convent drama; the devil is of course a very vividly realized figure in the plays of Hrotsvith of Gandersheim and in Hildegard of Bingen's *Ordo Virtutum*. This particular passage in the *testo breve* is clearly superior, as dramatization, to the parallel passages in the *testo minore* and other versions of the MVC. Here, there is vivid direct dialogue between the devil and Christ—dialogue taken in part from the gospels ("Get away, Satan!"), but including a comic retort by Christ as well: "Se io posso andare çò per la scala, perché mi debo io butare çoso?" The version in the *testo minore*, in contrast, lacks direct dialogue altogether; it presents a brief, flat summary of the episode instead: "E puoselo in sul tempio, nel più alto luogo che vi fosse e quivi lo tentò di vanagloria. E anche ora è vinto come prima, e defraudato della sua intenzione" (Sarri, 83; cf. Taney et al., 76).

77. **Saint Bernard says that . . . the devil believed he was pure man.** Bernard of Clairvaux, *Sermones* (Leclercq et al., *Sancti Bernardi Opera* 5:88).

78. **Saint Bernard says that nothing specific is written about the fourth time.** Bernard of Clairvaux, De Psalmo "Qui Habitat" 14, 4 (Leclercq et al., *Sancti Bernardi Opera* 4:471).

79. **And the apostle says . . . without sin.** Hebrews 4:15.

80. **But if you ask me what kind of food the angels served him . . . we may imagine this as we please.** In the *testo breve*, the author imagines the reader asking this question ("se tu me a dimandi di che vivanda li angeli lo servisse"). This way of phrasing the matter is similar to the formula used in contemporary romances, as indicated above (n64). The phrase also conveys a sense of the text as a response to an ongoing conversation between author and reader and mutual curiosity about the life of Christ—in this case, about something of such ordinary, human interest as what Christ ate. In the *testo minore*, the parallel phrase is one in which the author alone speculates on this question: "E addomando in prima di che gli angeli li servivano" (Sarri, 84; cf. Taney et al., 76). As for the phrase, "we may imagine this as we please," and the ensuing scene: this has been recognized as one of the most charming and imaginative episodes in the MVC, and it appears to have

no precedent. For illustrations, in which the angels carry the food wrapped in a cloth, as well as a pitcher of wine, and return the dishes to Joseph to be washed, see Ragusa and Green, *Meditations*, 124–27.

81. **food prepared as it was for the prophet Daniel.** Daniel 14:33–38.

82. **"Give my greetings to my most sweet son."** Here too, the *testo breve*'s version is more dramatic, as it includes direct speech; in the *testo minore*, in contrast, the Virgin is pleased ("tutta rallegrata del Figliulo," Sarri, 86), but silent. In the Latin, even her emotional response to the news of her son's request is not present (Taney et al., 77). This is part of a larger pattern in which the Virgin's words and feelings are more prominent in the *testo breve* than in other versions of the MVC. "Give my greetings" is an imperfect translation; English cannot capture the specific flavor of Italian salutation formulas, but here the sense is similar to "entrust me to my most sweet son."

83. **Now up to this point, by the grace of God. . . . And we will begin with Palm Sunday.** This transition provides a graceful bridge to the chapters on the Passion. On the central importance of this passage for determining the sequence in which the various versions of the MVC were composed, see above "Textual History," xlvi–li; lxvi.

84. **carry always the words and deeds of our sweet spouse Lord Jesus in our hearts.** This passage has significant implications for understanding the origins of the MVC. In particular, it appears to present indirect evidence that the author of the *testo breve*, who speaks of Christ as "nostro dolce spoxo miser Iesù," may have been a nun. See above, "Authorship," cii–cvii, for a discussion of this phrase. The phrase is absent in the *testo minore*. As I have suggested (see "Authorship," above), the most reasonable explanation for its absence in the *testo minore* would seem to be that it was suppressed at a secondary stage by the author of the *testo minore*, who was not a nun but a friar, and therefore not socially and legally bound to Christ in a relationship of marriage, as nuns were; the phrase, therefore, which is implicitly self-descriptive, would not have applied to him, and it would have been odd to preserve it.

85. **when he was in Bethany.** Bethany, located on the east side of Jerusalem on the Mount of Olives, is mentioned in the Gospels as the place where Martha, Mary, and Lazarus lived (John 12:1). It is also the location of the house of Simon the leper, where Christ first encountered the woman who anointed his feet (Mt 26:6). John's Gospel identifies this woman as Mary, sister of Lazarus (11:1), and later tradition identifies her further as Mary Magdalene. On Magdalene and the development of her cult, especially in the later Middle Ages, see Jansen, *The Making of the Magdalen*.

86. **a female donkey tethered with her young colt.** The Gospels (Mk 11 and Lk 19) mention only a colt, not a colt with its mother. The *Historia scholastica* appears to be the source for the introduction of a female donkey with her colt—both, it is implied, unsuitable beasts for riding and kept for the use of the poor

(Peter Comestor, *Historia scholastic,* col. 1598). In the *testo breve*, it is clear that the disciples put their cloaks on the female donkey (*asinela*), and that Christ rides on her; this makes his entry into Jerusalem a very humble entry. In other versions, the humiliation implied here is mitigated. In the *testo minore*, the disciples put their vestments on both the mother and the male colt (*poltruccio*), and it is not clear which one Christ rides ("i discepoli puosero le vestimenta loro in su queste bestie. E poi Messer Jesù vi salì suso," Sarri, 285). In the Latin text, the author has Christ ride on one, then the other: "When this was done the Lord Jesus first humbly mounted the she-ass and a little later the colt, on which the disciples draped their clothing" (Taney et al., 223).

87. **"Master, I want to ask you a favor, and I beg you not to deny it."** On the topos of the "dialogue on Holy Wednesday" as a framework used to present scholastic arguments for the necessity of Christ's death, see Tóth, "Pseudo-Apocryphal Dialogue." For an argument that this episode from the MVC is quoted by the Augustinian Michael of Massa, and that Massa's sermons may in turn shed light on the authorship of the MVC, see Tóth and Falvay, "New Light." Note, however, that while Tóth and Falvay assert that Michael of Massa's sermons incorporate "quotations" from this chapter of the MVC, they produce no evidence of direct citation; the parallels are loose and inexact. It is possible, then, that an independent source lies behind Michael of Massa's sermons and the MVC.

88. **Oh, what a union is theirs!** It is difficult to capture in English the meaning of the medieval Italian *compagnia*; for a range of meanings, which include a strong sense of *rapporto* between people, see L. Leonardi et al., *Tesoro della Lingua Italiana delle Origini, compagnia,* s.f. Because the term often implies a large group or association, this sense hovers around the exclamation here. That just two people make up this particular *compagnia* gives the term an interesting twist: the intimate bond between Christ and his mother, and the conversation between them, makes them a rare society unto themselves.

89. **Now if you had seen the mother, and Magdalene too, weep with great sighs, perhaps you would not hold back from weeping with them.** At this moment, the *testo minore* characterizes the weeping differently, depicting the Virgin weeping "modestly and softly" and giving more dramatic lamentation to Magdalene: "Or se tu vedessi infra queste parole piagnere la Madre modestamente e pianamente, e vedessi la Maddalena, come ebbra del maestro suo, piangere fortemente e con grandi singhiozzi, forse che tu non ti potresti ritenere di piagnere con esso loro" (Sarri, 289; cf. Taney et al., 227).

90. **let's go with him to Jerusalem, to our house.** This second home of Magdalene and her female companions has no scriptural basis.

91. **When the days of the feast of unleavened bread approached.** In this passage on the preparation of the meal, the *testo breve* contains direct dialogue and dramatic action that follow the gospel very closely (Mk 14:12–16); these are not present in the *testo minore* (Sarri, 291; cf. Taney et al., 228). This is part of a more

general pattern in which the *testo breve* gives close translations from scripture which do not appear in the other versions of the MVC; see n98 below.

92. **the seventy-two disciples, who had come there to serve Lord Jesus and his disciples.** The seventy-two disciples are mentioned in Luke 10:1–24. It is not clear what the author's source was for this comment that disciples from among this group of the seventy-two helped to prepare the Last Supper. In the *testo minore*, an additional source, with more specific details, is introduced at this point: "E ho trovato nella leggenda di santo Marziale, che egli con alquanti di lxxii discepoli fuoro in quella sera a servire a Cristo, quando elli lavava li piedi delli apostoli. E apparecchiato che fu ogni cosa per la cena, santo Joanni prezioso, il quale sollicitamente andava e tornava a vedere e aiutare apparecchiare, venne a Jesù e disse: Messere, voi potete oggimai cenare quando vi piace, imperò che ogni cosa è apparechiato" (Sarri, 291; cf. Taney et al., 228).

93. **And this table, or rather board, was square in shape, and made of several pieces; and I have seen it in Rome, in the church of Saint John Lateran, and I took its measure, and each side is the length of one arm and one palm and three fingers; so it could seat three per side.** Fragments from what is said to be the table used at the Last Supper were enshrined above the Altar of the Holy Sacrament at Saint John Lateran in the Middle Ages. On the author's interest in this relic, the impulse to measure it in order to recreate the most plausible seating arrangement at the Last Supper, and the possibility that the occasion for the author's visit to Rome may have been the Jubilee year of 1300, see "Authorship," above, cxiv–cxvi. The speculation that the table was square is distinctive. I have found no parallels in other texts or images from the Trecento; typically the table's shape is long and rectangular or shaped like a horseshoe. In suggesting that the apostles and Christ could sit three per side, with Christ sitting at one of the corners, the author locates Christ at the humblest place while also manifesting a less hierarchical mentality than is typically evident in Last Supper scenes. This description may register a "gendered perception," of the kind described by Hiller; see her *Gendered Perceptions*. Author A's interest in Jewish customs is evident in the comment that "it should be known that this table was placed on the floor, according to the custom of the ancients, who sat on the floor."

94. **And then the Passover lamb was brought out.** This is another textual moment where the priority of the *testo breve* in the sequence of composition appears to be evident. The *testo minore* reads, "Fue dunque recato l'agnello pasquale, e colui ch'è vero e immaculato Agnello, cioè Cristo benedetto, il qualle stava in mezzo di loro, sì come persona che serviva, sì 'l tolse e dividelo" (Sarri, 293; cf. Taney et al., 230). In my view, it is easy to see why a reviser would wish to insert Christ's allegorical title *immaculato Agnello* into the scene at this moment when the literal lamb is brought out. If we consider the alternative, positing for the sake of argument that the *testo breve* could be a revision and condensation of the *testo minore*, it is not easy to identify a reason for the excision of the image of Christ as

Lamb. The phrase takes up minimal space, and it is not offensive or irrelevant. In-deed, the deliberate removal of the phrase seems to me to be implausible; it is a re-minder of Christ's divine nature, and its excision would be a risky, irreverent move. Moreover, as I have noted elsewhere, this type of textual difference between the *testo breve* and the *testo minore* is systematic: reminders of Christ's divinity appear more frequently in the *testo minore*. See above,"Textual History," lxxvii–lxxix, for further comment.

95. **according to what Saint Augustine says, if Peter had known, he would have torn him apart with his teeth.** This detail appears in the *Legenda aurea*; see Ryan, *Jacobus de Voragine* 2:340.

96. **Thus one reads of Saint Francis that he did not disclose secret revela-tions.** Bonaventure, *Legenda maior*, 603.

97. **to another room . . . according to those who have seen it.** This detail may have been orally communicated by the friar who has been to the Holy Land (see above, n31), and this may be the most likely source given the wording of the phrase ("according to those who have seen it"). The house on Mount Sion said to be the place where the Last Supper was celebrated in the upper room, the cenacle, was a site of particular interest to Franciscans, to whom it was officially granted in 1333 (Morris, *The Sepulchre of Christ and the Medieval West*, 303); it became the locus of the Franciscan "custody of the Holy Land" thereafter. Burchard of Mount Sion, a Dominican who lived in the Holy Land from about 1275 to 1285, gives de-tailed descriptions of the cenacle and other sites in Jerusalem and emphasizes that he only records what he has "seen with his own eyes," an emphasis present in the *testo breve* (Morris, *The Sepulchre of Christ and the Medieval West*, 275). In the *Historia scholastica*, the detail that the dining room, the *coenacula*, was above another room, the *cubicula*, is mentioned (Peter Comestor, *Historia scholas-tica*, col. 1615B).

98. **Of the beautiful sermon that Lord Jesus Christ gave to his disciples after communion, and the departure of Judas.** This chapter is essentially a close translation of passages selected from John 13:31–17:23, without imaginative elabo-rations or commentary by the author. Its genre as a *bel sermone* is emphasized. The parallel section in the *testo minore* is very different: the sequence and flow of the scriptural base is broken up; there are only a few direct citations from scripture; and the voice and style of the medieval preacher take over, along with the orderly structure found in many medieval sermons: "Del quale cinque cose principalmente ne sono da pensare. La prima . . . La seconda . . . La terza cosa," etc. (Sarri, 297–98; cf. Taney et al., 233–34). This difference between the two texts is another impor-tant site for evaluating the sequence in which the *testo breve* and *testo minore* were composed, as well as the divergent aims of the authors of the two texts. The *testo breve*'s version assumes that the act of translating directly from scripture need not be rationalized or explained; and in literary terms, it is as if the author recognized that the beauty and poignancy of this particular stretch from the Gospel of John, re-

lated directly in the voice of Christ, could not be improved upon as dramatic material for affective meditation. The author of the *testo minore* appears to have had different aims and concerns. The most likely explanation for the difference between the two texts, in my view, is that the author of the *testo minore* may have been concerned about the practice of translating scripture into the vernacular, given the dangers, as many saw it, that unmediated access to the scriptures could lead to error and heresy; he therefore substituted his own sermon for Christ's. See "Authorship," above, cix–cx, for further comment on efforts to curtail and control what was apparently a burgeoning practice of scriptural *volgarizzamento* by laypeople and women—one condemned in no uncertain terms by Giordano of Pisa, among others. On biblical translation in the period more generally, see L. Leonardi, *La Bibbia in italiano*, and esp. Asperti, "I Vangeli in volgare italiano." As the essays in Leonardi's volume indicate, objections to biblical translation were not universal in the later Middle Ages; moreover, such objections appear to have been made in the context of large-scale translations rather than individual passages. The issue is complex; the question of the *testo breve*'s translations from the Bible thus merit further attention.

99. **as if to say, this humanity was your food and comfort.** The meaning of this phrase is not immediately obvious; it has the ring of an allusion, but I have not been able to trace it.

100. **They all strove to draw near him, like chicks do around the hen when they are afraid of some bird of prey. Like this the disciples gathered around Lord Jesus, because they did not know where he was going.** This is one of the most interesting lines in the *testo breve*, and potentially one of the most telling regarding the textual history and authorship of the MVC. The line is unique to the *testo breve*. Christ refers to himself in the gospels as a mother hen wishing to protect her chickens under her wings (Mt 23:37, Lk 13:34); the author of the *testo breve* has developed this image of maternal comfort and protection further by placing it at a point in the emotional arc of the narrative where it makes good sense, at a moment of heightened suspense and anxiety. The parallel passage in the *testo minore*, in contrast, lacks the element of protective comfort. It reads, "Vedi ora i discepoli come li vanno dietro ragunati insieme; e chi più puote più li s'appressa, come fanno i pulcini dietro alla gallina, incalciandolo ora l'uno ora l'altro, per lo desiderio ch'hanno d'accostarlisi e d'udire le sue parole. E come elli volentieri sosteneva questa ingiuria da loro" (Sarri, 300; cf. Taney et al., 235). The *testo minore*'s use of the image imbues the chicks with a higher degree of intellectual curiosity, but at the cost of affect logic and momentum. The chickens have become competitive—like eager young scholars trying to catch the words from the lips of the master, and annoying him in the process; for in the *testo minore*, Christ is cast as "putting up with" the way they are crowding around him, a crowding that he perceives as "ingiuria." In effect, the *testo minore* not only suppresses the element of affective poignancy but the maternal image itself, displacing it with an image of

Christ as teacher whose words are more important than his comforting physical presence. This is consistent with other indications that the *testo minore* is likely to be the work of a redactor who sought, among other things, to enhance the image of Christ as teacher or preacher.

101. **And here Saint Jerome says . . . contrary to the opinion of many heretics.** The details that Christ's suffering showed his humanity, contrary to the opinion of heretics, and that he grieved for Judas, the Jews, and Jerusalem, appear in St. Jerome's *Commentary on Matthew* (Scheck, *St. Jerome*, 300). It is not necessarily the case, however, that the author drew directly on this *Commentary*. Given the absorption of parts of Jerome's *Commentary* into the *Glossa Ordinaria*, it is possible, perhaps more likely, that the latter was the author's direct source.

102. **he grieved also for his desolate companions.** I have offered the term "companions" here, and elsewhere, for the Italian *fameglia* ("per la desolata fameglia," f. 69v), but the Italian often carries the specific inflections of a more closely defined group: members of a family and household, including servants, who live together. "Familiars" is a closer cognate in English, but a bit too dated to use here. See L. Leonardi et al., *Tesoro della Lingua Italiana delle Origini, famiglia,* s.f., for fourteenth-century uses of the term. It is interesting that Christ suffers here in the MVC at the thought of his *fameglia* being desolate; he suffers because he knows they will suffer when they are bereft of his presence. In Jerome's *Commentary on Matthew*, Christ suffers because he will be abandoned by his apostles—i.e., from self-pity, on account of the "falling away of all the apostles, who were scandalized" (Scheck, *St. Jerome*, 300). It is not clear that this shift was the invention of the author of the *testo breve*, but the difference itself is worth noting.

103. **And wise commentators also say that Lord Jesus prayed to the Father more out of compassion for the Jewish people than from his own fear.** Peter Comestor, *Historia scholastica*, col. 1621. Jeremy Cohen, in *The Friars and the Jews*, argues that the Dominicans and Franciscans were key sources of oppression against the Jews in the thirteenth and fourteenth centuries, but this view has remained controversial; see also Synan, *The Pope and the Jews*.

104. **And while he was in such agony and anguish, the angel Michael came and comforted him.** An angel is mentioned as comforting Christ in Gethsemane (Lk 22:43), but he is not named as Michael. It is not clear what the author's source was for this exchange with Michael, but among Michael's attributes was that of comforter of the sick, especially at the hour of death. On the role of angels generally as intermediaries with God—beings who "present our prayers before God" and "plead our cause for us"—see the description in "Saint Michael, Archangel" in the *Legenda Aurea* (Ryan, *Jacobus de Voragine* 2:210).

105. **And it should be known that in Christ Jesus there were four kinds of will.** I have not been able to trace the author's direct source for the four kinds of will in Christ, but it is interesting to observe that the author presents a theory of the will that begins by recognizing the "will of the flesh" and the "will of the emotions"

and seeing both fully embodied in Christ. Aquinas, in contrast, identifies just two kinds of will in Christ, the will of reason and the will of divinity (Aquinas, *Summa theologiae* III, 9, 19, a, 6).

106. **And they all fell to the ground; and they did so three times.** John's Gospel includes this incident in which those who arrested Jesus fell to the ground on hearing "I am he" (Jn 18:6). This detail is not present in the *testo minore*, which does not follow the Gospel account as closely as the *testo breve*.

107. **And then all of the disciples fled, and left Lord Jesus, the most innocent lamb, among those wolves and greedy dogs.** The stark juxtaposition of opposites here—*agnelo innocentissimo / lupi et cani affamati*—is a characteristic rhetorical move in late-medieval Passion narratives, and one with far-reaching consequences. See Bestul's perceptive treatment of the "hidden alliances" between images that elicit compassion for Christ and the creation of more virulent forms of anti-Jewish sentiment in the later Middle Ages (Bestul, *Texts of the Passion*, 69–110), and for a broader historical treatment of such rhetoric, see Nirenberg, *Anti-Judaism*.

108. **Annas, who was the father-in-law of Caiphas.** Peter Comestor, *Historia scholastica,* appears to have been the source for this and many other details signalling an interest in the historical facts and figures from the Bible; Josephus, in turn, lies behind much of what Peter Comestor offers.

109. **And as Peter was in the hall below, warming himself, a serving woman of the high priest came.** Given the potential for poignancy and pathos in the story of Peter's denial of Christ, it is striking that the entire episode of Peter's denial is not present in the *testo minore* and other versions of the MVC. The story, including the affective drama inherent in the dialogue between Peter and the servants, is preserved fully here in the *testo breve*, and the author ends the story with an additional detail, rich in affective power, on the merciful gaze of God.

110. **And here a saint says that the gaze of Our Lord is as good as a pardon.** I have not been able to trace this source. The vague quality of this allusion is consistent with the author's more general practice of referring to sources very loosely, which may itself be an indication that the author did not have training in the standard citation practices of an educated Franciscan of the fourteenth century; see "Authorship," above, for further comment on citation practices and their potential value for the question of determining the authorship of the *testo breve*.

111. **And having prayed, she left the house. . . . Oh how bitter was this moment as they set forth!** This dramatic moment, in which Mary and her companions leave the house, is not present in the *testo minore*; there, Mary simply remains in prayer (Sarri, 314). In literary terms, this unique reading in the *testo breve* would seem to be the better reading. It is a simple but poignant moment of dramatic action, one that heightens the narrative suspense at the end of the chapter. The term *partimento*—departure from a place—underscores this narrative moment as a liminal moment, as Mary and her companions cross the *limen* or threshold, leaving the security and comfort of Magdalene's house to enter into the painful

unknown. But the term may also carry a more specific historical and ritual resonance applicable to women's lives, since *partimento* can also refer to the moment when a woman leaves the family home to be married (Battaglia, *Grande dizionario, partimento*, s. m.). Whether or not a suggestion of that sense of leaving the security of the home is embedded in the term *partimento* in this instance, this is clearly a moment of great uncertainty and heightened vulnerability for the women, and in this sense it is part of the larger pattern in the *testo breve* in which women's actions, perspectives, and emotions receive more astute narrative treatment than they do in the other versions of the MVC.

112. **at the hour of prime, the princes and Pharisees had Jesus brought before them.** Although "prime" can simply mean the first hour of the day, in this context it appears to refer to the liturgical or canonical hours. See n132 below for the tradition of narrating the Passion of Christ according to the canonical hours, a tradition that preceded the composition of the *Meditations*.

113. **And when they reached Pilate, they began to accuse him falsely of many things.** Like several other chapters on the Passion, this chapter of the *testo breve* adheres far more closely to the language of the Gospels, including the dramatic dialogue of the Gospels, than does the *testo minore*. Compare this chapter with that in Sarri, 314–16, where Christ's dialogue with Pilate is omitted and indirect speech is substituted for direct speech, rendering the *testo minore* less vibrant and moving than the *testo breve*.

114. **Now I have become the *maistra* of lament.** An allusion to the genre of Marian lament seems to be embedded in this phrase. As the popularity of Marian laments such as the *Quis dabit* and the *Dialogus beatae Mariae et Anselmi de Passione domini* indicates, Mary did indeed serve as the model for imitation for the *pianto* or *planctus* on the death of Christ. Often she is explicitly cast as one from whom grief and lamentation must be learned; the interlocutor in both the *Quis dabit* and *Dialogus* seek to learn from her (Bestul, *Texts of the Passion*, 165–85). The title, *maistra*, is, however, highly unusual; I have found no parallels. The designation may be unique to the *testo breve*. It is not present in the *testo minore* and other versions of the MVC. In asserting a type of female authority, this passage is akin to others in the *testo breve* that present women as possessing authority in ways that other versions of the MVC do not.

115. **O soul who desires to have compassion. . . . O Jesus, how great is your love!** The *testo breve* is far more replete with exclamations than the *testo minore* in this chapter (cf. Sarri, 316–18), as it is in general throughout the Passion chapters. There is also a greater frequency of the invitation to "behold" (*guardalo, risguarda*) in the *testo breve* than in the *testo minore*, in this chapter and elsewhere, which is in keeping with its more obvious designs to engage the reader as active and feeling participant in the drama.

116. **"We have no king but Caesar" . . . ungrateful people!** This passage does not appear in the *testo minore* or other versions of the MVC. I have not iden-

tified a source. In its rhetorical intensity, the passage bears an affinity to the kind of anti-Jewish rhetoric found in so many texts of the period, including Chaucer's *Prioress's Tale*. See Bestul, *Texts of the Passion*; Nirenberg, *Anti-Judaism*; and Bale, *Feeling Persecuted*, for rich and compelling treatments of one of the most problematic and troubling aspects of the rise of affective piety and the dynamics of violence and compassion within it.

117. **And when she saw him, she could hardly recognize him. And as they beheld each other, she was filled with sorrow.** This scene was widely recognized for its poignant dramatic potential and was richly developed in the visual arts. Early Trecento examples include Giotto's fresco at the Scrovegni Chapel, 1305; Duccio's *Maestà*, 1311; and Simone Martini's *Road to Calvary* from the Orsini polyptych, ca. 1340.

118. **Then she said to the Magdalene, "O Magdalene, which one is my son?" ... "That one is your son, my lady."** This exchange between Mary and Magdalene is not present in the *testo minore* and other versions of the MVC (cf. Sarri, 321). It is a tender and poignant moment of affective drama unique to the *testo breve*. It may have been excised by Author B because it is manifestly illogical: of course Mary knows which one is her son. Yet it underscores the disfiguration of Christ as well as Mary's affective response of disbelief, while enhancing Magdalene's role with her delicate statement of the inevitable truth, "quello è il vostro figliolo, Madona mia."

119. **O soul who desires to have compassion for your Creator, and to feel the pain that his Mother feels and to share in her weeping.** On *imitatio Mariae* as a primary technique offered in late medieval meditative writings for eliciting feelings of compassion, see McNamer, *Affective Meditation and the Invention of Medieval Compassion*.

120. **And then behold his glorious face.... Where is the beautiful beard? Where is the beautiful hair ... your face? O most sweet Jesus, what pain you bore for us!** This visual and affective sequence is not present in the *testo minore* (cf. Sarri, 321). The author uses a similar kind of rhetoric to elicit pathos (akin to the *ubi sunt* motif in Latin poetry) in chap. 12; see n69, above.

121. **according to the opinion of certain scholars, was fifteen feet long.** Peter Comestor, *Historia scholastica*, col. 1634.

122. **O soul who desires to glory in the Passion of your Lord.** *Mihi absit gloriari nisi in cruce Domini* [Far be it from me to glory except in the cross of the Lord] (Gal 6:14) was adopted by the Franciscans as the motto of their Order. For the development of the language of "glorying in the Passion," especially among Cistercians and Franciscans, see "Excursus: *Gloria Passionis*," in Auerbach, *Literary Language and its Public,* 67–81.

123. **Now one gets the cross ready, and one the nails. ...** The use of the historical present at key moments is a notable aspect of the style of the *testo breve*; it is deployed in scenes that have heightened potential for the reader's affective

involvement, affording a greater sense of immediacy and sensory vividness. On the switching of tenses as a feature of medieval narrative, especially Old French narrative, see Fleischman, *Tense and Narrativity*, esp. 7–10.

124. **strip him naked . . . to increase his shame.** On the theme of the naked-ness of Christ, its attendant shame, and the role of the Franciscans in promoting this theme, see Derbes, *Picturing the Passion*, 138–42.

125. **took the veil from her head and wrapped it around Lord Jesus Christ with bitter sorrow.** A fresco from the Clarissan church of Santa Maria Donnaregina in Naples depicts this scene; see Derbes, *Picturing the Passion*, 141.

126. **And then he was led to the place where the cross was laid out. . . . And at this, the cross was raised up and affixed in the earth.** This is one of the most significant passages in the *testo breve*, not only in itself—as perhaps the cli-mactic moment of the narrative, and the scene of greatest violence and pathos—but for its potential to illuminate the textual history of the MVC. It depicts the cru-cifixion in the style known as *jacente cruce*: Christ is nailed to the cross as it lies prone on the ground. The other style, *erecta cruce*, is one in which Christ ascends a ladder to an upright cross, and then is nailed to it in the sight of all. Here in the *testo breve*, the author's decision to offer to the meditator the scene *jacente cruce* is of a piece with what appears to be the work's primary aim throughout: to elicit com-passion for a very human, vulnerable Christ, and to imbue his sufferings with great pathos. In the *testo minore* and other versions of the MVC, there are, in contrast, two versions of the crucifixion, *erecta cruce* and *jacente cruce*, with the former, which depicts Christ as heroic martyr, cast as the preferred image and elaborated at greater length. See Sarri, 323–25; Taney et al., 252–53. For a more extended dis-cussion of this difference between the texts, and the way it contributes to the evi-dence that the *testo breve* is likely to have come first in the sequence of MVC ver-sions, see McNamer, "The Origins of the *Meditationes Vitae Christi*." In short, it appears that the scene of crucifixion *erecta cruce* was added by a redactor who sought to correct the *testo breve*'s depiction of an utterly humiliated Christ, de-prived here even of the agency of ascending a ladder, and to promote a Franciscan ideology linked to the theme of the Ascent of the Cross.

127. **O soul who seeks revenge.** Given the prominence of seeking revenge for perceived offenses as an accepted and honored practice among social groups in fourteenth-century Italy, the phrase "O anima la qualle cerchi de vendicharte" may have had special resonance for contemporary readers.

128. **Now when they had crucified him . . . place hope in his mercy.** The account of the death of Christ in the remainder of this chapter follows the Gospels far more closely than the parallel chapter in the *testo minore*, which compresses the events and omits most of the dialogue found in the Gospel accounts; cf. Sarri, 324–29.

129. **And these were the seventh words that our Savior said.** The theme of the seven words spoken from the cross has liturgical origins. Here in the *testo breve*, the seven words are interwoven with the narrative of Christ's death. In the

*testo minore*, the seven words are gathered together into a separate segment and prefaced by a note characterizing Christ as a kind of preacher, one who was not "lazy" even as he was dying on the cross: "Ma lo Segnore stando in su la croce, eziandio insino che lo spirito ne penò ad uscire, non istette ozioso: ma faceva e diceva quelle cose ch'erano utile per noi. Onde disse sette parole" (Sarri, 326).

130. **And as soon as Christ died, his soul descended into limbo to the Holy Fathers. . . . And this is the banner with which the sinner wins all battles.** The theme of Christ's descent into limbo and the harrowing of hell derives from early apocryphal gospels; see the Gospel of Nicodemus, in Ehrman and Pleše, *The Other Gospels*. This rhythmic, resonant passage, structured as the repetition and variation of praises of the banner of paradise, has the ring of a liturgical canticle, but I have not been able to identify a specific source. It is not present in the *testo minore* or other versions of the MVC.

131. **And this opening seems to me to signify three notable and worthy things.** The repetition in this passage of the phrase "it seems to me" suggests that the author of the *testo breve* is experimenting with original scriptural interpretation. The passage is not present in the *testo minore*. Although each of the insights here has parallels elsewhere, and none appear to be risky or heretical, the passage is openly engaging in the act of scriptural interpretation and grounding this in personal opinion alone ("me pare comprehendere tre notabele e degne cose"; "me pare intendere") rather than in the authority of the church and learned exegetes.

132. **And Lord Jesus remained on the cross like this until after vespers.** This temporal designation, "after vespers," would have been familiar to a contemporary religious audience to mean simply "after sunset"; but like other references to the liturgical hours in the Passion chapters, it is also conflated with the long-established meditative practice of telling the story of Christ's Passion according to the liturgical hours. See "The Ideal of the Imitation of Christ," in Constable, *Three Studies*, 145–248, esp. 205–6.

133. **Now pay close attention here as you imagine this. . . . she held it until Joseph had descended the ladder.** The images here, including the resting of the body of Christ on the shoulders of Joseph and Mary's taking of the hand, have gestural parallels in scenes from the visual arts of the early Trecento; cf. Duccio's *Deposition* from the Maestà (1308–11) and Simone Martini's rendering of the scene in the Orsini Polyptych (ca. 1330). The detail of the hiding of the nail so that Mary will not see it appears to be of Byzantine origin. The author's linking of these scenes into such delicately choreographed action, however, seems to be without narrative precedent. Contemporary Passion plays and liturgical drama may have inspired the author, but the evanescent character of live drama, and the paucity of stage directions even in those playbooks that do survive, has left no traces of a sequence of moving images like this.

134. **Then the mother sat on the ground, and Joseph put her most sweet Son in her lap.** In the *testo breve*, the full body of Christ is laid in the mother's lap, in a pose similar to that of the sculptural image of the *pietà*; in the *testo minore*, the

body is laid on the ground, and only Christ's head is laid in his mother's lap ("E la Madre si pone a sedere in terra, e riceve lo capo nel grembo suo con grande sospiri," Sarri, 334; cf. Taney et al., 260). Images of the *Lamentation* from the eleventh through the fourteenth centuries sometimes depict Mary holding the body, sometimes only the head; see Schiller, *Iconography of Christian Art*, vol. 2, figs. 593–606. The difference between the *testo breve* and the *testo minore* appears to be an interesting site of tension, one deserving of further study, regarding tactility and the body of Christ in the early Trecento and in the making of the MVC. On the prominence of the sculptural image of the *pietà* in women's convents, see Ziegler, *Sculpture of Compassion*. On the richness of the *pietà* as a site for investigating the rich confluence of aesthetics, affect, and gender, see Hamburger, "To Make Women Weep."

135.  **And now she kissed his most holy mouth. . . . and she was not able to stop kissing him.** This passage is unique to the *testo breve*. It is notable for the way the repetitions and delicate pacing lend a ritualized element to the scene that allows for the steady building of pathos without crossing into unrestrained emotionalism. The systematic kissing of Christ's body from head to toe is, to my knowledge, without textual precedent. Angela Foligno, however, imagines herself holding and kissing the breast and mouth of Christ in the tomb: "She said she had first of all kissed Christ's breast—and saw that he lay dead, with his eyes closed—then she kissed his mouth, from which, she added, a delightful fragrance emanated" (Lachance, *Angela of Foligno,* 182). In the *Quis dabit*, Mary "did not grow tired of kissing his brow and cheeks, his mouth and also his eyes" (Bestul, *Texts of the Passion*, 180–81). In the *testo minore*, Mary is described only as "looking at" Christ's body: "Guardava le fedite delle mani . . . guardando e piagnendo non si potea saziare" (Sarri, 335; cf. Taney et al., 261).

136.  **And she said, "O my most sweet son, O King of Glory, how is it that you are crowned with thorns?. . . This is your son and my Master."** This passage, too, poetic and moving as it is, is not present in the *testo minore*. Note the way the exchange between Mary and Magdalene picks up and repeats their exchange on the road to Calvary (chap. 26), registering, at this later stage in the narrative, their even greater grief at seeing Christ *così crudelmente vulnerato* and lifeless.

137.  **do not take him from me—or else bury me with him!** The topos of Mary's desire to be buried with her son is found in other texts of the period, including the *Quis dabit*; see Bestul, *Texts of the Passion*, 182–83.

138.  **I have found in a certain source that Our Lord revealed to one of his devoted ones that through derision he was shorn.** This allusion has implications for the dating of the MVC; see above, "Date and Place of Composition," cxx–cxxv. It is likely to be an allusion to Angela of Foligno's *Memoriale*; see Menestò, *Angela da Foligno*, 7. The English translation of Angela's text by Lachance—"He even showed me how his beard, eyebrows, and hair had been plucked out " (*Angela of Foligno*, 127)—renders the Latin as accurately as possible in English, but the English term "plucked" does not fully capture the brutality and shame of the Italian

phrase, *per derisione lui fo tosato. Tosato*, in this context, suggests a rough shearing or shaving of the head and face—an act of punishment and humiliation so gruesome that the author cannot quite believe it ("S'el fu vero, non so"). The author's inclusion of this passage merits consideration within the context of "ugly art" made for and by women religious; see Hamburger, "To Make Women Weep." In the *testo minore*, the passage reads, "Ho trovato scritto in alcuno luogo che 'l Segnore revelò a una sua devota che li fuoro tosolati i capelli e pelata la barba; ma i Vangelisti non scrissero ogni cosa. E certo ch'elli fosse tosolato, no 'l saperia pruovare per la Scrittura; ma che la barba li fosse divelta ben si potrebbe provare. Onde dice Isaia profeta in persona del Signore" (Sarri, 335).

139. **pressed her face against that of her son with much weeping.** Of Byzantine origin, this moving image, face pressed against face, became widespread in early Trecento art; examples include Duccio's *Burial* in the Maestà (1308–11), Pietro Lorenzetti's *Entombment* in the lower church at the Basilica of San Francesco, Assisi (ca. 1320), and Simone Martini's *Entombment* from the Orsini Polyptych (ca. 1330).

140. **our life together was most sweet.** I have translated the Italian *conversatione* as "life together" because *conversatione* in this context means more than the English word "conversation" implies: it carries a more general sense of exchanges between familiars, including not only words but the gestures and ways of being together that create relationships (see L. Leonardi et al., *Tesoro della Lingua Italiana delle Origini, conversazione* [1], s.f.). In religious contexts of the period, it often signifies exchanges of a spiritually edifying kind, including wordless conversations; the topos of Mary's holding of the infant Christ in Italian art is often referred to as *sacra conversazione*. In secular culture, too, the concept and practice of *conversatione* was cultivated and valued. On the latter, see Robiglio, "Between Language and Likemindedness."

141. **And then she kissed the precious blood with which it was completely bathed, and the other women who were there with her did the same.** This action is not present in the *testo minore*, which reads: "E quando giunsero alla croce, ella s'inginocchiò e disse: Qui si riposò lo Figliuolo mio, e qui è lo sangue suo prezioso. E tutti quanti fecero lo simigliante. Puoi pensare ch'ella fu la prima persona che adorasse la croce" (Sarri, 340). It would appear, then, that here, too, the redactor responsible for the *testo minore* deliberately omitted this detail. Like the mother's holding and kissing of her dead son in her lap in this chapter, her kissing of her son's blood is a very potent image, one that appears to be an allusion to ritual practices. The omission of this dramatic action in the *testo minore* could be seen as an effort to tone down the more carnal and tactile character of the gestures depicted in the original text, in ways that bear comparison to broader patterns concerning women's devotional practices and attempts to control or contain them. On the religious and cultural significance of blood, see Bildhauer, *Medieval Blood*, and Bynum, *Wonderful Blood*.

142. **And many women, out of compassion, accompanied her to comfort her.** In the *testo minore*, it is not only women, but also men who weep with Mary. The passage there reads: "Intrando loro nella città, incontanente vennero vergine e altre donne da bene, e accompagnarsi co' lei, e consolavanla per la via; e levossi uno grande pianto. E anche alquanti buoni uomini che trovavano per la via, abbiendole compassione, sì si moveano a piangere, e diceano: Certo grandi injustizia è fatta oggi" (Sarri, 340–41). This is one of the small differences between the *testo breve* and the *testo minore* that appears to point towards a sequence of revision. In my view, it is easier to understand why a redactor would wish to add men to the picture than to supply a potential motive for deliberately excising men from the scene. For this reason alone, this difference between the two texts would seem to suggest that the *testo minore* is an expansion and adaptation of the *testo breve*. But there is another reason, too, why it seems more reasonable to conclude that the men were added by the author of the *testo minore*, rather than subtracted by the author of the *testo breve*. For the men, in short, are imperfectly integrated into the *testo minore*. When Mary turns to bid thanks and farewell to those who have accompanied her, the assembled group consists of women only, in *both* texts ("Et rivoltandosi la Donna Nostra indrieto sì regraciò le donne che l'avea acompagnata," *testo breve* f. 107r; "E quando giunsero alla casa, volsesi inverso le donne, e umilemente le ringraziò," Sarri 341; cf. Taney et al., 264). The dramatic inconsistency in the *testo minore*, then (in which men, too, are said to be present, yet Mary does not bid farewell to them, only to the women), would seem to be a relic from an earlier state of the text, a telltale sign that Author B added men to the narrative but did not finish the work of aligning the details in the very next scene.

143. **And last night my son was betrayed by Judas . . . and at the hour of compline he was shrouded by us and placed in a tomb.** In recollecting the events of the Passion in sequence, linking them to the canonical hours, and responding with exclamations of compassion, Mary is depicted here as modelling the practice of affective meditation on the Passion.

144. **And she alone was the keeper of the faith on Holy Saturday, and for that reason, Saturday is dedicated to her.** The tradition of Mary as keeper of the faith on Holy Saturday is conflated here with her maternal authority over the disciples who would become the leaders of the church. Mary also has authority over narrative in this chapter: she wants to hear the full story of the Passion, and facilitates the telling and hearing of it by the assembled group. Magdalene and Mary then model emotional response to the Passion narrative with their exclamations of sorrow and loss, functioning as inscribed readers who perform ideal reader response.

145. **how the soul of Lord Jesus Christ descended into limbo to rescue the Holy Fathers.** The Gospel of Nicodemus served as indirect source for many medieval depictions of the Harrowing of Hell; see Ehrman and Pleše, *The Other Gospels*, 260–66. Much of the episode from the Gospel of Nicodemus is presented in the *Golden Legend* (Ryan, *Jacobus de Voragine* 1:222–24).

146. **the demons sensed his approach . . . he kicked the gates open, and he entered carrying the banner of the cross.** These colorful dramatic details are not present in the *testo minore* (cf. Sarri, 345–46; cf. Taney et al., 267–68). Their presence in the *testo breve* is of a piece with the author's keen interest in vivid dramatization.

147. **the paradise of delights.** In contemporary cosmography, *paradiso deliciano* was another name for the earthly paradise, often conflated with the Garden of Eden; cf. Dante, *Purgatorio*, cantos 28–33.

148. **And as she was praying with this desire, suddenly Lord Jesus appeared and said, "God be with you, my dearest mother."** The *Legenda Aurea* has Jesus appear first to his mother, and presents both a source and reasons for believing this: "The third apparition was to the Virgin Mary and is believed to have taken place before all the others, although the evangelists say nothing about it. The church at Rome seems to approve this belief, since it celebrates a station at the church of Saint Mary on Easter Sunday. Indeed, if this is not to be believed, on the ground that no evangelist testifies to it, we would have to conclude that Jesus never appeared to Mary after his resurrection because no gospel tells us where or when this happened. But perish the thought that such a son would fail to honor such a mother by being so negligent! . . . Christ must first of all have made his mother happy over his resurrection, since she certainly grieved over his death more than the others. He would not have neglected his mother while he hastened to console others" (Ryan, *Jacobus de Voragine* 1:221). Ryan notes that the church in Rome was Santa Maria Maggiore, and that the pope would have led the celebration of the feast (221n6). Worth noting here too is the specific language of the Italian text, *madre mia carissima*. This simple, tender greeting registers another textual difference between the *testo breve* and the *testo minore*. Here, the greeting is the kind of greeting any loving Italian son would bestow on his mother, and as such, it generates a poignant affective moment through its domestic realism; indeed the dramatic irony here (for this is no ordinary mother, ordinary son, or ordinary reunion) is fundamental to the affective power of the passage. In the *testo minore*, in contrast, Christ greets his mother as "Madre santa" (Sarri, 347; cf. Taney et al., 280). Moreover, he is, in the *testo minore*, wearing dazzling white garments—*vestimenti bianchissimi*; there is no mention of his dazzling garments in the *testo breve*. This is part of a larger pattern of difference between the two texts, in which the *testo minore* places greater emphasis on the divinity and majesty of Christ and his mother, often at the cost of disrupting a sense of affective intimacy between these figures or in the reader's relation to them. Cf. chap. 4, "Now you, too, go to the manger and kneel," and n26.

149. **And in all the places in which some harm had been done to their Master, they would fall to their knees.** In performing the Stations of the Cross here, the three Marys serve as foundational exemplars of that practice. Devotion to the sites of the Passion in Jerusalem is documented from the fourth century; see Morris, *The Sepulchre of Christ and the Medieval West*. On the practice of the

Stations of the Cross in convent settings, see esp. Rudy, *Virtual Pilgrimages in the Convent.*

150. **Now watch how, with a face full of tears, she beseeches the good gardener, who knows all the roots of our hearts.** The phrase "el qualle cognosce tute le radice degli cuori nostri" is unique to the *testo breve*.

151. **And I can hardly believe that she did not touch him in a familiar way and kiss his feet and hands before he left her.** Christ's injunction to Mary, *Noli me tangere* (Jn 20:17) was one of the most rich and vexed sites of scriptural interpretation in the later Middle Ages. The apparent harshness of the phrase is mitigated here in the *testo breve* not only through the author's citation of Bernard's "compassionate explanation" (see next note), but more radically through this expression of the author's personal belief: "I can hardly believe that she did not touch him in a familiar way."

152. **And according to the common interpretation . . . according to what Saint Bernard says.** Bernard of Clairvaux, *Sermones super Cantica Canticorum* 28 (Leclercq et al., *Sancti Bernardi Opera* 1:199). There is in fact a significant difference between Bernard's interpretation, which gives "touch" a spiritual meaning, and that of the author of the *testo breve*, who validates physical touch in this scene. Bernard allows Magdalene to touch the risen Christ "manu fidei, desiderii digito, devotionis amplexu" (1:199) ["with the hand of faith, the finger of desire, the embrace of love" (Walsh, *Bernard of Clairvaux*, 93)]. The reading in the *testo minore* is similar to that of the *testo breve* here.

153. **So it was in a simple, matter-of-fact way, and not to be obstinate, that he said those words, "Do not touch me."** The Italian phrase *materialmente et non pertinacemente* presents a challenge to the translator. Indeed it manifestly presented challenges to scribes of early copies of the Italian MVC: this is a site of considerable confusion and variation in manuscripts of the *testo minore*. The term *pertinacemente* remains stable, but variants for the first word include *misterialmente* (e.g., Florence, Biblioteca Riccardiana MS 1273, f. 53r; Biblioteca Riccardiana MS 1286, f. 38; Biblioteca Riccardiana MS 1346, f. 150r; Biblioteca Riccardiana MS 1348, ff. 52r–52v; Bibilioteca Riccardiana MS 1378, f. 55r; Biblioteca Riccardiana MS 1357, f. 37r; Florence, Biblioteca Medicea Laurenziana MS Ashburnham 458, f. 104r; and, with the variant spelling *mesterialmente*, Biblioteca Nazionale Centrale di Firenze MS II.IX.164, f. 83r; Biblioteca Nazionale Centrale di Firenze MS II.III.414, f. 58v; Biblioteca Medicea Laurenziana MS Ashburnham 544, f. 53v); *maestralmente* (Biblioteca Nazionale Centrale di Firenze MS II.III.415, f. 118v); *miseriandosamente* (Biblioteca Nazaionale Centrale di Firenze MS Conv. Sopp. G. 2. 1585, f. 77r). In one instance, the word *misericordievoleme* [*sic*] is crossed out, and *misterialmente* written above it in a later hand (Biblioteca Medicea Laurenziana MS Ashburnham 430, f. 106r). The existence of these variants forces closer scrutiny of the *testo breve*'s reading, *materialmente*—the meaning of which is not immediately obvious. This is a significant crux, given the im-

portance of the scene of Christ's appearance to Magdalene in late-medieval culture, and it is a crux that merits further discussion. But in my view, *materialmente* is a *lectio difficilior*, and supplies the best reading of the passage. It is not only attested in the *testo breve*, but in one manuscript of the *testo minore* that I have examined, Bibliotoca Riccardiana MS 1358: "dunque materialmente et non pertinacemente disse quella parola. Impero che lo signore benignissimo non e duro ne crudele e specialmente a coloro che llamanano" (f. 35v). Biblioteca Riccardiana MS 1358 is one of the earliest manuscripts of the *testo minore*; see above, "Date and Place of Composition," cxxviii–cxxix. This may suggest that *materialmente* survived the initial transition from the *testo breve* to the *testo minore* but was eclipsed by the more dominant reading *misterialmente* at an early stage. One valuable guide to evaluating whether *materialmente* makes good sense in this context is the parallel phrase in the sentence directly preceding this, the assertion that Christ spoke to Magdalene "per consolarla et non per turbarla." If x is to *consolarla* as *non pertinacemente* is to *non per turbarla*, then x is evidently a manner of speaking that gives comfort. *Misterialmente* is not, in an obvious way, a mode of speaking that gives comfort. *Maestralmente*—in the manner of a master or teacher—does carry this potential meaning, especially since Magdalene regularly refers to Christ as *maestro*. But one of the meanings of *materialmente* attested in the first half of the fourteenth century is, according to Battaglia, *Grande dizionario*, "Semplicemente, all buona; ingenuamente" (*materialmente*, avv.). This definition lies behind my decision to translate the phrase as "in a simple, matter-of-fact way."

154. **"Your speech pleases me; it is so sweet that it surpasses all sweetnes." And meditating on God is like this.** On the rich associations of "sweetness" in the context of meditation in the high and late Middle Ages, see Carruthers, "Sweetness."

155. **Now you know that in the Gospels. . . . But not one of the Gospels tells how he appeared to his mother.** This short passage, unique to the *testo breve*, provides evidence of the author's knowledge of sources (it suggests, for instance, that the author drew on the Gospel of Nicodemus directly, rather than through an intermediary source) even as it crystallizes the MVC's fundamental attitude to authority—i.e., that the Gospels and other textual sources are not the only means of knowing the truth, for "in a spirit of devotion we may imagine."

156. **his beloved disciple, that is, Magdalene.** The phrase *sua dillecta discipula, çioè Magdalena* is unusual. While Magdalene is regularly described as being beloved of Christ, and became known as "the apostle to the apostles" in the Middle Ages because of her role in announcing the resurrection to the disciples, the phrase here, *sua dillecta discipula*, recalls the designation given to John in the Gospels as Christ's (one and only) "beloved disciple." In doing so, it may be yet another indication of the *testo breve*'s tendency to put women front and center in its retellings of the Gospels. On Magdalene as a figure through whom contested ideas played out in the later Middle Ages, see Jansen, *The Making of the Magdalene*.

157. **we should pay close attention to this feast of the Ascension of Our Lord.** A phrase appears to have been dropped from the Canonici copy at the end of this sentence; the original is likely to have asserted that we should be very attentive to this feast because it surpasses all the others. This can be deduced from a cross-reference on f. 124v, "And so, as I told you at the beginning, this feast is greater than all the others" ["sì come io te dissi nel principio che questa solenitade era sopra tute le altre"], as well as from the reading at the beginning of the parallel chapter in the *testo minore*: "ora lo ti conviene fare molto maggiormente, imperciò che questa solennitade avanza tuttle l'altre" (Sarri, 369).

158. **the Mount of Olives.** In the *testo minore*, the location of this mountain is mentioned: "lo quale è presso a Jerusalem a uno miglio" (Sarri, 372). This is one of the small differences between the *testo minore* and the *testo breve* that has potential value for determining the sequence in which the two were composed. As discussed above (lxviii–lxix), it seems to me that the likeliest explanation for the presence of specific distances in the *testo minore* is that these were added at a secondary stage in the composition of the text. This theory, that the distances were added, is compatible with a well-attested practice of glossing texts throughout the medieval period; the systematic removal of references to distances between holy places in a religious text is not a widespread practice (I know of no parallel examples).

159. **But it seems to me that the greatest feast is the Ascension.** The chapter's argument that the Ascension is the greatest of feast days derives in part from Bernard of Clairvaux (see below, n161); but on the whole it seems to be the author's own argument. As such, it merits consideration as a striking instance of early vernacular theology in Italian, one in which the phrase "it seems to me" (*me pare*) is lucidly and repeatedly offered as sufficient justification for a novel argument. Interestingly, the author also enlists the reader's reason and capacity for independent judgment: "Consider this, then, and examine all the reasons well, and you will see that I tell you the truth" (193). The author thus advances a steady, rational argument and asks the nun for whom the work was intended to participate in a process of reasoning.

160. **See, then, how magnificent today's feast day is.** The prominence given to the Ascension in the *testo breve* may suggest that the work was composed in conjunction with a particular feast of the Ascension, or that the nuns for whom it was composed had a special dedication to this feast.

161. **And to confirm my argument, I give you the testimony of St. Bernard.** Bernard of Clairvaux, *In Ascensione Domini* 2, 1 (Leclercq et al., *Sancti Bernardi Opera* 5:126). The particular wording of this phrase is interesting: "Et per confirmatione del mio ditto, io ti do per testimonio sancto Bernardo." First, it privileges the author's argument over that of Bernard, who is cast here merely as a supporting witness. Second, the phrase has an experimental ring, as if the author is not used to putting forward original theological ideas but feels strongly compelled to do so here.

162.  **I have shown you clearly . . . I am not writing about . . . that I do not write about in this book.** The use of the first person singular is more prominent in this concluding chapter than in the others.

163.  *I ask you, sisters, for charity, that when you read in this book, you pray to Lord Jesus for me, so that he might grant me recognition.* It is not clear whether this final request is that of a scribe or of the author. It is rubricated in the manuscript, and this indicates that it stands at one remove from the work itself; but this does not settle the question. The Italian phrase *che me doni cognoscimento* has several meanings, including to give knowledge (to illuminate, grant wisdom) or to acknowledge or recognize. See L. Leonardi et al., *Tesoro della Lingua Italiana delle Origini*, *conòscere*, v., 5.1 and 6. Implicit in the second of these is the sense that God will recognize one on the Day of Judgment, or acknowledge the value of virtuous labor, including the composition or copying of a meditative book, on that Day.

# BIBLIOGRAPHY

## MANUSCRIPTS CITED

Florence, Biblioteca Nazionale Centrale di Firenze MS II.IX.164
Florence, Biblioteca Nazionale Centrale di Firenze MS II.III.414
Florence, Biblioteca Nazionale Centrale di Firenze MS II.III.415
Florence, Biblioteca Nazionale Centrale di Firenze MS Conv. sopp. G.2.1585
Florence, Biblioteca Medicea Laurenziana MS Ashburnham 544
Florence, Biblioteca Medicea Laurenziana MS Ashburnham 458
Florence, Biblioteca Medicea Laurenziana MS Ashburnham 430
Florence, Biblioteca Riccardiana MS 1273
Florence, Biblioteca Riccardiana MS 1286
Florence, Biblioteca Riccardiana MS 1346
Florence, Biblioteca Riccardiana MS 1348
Florence, Biblioteca Riccardiana MS 1357
Florence, Biblioteca Riccardiana MS 1358
Florence, Biblioteca Riccardiana MS 1378
Oxford, Bodleian Library MS Canonici Italian 174
Oxford, Corpus Christi College MS 410
Paris, Bibliothèque nationale de France MS italien 115
Rome, Biblioteca Angelica, MS 2213

## PRINTED TEXTS AND WEB SOURCES

Ahl, Diane Cole. "Camposanto, Terra sancta: Picturing the Holy Land in Pisa." *Artibus et Historiae* 24 (2003): 95–122.

Alberzoni, Maria Pia. *Clare of Assisi and the Poor Sisters of the Thirteenth Century*. Translated by Jean-François Godet-Calgeras. St. Bonaventure: Franciscan Institute Publications, 2004.

Allaire, Gloria, and F. Regina Psaki, eds. *The Arthur of the Italians: The Arthurian Legend in Medieval Italian Literature and Culture*. Cardiff: University of Wales Press, 2014.

Andrews, Frances. *The Early Humiliati*. Cambridge: Cambridge University Press, 1999.

Aquilecchia, Giovanni, ed. *Giovanni Villani: Cronica; Con le continuazioni di Matteo e Filippo*. Turin: Einaudi, 1979.

Aquinas, Thomas. *Summa theologiae*. New York: McGraw-Hill, 1964–1981.

Armstrong, Regis J., ed. and trans. *Clare of Assisi: Early Documents*. Saint Bonaventure, NY: Saint Bonaventure University, Franciscan Institute Publications, 1993.

Armstrong, Regis J., Wayne Hellmann, and William J. Short, eds. *Francis of Assisi: Early Documents*. 3 vols. New York: New City Press, 1999–2001.

Arosio, Marco. "Giovanni de' Cauli," *Dizionario Biografico degli Italiani* 55 (2001); http://www.treccani.it/enciclopedia/giovanni-de-cauli_(Dizionario-Biografico)/.

Asperti, Stefano. "I Vangeli in volgare italiano." In Leonardi, *La Bibbia in italiano*, 119–44.

Auerbach, Erich. *Literary Language and Its Public in Late Latin Antiquity and in the Middle Ages*. Translated by Ralph Manheim. Princeton: Princeton University Press, 1993.

——. *Mimesis: The Representation of Reality in Western Literature*. Translated by Willard R. Trask. Princeton: Princeton University Press, 1953.

Auzzas, Ginetta. "Dalla predica al trattato: Lo *Specchio della vera penitenzia* di Iacopo Passavanti." *Lettere Italiane* 54 (2002): 325–42.

——, ed. *Iacopo Passavanti: Lo Specchio della vera penitenzia*. Florence: Accademia della Crusca, 2014.

Baier, Walter. *Untersuchungen zu den Passionsbetrachtungen in der* Vita Christi *des Ludolf von Sachsen*. 3 vols. Analecta Cartusiana 44. Salzburg: Institut für Englische Sprache und Literatur, 1977.

Bale, Anthony. *Feeling Persecuted: Christians, Jews and Images of Violence in the Middle Ages*. London: Reaktion, 2010.

Banfi, Florio. *Santa Elisabetta d'Ungheria, Landgravia di Turingia*. Assisi: S. Maria degli Angeli, 1932.

Barasch, Moshe. *Giotto and the Language of Gesture*. Cambridge: Cambridge University Press, 1987.

Barbieri, Edoardo. "Domenico Cavalca volgarizzatore degli *Actus Apostolorum*." In Leonardi, *La Bibbia in italiano*, 291–328.

Barratt, Alexandra. "'The Flower and the Leaf' and 'The Assembly of Ladies': Is There a (Sexual) Difference?" *Philological Quarterly* 66 (1987): 1–24.

——. "*The Revelations of Saint Elizabeth of Hungary*: Problems of Attribution." *The Library*, 6th ser., 14:1 (1992): 1–11.

——. "The Virgin and the Visionary in the *Revelation of St. Elizabeth*." *Mystics Quarterly* 17 (1991): 125–36.

————, trans. *The Revelations of St. Elizabeth (of Töss)*. *Vox Benedictina: A Journal of Translations from Monastic Sources* 10:1 (1993): 75–114.

Bartal, Renana. "Repetition, Opposition, and Invention in an Illuminated *Meditationes Vitae Christi*, Oxford, Corpus Christi College MS 410." *Gesta* 53 (2014): 155–74.

Battaglia, Salvatore. *Grande dizionario della lingua italiana*. Turin: Unione tipografico-editrice torinese, 1973

Bellorini, T., and E. Hoade, trans. *Niccolò da Poggibonsi: A Voyage Beyond the Seas, 1346–1350*. Jerusalem: Franciscan Press, 1945.

Belting, Hans. "The New Role of Narrative in Public Painting of the Trecento: Historia and Allegory." In *Pictorial Narrative in Antiquity and the Middle Ages*, edited by Herbert L. Kessler and Marianna Shreve Simpson, 151–70. Washington, DC: National Gallery of Art, 1985.

Benson, Pamela Joseph, and Victoria Kirkham, eds. *Strong Voices, Weak History: Early Women Writers and Canons in England, France, and Italy*. Ann Arbor: University of Michigan Press, 2005.

Bertaux, Émile. *Santa Maria di Donna Regina e l'arte senese a Napoli nel secolo XIV*. Naples: F. Giannini, 1899.

Bertelli, Sandro. "Il copista del *Novellino*." *Bollettino Annuale dell'Accademia della Crusca* 56 (1998): 31–45.

————, ed. *I manoscritti della letteratura italiana delle origini: Firenze, Biblioteca Medicea Laurenziana*. Florence: SISMEL Edizioni del Galluzzo, 2011.

————, ed. *I manoscritti della letteratura italiana delle origini: Firenze, Biblioteca Nazionale Centrale*. Florence: SISMEL Edizioni del Galluzzo, 2002.

Bestul, Thomas. *Texts of the Passion: Latin Devotional Literature and Medieval Society*. Philadelphia: University of Pennsylvania Press, 1996.

*Bibliotheca Sanctorum*. Rome: Istituto Giovanni XXIII nella Pontificia Università Lateranense, 1961–70.

Bildhauer, Bettina. *Medieval Blood*. Cardiff: University of Wales Press, 2006.

Boccali, Giovanni, ed. *Mariano da Firenze: Libro delle degnità et excellentie del Ordine della seraphica madre delle povere donne sancta Chiara da Asisi*. Florence: Edizioni Studi Francescani, 1986.

Bonaventure. *Legenda maior*. Analecta Franciscana 10. Quarrachi: Ex Typographia Collegii S. Bonaventurae, 1885–1941.

————. *On the Perfection of Life, Addressed to Sisters*. In *The Works of Bonaventure*, translated by José de Vinck, 1:209–55. Paterson, NJ: St. Anthony Guild Press, 1960.

Bornstein, Daniel, ed. and trans. *Life and Death in a Venetian Convent: The Chronicle and Necrology of Corpus Domini, 1395–1436*, by Bartolomea Riccoboni. Chicago: University of Chicago Press, 2000.

Bornstein, Daniel, and Roberto Rusconi, eds. *Women and Religion in Late Medieval Italy*. Translated by Margery J. Schneider. Chicago: University of Chicago Press, 1996.

Botterill, Steven. "Minor Writers." In *The Cambridge History of Italian Literature*, edited by Peter Brand and Lino Pertile, 108–27. Cambridge: Cambridge University Press, 1997.

————, ed. and trans. *Dante Alighieri: De vulgari eloquentia*. New York: Cambridge University Press, 1996.

Boulton, Maureen Barry McCann. *Sacred Fictions of Medieval France: Narrative Theology in the Lives of Christ and the Virgin, 1150–1500*. Woodbridge: D. S. Brewer, 2015.

Branca, Vittore, ed. *Giovanni Boccacio: Decameron*. Florence: Accademia della Crusca, 1976.

————. *Merchant Writers of the Italian Renaissance*. Translated by Murtha Baca. New York: Marsilio Publishers, 1999.

Briquet, C.-M. *Les filigranes: Dictionnaire historique des marques du papier dès leur apparition vers 1282 jusqu'en 1600*. 2nd ed. New York: Hacker Art Books, 1966.

Brundage, James A. *Law, Sex, and Christian Society in Medieval Europe*. Chicago: University of Chicago Press, 1988.

Bruzelius, Caroline. *The Stones of Naples: Church Building in the Angevin Kingdom, 1266–1343*. New Haven: Yale University Press, 2004.

Burr, David. *The Spiritual Franciscans: From Protest to Persecution in the Century after Saint Francis*. University Park: Pennsylvania State University Press, 2001.

Bynum, Caroline Walker. *Wonderful Blood: Theology and Practice in Late Medieval Northern Germany and Beyond*. Philadelphia: University of Pennsylvania Press, 2007.

Canaccini, Federico. *Al cuore del primo Giubileo: Bonifacio VIII e l'Antiquorum habet*. Vatican City: Lateran University Press, 2016.

Cannon, Joanna. "Duccio and Devotion to the Virgin's Foot in Early Sienese Painting." In *A Wider Trecento: Studies in Thirteenth- and Fourteenth-century European Art Presented to Julian Gardner*, edited by Louise Bourdua and Robert Gibbs, 39–61. Leiden and Boston: Brill, 2012.

————, and André Vauchez. *Margherita of Cortona and the Lorenzetti: Sienese Art and the Cult of a Holy Woman in Medieval Tuscany*. University Park: Pennsylvania State University Press, 1998.

Carruthers, Mary. *The Book of Memory: A Study of Memory in Medieval Culture*. 2nd ed. Cambridge: Cambridge University Press, 2008.

————. "Sweetness." *Speculum* 81.4 (2006): 999–1013.

Cellucci, Luigi. "Le *Meditationes vitae Christi* e i poemetti che ne furono ispirati," *Archivum Romanicum* 22 (1938): 30–98.

Cerquiglini, Bernard. *In Praise of the Variant: A Critical History of Philology.* Translated by Betsy Wing. Baltimore: Johns Hopkins University Press, 1999.

Chareyron, Nicole. *Pilgrims to Jerusalem in the Middle Ages.* Princeton: Princeton University Press, 2005.

Cherubini, Giovanni. *Pellegrini, pellegrinaggi, giubileo nel Medioevo.* Naples: Liguori, 2005.

Cignoni, Arianna Pecorini. "Gregorio IX e il francescanesimo femminile: Il Monastero di Ognissanti in Pisa." *Studi Francescani* 95 (1998): 383–406.

Clear, Matthew J. "Maria of Hungary as Queen, Patron, and Exemplar." In Elliott and Warr, *The Church of Santa Maria Donna Regina,* 45–60.

Cohen, Jeremy. *The Friars and the Jews: The Evolution of Medieval Anti-Judaism.* Ithaca: Cornell University Press, 1984.

Colledge, E. "'Dominus cuidam devotae suae': A Source for Pseudo-Bonaventure," *Franciscan Studies* 36 (1976): 105–7.

Connolly, Thomas. *Mourning into Joy: Mourning, Raphael, and Saint Cecilia.* New Haven: Yale University Press, 1994.

Constable, Giles. *Three Studies in Medieval Religious and Social Thought.* Cambridge: Cambridge University Press, 1995.

Cook, William R. *Francis of Assisi: The Way of Poverty and Humility.* Wilmington, DE: M. Glazier, 1989.

Corbari, Eliana. *Vernacular Theology: Dominican Sermons and Audience in Late Medieval Italy.* Boston: Walter de Gruyter, 2013.

Corner, Flaminio. *Notizie storiche delle chiese e monasteri di Venezia e di Torcello.* Padua: Nella stamperia del Seminario appresso Giovanni Manfré, 1758. Reprinted with introduction by Ugo Stefanutti, Collana di bibliografia e storia veneziana 18. Bologna: A. Forni, 1990.

Cornish, Alison. *Vernacular Translation in Dante's Italy: Illiterate Literature.* New York: Cambridge University Press, 2011.

Dalarun, Jacques. *La Vie retrouvée de François d'Assise.* Paris: Éditions franciscaines, 2015. Translated by Timothy J. Johnson as *The Rediscovered Life of St. Francis of Assisi.* St. Bonaventure, NY: Franciscan Institute Publications, 2016.

D'Ancona, Alessandro. *Origini del teatro italiano.* Rome: Bardi, 1971. Orig. pub. 1877.

Davis, Charles T., ed. *Ubertino da Casale: Arbor vitae crucifixae Jesu.* Turin: Bottega d'Erasmo, 1961.

De Bartholomaeis, Vincenzo, ed. *Laude drammatiche e rappresentazioni sacre.* 3 vols. Florence: Felice Le Monnier, 1943; repr. 1967.

de Hamel, Christopher. *The Book: A History of the Bible.* New York: Phaidon, 2001.

Delcorno, Carlo. "Cavalca, Domenico." *Dizionario Biografico Degli Italiani.* Vol. 22. 1979, http://www.treccani.it/biografie/.

————. "Diffusione del volgarizzamento." In Carlo Delcorno, *La tradizione delle "Vite dei Santi Padri,"* 515–32. Venice: Istituto Veneto di Scienze, Lettere ed Arti, 2000.

————. "Predicazione volgare e volgarizzamenti," *Mélanges de l'École francaise de Rome: Moyen-Âge, Temps modernes,* 89.2 (1977): 679–89.

————, ed. *Domenico Cavalca: Vita dei santi padri.* Florence: Edizioni del Galluzzo per la Fondazione Ezio Franceschini, 2009.

————, ed. *Giordano da Pisa: Quaresimale fiorentino, 1305–1306.* Florence: Sansoni, 1974.

de Luca, Giuseppe. *Introduzione alla storia della pietà.* Rome: Edizioni di Storia e Letteratura, 1962.

————, ed. *Prosatori minori del Trecento,* vol. 1, *Scrittori di religione.* Milan, Naples: Riccardo Ricciardi Editore, 1954.

Derbes, Anne. *Picturing the Passion in Late Medieval Italy: Narrative Painting, Franciscan Ideologies, and the Levant.* New York: Cambridge University Press, 1996.

De Robertis, Teresa, and Rosanna Miriello, eds. *Manoscritti datati della Biblioteca Riccardiana di Firenze.* Florence: SISMEL Edizione del Galluzzo, 1997–2013.

De Sanctis, Francesco. *Storia della letteratura italiana.* Edited by Niccolò Gallo. Milan: Mondadori, 1991.

Doležalová, Lucie, ed. *The Making of Memory in the Middle Ages.* Leiden: Brill, 2010.

Donadelli, Giuseppe, ed. *Meditazioni della vita di Gesù Cristo: Testo inedito del buon secolo della lingua.* Milan: Presso Secondo Brambilla libraio Piazza de' Mercanti, 1823.

Dronke, Peter. *Women Writers of the Middle Ages: A Critical Study of Texts from Perpetua (d. 203) to Marguerite Porete (d. 1310).* Cambridge: Cambridge University Press, 1984.

Ehrman, Bart D., and Zlatko Pleše, eds. and trans. *The Other Gospels: Accounts of Jesus from Outside the New Testament.* New York: Oxford University Press, 2014.

Elliott, Dyan. *Spiritual Marriage: Sexual Abstinence in Medieval Wedlock.* Princeton: Princeton University Press, 1995.

Elliott, Janis, and Cordelia Warr, eds. *The Church of Santa Maria Donna Regina: Art, Iconography and Patronage in Fourteenth-Century Naples.* Burlington VT: Ashgate, 2004.

Ertl, Péter, Eszter Konrád, Anikó Ludmann, and Dávid Falvay. "The Italian Variants of the *Meditationes Vitae Christi*: A Preliminary Structural Collation." *Italogramma* 6. Available at http://italogramma.elte.hu/?cat=15.

Falvay, Dávid. "Le rivelazioni di Santa Elisabetta d'Ungheria." In *Annuario dell'Accademia d'Ungheria in Roma 2002–2004*, ed. Laszlo Csorba and Gyongyi Komlossy, 248–63. Rome: Accademia d'Ungheria di Roma, 2005.

————. "St. Elizabeth of Hungary in Italian Vernacular Literature: *Vitae*, Miracles, Revelations, and the *Meditations on the Life of Christ*." In *Promoting the Saints: Cults and Their Contexts from Late Antiquity Until the Early Modern Period; Essays in Honor of Gábor Klaniczay for His Sixtieth Birthday*, ed. Ottó Gescer, 137–50. New York: Central European University Press, 2011.

————, and Péter Tóth. "L'Autore e la trasmissione delle *Meditationes Vitae Christi* in base a manoscritti volgari italiani." *Archivum Franciscanum Historicum* 108 (2015): 403–30.

Field, Sean L. *Isabelle of France: Capetian Sanctity and Franciscan Identity in the Thirteenth Century*. Notre Dame, IN: University of Notre Dame Press, 2006.

Field, Sean L., Larry F. Field, and Lezlie S. Knox. *Visions of Sainthood in Medieval Rome: The Lives of Margherita Colonna by Giovanni Colonna and Stefania*. Notre Dame, IN: University of Notre Dame Press, 2017.

Findlay, Alison. *Playing Spaces in Early Women's Drama*. New York: Cambridge University Press, 2006.

Fischer, Columban. "Die *Meditationes vitae Christi*: Ihre handschrifliche Überlieferung und die Verfasserfrage." *Archivum Franciscanum Historicum* 25 (1932): 3–35, 175–209, 305–48, and 449–83.

Fleck, Cathleen A. "'To exercise yourself in these things by continued contemplation': Visual and Textual Literacy in the Frescoes at Santa Maria Donna Regina." In Elliott and Warr, *The Church of Santa Maria Donna Regina*, 109–28.

Fleischman, Suzanne. *Tense and Narrativity*. Austin: University of Texas Press, 1990.

Fleming, John. *An Introduction to the Franciscan Literature of the Middle Ages*. Chicago: Franciscan Herald Press, 1977.

Flora, Holly. *The Devout Belief of the Imagination: The Paris* Meditationes Vitae Christi *and Female Franciscan Spirituality in Trecento Italy*. Turnhout: Brepols, 2009.

————, and Arianna Pecorini Cignoni. "Requirements of Devout Contemplation: Text and Image for the Poor Clares in Trecento Pisa," *Gesta* 45.1 (2006): 61–76.

Foucault, Michel. "What is an Author?" In *Rethinking Popular Culture: Contemporary Perspectives in Cultural Studies*, edited by Chandra Mukerjee and Michael Schudson, 446–64. Berkeley: University of California Press, 1991.

Fraknói, Vilmos, ed. *Inquisitio super vita, conversatione et miraculis beatae Margarethae virginis, Belae IV: Hungarorum regis filiae, sanctimonialis monasterii virginis gloriosae de insula Danubii, Ordinis Praedicatorum, Vesprimiensis diocesis*. In *Monumenta Romana episcopatus Vesprimiensis* I, 162–383. Budapest, 1896.

Franco, Bradley R., and Beth A. Mulvaney, eds. *The World of Saint Francis of Assisi: Essays in Honor of William R. Cook*. Leiden: Brill, 2015.

Frugoni, Chiara. *Francesco e l'invenzione delle stimmate: Una storia per parole e immagini fino a Bonaventura e Giotto*. Torino: Einaudi, 1993.

Fulton, Rachel. "'Taste and See that the Lord is Sweet' (Ps. 33:9): The Flavor of God in the Monastic West." *Speculum* 86.2 (2006): 164–209.

Gaddoni, Serafino. "Inventaria Clarissarum (1317–1341)." *Archivum Franciscanum Historicum* 9 (1916): 294–346.

Gardner, Edmund. *Dante and the Mystics.* New York: E. P. Dutton, 1913.

Gasca Queirazza, Giuliano. "Intorno ad alcuni codici delle *Meditationes vitae Christi.*" *Archivum Franciscanum Historicum* 55 (1962): 252–58.

———, ed. *Meditacioni di la vita di Christu.* Palermo: Centro di studi filologici e linguistici siciliani, 2008.

Gilbert, Creighton E. "The Pisa Baptistry Pulpit Addresses Its Public." *Artibus et Historiae* 21:41 (2000): 9–30.

Gill, Katherine. "Women and the Production of Religious Literature in the Vernacular, 1300–1500." In *Creative Women in Medieval and Early Modern Italy: A Religious and Artistic Renaissance,*" edited by E. Ann Matter and John Coakley, 64–85. Philadelphia: University of Pennsylvania Press, 1994.

Ginzburg, Carlo. "Morelli, Freud, and Sherlock Holmes: Clues and Scientific Method." *History Workshop* 9 (1980): 5–36.

Graboïs, Aryeh. "Christian Pilgrims in the Thirteenth Century and the Latin Kingdom of Jerusalem." In *Outremer: Studies in the History of the Crusading Kingdom of Jerusalem Presented to Joshua Prawer,* ed. B. Z. Kedar, H. E. Mayer, and R. C. Smail, 285–96. Jerusalem: Yad Izhak Ben-Zvi Institute, 1982.

Gramigni, Tommaso. *I manoscritti della letteratura italiana delle origini.* M.A. thesis, Università di Firenze, 2003–04.

Greetham, D. C. *Textual Scholarship: An Introduction.* New York: Garland Publishing, 1994.

Griesbach, Johann Jacob, ed. *Novum Testamentum graece: Textum ad fidem codicum versionum et Patrum recensuit et lectionis varietatem adiecit.* 3rd. ed. Edited by D. David Schulz. Berlin: Friedrich Laue, 1827.

Gura, David. *A Descriptive Catalogue of the Medieval and Renaissance Manuscripts of the University of Notre Dame and Saint Mary's College.* Notre Dame, IN: University of Notre Dame Press, 2016.

Habig, Marion A., ed. *St. Francis of Assisi: Writings and Early Biographies; English Omnibus of the Sources for the Life of St. Francis.* 4th rev. ed. 2 vols. Chicago: Franciscan Herald Press, 1983.

Hale, Rosemary Drage. *Imitatio Mariae: Motherhood Motifs in Late Medieval German Spirituality.* Ph.D. dissertation, Harvard University, 1992.

———. "Rocking the Cradle: Margaretha Ebner (Be) Holds the Divine." In *Performance and Transformation: New Approaches to Late Medieval Spirituality,* edited by Mary A. Suydam and Joanna E. Zeigler, 211–39. New York: St. Martin's Press, 1999.

Halligan, Theresa A., ed. *The Booke of Gostly Grace of Mechtild of Hackeborne.* Toronto: Pontifical Institute of Medieval Studies, 1979.

Hamburger, Jeffrey. *The Rothschild Canticles: Art and Mysticism in Flanders and the Rhineland circa 1300.* New Haven: Yale University Press, 1990.

———. "To Make Women Weep: Ugly Art as 'Feminine' and the Origins of Modern Aesthetics." *RES: Anthropology and Aesthetics* 31 (1997): 9–33.

Head, Thomas. "The Marriages of Christina of Markyate." *Viator* 21 (1990): 75–101.

Heijkant, Marie-José. "From France to Italy: The Tristan Texts." In Allaire and Psaki, *The Arthur of the Italians*, 41–68.

Herlihy, David. *Women, Family and Society in Medieval Europe: Historical Essays, 1978–1991.* Edited with an introduction by A. Molho. Providence, RI: Berghahn Books, 1995.

Hiller, Diana. *Gendered Perceptions of Last Supper Frescoes, c. 1350–1490.* Burlington, VT: Ashgate, 2014.

Hoch, Adrian S. "The 'Passion' Cycle: Images to Contemplate and Imitate Amid Clarissan *Clausura*." In Elliott and Warr, *The Church of Santa Maria Donna Regina*, 129–53.

Houston, Kerr. "Painted Images and the Clarisse, 1212–1320: Aspects of Production and Reception, and the Idea of a Nunnery Art." Ph.D. dissertation, Yale University, 2001.

Hudson, Anne. "The Variable Text." In *Crux and Controversy in Middle English Textual Criticism*, edited by A. J. Minnis and Charlotte Brewer, 49–60. Cambridge: D. S. Brewer, 1992.

Jacobus, Laura. "Giotto's *Annunciation* in the Arena Chapel, Padua." *Art Bulletin* 81:1 (March 1999): 93–107.

James, Montague Rhodes. *The Western Manuscripts in the Library of Trinity College Cambridge: A Descriptive Catalogue.* 4 vols. Cambridge: Cambridge University Press, 1900–1904.

Jansen, Katherine Ludwig. *The Making of the Magdalen: Preaching and Popular Devotion in the Later Middle Ages.* Princeton: Princeton University Press, 2001.

Johnson, Ian, and Alan F. Westphall, eds. *The Pseudo-Bonaventuran Lives of Christ: Exploring the Middle English Tradition.* Turnhout: Brepols, 2013.

Jotischky, Andrew. *The Carmelites and Antiquity: Mendicants and Their Pasts in the Middle Ages.* Oxford: Oxford University Press, 2002.

Kaftal, George. *Iconography of the Saints in Tuscan Painting.* Florence: Sansoni, 1952.

Karnes, Michelle. *Imagination, Meditation, and Cognition in the Middle Ages.* Chicago: University of Chicago Press, 2011.

———. "Nicholas Love and Medieval Meditations on Christ." *Speculum* 82.2 (2007): 380–408.

Kelly, Samantha. "Religious Patronage and Royal Propaganda in Angevin Naples: Santa Maria Donna Regina in Context." In Elliott and Warr, *The Church of Santa Maria Donna Regina*, 27–44.

Kelly, Stephen, and Ryan Perry, eds. *Devotional Culture in Late Medieval England and Europe: Diverse Imaginations of Christ's Life*. Turnhout: Brepols, 2014.

Kemper, Tobias. *Die Kreuzigung Christi: Motivgeschichtliche Studien zu lateinischen und deutschen Passionstraktaten des Spätmittelalters*. Tübingen: Niemeyer, 2006.

Kessler, Herbert L., and Johanna Zacharias. *Rome 1300: On the Path of the Pilgrim*. New Haven: Yale University Press, 2000.

Kirchner, Julius. "Family and Marriage: A Socio-Legal Perspective." In *Italy in the Age of the Renaissance: 1300–1550*, edited by John Najemy, 82–102. Oxford: Oxford University Press, 2004.

Klaniczay, Gábor. *Holy Rulers and Blessed Princesses: Dynastic Cults in Medieval Central Europe*. New York: Cambridge University Press, 2002.

Klaniczay, Tibor. "Attività letteraria dei Francescani e dei Domenicani nell'Ungheria Angioina." In *Gli Angionini di Napoli e di Ungheria: Atti del Colloquio italo-ungherese*, 27–40. Rome: Accademia Nazionale dei Lincei, 1974.

Klapisch-Zuber, Christiane. *Women, Family, and Ritual in Renaissance Italy*. Translated by Lydia Cochrane. Chicago: University of Chicago Press, 1985.

Kloppenborg, John S., and Judith H. Newman. *Editing the Bible: Assessing the Task Past and Present*. Atlanta: Society of Biblical Literature, 2012.

Knox, Lezlie. *Creating Clare of Assisi: Female Franciscan Identities in Later Medieval Italy*. Boston: Brill, 2008.

Lachance, Paul, trans. *Angela of Foligno: Complete Works*. Classics of Western Spirituality. Mahwah, NJ: Paulist Press, 1993.

Lambert, Malcolm. *Franciscan Poverty: The Doctrine of Absolute Poverty of Christ and the Apostles in the Franciscan Order, 1210–1323*. London: S.P.C.K., 1961.

Lansing, Carol. *The Florentine Magnates: Lineage and Faction in a Medieval Commune*. Princeton: Princeton University Press, 1991.

————. *Passion and Order: Restraint of Grief in the Medieval Italian Communities*. Ithaca: Cornell University Press, 2008.

Lanza, Antonio, and Marcellina Troncarelli, eds. *Pellegrini scrittori: Viaggiatori toscani del Trecento in Terrasanta*. Florence: Ponte alle grazie, 1990.

Lavin, Marilyn Aronberg. "Giovanni Battista: A Study in Renaissance Religious Symbolism." *Art Bulletin* 37 (1955): 85–101.

————. "Giovanni Battista: A Supplement." *Art Bulletin* 43 (1961): 319–26.

Leclercq, J., et al., eds. *Sancti Bernardi Opera*. 8 vols. Rome: Editiones Cistercienses, 1957–77.

Leonardi, Claudio, ed. *La letteratura francescana*. 4 vols. Milan: Mondadori, Fondazione L. Valla, 2004–13.

Leonardi, Lino, ed. *La Bibbia in italiano tra Medioevo e Rinascimento: Atti del convegno internazionale, Firenze, Certosa del Galluzzo, 8–9 novembre 1996*. Florence: SISMEL, 1998.

Leonardi, Lino, et al. *Tesoro della Lingua Italiana delle Origini*. Available at http://tlio.ovi.cnr.it/TLIO/.

Lewis, Gertrud Jaron. *By Women, for Women, about Women: The Sister-books of Fourteenth-Century Germany*. Toronto: Pontifical Institute of Medieval Studies, 1996.

Little, Lester K. "*Imitatio Francisci*: The Influence of Francis of Assisi on Late Medieval Religious Life." In *Defenders and Critics of Franciscan Life: Essays in Honor of John V. Fleming*, edited by Michael F. Cusato and Guy Geltner, 195–218. Leiden: Brill, 2009.

Maas, Paul. *Textual Criticism*. Translated by Barbara Fowler. Oxford: Clarendon Press, 1958.

MacCullough, J. A. *The Harrowing of Hell: A Comparative Study of Early Christian Doctrine*. Edinburgh: T. & T. Clark, 1930.

Macray, William Dunn, and the Bodleian Library. *Annals of the Bodleian Library, Oxford: With a Notice of the Earlier Library of the University*. 2nd ed. Enlarged and continued from 1868 to 1880. Oxford: Bodleian Library, 1984.

Maggioni, Giovanni Paolo, ed. *Legenda aurea: Con le miniature del codice Ambrosiano C 240 inf.* Florence: SISMEL Edizioni del Galluzzo; Milan: Biblioteca Ambrosiana, 2007.

Maginnis, Hayden B. J. *The World of the Sienese Painter*. University Park: Pennsylvania State University Press, 2001.

Magli, Ida. *Gli uomini della penitenza: Lineamenti antropologici del medioevo italiano*. Padua: F. Muzzio, 1995.

Makowski, Elizabeth. *Canon Law and Cloistered Women: Periculoso and Its Commentators*. Washington, DC: Catholic University of America Press, 1999.

Malato, Enrico, ed. *Storia della letteratura italiana*. 14 vols. Rome: Salerno Editrice, 1995–2004.

Mâle, Émile. *L'art religieux de la fin du moyen âge en France*. 3rd ed. Paris: Librairie Armand Colin, 1925.

Manni, Domenico Maria, ed. *Volgarizzamento delle vite de' Sante Padri: Con vite di alcuni altri santi scritte nel buon secolo della vita toscana*. Florence: Domenico Maria Manni, 1734–35.

Mantzavinos, C. "Hermeneutics." *Stanford Encyclopedia of Philosophy*. June 22, 2016. Available at http://plato.stanford.edu/entries/hermeneutics/.

Matter, E. Ann, and John Coakley, eds. *Creative Women in Medieval and Early Modern Italy: A Religious and Artistic Renaissance*. Philadelphia: University of Pennsylvania Press, 1994.

McGann, Jerome. *A Critique of Modern Textual Criticism*. Chicago: University of Chicago Press, 1983.

McGinn, Bernard. *The Flowering of Mysticism: Men and Women in the New Mysticism (1200–1350)*. New York: Crossroad, 1998.

McNamer, Sarah. *Affective Meditation and the Invention of Medieval Compassion.* Philadelphia: University of Pennsylvania Press, 2010.

————. "The Author of the Italian *Meditations on the Life of Christ.*" In *New Directions in Medieval Manuscript Studies and Reading Practices: Essays in Honor of Derek Pearsall,* edited by Kathryn Kerby-Fulton, John J. Thompson, and Sarah Baechle, 119–37. Notre Dame, IN: University of Notre Dame Press, 2014.

————. "The Debate on the Origins of the *Meditationes Vitae Christi*: Recent Arguments and Prospects for Future Research." *Archivum Franciscanum Historicum* 110, forthcoming.

————. "Further Evidence for the Date of the Pseudo-Bonaventuran *Meditationes vitae Christi.*" *Franciscan Studies* 50 (1993 for 1990): 235–61.

————. "The Origins of the *Meditationes Vitae Christi.*" *Speculum* 84 (2009): 905–55.

————. Review of *Iohannes de Caulibus: Meditaciones Vite Christi,* edited by M. Stallings-Taney. *The Journal of Theological Studies,* n.s., 50:1 (1999): 378–85.

————, ed. *The Two Middle English Translations of the Revelations of St. Elizabeth of Hungary.* Middle English Texts 28. Heidelberg: Universitätsverlag C. Winter, 1996.

Menestò, Enrico, ed. *Angela da Foligno: Il Memoriale.* Edizione Nationale dei Testi Mediolatini d'Italia, 29. Florence: SISMEL Edizione dal Galluzzo, 2013.

Merolle, Irma. *L'abate Matteo Luigi Canonici e la sua biblioteca: I manoscritti Canonici e Canonici-Soranzo delle biblioteche fiorentine.* Rome: Institutum historicum Soc. Jesu; Florence: Biblioteca Mediceo-Laurenziana, 1958.

Metz, René. *La consécration des vierges dans l'église romaine: Étude d'histoire de la liturgie.* Paris: Presses Universitaires de France, 1954.

Mews, Constant J. *The Lost Love Letters of Heloise and Abelard: Perceptions of Dialogue in Twelfth-Century France.* 2nd ed. New York: Palgrave Macmillan, 2008.

Middledorf, Ulrich. *Sculptures from the Samuel H. Kress Collection: European Schools, XIV–XIX Century.* London: Phaidon Press for the Samuel H. Kress Foundation, 1976.

Minnis, Alastair. *Medieval Theory of Authorship: Scholastic Literary Attitudes in the Later Middle Ages.* 2nd ed. Philadelphia: University of Pennsylvania Press, 2009.

Mitchell, J. B. "Trevisan and Soranzo: Some Canonici Manuscripts from Two Eighteenth-Century Venetian Collections." *The Bodleian Library Record* 8.3 (1969): 125–35.

Mooney, Canice [Cainneach ó Maonaigh], ed. *Smaointe Beatha Chríost. i. Innsint ghaelge a chuir Tomás Gruamdha ó Bruachain (fl. c. 1450) ar an Meditationes vitae Christi.* Dublin: Dublin Institute for Advanced Studies, 1944.

Mooney, Catherine. *Clare of Assisi and the Thirteenth-Century Church: Religious Women, Rules, and Resistance*. Philadelphia: University of Pennsylvania Press, 2016.

Moorman, John. *A History of the Franciscan Order*. Oxford: Clarendon Press, 1968.

———. *Medieval Franciscan Houses*. St. Bonaventure, NY: Franciscan Institute, St. Bonaventure University, 1983.

Morey, James H. "Peter Comestor, Biblical Paraphrase, and the Medieval Popular Bible." *Speculum* 68 (1993): 6–35.

Morpurgo, Salomone. *I Manoscritti della R. Biblioteca Riccardiana di Firenze: manoscritti italiani*, vol. 1. Rome, 1900.

Morris, Colin. *The Sepulchre of Christ and the Medieval West: From the Beginning to 1600*. New York: Oxford University Press, 2005.

Mortara, Alessandro. *Catalogo dei manoscritti italiani che sotto la denominazione di codici Canoniciani italici si conservano nella Biblioteca Bodleiana a Oxford*. Oxford: Clarendon Press, 1864.

*Movimento religioso femminile e francescanesimo nel secolo XIII: Atti del vii convegno internazionale, Assisi, 11–13 ottobre 1979*. Assisi: Società Internazionale di Studi Francescani, 1980.

Mueller, Joan. *The Privilege of Poverty: Clare of Assisi, Agnes of Prague, and the Struggle for a Franciscan Rule for Women*. University Park: Pennsylvania State University, 2006.

Murphy-O'Connor, Jerome. *The Holy Land: An Oxford Archaeological Guide from Earliest Times to the Present*. Oxford: Oxford University Press, 2005.

Musa, Mark, and Peter Bondanella, trans. *Giovanni Boccaccio: Decameron*. New York: Signet Classics, 2010.

Newhauser, Richard. "Jesus as the First Dominican." In *Christ Among the Medieval Dominicans: Representations of Christ in the Texts and Images of the Order of Preachers*, edited by Kent Emery, Jr., and Joseph Wawrykow, 238–55. Notre Dame, IN: University of Notre Dame Press, 1998.

Newman, Barbara. *From Virile Woman to WomanChrist: Studies in Medieval Religion and Literature*. Philadelphia: University of Pennsylvania Press, 1995.

———. "Intimate Pieties: Holy Trinity and Holy Family in the Late Middle Ages." *Religion and Literature* 31 (1999): 77–101.

———. "Latin and the Vernaculars." In *The Cambridge Companion to Christian Mysticism*, edited by Amy Hollywood and Patricia Beckman, 225–39. Cambridge: Cambridge University Press, 2012.

———. *Making Love in the Twelfth Century: "Letters of Two Lovers" in Context*. Philadelphia: University of Pennsylvania Press, 2016.

———. "Mechthild of Hackeborn and Dante's Matelda." Forthcoming in *A Companion to Mechthild of Hackeborn*, edited by Anne Mouron and Naoë Kukita Yoshikawa.

————, trans. *Mechthild of Hackeborn: The Book of Special Grace*. Classics of Western Spirituality. Mahwah, NJ: Paulist Press, 2017.

————. Review of *Affective Meditation and the Invention of Medieval Compassion*. *Journal of English and Germanic Philology* 110:4 (October 2011): 523–26.

Nicolini, Ugolino. "I minori osservanti di Monteripido e lo 'scriptorium' delle clarisse di Monteluce in Perugia nel secoli XV e XVI." *Picenum seraphicum* 8 (1971):100–130.

Nirenberg, David. *Anti-Judaism*. New York: W. W. Norton, 2013.

Oliger, Livario. "Le *Meditationes vitae Christi* del Pseudo-Bonaventura." *Studi Francescani* 7 (1921): 143–83; 8 (1922): 18–47.

————. "*Revelationes B. Elisabeth*: Disquisitio critica una cum textibus latino et cataleaunensi." *Antonianum* 1 (1926): 14–83.

Oliver, Judith. "A Bundle of Myrrh: Passion Meditation in French Vernacular Poems and Images and Some Liège Psalters." In *Tributes in Honor of James H. Marrow: Studies in Painting and Manuscript Illumination of the Late Middle Ages and Northern Renaissance*, edited by Jeffrey H. Hamburger and Anne S. Korteweg, 361–73. London: Harvey Miller, 2006.

Olson, Linda, and Kathryn Kerby-Fulton, eds. *Voices in Dialogue: Reading Women in the Middle Ages*. Notre Dame, IN: University of Notre Dame Press, 2005.

Pächt, Otto. Review of *Meditations on the Life of Christ: An Illustrated Manuscript of the Fourteenth Century*, edited and translated by Isa Ragusa and Rosalie Green. *Medium Aevum* 32.3 (1963): 234–35.

Palladino, Pia. *Treasures of a Lost Art: Italian Manuscript Painting of the Middle Ages and Renaissance*. New York: Metropolitan Museum of Art, 2003.

Papi, Anna Benvenuti. "*In castro poenitentiae*": Santità e società femminile nell'Italia medievale*. Rome: Herder, 1990.

Pasquali, Giorgio. *Storia della tradizione e critica del testo*. Milan: Mondadori, 1974. Orig. pub. Florence: F. Le Monnier, 1952.

Pecoraro, Paolo. "L'ora di Citerea: Una interpretazione della Matelda dantesca." *Critica letteraria* 11 (1983): 419–44.

Pecori, Luigi. *Storia della terra di San Gimignano*. Florence: Tipografia Galileiana, 1853.

Perry, Ryan. "'Thynk on God, as we doon, men that swynke': The Cultural Locations of *Meditations on the Supper of Our Lord* and the Pseudo-Bonaventuran Tradition." *Speculum* 86 (2011): 419–54.

Peter Comestor. *Historia scholastica*. In *Patrologia Latina*, edited by J.-P. Migne, vol. 198 (1844): cols. 1053–1722.

Petrocchi, Giorgio. "Sulla composizione e data delle *Meditationes vitae Christi*." *Convivium*, n.s., 4 (1952): 757–78.

Pfaff, Richard W. "James, Montague Rhodes (1862–1936)." *Oxford Dictionary of National Biography*. Oxford: Oxford University Press, 2004. Available at http://www.oxforddnb.com/view/article/34152.

Phillips, Dianne. "The *Meditations on the Life of Christ*: An Illuminated Fourteenth-Century Italian Manuscript at the University of Notre Dame." In *The Text in the Community: Essays on Medieval Works, Manuscripts, Authors and Readers*, edited by Jill Mann and Maura Nolan, 237–81. Notre Dame, IN: University of Notre Dame Press, 2006.

Pignatti, Franco. "Girolamo da Siena." *Dizionario Biografico degli Italiani*, 56 (2001), Treccani. Available at http://www.treccani.it/enciclopedia/girolamo-da -siena.

Poirel, Dominique. "The Death of Angela of Foligno and the Genesis of the *Liber Angelae*." In Robins, *Textual Cultures of Medieval Italy*, 265–94.

Poor, Sara. *Mechthild of Magdeburg and Her Book*. Philadelphia: University of Pennsylvania Press, 2004.

Pozzi, Giovanni, and Claudio Leonardi, eds. *Scrittrici mistiche italiane*. Genoa: Marietti, 1988.

Psaki, F. Regina, ed. and trans. *Italian Literature II: Tristano Riccardiano*. Arthurian Archives 12. Cambridge: D. S. Brewer, 2006.

Raby, F. J. E. *A History of Christian Latin Poetry*. 2nd ed. Oxford: Oxford University Press, 1953.

Ragusa, Isa. "L'autore delle *Meditationes vitae Christi* secondo il Codice MS. ital. 115 della Bibliothèque Nationale di Parigi." *Arte medievale* 11 (1997): 145–50.

———, and Rosalie B. Green, trans. *Meditations on the Life of Christ: An Illustrated Manuscript of the Fourteenth Century*. Princeton: Princeton University Press, 1961.

Robiglio, Andrea A. "Between Language and Likemindedness: Some Aspects of the Concept of *Conversatio Civilis* from Aquinas to Guazzo." In *Language and Cultural Change: Aspects of the Study and Use of Language in the Later Middle Ages and the Renaissance*, edited by Lodi Nauta, 113–32. Leuven: Peeters, 2006.

Robins, William, ed. *Textual Cultures of Medieval Italy*. Toronto: University of Toronto Press, 2011.

Roest, Bert. "*Ignorantia est mater omnium malorum*: The Validation of Knowledge and the Office of Preaching in Late Medieval Female Franciscan Communities." In *Saints, Scholars, and Politicians: Gender as a Tool in Medieval Studies*, edited by Mathilde van Dijk and Renée Nip, 65–83. Turnhout: Brepols, 2005.

———. *Order and Disorder: The Poor Clares between Foundation and Reformation*. Leiden: Brill, 2013.

Ronzani, Mauro. "Il francescanesimo a Pisa fino alla metà del Trecento." *Bollettino storico pisano* 54 (1985): 1–55.

———. *Penitenti e Ordini Mendicanti a Pisa sino all'inizio del Trecento. Mélanges de l'École française de Rome: Moyen-Âge, Temps moderns*, 89.2 (1977): 733–41.

Rose, Mark. *Authors and Owners: The Invention of Copyright.* Cambridge, MA: Harvard University Press, 1995.

Rossi, Adamo, ed. *Edizione principe di quattordici scritture italiane.* Perugia, 1856.

Rossi, Giancarlo. "La 'redazione latina' dello *Specchio della vera penitenza.*" *Studi di filologia italiana* 49 (1991): 29–58.

Rudy, Kathryn M. *Virtual Pilgrimages in the Convent: Imagining Jerusalem in the Late Middle Ages.* Turnhout: Brepols, 2011.

Ruh, Kurt. *Bonaventura deutsch: Ein Beitrag zur deutschen Franziskaner-Mystik und -Scholastik.* Bern: Francke, 1956.

Ryan, William Granger, trans. *Jacobus de Voragine: The Golden Legend.* 2 vols. Princeton: Princeton University Press, 1993.

Salter, Elizabeth. *English and International: Studies in the Literature, Art and Patronage of Medieval England.* Edited by Derek Pearsall and Nicolette Zeeman. Cambridge: Cambridge University Press, 1988.

———. *Nicholas Love's "Myrrour of the Blessed Lyf of Jesu Christ."* Analecta Cartusiana 10. Salzburg: Institut für Englische Sprache und Literatur, Universität Salzburg, 1974.

"S. Alvise (Venezia)" Archivio di Stato di Venezia. Available at http://www .archiviodistatovenezia.it/siasve/cgi-bin/pagina.pl?Tipo=ente&Chiave=724.

Sansone, Giuseppe E., ed. *Francesco da Barberino: Reggimento e costumi di donna.* Rome: Zauli, 1995.

Santi, Francesco, ed. *La letteratura francescana,* vol. 5: *La mistica.* Milan: Mondadori, Fondazione L. Valla, 2016.

Sapegno, Natalino. *Storia letteraria del Trecento.* Milan: Riccardo Ricciardi Editore, 1963.

Sargent, Michael, ed. *Nicholas Love: The Mirror of the Blessed Life of Jesus Christ; A Full Critical Edition.* Exeter: University of Exeter Press, 2005.

Sarri, Francesco, ed., *"Le meditazioni della vita di Cristo" di un frate minore del secolo XIV.* Milan: Vita e pensiero, 1933. Adapted as a digitized edition of the *testo minore* on the Digital Georgetown site: https://repository.library .georgetown.edu/handle/10822/1042297.

Savage, Anne, and Nicholas Watson, trans. *Anchoritic Spirituality: Ancrene Wisse and Associated Works.* New York: Paulist Press, 1991.

Scheck, Thomas P., trans. *St. Jerome: Commentary on Matthew.* Fathers of the Church. Washington, DC: Catholic University of America Press, 2008.

Schiaffini, Alfredo, ed. *Paolo da Certaldo: Libro di buoni costumi.* Florence: F. Le Monnier, 1945.

Schiller, Gertrud. *Iconography of Christian Art.* 2 vols. London: Lund Humphries, 1971–72.

Schmidt, Margot. "Mechthild von Hackeborn." In *Die deutsche Literatur des Mittelalters Verfasserlexicon,* 2nd ed., edited by Kurt Ruh et al., 6:251–60. Berlin: de Gruyter, 1987.

Şenocak, Neslihan. *The Poor and the Perfect: The Rise of Learning in the Franciscan Order, 1209–1310*. Ithaca: Cornell University Press, 2012.

———. "Voluntary Simplicity: The Attitude of Francis towards Learning in the Early Biographies." In *The Cambridge Companion to Francis of Assisi*, edited by Michael J. P. Robson, 84–100. Cambridge: Cambridge University Press, 2012.

Serventi, Silvia, ed. *Girolamo da Siena: Epistole*. Venice: Istituto Veneto di Scienze, Lettere ed Arti, 2004.

Smalley, Beryl. *The Study of the Bible in the Middle Ages*. Oxford: Basil Blackwell, 1952.

Smith, Lesley. *The Glossa Ordinaria: The Making of a Biblical Commentary*. Boston: Brill, 2009.

Sorio, Bartolommeo, ed. *Cento meditazioni di S. Bonaventura sulla vita di Gesù Cristo*. Rome, 1847. Available at https://archive.org/details/centomeditazioni 00bona.

Stallings, Sister M. Jordan, ed. *Meditaciones de passione Christi, olim Sancto Bonaventura attributae*. Washington, DC: Catholic University of America Press, 1965.

Stallings-Taney, C. Mary. "The Pseudo-Bonaventure *Meditaciones vite Christi*: *Opus Integrum*." *Franciscan Studies* 55 (1998): 253–80.

———, ed. *Iohannes de Caulibus: Meditaciones vite Christi*. Corpus Christianorum, Continuatio Mediaevalis, 153. Turnhout: Brepols, 1997.

Stoppino, Eleonora, trans. "The Italian *Reggimento e costumi di donna* (Selections) and *Documenti d'amore* (Selections) of Francesco da Barberino" In *Medieval Conduct Literature: An Anthology of Vernacular Guides to Behavior for Youths, with English Translations*, ed. Mark D. Johnston, 127–59. Toronto: University of Toronto Press, 2009.

Synan, Edward. *The Popes and the Jews*. New York: Macmillan, 1965.

Taney, Francis X., Sr., Anne Miller, and C. Mary Stallings-Taney, trans. *Meditations on the Life of Christ*. Asheville, NC: Pegasus Press, 2000.

Tarrant, R. J. "Toward a Typology of Interpolation in Latin Poetry." *Transactions of the American Philological Association* 117 (1987): 281–98.

Testi Cristiani, Maria Laura. *Arte Medievale a Pisa*. Rome: Consiglio Nazionale delle Ricerche, 2005.

Thomson, R. M. *A Descriptive Catalogue of the Medieval Manuscripts of Corpus Christi College Oxford*. Cambridge: D. S. Brewer, 2011.

Tóth, Péter [Peter]. "Pseudo-Apocryphal Dialogue as a Tool for the Memorization of Scholastic Wisdom: The Farewell of Christ to Mary and the *Liber de Vita Christi* by Jacobus." In Doležalová, ed., *The Making of Memory in the Middle Ages*, 161–96.

———, and Dávid Falvay. "New Light on the Date and Authorship of the *Meditationes Vitae Christi*." In *Devotional Culture in Late Medieval England: Diverse Imaginations of Christ's Life*, edited by Stephen Kelly and Ryan Perry, 17–105. Turnhout: Brepols, 2014.

Trexler, Richard. *Naked before the Father: The Renunciation of Francis of Assisi.* New York: Peter Lang, 1989.

Turner, James. *Philology: The Forgotten Origins of the Modern Humanities.* Princeton: Princeton University Press, 2014.

Vaccari, Alberto. "Le 'Meditazioni della vita de Cristo' in volgare." *Scritti di erudizione e di filologia* 1 (1952): 341–78.

Varanelli, E. S. "*Le Meditationes Vitae Nostri Domini Jesu Christi* nell'arte del Duecento italiano." *Arte Medievale* 6 (1992): 137–48.

Varanini, Giorgio, ed. *Cantari religiosi senesi del Trecento.* Scrittori d'Italia 230. Bari: Laterza, 1965.

Vauchez, André. *Francis of Assisi: The Life and Afterlife of a Medieval Saint.* Translated by Michael F. Cusato. New Haven: Yale University Press, 2012.

Vavalà, Evelyn Sandberg. *La croce dipinta italiana e l'iconografia della passione.* Verona: Casa editrice Apollo, 1929.

Vidal, Jaime. *The Infancy Narrative* in Pseudo-Bonaventure's 'Meditationes Vitae Christi': A Study in Medieval Franciscan Christ-Piety (c. 1300)." Ph.D. dissertation, Fordham University, 1984.

Walker, Greg, ed. *Medieval Drama: An Anthology.* Oxford: Blackwell Publishers, 2000.

Walsh, Katherine, and Diana Wood, eds. *The Bible in the Medieval World: Essays in Memory of Beryl Smalley.* Oxford: Basil Blackwell, 1985.

Walsh, Killian, trans. *Bernard of Clairvaux: On the Song of Songs.* 4 vols. Kalamazoo, MI: Cistercian Publications, 1980.

Watson, Nicholas. "Censorship and Cultural Change in Late-Medieval England: Vernacular Theology, the Oxford Translation Debate, and Arundel's Constitutions of 1409." *Speculum* 70 (1995): 822–64.

Webber, T. "The Books of Leicester Abbey." In *Leicester Abbey: Medieval History, Archaeology, and Manuscript Studies,* edited by Joanna Story, Jill Bourne, and Richard Buckley, 127–46. Leicester: The Leicestershire Archaeological Society, 2006.

————. "Latin Devotional Texts and the Books of the Augustinian Canons of Thurgarton Priory and Leicester Abbey in the Late Middle Ages." In *Books and Collectors, 1200–1700: Essays Presented to A. G. Watson,* edited by James Carley and Colin Tite, 27–41. London: British Library.

————, and A. G. Watson, eds. *The Libraries of the Augustinian Canons.* Corpus of British Medieval Library Catalogues 6. London: The British Library, 1998.

Wileumier-Schalij, J. M. "Is Michael de Massa de auteur van de latijnse grondtekst van het zgn. Pseudo-Bonaventura-Ludolphiaanse Leven van Jezus?" *Nederlands Archief voor Kerkgeschiedenis* 60 (1980): 1–10.

Winroth, Anders. *The Making of Gratian's Decretum.* Cambridge: Cambridge University Press, 2000.

Wood, Jeryldene M. *Women, Art, and Spirituality: The Poor Clares of Early Modern Italy.* Cambridge: Cambridge University Press, 1996.

Yakou, Hisashi. "Contemplating Angels and the 'Madonna of the Apocalypse.'" In Elliott and Warr, *The Church of Santa Maria Donna Regina,* 93–107.

Young, Karl. *The Drama of the Medieval Church.* 2 vols. Oxford: Clarendon Press, 1933.

Zangirolami, Cesare. *Storia delle chiese, dei monasteri, delle scuole di Venezia rapinate e distrutte da Napoleone Bonaparte.* Venice: Fillippi, 2007.

Ziegler, Joanna. *Sculpture of Compassion: The Pietà and the Beguines in the Southern Low Countries c. 1300–c. 1600.* Brussels: Institut historique belge de Rome, 1992.

Zorzi, Marino. "Dal manoscritto al libro." In *Storia di Venezia: Dalle origini alla caduta della Serenissima,* 14 vols., edited by Gino Benzoni and Antonio Menniti Ippolito. Rome: Istituto della Enciclopedia Italiana, 1992–2002; vol. 4, *Il Rinascimento: Politica e cultura,* ed. Alberto Tenenti and Ugo Tucci, 817–958.

Zumthor, Paul. *Towards a Medieval Poetics.* Translated by P. Bennett. Minneapolis: University of Minnesota Press, 1992.

# INDEX

Abbey of Leicester, xci–xcii

Abbey of San Pietro a Castello, Naples, cxliii

adaptation, xxxixn14; devotional texts and, xxxiv; five stages of MVC's, cxxxviiin51; mystery plays and, xlvn26; *testo minore* as, lxvi–lxxxvi

Angela of Foligno, xxx, lxv, cn12, cix, cxi, cxvii, cxxiv, cxxv, 230n135; and Brother A, cxxiv

anonymity (authorial), xxviii, xxx, xxxiv, xl

Aquinas, Thomas, 199n1

Aristotle, 199n1

art: affective devotion and, l–li; devotional, cxlviii, 206n27, 231n140; intermediality and, xxxi–xxxii; Pisan, cxlvii–cxlviii; Trecento, xxxi, cxix, cxxxn32, 202n12, 231n139; ugly, cxxvn15, 231n138

Auerbach, Erich, xxxiin24

Augustine, Saint, lxxvii, cxi, cliii, 209n39

authority: female, 226n114, 232n144; learned, xliv, ciin16, 211n46; parental, 216n68; reader and, 201n8; scriptural, cxiv; spiritual, xli, cxvii–cxviii; textual, xxii–xxiii, xxxviii, c

Baier, Walter, cxxxivn43

Barasch, Moshe, 166n12

Barbarino, Francesco da, 202n10

Barratt, Alexandra, xcivn100, cxl, cxliin64

Bartal, Renana, cxxx, 207n27

Bartolomeo da San Concordio, lxv, clxxv

Basilica of San Francesco, Assisi, lxxix, 231n139

Beatrice of Nazareth, lxv

Bernard of Clairvaux: xli, xliii–xlvi, lii–liii, lxiii, lxxx, lxxxviii, lxxxix, cxi, 203n12; 215n65; sermon on the Nativity, 206n25; *Sermons on the Song of Songs*, xliii, ciii, cxi, 200n5, 201n7, 209n37

Bertelli, Sandro, cxxvii–cxxviii

Boccaccio, Giovanni, lxi, cxiiin10

Bodleian Library, xix, xx, cli

Bojanni, Benevenuta, xxxn18, cix

Bonaventure, Saint: adaptation of Thomas of Celano's lives of Francis, cn12; *Legenda maior*, cxi, 222n96; *Lignum Vitae*, li; MVC attributed to, xix, xxxix, lvii, xciii, xciv, cxxx; views of control over female monastic life of, lxxxvii

Boniface VIII, cxv

SARAH  McNAMER

is associate professor of English and medieval studies
at Georgetown University. She is the author of *Affective Meditation
and the Invention of Medieval Compassion* (2010).

CPSIA information can be obtained
at www.ICGtesting.com
Printed in the USA
LVOW12*0627140218
566544LV00006B/29/P